EFFECTIVE PUBLIC RELATIONS

9TH EDITION

SCOTT M. CUTLIP, APR, PRSA FELLOW
Dean Emeritus
Henry W. Grady College of Journalism and Mass Communication
The University of Georgia

ALLEN H. CENTER, APR, PRSA FELLOW
Distinguished Resident Lecturer
San Diego State University
Vice President of Public Relations (retired)
Motorola, Inc.

GLEN M. BROOM, PH.D.
Professor, School of Communication
San Diego State University
Adjunct Professor, Queensland University of Technology
Brisbane, Australia

PEARSON
Prentice
Hall

PEARSON EDUCATION INTERNATIONAL

Editorial Director: *Leah Jewell*
Executive Editor: *Deirdre Anderson*
Production Liaison: *Fran Russello*
Full-Service Project Management:
   Katie Ostler and Sue Katkus, Schawk, Inc.
Prepress and Manufacturing Buyer:
   Brian Mackey

Director of Marketing: *Brandy Dawson*
Marketing Manager: *Kate Mitchell*
Marketing Assistant: *Kara Pottle*
Editorial Assistant: *Christina Walker*
Cover Design: *Bruce Kenselaar*
Interior Design: *Van Mua, Schawk, Inc.*
Cover Photo: *Getty Images*

This book was set in 10/12 Times Ten Roman by Schawk, Inc., and was printed and bound by Bind-Rite Graphics. The cover was printed by Phoenix Color Corp.

Pearson Education LTD.
Pearson Education Singapore, Pte. Ltd
Pearson Education Canada, Ltd.
Pearson Education—Japan
Pearson Education Australia PTY, Limited

Pearson Education North Asia Ltd
Pearson Educación de México, S.A. de C.V.
Pearson Education Malaysia, Pte. Ltd
Pearson Education, Upper Saddle River, NJ

10 9 8 7 6 5 4 3 2
ISBN: 0-13-123014-X

In memory

Of

Scott M. Cutlip

(1915–2000)

In memory of one of the pathfinders who gave the
emerging profession of public relations both
its intellectual foundation and its moral compass.

BRIEF CONTENTS

CONTENTS

Effective Public Relations (*EPR*) has earned a legacy matched by few books in any field. Since the first edition was published in 1952, **Scott M. Cutlip** and **Allen H. Center** have played leading roles in advancing public relations toward professional status. This ninth edition continues almost six decades of defining public relations as a profession, schooling its practitioners, and serving as a reference for those in the calling worldwide.

CUTLIP AND CENTER

Scott M. Cutlip

For many of those years *EPR* has been viewed as "the bible of public relations," often referred to as simply "Cutlip and Center." "After all," as one long-time counselor and consultant said, "it was Cutlip and Center, as much as anyone, who gave those of us who strayed or wandered into the profession from journalism and other professional pursuits, a sense of substance and legitimacy about practicing our adopted craft."[1]

Many of their ideas and ambitions in the first edition still serve as beacons leading public relations practice and study. The role and function of *EPR* has changed however. No longer can it serve as the comprehensive encyclopedia of public relations—the body of knowledge has outgrown the bounds of a single book. No longer is it the only credible academic textbook or professional reference. Public relations education and professional preparation have progressed beyond the limits of a single book or course. All the same, *EPR* is the basic reference for the field worldwide. It is the book used by those preparing for accreditation exams, it is the book most frequently cited in public relations literature, and it has been translated for study in Chinese, Italian, Korean, Latvian, Russian, and Spanish. As one reviewer said, "'Cutlip, Center, and Broom' …[is] the standard against which all basic public relations textbooks are measured."[2]

Allen H. Center

CONTENTS

What will you learn from the ninth edition of *EPR?* First, you will learn basic concepts necessary to understand what public relations is and how it is practiced in various settings. Second, you will learn the concepts, theory, principles, and processes that guide the practice. (Other public relations books and courses cover writing techniques and case studies.) Third, you will learn updated information and examples to help you understand contemporary public relations practice. To help facilitate this learning process, each chapter begins with a study guide that outlines specific learning objectives to help you study and master the material.

This ninth edition is divided into four parts. Part I describes the field and defines basic concepts; it also describes what practitioners do and where they work, and identifies historical leaders and traces the origins of current practice. Part II introduces the principles and theory that underpin and guide the practice, including the professional, ethical, legal, and internal and external contexts, and media and media relations. Within a systems theory framework, chapters also present communication and public opinion theory essential to understanding the function of public relations. Part III applies theory to practice by detailing the "four-step public relations process." Four chapters outline the strategic planning steps necessary for managing public relations programs. Part IV gives context to the practice by illustrating what public relations does and how it functions in business and industry; government, military, and politics; nonprofit organizations, trade associations and professional societies, and other nongovernmental organizations.

In short, the book covers much about the theory and practice of public relations. *EPR* does not trivialize public relations by presenting brief, oversimplified case studies. Rather, *EPR* gives you a foundation for subsequent courses and books devoted to implementing public relations programs and developing program tactics. You should be wary of how-I-saved-the-day books that claim to show how to succeed in public relations without first providing a foundation based on the body of knowledge.

CONTRIBUTORS

This ninth edition contains new data, ideas, examples, and contributions from many people who influenced both the substance and style of what you are about to read. More colleagues than I can name here provided valuable reactions and useful suggestions on drafts of chapters. They will recognize how their feedback changed and improved the book. Others either responded to my requests for help or through their own publications made significant contributions to this edition. At the risk of offending those not named, the following deserve special mention: **James E. Grunig**, Ph.D., University of Maryland, College Park, and his colleagues in the IABC Foundation's Excellence Project; **Ray E. Hiebert**, Ph.D., University of Maryland, College Park, the long-time editor of the field's first scholarly journal, *Public Relations Review*; **Elizabeth L. Toth**, Ph.D., APR, then of Syracuse University, now at the University of Maryland; and **Linda Childers Hon**, Ph.D., University of Florida, the two most recent editors of the scholarly *Journal of Public Relations Research*, which records the body of knowledge that serves as a foundation for this and other books. Among colleagues also deserving credit here are the many authors of other textbooks who keep raising the standards of excellence in books serving our common interest in public relations.

Former and current students form a pipeline of new information and examples, for which I am grateful and in their debt. **MaryLee Sachs**, Chairman, Hill & Knowlton USA, New York, heads that list. Others include **Vicki Hoffman Beck**, Director–Hollywood, Health & Society, USC Annenberg Norman Lear Center, Beverly Hills, California; **Marilyn Kern-Foxworth**, Ph.D., APR, President, Kern Foxworth International, LLC, Silver Spring, Maryland; **Suman Lee**, Ph.D., Assistant Professor, Iowa State University; **Tom Magnetta**, Assistant Account Executive, 21PR, Santa Monica, California; and Rear Admiral **Terry L. McCreary**, Chief of Information,

U.S. Navy, Washington, D.C. In addition, students in my classes suggested changes that made their way into the ninth edition. I want to thank them all and hope that you will be as generous with your feedback and suggestions.

Likewise, I cannot list all the colleagues in education and the practice who contributed to this edition. I pretested many of the ideas on them in presentations, in discussions or debates, and over extended lunches and dinners. Several responded to my requests for help or served unwittingly as helpful critics. You cannot write a book like this without the support, suggestions, and critical analysis of such friends and colleagues. That long list includes **Francisco J. Agraz**, J.D., Public Affairs Specialist, Federal Bureau of Investigation, Houston; **Ming Anxiang**, Professor and Director, Institute of Journalism and Communication, Beijing, China; **James Everett**, Ph.D., Associate Professor, Queensland University of Technology, Brisbane, Australia; **Melissa Koski**, Specialist, Fleishman Hillard, St. Louis; **Robert Masters**, FPRIA, Director, Robert Masters & Associates Pty Ltd., Melbourne; **Jim R. Macnamara**, FPRIA, CEO, CARMA International, Chippendale, NSW, Australia; **David B. McKinney**, APR, ABC, Public Affairs Manager, Shell Chemical Company, Deer Park, Texas; **Kerry Tucker**, Chairman and CEO, Nuffer, Smith, Tucker, San Diego; **Kenn Ulrich**, APR, Fellow, Instructor, San Diego State University.

Six colleagues made major contributions to the ninth edition: **Shannon A. Bowen**, Ph.D., University of Houston, collaborated on the new Chapter 9 (Internal Relations and Employee Communication), and contributed to Chapters 2, 3, 5 and 8; **George D. Lennon**, USDA Forest Service, Washington, D.C., collaborated on updating Chapter 16 (Government and Public Affairs); **Richard K. Long**, Brigham Young University, collaborated on the new Chapter 15 (Business and Industry Public Relations); **Jim F. McBride**, McBride Group and San Diego State University instructor, collaborated on the updated Chapter 17 (Nonprofits, Trade Associations, and Nongovernmental Organizations); **Barbara K. Petersen**, Ph.D., University of South Florida, collaborated on the new Chapter 6 (Legal Considerations); and **Bey-Ling Sha**, Ph.D., San Diego State University, helped update Chapters 11 through 14 on the management process.

Prentice Hall editors provided able assistance and firm direction in getting the ninth edition produced: **Deirdre Cavanaugh Anderson**, Executive Editor–Communication, replaced previous editor, **Bruce Kaplan**. Bruce had patiently guided the book through the early phases, providing support and guidance on how to take the book into the twenty-first century. Deirdre, however, assumed the task of moving the concept to reality. In the final stages, **Craig Campanella**, Executive Editor–English, ably filled in for Deirdre during her maternity leave. In spite of their seemingly unrelenting pressure to meet what often seemed like unrealistic deadlines (I do have a day job!), I am grateful to all three for their support and encouragement.

Katie Ostler, Editorial Project Manager, and copy editor **Karen Slaght**, at Schawk, Inc., turned the many thousands of words into the pages you will read. I appreciate their help in producing the ninth edition…and relieve them of any responsibility for typos and wording problems created by yours truly.

I am also grateful for the love and support of my wife, Betty, a professor of nursing with a demanding schedule teaching students how to help families bring healthy babies into the world. She has been my attentive audience as I talked through ideas on the pages that follow, my proofreader and reviewer of my attempts to put those ideas on paper, and my constant role model for staying on task.

All of these people and others played important roles in producing this ninth edition, but **you** are the most important person. This book is for you. It introduces you to the challenging and rewarding calling of building organization–public relationships in an era of instantaneous global communication. I hope the pages that follow help you achieve success and satisfaction in your public relations career.

Glen M. Broom

Glen M. Broom

POSTSCRIPT

Unfortunately, some important colleagues will not see the fruits of their effort in this edition. First, senior coauthor **Scott M. Cutlip** died shortly after the eighth edition was published. Much has been written about this dean of public relations education and his many contributions to our field.[3] His contributions in this book and his scholarly research made public relations an area of academic study on university campuses, and earned him the Association for Education in Journalism and Mass Communication's highest honor, the Paul J. Deutschmann Award for Excellence in Research. He was awarded the Public Relations Society of America's first Outstanding Educator Award in 1970 and was the third person inducted into the Arthur W. Page Society's Hall of Fame in 1987. It is not a stretch to say that Scott Cutlip was the father of public relations education—worldwide.

In March 2003, the field lost one of its most energetic leaders—**William C. Adams**, APR, Fellow, Associate Professor, Florida International University. He collaborated on writing the business and industry chapter for both the seventh and eighth editions. He drew on his 25 years of corporate practice at Amoco and Phillips Petroleum to build a 13-year teaching career that inspired students to pursue excellence in public relations. Of course, he was their best role model.

To fill the void for expertise in preparing the corporate practice (Chapter 15), I turned to **Richard K. Long**, Professor, Brigham Young University. He had spent 30 years in executive positions in corporate public relations—at Dow Chemical Company (24 years) and Weyerhaeuser Company (6 years)—before joining the faculty at BYU. He published frequently in professional publications and, like Professor Adams, cared deeply for his students and their success in public relations. He provided me assistance far beyond Chapter 15, with his counsel, editing, and enthusiastic support. He died in January 2005 at age 60. (See Chapter 15 and Exhibit 16.2 in Chapter 16.)

I surely wish you could have known them, but I am pleased to know that you will learn from them in the pages that follow.

NOTES

[1] Stephen H. Baer, Fellow, PRSA, writing in a book review published in *Public Relations Review*, Vol. 18, No. 4 (Winter 1992), 392.

[2] Donald K. Wright, "Review of Public Relations Literature: Basic Textbooks," *Public Relations Review* 22, no. 4 (Winter, 1996): 380.

[3] For a summary of Scott Cutlip's career achievements and contributions, see the special edition of *Public Relations Review* (Volume 17, no. 4 [Winter 1991]: 331–412), featuring articles for the Paul J. Deutschmann Award for Excellence in Research presentation.

1 INTRODUCTION TO CONTEMPORARY PUBLIC RELATIONS

Public relations is the management function that establishes and maintains mutually beneficial relationships between an organization and the publics on whom its success or failure depends.

STUDY GUIDE

After studying Chapter 1, you should be able to

- Write a definition of public relations that emphasizes building and maintaining relationships between organizations and their publics.

- Distinguish between the public relations and marketing functions of organizations, identifying the exchange between provider and customer as the distinguishing characteristic of marketing relationships.

- Define and differentiate among related concepts, including publicity, advertising, press agentry, public affairs, issues management, lobbying, investor relations, and development.

- Outline how public relations helps improve organizations and society.

Individuals and groups have always entered into relationships with others to satisfy mutual wants and needs. In the interconnected global community, however, increasing interdependence requires even more complex social, political, and economic interaction. As a result, establishing and maintaining relationships at all levels of social systems have become important areas of scholarly study and professional practice.

For example, *human relations, marriage relations,* and *interpersonal relations* are terms used to describe the study and management of relationships between individuals. At the other extreme, international relations deals with relationships among nations in the largest social system. Courses and books are devoted to the study of all these relationships, as well as relationships in families, work teams, groups, organizations, and other social entities.

1

This book is about *relationships between organizations and their stakeholder publics*—people who are somehow mutually involved or interdependent with these organizations. The term *public relations* refers to the management of organization–public relationships and is one of the fastest-growing fields of professional employment worldwide.

In everyday conversation and in the media, however, people use the term *public relations* to refer to many things, and often their definition is not positive. For example, some use "it's just public relations" as a pejorative description for what they consider to be an insincere public gesture. Public relations, according to critics, is "an industry designed to alter perceptions, reshape reality and manufacture consent."[1] Others say something is "good public relations" or "great PR" if it appears in the media. They equate public relations with anything that attracts media coverage: "We encourage that feeling because that's what we do."[2] Some see public relations as trying to hide the truth or putting a positive "spin" on bad news. One author suggests that "the terms PR and public relations have become widely accepted shorthand for subterfuge and deception."[3] Even more disturbing is the long-held view that public relations people "pull the wires which control the public mind, who harness old forces and contrive new ways to bind and guide the world."[4]

This book is not *about these jaundiced views of public relations.* Rather, this chapter introduces public relations as the management art and science of building and maintaining relationships between organizations and their stakeholder publics. We define public relations as an organizational management function, discuss its parts and specializations, and distinguish it from other management functions and activities. The discussion begins with a review of how the concept of public relations has changed over the years.

■

EVOLUTION OF THE CONCEPT

Changing views of public relations reflect the evolution of the practice in organizations and in society. They also portray an emerging profession seeking its own identity and professional recognition. Highlights of the evolution illustrate how the function became a part of organizational management. (See Chapter 4 for a more detailed historical analysis.)

Powerful business interests in the early 1900s employed public relations to defend themselves and their monopolies against muckraking journalists and increasing interest in government regulation. The emphasis was on telling their side of the story and on counterattacks designed to influence public opinion and to prevent increased governmental regulation of business.

One-way persuasive communication dominated as the United States entered World War I and President Woodrow Wilson created the Committee on Public Information. Headed by George Creel and staffed by young propagandists, some of whom would later establish public relations firms, the committee's goal was to unite public opinion behind the war through a nationwide propaganda campaign. During those early years, public relations took the form of publicity designed to influence others—often referred to simply as "propaganda."

Many still define public relations as merely persuasion. For example, one dictionary defined public relations as "**inducing** the public to have understanding for and goodwill" (emphasis added). This definition reflects the writings of Edward L. Bernays—one of the founders of public relations—in his influential book, *The*

FIGURE 1.1

"OLD SCHOOL "PR""

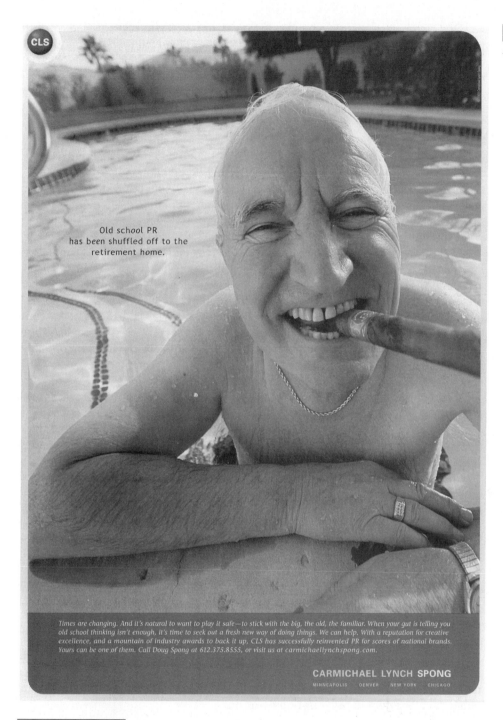

Courtesy Carmichael Lynch Spong, Minneapolis

Engineering of Consent (1955). Even today, many practitioners work with managers and clients who see public relations as simply one-way communication to persuade others.

During the decades following World War II, our understanding of media effects became more sophisticated. Consequently, definitions evolved to include notions of two-way communication and relationships. Definitions included words such as **reciprocal**, **mutual**, and **between**, indicating a maturing view of the function. This interactive concept appeared in *Webster's Third New International Dictionary*'s definition: "The art or science of developing reciprocal understanding and goodwill." The British Institute of Public Relations defined the function as an effort to establish and maintain "mutual understanding between an organization and its publics."

Early editions of this text also defined public relations as an interactive concept, "the planned effort to influence opinion through good character and responsible performance, based on mutually satisfactory two-way communications." Another influential text published in 1984 also emphasized communication in another version of this interactive concept, "the management of communication between an organization and its publics."[5]

Yale professor and *Public Opinion Quarterly* founder Harwood L. Childs had introduced an even more advanced concept in the late 1930s. Going against the conventional wisdom, Childs concluded that the essence of public relations "is not the presentation of a point of view, not the art of tempering mental attitudes, nor the development of cordial and profitable relations." Instead, he said, the basic function "is to reconcile or adjust in the public interest those aspects of our personal and corporate behavior which have a social significance."[6] Childs saw the function of public relations as helping organizations adjust to their social environments, a concept that reemerged many years later in contemporary public relations.

Organizational adjustment as the outcome for public relations suggests a management-level, policy-influencing role and calls for corrective action in addition to communication. The International Public Relations Association (IPRA) adopted these elements by including "counseling organization leaders" and implementing "planned programs of action" in its definition of public relations.

In summary, the one-way concept of public relations relies almost entirely on propaganda and persuasive communication, typically in the form of publicity. The two-way concept emphasizes communication exchange, reciprocity, and mutual understanding. Additionally, the two-way concept includes counseling management on **change** needed within the organization. You will find all these concepts reflected in today's practice.

DEFINING THE CONCEPT IN PRACTICE

Describing public relations practice is yet another way to define the function. *Public Relations News*, one of several commercial newsletters serving the field, defines public relations operationally. Notice how the newsletter's definition describes what public relations **does** in organizational settings:

> Public relations is the management function which evaluates public attitudes, identifies the policies and procedures of an individual or an organization with the public interest, and plans and executes a program of action to earn public understanding and acceptance.

Hundreds have written definitions attempting to capture the essence of public relations by listing the major activities that make up the practice. A longtime public relations scholar and professional leader, the late Rex F. Harlow, collected almost 500 definitions written between the early 1900s and 1976. He then identified their major elements in order to say what public relations **is**, not just what it **does**. His definition includes both conceptual and operational elements:

> Public Relations is the distinctive management function which helps establish and maintain mutual lines of communication, understanding, acceptance and cooperation between an organization and its publics; involves the management of problems or issues; helps management to keep informed on and responsive to public opinion; defines and emphasizes the responsibility of management to serve the public interest; helps management keep abreast of and effectively utilize change, serving as an early warning system to help anticipate trends; and uses research and sound and ethical communication as its principal tools.[7]

The Public Relations Society of America (PRSA) adopted an even longer "Official Statement on Public Relations." The authors, a blue-ribbon panel of PRSA leaders, attempted to provide society members a definition of the field that stressed public relations' contributions to society. In addition to this conceptual aspect of the definition, the panel included activities, results, and knowledge requirements of public relations practice. (See Exhibit 1.1 on page 6.)

Elements common to many definitions suggest that public relations:

1. Conducts a planned and sustained program as part of an organization's management.
2. Deals with the relationships between an organization and its stakeholder publics.
3. Monitors awareness, opinions, attitudes, and behavior inside and outside the organization.
4. Analyzes the impact of policies, procedures, and actions on stakeholder publics.
5. Identifies policies, procedures, and actions that conflict with the public interest and organizational survival.
6. Counsels management on the establishment of new policies, procedures, and actions that are mutually beneficial to the organization and its publics.
7. Establishes and maintains two-way communication between the organization and its publics.
8. Produces measurable changes in awareness, opinion, attitude, and behavior inside and outside the organization.
9. Results in new and/or maintained relationships between an organization and its publics.

PUBLIC RELATIONS DEFINED

As one scholar observed, definitions serve at least two purposes: to help us understand the world around us and to argue for a particular worldview of how one concept relates to other concepts.[8] Consequently, a definition of **public relations** should help us understand what public relations is and does, as well as how it relates to other organizational activities.

Public relations is the management function that establishes and maintains mutually beneficial relationships between an organization and the publics on whom its success or failure depends.

EXHIBIT 1.1

PUBLIC RELATIONS SOCIETY OF AMERICA'S "OFFICIAL STATEMENT OF PUBLIC RELATIONS"

Public relations helps our complex, pluralistic society to reach decisions and function more effectively by contributing to mutual understanding among groups and institutions. It serves to bring private and public policies into harmony.

Public relations serves a wide variety of institutions in society such as businesses, trade unions, government agencies, voluntary associations, foundations, hospitals, schools, colleges, and religious institutions. To achieve their goals, these institutions must develop effective relationships with many different audiences or publics such as employees, members, customers, local communities, shareholders, and other institutions, and with society at large.

The management of institutions needs to understand the attitudes and values of their publics in order to achieve institutional goals. The goals themselves are shaped by the external environment. The public relations practitioner acts as a counselor to management and as a mediator, helping to translate private aims into reasonable, publicly acceptable policy and action.

As a management function, public relations encompasses the following:

- Anticipating, analyzing, and interpreting public opinion, attitudes, and issues that might impact, for good or ill, the operations and plans of the organization.

- Counseling management at all levels in the organization with regard to policy decisions, courses of action, and communication, taking into account their public ramifications and the organization's social or citizenship responsibilities.

- Researching, conducting, and evaluating, on a continuing basis, programs of action and communication to achieve the informed public understanding necessary to the success of an organization's aims. These may include marketing, financial, fund raising, employee, community or government relations, and other programs.

- Planning and implementing the organization's efforts to influence or change public policy.

- Setting objectives, planning, budgeting, recruiting and training staff, developing facilities—in short, managing the resources needed to perform all of the above.

- Examples of the knowledge that may be required in the professional practice of public relations include communication arts, psychology, social psychology, sociology, political science, economics, and the principles of management and ethics. Technical knowledge and skills are required for opinion research, public-issues analysis, media relations, direct mail, institutional advertising, publications, film/video productions, special events, speeches, and presentations.

In helping to define and implement policy, the public relations practitioner uses a variety of professional communication skills and plays an integrative role both within the organization and between the organization and the external environment.

———————————

—Courtesy of Public Relations Society of America

The definition of public relations (see right margin on page 5) positions the practice of public relations as a **management function**, meaning that management in all organizations must attend to public relations. It also identifies building and maintaining **mutually beneficial relationships** between organizations and publics as the moral and ethical basis of the profession. At the same time, it suggests criteria for determining **what is** and **what is not** public relations. And finally, it defines the concept of the practice that is the subject of this book. Public relations is the management function that establishes and maintains mutually beneficial relationships between an organization and the publics on whom its success or failure depends.

CONFUSION WITH MARKETING

Many people confuse public relations with another management function—**marketing.** Job openings for "public relations representatives" turn out to be positions as door-to-door sales representatives or telephone solicitors. In some organizations, the same person does both public relations and marketing, often without distinguishing between the two. Because of such confusion, some mistakenly conclude that there is no difference.

Confusion also occurs in nonprofit organizations and government agencies in which "nonprofit marketing" and "social marketing" often refer to building and maintaining relationships with members, patients, donors, and other constituencies. In one such case, a practitioner who worked for a large hospital arrived on a Monday morning to find a new sign on her office door—"Marketing Communication Department." Much to her surprise, management had changed the title of the "Public Relations Department" without telling her! Hospital administration apparently saw no problem with putting a marketing title on the public relations department. After all, in their view, they were not changing anything but the title.

Those in the practice also add to the confusion. Some public relations practitioners' business cards say that they do "marketing communications" or "integrated marketing communications." Some public relations firms have "marketing communications" or "marketing public relations" in their titles and on their letterheads. A former principal of one such firm wrote a book describing "marketing public relations" as "programs that encourage purchase and consumer satisfaction through credible communication of information and impressions . . . ."[9]

In fact, many hired into "public relations" jobs spend much of their time supporting marketing, introducing new products and services, publicizing their uses, and generally supporting the marketing strategy. For many firms, marketing support pays the bills. As one firm owner said, "Take away our work in marketing and you take away more than half our business." After considering the distinction between public relations and marketing, the CEO of another public relations firm concluded that "75 percent of public relations people are really in marketing." Paul Holmes, president of The Holmes Group and columnist for *PRWeek,* described the confusion:

> Someone once told me he was changing his firm's name from XYZ Public Relations to XYZ Marketing Communications because "we've broadened our portfolio of services." But marketing (managing the relationship between a company and its customers) is a much narrower discipline than PR (managing the relationship between a company and all stakeholders), though it's not narrower than publicity, which is probably what the firm was doing.[10]

Some marketing authors add to the confusion by suggesting that public relations (read "publicity") is really just a tactic used in marketing:

> No exciting product to talk about? Get one. This is the job of the PR strategist today. Find an idea that will generate publicity. And not any kind of publicity either. Publicity that will build a brand.[11]

If not always clearly defined in practice, public relations and marketing can be distinguished conceptually and their relationship clarified. First, people's wants and needs are fundamental to the concept of marketing. What people want or need gets translated into consumer demand. Marketers offer products and services to satisfy

Marketing is the management function that identifies human needs and wants, offers products and services to satisfy those demands, and causes transactions that deliver products and services in exchange for something of value to the provider.

the demand. Consumers select the products and services that provide the most utility, value, and satisfaction. Finally, the marketer delivers the product or service to the consumer in exchange for something of value. According to marketing scholar Philip Kotler: "Exchange, which is the core concept of marketing, is the process of obtaining a desired product from someone by offering something in return."[12] **This transaction distinguishes the marketing function—two parties exchanging something of value to each other.**

In short, marketing creates quid pro quo relationships in which an exchange occurs—ownership changes hands. The goal of marketing is to attract and satisfy customers on a sustained basis in order to secure "market share" and to achieve an organization's economic objectives.

To that end, product publicity and media relations are used to support marketing. Because public relations specialists typically know how to write for the news media, how to work with journalists, and how to plan and implement internal communication programs, marketers call on them to help in the marketing effort. For example, Apple Computer uses publicity to launch new models and operating systems—even getting Steve Jobs on the cover of *Time* magazine when it introduced the iMac. WD-40 uses publicity and its Web site to discover and promote new uses of its major product. The dairy industry uses media events and publicity—in addition to its "Got Milk?" advertising campaign—to promote the health benefits of drinking milk. Ford used press conferences and other press releases to defend the Explorer SUV during the rollover crisis associated with Firestone tire tread separation and recall. Likewise, Coca-Cola in Belgium engaged crisis communication specialists when facing charges that its product was contaminated.

A few organizations see marketing relationship with customers as only one of many organizational relationships. On their organization charts, marketing is part of the larger public relations function. Many other organizations view marketing as the major function, viewing all noncustomer relationships (with employees, investors, neighbors, government, media, etc.) as necessary only in the context of supporting marketing. In these organizations, typically, the top public relations officer reports to marketing. A few organizations identify "consumer relations" as part of public relations, making the public relations department responsible for communications with customers and other consumers regarding instructions for using products, safety, complaints, and repair services. In the majority of organizations, however, marketing and public relations are separate management functions with different but overlapping and complementary goals.

In summary, effective public relations contributes to the marketing effort by maintaining a hospitable social and political environment. For example, a hospital that maintains good relationships with volunteers, nurses, physicians, local employers, local government, and community groups will likely enjoy success in the marketing effort to attract patients, physicians, and referrals. Likewise, successful marketing and satisfied customers help build and maintain good relations with other publics, such as employees, investors, government regulatory agencies, and community leaders.

On the other hand, misguided marketing strategies and gimmicks illustrate how these efforts can backfire and create public relations problems. The classic—"Joe Camel"—may have been an effective marketing tactic for reaching children and teenagers, but it may have been the straw that broke the camel's back for the tobacco industry as it defended itself in numerous court cases. Nestlé's successful marketing of Nan™ baby formula—apparently ignoring the intent of the World Health Organiza-

tion's Code of Marketing Milk Substitutes—prompted the National /
Breastfeeding Advocacy to charge Nestlé with "using a vulnerable pop
grab at market share. . ." as quoted in *The Wall Street Journal*.[13] How's tr
press?"

Do you remember the negative press coverage of Abercrombie &
troversial "magalog" featuring nudity that some claimed promoted
sumption and group sex? Apparently not daunted by public reacti(
marketed thongs to 7- to 14-year-old girls. That led to protest grour
Web sites, such as www.boycott-af.com. Add outrage over A&F's mar
featuring gag slogans clearly offensive to Asian Americans and res
Virginia. Asian youth picketed A&F stores carrying placards urging customers ιο
"Throw out your trash. Don't wear clothes that bash." The governor of West Virginia wrote a letter to A&F's chairman protesting the company's stereotyping of
West Virginia as "a haven of incest." As protests increased nationwide, A&F
removed the controversial T-shirts from store shelves.[14]

These examples illustrate that organizations must attend to both public relations and marketing in order to achieve organizational goals. Each makes unique
but complementary contributions to building and maintaining the many relationships essential for organizational survival and growth. To ignore one is to risk failure
in the other.

PARTS OF THE FUNCTION

Some confuse public relations with its activities and parts. For example, many think
that "publicity" is simply another way of saying "public relations." Publicity is often
the most visible part, but seldom the only program tactic. Similarly, "lobbying" may
be the most noticeable public relations activity in Washington, D.C., and in state
capitals, but it usually is only one part of an overall public relations strategy. Likewise, employee communication may dominate in some organizations, but it represents the public relations effort within the organization that is necessary before
dealing with relationships outside the organization.

The contemporary meaning and practice of public relations includes all the following activities and specialties.

Internal Relations

Critical to the success of any organization, of course, are its employees. Before any
relationships can be maintained with customers, consumers, neighbors, investors,
and others outside the organization, management must attend to those who do the
work—the employees. Hence, CEOs in organizations talk about employees as their
"number one public" or as "the organization's most important asset," and they try to
create an "organizational culture" that attracts and retains productive workers. This
part of public relations practice is **internal relations.**

Internal relations specialists work in departments of "employee communication," "employee relations," or "internal relations." They plan and implement programs of internal communication to keep employees informed and motivated, and
to promote the organization's culture. According to Jon Iwata, senior vice president
of communications at IBM, "When we talk about employee communications, we

Internal relations is the specialized part of public relations that builds and maintains mutually beneficial relationships between managers and the employees on whom an organization's success depends.

really think of it in terms of corporate culture—how work gets done in our company, how we view things here." He points out that the CEO plays a critical role: "The CEO has to get his or her business to perform, and that is down to the workforce. The realization is that in order to drive any business results, the employees have to be with you...."[15]

According to Alvie Smith, former director of corporate communications at General Motors, two factors explain management's respect for this part of the public relations function:

1. The value of understanding, teamwork, and commitment by employees in achieving bottom-line results. These positive aspects of worker behavior are strongly influenced by effective, way-of-life interactive communications throughout the organization.

2. The need to build a strong manager–communication network, one that makes every supervisor at every level accountable for communicating effectively with his or her employees. This needs to be more than just job-related information and should include key business and public issues affecting the total organization.[16]

Newsletters have long dominated the practice of employee communication, but technology is changing the mode of delivering messages within organizations. At IBM, for example, the intranet has replaced the traditional coworker grapevine and immediate supervisor as the preferred and most credible source for employees.[17]

Internal relations staff work closely with the human resources department to communicate about benefits, training, safety, and other topics important to employees. They work with the legal department in communication related to labor relations during contract negotiations and work stoppages. And internal relations staff work with external relations staff to coordinate messages so the organization speaks with "one voice." (Chapter 9 discusses internal relations and employee communication in greater detail.)

Publicity

Much of the news and information in the media originates from public relations sources. Because the sources do not pay for the placement, however, they have little or no control over **if** the information is used, **when** it is used, and **how** it is used, or misused, by the media. Public relations sources provide what they judge to be newsworthy information, **publicity**, with the expectation that editors and reporters will use the information. Media decision makers may or may not use the information, based on their judgment of its news value and interest to their audiences. They may use the information as provided, change the original information, or change how it is presented, usually without identifying a publicity specialist as the original source. In the eyes of readers, listeners, or viewers, the medium carrying the information is the source.

Examples of publicity include a story in the financial section about increased earnings for a corporation, a photo and caption on the business page announcing a new product launch, a columnist's item on the progress of a charity fund-raising campaign, a feature story in the city magazine outlining the latest scientific findings from a cancer research center, an entertainment tabloid listing of the local concert of your favorite music group, and television news coverage of the new civic center

Publicity is information provided by an outside source that is used by the media because the information has news value. It is an *uncontrolled* method of placing messages in the media because the source does not pay the media for placement.

dedication ceremony. Typically, such stories came from the corporation's public relations department, the charitable organization's director of donor relations and development, the university medical school's news bureau, the music group's publicist, or the mayor's director of media relations (sometimes called press secretary).

Print media usually receive a press release, feature story with photographs, or press kit including detailed background information. Broadcast media typically receive a broadcast-style news script, recorded interview or "sound bites," video news release (VNR), or press kit including material suitable for broadcast (see Figure 1.2). To generate publicity, the source must know what information will attract media attention, identify a newsworthy angle and lead, and write and package the information appropriately for each medium. It also helps to have journalists think of you as a trustworthy news source.

Newsworthy **events** also generate publicity by attracting media coverage. Groundbreaking ceremonies, ribbon cuttings, open houses, reunions, dedications, telethons, marathons, ceremonial appointments, honorary degrees, contract and legislation signings, organized protests, press conferences, and other "media events" are designed to be "news." An amusement park makes news, for example, when the 500-millionth "guest" enters the park. Network news crews cover the president signing health-care reform legislation as leaders of health-care groups pose with him on the White House lawn. Those staging and managing such events hope to attract media coverage and to gain some control over what is reported. Successful publicity events have real news value; appeal to media gatekeepers; offer photo, video, or sound opportunities; and communicate the source's intended message.

The publicity model of practice also operates under the "public information" title. "Telling our story" remains one of the most frequently practiced models in practice. Many top managers and clients hire public relations specialists to secure

FIGURE 1.2

PUBLICITY MATERIALS

Courtesy Nuffer, Smith, Tucker, Inc., San Diego

media coverage that will put the organization in a favorable light. Those operating under the publicity model typically began their careers as journalists and use their understanding of the media to craft newsworthy messages and events that will attract media coverage.

Publicity produced by former journalists dominated public relations practice in its infancy, so it is not surprising that some still confuse publicity with the broader concept of public relations. There is much more to public relations than publicity, however.

Advertising

Unlike when using publicity, advertisers control content, placement, and timing by paying for media advertising time and space. Although both publicity and **advertising** are mediated communication, advertising gives the source control over content and placement.

Many associate advertising with marketing goods and services, but it is not limited to that purpose. Other parts of the organization also use this controlled means of placing messages in the mass media for nonmarketing purposes. For example, human resources departments place advertisements in newspaper classifieds and Sunday business sections to announce job openings. Legal departments place advertisements in "newspapers of record" to conform with public notification requirements when corporations issue new bonds or sell shares, when recalling a defective product, or when complying with a court settlement.

Public relations uses advertising to reach audiences other than the customers targeted by marketing. When Andersen Consulting changed its name to Accenture, the company placed advertisements in business publications announcing the new name. Investor relations at another company placed advertisements to assure stockholders and financial analysts that the corporation had thwarted a hostile takeover attempt. Advertisements announced that Boeing Company was moving corporate headquarters from Seattle to Chicago. The Embassy of Kuwait purchased full-page advertisements in major U.S. newspapers to announce that "America is our ally" and support for "the international effort to eradicate terrorism" following the 9/11 World Trade Center catastrophe. An aerospace company's community relations department placed an advertisement announcing its gift to the local symphony, yet not a single member of the intended audience buys the wing assemblies and air frames manufactured by the company. A local charity's public relations committee bought a full-page advertisement to thank contributors who funded a new center for the homeless. Merck & Company used advertising to announce its withdrawal of VIOXX™ from the market in 2004 (see Figure 1.3).

Mobil Oil (now Exxon Mobil) began the practice of using "advertorials" on op-ed pages and in magazines in 1970 "to speak out on a variety of issues designed to reach opinion makers."[18] According to Mobil's then–public relations vice president, Mobil's chairman wanted to make the company's positions on economic and political issues part of public debate. The advertisement did not sell Mobil products. The *Minnesota Law Review* described such corporate advertising as "a hybrid creature designed to use the means of paid advertising to accomplish the goals of PR."

Organizations use advertising for public relations purposes when they want to address criticism in the media—over which they have no control, when they feel that their point of view is not being reported fairly, when they feel that their publics do not understand the issues or are apathetic, or when they are trying to add their

> **Advertising is information placed in the media by an identified sponsor that pays for the time or space. It is a *controlled* method of placing messages in the media.**

**IMPORTANT INFORMATION
FOR PATIENTS TAKING VIOXX®(rofecoxib)**

 MERCK

September 30, 2004

Merck Voluntarily Withdraws VIOXX

Dear VIOXX Patient:

Merck & Co., Inc. announced today a voluntary withdrawal of VIOXX®

This decision is based on new data from a three-year clinical study. In this study, there was an increased risk for cardiovascular (CV) events, such as heart attack and stroke, in patients taking VIOXX 25 mg compared to those taking placebo (sugar pill). While the incidence of CV events was low, there was an increased risk beginning after 18 months of treatment. The cause of the clinical study result is uncertain, but our commitment to our patients is clear.

Patients who are currently taking VIOXX should contact their health care providers to discuss discontinuing use of VIOXX and possible alternative treatments. In addition, patients and health care professionals may obtain information from merck.com and vioxx.com or may call 1-888-368-4699.

Merck will reimburse all patients for their unused VIOXX. All dosage strengths and formulations of VIOXX are affected by this voluntary withdrawal. Information can be found at vioxx.com or at 1-888-368-4699.

Merck is notifying physicians and pharmacists and has informed the Food and Drug Administration of this decision.

We are taking this action because we believe it best serves the interests of patients. That is why we undertook this clinical trial to better understand the safety profile of VIOXX. And it's why we instituted this voluntary withdrawal upon learning about these data.

Be assured that Merck will continue to do everything we can to maintain the safety of our medicines.

Raymond V. Gilmartin,
Chairman, President & CEO

Please read the Patient Prescribing Information for VIOXX.

Where patients come first 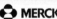 MERCK

Merck & Company, Inc.

voices to a cause. For example, Nike ran full-page newspaper advertisements denying that the company used unfair labor practices in its Asian factories. Advertising messages attempted to counter the critical news coverage of "Asian sweatshops" and to deflect attention from editorial criticism and ridicule by editorial cartoonists, including the *Doonesbury* cartoon strip. Subsequent advertisements reported the results of Ambassador Andrew Young's six-month investigation of Nike labor practices overseas.

In the final analysis, given adequate budget, *organizations use advertising to control content, placement, and timing for placing public relations messages in the media.*

Press Agentry

In *Walking the Tightrope*, the late Hollywood publicist Henry Rogers summarized the essence of press agentry, "When I first started, I was in the publicity business. I was a press agent. Very simply, my job was to get the client's name in the paper."[19] He candidly reported that he had lied to the West Coast editor of *Look* magazine about Rita Hayworth's "fabulous" wardrobe. The magazine devoted its cover and 10 pages of photographs to the then-relatively unknown actress and her hastily borrowed clothes. Following such attention in a major national magazine, she became the talk of Hollywood, and Columbia Pictures extended her contract. To the extent that mass media coverage confers status, Rita Hayworth's early stardom can be attributed in part to her press agent's lies about the size and worth of her wardrobe.

Press agents attempt to attract public notice more than to build public understanding. Publicity is their major strategy. They base their approach on agenda-setting theory, which says that the amount of mass media coverage subsequently determines public perception of the relative importance of topics and people. They attract attention through the practice of **press agentry.**

> **Press agentry is creating newsworthy stories and events to attract media attention and to gain public notice.**

And the press coverage does not have to be positive, according to some. For example, the Swedish pharmaceutical company Astra AB's announcement that it had fired the head of Astra USA operations and several other U.S. executives received wide media coverage. The fired executives had been charged with "an organized pattern of sexual harassment" and embezzlement! An Astra board member was quoted in the Swedish magazine *Maanadens Affaaerer* as having said of the publicity, "Of course it's not good with sex scandals, but in the United States this has helped us get out Astra's name without having to pay expensive advertising fees."[20] The *New York Times* quoted a spokesperson for Bruno Magli shoes—featured as evidence in the O. J. Simpson trial—taking a similar view of negative publicity, "It's certainly not the best way to get the name out there, but it's effective. Now we have a bigger audience of people who know about our shoes."[21]

Press agentry plays a major role in the music recording industry, professional sports, tourist attractions, motion picture studios, television, concert and theater performances, and business enterprises headed by celebrities. For example, press agents gave us the legends of Davy Crockett and Courtney Love; promoted the Indianapolis 500 Memorial Day auto race and the Super Bowl into national events; turned Miami Beach and Puerto Vallarta into internationally known resorts; positioned Florida's Disney World and Euro Disney as vacation destinations even before opening days; and made the *Spiderman* movies and each new Disney animated release must-see movies even before finishing the editing. Press agentry also is an important factor in political campaigns and national political party conventions attempting to build name recognition and attract voters through media exposure.

In the candid words of a veteran press agent, "We stoop to anything, but our stuff gets printed." And it can pay off. A musical group's earning power may be as much a tribute to the skill of its press agent to get publicity as to its musical abilities. A career-launching appearance on a popular talk show may reflect the work of a press agent more than the talent of the guest. Likewise, a good press agent can make a new club or restaurant the "in place" even before a single customer experiences the ambiance, food, or entertainment of the place itself. A favorable review by a restaurant reviewer or entertainment critic may jump-start a new bistro or band. For example, the young press agent who worked for a struggling band later admitted that he reported that the band "sold 50,000 albums this week when I knew it was 5,000, but it made a better story."[22] By the way, the "struggling band" was the Beatles.

There are full-time press agents, or celebrity publicists, but many public relations practitioners have used press agentry tactics at some time or another to attract media attention to their clients, causes, or organizations. This was the case when Internet portal designer Verity, Inc., hired Edelman PR Worldwide "to raise our visibility." There is more to public relations than press agentry, however.

Confusion results when press agents describe what they do as "public relations" or use that term to give their agencies more prestigious, but less-accurate, titles. Hence, many journalists mistakenly refer to all public relations practitioners as "flacks," even though the *Associated Press Stylebook* defines "flack" as "slang for press agent." In fact, consumer press writers often use "flak" or "flack" when referring to public relations people (30 percent of 1,350 articles in one study). Only "spin doctor" was used more often—in 56 percent of the stories.[23]

Public Affairs

The armed services, many governmental agencies, and some corporations use the title "public affairs" as a substitute for public relations. In the military and government, this title is part of a name game dating back to the 1913 Gillett Amendment to an appropriation bill in the U.S. House of Representatives. The amendment stipulates that federal agencies cannot spend money for **publicity** unless specifically authorized by Congress. This legislative hostility was reaffirmed in Public Law 93–50, Section 305, enacted July 1, 1973. This law expressly prohibits government spending on "publicity or propaganda purposes designed to support or defeat legislation pending before the Congress." Historian J. A. R. Pimlott concluded that limitations imposed on government public relations "springs from the fear lest programs undertaken in the name of administrative efficiency should result in an excessive concentration of power in the Executive."[24]

Neither the 1913 amendment nor the 1973 law actually refers to public relations. Nevertheless, many federal, state, and local governmental officials apparently confuse publicity with the larger concept of public relations. As a result, governmental agencies typically use other terms to describe building and maintaining relationships with their constituents. It is nothing more than a label switch, however, as thousands of public relations specialists work in local, state, and federal government under titles such as "public affairs," "public information," "communications," "constituent relations," and "liaison."

Recognizing the obvious need for building and maintaining relations with citizens, beginning in the Johnson administration, the federal government created Federal Information Centers (now Federal Citizen Information Centers) to give citizens a single place to get information about federal programs and services. As summarized by Mordecai Lee:

First, they perform a marketing function, helping increase the utilization of public-sector services and products. Second, as a medium for answering questions about the federal government that aren't related to obtaining a service, FICs accomplish democratic accountability to the public. They contribute to an informed citizenry, the sine qua non of democracy.[25]

In corporations, "public affairs" typically refers to public relations efforts related to public policy and "corporate citizenship." Corporate public affairs specialists serve as liaisons with governmental units; implement community improvement programs; encourage political activism, campaign contributions, and voting; and volunteer their services in charitable and community development organizations (see Figure 1.4). Hewlett-Packard's public affairs department states its mission as to "shape public policy to foster an environment that allows HP to achieve its business objectives."[26] Likewise, public relations counseling firms use the public affairs label for their lobbying and governmental relations services.

A public affairs specialist described the relationship between public relations and public affairs as follows: "**Public affairs** is the public relations practice that addresses public policy and the publics who influence such policy."[27] An association executive based in Washington, D.C., defined public affairs as "PR tactics applied to GR (government relations) strategies to produce 'excellent public policy.'"[28] A survey of public affairs officers identified major public affairs responsibilities as including (in descending order) federal government affairs, state government affairs, local government affairs, community relations, political action committees, contributions, grassroots support, and issues management. Forty-three percent of their departments use the title "public affairs." Other public affairs specialists operate in departments called "corporate affairs," "corporate relations," "government relations," and "external affairs."[29]

Growing interest in public affairs parallels high turnover in government, changes in communication, increasing importance of state and local governments, and a more complex regulatory environment. For example, term limits imposed on elected officials and voter dissatisfaction with those in office produced unprecedented levels of turnover in all levels of government. Turnover increases the power of staff members, who often outlast the elected officials they serve, and increases the need to provide information to newly elected officials. The Internet, 24-hour news channels, C-SPAN, and satellite links worldwide give constituencies instant access to events around the globe. As one public affairs practitioner observed, "Before C-SPAN, the only people who got to see the action on the House floor were high school seniors and a few ambitious tourists."[30] In short, public affairs work occurs in an increasingly complex and democratic environment, leading to a major role for public relations in the formulation of public policy.

Lobbying

Lobbying, an even more specialized—and criticized—part of public affairs, attempts to influence legislative and regulatory decisions in government. Even though the U.S. Constitution protects the right to petition the government, some view lobbying as an attempt to manipulate government for selfish ends. Movies and television programs depicting smoke-filled rooms and payoffs by lobbyists working for powerful corporate and special interests perpetuate this cynical view of lobbying. News stories sometimes report illegal or questionable cash contributions to legislators, lavish fundraising parties, and hosted weekends at exotic golf resorts. However, lobbying more often takes the form of open advocacy and discussion on matters of public policy.

Public affairs is a specialized part of public relations that builds and maintains governmental and local community relations in order to influence public policy.

Lobbying is a specialized part of public relations that builds and maintains relations with government primarily for the purpose of influencing legislation and regulation.

Public Affairs Job Description

FIGURE 1.4

PUBLIC AFFAIRS JOB DESCRIPTION

Public Affairs Managers

Times Mirror Cable Television, one of the largest multi-cable systems in the nation, has maintained its commitment to bring quality entertainment and services to the marketplace. This continued demand for excellence coupled with new growth has created 3 additional openings for Public Affairs Managers.

The successful candidates will work with field management to develop and implement broad-based public affairs programs at subsidiary cable TV systems nationwide. Other responsibilities will include insuring franchise compliance, producing press releases and other media, developing and implementing strategies to resolve regulatory problems, and conducting a community relations program. In addition, to be effective in this position, it is crucial that applicants are willing to work in a staff support role.

For this position, we are seeking public policy-oriented individuals with a BA degree and a minimum of 5 years direct hands-on experience in at least 2 of the following: government relations, public relations, community affairs or the cable industry. Grad work and/or a law degree would be a definite plus. Other requirements include: strong oral and written communications skills as well as knowledge of local government and/or public sector regulatory functions.

We are a subsidiary of The Times Mirror Company and offer an attractive compensation and benefits package including free dental insurance and a company paid pension plan. If you are a talented, assertive and skilled professional, we encourage you to explore our career opportunities. For immediate consideration, please send your resume and salary requirements to the **Human Resources Department, Times Mirror Cable Television, P.O. Box 19398, Irvine, CA 92713. (No phone calls please.)**

TIMES MIRROR CABLE TELEVISION

We are an equal opportunity employer and encourage women and minorities to apply.

Courtesy Times Mirror Cable Television

Courtesy Times Mirror Cable Television

Registration laws and their enforcement vary from state to state, but all who engage in lobbying the U.S. Congress are required to report their activities and expenditures under the Federal Regulation of Lobbying Act (see Chapter 6). Despite occasional abuse and public rebuke, lobbying remains a legal and accepted way for citizen groups, associations, labor unions, corporations, and other special-interest groups to influence government decision making. Although clearly labeled and monitored at national and state levels, similar lobbying efforts on county and municipal issues often are part of and undifferentiated from public affairs, community relations, or other public relations efforts.

Lobbyists at all levels of government must understand the legislative process, know how government functions, and be acquainted with individual lawmakers and officials. Because these are not part of many public relations practitioners' educational preparation, lobbyists typically have backgrounds as well-connected lawyers, governmental administrators, elected officials' important staff members, or other insiders with good relationships with governmental decision makers. In fact, critics of "the public–private revolving door" say that lobbyists "cash in" on the access and credibility they earned while working in government to work for special interests.

The number of lobbyists has increased dramatically. One directory lists more than 32,000 individuals and almost 3,000 firms who represent more than 29,000 domestic and foreign businesses, trade associations, unions, and other advocacy groups.[31] A Washington watchdog group estimates that lobbyists spend an average of more than $3 million per legislator lobbying Congress.[32]

In practice, lobbying must be closely coordinated with other public relations efforts directed toward nongovernmental publics. Sophisticated lobbyists mobilize like-minded constituents so that their voices will be heard by lawmakers and officials in government. Computerized mailing lists, high-speed printers, and software for individualizing letters can produce a flood of mail, phone calls, faxes, and personal visits from constituents. Customized e-mail address lists; online news groups, forums, and blogs; and "blast" or broadcast faxing provide even faster ways to mobilize constituents.

Getting the folks "back home" to take up the cause is referred to as "grassroots lobbying" and is part of many coordinated public relations efforts to influence public policy. In some cases, however, responses actually come from "front" groups created to deceive or mislead policy makers about public sentiment on the issue at hand. Some refer to these pseudo-grassroots movements as "Astroturf lobbying." Examples of such front groups include "Citizens for Riverboat Gambling," funded by a gambling organization trying to pass a local referendum, and numerous "pro-gun ownership "grassroots networks" formed by National Rifle Association of America (NRA) members at the encouragement of the NRA's lobbying arm, the Institute for Legislative Action. Such front organizations are designed to give the appearance of widespread citizen support, when in reality they were created by their sponsors to promote narrow interests.

In its primary roles as credible advocate and reliable source of information, however, lobbying takes the form of information designed to educate and persuade (see Exhibit 1.2). Lobbyists succeed or fail in part based on their traditional public relations skills—researching legislators' positions on issues and information needs, and communicating persuasive information to government officials, to grassroots constituencies, and to their clients. In addition to those abilities, lobbyists need sophisticated knowledge of government, legislative process, public policy, and public opinion. Stereotypical images of the cigar-chomping insider dispensing stacks of cash no longer apply to most lobbyists and their work:

> Indeed, lobbyists spend substantially more time collecting information from government than they do communicating to it, since sound lobbying strategies, tactics, and positions are highly dependent on a strong base of information.[33]

Lobbying is an outgrowth of our democratic system in a pluralistic society, keeping government open to those affected by proposed legislation and govern-

EXHIBIT 1.2

LOBBYING

"Lobbying involves much more than persuading legislators. Its principal elements include researching and analyzing legislation or regulatory proposals; monitoring and reporting on developments; attending congressional or regulatory hearings; working with coalitions interested in the same issues; and then educating not only government officials but also employees and corporate officers as to the implications of various changes. What most lay people regard as lobbying— the actual communication with government officials— represents the smallest portion of a lobbyist's time; a far greater proportion is devoted to the other aspects of preparation, information and communication."

American League of Lobbyists, Alexandria, VA
(www.alldc.org/resources.htm)

ment regulation. In Washington, D.C., and state capitals, the role of lobbying and other public affairs efforts will play increasingly important roles in formulating and implementing public policy. The challenge continues to be how to more effectively regulate campaign finance and lobbying. In the end, however, the role of lobbyists remains to ethically present the interests of their clients in the public policy debate.

Issues Management

Two points capture the essence of **issues management:** (1) early identification of issues with potential impact on an organization, and (2) a strategic response designed to mitigate or capitalize on their consequences. For example, in the context of public opinion, issues management "attempts to discern trends in public opinion so that an organization can respond to them before they amplify into serious conflict.[34]"

As originally conceived by the late public relations consultant W. Howard Chase in 1976, issues management includes identifying issues, analyzing issues, setting priorities, selecting program strategies, implementing programs of action and communication, and evaluating effectiveness. He said the process "aligns corporate principles, policies and practices to the realities of a politicized economy."[35] More recently, Chase defined issues management as the process of closing the "gap between corporate action and stakeholder expectation."[36] A panel of experts expanded the definition to include:

> ...anticipating, researching and prioritizing issues; assessing the impact of issues on the organization; recommending policies and strategies to minimize risk and seize opportunities, participating and implementing strategy; evaluating program impact."[37]

Even though issues management was originally touted as a new approach that would give practitioners elevated status, many do not see it as anything different from what they already do. Others express concern that the term suggests something unlikely and unacceptable because it sets up visions of manipulation—that an organization can "manage" major public issues. Many major corporations, however, have created issues management units or "task forces," either by establishing specialized sections or by renaming existing sections of the public relations department. They focus on how to respond to public concerns about terrorism, deregulation, offshore "outsourcing,"

Issues management is the proactive process of anticipating, identifying, evaluating, and responding to public policy issues that affect organizations' relationships with their publics.

globalization, biotechnology (genetic engineering), global warming, toxic waste disposal, managed care, an aging population, and corporate influence in politics.

Conceptually, if not always administratively, issues management is part of the public relations function. When viewed merely as persuasive communication, however, it becomes a tactic to influence public policy, not part of an organization's strategic planning. When concerned with adjusting the organization and building relationships with stakeholders to achieve mutual goals, "public relations and issues management are quite similar and result in similar outcomes."[38]

Investor Relations

> **Investor relations** is a specialized part of corporate public relations that builds and maintains mutually beneficial relationships with shareholders and others in the financial community to maximize market value.

Also referred to as "IR" and "financial relations," **investor relations** is another specialized part of public relations in publicly held corporations. Investor relations specialists work to enhance the value of a company's stock. This reduces the cost of capital by increasing shareholder confidence and by making the stock attractive to individual investors, financial analysts, and institutional investors.

Investor relations specialists keep shareholders informed and loyal to a company in order to maintain a fair valuation of a company's stock. Their work involves tracking market trends, providing information to financial publics, counseling management, and responding to requests for financial information. Annual and quarterly reports, SEC-required 10-K forms, e-mailed earnings reports, and home page links to "material" financial information are methods used to disseminate timely information to analysts, investors, and the financial press. Here is an example of how it works to benefit both a company and its investors:

A new biotechnology company has 10 million shares outstanding, with each share selling for $20. This means the company has a "market capitalization" of $200 million. Assume that the stock becomes more attractive to institutional investors, financial analysts, and individual investors as they learn more about the company's products, its management, "financials," and plans. If the share price increases to $25, the market value of the company increases to $250 million! Now assume that the company needs $10 million to pursue research on promising new products. At $25 a share, it needs to sell only 400,000 company-held shares, versus 500,000 shares at $20, to raise the $10 million to finance the research. Not only are investors' holdings worth more, but it also takes fewer shares to raise additional capital.

On the other hand, consider what happens to the value of stockholder investments and the cost of new capital when a corporation loses shareholder confidence, fails to respond to analysts' concerns about the latest quarterly earnings report, or receives negative coverage in the financial press. For example, when Compaq Computer merged with Hewlett-Packard, H-P stock lost almost one fifth of its premerger value and Compaq stock fell about 10 percent. Some specialists criticized how the investor relations staffs had failed to address investors' concerns that had been extensively reported in the financial press before the rumored merger.

Investor relations specialists must know corporate finance, accounting, Wall Street, international equities trading (the Tokyo Stock Exchange is the world's largest), international business trends, business journalism, and much more. Most of all, however, they must know Securities and Exchange Commission and stock exchange financial reporting requirements. These requirements became much more rigorous in 2002 with the passage of the Sarbanes–Oxley Act. Passed on the heels of corporate scandals (Enron, WorldCom, HealthSouth, Imclone, and Martha Stewart Living Omnimedia, to name just a few), this act requires disclosure "on a rapid and current basis" of "material information" that might be useful to investors and others. "Public relations practitioners who do not have solid training and experience in business, management, and law will apparently be unable to fill even entry level positions in investor relations," according to researchers who studied CEO perceptions of the function.[39]

As a result, those aspiring to careers in investor relations should combine studies in public relations with coursework in finance and business law. An MBA degree is often necessary preparation (see Figure 1.5). It also helps to know more than one language, to study economics and corporate finance, to be widely traveled, and to have studied the rapidly changing international political scene. Corporations and investor relations specialists increasingly deal in a global economy. Because few practitioners have the required background in corporate finance and the competition for those who do is great, investor relations practitioners are among the highest paid in public relations.

Finance

INVESTOR RELATIONS

The Titan Corporation, a high-tech San Diego-based NYSE company, is currently seeking a seasoned professional to manage the company's investor relations programs. Reporting to the CEO, the successful candidate must be able to effectively communicate company information to all audiences, including shareholders, brokers, analysts, media and employees. Responsibilities include: liaison to the financial community; preparation of financial press releases; assisting CEO with shareholder and road show meetings; development and distribution of investor materials and company story; review of SEC filings; and maintenance of current shareholder, mailing and fax lists.

The ideal candidate will possess 10 years' direct experience in investor relations and corporate communications, excellent verbal/written communication skills, ability to deal with Board of Directors and Executive Staff, computer skills, and the highest standards of ethics and integrity. MBA preferred.

In return for your expertise, we offer an excellent salary and benefits package, including bonus and stock option programs. To take advantage of this excellent opportunity, please submit resume, including salary history in confidence to: The Titan Corporation, 3033 Science Park Rd., San Diego, CA 92121. Fax (619) 552-9745, Via E-mail to: resumes@titan.com We are an equal opportunity employer.

http://www.titan.com

TITAN
Technology for Changing Times

FIGURE 1.5

INVESTOR RELATIONS JOB DESCRIPTION

Courtesy Titan Corporation, San Diego

Development

Just as investor relations helps finance publicly held corporations, fund-raising and membership drives provide the financial support needed to operate charitable and nonprofit organizations. These organizations typically use the title **"development"** or "advancement" for this aspect of public relations. Nonprofit hospitals, social welfare groups, disease research foundations, service charities, and universities have directors of development. Organizations that rely on membership fees for some or all of their revenues—museums, zoos, theaters, symphony orchestras, professional societies, unions, trade associations, and citizen-action groups—often have a "director of member services and development."

Development specialists work for public broadcasting stations, disease research foundations, community arts groups, museums and zoos, youth clubs, universities, special-interest groups, and religious organizations. Because these groups depend on donations, membership fees, or a combination of the two, they rely heavily on annual campaigns and special events to call attention to their needs and to solicit public support and contributions.

An annual telethon, 10K run, open house, homecoming, and celebrity auction, however, represent only a few of the activities in a yearlong program to establish and maintain relationships with volunteers, alumni, members, and donors, as well as prospective members and donors. Fund-raising activities and membership services make up a major part of the overall program. This makes development a significant part of the larger management function—public relations—in nonprofit organizations.

CONFUSION OF TERMS

The terms discussed in the preceding sections all deal with various organizations' relationships with specific groups or publics. They are all parts of the broader organizational management function known as public relations. Some organizations divide the function on the basis of **internal** and **external** publics. Internal relations deals with publics concerned about or involved in the internal workings of the organization, such as employees, families of employees, and volunteers. Relations with publics outside the organization—neighbors, consumers, environmentalists, investors, and so forth—are the responsibility of external relations.

Title confusion is further complicated when the total function is given one of many other labels such as corporate relations, corporate communications, university advancement, hospital relations, public affairs, and public information. Whatever name is used, the basic concept and function of public relations are similar from one organization to the next—large or small, local or global. **All effective organizations establish and maintain relationships identified as important to survival and growth.**

In practice, however, too often employers and clients define public relations narrowly or wrongly by the various tasks they assign to it. In one organization, public relations takes the form of candid, open communication with many publics. In another, it attempts to maintain a silent, low profile. In one organization the purpose can be to provoke controversy and to maintain an adversarial relationship that motivates and activates members. In yet another, public relations tries to reconcile and compromise with an important public; for example, management may attempt to reconcile differences with a labor union.

Likewise, practitioners define public relations every day by the limits of what they do and by what they call "public relations." For example, many do product publicity because that is what they are paid to do under the rubric of public relations. Others see it as "getting ink" or "hits" (exposure in the mass media), because that is their experience as former journalists now attempting to be public relations practitioners.

Concerned citizens see frequent references to "PR," "public relations," and "flacks" in press coverage of oil spills, industrial toxic waste leaks, political campaign shenanigans, city hall corruption, and so forth. Movies and television programs featuring public relations practitioners do not present accurate portrayals. Media coverage seldom associates public relations with positive stories of organizations and their accomplishments. Books such as *PR! A Social History of Spin* and *Toxic Sludge Is Good for You* selectively report post hoc analyses of press agentry and advocacy on behalf of clients and causes later proven to be of dubious merit. There is little market for books that report all the good work done by public relations on behalf of clients and causes judged to be worthy of public support, such as raising public awareness of cancer prevention and detection. In other words, it depends on whose side you are on, much as it depends on which side lawyers represent in controversial cases.

In short, most people know public relations by what they see organizations and practitioners do, or by what media report as "public relations." Few study the concept itself or the roles public relations plays in organizations and society. The challenge for practitioners is to define and perform public relations in ways consistent with the contemporary meaning of this necessary organizational and social function.

TOWARD RECOGNITION AND MATURITY

Some scholars credit public relations for the heightened attention to public accountability and social responsibility among government administrators and business executives (see Exhibit 1.3 on page 24). Others point to the function's role in making organizations responsive to public interests and to its contribution to the public information system that is essential to a democratic society and organizational survival. For example, *PRWeek* reported corporate social responsibility (CSR) as essential to organizational survival:

> The new era of transparency is part of an offshoot movement in CSR that's been dubbed "sustainability." Sustainability proponents argue that companies that are consistently indifferent to their impact on the environment and its various stakeholders—such as employees and customers—are threatening their own long-term sustainability.[40]

As the dust jacket of *The Naked Corporation: How the Age of Transparency Will Revolutionize Business* says, "If you have to be naked, you had better be buff.[41]"

EXHIBIT 1.3

PUBLIC RELATIONS IN THE TYLENOL CRISES

Lawrence G. Foster
Corporate Vice President—
Public Relations (retired)
Johnson & Johnson

A different form of terrorism was unleashed on America in 1982 with the grim news of cyanide-laced Tylenol poisonings in the Chicago area. Seven people died. Because the extent of the contamination was not immediately known, there was grave concern for the safety of the estimated 100 million Americans who were using Tylenol.

The first critical public relations decision, taken immediately and with total support from company management, was to cooperate fully with the news media. The press was key to warning the public of the danger. The poisonings also called for immediate action to protect the consumer, so the decision was made to recall two batches of the product and later to withdraw it from store shelves nationally.

During the crisis phase of the Tylenol tragedy, virtually every public relations decision was based on sound, socially responsible business principles, which is when public relations is most effective.

Johnson & Johnson's corporate Credo strongly influenced many of the key decisions. Robert Wood Johnson, son of the company founder and, at the time, chairman of the company, wrote the one-page Credo in 1943. The Credo lists four responsibilities. The customer is placed first and foremost, followed by responsibility to employees, to the communities where they work and live, and finally, responsibility to the stockholders. (See complete Credo in Chapter 12.)

At Johnson & Johnson, Lawrence G. Foster, Corporate Vice President of Public Relations, reported directly to Chairman and CEO James E. Burke, who promptly formed a seven-member strategy committee to deal with the crisis. Foster and five other senior executives on the committee met with Burke twice daily for the next six weeks to make key decisions, ranging from advertising strategy and network television interviews to planning Tylenol's comeback in tamper-resistant packaging.

In the weeks following the murders, Foster and his three senior staff members, all former journalists, responded to more than 2,500 calls from the press. They were helped by the smaller public relations staff at McNeil Consumer Products (manufacturers of Tylenol). While the corporate staff was dealing with the press, Burson-Marsteller, which had the product publicity account for Tylenol, began planning a unique 30-city video press conference via satellite to reintroduce the product. Polls showed that 90 percent of Americans did not fault the company, and 79 percent said they would again purchase Tylenol. The satellite relaunch took place in just six weeks. Later, sales of Tylenol began soaring to new highs.

The *Washington Post* wrote: "Johnson & Johnson has effectively demonstrated how a major business ought to handle a disaster."

The unthinkable happened four years later. A woman in Westchester County, New York, died after ingesting a Tylenol capsule that contained cyanide. A second contaminated bottle was found in a nearby store a few days later. Chairman Burke reconvened the strategy committee, and the Credo was at the center of the discussions. The next day, Johnson & Johnson announced that, henceforth, no J&J company worldwide would market any over-the-counter capsule product because the safety of customers could no longer be assured, even when the capsules were in the new safety packaging. The public made Tylenol caplets a best seller soon after, and to this day Johnson & Johnson has kept its pledge not to market an over-the-counter capsule product anywhere in the world.

Once again, Robert Wood Johnson's Credo had shown the way. The Tylenol tragedies demonstrated that public relations is a business of basics and that the best public relations decisions are closely linked to sound business practices and a socially responsible corporate philosophy.[42]

—Courtesy Lawrence G. Foster
Corporate Vice President—Public Relations (retired)
Johnson & Johnson

Public relations deserves credit for establishing and sustaining the connection between public support and organizational management's heightened attention to social responsibility and to leadership in personal standards of behavior. As one business leader long ago said:

> We know perfectly well that business does not function by divine right, but, like any other part of society, exists with the sanction of the community as a whole....Today's public opinion, though it may appear as light as air, may become tomorrow's legislation for better or worse.[43]

Public relations also helps organizations anticipate and respond to public perceptions and opinions, to new values and lifestyles, to power shifts among the electorate and within legislative bodies, and to other changes in the environment. This dialogue contributes to making the democratic process—as well as the social, economic, and political systems—more effective in meeting social needs. Without effective public relations, organizations tend to become insensitive to changes occurring around them and to become dysfunctional as they grow increasingly out of step with their environments.

Public relations also makes information available through the public information system. Practitioners increase public knowledge and understanding by promoting expression and debate in the competitive marketplace of ideas regarding, for example, the need for health-care reform, the causes of global warming, the value of a new public transportation system, the impact of international trade barriers, or the need for blood and organ donations. Public relations serves the public interest by providing a voice in the public forum for alternative points of view, including the views of those—such as the homeless and powerless—who would not otherwise be heard because of limited media attention.

The practice serves society by mediating conflict and by building the consensus needed to maintain social order. Its social function—its mission—is accomplished when it replaces ignorance, coercion, and intransigence with knowledge, compromise, and adjustment. In other words, ***public relations* facilitates adjustment and maintenance in the social systems that provide us with our physical and social needs.**

In the final analysis, an organization's relationships are the responsibility of top management. As public relations counselor Henry DeVries rephrased our definition of public relations, "Public relations is the boss's job to build and keep strong bonds with key groups that the organization needs to grow and thrive." Once this concept of public relations is embraced at the top, it spreads and becomes part of an organization's culture.

In the short term, the policies and activities of employers, clients, and practitioners often define the day-to-day practice. The evolution of the concept and the professional calling, however, reflects the changing needs of organizations adjusting to multicultural, global environments. In its advanced form, the function responds to long-term social needs, not to immediate special interests. As practitioners accept their social responsibility and act accordingly, others will understand and value public relations' contributions to organizations and society.

Public relations professionals who help organizations establish and maintain mutually beneficial relationships perform an essential management function that has an impact on the larger society. They encourage social responsibility in organizations and promote public relations' essential role in maintaining social order. Inherent in this concept of public relations is a moral commitment to mutual adjustment among interdependent elements of society. That calling motivates the following chapters.

NOTES

[1] John Stauber and Sheldon Rampton, *Toxic Sludge Is Good for You! Lies, Damn Lies and the Public Relations Industry* (Monroe, ME: Common Courage Press, 1995), 2.

[2] Thomas J. Madden, *Spin Man: The Topsy-Turvy World of Public Relations...a Tell-All Tale* (Boca Raton, FL: TransMedia Publishing, Inc., 1997), 1.

[3] Stuart Ewen, *PR! A Social History of Spin* (New York: Basic Books, 1996), viii.

[4] Edward L. Bernays, *Propaganda* (New York: Horace Liveright, 1928), 9–10, as quoted by Larry Tye in *The Father of Spin: Edward L. Bernays & the Birth of Public Relations* (New York: Crown Publishers, Inc., 1998), 92.

[5] James E. Grunig and Todd Hunt, *Managing Public Relations* (New York: Holt, Rinehart and Winston, 1984), 6.

[6] Harwood L. Childs, *An Introduction to Public Opinion* (New York: John Wiley and Sons, 1940), 3, 13.

[7] Rex F. Harlow, "Building a Public Relations Definition," *Public Relations Review* 2, no. 4 (Winter 1976): 36.

[8] Joye C. Gordon, "Interpreting Definitions of Public Relations: Self Assessment and a Symbolic Interactionism-Based Alternative," *Public Relations Review* 23, no. 1 (Spring 1997): 57–66.

[9] Thomas L. Harris, *The Marketer's Guide to Public Relations* (New York: John Wiley and Sons, 1991), 12. This book is not about public relations. Rather, it describes how public relations practitioners apply their knowledge and skills to support marketing.

[10] Paul Holmes, "To Overcome Its Identity Crisis, the Industry Has to Define and Defend 'Public Relations.'" *PRWeek*, 17 March 2003, 9.

[11] Al Ries and Laura Ries, *The Fall of Advertising & the Rise of PR* (New York: Harper-Collins Publishers, Inc., 2002), 129.

[12] Philip Kotler, *Marketing Management*, 11th ed. (Upper Saddle River, NJ: Prentice Hall, 2003), 12.

[13] Miriam Jordan, "Nestlé Markets Baby Formula to Hispanic Mothers in U.S.," *Wall Street Journal*, 4 March 2004, www.breastfeedingtaskforla.org/media/WSJ%2003%2004%2004%20Nestle%20Formula.pdf.

[14] Associated Press, "West Virginia governor seeks halt of Abercrombie T-shirts," *USA Today,* 23 March 2004, http://www.usatoday.com/news/nation/2003-03-23-tshirts_x.htm. See also "Offensive Ads," *USA Today*, 15 September 2003, www.usatoday.com/news/opinion/editorials/2003-09-15-edit_x.htm.

[15] "Employee Comms Vital to How IBM's Work Gets Done," *PRWeek*, 17 May 2004, 7.

[16] Alvie L. Smith in letter to authors, March 28, 1993.

[17] "Employee Comms Vital," 7.

[18] Gerri L. Smith and Robert L. Heath, "Moral Appeals in Mobil Oil's Op-Ed Campaign," *Public Relations Review* 16, no. 4 (Winter 1990): 49.

[19] Henry C. Rogers, *Walking the Tightrope: The Private Confessions of a Public Relations Man* (New York: William Morrow, 1980), 14.

[20] Associated Press, "Astra Exec Fired in Sex, Theft Scandal," *San Diego Union-Tribune*, 27 June 1996, Business Section, 2.

[21] "A Shoe-In for Product Publicity," *Public Relations Tactics*, 4, no. 1 (January 1997), 3.

[22] Robert Barr (Associated Press), "King of the Tabloid Publicists Usually Holds the Smoking Gun," *San Diego Union-Tribune*, 1 January 2000, A-33.

[23] "Preach What We Practice," *PRWeek*, 18 February 2002, 21.

[24] J. A. R. Pimlott, *Public Relations and American Democracy* (Princeton, NJ: Princeton University Press, 1951/1972), 76.

[25] Mordecai Lee, "A Public Relations Program Even Congress Could Love: Federal Information Centers," *Public Relations Review* 30, no. 1 (March 2004): 62.

[26] Raymond L. Hoewing, "The State of Public Affairs: A Profession Reinventing Itself," in *Practical Public Affairs in an Era of Change*, ed. Lloyd B. Dennis (Lanham, MD: University Press of America, 1996), 45.

[27] John L. Paluszek, "Editorial Note: Defining Terms," in *Practical Public Affairs*, xviii.

[28] Rich Long, "PR and GR: So Happy Together?" *The Public Relations Strategist* 8, no. 3 (Summer 2002), 17.

[29] Hoewing, "The State of Public Affairs," 34.

[30] Long, "PR and GR: So Happy Together?" 16.

[31] *Federal Lobby Directory* (Online), PoliticalMoneyLine®, Washington, DC, politicalmoneyline.com/cgi-win/lb_directory.exe?DoFn=, (July 6, 2004).

[32] "How the Feds Stack Up," The Center for Public Integrity (Online),15 May 2003, www.publicintegrity.org/hiredguns/printer-friendly.aspx?aid=167, (July 6, 2004).

[33] Charles S. Mack, "Lobbying and Political Action," in *Practical Public Affairs*, 105.

[34] Priscilla Murphy, "Chaos Theory as a Model for Managing Issues and Crises," *Public Relations Review* 22, no. 2 (Summer 1996): 103.

[35] W. Howard Chase, "Public Issue Management: The New Science," *Public Relations Journal* 33, no. 10 (October 1977): 25–26.

[36] W. Howard Chase and Teresa Yancey Crane, "Issue Management: Dissolving the Archaic Division between Line and Staff," in *Practical Public Affairs*, 130–31.

[37] Kerry Tucker and Glen Broom, "Managing Issues Acts as Bridge to Strategic Planning," *Public Relations Journal* 49, no. 11 (November 1993): 38–40.

[38] Martha M. Lauzen, "Understanding the Relation between Public Relations and Issues Management," *Journal of Public Relations Research* 9, no. 1 (1997): 80. For a theoretical basis of issues management, see Robert L. Heath, *Strategic Issues Management: Organizations and Public Policy Challenges* (Thousand Oaks, CA: Sage Publications, Inc., 1997).

[39] Barbara K. Petersen and Hugh J. Martin, "CEO Perceptions of Investor Relations as a Public Relations Function: An Exploratory Study," *Journal of Public Relations Research* 8, no. 3 (1996): 205–6.

[40] "CSR: Beyond Lip Service," *PRWeek*, 6 January 2003, 17.

[41] Don Tapscott and David Ticoll, *The Naked Corporation: How the Age of Transparency Will Revolutionize Business* (New York: The Free Press, 2003).

[42] For more detailed discussion of the Tylenol crises, see Lawrence G. Foster, "Tylenol: 20 Years Later," *The Public Relations Strategist* 8, Issue 4 (Fall 2002), 16–20; and Foster's *Robert Wood Johnson: The Gentleman Rebel* (Ashland, OH: Lillian Press, 1999).

[43] Quote from former General Electric Company President Ralph J. Cordiner, as reported in Scott M. Cutlip and Allen H. Center, *Effective Public Relations*, 2nd ed. (Upper Saddle River, NJ: Prentice Hall, 1958), 6.`

ADDITIONAL SOURCES

Center, Allen H., and Patrick Jackson. *Public Relations Practices: Managerial Case Studies and Problems*, 6th ed. Upper Saddle River, NJ: Prentice Hall, 2003. Collection of classic case studies illustrating management problems and opportunities in public relations.

Grunig, James E., ed. *Excellence in Public Relations and Communication Management*. Hillsdale, NJ: Lawrence Erlbaum Associates, 1992. Influential summary of public relations theory and research literature produced with the support of International Association of Business Communicators (IABC) Research Foundation.

Grunig, Larissa A., James E. Grunig, and David M. Dozier. *Excellent Public Relations and Effective Organizations: A Study of Communication Management in Three Countries*. Mahwah, NJ: Lawrence Erlbaum Associates, 2002. The third in the series of "excellence study" reports.

Kelly, Kathleen S. *Effective Fund-Raising Management*. Mahwah, NJ: Lawrence Erlbaum Associates, 1997. Introduces history, theory, ethics, legal issues, and techniques of expanding practice of fund-raising and development in not-for-profit settings.

Kotler, Philip. *Marketing Management*, 11th ed. Upper Saddle River, NJ: Prentice Hall, 2003. A marketing expert's view of public relations as one of "four promotional tools."

Lattimore, Dan, Otis Baskin, Suzette T. Heiman, Elizabeth L. Toth, and James K. Van Leuven. *Public Relations: The Profession and the Practice*. New York: McGraw-Hill, 2004. Recent addition to the list of useful introductory textbooks for the field.

Newsom, Doug, Judy VanSlyke Turk, and Dean Kruckeberg. *This Is PR: The Realities of Public Relations*, 7th ed. Belmont, CA: Wadsworth /Thomson Learning, 2000. Another useful introduction to the field.

Schultz, Don, and Heidi Schultz. *IMC: The Next Generation* (New York: McGraw-Hill, 2003). Updates and expands concept of integrated marketing communication (IMC), but reaffirms IMC's focus on **customers** and **prospects** (pp. 48 and 69) and "a customer-centric organization" (p. 52)—in other words, **marketing**.

White, Jon, and Laura Mazur. *Strategic Communications Management: Making Public Relations Work*. Wokingham, UK: Addison-Wesley, 1995. British perspective on rapidly growing public relations practice in Europe.

Wilcox, Dennis L., Glen T. Cameron, Phillip H. Ault, and Warren K. Agee. *Public Relations: Strategies and Tactics*, 7th ed. Boston: Allyn & Bacon, 2003. Yet another useful introductory text.

2   PRACTITIONERS OF PUBLIC RELATIONS

The way to gain a good reputation is to endeavor to be what you desire to appear.

—Socrates

STUDY GUIDE

After studying Chapter 2, you should be able to

- Describe practitioners' characteristics and work assignments.

- Define the four major roles played by practitioners, discuss the major differences among the roles, and distinguish among them in practice.

- List the five criteria for evaluating the professional status of public relations and discuss the extent to which public relations measures up on each of the criteria.

- Outline the major requirements for success in public relations, identifying writing as the primary requirement for entry to the field and success in the practice.

This chapter discusses public relations practitioners—who they are, what they do, the roles they play, and their professional aspirations. Compared to accounting, law, and medicine, the relatively young practice of public relations is an *emerging profession*. Unlike the more established professions, public relations does not require a prescribed educational preparation, government-sanctioned qualifying exams, and peer review to ensure competent and ethical practice. Nor do its practitioners operate in clearly defined roles recognized as essential for the common good. And because there are no complete official lists, the number how many practice public relations is an estimate that takes into account membership data from the major professional societies and statistics from the U.S. Department of Labor.

NUMBER AND DISTRIBUTION

The number of practitioners continues to increase as organizational, social, economic, and political forces change the role and stature of the public relations practitioners worldwide. For example, a professor in the Netherlands estimated that there are 1.5 million public relations professionals worldwide.[1] Reed's Worldwide Directory of Public Relations Organizations reports that approximately 150,000 members belong to 215 public relations associations, societies, clubs, and other groups worldwide.

Different organizational titles and job descriptions, however, make accurate counts difficult, even in the United States, let alone worldwide. As noted in Chapter 1, what one organization calls "marketing communication" may actually describe a public relations position. What another organization calls a "public relations representative" would be more accurately titled "sales" or "customer service representative." Little agreement on the underlying concept and inconsistent use of titles complicate attempts to count how many really work in public relations.

The U.S. Department of Labor reports public relations employment statistics in its monthly Employment and Earnings under the occupational headings "managers: marketing, advertising, and public relations" and "public relations specialists." Unfortunately, these categories do not include all who work in the field. For example, public relations managers are counted along with other managers, so separate counts are not available. Artists, graphic designers, photographers, videographers, lobbyists, receptionists, researchers, and other specialists who work in public relations departments and firms may be counted in other categories. As a result, the Labor Department's figures probably include fewer than half of all those working in public relations. Even though the data are incomplete, magazines like *Fortune* and *U.S. News & World Report* typically rate public relations among the most rapidly growing and "best jobs" during the 1990s. Then things changed.

Instead of increasing, the number reported by the Labor Department for 2000 had dropped to 129,000, reflecting the collapse of the ".com" high-tech sector and the economic downturn of the early 2000s. By 2003, however, the reported total of 150,000 indicated a recovery in public relations employment.[2] These figures do not include all those practitioners who had been terminated because of downsizing then retrained as outside vendors when the services they had provided became outsourced. In fact, the number of people engaged in public relations work has continued to increase, but the nature of their employment arrangements has changed, just as similar changes occurred in other occupations.

Where They Work

Employment opportunities for public relations specialists exist in almost every community but are concentrated in major population centers. For example, the greatest numbers of Public Relations Society of America (PRSA) members are in California, New York, Texas, Ohio, Michigan, Pennsylvania, and Illinois. Washington, D.C., however, has the largest PRSA chapter, with almost 1,000 members. New York is a close second, with almost 920. The Atlanta, Georgia, chapter has more than 700 members; the Chicago chapter, 560; Detroit, 500; Denver, Colorado, 480; and Los Angeles, 465.

About 40 percent of practitioners work in business and commercial corporations: manufacturing, financial, industrial, consumer goods, media, utilities, transportation, and entertainment; 27 percent in public relations firms, advertising agencies, and individual consultancies; 14 percent in associations, foundations, and educational institutions; 8 percent in health care: hospitals, medical agencies, and other health services; 6 percent in federal, state, and local government; and 5 percent in charitable, religious, and other nonprofit organizations (see Table 2.1).

The single largest employer for public relations is the federal government. According to the U.S. Office of Personnel Management, 4,400 "public affairs" specialists work under various titles. The total jumps to almost 20,000 in the "information and arts" category, however, when the count includes photographers, writers and editors (not including technical writers and editors), visual information specialists, and others working in public communication for the government.[3] Presumably, this figure includes the 6,567 persons working for the former U.S. Information Agency: 3,323 in the United States and 3,244 abroad.[4] However, because the function is often camouflaged to hide it from Congress and the press, reliable figures on the number of public relations specialists in government are not available.

The growing number of public relations firms range in size from an individual counselor (who may use "and Associates") to a large national and international firm with a staff of several hundred. For example, each of the three largest international firms—New York-based Burson-Marsteller, London-based Shandwick, and New York-based Hill & Knowlton—employ close to 2,000. The largest independently owned firm—Edelman Public Relations Worldwide (with headquarters offices in New York and Chicago)—employs 1,800. Ruder Finn has more than 300 in its New York office, and high-tech firm Waggener Edstom employs almost 200 in its Seattle

Organization	Estimated Percentage of Practitioners[a]
Corporations: manufacturing, industrial, consumer goods, financial, insurance media, and entertainment	40
Public relations firms, advertising agencies, marketing communication firms, and individual practitioners	27
Associations, foundations, and educational institutions	14
Health care: hospitals, health maintenance organizations, clinics, home health-care agencies, and mental health facilities	8
Government: local, state, and federal	6
Charitable, religious, and social welfare organizations	5

TABLE 2.1

PUBLIC RELATIONS EMPLOYERS

[a] Estimates based on PRSA and IABC membership profiles and descriptive statistics from other surveys of practitioners.

office. Agricultural specialist Morgan & Myers has more than 50 practitioners in its Jefferson, Wisconsin, main office.[5]

Several major corporations have 100 or more public relations specialists in headquarters and branch offices. Downsizing during the 1990s greatly reduced the number of large staffs and shifted work (outsourcing) to a growing number of increasingly specialized external firms and individual practitioners. For example, *Fortune* 500 company Goodrich Corporation has more about 23,000 employees worldwide, but only seven in its public relations function—vice president Lisa Bottle and staffs of three in the U.S. and three in the U.K.[6] Similarly, Elise Eberwein, vice president of corporate communication at America West Airlines, supervises a staff of seven. Her team handles corporate relations, media relations, investor relations, and communications with 13,000 employees, most of whom "work at 30,000 feet."[7]

The New Majority: Women

According to 1968 U.S. Department of Labor statistics for the "public relations specialists" occupational category, only 25 percent were women. By the end of 1983, women held more than 50 percent of public relations jobs. In the 1990s, more than 66 percent were women.[8]

When the late Rea Smith wrote "Women in Public Relations: What They Have Achieved" in 1968, only one in ten members of PRSA was female.[9] The ratio was one in seven in 1975 when Sondra Gorney concluded that "the walls of the traditional 'man's world' have not tumbled yet."[10] Apparently the walls had tumbled by 1990, when PRSA membership was 54 percent female, and International Association of Business Communicators (IABC) membership was 60 percent female.[11] Current professional society membership profiles show that almost 65 percent are female, and data from colleges and universities indicate that twice as many female students major in public than do males.[12]

EDUCATION AND PREPARATION

More than 92 percent of practitioners are college graduates, including almost 23 percent with some postgraduate studies without a graduate degree completed, 25 percent with master's degrees, and 2 percent with doctoral degrees. Surveys historically show that practitioners entered the field from many academic majors and work experiences. Approximately 40 percent had majored in journalism, with news-editorial graduates outnumbering public relations graduates two to one. English, speech, communication, and business (in that order) follow journalism as college majors of those entering public relations.

Increasingly, however, employers look for specialized public relations degrees and advanced degrees emphasizing research and social science. The Commission on Public Relations Education quoted former University of California at Berkeley chancellor, Clark Kerr, who suggested that requiring such specialized education indicates progress as a profession:

> Some new professions are being born; others are becoming more professional....The university becomes the chief port of entry for these professions, In fact a profession gains its identity by making the university the port of entry.[13]

In addition to the more than 300 colleges and universities offering public relations undergraduate and graduate programs, PRSA, IABC, Arthur W. Page Society, and other professional groups sponsor continuing education courses, institutes, seminars, and conferences. These professional development programs—now seen as essential for maintaining cutting-edge skills and knowledge—attract increasing numbers of working practitioners.

Journalism experience is no longer required preparation for public relations employment. On the other hand, journalistic media experience gives practitioners an understanding of media gatekeepers' values and ways of working. If that experience leads to a "journalist-in-residence" approach, however, public relations will be limited to news dissemination and media relations. Older and more experienced practitioners have typically worked in the media prior to their career in public relations. Fewer than one out of four younger practitioners have worked for newspapers, magazines, radio stations, or television stations before being hired in public relations. More and more employers and public relations managers consider public relations education desirable preparation, making it easier to move directly into the field after graduation. Given the choice, however, employers still value media experience, even if only with the school newspaper or radio station.

Many employers also look for education or experience in a specialized field in addition to public relations. The most difficult positions to fill are those that require specialized preparation and backgrounds such as computer technology, corporate finance, health care, and agriculture. For example, students who combine public relations education with a minor in health care or hospital administration have a clear advantage when applying for hospital public relations openings. Likewise, graduates who minored in computer science while completing their public relations education have a competitive advantage in the world of high-tech public relations.

SALARIES

Salary survey reports typically show that the highest salaries are paid to practitioners working for corporations, particularly those in industry and manufacturing, followed closely by those in high-tech and power utilities. The highest paid specialties are financial/investor relations and crisis management, followed by issue/reputation management.[14]

Many experienced practitioners earn $100,000, $200,000, or more. These practitioners typically work for multibillion-dollar corporations in which the top public relations executives often are corporate officers, either elected or appointed. Officers typically receive stock options, bonus or profit-sharing checks, and lucrative retirement programs in addition to their six-figure salaries. Fringe benefits and perquisites add considerable value to their positions. Employers do not frivolously dispense high salaries or extra benefits, however. Just as when recruiting other top executives, employers must compete for top public relations professionals and managers. For example, compensation packages for the top public relations post at major corporations often are in the $1 million range.

Competition for management-level talent is so intense that executive search firms (sometimes called "headhunters") are retained to identify, screen, and recruit finalists for top public relations positions. Executive recruiters report that top corporate PR posts are now paying $500,000+, and companies have a hard time filling them. Searches may last a year.

Salaries tend to be highest in the Northeast and Middle Atlantic states, led by New York and Washington, D.C. The West also pays relatively high salaries, with northern California's Silicon Valley leading that part of the country. Salaries in the Midwest and South are below the national median. Recent Department of Labor data indicate that for all "public relations specialists" the **median** salary in 2003 was $48,590, with a **mean** salary of $42, 590.[15]

Salary survey results show a pay difference in public relations that deserves special attention: Surveys consistently find that salaries paid to women are below those paid to men. For example, comparisons of men's and women's salaries over time indicate "gaps" in the range of $10,000 to 20,000.[16]

One series of studies tracked practitioner salaries from 1979 to 1985 to 1991. Between 1979 and 1985, the salary gap between men and women increased. The results showed that women earned less than men even when they had equal education, professional experience, and tenure in their jobs.[17] The disparity appears to be diminishing, however. When researchers compared 1979 salaries with 1991 salaries and controlled for years of professional experience, role in management, and participation in decision making, salary differences between men and women were not statistically significant.

> The relation between gender and salary is not statistically significant…after controlling for the influences of professional experience, manager role enactment, and decision-making participation…[which] suggests that patterns of gender salary discrimination and gender role segregation may be breaking down in public relations work.[18]

The researchers cautioned, however, that although this one study indicates progress toward gender equity, it does not mean that the glass ceiling has been removed.

There are other positive signs. Newsletters and publications covering public relations increasingly reflect the pattern of women being promoted to the top public relations positions in all types of organizations. Of course, this not surprising, given the gender makeup of the students in the major and those in the practice. Public relations is a female-dominated profession. Just as in many other fields, however, the overall pattern is that women in public relations still make less than do their male counterparts.

WORK ASSIGNMENTS

Some describe public relations work by listing the specialized parts of the function: media relations, investor relations, community relations, employee relations, government relations, and so forth. Such labels do not describe the many activities and diverse assignments in the day-to-day practice, however. The following ten categories summarize what public relations specialists do at work:

1. *Writing and Editing:* Composing print and broadcast news releases, feature stories, newsletters to employees and external stakeholders, correspondence, Web site and other online media messages, shareholder and annual reports, speeches, brochures, film and slide-show scripts, trade publication articles, institutional advertisements, and product and technical collateral materials.

2. *Media Relations and Placement:* Contacting news media, magazines, Sunday supplements, freelance writers, and trade publications with the intent of getting

them to publish or broadcast news and features about or originated by an organization. Responding to media requests for information, verification of stories, and access to authoritative sources.

3. *Research:* Gathering information about public opinion, trends, emerging issues, political climate and legislation, media coverage, special-interest groups, and other concerns related to an organization's stakeholders. Searching the Internet, online services, and electronic government databases. Designing program research, conducting surveys, and hiring research firms.

4. *Management and Administration:* Programming and planning in collaboration with other managers; determining needs, establishing priorities, defining publics, setting goals and objectives, and developing strategy and tactics. Administering personnel, budget, and program schedules.

5. *Counseling:* Advising top management on the social, political, and regulatory environments; consulting with the management team on how to avoid or respond to crises; and working with key decision makers to devise strategies for managing or responding to critical and sensitive issues.

6. *Special Events:* Arranging and managing news conferences, 10K runs, conventions, open houses, ribbon cuttings and grand openings, anniversary celebrations, fund-raising events, visiting dignitaries, contests, award programs, and other special observances.

7. *Speaking:* Appearing before groups, coaching others for speaking assignments, and managing a speakers' bureau to provide platforms for the organization before important audiences.

8. *Production:* Creating communications using multimedia knowledge and skills, including art, typography, photography, layout, and computer desktop publishing; audio and video recording and editing; and preparing audiovisual presentations.

9. *Training:* Preparing executives and other designated spokespersons to deal with media and to make other public appearances. Instructing others in the organization to improve writing and communication skills. Helping introduce changes in organizational culture, policy, structure, and process.

10. *Contact:* Serving as liaison with media, community, and other internal and external groups. Listening, negotiating, managing conflict, and reaching agreement as mediator between an organization and its important stakeholders. Meeting and entertaining as host to guests and visitors.

Although last on this list, being "good with people" is often the first thing many attribute to public relations. True enough, public relations people often find themselves dealing with people problems and sensitive relationships, but it would be misleading to limit one's view of public relations work to this commonly held stereotype.

The mix of assignments and responsibilities varies greatly from organization to organization, but one task is the common denominator: writing. (Study the job descriptions in Exhibit 2.1.) Writing skills remain a requirement throughout one's career. Daily logs in Exhibits 2.2, 2.3, and 2.4 illustrate the central role of writing in public relations work. To manage their jobs, individual practitioners devise and apply similar strategies and approaches day in and day out. In other words, they develop and play roles.

EXHIBIT 2.1

JOB DESCRIPTIONS

Director–University Relations

Director will report directly to university president and lead program of media relations, publications, electronic media and issues management. Responsible for researching, writing and editing news releases, feature stories, fact sheets and other materials about the university to national news media. Must be hands-on leader with knowledge of strategic management, publication production and new media design.

VICE PRESIDENT
INVESTOR RELATIONS

International pharmaceutical company seeks experienced investor/financial relations executive. New VP reports directly to CEO/president and serves on the exec. committee. VP manages IR web site; maintains institutional, broker and retail investor contacts; coordinates financial reporting; and produces annual reports. Corp./IR communication exp.; and strong analytical, writing and management skills; and working knowledge of SEC disclosure requirements. MBA preferred and prior exp. in pharm./health care necessary.

PUBLIC RELATIONS

Software company seeks PR
writir
article
ade
s
nd
ce dire
her
or

COORDINATOR—INTERNAL
COMMUNICATIONS

Medical center Communications Division opportunity for leader with 8-10 years significant supervisory experience in organizational communication. Coordinator will supervise internal publications, staff communications and recruiting outreach support. Must have extensive writing, planning, consulting and project management experience. Experience and knowledge of new communication technology required. Master's degree preferred.

public relations account executive

Requires minimum five years experience in tourism / hospitality industry account service, travel writing background and strong media contacts. Fluency in Spanish helpful. Portfolio of results-oriented work and strong reference letters from previous clients required for interview.

COMMUNICATION DIRECTOR

Laser systems company seeks accomplished professional to direct government/community relations and public affairs. You also will direct institutional advertising, environmental communications, customer relations, employee
____ and plant tours.

Public Relations Director

Health care provider seeks senior manager to plan strategic public relations activities and collaborate with other departments heads to maintain relationships with payors, physicians, area consumers, and employees. Must have top-level media and community contacts.

Director of Campaign Communications

Major charitable foundation seeks pro to direct media relations, special events, donor relations and campaign communications. Requires significant experience in fund raising; proven record of establishing program goals, identifying target publics, and setting specific communication objectives; significant experience managing multi-media communications program; and strong presentation skills. Successful candidate will plan, manage and direct implementation of a $5-million capital campaign. Position reports directly to Executive Director.

EXHIBIT 2.2

DAY IN THE LIFE OF A PUBLIC RELATIONS DIRECTOR (NONPROFIT ORGANIZATION)

Andrea Lacy, Public Relations Specialist San Diego Urban League

8:00 A.M.   Scan local newspapers for articles relevant to the League. Photocopy and file pertinent articles.

8:30   Review personal calendar to determine upcoming deadlines and tasks.

8:35   Check e-mail and incorporate new tasks into personal calendar.

8:45   Call printing company to arrange delivery of Life Member Reception invitations. Hosted by the League's board of directors and the president and CEO, the reception is an opportunity for contributors to mingle with each other and the organization's department heads.

9:00   Conference call with supervisor and graphic artist to discuss newsletter design and timeline.

9:40   Draft newsletter timeline, send it to supervisor for review, and fax to graphic artist. The newsletter will be distributed to board members and corporate and private contributors, as well as key locations within the community.

10:15   Call League supervisors to request lists needed for research. (A board member who is the president of a local research firm will survey key publics identified by the public relations plan. The research will be used as a benchmark.) Call research firm to discuss status of lists and future deadlines.

11:05   Gather press releases, letters of correspondence, and photos for newsletter articles. Prepare questions for interviews. Draft short article.

12:30 P.M.   Read weekly business journal and daily business newspaper at lunch.

1:30   Check e-mail and in box for messages and today's mail.

1:45   Return call to graphic artist. She wants to discuss changes to the newsletter timeline. Edit timeline per discussion and send copy to supervisor.

2:20   Receive disk containing one of the lists needed for the research project. Reformat the list and set aside.

2:50   Draft calendar announcement for Life Member Reception and select appropriate media. Prepare envelopes for mail. Send announcement to supervisor for approval.

3:20   Return to newsletter activities. Draft calendar of events and outlines for several articles. Search the National Urban League Web page to gather information for a feature article on the Thurgood Marshall Achievers Society, a group founded in part by the League to increase the number of African-American students entering college.

4:55   Send e-mail to supervisor to inform her about the day's activities and any upcoming deadlines.

5:10   Send e-mail to League department heads requesting clerical assistance with handwritten invitation envelopes.

5:20   Note tomorrow's activities on personal calendar. Pick up weekly community periodical from convenience store on the way home.

ROLES

Over time, practitioners adopt patterns of behavior to deal with recurring situations in their work and to accommodate others' expectations of what they should do in their jobs. Four major public relations roles describe much of the practice. At one

EXHIBIT 2.3

DAY IN THE LIFE OF AN ASSISTANT ACCOUNT EXECUTIVE

Tom Magnetta, Assistant Account Executive, PR21, Santa Monica, CA

8:30 A.M. Arrive at office 30 minutes ahead of supervisors. Check and respond to e-mails and voice mail in order of importance. Complete any outstanding tasks from the previous day.

9:00 Scan media for news stories relevant to each client, and determine how clients are or could be affected, keeping in mind how clients could capitalize or respond to changes in the external environment. Prepare a daily clip report on each client and submit—with stories—to the respective supervisor.

10:30 Research event location and determine logistics for an upcoming public health presentation sponsored by health-care client.

11:00 Draft newsletter cover story—as assigned by supervisor—for auto show client and submit for edits.

12:30 P.M. Attend lunch staff meeting in the conference room. Help other team brainstorm ideas for existing client and hear updates from each account team.

1:30 Follow up on new e-mails and voice mail received during lunch, including a message left by a technology reporter regarding a news release sent yesterday. Forward requested materials—hi-resolution pictures and client fact sheet—for story the reporter is writing.

2:30 Receive from print shop an order of approved media kit materials for next week's mailing for consumer client. Check quality and ensure there are enough materials and product to cover last-minute additions of media to contacts. Place an order to client for two additional cases of product.

3:30 Help another team with a not-for-profit client do follow-up pitching to Los Angeles media asking them to cover a high-profile benefit dinner raising funds to support controversial medical research.

5:00 Health-care account team meeting: Review task list for upcoming public health presentation. Provide team information gathered from location and logistics research. Present event media list put together last week and solicit changes and additions. Discuss recent news stories relevant to client and industry and develop list of topics for next week's client phone conference.

6:30 Return to desk to check and respond to afternoon's e-mail and voice mail. Make a to-do list for tomorrow before heading home.

time or another, however, practitioners play all these and other roles to varying degrees, even though a dominant role emerges as they go about their day-to-day work and dealings with others.

Communication Technician

Most practitioners enter the field as communication technicians. Entry-level job descriptions typically list communication and journalistic skills as requirements. Communication technicians are hired to write and edit employee newsletters, to write news releases and feature stories, to develop Web site content, and to deal

EXHIBIT 2.4

WEEK IN THE LIFE OF A GOVERNMENT PUBLIC AFFAIRS SPECIALIST

Francisco J. Agraz,
Public Affairs Specialist;
FBI Houston Division

Monday

- Begin day by reviewing e-mails on FBINET (secure) and public (Internet) computers. Summarize weekly Community Relations activities for management report.

- Attend weekly branch meeting of administrative supervisors.

- Consult with Special Agent Supervisor in preparation for an upcoming speech to a town hall meeting requested by local legislator regarding counterterrorism issues.

Tuesday

- Special Agent in Charge (SAC) appoints Agraz to serve as Combined Federal Campaign (CFC) Employee Coordinator. Confer regarding campaign expectations for this year. Draft CFC Plan and Goals. Draft EC (FBI memorandum) for file. Calendar dates for Campaign Kick Off Rally, reserve building meeting areas for event, confer with CFC staff regarding campaign materials and schedule.

- Review prior evening's TIVO recordings of local news broadcasts and newspaper.

Wednesday

- EC (FBI Memorandum) from FBI HQ Office of Public Affairs, Washington, D.C., requesting that Houston Division nominate a local community leader to receive the **FBI Director's Community Leadership Award** in the Houston area. Review list of community contacts. Confer with Public Affairs Specialists in other local federal agencies. Draft EC with suggested name, for approval. Submit name to HQ via EC, reserve conference room for presentation of award. Coordinate with Media Representative about news release to announce event.

- Assist Crisis Management Squad in preparation of Power-Point and other presentation materials regarding upcoming Table Top Exercise (TTX). A TTX explores "what-if" scenarios with local, state, and federal agencies. Attend, assist, and participate in TTX regarding Community Relations.

Thursday

- Finish semiannual budget report to HQ Community Relations Unit concerning expenses incurred to date, as well as to report speech and public appearance statistics by Houston Field Office executives, agents, and other employees.

- Respond to letters, faxes, e-mails, and telephone calls requesting FBI Special Agents as speakers.

- Make follow-up calls to community leaders who received earlier invitation letters from SAC to the FBI Houston Citizens' Academy. The Academy provides an inside look at FBI mission and priorities during eight weekly class sessions. Coordinate with Security Officer regarding clearances for proposed Academy attendees.

Friday

- Prepare a three-day program of presentations and tours for visiting foreign police executives. Coordinate with FBI executives as to topics, hosting duties, venues, and list of proposed presenters.

- Telephone conference with I Have A Dream-Houston® regarding FBI Junior Special Agent Program for elementary school students, and mentor possibilities and career day presentations for middle and high school students. Draft EC to memorialize plans. Send an All Employee e-mail soliciting volunteer teachers and mentors.

- Travel to Houston DEA Field Office for meeting to plan Anti-Drug Red Ribbon Rally for 1,000 Texas students from Houston, Dallas, San Antonio, and Austin, held every October.

- Support a Bank Robbery investigation by preparing a "Wanted by the FBI" poster using bank surveillance photos. Publish poster via e-mail to local news media. Alert FBI Media Representative that there may be media inquiries.

with media contacts. Practitioners in this role usually are not present when management defines problems and selects solutions. They are brought in later to produce the communications and implement the program, sometimes without full knowledge of either the original motivation or the intended results. Even though they were not present during the discussions about a new policy or management decision, they are the ones given the job of explaining it to employees and to the press.

Practitioners not only begin their careers in this role but also spend much of their time in the technical aspects of communication, as illustrated by the list of work assignments presented in the preceding section and by the job descriptions in Exhibit 2.1. When limited to this role, however, practitioners typically do not participate significantly in management decision making and strategic planning. They complain that they are not part of the management team and that they are "the last to know."

Expert Prescriber

When practitioners take on the expert role, others see them as the authority on public relations problems and solutions. Top management leaves public relations in the hands of the expert and assumes a relatively passive role. Practitioners operating as expert practitioners define the problem, develop the program, and take full responsibility for its implementation. Other managers may want to keep public relations as the sole responsibility of practitioners so they can get back to business as usual, content that things will be handled by the "PR experts."

The expert prescriber role seduces practitioners because it is personally gratifying to be viewed as the authority on what needs to be done and how it should be done. It seduces employers and clients because they want to feel sure that public relations is being handled by an expert. They also erroneously assume that they will no longer have to be involved once the expert is on the job. Limited participation by key top managers, however, means that their relevant knowledge does not get factored into the problem-solving process. Public relations becomes compartmentalized and isolated from the mainstream of the enterprise.

By not participating themselves, managers become dependent on the practitioner any time public relations issues arise. Managers also develop little or no commitment to public relations efforts and do not take responsibility for the success or failure of programs. In effect, other managers in the organization assume an it's-not-my-job stance on public relations matters. They see public relations as a sometimes-necessary job handled by support staff not directly involved in the organization's main line of business.

Whereas the expert prescriber role is called for in crisis situations and periodically throughout any program, in the long run it hinders the diffusion of public relations thinking throughout the organization. It also leads to the greatest dissatisfaction with practitioners, because they are held solely accountable for program results even though they had little or no control over critical parts of the situation and the factors that led to public relations problems in the first place. Top management often responds by simply replacing one expert with another, endlessly searching for someone who can make public relations problems go away without having to make needed changes in organizational policy, products, or procedures.

Communication Facilitator

The communication facilitator role casts practitioners as sensitive listeners and information brokers. Communication facilitators serve as liaisons, interpreters, and mediators between an organization and its publics. They maintain two-way communication and facilitate exchange by removing barriers in relationships and by keeping channels of communication open. The goal is to provide both management and publics the information they need for making decisions of mutual interest.

Practitioners in the communication facilitator role find themselves acting as information sources and the official contacts between organizations and their publics. They referee interactions, establish discussion agendas, summarize and restate views, call for reactions, and help participants diagnose and correct conditions interfering with communication relationships. Communication facilitators occupy boundary-spanning roles and serve as links between organizations and publics. They operate under the assumption that effective two-way communication improves the quality of decisions that organizations and publics make about policies, procedures, and actions of mutual interest.

Problem-Solving Facilitator

When practitioners assume the role of problem-solving facilitator, they collaborate with other managers to define and solve problems. They become part of the strategic planning team. Collaboration and consultation begin with the first question and continue until the final program evaluation. Problem-solving practitioners help other managers and the organization apply to public relations the same management step-by-step process used for solving other organizational problems.

Line managers play an essential part in analyzing problem situations, as they are the ones most knowledgeable of and most intimately involved with the organization's policies, products, procedures, and actions. They are also the ones with the power to make needed changes. As a result, they must participate in the evolutionary thinking and strategic planning behind public relations programs. When line managers participate in the public relations strategic planning process, they understand program motivations and objectives, they support strategic and tactical decisions, and they are committed to making the changes and providing the resources needed to achieve program goals.

Problem-solving facilitators get invited to the management team because they have demonstrated their skill and value in helping other managers avoid and solve problems. As a result, public relations thinking is factored into management decision making.[19]

WHAT ROLES RESEARCH TELLS US

Researchers have studied what leads practitioners to play different roles, as well as what happens when they enact different roles in their organizations. Their findings have isolated factors that influence role selection and enactment, salary and career advancement, and participation in organizational decision making. Other scholars have used the role models to describe similarities and differences in the practice internationally.

Technicians Versus Managers

Research findings show that practitioners play several roles, but that over time one emerges as the dominant role. For example, in a study of PRSA and IABC members in the United States, 37 percent rated themselves dominant in the expert prescriber role and 37 percent scored communication technician as their dominant role. Another 21 percent scored the problem-solving facilitator role as dominant, and only 5 percent put themselves in the dominant role of communication facilitator.[20]

In a similar study of Canadian Public Relations Society and Canadian IABC members, 42 percent rated themselves in the dominant role of communication technicians, 16 percent as expert prescribers, 15 percent as problem-solving facilitators, and 12 percent as communication facilitators. Fifteen percent weighted two or three roles equally.[21]

Not surprisingly, survey results indicate that practitioners' dominant roles are associated with sex, age, and years of experience. For example, comparisons of PRSA and IABC members' dominant roles produce different profiles: Whereas 44 percent of PRSA members practice in the dominant role of expert prescribers, only 27 percent of IABC members operate primarily in that role. On the other hand, 50 percent of IABC members, but only 29 percent of PRSA members, act in the communication technician dominant role.

High scores on the communication technician role tend to stand alone. For the other three roles, however, high scores on one tend to go with high scores on the other two. In other words, practitioners who play the dominant role of expert prescriber, communication facilitator, or problem-solving process facilitator also tend to play the other two roles. High correlations among the three roles suggest that they go together to form a single, complex role that is distinct from the communication technician role. As a result, **two major dominant roles occur in practice: public relations technician and public relations manager**.

Public relations technicians are primarily concerned with writing, producing, and disseminating communications, such as press releases, speeches, Web sites, feature stories, and annual reports. They tend to be creative, artistic, and technically proficient; see themselves as their organization's "wordsmith"; and exhibit little inclination or aptitude for strategic planning and research. For the most part they focus on communications and other activities in the process. Those in this dominant role typically make less and are not part of the management inner circle but enjoy high levels of job satisfaction if they remain in the technician role by choice. This role constitutes the traditional core of public relations work—writing news releases and other mediated communications and doing media relations.

The public relations manager role casts practitioners as part of organizational management. This role calls for research skills, an aptitude for strategic thinking, and a tendency to think in terms of the **outcomes or impact** of public relations activities. Practitioners in the public relations manager role do not limit their tactics to communications. They use environmental scanning and organizational intelligence, negotiation and coalition building, issues management, program evaluation, and management counseling as public relations tools. Accountability and participation in organizational management earn these practitioners high salaries, as well as high stress and responsibility. Researchers who studied 321 organizations in the United States, Canada, and the United Kingdom, however, found that the major predictor of public relations excellence was the extent to which the organization's top public relations executive was able to enact the manager role versus the technician role.[22]

Environmental Influences

Important distinctions are lost when the three managerial roles are combined. For example, as Table 2.2 illustrates, a practitioner's dominant role is a function of an organization's environment. Communication technicians tend to work in organizations with relatively stable, low-threat environments, such as many nonprofit organizations and charities. Communication facilitators predominate in organizations with relatively turbulent settings that pose little threat, such as school districts and some governmental agencies. Problem-solving process facilitators and expert prescribers work in organizations with threatening environments. In relatively stable settings, including some utilities and associations, the problem-solving process facilitator role dominates. Expert prescribers dominate in rapidly changing environments, particularly in public relations firms that specialize in crisis communication and in consumer products companies subject to high levels of competition and government regulation.[23]

In short, the expert prescriber role appears when immediate action is imperative, whereas the problem-solving process facilitator dominant role is preferred when there is time to go through a process of collaboration and joint problem solving. Highly paid problem-solving process facilitators and expert prescribers tend to work for organizations most threatened by competition, government regulation, labor conflicts, and public scrutiny, such as financial and insurance companies, utilities, and the public relations firms who work for these companies. By contrast, lower-paid communication technicians and communication facilitators typically work as promotional publicists for media and advertising agencies or for educational and religious organizations and charities.

Scanning and Evaluation

The various studies of public relations roles have consistently demonstrated the impact of using research to manage the function. In the three-phase study of roles reported previously, practitioners who use all types of research and information gathering were the ones most likely to operate in the management roles. The relationship between research and managerial roles also appears in the findings of an international sample of IABC members.[24] Operating in the manager role correlates with the use of scientific, informal, and mixed approaches to research, whereas operating in the technician role does not. Canadian researchers found a similar pattern when they surveyed members of the Canadian Public Relations Society (CPRS) and Canadian members of IABC, but the highest correlations were for communication facilitators. The researchers concluded, "Perhaps communication facilitators

	Low Threat	High Threat
Little Change	Communication technician	Problem-solving facilitator
Much Change	Communication facilitator	Expert prescriber

TABLE 2.2

ORGANIZATIONAL ENVIRONMENTS AND ROLES

require more objective information than the others in order to keep channels of communication open between various parties."[25]

Research shows that all types of information gathering help practitioners move into management roles. The obvious conclusion is that practitioners must be actively gathering information useful in decision making before they are invited to the management table. Furthermore, becoming part of the management team does not happen simply because of years on the job. Rather, how much research practitioners do determines the likelihood that they have a role in management decision making.[26] Moving into the management role, however, "does not immediately ensure that practitioners have the knowledge or expertise to enact the manager role," according to Lauzen and Dozier.[27] Simply put, practitioners long accustomed to operating in the technician role may not be able to make the adjustment to the strategic manager role.

Many factors influence practitioner roles, including education, professional experience, personality, supervision, and organizational culture and environment. Practitioners who understand the causes and consequences of playing different roles can develop strategies for dealing with a variety of situations and with others' views of practitioner roles. This understanding may be particularly important for women because role differences are associated with both salary and participation in management decision making.

THE GLASS CEILING

Studies of women in public relations historically have found both a salary gap and a "glass ceiling" on promotions to management positions. As one researcher put it, there is a "million-dollar penalty for being a woman," noting the effects of male–female salary differences and limited advancement opportunities over the course of a career.[28]

Those who study the glass-ceiling problem suggest the following strategies:

1. Women aiming for top management must develop career plans and select employers with care and not plan on "being in the right place at the right time." "Women have to get into the game and be as aggressive and determined as any male counterpart."

2. Women must develop management skills: goal setting, analysis, planning, research, program execution, measurement, and evaluation. They must also know how to communicate with managers. As one female manager put it, "I think as time goes on, and this is especially critical for women, communicators are going to have to think like managers, talk like managers, and communicate with other managers."

3. Women must aim higher. One study found that when women are asked to estimate what salary they will be making in 10 years, they project only 60 percent of what men project. Rather than undervalue themselves, they should research salaries in the area and in comparable organizations before accepting an offer. Researchers also found that women may forget to negotiate perks: professional dues, conference expenses, and other benefits in addition to salary.[29]

The transition of women into the workplace appears to be moving from the crisis stage of the 1980s into a genuine negotiation stage from which the profession and the workplace will eventually emerge stronger and, perhaps, with a different set of values that combines the best of both.[30]

Much of the credit for progress goes to women in public relations who have struggled to break through the managerial glass ceiling and to feminist scholars who have explicated and documented the process and effects of gender discrimination. Although the glass ceiling and gender discrimination have not been eliminated, as the authors quoted earlier put it, "Watch for falling glass."

MINORITIES

Surveys of public relations workforces show that people of color are severely underrepresented in public relations practice. U.S. Department of Labor statistics show a marked increase of minorities in the "public relations specialists" category, from about 3 percent in 1979 to almost 15 percent Black and Hispanic origin by the late 1990s.[31] Membership profiles of PRSA and IABC indicate that minorities represent a little more than 7 percent of membership in these two professional societies. These figures do not compare favorably, however, with estimates that minorities represent 25 percent of the U.S. population and are growing as a percentage of the overall population.[32]

Demographic trends and the increasing marketplace power of minorities call for an even greater presence in the years to come, according to public relations scholar and diversity consultant Marilyn Kern-Foxworth[33] (see Exhibit 2.5). Recognition of the importance of building and maintaining relationships with all racial and ethnic segments of the community has increased opportunities for individual practitioners as well as for minority-owned firms. Globalization has also increased demand for skilled practitioners able to bridge cultural and communication gaps.[34] For example, when MaryLee Sachs became Hill & Knowlton USA's president and CEO, she made diversity a priority: "We should be reflective of the cities in which we operate, and reflective of our clients, our clients' businesses, what they're trying to do, and the types of audiences they're trying to reach."[35]

However, surveys continue to show that minorities are underrepresented in corporate departments, firms, and other major organizations' public relations staffs. Educational programs in public relations continue to recruit minority students, scholarships and internship programs encourage participation, and employment opportunities reward those who take advantage of them. Minority practitioners with public relations training and skills will continue to be in demand because all organizations need to communicate with the many publics in an increasingly pluralistic society. Ketchum's Raymond Kotcher succinctly summarized the challenge: "The public relations profession should aspire to be representative of the communities served by our companies, clients and organizations across the nation."[36]

PROFESSIONALISM

When practitioners assemble at professional meetings, discussions typically turn to the extent to which public relations qualifies as a profession. The topic of professionalism dominates many conferences. The many publications and newsletters

EXHIBIT 2.5

THE CASE FOR DIVERSITY IN PUBLIC RELATIONS

*Marilyn Kern-Foxworth, Ph. D.,
APR, President
*Kern Foxworth International,
LLC; Silver Spring, Maryland*

"I believe with all my heart and soul that diversity makes companies perform better; in fact, I know it does. Enlightened businesses understand that diversity is absolutely and unequivocally a business imperative that is critical to its long-term success."

—Ann Fudge, Chair
Young & Rubicam
National Urban League Convention
(July 23, 2004)

This is your wake-up call. The faces, values, and heritage of America have changed significantly over the past two decades. These demographic changes—especially **diversity**—create challenges for the public relations practice.

At the beginning of the 20th century, 1 in 8 U.S. citizens represented a race other than white. By the beginning of the 21st century, that had changed to 1 in 4; more than 82 million people of color now make up the multicultural market in a total population of 291 million people. Furthermore, futurists predict that by 2050 multiracial groups will outnumber the white population by 13 million.

Successful public relations practitioners recognize these realities. They know that their organizations' stakeholder bases now include distinct multicultural clients, employees, patrons, donors, investors, customers, viewers, readers, and media. They also know that public relations must take into account the diversity of the communities and stakeholders they serve:

- **Human resources** must consider diversity if it wants workplaces to have more diverse employees, officials, and staffs making decisions regarding hiring, firing, and promotions.

- **Community relations** must reach out to communities that include multiracial audiences and participants when planning events and selecting sponsorship partners. For

example, research findings are consistent on one crucial point: stakeholders of color are more likely to support and have favorable opinions of companies that invest in their communities. This can include sponsoring social action programs that demonstrate understanding of the heritages of various community groups, and seeking constituents' input on issues that affect their communities.

- **Crisis communication** must consider the possibility of diversity-related problems and how to effectively manage such situations. Organizations' reputations are maligned when media report instances of blatant discrimination or stereotyping. Most racial groups have been disappointed at times when brands known worldwide have been exposed for not hiring or promoting employees of color, or for devaluing their culture and heritage. Some of the most visible cases have involved Avis, Abercrombie & Fitch, Coca-Cola, Denny's, Taco Bell, Texaco, and Washington Redskins.

- **Investor relations** must take into account that the aggregate disposable income of multicultural groups has grown to $1.3 trillion. That income, if considered a separate nation-state, would rank the multicultural consumer market sixth in the world economically, higher than Italy, China, Brazil, Canada, and Spain. Investor relations professionals who have not cultivated financial markets among multicultural populations will lose ground in the competition for investment dollars.

- **Media relations** strategies must incorporate the new media and Internet use by multicultural audiences. Multiracial audiences on the web are currently growing faster than any other market segment. In 2005, Internet usage by African-American and Hispanic consumers reached parity with the general U.S. market.

Recognizing the diversity of groups traveling the information super highway and the opportunity to add new African-American, Latino, Asian American, and Native American subscribers, AOL created two new products—AOL Black Forum and AOL Latino. In 2004, Comcast and Radio One partnered in a venture to create TV One to compete with Black Entertainment Network (BET), ultimately creating two networks targeting African Americans. The Latino Newswire now disseminates news specifically of interest to this audience segment. There are many other multicultural media,

EXHIBIT 2.5 *continued*

online and offline, used by public relations professionals to reach their increasingly diverse stakeholders.

Multicultural audiences are more public relations savvy today than at any other time. They notice when companies put money back into their neighborhoods, understand their culture, and respect their differences. To keep pace with the challenges of diversity, corporations, nonprofit agencies, and other institutions must adjust to ensure that all facets of their operations account for diversity. Public relations must take a

leadership role in making those changes happen. Otherwise, their organizations will not keep pace with changing social and cultural environments.

_____

*Kern Foxworth International, LLC, a communications consulting firm that conducts diversity training for *Fortune* 500 companies, governmental agencies, and universities.

serving the field all address the professionalization of public relations. Concern about professionalism prompted PRSA to require accredited members to complete continuing education in order to maintain their accredited status.

Criteria for assessing the professional status of a field date back to preindustrial England. Sons of wealthy landowners went to either Cambridge or Oxford to receive a liberal arts education before taking exams to enter the practices of law and medicine. Wealth was a prerequisite because professional practice provided little, if any, remuneration.

By the late 1800s the "status professionalism" of England began to give way to "occupational professionalism." Specialized skills and knowledge became the basis for entry, opening the way for the growing middle class. Although being challenged in some fields, many of the values associated with the origins of professions persist today: "personal service, a dislike of competition, advertising and profit, a belief in the principle of payment in order to work rather than working for pay and the superiority of the motive of service."[37]

Many have attempted to define contemporary professions, but no single definition fits all fields. Typically, disagreement results when an occupational group argues for a specific and unique characteristic designed to exclude others. There is general agreement, however, that the following criteria apply to all professions:

1. Requires specialized education to acquire a body of knowledge and skills based on theory developed through research. The practice is based more on unique knowledge than on performance skills.

2. Provides a unique and essential service recognized as such by the community. Practitioners are identified with their profession: "She's a lawyer" or "He's the accountant."

3. Emphasizes public service and social responsibility over private interests. Private economic gain and special interests are subordinate to the public good. There is "nobility of purpose."

4. Gives autonomy to and places responsibility on practitioners. Freedom to decide and act means individuals are held accountable.

5. Enforces codes of ethics and standards of performance through self-governing associations of colleagues. Values are interpreted and enforced by disciplining those who deviate from accepted norms and prescribed behaviors. Professional societies set standards for specialized educational preparation, determine who is admitted into practice, monitor practitioner performance against agreed-upon standards, and confer different levels of status on practitioners.

Any discussion of practitioners' educational backgrounds makes it clear that entry into public relations does not require specialized educational preparation. A small percentage of practitioners belong to the major professional associations. An even smaller number are "accredited" or "certified," meaning that they have passed a battery of tests and been judged to be competent practitioners by a panel of their professional peers. No state requires a license to practice public relations. Not only are there varied and often bizarre notions held by others about what constitutes public relations, there is also disagreement within the field.

Frequent examples of self-serving behavior and advocacy on behalf of special interests bring into question the extent to which public service and social responsibility guide the practice. News reports expose "public relations spin doctors" or "damage control specialists" retained by clients charged with unethical or illegal activities. Only a small percentage of practitioners work as truly independent counselors. In fact, most function in staff positions accountable to line management, so autonomy and personal responsibility are not commonly associated with their roles. And because only a small proportion of practitioners belongs to strong professional associations, the vast majority is not subject to enforced codes of conduct.

These issues are discussed more fully in Chapter 5, but it is obvious that a strict interpretation of the criteria precludes qualifying public relations as a profession. In fact, if required to completely adhere to the standards, few, if any, fields could pass the test. Many practicing public relations, on the other hand, qualify as professionals, on the basis of their commitment to meeting professional standards. Widespread efforts in education and the professional associations advance the calling and professionalize the field. Professionalism is an important concern and goal for those entering the emerging profession of public relations.

REQUIREMENTS FOR SUCCESS

Surveys of top public relations executives show that they think communication skills, knowledge of media and management, problem-solving abilities, motivation, and intellectual curiosity are needed for success. Exhibit 2.6 presents Bill Cantor's list of personality traits required for success in public relations. Public relations consultant Richard Long lists five qualities of those on the career "fast track":

1. *Results*. The single most important key to success is a reputation for getting results, being goal oriented. Employers and clients pay for results, not hard work and effort.

2. *Conceptualizing*. Those on the fast track have an ability to focus on the employer's or client's needs. The strong conceptualizer is a "quick study" who is a good listener and thorough note taker.

EXHIBIT 2.6

CANTOR'S TRAITS FOR SUCCESS

1. *Response to tension.* Most successful public relations executives are intense people, although it may not always be evident even to themselves. Often they are at their best under fire, and rather than solving problems by abstract analysis, they will reach practical solutions by direct action.

2. *Individual initiative.* Successful public relations executives will usually take immediate action before a situation becomes blown out of proportion. They usually will not wait for instructions but take the initiative to solve the problem; seek to anticipate and adjust to change; lead the public relations effort.

3. *Curiosity and learning.* The public relations professional should have an inquiring mind, should want to learn everything possible about the product, service, client or organization, and the competition. Because public relations is not an exact science, frequently the public relations executive must try a number of approaches in order to solve a problem, some of which might not work. If and when they don't work, professionals regard them not as personal blunders but as learning opportunities. They solve problems by persistence and intelligence. They never stop learning.

4. *Energy, drive, and ambition.* Successful public relations people have energy, drive, and ambition. They work rapidly and are not afraid to take a calculated risk. This is a very important element in the personality of public relations executives. Most of the top practitioners are stimulated by the problems to be solved and are willing to work the hours it takes to reach their goals.

5. *Objective thinking.* Public relations executives must be as objective and factual as possible and above all have excellent judgment. They must know what to do and say and when. They must have a sense of timing. They must have a capacity for intense concentration, attention to intricate detail, and keen powers of observation. This is especially critical in counseling.

6. *Flexible attitude.* It is crucial that public relations executives have the ability to see things from someone else's viewpoint, for example, executive management's, a publication editor's, or a hostile audience's.

7. *Service to others.* Most successful public relations executives have a natural desire to help people. Pleasure in the success of others is a major motivation for the service behavior.

8. *Friendliness.* Public relations people generally are perceived as likable, friendly, and genuinely interested in others, rarely as resentful, bitter, or hostile. They develop and maintain a wide range of personal contacts.

9. *Versatility.* Successful public relations executives are often able to perform well in a variety of areas because they have a venturesome spirit and a lively interest in the world at large. The best practitioners are generalists with a specialty. The desire to learn and the ability to focus on varied subjects helps them adjust rapidly to new tasks and multiple client problems and needs.

10. *Lack of self-consciousness.* Successful public relations executives are much less self-conscious than other executives, perhaps because they often function as catalysts. Although some practitioners have large egos, they often are self-effacing, functioning in the background while projecting others into the limelight. This trait is indigenous to the public relations professional.

Courtesy Bill Cantor and reprinted with permission from *Public Relations Journal.*

3. *Human Relations.* Persons on the fast track are team players who balance personal goals with those of the organization. These persons also know how to deal with management, including when they do not agree with the boss.

4. *Style.* The most important style-related trait is a "can-do" attitude. Another is constructive competitiveness. Those on the fast track translate confidence into persuasive advocacy and substantive public relations contributions.

5. *Intangibles.* This quality almost defies description, but charisma, presence, and moxie affect the way other managers evaluate people in public relations. Go to school on the boss. The bottom line with bosses, however, is to find ways to make their jobs easier. Know what your boss expects of you.[38]

Among other traits sought by employers are an understanding of how the business works (whatever a particular organization's business is), skill with computer software and new media technology, being well read and informed on current events, and having an ability to deal with frustration and to improvise. One trait tops every list, however. Ability to write is number one by a wide margin. As one executive put it:

> Too often, clear writing is not stressed sufficiently and the public relations professional goes through his or her career with one hand tied behind. Learn how to write before you start to climb the public relations ladder.[39]

Another said, "If our experience is typical, writing is one of the very weakest areas of most new graduates. That's probably being kind . . . 'appalling' is what's really crossing my mind."[40]

In short, both entry-level employment and long-term career success require the ability to write grammatically correct, easy-to-read, forceful, informative, and persuasive copy for publication and speech.

NOTES

[1] Anne van der Meiden, Foreword to Milenko D. Djuric, *Public Relations: The Key to a Successful Appearance on the Market* (Belgrade, Yugoslavia: Marketing Research Institute, 1992), 203. The first book written on the state of the emerging profession in Yugoslavia. English overview summarizes seven chapters.

[2] U.S. Department of Labor, Bureau of Labor Statistics (www.bls.gov/oes), 2003. Check under Specific Occupational Code 27-3031 ("Public Relations Specialists").

[3] U.S. Office of Personnel Management, Office of Workforce Information, *Federal Civilian Workforce Statistics: Occupations of Federal White-Collar and Blue-Collar Workers* (Washington, DC: Government Printing Office, September 30, 1995), 34.

[4] U.S. Office of Personnel Management, Statistical Analysis and Services Division, *Federal Civilian Workforce Statistics: Employment and Trends* (Washington, DC: Government Printing Office, August 1997), 37.

[5] For data on employee numbers, see current editions of "Jack O'Dwyer's Newsletter" and *O'Dwyer's Directory of Public Relations Firms*.

[6] John N. Frank, "Goodrich Brings in New PR Head after TRW Acquisition," *PRWeek* (January 13, 2003): 5.

[7] "America West's Turnaround Is Down to Its Employees," *PRWeek* (June 14, 2004): 8.

[8] U.S. Department of Labor, Bureau of Labor Statistics, *Employment and Earnings* (Washington, DC: U.S. Government Printing Office, January 1998), 175.

[9] Rea W. Smith, "Women in Public Relations," *Public Relations Journal* 24 (October 1968): 26, 27, and 29.

[10] Sondra K. Gorney, "Status of Women in Public Relations," *Public Relations Journal* 31 (May 1975): 10–3.

[11] David Y. Jacobson and Nicholas J. Tortorello, "Salary Survey," *Public Relations Journal* 46, no. 6 (June 1990): 18–25; and *Profile '89* (San Francisco: International Association of Business Communicators and IABC Research Foundation, 1989).

[12] Lee B. Becker, Tudor Vlad, Jisu Huh, and Nancy R. Mace, "Annual Enrollment Report: Graduate and Undergraduate Enrollments Increase Sharply," *Journalism & Mass Communication Educator* (Autumn 2003): 284.

[13] John L. Paluszek, "Public Relations Students: Today Good, Tomorrow Better," *The Public Relations Strategist* 5, no. 4 (Winter 2000): 29.

[14] For current salary figures, see the "Annual Salary Survey" published by *PRWeek* (www.prweek.com).

[15] U.S. Department of Labor, Bureau of Labor Statistics (www.bls.gov/oes/2003.may/oes273031.htm).

[16] Larissa A. Grunig, Elizabeth L. Toth, and Linda C. Hon, *Women in Public Relations: How Gender Influences Practice* (New York: The Guilford Press, 2001), 206–208.

[17] Glen M. Broom and David M. Dozier, "Advancement for Public Relations Role Models," *Public Relations Review* 12, no. 1 (Spring 1986): 37–56.

[18] David M. Dozier and Glen M. Broom, "Evolution of the Managerial Role in Public Relations Practice," *Journal of Public Relations Research* 7, no. 1 (1995): 17–18.

[19] For the original conceptual definitions of the roles, see Glen M. Broom and George D. Smith, "Testing the Practitioner's Impact on Clients," *Public Relations Review* 5, no. 3 (Fall 1979): 47–59.

[20] Jennie M. Piekos and Edna F. Einsiedel, "Roles and Program Evaluation Techniques Among Canadian Public Relations Practitioners," *Public Relations Research Annual* 2 (1990): 95–113.

[21] David M. Dozier (with Larissa A. Grunig and James E. Grunig), *Manager's Guide to Excellence in Public Relations and Communication Management* (Mahwah, NJ: Lawrence Erlbaum Associates, 1995): 23–37.

[22] Lalit Acharya, "Public Relations Environments," *Journalism Quarterly* 62, no. 3 (Autumn 1985): 577–84.

[23] David M. Dozier, "The Innovation of Research in Public Relations: Review of a Program of Research," *Public Relations Research Annual* 2 (1990): 16–21.

[24] Piekos and Einsiedel, "Roles and Program Evaluation Techniques," 109.

[25] Glen M. Broom and David M. Dozier, "Advancement for Public Relations Role Models," *Public Relations Review* 12, no. 1 (Spring 1986): 37–56.

[26] Martha M. Lauzen and David M. Dozier, "Issues Management Mediation of Linkages Between Environmental Complexity and Management of the Public Relations Function," *Journal of Public Relations Research* 6, no. 3 (1994): 180.

[27] Carolyn Garret Cline, "Public Relations: The $1 Million Penalty for Being a Woman," in *Women in Mass Communication: Challenging Gender Values*, ed. Pamela J. Creedon (Newbury Park, CA: Sage Publications, 1989), 263–75.

[28] Adapted and quoted from Cline, "The $1 Million Penalty for Being a Woman," 272–74.

[29] Shirley A. Serini, Elizabeth Toth, Donald K. Wright, and Arthur G. Emig, "Watch for Falling Glass . . . Women, Men, and Job Satisfaction in Public Relations: A Preliminary Analysis," *Journal of Public Relations Research* 9, no. 2 (1997): 116.

[30] Employment and Earnings (Washington, DC: U.S. Department of Labor, Bureau of Statistics, January 1980 and January 1998): 175.

[31] For a discussion of the three major minority publics—African Americans, Asian Americans, and Hispanic Americans—see Linda P. Morton, "Targeting Minority Publics," *Public Relations Quarterly* 42, no. 2 (Summer 1997): 23–27.

[32] Marilyn Kern-Foxworth, "Status and Roles of Minority PR Practitioners," *Public Relations Review* 15, no. 3 (Fall 1989): 39–47.

[33] Marilyn Kern-Foxworth, "Black, Brown, Red, and Yellow Markets Equal Green Power," *Public Relations Quarterly* 36, no. 1 (Spring 1991): 30.

[34] Raymond L. Kotcher, "Diversity in Today's Workplace and Marketplace," *Public Relations Quarterly* 40, no. 1 (Spring 1995): 7.

[35] "Diversity Survey 2003—Wanted: A More Diverse Workforce," *PRWeek* (December 1, 2003):19.

[36] Kotcher, "Diversity in Today's Workplace," 8.

[37] Philip Elliott, *The Sociology of Professions* (London: Macmillan, 1972), 52–3. Useful reference on the origins and evolution of professions.

[38] Adapted from a speech by Richard K. Long, LONG-term Solutions, Federal Way, WA. Long formerly served as public relations executive at Dow Chemical Company, Midland, MI, and Weyerhaeuser, Tacoma, WA. Used with permission of the author.

[39] From speech to Black Public Relations Society of Greater New York by Kenneth R. Lightcap, managing director, Manning Selvage and Lee, New York, April 17, 1991.

[40] James E. Lukaszewski, Chairman, The Lukaszewski Group, Inc., as quoted in Jack Haberstroh, "PR Graduates Don't Measure Up as Writers," *Public Relations Quarterly* 39, no. 4 (Winter 1994–95): 22.

ADDITIONAL SOURCES

Bowen, Shannon A. "I Thought It Would Be More Glamorous: Preconceptions and Misconceptions of Public Relations among Students in the Principles Course." *Public Relations Review* 29 (2003): 199–214.

Bivins, Thomas H. *Handbook for Public Relations Writing*, 3rd ed. Lincolnwood, IL: NYC Business Books, 1995. Provides an introduction to the wide range of writing assignments in public relations practice.

Center, Allen H., and Patrick Jackson. *Public Relations Practices: Managerial Case Studies and Problems*, 6th ed. Upper Saddle River, NJ: Prentice Hall, 2003. Case studies illustrate how practitioners apply public relations theory and principles.

Creedon, Pamela J., ed. *Women in Mass Communication*, 2nd ed. Newbury Park, CA: Sage, 1993. Essays explore feminist theory and the women's movement in mass communication.

Grunig, Larissa A., Elizabeth L. Toth, and Linda C. Hon, *Women in Public Relations: How Gender Influences Practice*. New York: The Guilford Press, 2001. Authoritative synthesis of almost two decades of scholarly inquiry on gender issues in public relations.

Hon, Linda Childers, Larissa A. Grunig, and David M. Dozier. "Women in Public Relations: Problems and Opportunities." In *Excellence in Public Relations and Communication Management*, edited by James E. Grunig, 419–38. Mahwah, NJ: Lawrence Erlbaum Associates, 1992.

3 ORGANIZATIONAL SETTINGS

Public relations people, if they are to be truly respected by management colleagues, must merit "a seat at the management table."

—The Public Relations Strategist[1]

STUDY GUIDE

After studying Chapter 3, you should be able to

- Discuss top management's impact on determining the relative importance and role of public relations.

- Distinguish between line and staff functions, and explain why public relations is a staff function in most organizations.

- Outline major advantages and disadvantages of internal departments and outside counseling firms for serving an organization's public relations needs.

- Describe working relationships between the public relations unit and other departments in organizations.

- Outline four approaches public relations firms use for billing clients.

Years of acquisitions, divestitures, downsizing, globalization, reengineering, and mergers have produced great changes in the structure of organizations. Budget cuts and deficits, taxpayer revolts, and deregulation have led to reorganization, decentralization, and staff cuts in all levels of government. Nationally publicized scandals, embarrassing revelations about executive salaries and benefits, increasing demand for social services, and vigorous competition for funds have forced changes in the missions and fund-raising methods in many nonprofit organizations. Employees at all levels have learned to live and work with sometimes contradictory rhetoric saying that their organization was trying to become "lean and mean," that reorganization and retraining meant "empowerment," that layoffs and plant closings were aimed at "right-sizing," and that high overhead and budget cuts had forced "outsourcing." In short, organizational changes have transformed much in public relations practice.

Many, if not most, organizations reorganized the public relations function, reduced department staff size, and tried to do more with fewer people. Many shifted part or all of the workload to outside counseling firms and agencies, producing dramatic increases in cash flow and profitability. Small public relations firms merged; acquired others; or affiliated to form regional, national, and international networks. Large national public relations firms became international by opening or acquiring branches outside their headquarters country or by merging with firms in other countries.

In other words, practitioners work in turbulent organizational settings, dealing with both internal and external change. Many work at the highest levels of management, helping chief executive officers (CEOs) and others manage organizational change. This chapter discusses the origins and place of public relations in organizations, its responsibilities, and its working relationships with other departments.

ORIGINS WITHIN ORGANIZATIONS

Public relations in organizations often can be traced back to unintended and humble beginnings. It can begin with someone simply answering letters from customers or members; with someone writing copy for direct mail, institutional advertising, or the annual report; with someone handling visitors, conducting tours, or arranging the annual meeting; or with someone serving as an organization's ombudsman for employees or neighbors. In other organizations, public relations starts as product and service publicity, as news support for a national advertising campaign, or as a fund-raising or membership drive.

Public relations' creation, however, does not always spring from a welcome opportunity. For example, emergencies or crises such as accidents, product recalls, and layoffs attract public and media attention. If no one on the staff is qualified to deal with the media and to handle public information, the function begins under crisis conditions. Media specialists or outside public relations counsel brought in on a short-term basis to help with the immediate crisis subsequently may be hired or retained on a continuing basis. Long after the emergency or crisis subsides, public relations is defined and redefined to fit changing missions, new problems and opportunities, and the values and views of a succession of CEOs.

Because so many factors influence how public relations begins in organizations, even some large organizations have small public relations departments. Conversely, some relatively small enterprises employ many practitioners, in some cases supplementing their work with outside counsel. Many departments report directly to the CEO, whereas others report to the top human resources or marketing officer. In a few organizations, public relations reports to the top legal officer. Some organizations retain outside counselors, even though setting up their own internal staff would be logically the more appropriate choice. In others, internal staffers are assigned tasks that could be better handled by outside counsel.

Public relations departments in some organizations have large staffs and generous budgets, even though the original motivations for the function have long been forgotten and their mission is not clearly defined. Departments in other organizations strain to marshal public support, to neutralize well-organized public opposition, or to build new relationships across international borders without either the staff or the funds necessary to achieve program goals.

Such mismatches often represent nothing more than delays in adapting to change. But even practitioners disagree about what is the best structure and place for the function in various types of organizations. As a consequence, each internal public relations department is tailor-made to suit a particular organization and its unique circumstances, particularly the expectations of the CEO.

Establishing a Public Relations Department

The position of public relations on the organization chart and its relationship to top management often can be explained by how the function came into being. For example, top managers in a rapidly growing corporation discover that they have lost touch with employees, and their former face-to-face communications with all employees are no longer possible. The CEO then directs the human resources department to hire a writer–editor to create a weekly news update for the company's intranet and to publish a quarterly employee newsletter. On the basis of the success of the employee communication efforts, top managers soon ask the energetic and ambitious communication specialist to write occasional news releases about employee achievements and corporate successes. Shortly after, the job expands to include duties such as speechwriter for the CEO and the corporation's media contact. The communication specialist hires an assistant to handle a growing number of internal and external communication needs.

Because the function expanded beyond its original employee communication origins, top management moves it out of the human resources department and gives it a new title—"Public Relations Department." The new department's manager reports directly to the CEO. Its missions are to improve communication and to build better relationships with all the corporation's major internal and external stakeholders.

As the corporation grows, the public relations department takes on responsibilities for maintaining relationships with investors and financial analysts, government agencies at all levels, community groups, environmental and other special-interest groups, and an increasingly diverse workforce. The public relations manager gets promoted to vice president and appoints managers for each of the specialized department areas. In some instances, the new vice president is elected to the executive committee and participates in corporate decision making at the highest level.

From its origin as a low-level communication support function in the human resources department, the role evolved to become an integral part of the management team. To stay on the management team, however, it must contribute to achieving organizational goals and demonstrate accountability through measurable results.

Retaining Outside Counsel

Client relationships with outside counseling firms also can begin in simple and unexpected ways. For example, an organization retains an outside firm (sometimes called an "agency") to conduct a survey of community public opinion regarding a proposed trash-to-energy recycling plant. After receiving the survey results, client management asks the firm to help interpret the findings "from an outsider's perspective" and to help solve a public opinion problem identified by the survey. Success in the follow-up project leads to a continuing and expanding relationship as the client draws on the full range of the firm's public relations capabilities.

The client pays the firm a monthly retainer fee, ensuring access to outside counsel and covering a set number of hours of service each month. Above and beyond regular counsel and services, the firm takes on special projects such as producing the annual report, designing and creating the organization's home page on the World Wide Web, and special-event planning for the grand opening and dedication of the new facility. The firm bills the client an agreed-upon hourly fee or a fixed fee to cover all costs associated with the additional projects.

The firm's account executive and the internal department's management work as a team to plan and carry out the public relations program. The account executive meets periodically with the client's senior management and public relations staff to discuss plans and to assess progress. The client–firm relationship becomes so close that the firm's account executive sits in on many of the client's internal planning meetings.

Friction sometimes develops, however, when the account executive is not available because of travel and work demands from other clients or, more commonly, when the firm charges for more hours than the client's management anticipates. A hastily called meeting to discuss the invoice reminds both the account executive and internal public relations management that outside counsel is a variable cost and that the outside firm has its own economic goals. The relationship continues but with frequent reminders that clients and outside counselors work from different perspectives. That outsider's perspective was, after all, why the client organization retained the counseling firm in the first place.

PUBLIC RELATIONS STARTS WITH TOP MANAGEMENT

One of the few safe generalizations in public relations is that an organization's public reputation derives in substantial part from the behavior of its senior officials. As those in top management act and speak, so go the interpretations and echoes created by the public relations function. Thus, public relations is inescapably tied, by nature and by necessity, to top management, with public relations staff providing counsel and communication support.

For example, when traces of benzene were found in its bottled water, Source Perrier's top management first suggested that it resulted from a single, isolated cleaning accident and that contaminated bottles were limited to only the few being recalled in North America. The next installment of top management's story came when scientists found benzene-tainted products in Europe. This time, management attributed the benzene to a simple problem with the filter system. Finally, red-faced Perrier management announced a worldwide recall. Tests showed that consumers around the world had been drinking contaminated products for months. The media blasted Perrier, questioning management's integrity and raising concern for public safety. Perrier lost and has not regained its former share of the bottled water market.

Likewise, Exxon's CEO did not go to Alaska after the tanker Exxon *Valdez* spilled millions of gallons of crude oil into the environmentally sensitive Prince William Sound. TWA's (airline now merged into American Airlines) CEO resigned three months after 230 people lost their lives in the crash of Flight 800. He had been criticized for delaying 13 hours before leaving London to go to the crash site and for not immediately expressing concern about crash victims and their families. Both companies have struggled to regain public confidence and respect.

Johnson & Johnson's handling of the Tylenol tampering crisis, however, stands in stark contrast. Top management put customer safety first, immediately pulling the product off retail shelves and recalling capsules in the United States and abroad. Management took these dramatic steps even though the only known tampering cases were limited to the Chicago area. Media coverage praised the company's socially responsible actions, reported the company's cooperation with federal agencies, and gave full coverage to later announcements of new tamper-resistant packaging.

Similarly, then-Texaco's CEO quickly apologized when taped recordings were released that exposed senior managers discussing past racial discrimination and the planned destruction of evidence for a civil rights case. He then announced the formation of an independent task force to help the company implement its plan to increase diversity in its employees and management and among the outside firms hired by Texaco. Unlike the crises at Perrier, Exxon, and TWA, Johnson & Johnson's crisis became a classic case study in crisis communication management, and Texaco's embarrassing revelation motivated long-overdue change. In these cases, the CEO set the course and became the public face in responding to the crisis.

Crises potentially involve and affect many stakeholder groups: customers, employees, wholesalers and retailers, consumer action groups, government agencies, stockholders and investment analysts, international media, and concerned citizens around the world. The Perrier case probably contributed to the subsequent series of investigations and media disclosures about the quality and purity of all bottled waters, so even competing brands were affected. Exxon credit card holders cut up and returned their cards, quit buying Exxon products, and even protested the use of single-hull tankers. TWA lost its CEO and media relations director, suffered a major setback in consumer confidence, and had to play down rumors of impending bankruptcy. A few years later, the airline went bankrupt and was acquired by American Airlines.

By contrast, Johnson & Johnson's response positioned it as a leader in safe packaging, forcing competing brands to follow suit; led to Johnson & Johnson's ranking among the most respected corporations; and helped the company retain market share for Tylenol. Texaco's quick apology, immediate corrective actions, and announced long-term strategy for organizational change cut short public criticism and made the company's responses part of the story. Each crisis provides an example of top management's key role in an organization's public relations.

These cases illustrate that public relations credibility starts with management's integrity and socially responsible actions. In addition, long-term success in public relations calls for the following from top management:

1. Commitment to and participation in public relations
2. Retention of competent public relations counsel
3. Incorporation of public relations perspectives in policy making
4. Two-way communication with both internal and external publics
5. Coordination of what is done with what is said
6. Clearly defined goals and objectives

The first and continuing task for public relations is to earn and hold support from top management. Johnson & Johnson's former public relations head reports that such support is not easily earned and requires mutual respect:

> Perhaps in more than any other relationship among senior executives in a company, the chemistry that exists between the CEO and the senior public relations executive is most

critical. If things are working as they should, the public relations person is given the unique opportunity to become the CEO's "loyal opposition," the one who, behind closed doors, can say, "If you do this, you are making a huge mistake."[2]

STAFF ROLE

Public relations is one of several staff functions, meaning that it advises and supports line managers who have responsibility and authority to run the organization. Practitioners therefore need to understand the staff role.

The line–staff management model originated in the military but now is used in most large organizations. **Line functions** in industry include the product- and profit-producing functions: engineering, production, and marketing. **Staff functions** include those that advise and assist line executives: finance, legal, human resources (formerly personnel), and public relations. Iowa-based publisher and broadcaster Meredith Corporation makes the staff role explicit in the position title—"Staff Vice President/Director of Public Relations."

Staff support becomes increasingly necessary as an organization increases in size and complexity. Line executives have the authority and responsibility to set policy and to oversee the operations, but they need assistance in the form of plans, advice, support services, and suggestions from staff executives. Staff officers advise top executives and provide support to line officers.[3] Many years ago, a management expert made the distinction rather bluntly: "Specialists are necessary, but 'they should be on tap—not on top.'"[4]

Line management and public relations staff should be able to count on each other for support. Management reasonably expects the following from the public relations staff:

1. Loyalty
2. Counsel on the public relations aspects of decisions
3. Skill in articulating principles and in enhancing public understanding of the organization
4. Inspiration to help all members do their best
5. Influence in restraining other members from saying or doing anything detrimental to the organization's welfare
6. Character—honesty, trustworthiness, and discretion

One CEO defines the ideal public relations officer as

Honest, trustworthy, discreet, with solid analytical skills, and a total comprehension and understanding of the core business and the key publics. He or she will have the ability to listen, the ability to counsel, and the ability to help the CEO manage competing priorities. The most important qualities, however, are chemistry, trust, and respect. Without them, it's impossible for the CEO and chief communication officer to establish a productive long-term relationship.[5]

Public relations staff expect the following from line management:

1. Positive public relations leadership
2. Support of approved communication policy

3. Strategic plans embracing all policies and programs

4. Adequate budget to do the job, including funds for adequate public opinion research, analysis, and program evaluation

5. Reasonable availability for consultation and for public appearances

Each also has the right to expect of the other character and performance that will stand public scrutiny and fulfill the organization's social responsibility.

Differences between line and staff management, however, call for different roles in the relationship. Line management determines the ground rules and sets the course. Once all points of view have been aired and debated, the resulting decisions may result from a consensus or from choices made by line management. Both line and staff managers must participate, but final decisions are the province of senior line management. Public relations works within those rules on matters having an impact on the organization's internal and external relationships.

Public relations practitioners typically applaud when public relations executives move into line management but view the reverse with alarm. In a bit of semantic tyranny, the Task Force on the Stature and Role of Public Relations labeled movement into public relations management from other staff or line units as "encroachment," identifying it as a threat to the profession.[6] Their concern centers on who will make public relations program decisions and recommendations and who will be left with the tasks of implementing programs.[7] On the other hand, not all agree that there is an encroachment problem, pointing out that executives who have public relations experience move on to other assignments with a greater understanding of the function.

Line managers often rotate through a variety of assignments before reaching the top. Not many, however, include public relations in their regular rotation of assignments. Public relations experience would add to the credibility of public relations as a management function, demystify the function for other managers, and expand career opportunities for those now viewed as communication technicians with no role in management.[8] In most organizations, however, the demarcation between line and staff management continues to guide decision making.

ROLE IN DECISION MAKING

Traditional and somewhat rigid distinctions between line and staff managers—giving orders versus giving advice—do not always represent their respective roles in decision making. For example, practitioners operating in the expert prescriber role often have the power to choose among public relations program alternatives, with line management later endorsing the selections or exercising veto power. Practitioners, when in a problem-solving process facilitator role, often collaborate with line managers to make decisions. Increasingly, practitioners are assuming positions in the policy-setting and decision-making "dominant coalition," a term used to describe those who hold power in organizations.[9]

Proximity and **access** are important factors influencing the role of public relations in management decision making. For example, when faced with bankruptcy, Federated Department Stores expanded its dominant coalition to include the vice president of corporate communication:

> They moved the corporate communications function to the 20th floor; the 20th floor is where the senior management offices are located. So we were literally right in the midst of things….It's a very informal communications process. There was an amazing amount

of contact that occurred in the hallway. The president would just walk down the hall and come in my office. It is casual in that respect, but really is an important component of the access to the thought process, access to the person, access to judgment calls when they need to be made.[10]

Organizational changes also can enhance or diminish the role of public relations in management. For example, Volvo's CEO, upon appointment at the Sweden-based manufacturer, elevated the senior communication and government relations officers to the top management team. At United Airlines, the establishment of an employee stock option plan led to an expanded role for public relations in corporate decision making. Then-vice president of corporate communication John Kiker said that since that change, United's CEO and other managers increasingly seek public relations input and counsel before making decisions, rather than "make decisions first, and communicate the decisions afterwards."[11] When Boeing Company acquired McDonnell Douglas Aircraft Company, it restructured its management team, forming an executive council that reports to the chairman's office. The vice president of communications and investor relations and the vice president of ethics report to the council, placing these staff management executives in positions to influence decision making.[12]

In addition, **characteristics of the practitioners** themselves—particularly **personal credibility**—contribute to their inclusion or exclusion from the dominant coalition. Researchers have identified practitioners' lack of broad business experience, passivity, naïveté about organization politics, technical education, gender, and tenure in their organizations as factors contributing to the relatively limited power of public relations in organizations.[13]

Public relations participation in organizational decision making also depends on **the extent to which the function conducts various kinds of research.** Researchers have called such research "organizational intelligence gathering," "environmental scanning," "scanning for planning," and "formal versus informal research." Regardless of labels, survey results consistently show that when the function engages in various types of research, there is a greater likelihood that public relations staff will be involved in decision making and other management planning activities.[14]

The major determinant of public relations' role in organizational decision making, however, is **the degree to which line managers and practitioners themselves view the function as part of the management team.** When top management views the function as marginal and outside the main line of business, it remains outside the dominant decision-making coalition. The Excellence Study researchers discovered that CEOs in the top 10 percent of organizations were almost three times more supportive of the public relations function than were CEOs in other organizations. Likewise, top public relations executives in the top 10 percent of organizations in the study rated the dominant coalition as more than three times more supportive than did public relations executives in other organizations.[15]

When public relations operates in the realm of programmed decisions, it is seen as part of organizational routine and overhead. When it participates in nonprogrammed decision making, on the other hand, it is seen as playing an important role in achieving organizational goals and contributing to the bottom line. When public relations employs management by objectives (MBO), management by objectives and results (MOR), or management by key results to guide program planning and management, then the focus shifts from producing communications (process) to results and consequences (impact). It also makes public relations more a part of the management team held accountable for achieving organizational goals.

According to Robert Dilenschneider, former president and CEO of Hill & Knowlton and now chairman of the Dileschneider Group of New York and Chicago, "seven deadly sins in this business" threaten progress in integrating the function:

1. Overpromising, making commitments for things they know they cannot deliver
2. Overmarketing, or overselling the client on the capabilities or expertise of public relations
3. Underservicing (sometimes referred to as "bait-and-switch"), listing senior people as part of the account team but using junior staff to do the work
4. Putting the firm's financial results ahead of performance and results for the client
5. Using the quick fix, when public relations takes the form of shortsighted responses to complex problems that require long-lasting solutions (Note: It is easy to fall into the trap of client or management expectations that public relations has the power to fix problems without having to make changes in the organization.)
6. Treating public relations as simply a support function charged with implementing strategies formulated by lawyers, financial officers, and top-line managers
7. Violating ethical standards, thereby damaging the function's reputation for ethical conduct and concern for social responsibility[16]

As a management function, public relations is part of an organization's structure and process for adapting to change. Its responsibilities include helping organizations identify, assess, and adjust to their turbulent economic, political, social, and technological environments. In the words of one corporate CEO,

> I believe the public relations field will continue to be pressed by the dynamics of public media and special interest group scrutiny, and the acceleration of global telecommunications technologies. The public relations profession needs to anticipate social, political, and economic issues that have the potential of impacting business plans, instead of being only reactive.[17]

In the final analysis, however, as Pacific Gas and Electric's former CEO Richard A. Clarke said, "The only way CEOs can get what they need from their public relations advisers is to have them at the table when the policies, strategies, and programs are being hammered out."[18]

THE INTERNAL DEPARTMENT

The internal department is the most common structure for serving the public relations needs of organizations. The department may consist of only one person, as in a small hospital, or a staff of almost 1,500, as in the U.S. Army. There is probably even more work in public relations in the Department of Defense, but the actual number there remains difficult to determine. A public relations department may be concentrated in the organization's headquarters or scattered among many locations. The department's size, role, and place in the organization chart vary from one organization to the next.

The Department's Advantages

An internal department has at least four factors working in its favor:

1. Team membership
2. Knowledge of the organization
3. Economy to the organization for many ongoing programs
4. Availability to associates

Team membership is the department's greatest advantage over outside counsel. In some organizations the top public relations executive's office is next door to the chief executive's office. As an example of the close working relationship, for years the top public relations executive at Eastman Kodak began most workdays by meeting with the CEO. Federated Department Stores moved the public relations function to the 20th floor where other senior management offices are located because "it's a more complicated, complex, interrelated … involvement than ever before."[19]

Frequent contact between the public relations department and top-line management is the rule rather than the exception. According to *pr reporter* newsletter, 60 percent of public relations executives meet with their CEOs at least once each week. Such a close working relationship between the public relations department and the CEO builds confidence, trust, and support. It can also position public relations as a key player on the management team.

Knowledge of the organization means an intimate, current knowledge that comes from being an insider. Staff members know the relationships among individuals and departments and are fully aware of the undercurrents of influence and internal politics. They can call on key people to make decisions and avoid those who put personal ambition and expedience above organizational and public interests. They are aware of who can serve as able and articulate spokespersons as opposed to those who become tongue-tied or are media-shy persons who do not perform well on camera.

Occasionally a trusted outside counselor is able to acquire such knowledge, but insiders are in the better position to do so and to apply their knowledge on a continuous basis. Because they are part of the organization, internal departmental staff are able to advise, conciliate, and provide services while taking into account organizational history and culture. They know who and what to avoid, as well as who and what to include.

Economy can occur from typically lower overhead costs and efficient integration in an organization. When the need for public relations is continuous—and in most organizations it is—then a full-time, permanent staff is typically more cost effective than outside counsel and services. For example, the marginal costs of the department's space, heat, and light are typically a small portion of overhead costs in a large organization. The outside firm's overhead might be higher than that of an internal department simply because outside firms are typically smaller than the client organizations they serve, so economies of scale on overhead, such as the costs of facilities, employee benefits programs, and supplies, are lost.

Start-up costs for projects can be less, because internal staff members already have the necessary background, access, and understanding. Routine aspects of the work, such as weekly news releases, monthly publications, quarterly reports, and so forth, are efficiently handled by those closest to the sources and other departments in the organization. Efficiency contributes to cost effectiveness.

Availability of staff practitioners has many facets. When things go wrong, practitioners are only a minute away from a face-to-face meeting with the organization's officers. And as deputies, they can be entrusted with delicate matters. For example, if a senior executive defects in a huff, the CEO wants a public relations specialist on the spot who knows the background, understands the dangers of mishandling the news, and has credibility with the news media and other key players.

Availability also means being on call for all other departments, divisions, and operating units. Staff members can be called into meetings on short notice. In some organizations, public relations is decentralized, with specialists assigned to each operating unit. In others, a centralized function operates from headquarters much in the fashion of an outside firm, treating operating units and other departments as clients. The difference, of course, is that the on-site internal staff members are relatively handy for consultation.

The Department's Disadvantages

Team membership can be a problem when a person sacrifices objectivity and perspective in order to be a team player. If people are too loyal, they may be exploited when friendships and collegiality lead to subservience. Availability can cast the function as a catchall if it does not have a clearly defined mission and specified roles.

A **loss of objectivity** can happen ever so slowly and unwittingly as practitioners are subjected to day-to-day pressure and politics in the workplace. In supporting and being supported, they tend to be absorbed and compromised by group views. Their ability to see other points of view gives way to the subjectivity that afflicts those they were hired to counsel. They lose their ability to do the boundary spanning needed to avoid or solve problems in the organization's relationships with others. In effect, practitioners run the risk of becoming part of the problem. After all, they work hard to become part of the management team.

Domination and **subservience** result when the function becomes co-opted, resulting in a group of yes-men and -women. Being team players and helping others is one thing; being diverted from goals, planning, and strategy to run errands for others is another. Practitioners walk a narrow line between rendering professional services that are valuable, helpful, and appreciated and rendering low-level support that is easily replaced. Successfully making this distinction in practice tends to sort out potential staff managers from those who will remain in technical support staff roles. There is much more to the position than simply knowing organizational politics or playing the political game. The key is being a team player providing staff support based on public relations knowledge and skills while retaining one's unique role and professionalism. Inaction based on fear of making a career-threatening move or decision renders the function powerless and undermines its role as counselor to top management.

Confused mission and roles can result from being readily available. Practitioners find themselves serving as stand-ins for top executives who make commitments but do not or cannot follow through themselves. For example, a CEO accepts an invitation to serve on a community organization board or committee but finds it difficult to attend the meetings. The practitioner gets a call to attend in the CEO's place. One could argue this indicates that the CEO trusts the public relations officer to effectively represent the organization. External constituencies are seldom pleased to have a public relations representative instead of the CEO, however. They accept the switch in order to maintain the organization's support and permission to use the CEO's name on the letterhead and in other public communications.

The dilemma of a state bar association public relations director illustrates confusion about mission and roles. Among many miscellaneous duties, he was put in charge of the housekeeping staff and was directed to deal with the homeless and others who entered the main reception area to use restroom facilities and to seek refuge from the cold and rain. How did the practitioner get such duties? Being the only nonlawyer at the director level probably did not help, but a vague and open-ended job description made the function vulnerable. The public relations director also was the most available, because other directors were often out of the office conducting programs and providing direct services to members. It became a vicious cycle: The more miscellaneous assignments the director had, the less time he had for the association's public relations efforts and publications. Not surprisingly, the executive director eventually questioned the public relations director's effectiveness and criticized him for missing publication deadlines.

Titles and Reporting Relationships

Titles and positions of departments in organizations vary greatly. *O'Dwyer's Directory of Corporate Communications*—2004 lists titles for 7,800 departments in companies, associations, and governmental units. Recent editions of this annual directory show that "public relations" is the most commonly used title across all organizations. Many corporations use "corporate communications" or "communications," with about one in ten using "public affairs." Other commonly used titles include "corporate relations" and "public information." Among *Fortune* 500 companies, however, only about one in five use "public relations" titles (alone or in combination with other names).

There is no compelling reason to conclude that some other title will replace "public relations." To the contrary, "public relations" has survived almost a century despite the many attempts by practitioners themselves to find an alternative, despite the occasional taint of malpractice by individual practitioners, and despite public relations bashing by the media. Both news media and publics worldwide have come to understand the term and to use it to describe this function in organizations. Switching labels does not change more than 100 years of history.

More significant than the department's title, however, is the top public relations executive's place on the organizational chart and reporting relationship to the CEO. Too often, public relations is not included in the CEO's decision-making circle, the executive committee. In a corporation, for example, that group typically brings together the CEO, the president (if someone other than the CEO), and the heads of manufacturing, finance, marketing, engineering and R&D, and legal. If public relations is not included, then implications of decisions on the organization's relationships with key stakeholders and communication needs may not be part of the discussion when decisions are made.[20] Even if not included in the decision circle meetings, however, the top public relations executive typically reports directly to the CEO.

Reporting relationships and job functions are included in organization charts and job descriptions. These lay the groundwork for division and specialization of work, communication up and down the chain of command, and acceptance of various functions throughout the organization. Some practitioners, however, become preoccupied with trying to change the charts and edit their job descriptions, as though these, with no other changes, will elevate the public relations function or somehow change how it is performed. As one long-standing opponent of organization charts—the late Clarence Randall, a management innovator when he headed Inland Steel—pointed out,

To know who is to do what and to establish authority and responsibility within an institution are the basic first principles of a good administration, but this is a far cry from handing down immutable tablets of stone from the mountaintop....It is not the preparation of the organization chart that I condemn, but its abuse: this blowing up its significance to a point where guidance ceases and inhibition sets in.[21]

Organization charts are, at best, approximations, but they do help clarify the role and relationships of various functions. Figure 3.1, for example, illustrates how public relations and legal *staff* functions report to the CEO differently than do the *line* managers. Figure 3.2 and 3.3 detail reporting relationships within public relations departments at a university and a corporation.

FIGURE 3.1

LINE AND STAFF ORGANIZATION CHART

FIGURE 3.2

UNIVERSITY PUBLIC RELATIONS DEPARTMENT

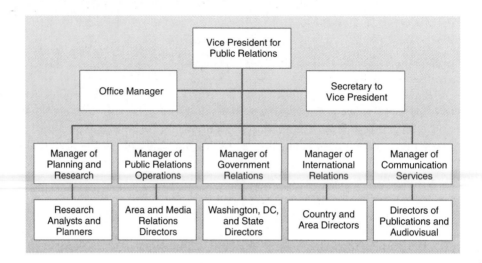

Determinants of Excellence

The landmark "Excellence Study," funded by the International Association of Business Communicators (IABC) Research Foundation, identified the major factors that make public relations an effective management function in organizations. These characteristics provide a guide for how to structure and manage the public relations function. A summary of the research findings follows.

1. Empowerment of the Public Relations Function
- The senior public relations executive is involved with the strategic management processes of the organization, and communication programs are developed for strategic publics identified as a part of this strategic management process.
- The senior public relations executive is a member of the dominant coalition of the organization, or the senior public relations executive has a direct reporting relationship to senior managers who are part of the dominant coalition.
- Diversity is embodied in all public relations roles.

2. Communicator Roles
- The public relations unit is headed by a manager rather than a technician.
- The senior public relations executive or others in the public relations unit must have the knowledge needed for the manager role, or the communication function will not have the potential to become a managerial function.
- Both men and women must have equal opportunity to occupy the managerial role in an excellent department.

3. Organization of the Communication Function, Relationship to Other Functions, and Use of Consulting Firms
- An excellent public relations function integrates all public relations programs into a single department or provides a mechanism for coordinating programs managed by different departments.
- Public relations should be a management function separate from other functions.

4. Models of Public Relations

- The public relations department and the dominant coalition share the worldview that the communication department should reflect the two-way symmetrical, or mixed-motive, model of public relations.

- Communication programs developed for specific publics (including employees) are based on the two-way symmetrical, mixed-motive model.

- The senior public relations executive or others in the public relations unit must have the knowledge needed for the two-way symmetrical model, or the communication function will not have the potential to practice that excellent model.[22]

The Excellence theory provides guidelines for how public relations should be conducted, structured, and implemented in order to contribute to overall organizational excellence. The Excellence Study also produced evidence demonstrating how the organizational context nurtures or impedes the effectiveness of public relations departments.

WORKING WITH OTHER DEPARTMENTS

Public relations staff work most closely with the marketing and finance units. They also collaborate with the human resources, industrial or employee relations, and legal departments. All these functions overlap with public relations in varying degrees, occasionally leading to unavoidable confusion about or even outright conflict over their respective roles. Disruptive and costly friction occurs particularly in relations with marketing, legal counsel, human resources, and development. To discharge obligations effectively, each function needs the support and cooperation of the others.

Marketing

As Chapter 1 pointed out, public relations is most often confused with marketing. These two major communication and outreach functions must work in harmony in dealing with an organization's many publics. Conflict usually arises in corporations over which function should be responsible for institutional advertising and product publicity. In nonprofit organizations, the two functions struggle over responsibility for and resources—budget and people—for fund-raising, membership drives, or public education and persuasion campaigns. Confusion often results from differing views of the roles of marketing versus public relations, with marketing specialists typically defining "public relations" as simply publicity or, even more mistakenly, as "journalism." Some holding this view also define any goal-driven strategic plan as "marketing."

Confusion also results from the mistaken notion that advertising is the sole province of marketing. Advertising designed to establish, change, or maintain relationships with key publics (usually by influencing public opinion) should, by its objectives and strategic nature, be supervised by the public relations department. Advertising for public relations purposes—causes and issues, corporate reputation, financial, or special events—may require the advertising department's expertise to produce and place the advertisements, but the outcome sought has more to do with public relations than with selling goods or services, in other words, marketing.

Conversely, publicity about products and services designed to increase sales is clearly directed to achieving marketing outcomes. Because public relations staff members are typically more skilled at writing and placing publicity, they often are enlisted to help publicize new products, product changes, price changes, product recalls, and special promotional activities as part of the marketing effort. Microsoft used national publicity efforts, along with advertising, to help introduce each edition of Windows. Even though it may have had an impact on publics other than customers—such as investors, competitors, government regulators—the publicity was designed primarily to support the marketing effort.

Advertising and publicity produced by either public relations or marketing should be coordinated with the other's communications. For example, public relations should not tell environmental groups about the company's commitment to protecting the environment when marketing is running a nationwide sale of "non-green" products that cause environmental damage. Backlash is an ever-present danger. The growth of articulate protest and consumer groups, widespread use of the Internet globally, investigative and consumer reporting, and government scrutiny all make cooperation between public relations and marketing essential.

Competition, even conflict, between these two functions is understandable. Practitioners often compete on parallel career tracks for recognition, job advancement, and budgets. For example, a public relations author published an article with the subtitle "How to Steal Budget from Those Folks in Advertising." In some organizations, marketing and public relations report to the same executive, who is charged with coordinating efforts. Usually, however, they are separate departments, with public relations in a staff relationship to the chief executive officer and marketing in the line management chain of command.

Legal Counsel

The conflict between public relations and legal staffs is an old one. In the days of the muckrakers, corporate executives turned first to their lawyers to fix things. Some still do. One of the founders of public relations, Ivy Lee, felt strongly about this in 1925:

> I have seen more situations which the public ought to understand and which the public would sympathize with, spoiled by the intervention of the lawyer than in any other way. Whenever a lawyer starts to talk to the public, he shuts out the light.[23]

Traditionally, legal and public relations counselors approach situations from different perspectives. Lawyers tend to favor "no comment," pointing out that what you say may come back to haunt you (be used as evidence in court) and reminding that you are not legally obliged to say anything. Public relations practitioners, on the other hand, espouse the virtues of openness, of sharing information as soon as possible, of cooperating with the media, and of responding to people's claims to a right to know. Lawyers are accustomed to getting extensions, to protracting the process in private, and to delaying responses as long as possible. Public relations specialists routinely meet deadlines, recognize media time constraints as real, and respond immediately to media requests.

Public relations practitioners work to build and maintain mutuality and harmony in relationships. If public relations succeeds, then top management assumes that things are going smoothly and that there is no need for counsel. Lawyers, on the other hand, are called on when conflict and discord dominate an organization's relationships. Under conditions of threatened or actual legal action, top management turns to legal counsel for advice and protection. Hence lawyers gain power when organizations face conflict and discord with publics that turn to the courts for redress.

Under more positive conditions, public relations practitioners with good writing skills can help make legal documents more understandable. In doing so, they can save organizations the costs of being misunderstood or of being offensive because of obscure or needlessly harsh language. Cooperation between these two functions can protect the organization legally while at the same time serving the public interest, as when Sentry Insurance led the way in the insurance industry by rewriting policies and literature in plain English. The new policy descriptions meet the test of legal counsel and greatly increase information value to policyholders and prospective customers.

Close cooperation between legal and public relations counsel also is critical during labor contract negotiations, product recalls, layoffs or other sensitive personnel matters, consumer protests or boycotts, and other legally based or explosive situations. Additionally, legal and public relations counsel must be coordinated on such matters as booklets explaining benefits to employees, the legality of advertising or publicity claims, plant security, and disclosure of financial information.[24]

Once a concern primarily in business and industry, close cooperation between legal and public relations counselors now is necessary in most organizations. Examples from various settings illustrate the need: Universities defend themselves both in the courts of justice and public opinion when fraternity hazing deaths, date rapes, or discrimination charges in tenure decisions become national news. The presidents of Stanford, MIT, and other major universities called in both lawyers and public relations specialists when excessive overhead charges on federally funded research projects made headline news.

Increasingly, legal and public relations specialists collaborate when counseling CEOs and coordinate their responses in courts of law and in courts of public opinion. Additionally, more and more CEOs began their careers as lawyers; one survey of CEOs found that almost one-third had law degrees.[25] As one lawyer advised fellow legal counselors, however, "Make sure you are the lawyer and that public relations is handled by a public relations professional."

Human Resources

The American Society of Personnel Administrators changed its 40-year-old name to the Society for Human Resources Management in 1989. Some predicted that the emerging conflict between public relations and human resources would become a turf war similar to the one public relations and marketing experienced in the 1980s and early 1990s. Lines were blurred, and opportunity for friction was high. They still are.

Fundamental problems include (1) whether human resources' role in strategic planning in personnel matters during downsizing (read "layoffs"), reengineering, mergers, and acquisitions extends to areas outside employee relations; (2) the extent to which communication efforts within the community constitute an extension of the organization–employee relationship; and (3) whether programs directed to the employee public draw more on public relations concepts than on those developed from the traditions of personnel and extended to the new function of human resources. Control of employee communications (not the whole of employee relations) is the most frequent source of conflict between these two functions. Compromise comes when practitioners and human resource specialists realize that internal relationships inevitably reverberate externally.

Recognizing that the workforce has been and is changing, many organizations have increased efforts to develop their major resource, people. Concerns about employee loyalty and mobility, "virtual organizations," quality-of-life issues, and employee education and training are seen as directly affecting the bottom line.

> Change is now probably the only corporate constant. And if employees are expected to go along with the new programs, who better to collaborate and strategize about workforce changes than human resources and public relations?[26]

To help manage change, organizations are reorganizing, restructuring, and reengineering communication units, according to Paul Sanchez , formerly with Watson Wyatt Worldwide:

> Many communicators, once identified as part of the human resources or public relations function, are now a separate and distinct communication department, reversing a trend from the late 1980s. As senior management looks for more strategic integrated communication programming, they are finding that other staff agencies often lack the expertise or time to provide the required focus or skills spectrum. This is especially true for the types of broad communication initiatives that organizations must undertake to support organizational change.[27]

Strategic management of human resources and organizational change requires close cooperation and collaboration between public relations and human resources specialists. Otherwise, it is apparent that top management will create new units to conceive and implement internal and external communication strategy to achieve organizational goals.

THE OUTSIDE COUNSELING FIRM

Beginning in the 1980s, many "public relations agencies" changed their titles to "public relations firms." The change reflects an increased emphasis on counseling and strategic planning services, viewed as more professional than the communication tactics produced by press agents and publicity agencies. Another reason for the switch is to position the firm as something different from advertising agencies and other vendors of services working on commissions. Although some still refer to "agencies" in unguarded moments, most in the field prefer to be seen as similar to law firms, management consulting firms, certified public accounting firms, architectural firms, and consulting engineering firms.

Public Relations Firms

Public relations counseling firms in the United States range widely in size and scope. *O'Dwyer's Directory of Public Relations Firms,* which is the most complete, lists 2,275 U.S. firms by location and specialty, plus 625 in 88 other countries. New York leads all cities in the number of firms, followed closely by Chicago and Washington, D.C. The largest New York–based firm—Burson-Marsteller—employs more than 2,000 people worldwide in 47 office in 24 countries, with affiliates in seven other countries. In contrast, worldwide there are uncounted thousands working as independent self-employed counselors. Many work as "_____ and Associates," often meaning, "If I can't handle a project myself, I know other practitioners I can bring in on the project."

With the growing recognition of the global economy and formation of the European Union, the public relations capital has shifted from New York to London. According to London-based *Marketing* magazine, the leading professional publication in London, Weber Shandwick Worldwide—the largest public relations firm worldwide—has more than 2,000 employees in a rather loose network of offices built through acquisition, rather than formed by the parent firm. U.S.–based (New York) Hill & Knowlton has a network of 27 offices in Europe, 11 in the Asia-Pacific region, and 7 in Latin America.[28] H&K's London office is bigger than its New York headquarters in both size and billings. Business in Europe could increase dramatically with the new common currency and decreased international barriers to commerce. In the meantime, business in China and the rest of Asia is drawing global firms and inspiring local start-ups.

Phone directories in every major city list firms under "Public Relations" and "Publicity." For example, the London yellow pages directory contains listings under "Public Relations Consultancies" (outside the United States, "consultancy" is typically used instead of "firm.") and "Publicity Consultants."

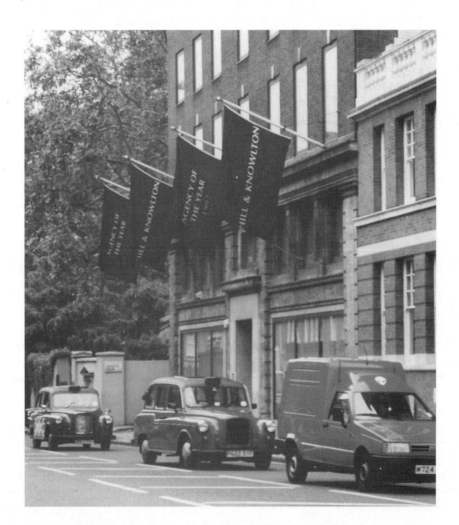

FIGURE 3.4

HILL & KNOWLTON'S LONDON OFFICE

As markets and economies became global, as global alliances formed, and as global media delivered messages around the world within seconds, public relations and every other aspect of corporate business became global enterprises. As a result, public relations firms in most major cities operate transnationally, either through affiliates or by subcontracting with local firms in other countries. For example, Sumner Rider & Associates, based in New York and Washington, D.C., used local firms in Germany, Japan, Mexico, and Italy for a program directed to the automotive industries in those countries. According to SR&A president Peter Rush,

> We demand the same things of firms in other countries that we demand of ourselves—credibility, accountability, expertise, experience, ethics, and, most important, results—although we fully understand that we have to allow them to execute the work in keeping with their cultural norms, especially as they relate to media relations.[29]

Whatever the approach, public relations firms now serve clients with new approaches to communication and sophisticated counsel in a global village.

Standards of practice for public relations firms are more closely monitored and enforced in Europe than in the United States and Asia. More than 200 firms belong to the Public Relations Consultants Association, which requires member consultancies to follow specific guidelines for dealing with the media, clients, and competitors; for conducting investor relations for publicly traded companies; and for enforcing the "Professional Charter" through arbitration and settlement. Strict enforcement forced Ogilvy Adams & Rinehart to withdraw from PRCA when it refused to list all of its clients in the association's confidential "Annual Register" as required in the PRCA Professional Charter. The first such association of firms in the United States was formed in 1998 after 38 founding firms, representing most of the major national and international firms, contributed $200,000 to establish the American Association of Public Relations Firms (AAPRF).

Advertising Agency Ownership

Many of the largest firms are subsidiaries of large advertising agencies. Many were acquired as advertising agencies bought out retiring founders and principals of closely held public relations firms. The trend began in 1978, when Foote, Cone and Belding purchased Carl Byoir and Associates. The largest U.S.–based firms are now owned by advertising agencies: Burson-Marsteller, Cohn & Wolfe, and Hill & Knowlton, Inc., by London-based WPP Group PLC; and Ketchum Public Relations Worldwide, Porter Novelli International, and Fleishman-Hillard by Omnicom Group Inc. Edelman Public Relations Worldwide, with almost 1800 employees in an international network of offices, is the largest independently owned firm.

Those who work in firms owned by large advertising agencies point to greater cooperation between the marketing and public relations functions being served by the "full-service" team, better research provided by the more experienced and sophisticated research departments of advertising agencies, greater communication production resources and capabilities, and better management.

Critics of advertising agency ownership believe that public relations firms lose their independence and clients lose the benefit of the counselor's alternative view in communication planning. They also point to diminished budgets and power for public relations, as it inevitably becomes subservient to the marketing-driven budgets and goals of the advertising team. Problems also arise when two strong institutions with different histories and cultures try to perform as a team, especially when historically they were competitors. Even though they are under the umbrella of common ownership, they remain competitors for the client's budget. Because each unit of a large conglomerate is rewarded on the basis of how much business it generates, in effect advertising and public relations units compete for the client's business. Moreover, critics question the value of the offer of one-stop shopping. Few clients use the firms as communication supermarkets. Rather, most large clients prefer to spread their business over several agencies and firms, expanding the range of perspectives and client experiences.

History suggests that forces work against the advertising agency–public relations subsidiary arrangement. Advertising agencies have found it difficult to determine what public relations services to offer, how to organize the function effectively, and how to sustain it apart from the advertising side of the shop, from which it derives the vast majority of dollar billings.

Specialization

Most firms claim to be "full-service" firms, but some carve out specialized client–service market niches. Although there are many specialties, the most dramatic growth has occurred in Washington, D.C., firms that specialize in government relations—lobbying, public affairs, and legislative affairs. Clients retain these firms primarily to participate in the public policy process and to have influence on those who formulate and implement public policy.

Client lists at many such firms also include foreign governments and foreign corporations who follow developments in the U.S. capital and who want their points of view to be considered in the White House, Congress, or federal agencies. The service can be nothing more than putting out news releases about a visiting dignitary or providing updates on legislation of interest to a foreign client. Regardless of the assignment, individuals who represent foreign interests must register with the U.S. Department of Justice. The Foreign Agents Registration Act of 1938 requires registration by any "public relations counsel, publicity agent, information-service employee, or political consultant that acts within the United States in the interest of a foreign principal." Globalization and increased international commerce of all kinds suggest that this will continue as a growth area for public relations firms specializing in government relations.

Unfortunately, the Beltway (Washington, D.C.) set also includes influence-peddling operations that rise and fall with administrations and as the public-service–private-sector revolving door produces more and more insiders with connections in their former government employers. Commenting on the antics of those who turned government service into profitable public relations and lobbying practices, one editorial writer asked, "Has the murky 'profession' of public relations turned to sleaze?" In fact, for some who abused their positions of public trust, it meant prison time and hefty fines for illegal lobbying. Those exceptions aside, there remains a large and growing need for legitimate public relations counsel on legislative affairs and lobbying in the nation's capital, as well as in every state capital and major city.

Other specialties include agriculture, financial public relations and investor relations, health care, high tech, sports, and travel and tourism, to name only a few. In agriculture, for example, Morgan & Myers in Jefferson, Wisconsin, serves clients such as the American Dairy Association, Asgrow Seed Company, and the National Pork Producers Council (see Figure 3.5). Financial Dynamics (New York) serves clients such as Coca-Cola, Renaissance Capital, and Exclusive Resorts. The client list at InterScience (New York) includes health-care, pharmaceutical, and biotechnology

FIGURE 3.5

MORGAN & MYERS

**Moving from one end of the food market
to the other requires skillful navigation.**

Whether your target is at the helm of a tractor
or the head of the kitchen table,
we'll help steer you in the right direction.

**Morgan
&Myers**   *Public
Relations
Counselors*

Phone: 414-674-4026 · **Fax:** 414-674-6670 · **E-mail:** *gmyers@morganmyers.com*

Member
The
WORLDCOM
Group, Inc.

JEFFERSON, WISCONSIN · MILWAUKEE · MINNEAPOLIS · WATERLOO, IOWA

Courtesy Morgan & Myers.

organizations such as the American Association of Clinical Endocrinologists, Bristol Myers Squibb, SB Health Services, and the National Institutes of Health. In the high-tech setting of Silicon Valley, California, Citigate Cunningham serves clients such as Apple, Cisco Systems, Hewlett-Packard, and Oracle.

In addition to industry specialization, a few firms provide specialized services to help clients target particular communities. For example, when retailer Eddie Bauer was threatened with a national boycott after a nationally publicized security guard's questionable accusation that a Black customer had shoplifted, the company retained the Black-owned firm Robinson Associates (Washington, D.C.) for counsel on community relations.

Reasons for Retaining Outside Counsel

Chester Burger, longtime consultant to the public relations industry, lists six reasons why organizations retain firms.

1. Management has not previously conducted a formal public relations program and lacks experience in organizing one.
2. Headquarters may be located far from communications and financial centers.
3. The firm has a wide range of up-to-date contacts.
4. An outside firm can provide the services of experienced executives and creative specialists who would be unwilling to move to other cities or whose salaries a single organization could not afford.
5. An organization with its own public relations department may need highly specialized services that it cannot afford or does not need on a full-time, continuous basis.
6. Crucial policy matters require the independent judgment of an outsider.

As an example, GTE Diversified Products retained Hill & Knowlton to help plan and conduct the global public relations program for its joint venture with Siemens A.G., Germany. Charged with coordinating internal and external communication operations in the United States and 22 other countries, the vice president of public affairs enlisted experienced outside help:

> By retaining their (Hill & Knowlton) services, we benefited from an existing network of media contacts, saving us some of the trouble of tracking down outlets we needed to contact with news of the joint venture. We also used their capabilities in resolving problems in translating, designing, and delivering documents in a manner appropriate to each of our markets.
>
> If you don't have a structure in place, you should consider hiring the services of an outside firm that can provide you with the necessary expertise....In a global setting, doing all this requires more effort, more forethought, and more skills than ever. There are simply more variables to contend with. And this puts even greater demands on public affairs staff.[30]

Client–Firm Relationships

Sometimes counseling firms initiate contact with clients they think need help. More commonly, clients call counseling firms. For instance, an oil company may have a

EXHIBIT 3.1

CHECKLIST FOR SELECTING A FIRM

Competence and reputation

- Years in business
- Size—people and billings
- Full service—specialties
- Reach—local, regional, national, international
- Growth pattern/financial stability
- Types of accounts
- Experience with accounts similar to yours—any conflicts
- Samples of work
- Sample list of suppliers used

Clients

- Existing client list
- Past clients
- Average number of clients during past three years—retainer clients, project clients
- Oldest clients and length of service
- Average length of client–firm relationships
- Clients lost in last year

Staff

- List and qualifications of staff— full time, project clients, freelance/ consultants
- Names of several former employees
- Staff to be assigned to your account—qualifications and longevity with firm
- Percent of their time to be devoted to your account—other accounts they will handle
- Staff or personnel backup available
- Staff turnover in the past two years

Results and measurement

- Does firm understand your objectives/needs?
- How will progress be reported?
- How will results be measured?
- What will it cost—billing process, hourly rate, expenses billed, approval process?

Courtesy Harland W. Warner, APR, Fellow Warner Communication Counselors, Inc. Reprinted with permission of Public Relations Review.

persistent problem with government regulation of offshore drilling, a long-planned enterprise in which millions of dollars have been invested. However, plans are held up because of opposition to exploration by environmental groups, investor concern that stock value will drop because of unfavorable reports in the business press, and public skepticism that the oil company will protect fragile ocean ecosystems. All this is framed by memories of the Exxon *Valdez* oil spill off Alaska's Prince William Sound. The internal department convinces the chairman and CEO that it is time to seek the best outside help available to help design and manage a strategic plan to address these public relations problems. Unfortunately, it too often takes a *Valdez* oil spill, stock sell-off, or some other crisis to get top management's attention.

It is not uncommon for the client–firm relationship to begin with an emergency, as was the case when Arizona Economic Council officials called on Hill & Knowlton.

After Arizona voters defeated a ballot initiative establishing a state holiday honoring Martin Luther King Jr., the National Football League announced that it would move the Super Bowl game from the Tempe, Arizona. In such emergencies, counsel provides advice and helps the client manage the crisis. Depending on the outcome, the firm may be retained on a long-term basis to prevent such crises in the future. In the Arizona situation, however, the Super Bowl game was moved to the Rose Bowl in Pasadena, and Hill & Knowlton lost the Arizona Economic Council as a client.

Under more typical circumstances, a counseling firm begins its service after being invited to present a proposal. It begins by researching the client's problem situation and its relationships with the publics affected by or involved in the situation. Called a "public relations audit," this initial exploration can take several days or even weeks. After doing the research, the counselor may report that there is no real problem or threat that requires outside assistance, or that the problems disclosed by the research are outside the counselor's area of expertise. More likely, however, the counsel arranges to make a presentation outlining the following.

1. Research findings and situation analysis of the problem or opportunity
2. Potential harm or gain to the organization
3. Projected difficulties and opportunities, given various courses of action or non-action
4. Overall program goals, as well as objectives for various publics
5. Immediate action and communication responses, if needed to meet a crisis
6. Long-range plan for achieving the goals and objectives
7. Evaluation plans for monitoring the program and assessing impact
8. Staffing plans, budget, and timetable

Typically, competing firms make presentations (see Figure 3.6), and one is selected on the basis of its demonstrated capabilities and the presentation proposal. Once retained, the counselor usually functions in one of three ways:

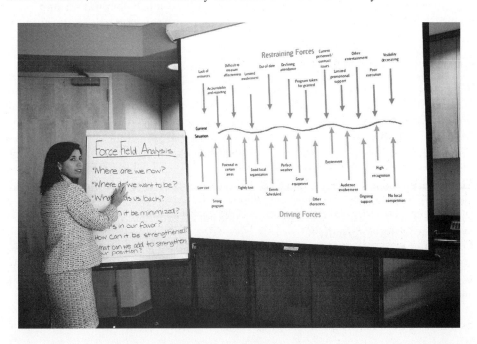

FIGURE 3.6

COUNSELOR'S PRESENTATION

Courtesy Mary Correia-Moreno, Vice President and COO, Nuffer, Smith, Tucker, Inc., San Diego.

1. Provides advice, leaving execution to the client's internal staff
2. Provides advice and works with the client's staff to execute the program
3. Provides advice and undertakes full execution of the program

Occasionally, client–firm relationships take a turn the client does not anticipate. To get the business (win the account), usually an "A-Team" of experienced professionals makes the presentation (new business pitch). The client is duly impressed by the talent and depth of experience they assume will be applied to their problems. In some instances, however, that is the last they see of many of these people. Instead, the account is assigned to staff members who do not have the range of experience represented by the new business development team. Critics justifiably refer to this practice as a "bait-and-switch" tactic. The firm's senior executives show up just often enough to assure the client, but in fact the work has been delegated to junior staff. Firms employ such a strategy at the risk of losing clients.

Clients occasionally call for a review of the firm's work or even reopen the selection process by requesting proposals from competing firms. A review may simply be a cover for having already decided to change firms. To soften the blow, the incumbent firm is given the "courtesy" of making the "short list" of finalists before another firm gets the account. In some cases, clients call for reviews and entertain proposals from competing firms simply to remind the incumbent firm that the client's business should not be taken for granted or given anything less than prime attention.

Some counselors suggest yet another reason why some clients conduct reviews and call for proposals: to get new ideas—free. The suspicion is that there is no real intention to replace the incumbent firm. The published request for proposals (RFP) or the invitation to selected firms represents an unethical search for new ideas without having to pay for the counsel. Consequently, some firms will not do speculative pitches unless the client pays a fee that covers the cost of preparing the presentation. Critics of the RFP selection process say that quality is often sacrificed when price considerations lead to choosing the low bidder.

For the most part, however, trust and respect characterize many client–firm relationships that are built on a foundation of cooperation, collaboration, and collegiality developed while working together through both the worst and best of times.

Counselors' Advantages

Nine out of ten major corporations responding to one survey reported using external counsel at corporate headquarters, with half also hiring local counseling firms to supplement corporatewide efforts and to handle regional problems and issues.[31] A Public Relations Society of America Counselors Academy survey found that almost three out of four corporations use outside counsel even though they have their own internal departments. Survey results from a wide range of organizations show increased use of outside counsel, even in government and nonprofit settings. The trend in the 1990s was to cut in-house staff and outsource work to external firms.[32] Clearly, external counsel provides valuable services not readily available internally.

Counselors rank **variety of talents and skills** as their greatest advantage over internal staffing. **Objectivity,** relatively untrammeled by the politics within an organization, ranks second. **Range of prior experience** is third; **geographical scope** of their operations, fourth; and the **ability to reinforce and upgrade a client's internal staff,** fifth.

Counseling firms with large staffs emphasize the **flexibility** of their personnel and operations as a prime advantage. In their offices, or no farther away than the telephone, are skilled researchers, artists, models, copy editors, magazine feature writers, media coaches and placement specialists, talk show experts, photographers, and legislative experts. A client can request a highly technical and specialized service, and an account executive can attend to the need immediately.

Flexibility is also tied to scope of operations and to range of experience. A firm based in New York, Washington, or Chicago can serve clients in Colorado, West Virginia, and California through its branches or affiliates. A global firm is as likely to have a network of branch offices or affiliated firms in London, Tokyo, and Melbourne as in Denver, Dallas, and Seattle.

In the course of a year, counselors work on many different problems for several different clients. In effect, a public relations firm is a repository of living case histories. Each project adds to its fund of knowledge. Experience and versatility of staff make this synergy possible. The counselor approaches each situation bolstered by experience with similar situations and knowledge of the success or failure that attended previous encounters.

The counselor's **reputation** can be a major advantage. Externally, a counselor's reputation among the press and government officials can work to the advantage of clients. Internally, outside experts often can introduce ideas that internal staffers have struggled unsuccessfully to place on the agenda. Apparently paying a hefty fee increases top management's attention to public relations counsel. And from the client's point of view, knowing that the counselor's reputation and subsequent referrals are on the line also helps ensure performance.

Counselors' Handicaps

With rare exceptions, intervention by outside counsel—and this applies to almost all consultants—meets with **internal opposition** ranging from **nonacceptance** to outright rejection. This is, at least in theory, the counselor's most serious handicap. Antagonism toward and resistance to outsiders are natural human traits. The old guard resists change—the new idea, new approach, new look—and sees it as a threat to security and established ways of doing business.

The counselor more often than not makes suggestions in the form of recommendations. Those originally responsible can take offense and be alienated by these suggestions. Their realm is being invaded; their judgment is being criticized. The offended ask, "What does this outsider know about our organization, our way of doing things?"

Counselors, however, do not rank this problem at the top. They overwhelmingly cite **questions of cost** as the most frequent problem with clients. They list **threat to old guard and set ways** as the second most persistent handicap. **Resistance to outside advice** comes in third, and **unforeseen conflicts of personality or conviction** is fourth.

Other problems expressed frequently by counselors include a stubborn **lack of understanding of public relations by clients** and **unavailability of clients—**

presumably the decision makers—at times when counselors want decisions. These suggest a problem of priorities on the part of clients.

Threatened insiders can create problems not related to the actual quality of service. Under the guise of scrutiny and concern, they raise questions about cost, return on investment, or qualifications. They point to the counselor's **superficial grasp of the organization's unique problems:** the local and historical angles on problems, the sacred cows, the things we never talk about. When those in the client organization raise such questions, it is an uphill battle for external counselors. Dealing with the internal staff and others in the client organization calls for special consulting skills.

Counseling Firm Costs

Clients retain the services of a counseling firm for specific projects or for an indefinite period of continuing service, reviewable and renewable at intervals. Fees for continuing services typically are established in one of four ways:

1. A monthly retainer covering a fixed number of hours and services
2. A minimum retainer plus monthly billing for actual staff time at hourly rates or on a per diem basis
3. Straight hourly charges, usually on a scale representing the range of experience and expertise
4. Fixed project fee, typically resulting from competitive bidding in response to a request for proposal (RFP)

Fees for specific projects, on the other hand, are paid on an hourly fee basis or as a negotiated fixed fee covering the entire project. In recent years, the project fee basis for paying firms has changed the nature of business. Now instead of having a stable client list and steady cash flow from retainers and hourly fees, firms have to compete for contracts to do specific and limited projects. As one firm's principal put it, instead of having 30 clients, the firm has to have 300 clients because so much of the work is piecemeal.

Out-of-pocket expenses are generally billed at cost and are exclusive of the retainer fee. In some cases, the client deposits an advance with the firm to cover such expenses. Some firms, however, mark up actual costs of certain expenses by 15 to 20 percent to cover overhead costs. One firm, for example, marks up advertising placements, photography, and printing by 20 percent but bills actual cost for entertainment, clipping services, and postage.

Fees vary widely. Large counseling firms have minimum retainer fees, usually in the range of $1,000 to $10,000, but up to $50,000 and more per month for major accounts. Wood products company Louisiana-Pacific (Portland) retained Fleishman-Hillard (St. Louis) for $60,000 per month, plus expenses. At the other end of the scale, a small client might pay as little as a $500 monthly retainer to write an occasional news release or as little as $100 for a single news release.

Hourly fees range from a low of $25 an hour for assistant account executives or other junior support staff to several hundred dollars for every hour worked by senior counselors and firm principals. Financial Relations Board (Chicago) reportedly charges $60 to $400 hourly for project staff. These rates typically reflect salary markups in the range of 2.5 to 3.5 times actual hourly staff costs. Figures differ from city to city, but four elements are reflected in counseling fees and charges:

1. Actual cost of staff time devoted to the project
2. Executive time and supervision
3. Overhead costs
4. Reasonable profit for doing the work, based on what the market will bear

The most common threat to client–firm relationships is conflict over the costs and hours billed. As a result, most firms use sophisticated accounting methods to record and track staff hours and project expenses. "Billable hours" often become a criterion for assessing employee productiveness. Some firms, formally or informally, expect each practitioner to bill a minimum number of hours each month, just as in most accounting and law firms. For example, it would not be unusual for an employee to "bill out" an average of more than 30 hours each week. In other words, the employee's time sheet—recorded in tenth- or quarter-hour units—documents 30 or more hours of work charged to specific client projects. (Exhibit 3.2 shows a typical form for recording hours.) Each client's monthly bill, then, reflects the total hours recorded on all staff time sheets designated to that account or project. The account executive monitors these time sheets and detailed expense records to keep costs in line with the client–firm agreement.

NEW APPROACHES

Increasingly, organizations are using a combination of internal departments and outside counsel to fulfill the public relations management function. Moreover, top management is increasingly recognizing how essential public relations is to organizational success. High-level practitioners are increasingly joining the executive decision-making group or at least are being consulted on major decisions. Practitioners in firms are increasingly serving as counselors and strategic planners, rather than acting merely as press agents and communication technicians. In short, public relations is changing and becoming an integral part of most organizations' management structure.

The president of one public relations firm predicts these changes will affect both internal departments and the firms serving them:

> Traditional, large, central PR departments will almost certainly become relics. Very tight, small and expert departments are likely to become the norm and outsourcing may be the word most commonly used. In many cases, the PR chief will use a broad array of consulting firms, rather than just one. He or she may conclude that it is far more effective to use a small, expert local company in a Third World country, rather than the local office of a U.S. multinational agency. The agencies, for their part, will need to find ways to demonstrate that they have significant comparative advantage relative to these small, local rivals.[33]

Former AT&T public relations executive Edward M. Block, who oversaw what was at the time the largest public relations department (before the 1984 breakup of

EXHIBIT 3.2

TIME SHEET

TIMESHEET Name _____ Employee # _____ Date _____

	Job #		Operation Code	Total Hours	Comments		Job #		Operation Code	Total Hours	Comments
	PFC	Job					PFC	Job			
7:00						11:00					
7:06						11:06					
7:12						11:12					
7:18						11:18					
7:24						11:24					
7:30	684	342	100		Plan product	11:30					
7:36					launch event	11:36					
7:42						11:42					
7:48						11:48					
7:54						11:54				2.0	
8:00						12:00					
8:06						12:06					
8:12						12:12					
8:18						12:18					
8:24						12:24					
8:30						12:30					
8:36				1.2		12:36	142	010	130		Follow up pitch
8:42	684	342	110		Meet w/ client	12:42					letter to Wall St.
8:48					re: special event	12:48					Journal
8:54						12:54					
9:00						1:00					
9:06						1:06					
9:12						1:12					
9:18						1:18					
9:24						1:24					
9:30						1:30					
9:36						1:36					
9:42						1:42					
9:48						1:48				1.4	
9:54				1.3		1:54	201	010	110		Call re: next
10:00	001	920	920		New business	2:00					year's program
10:06					hotel proposal	2:06				.3	
10:12						2:12	444	222	125		Brainstorm
10:18						2:18					special event
10:24						2:24					
10:30						2:30					
10:36						2:36				.5	
10:42						2:42	001	925	925		
10:48						2:48					
10:54						2:54					

Source: *The New PR Client Service Manual*, 4th ed. (San Diego, CA: PRSA Counselors Academy and GCS PR, 2001), Chapter 12, p. 7. Reprinted with permission.

AT&T), agrees that the smaller departments will increasingly work with outside firms:

> Given the choice, I would never have built anything so large....Rather than build huge staffs it (the firm) can be a cost-effective way to out-source noncritical functions. But the high priority, core responsibilities must remain in-house. A firm may even be a counselor, but not a substitute or surrogate for handling the vital pr roles.[34]

The trend to smaller public relations departments using outside firms is apparent in recent restructuring of major corporations: Hotel and gaming company ITT (New York) cut its corporate public relations staff from more than 180 in the mid-1980s to just two vice presidents in 1998. Likewise, Texaco (White Plains, New York), following the lead of competitor Mobil Oil (Fairfax, Virginia), cut 7 of the 39 staffers who had to "reapply" for 32 positions in the downsized department. The new CBS Corporation (New York) retained only the senior vice president of corporate relations and terminated five staffers when it closed the Pittsburgh headquarters of the former Westinghouse Electric Corporation (which had acquired CBS in 1995). In the mid-1980s, CBS and Westinghouse had separate public relations departments with about 30 staffers in each. The large AT&T public relations staff, already reduced to just more than 800 after the 1984 breakup, was down to half that number in 1998.

Global markets, strategic planning, and the convergence of communication and technology have attracted others to the public relations counseling field. Management consulting firms have added "communications specialists" to their staffs. Job descriptions read much like position descriptions in traditional public relations firms. Some large law firms also have started offering "public relations counsel" to complement legal counsel and services in high-profile cases that attract media coverage.

Regardless of the source of counsel and services, public relations has an impact in an organization when people begin to tell each other that candor in communication is the best policy and that socially responsible actions are in the best interest of the organization. This means that public relations consciousness is gaining ground and there is growing confidence in the staff and outside counselors.

Exposing a clean organization to public gaze and operating in the mutual interests of itself and its publics does not mean that everything about the organization should be made public. In business there are competitors to consider. In the military there are security considerations. In health institutions there are ethical limitations on disclosure of patient information. In government agencies there are political and regulatory factors. Everywhere there are legal pros and cons. Common sense helps, but organizations must have specialized staff or counsel to perform the public relations function in an ethical and professional manner. That is a lesson from public relations' history, the topic of the next chapter.

NOTES

[1] Quoted from introduction to David R. Drobis, "Stop Whining and Take a Seat! *The Public Relations Strategist* 2, no. 1 (Spring 1996): 37.

[2] Lawrence G. Foster, "10 CEOs Send a Message to Public Relations," *The Public Relations Strategist* 1, no. 1 (Spring 1995): 8.

[3] R. Wayne Pace, *Organizational Communication: Foundations for Human Resource Development* (Englewood Cliffs, NJ: Prentice Hall, 1983), 16–17.

[4] Henry H. Farquhar, "The Anomaly of Functional Authority at the Top," *Advanced Management* 7, no. 2 (April–June 1942): 51.

[5] Gary F. Grates, "Why the Coveted Top Spot Is Losing Its Allure," *Communication World* 14, no. 3 (February 1997): 26.

[6] Philip Lesly, "The Stature and Role of Public Relations," *Public Relations Journal* 37, no. 1 (January 1981): 15.

[7] Martha M. Lauzen, "Public Relations Roles, Intraorganizational Power, and Encroachment," *Journal of Public Relations Research* 4, no. 2 (1992): 61–80.

[8] Bruce R. Barstow, "An Insider's Outside View of Public Relations," in *Precision Public Relations,* ed. Ray Eldon Hiebert (New York: Longman, 1988), 65. First published in *Public Relations Review* 10, no. 1 (Spring 1984): 10–17.

[9] James E. Grunig, ed., *Excellence in Public Relations and Communication Management* (Hillsdale, NJ: Lawrence Erlbaum Associates, 1992). The term "dominant coalition" is introduced on p. 24 and used throughout the book.

[10] Adam Shell interview with Carol Sanger, Vice President of Corporate Communications, Federated Department Stores, "Talk from the Top: Communicating in Tumultuous Times," *Public Relations Tactics* 3, no. 4 (April 1996): 30–31.

[11] *Jack O'Dwyer's Newsletter* 29, no. 42 (October 23, 1996): 7.

[12] Jeff Cole, "Boeing Names New Managers, Alters Structure," *The Wall Street Journal,* August 5, 1997, p. B7.

[13] Larissa A. Grunig, "Power in the Public Relations Department," *Public Relations Research Annual* 2 (1990): 115–55.

[14] For a detailed analysis, see David M. Dozier, "The Innovation of Research in Public Relations Practice: Review of a Program of Studies," *Public Relations Research Annual* 2 (1990): 3–28.

[15] David M. Dozier, with Larissa A. Grunig and James E. Grunig, *Manager's Guide to Excellence in Public Relations and Communication Management* (Mahwah, NJ: Lawrence Erlbaum Associates, 1995), 78–80.

[16] Robert L. Dilenschneider, "The Seven Deadly Sins," *PR Week* (November 14–20, 1988): 11. For a similar perspective with extensive case examples, see Dilenschneider's edited book, *Dartnell's Public Relations Handbook,* 4th ed. (Chicago: Dartnell Corporation, 1997).

[17] Foster, "10 CEOs Send a Message," p. 11.

[18] Ibid., p. 9.

[19] Shell interview with Carol Sanger, "Talk from the Top," p. 31.

[20] Roy T. Cottier, "Communication: A Management Strategy, Not a Professional Technique," *Vital Speeches* 53, no. 18 (July 1, 1987): 556–59. Speech to International Association of Business Communicators, Toronto. Cottier is former senior vice president of corporate relations at Northern Telecom Limited.

[21] Clarence Randall, *The Folklore of Management* (Boston: Little, Brown, 1959), 24.

[22] Adapted and quoted from Larissa A. Grunig, James E. Grunig, and David M. Dozier, *Excellent Public Relations and Effective Organizations: A Study of Communication Management in Three Countries* (Mahwah, NJ: Lawrence Erlbaum Associates, 2002), 12–16.

[23] Ivy Lee, *Publicity: Some of the Things It Is and Is Not* (New York: Industries Publishing Company, 1925), 58–59.

[24] See Chapter 6 for a more detailed discussion of legal considerations.

[25] Ellen Joan Pollock, "Order in the Boardroom: Lawyers Rise to CEO," *The Wall Street Journal,* September 11, 1996, p. B1.

[26] Jean Cardwell, "Learning to Waltz with Human Resources," *The Public Relations Strategist* 2, no. 1 (Spring 1996): 44.

[27] Paul Sanchez, "Agents for Change," *Communication World* 14, no. 3 (February 1997): 53.

[28] Data reported here are from *The Holmes Report: PR Agency Report Card 2004* (New York: The Holmes Group, 2004). See current edition for updates (www.holmesreport.com).

[29] As quoted by Lee Levitt, "U.S. Firms Tap Foreign Shops for Client Work," *O'Dwyer's PR Services Report* 11, no. 6 (June 1997): 34.

[30] Geoffrey L. Pickard, "Bridging the Gap in Joint Venture Communications: Global Public Affairs," *Vital Speeches* 53, no. 5 (December 15, 1986): 145–48.

[31] *Corporate Communications Benchmark 1997,* Section II, C. Report prepared by Edelman PR Worldwide, Opinion Research Corporation, and Integrated Marketing Communications Department, Northwestern University.

[32] Thomas L. Harris & Co., Highland Park, IL, conducts an annual survey of clients using the largest public relations firms.

[33] Frank Vogl, "Expectations of the Chief Corporate Public Relations Officer in 2001," speech presented to Arthur W. Page Society, Annual Spring Seminar, New York, March 28, 1996.

[34] As reported in "john budd's plain talk" (a supplement to *pr reporter*), no. 14 (December 1, 1997): 3. (Unfortunately, *pr reporter* is no longer published.)

ADDITIONAL SOURCES

Dozier, David M., with Larissa A. Grunig and James E. Grunig. *Manager's Guide to Excellence in Public Relations and Communication Management.* Mahwah, NJ: Lawrence Erlbaum Associates, 1995. Deals with power and change in organizations, building linkages to and working with top management, and qualities of public relations excellence.

Grunig, Larissa A., James E. Grunig, and David M. Dozier, *Excellent Public Relations and Effective Organizations: A Study of Communication Management in Three Countries.* Mahwah, NJ: Lawrence Erlbaum Associates, 2002.

Hammer, Michael, and James Champy. *Reengineering the Corporation: A Manifesto for Business Revolution.* New York: HarperCollins, 1993. The book that drove the reengineering craze that led to changes in processes, structures, and cultures in all types of organizations in the 1990s.

Maister, David H. *Managing the Professional Service Firm.* New York: Free Press, 1993. Widely read guide for maximizing service, satisfaction, and success (profitability) in firms.

Miller, Katherine. *Organizational Communication: Approaches and Process,* 3rd ed. Belmont, CA: Wadsworth, 2005.

O'Dwyer, Jack, ed. *O'Dwyer's Directory of Corporate Communications* and *O'Dwyer's Directory of Public Relations Firms.* New York: J.R. O'Dwyer Co. Annual listings and descriptions of public relations executives and employers and firms and clients.

White, Jon, and Laura Mazur. *Strategic Communications Management: Making Public Relations Work.* Wokingham, England: Addison-Wesley Publishing Company, 1995. British perspective on many of the topics covered in this chapter.

WEB SITES FOR SELECTED PUBLIC RELATIONS FIRMS:

www.bm.com (Burson-Marsteller's award-winning Web site links users to information about the firm and a collection of public relations articles and sources.)

www.edelman.com (Address for Edelman Public Relations Worldwide—largest independent firm, with 35 offices and 1,300 staff.)

www.fleishman.com (Fleishman-Hillard International Communications)

www.hillandknowlton.com (Hill & Knowlton)

www.mslpr.com (Manning Selvage & Lee Public Relations)

www.ogilvypr.com (Olgilvy Public Relations Worldwide)

www.pninternational.com (Porter Novelli International)

www.ruderfinn.com (Ruder·Finn)

www.worldcom.com (The WORLDCOM Group, Inc., link to network of partner firms worldwide)

4 HISTORICAL ORIGINS

Those who cannot remember the past are doomed to repeat it.

—George Santayana
(*The Life of Reason*, Vol. 1, 1905)

STUDY GUIDE

After studying Chapter 4, you should be able to

- Use examples to illustrate how the development of public relations occurred during attempts to mobilize public opinion in struggles for power and to promote change.

- Name major historical leaders in public relations and describe their respective contributions to the development of public relations and to current practice.

- Trace the evolution of public relations from its American beginnings to modern practice.

- Cite the origins of some of today's principles and techniques that guide public relations practice.

Studying how public relations evolved provides insight into its functions, its strengths, and its weaknesses. Unfortunately, many practitioners do not have a sense of their calling's history and thus do not fully understand its place and purpose in society. Nor do they realize how history and the development of public relations are intertwined. Published histories typically oversimplify what is a complex and dramatic story by emphasizing novelty and a few colorful personalities. But understanding public relations' historical context is vital to the professionalization of today's practice.

Efforts to communicate with others and to deal with the force of public opinion go back to antiquity; only the tools, degree of specialization, breadth of knowledge, and intensity of effort are relatively new. This chapter highlights the evolution of the modern practice of public relations.[1]

ANCIENT GENESIS

Communicating to influence viewpoints and actions can be traced from the earliest civilizations. Archaeologists found a farm bulletin in Iraq that told farmers of 1800 B.C. how to sow their crops, how to irrigate, how to deal with field mice, and how to harvest their crops. Rudimentary elements of public relations also appear in descriptions of the king's spies in ancient India. Besides espionage, the spies' duties included keeping the king in touch with public opinion, championing the king in public, and spreading rumors favorable to the government.[2]

Greek theorists wrote about the importance of the public will, even though they did not specifically use the term *public opinion*. Certain phrases and ideas in the political vocabulary of the Romans and in writings of the medieval period relate to modern concepts of public opinion. The Romans coined the expression *vox populi, vox Dei*—"the voice of the people is the voice of God." Machiavelli wrote in his *Discoursi,* "Not without reason is the voice of the people compared to the voice of God," and he held that the people must be either "caressed or annihilated."

Public relations was used many centuries ago in England, where the kings maintained Lords Chancellor as "Keepers of the King's Conscience." Even kings acknowledged the need for a third party to facilitate communication and adjustment between the government and the people. So it was with the church, traders, and artisans. The word *propaganda* appeared in the seventeenth century, when the Catholic Church set up its *Congregatio de Propaganda Fide*—"Congregation for Propagating the Faith."

AMERICAN BEGINNINGS: BORN IN ADVERSITY AND CHANGE

The American beginnings of public relations appear in the American Revolution's struggle for power between the patriots' grassroots movement and the commercial, propertied Tories. Later efforts to gain public support included the conflict between the trade and property interests led by Hamilton and the planter-and-farmer bloc led by Jefferson, the struggle between Jackson's agrarian pioneers and the financial forces of Nicholas Biddle, and the bloody Civil War.

Before the Revolution

Using publicity to raise funds, promote causes, boost commercial ventures, sell land, and build box-office personalities in the United States is older than the nation itself. The American talent for promotion can be traced back to the first settlements on the East Coast in the seventeenth century. Probably the first systematic effort on this continent to raise funds was that sponsored by Harvard College in 1641, when that infant institution sent a trio of preachers to England on a "begging mission." Once in England, they notified Harvard that they needed a fund-raising brochure, now a standard item in a fund drive. In response to this request came *New England's First Fruits,* written largely in Massachusetts but printed in London in 1643, the first of countless public relations pamphlets and brochures.[3]

Independence

The tools and techniques of public relations have long been an important part of political weaponry. Sustained campaigns to shape and move public opinion go back to the Revolutionary War and the work of Samuel Adams and his cohorts. These revolutionaries understood the importance of public support and knew intuitively how to arouse and channel it. They used pen, platform, pulpit, staged events, symbols, news tips, and political organization in an imaginative, unrelenting way. Adams worked tirelessly to arouse and then organize public opinion, proceeding always on the assumption that "the bulk of mankind are more led by their senses than by their reason." Early on, he discerned that public opinion results from the march of events and the way these events are seen by those active in public affairs. Adams would create events to meet a need if none were at hand to serve his purpose.[4]

Far more than most realize, today's patterns of public relations practice were shaped by innovations in mobilizing public opinion developed by Adams and his fellow revolutionaries. In fomenting revolt against England, these propagandists, operating largely from the shadows, developed and demonstrated the power of these techniques:

1. The necessity of an organization to implement actions made possible by a public relations campaign: the Sons of Liberty, organized in Boston in January 1766, and the Committees of Correspondence, also born in Boston in 1775

2. The use of symbols that are easily identifiable and emotion arousing: the Liberty Tree

3. The use of slogans that compress complex issues into easy-to-quote, easy-to-remember stereotypes: "Taxation without representation is tyranny"

4. Staged events that catch public attention, provoke discussion, and thus crystallize unstructured public opinion: the Boston Tea Party[5]

5. The importance of getting your side of a story to the public first, so that your interpretation of events becomes the accepted one: the Boston Massacre

6. The necessity for a sustained saturation campaign using these techniques through all available channels of communication to penetrate the public mind with a new idea or a new conviction

The revolutionaries recognized the enormous difficulty of mobilizing public opinion to fight a war and to form a government:

> They knew that there was a wide gap between their public professions and American reality. They knew that there was bitter opposition to Independence and that the mass of the people were [sic] mostly indifferent. They knew, too, that there were deep rivalries and serious differences among the colonies.[6]

But neither the revolutionaries nor the anti-independents,

> …could have anticipated…the stunning effect of *Common Sense*. The little pamphlet had become a clarion call, rousing spirits within Congress and without as nothing else had. The first edition, attributed to an unnamed "Englishman" [Thomas Paine]…appeared January 9, 1776. By the time Adams had resumed his place in congress a month later, *Common Sense* had gone into a third edition and was sweeping the colonies. In little time more than 100,000 copies were in circulation.[7]

One history buff called Paine's *Common Sense* "the greatest PR act of the Revolution" and traced three additional principles of modern practice to tactics used by revolutionaries:

Swaying Early Adopters: Samuel Adams and "The Committees of Correspondence."

The White Paper: Thomas Paine and "Common Sense."

The Product Launch Press Release: Thomas Jefferson and the "Declaration of Independence."[8]

In weak contrast to the revolutionists' effective communication, the Tories, supporters of King George and the British Empire, relied not so much on propaganda as on legal and military pressures, to no avail. It is little wonder that an exuberant Sam Adams would exult when he heard the firing at Lexington, "Oh, what a glorious morning is this!" He and his fellow propagandists had done their work well.[9] The emotion-laden revolutionary campaign set patterns for the nation's political battles that were to follow.[10]

The next public relations landmark in the new nation came with publication of *The Federalist Papers*, 85 letters written to newspapers between 1787 and 1788 by Alexander Hamilton, James Madison, and John Jay. The letters urged ratification of the Constitution, in what one historian called the new nation's "first national political campaign":

The political ordeal that produced the Constitution in 1787 and brought about its ratification in 1788 was unique in human history. Never before had the representatives of a whole nation discussed, planned, and implemented a new form of government in such a manner and in such a short time.[11]

Another historian, Broadus Mitchell, wrote,

In parrying blows against and enlisting support for the Constitution, the authors of the *Federalist* did the best job of public relations known to history. Objectors were not so much repulsed as refuted. Honest fears were removed. Ignorance was supplied with information and illustration. The manner was earnest rather than passionate, was persuasive by a candor that avoided the cocksure. He [Hamilton] addressed his readers' judgment in a spirit of moderation.[12]

Historian Allan Nevins credited Alexander Hamilton with "history's finest public relations job":

Obtaining national acceptance of the Constitution was essentially a public relations exercise, and Hamilton, with his keen instinct for public relations, took thought not only to the product but to the ready acquiescence of thoughtful people; and he imparted his views to others....Once the Constitution came before the country, the rapidity with which Hamilton moved was a striking exemplification of good public relations. He knew that if a vacuum develops in popular opinion, ignorant and foolish views will fill it. No time must be lost in providing accurate facts and sound ideas.[13]

Growth and Change

Developments in public relations are directly tied to the **power struggles evoked by political reform movements**. These movements, reflecting strong tides of protest against entrenched power groups, were the catalytic agents for much of the growth of public relations practice, because the jockeying of political and economic groups for dominance created the need to muster public support.

Public relations also grew when there was a need to **gain public acceptance and utilization of swiftly advancing technology**. For example, when the Bell Telephone System switched to all-number telephone dialing, it ran into a storm of public opposition on the West Coast from the Anti-Digit Dialing League, organized by Carl May against what he called the "cult of technology."[14] The U.S. Postal Service encountered similar resistance when it introduced zip codes.

The first clear beginnings of presidential campaigns and of the presidential press secretary's function came in the era of President Andrew Jackson. In the late 1820s and early 1830s, the common man won the ballot and the free public school was started. Literacy increased greatly, and a burgeoning, strident party press stimulated political interest. As the people gained political power, it became necessary to campaign for their support. No longer was government the exclusive concern of the patrician few. With the rise of democracy in America came increasing rights for, and power of, the individual.[15] The ensuing power struggle produced an unsung pioneer in public relations—**Amos Kendall**.

As a key member of President Jackson's "Kitchen Cabinet," Kendall served as a pollster, counselor, ghostwriter, and publicist. The Kitchen Cabinet was unexcelled at creating events to mold opinion. On all vital issues that arose, Jackson consulted these key advisers, most of whom, like Kendall, were former newspapermen.

Jackson, unlettered in political or social philosophy, had difficulty getting his ideas across. Like many of today's executives, he needed a specialist to convey his ideas to Congress and the country. Jackson's political campaigns and his government policies clearly reveal the influence of Kendall's strategy, sense of public opinion, and skill as a communicator.[16]

Likewise, Bank of the United States president Nicholas Biddle and his associates were fully alert to the methods of influencing public opinion in their political battles with Jackson and Kendall. In fact, banks were the first businesses to use the press for this purpose; by loans to editors and placement of advertisements, they influenced many newspapers and silenced others. In March 1831, the bank's board authorized Biddle's publicist, Mathew St. Clair Clarke, to saturate the nation's press with press releases, reports, and pamphlets pushing the bank's case. But the pamphlets, the many articles planted in the press, and the lobbying efforts by Biddle and his associates did not prevail over the forces of Jackson and Kendall.[17]

The history of public relations makes sense only when viewed in the context of these crises of power conflicts and change. It is not mere coincidence that in the past, business interests took public relations most seriously when their positions of power were challenged or threatened. Nor is it a coincidence that labor's programs intensified when waning public support led to regulatory legislation or when trade agreements led to well-paid union jobs being lost to countries with cheap labor. Similarly, the most intense developments in public relations within government came in periods of crisis: World War I, the Great Depression and New Deal, World War II, the uneasy Cold War years with the Soviet Union, the Vietnam War, the Persian

Gulf War, and the continuing global war against terrorism following the 9-11 attack and the removal of Iraq's Saddam Hussein.

Press Agentry Origins

To say that public relations evolved from press agentry, although a gross oversimplification, contains a kernel of truth. Systematic efforts to attract or divert public attention are as old as efforts to persuade and propagandize. Much of what we define as public relations was labeled "press agentry" when it was being used to promote land settlement in the unsettled U.S. West or to build up political heroes.

Biddle and the Bank of United States effectively demonstrated the power of press agentry when Jackson's opponents created the myth of Davy Crockett. Biddle's press agent, Mathew St. Clair Clarke, decided to build up "a brash, loud-talking Tennessee Congressman, the colorful Colonel Davy Crockett and to build him up as a frontier hero to counter Old Hickory's [President Andrew Jackson] appeal to the frontiersmen."[18] As Scott Cutlip reported, "The transmogrification of Davy Crockett from a boorish, backwoods boob into a colorful frontier statesman was the work of several ghostwriters and press agents," when in fact Crocket "spent four years loafing and boasting at the Congressional bar."[19]

The ghostwritten Crockett campaign included books, printed and widely distributed speeches (which were not the words he actually spoke when he stood up!), theatrical plays, and letters to editors. Reality has a way of catching up, however, so the Crockett strategy failed to keep Jackson from winning a second term as president or to prevent the election of Jackson's choice as his successor, Martin Van Buren, in 1836. Crockett failed in his own reelection bid and headed to Texas, where he was killed by Santa Ana's troops in the Siege of the Alamo. It was Walt Disney, however, who revived the legend of Davy Crockett, further embellished the myth, and cashed in on the creative work done by press agents more than 100 years earlier.

But the master of embellishment was P. T. Barnum, and he knew it. Barnum lived from 1810 until 1891, a period of great importance in the evolution of public relations. His influence continues.

> Today's patterns of promotion and press agentry in the world of show business were drawn, cut, and stitched by the greatest showman and press agent of all time—that "Prince of Humbug," that mightiest of mountebanks, Phineas Taylor Barnum.[20]

Barnum's circus, now know as the Ringling Bros. and Barnum and Bailey Circus, put on display such oddities as the alleged 160-year old nurse of George Washington, fake mermaids, the midget Tom Thumb, and so many large oddities that he introduced the word *jumbo* to our language. Promoter Barnum even employed his own press agent, Richard F. "Tody" Hamilton, whom he credited with much of the success of the circus.[21]

Railroad publicists played an important role in settling our nation and in creating the romantic aura that still surrounds the West. Beginning in the 1850s, railroads and land developers used publicity and advertising to lure people westward. Charles Russell Lowell, who directed the Burlington Railroad's publicity campaign launched in 1858, wrote, "We are beginning to find that he who buildeth a railroad west must also find a population and build up business." He had good advice for today's practitioner: "We must blow as loud a trumpet as the merits of our position warrants."[22]

Success begot imitators. Barnum led the way, and others followed in ever-increasing numbers. During the two decades before 1900, press agentry spread from show business to closely related enterprises. But as press agents grew in number and their exploits became more outrageous—although successful, more often than not—it was natural that they would arouse the hostility and suspicion of editors and inevitable that the practice and its practitioners would become tainted.

Business Practices

The last two decades of the nineteenth century brought other discernible beginnings of today's practice. Frenzied and bold development of industry, railroads, and utilities in America's post–Civil War era set the stage for public relations in the twentieth century.

Between 1875 and 1900, America doubled its population and jammed its people into cities, went into mass production and enthroned the machine, spanned the nation with rail and wire communications, developed the mass media of press and magazines, and replaced the plantation owner with the head of industry and the versatile pioneer with the specialized factory hand. These 25 years laid the foundation for a mighty industrial machine.

The rise of powerful monopolies, the concentration of wealth and power, and the roughshod tactics of the robber barons brought a wave of protest and reform in the early 1900s. Contemporary public relations emerged from the melee of the opposing forces in this period of the nation's rapid growth. In this "the public be damned" era, exploitation of people and of natural resources was bound to bring, ultimately, protest and reform once people became aroused.

The prevailing hard-bitten attitude of businesspeople toward the public—be they employees, customers, or voters—was epitomized in the brutal methods used by Henry Clay Frick to crush a labor union in the Carnegie-Frick Steel Company's Homestead, Pennsylvania, plant in 1892. The Pennsylvania state militia helped break the employees' strike, and the union was destroyed. Cold-blooded power won this battle, but the employees eventually won the war.[23] Historian Merle Curti observed, "Corporations gradually began to realize the importance of combating hostility and courting public favor. The expert in public relations was an inevitable phenomenon in view of the need for the services he could provide."[24]

From 1897 on, the term *public relations* appeared with increasing frequency in railroad literature and in speeches of railroad tycoons. In the American Association of Railroads' 1897 *Year Book of Railway Literature,* the stated objective was "to put annually in permanent form all papers or addresses on the public relations of railways, appearing or being delivered during the year, which seem to have enduring value."[25] *The Railway Age Gazette* pleaded for "better public relations" in a 1909 editorial entitled, "Wanted: A Diplomatic Corps."

First Corporate Department

The first corporate public relations department was established in 1889 by George Westinghouse for his new electric corporation. Westinghouse had organized his company in 1886 to promote his revolutionary alternating-current system of electricity. Thomas A. Edison had earlier established Edison General Electric Company, which used direct current. The infamous "battle of the currents" ensued.

Edison, aided by the astute Samuel Insull, launched a scare campaign against the Westinghouse alternating-current system. As Forrest McDonald recorded,

> Edison General Electric attempted to prevent the development of alternating current by unscrupulous political action and by even less savory promotional tactics....The promotional activity was a series of spectacular stunts aimed at dramatizing the deadliness of high voltage alternating current, the most sensational being the development and promotion of the electric chair as a means of executing criminals.[26]

When the state of New York adopted electrocution in 1888, Westinghouse hired Pittsburgh journalist Ernest H. Heinrichs to get his story to the public. When Westinghouse's AC system won public acceptance despite the Edison–Insull propaganda scare campaign, it demonstrated "that performance and merit are the foundation stones of effective public relations."[27]

Professional groups also were paying attention to public opinion in the mid-1800s. In 1855, the American Medical Association (AMA) passed a resolution "urging the secretary of the Association to offer every facility possible to the reports of the public press to enable them to furnish full and accurate reports of the transactions."[28] And in 1884, the AMA launched the first of its many programs to counter antivivisectionists' attacks, a problem that persists to this day as animal rights groups protest using animals in research.

EVOLUTION TO MATURITY

Although the roots of today's practice lie far in the past, its definite beginnings date from the early 1900s, when the world entered the twentieth century, which spanned from the horse and buggy to the international space station. The dividing lines blur a bit, but the growth can be traced through seven main periods (see Figure 4.1) of development:

1. *Seedbed Era* (1900–1916) of muckraking journalism countered by defensive publicity and of far-reaching political reforms promoted by Theodore Roosevelt and Woodrow Wilson through the use of public relations skills.
2. *World War I Period* (1917–1918) of dramatic demonstrations of the power of organized promotion to kindle a fervent patriotism: to sell war bonds, enlist soldiers, and raise millions of dollars for welfare.
3. *Booming Twenties Era* (1919–1929), when the principles and practices of publicity learned in the war were put to use promoting products, earning acceptance for changes wrought by the war-accelerated technology, winning political battles, and raising millions of dollars for charitable causes.
4. *Roosevelt Era and World War II* (1930–1945), an era dominated by Franklin D. Roosevelt and his counselor, Louis McHenry Howe: the Great Depression: and World War II—events profound and far reaching in their impact on the practice of public relations.
5. *Postwar Era* (1946–1964) of adjustment as the nation moved from a war-oriented economy to a postindustrial, service-oriented economy, shouldered leadership of the "Free World," brought widespread acceptance of public relations—strong professional associations, the beginnings of public relations

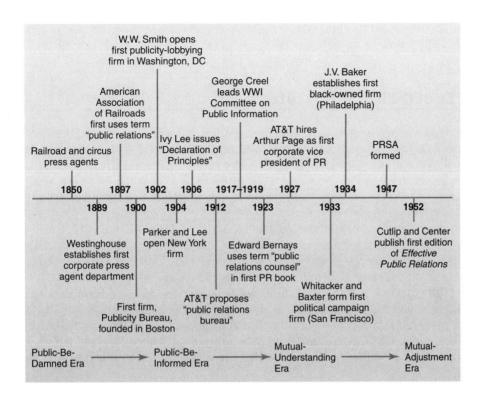

FIGURE 4.1

TIME LINE OF DEFINING EVENTS AND PEOPLE IN PUBLIC RELATIONS

education, and the emergence of television as a powerful communications medium.

6. *Period of Protest and Empowerment* (1965–1985) of student and activist protests against environmental pollution, racial and gender discrimination, concentration of special interest wealth and power, the Vietnam War, governmental abuse of the public trust, and consequently, an increasing recognition of social responsibility and more responsive organizations.

7. *Digital Age and Globalization (1986–present),* with accelerating technology; multiplying communication channels; and a world economy that features global competition, interdependence, instantaneous interaction, and terrorism.

These periods of development followed what Edward Bernays called the **"public-be-damned"** period of American enterprise, coming after the Civil War and lasting until about 1900. During public relations' seedbed era, Bernays suggested that the country had entered the **"public-be-informed"** period. He labeled the period following World War I as the time of **"mutual understanding,"** when the lessons of the behavioral sciences were being applied to public relations practice. Beginning in the late 1960s things changed.

Antiwar protests, the consumer movement, environmental activism, civil rights, and other demonstrations of the increasing power of citizens—including aroused minorities—challenged the status quo. Mutual understanding no longer satisfied those demanding **change**. Corrective **action** became the requirement, leading to the era of **"mutual adjustment."** This paradigm shift in society dramatically changed how public relations would be practiced in the latter part the twentieth century and into the twenty-first century. New technology accelerated the processes of adjustment. The following sections outline the key actors and events in that evolution.

SEEDBED ERA: 1900–1916

Muckraking journalists—David Graham Phillips, Lincoln Steffens, Charles Edward Russell, Upton Sinclair, Ida Tarbell, and others—effectively exploited the newly developed national forums made possible by popular magazines, national wire services, and feature syndicates. Regier says, "Muckraking…was the inevitable result of decades of indifference to the illegalities and immoralities attendant upon the industrial development of America."[29]

The reform and protest period extended roughly from 1900 to 1912. The muckrakers took their case to the people and got action. The agitation before 1900 had been primarily among farmers and laborers; now the urban middle class took up the cry against government corruption and the abuses of big business.

The muckrakers thundered out their denunciations in boldface in the popular magazines and metropolitan newspapers, which now had huge circulations. By 1900, there were at least 50 well-known national magazines, several with circulations of 100,000 or more. *The Ladies Home Journal,* founded only 17 years before, was approaching a circulation of one million. The impact of the mass media was growing.[30]

The work was begun dramatically by Thomas W. Lawson's "*Frenzied Finance*" series of articles in *McClure's* magazine in 1903. Ida Tarbell's *History of the Standard Oil Company,* described at the time as "a fearless unmasking of moral criminality masquerading under the robes of respectability and Christianity," and Upton Sinclair's book, *The Jungle,* which exposed the foul conditions in the meatpacking industry, both produced a violent public reaction. Public protest and reform brought regulatory legislation and a wave of trust busting. Businesses were forced to go on the defense.

Long accustomed to a veil of secrecy, business leaders felt the urge to speak out in self-defense but did not know how. Their first instinct was to turn to their advertising planners and lawyers. In the first stages of the muckraking era, many great corporations sought to silence the attacks from the press by the calculated placement and withdrawal of advertising. The strategy produced limited success.

Early Firms

The Publicity Bureau.   The nation's first publicity firm and forerunner of today's public relations firm was founded in Boston in mid-1900. George V. S. Michaelis, Herbert Small, and Thomas O. Marvin organized the Publicity Bureau "to do a general press agent business for as many clients as possible for as good pay as the traffic would bear." Michaelis, a Boston journalist once described by an associate as "a young man of many expedients," took the lead in organizing this new enterprise and was with it until 1909. One of the first people hired was James Drummond Ellsworth, who would later work with Theodore N. Vail in building the public relations program of American Telephone and Telegraph Company.[31]

Harvard University was the Publicity Bureau's first client. Michaelis, the firm's president, wrote to the president of Harvard boasting about the success of an early publicity effort: "We have met with very satisfactory success in publication of the articles, and I shall be glad to show you the clippings upon your return." And in a subsequent letter, he outlined what was surely the first fixed-fee plus expenses arrangement:

> In the matter of payment, we understand that you are to pay the Bureau $200 a month for our professional services, and those of an artist where drawings seem to be required. That this sum is to include everything except the payment of mechanical work, such as printings and the making of cuts, and the postage necessary to send out the articles themselves to the various papers, which items are to be charged to the University.[32]

The reorganized Publicity Bureau came into national prominence in 1906, when it was employed by the nation's railroads to head off adverse regulatory legislation then being pushed in Congress by President Theodore Roosevelt. Ray Stannard Baker reported,

> The fountainhead of public information is the newspaper. The first concern, then, of the railroad organization was to reach the newspaper. For this purpose a firm of publicity agents, with headquarters in Boston, was chosen. ...Immediately the firm expanded. It increased its Boston staff; it opened offices in New York, Chicago, Washington, St. Louis, Topeka, Kansas,...and it employed agents in South Dakota, California, and elsewhere.[33]

According to Baker, the Publicity Bureau operated secretly, "careful not to advertise the fact that they are in any way connected with the railroads." This firm effectively used the tools of fact-finding, publicity, and personal contact to saturate the nation's press, particularly weeklies, with the railroads' propaganda. The campaign was to little avail, however, because the Hepburn Act, a moderately tough regulatory measure, passed in 1906 after President Roosevelt used the nation's press and the platform to publicize a more persuasive case. Failure of their nationwide publicity effort caused railroad executives to reassess their public relations methods. Within a few years, many set up their own public relations departments. The Publicity Bureau faded into oblivion in 1911.[34]

Smith & Walmer.   The second firm also was the first to be based in Washington, D.C. William Wolff Smith quit his job as correspondent for the *New York Sun* and the *Cincinnati Enquirer* in 1902 to open a "publicity business" with a partner named Walmer in the capital. (Walmer's role and tenure with the firm are not known.) A *New York Times* reporter later recalled that the Smith & Walmer firm solicited "press-agent employment from anybody who had business before Congress."[35]

Smith closed the firm in 1916 and returned to law school, which he had quit in 1893 to take his first newspaper job. His "law practice," primarily devoted to lobbying the new regulatory agencies that resulted from the muckraking exposés, was the forerunner of the many law firms and public relations firms in Washington, D.C., and state capitals engaged in lobbying.

Parker & Lee.   Also during the seedbed era, former Buffalo reporter and veteran political publicist George F. Parker and young publicist Ivy Ledbetter Lee established the third firm in New York, Parker & Lee. They formed their partnership in 1904 after working together in the Democratic Party headquarters handling publicity for Judge Alton Parker's unsuccessful presidential race against Theodore Roosevelt. The firm lasted less than four years, but the junior partner—Lee—was to become one of the most influential pioneers in the emerging craft of public relations.

Hamilton Wright Organization, Inc.   The fourth firm—The Hamilton Wright Organization—was founded in 1908 when Hamilton Mercer Wright, a freelance journalist and publicist, opened a "publicity office" in San Francisco. Wright's first publicity work was for the California Promotion Committee, but he was also known for his promotion of Miami using publicity photographs. His agency's first account, however, was to promote the Philippine Islands on behalf of U.S. business interests, making his the first international firm.

He moved to New York City in 1917, after World War I cut short his work promoting tourism in Central America for the United Fruit Company. His son and grandson, both carrying the same name, followed in the founder's footsteps by specializing in promotion of foreign countries in the United States. The Wrights closed the firm in 1969.

Pendleton Dudley and Associates.   The fifth agency, started during the first decade of this century, lasted until 1988. Pendleton Dudley, who was to become an influential figure in public relations for half a century, took his friend Ivy Lee's advice and opened a publicity office in New York's Wall Street district in 1909. His first business client, AT&T, retained Dudley until his death at the age of 90 in 1966. He was among the few then in practice who saw the value of research and the need to measure program effectiveness. For all those 57 years, Dudley remained the active head of his firm, which in 1946 had become Dudley-Anderson-Yutzy Public Relations when Thomas D. Yutzy and George Anderson joined the firm. In 1970, sisters Barbara Hunter and Jean Schoonover acquired the firm and changed the name to D-A-Y. The firm became a subsidiary of Ogilvy & Mather in 1983, which dropped the separate D-A-Y identity and operation in 1988.[36]

Thomas R. Shipp and Co.   In 1914, Thomas R. Shipp organized the nation's sixth firm and the second located in Washington, D.C. Shipp, like William Wolff Smith, was a native of Indiana and a former reporter. He spent six years learning publicity and politics from two experts, Theodore Roosevelt and Gifford Pinchot. In 1909 they gave Shipp administrative and publicity responsibilities for the newly formed National Conservation Association (NCA)—"the center of a great propaganda for conservation." Historians credit the NCA with making "conservation" and "natural resources" powerful terms in the public vocabulary. Shipp opened his own "publicity company" when Smith closed his to return to law school. When the United States entered World War I, Shipp headed the first American Red Cross fund drive, raising an unprecedented $100 million. After the war, such corporations as General Motors, Standard Oil Company of New York, Swift & Company, and International Harvester retained Shipp as Washington public relations counsel.[37]

Early Pioneers

For the most part, big businesses hired former reporters to counter the muckrakers with whitewashing press agentry, demonstrating little grasp of the fundamental problems in the conflict. But there were exceptions. One was Georgia native Ivy Lee.

Ivy Ledbetter Lee.　Lee, a Princeton graduate and New York newspaper reporter covering business, saw the possibility of earning more money in the service of private organizations who were seeking a voice. After five years as a reporter, in 1903 Lee quit his low-paying job on the *World* to work in Seth Low's campaign for mayor of New York. This led to a job working with George F. Parker in the press bureau of the Democratic National Committee during the 1904 presidential campaign.

Ivy Lee

Parker had directed the publicity for Grover Cleveland's three campaigns for the presidency, but was not appointed as the nation's first press secretary.[38] Parker returned to political battle in 1904 to direct publicity for the Democratic National Committee in the unsuccessful campaign to unseat President Theodore Roosevelt. He hired Ivy Lee as his assistant.

Out of their campaign association came the decision to form the Parker and Lee partnership, which dissolved in 1908 when Lee went to work full time for one of the firm's clients, the Pennsylvania Railroad. He became director of the railroads' publicity bureau, which he had organized.[39]

When the anthracite coal mine operators hired Parker & Lee to tell management's side in the 1906 strike, Lee issued a "Declaration of Principles." Lee's statement of philosophy profoundly influenced the evolution of press agentry and publicity into public relations. Going against the prevailing feeling on Wall Street that "the public be damned," Lee's declaration made it clear that the public was no longer to be ignored, in the traditional manner of business, nor fooled, in the continuing manner of the press agent. It was to be informed. Lee mailed his newsworthy declaration to all city editors:

> This is not a secret press bureau. All our work is done in the open. We aim to supply news. This is not an advertising agency; if you think any of our matter ought properly to go to your business office, do not use it. Our matter is accurate. Further details on any subject treated will be supplied promptly, and any editor will be assisted most cheerfully in verifying directly any statement of fact….In brief, our plan is, frankly and openly, on behalf of business concerns and public institutions, to supply to the press and public of the United States prompt and accurate information concerning subjects which it is of value and interest to the public to know about.[40]

Lee's new approach greatly simplified the work of reporters assigned to cover the strike. Although reporters were not permitted to attend strike conferences, Lee provided reports after each meeting in the form of a "handout" (now called **press release** or **news release**). His success in generating favorable press coverage for the coal operators prompted the Pennsylvania Railroad to retain Parker and Lee in the summer of 1906. Lee handled the account.[41]

During this period Lee used the term *publicity* to describe what is now public relations; the concept and Lee's success grew steadily. In December 1914, Lee was appointed as a personal adviser to John D. Rockefeller Jr. The Rockefellers were being savagely attacked for the strikebreaking activities of their Colorado Fuel and Iron Company. Newspapers and other critics referred to the tragic event as "Bloody Ludlow" and "the Ludlow Massacre." Cartoonists and editorial writers called Rockefeller the biggest criminal of the time. Lee served the Rockefellers until John D. died in 1934, eulogized by the press as the great benefactor of society.

Ivy Lee did much to lay the groundwork for contemporary practice. Even though he did not use the term *public relations* until at least 1919, Lee contributed many of the techniques and principles that practitioners follow today. **He was**

among the first to realize the fallacy of publicity unsupported by good works and to reason that performance determines the publicity a client gets.

In his 31 years in public relations, Lee changed the scope of what he did from publicity to counseling clients. For example, he said, "If you issue an untruth in a public statement, it is going to be challenged just as soon as it sees the light."[42] His counsel extended beyond publicity, telling his audience at the 1916 Annual Convention of the American Electric Railway Association that "the actual relationship of a company to the people...involves far more than *saying*—it involves *doing*."[43]

Lee's record, although substantial, is not free from criticism. When he died, he was under fire for his representation of the German Dye Trust, controlled by I. G. Farben. Lee advised the cartel after Adolf Hitler came to power in Germany and the Nazis had taken control. Headlines at the time sensationalized his work—LEE GIVES ADVICE TO THE NAZIS and LEE EXPOSED AS HITLER PRESS AGENT. Although he never received pay directly from the Nazi government, Lee was paid an annual fee of $25,000 and expenses (a large sum at the time) by the Farben firm from the time he was retained in 1933 until his firm resigned the account shortly after his death in 1934.[44]

One of the craft's most forceful representatives, his practice and preachments made public relations an occupation. Ironically, however, as Lee biographer Ray Hiebert concluded, he was not able to do for himself what he had done so effectively for others:

> He was rarely able to explain his work adequately or to gain understanding for the underlying principles by which he operated. He often admitted that he did not know what to call himself, and that what he did was an art that he could not explain.
>
> When reporters reached him in Baden [Germany] after the news of his I. G. Farben work had been made public, he pulled within his shell and refused to make a statement.[45]

Theodore N. Vail.   The former American Telephone and Telegraph Company pioneered in public relations as well as in telephonic communications. Although public relations got short shrift when Theodore N. Vail was forced out in 1887 until he returned to power in 1902, the company did organize a "literary bureau" in Boston around 1890 and was one of the first clients of the Publicity Bureau. After Vail returned as a director, the policies that became identified with AT&T began to take shape, and they were brought to the fore when Vail became president in 1907. Vail hired James Drummond Ellsworth to begin a publicity and advertising program.

The company tried to eliminate public criticism through efficient operation and consideration for the needs of subscribers. A systematic method of answering complaints was put into effect. Unlike other utilities, Bell did not fight public regulation but accepted it as a price for monopoly. Vail and Ellsworth, in collaboration with the N. W. Ayer advertising agency, began an institutional advertising campaign that continued for decades[46] (see Exhibit 4.1).

Rex Harlow

Rex F. Harlow.   Others recognized the need for publicity services in other parts of the country. Rex F. Harlow began a lifetime career in 1912 in Oklahoma City when he was hired by an older brother to promote *Harlow's Weekly.* Harlow's career spanned the evolution of this young, uncertain calling to its maturity in the 1980s and helped shape today's practice. While teaching at Stanford University in 1939, he began teaching public relations courses and founded the American Council on Public Relations (ACPR). In 1945 he started the monthly *Public Relations Journal,* published until 1995 by the Public Relations Society of America. Harlow died April 16, 1993, at 100 years of age.

EXHIBIT 4.1

PROPOSAL FOR A PUBLIC RELATIONS BUREAU AT AT&T IN 1912

The establishment of a Public Relations Bureau in the American Telephone and Telegraph Company, in which all information concerning the relations of the telephone companies to the public should be concentrated and made available for use, would serve to coordinate much of the work now done independently by various departments of that company and the operating companies.

The bureau could bring together a large sum of material at present scattered, and a proper arrangement and collation of this would make it readily available and eliminate a considerable amount of duplication.

It would also be able to give its attention to the trend of public opinion and the drift of legislation, and by a study of these, bring to the attention of executive officers in a con-

densed form the broader lines of public sentiment in time to enable the telephone company to meet new phases of legislation and in many cases to forestall legislation by remedying conditions which have been the cause of trouble.

By employing a central organization to collect, analyze, and distribute material relating to these questions there will be a distinct saving in times of those actually engaged in work in the field and a broader and more efficient treatment of the problems.

All the available material can be brought together and everyone dealing with these questions be kept in touch with the trend of public opinion and action throughout the country...

Growth in Other Areas

Equally important public relations developments were taking place outside the business community. After Harvard retained the Publicity Bureau in 1900, the seedbed years brought innovative publicity programs to colleges and universities. The University of Pennsylvania's public relations program dates from 1904, when it set up the University Bureau of Publicity. That same year, Willard G. Bleyer, pioneer journalism educator, organized a press bureau at the University of Wisconsin at the direction of public relations–minded President Charles R. Van Hise. But it was William Rainey Harper, the dynamic builder of the University of Chicago, who did more than any other educator to harness the power of publicity to the cause of higher education. His methods and his resulting success were observed and copied by many others.[47]

The whirlwind high-pressure campaign to raise money for charitable causes was first fabricated in 1905 in Washington, D.C., by YMCA fund-raisers Charles Sumner Ward and Lyman L. Pierce. They were the first to use full-time publicists in a fund drive. The Y's successful techniques were soon used in the annual appeals of churches, colleges, civic centers, and health and welfare agencies.[48] The Ward–Pierce campaign format has endured the test of time and can be easily recognized in today's annual United Way drives.

WORLD WAR I PERIOD: 1917–1918

The contemporary practice of public relations first emerged as a defensive measure, but World War I gave it great offensive impetus. President Woodrow Wilson, who was keenly aware of the importance of public opinion, established The Committee on Public Information (CPI)—often referred to as the "Creel Committee." The CPI was charged with mobilizing public opinion in support of the war effort and Wilson's peace aims in a country in which opinion was divided when war was declared. Wilson appointed George Creel chairman.

George Creel.   George Creel and his CPI demonstrated as never before the power of publicity to mobilize opinion. Without a campaign manual to guide him, Creel improvised as he went along. For example, he had no national radio or television to reach the nation quickly, so he created the Four Minutemen, a network of 75,000 civic leaders covering the nation's some 3,000 counties. These volunteers, alerted by telegrams from Washington, would fan out to speak to schools, churches, service clubs, and other gatherings. By the war's end nearly 800,000 of these four-minute messages had been delivered.

Creel assembled as brilliant and talented a group of journalists, scholars, press agents, editors, artists, and other manipulators of the symbols of public opinion as America had ever seen united for a single purpose. The breathtaking scope of the huge agency and its activities were not to be equaled until the rise of the totalitarian dictatorships after the war. Creel, Byoir, and their associates were public relations counselors to the U.S. government, carrying first to the citizens and then to those in distant lands the idea that gave motive power to the wartime undertaking of 1917–1918.[49]

Analyzing the influence of the Creel Committee, *The New York Times* commented in 1920:

> Not only did he have a staff of press agents working immediately under him in a central office, but Creel decentralized the system so that every type of industry in the country had its special group of publicity workers. In this manner, more than in any other, were the heads and directors of movements of every type introduced to and made cognizant of the value of concentrating on publicity in so-called "drives."[50]

To illustrate the *Times*'s point, when America entered the war, the American Red Cross had a membership of fewer than 500,000 in 372 chapters scattered across the nation and $200,000 in working funds. In September 1918, as the war neared its end, the Red Cross had 20 million members in 3,864 chapters and had raised more than $400 million in gifts and membership dues. Another example: On May 1, 1917, there were only some 350,000 holders of U.S. bonds; six months later, after two organized publicity and sales drives for "Liberty Bonds," there were 10 million bondholders.

After the war, many held an overly optimistic belief in the power of mass communication. A noted political scientist, Harold D. Lasswell, observed, "When all allowances have been made, and all extravagant estimates pared to the bone, the fact remains that propaganda is one of the most powerful instrumentalities in the modern world."[51]

Carl Byoir

Carl Byoir.   The Creel Committee trained a host of practitioners who took their wartime experiences and fashioned a profitable calling. Among these was Carl Byoir, who at age 28 had been associate chairman of the CPI. After a decade's tour into other endeavors, Byoir founded a publicity firm in 1930 to promote tourism in Cuba. The firm would become one of the country's largest public relations firms, Carl Byoir & Associates (CB&A). Some of the nation's largest corporations retained CB&A, including B.F. Goodrich, Honeywell, Kimberly Clark, John Deere,

The Atlantic & Pacific Tea Company (A&P), Woolworth, and Swift. Long-term clients included Hughes Aircraft, a client for 40 years; Hallmark, 37 years; RCA, 34 years; and Borg Warner, 20 years.

Noted for its high standards of client service, Byoir and his associates are credited with introducing grassroots advocacy groups and the third-party endorsement, popularizing the Jeep, helping make the tubeless tire acceptable to consumers, and using the full-page editorial advertisement.[52] Byoir also devoted his own time and CB&A resources to social causes, such as raising money for the March of Dimes to fund research that ultimately eliminated the feared infantile paralysis—polio. Byoir died in 1957 at 68.[53]

BOOMING TWENTIES ERA: 1919–1929

Vigorously nourished by wartime developments, the public relations specialty quickly spread. It showed up in government, business, education, churches, social work—now burgeoning in the war's aftermath, the labor movement, and social movements. The victory of the Anti-Saloon League in achieving national prohibition and the triumph of the women's suffrage movement, both in 1920, provided fresh evidence of the newly found power of public relations.

This period also saw increased use of public relations advertising as a tool. Illinois Central Railroad started a campaign in 1920 that sought "promotion of a better understanding and closer relationship with the patrons of our lines." In 1922, Metropolitan Life Insurance Company started a good-health campaign. In 1923, General Motors (GM) began to use advertising to sell itself as an institution.

Edward L. Bernays and Doris E. Fleischman.   Among those vying with Ivy Lee for prominence and for business in the 1920s was Edward L. Bernays. Prior to World War I, Bernays had worked as a press agent. While he worked for the Creel Committee during the war, his busy mind envisioned the possibility of making a life's work of what he called "engineering public consent." Many have credited Bernays with introducing the term *public relations counsel* in *Crystallizing Public Opinion (1923)*, the first book on public relations. In fact, Bernays said that he and his wife and business partner, Doris E. Fleischman, came up with the term after opening his first office in 1919.[54]

Doris Fleischman

Bernays married Fleischman in 1922. Together they ran their firm—Edward L. Bernays, Counsel on Public Relations—until formally retiring from active practice in 1962. She died in 1980. They counseled major corporations, government agencies, and U.S. presidents from Calvin Coolidge through Dwight Eisenhower, with Bernays taking the spotlight for most assignments. Although credited with being an equal partner with Bernays in the firm, with creating the first public relations newsletter, and with collaborating with Bernays to develop the term *public relations counsel*, Fleischman struggled for professional equality because of her sex.[55] For example, in one of her two books she wrote,

Edward Bernays

> Many men resented having women tell them what to do in their business. They resented having men tell them, too, but advice from a woman was somewhat demeaning. I learned to withdraw from situations where the gender of public relations counsel was a factor or where suggestions had to be disassociated from gender. If ideas were considered first in terms of my sex, they might never get around to being judged on their own merits.[56]

Fleischman was an early feminist, who, after marrying Bernays, retained her birth name long before it was socially acceptable:

> During the next three decades, Fleischman continued to sign into hotels—and twice into maternity hospitals—as "Miss Doris E. Fleischman," and in 1925 she received the first U.S. passport granted to a married woman under her birth name. That was her name on the 1928 book she edited on careers for women and on the seven magazine articles and book chapters she published between 1930 and 1946.[57]

Bernays's first book on public relations followed Walter Lippmann's 1922 *Public Opinion,* a book that reflected the growing interest in power and nature of public opinion. In all the years prior to 1917, only 18 books on public opinion and publicity were printed. At least 28 titles appeared between 1917 and 1925.

Scholarly interest also dates from this period. Social scientists began to explore the nature of public opinion and the role of mass communication in its formation. Although sophisticated opinion-measurement methods did not appear until the 1930s, the postwar work of social scientists contributed much to the development of market research, public opinion polls, and communication science. Bernays broke more new ground in 1923 when he taught the first public relations course at New York University.

Bernays continued in his roles as author, lecturer, advocate, and critic into the 1990s. *Life Magazine* included Bernays in its 1990 special issue, "The 100 Most Important Americans of the 20th Century." He died March 9, 1995, at age 103.

John Hill

John W. Hill.   Despite a booming economy and rapidly growing media, there were only six public relations firms listed in the Manhattan telephone directory in 1926. In 1927, John W. Hill, a Cleveland journalist, started a firm in that city. In 1933, he formed a partnership with Don Knowlton and shortly thereafter moved to New York to found Hill & Knowlton, Inc. (H&K). Knowlton remained to run the Cleveland office. The two firms, connected only by overlapping ownership, operated independently until 1964, when Knowlton retired and the Cleveland office was sold to a successor firm. Hill died in 1977. In 1980, JWT Group, the holding company that owned the J. Walter Thompson Company advertising agency, acquired H&K for $28 million. The JWT Group of companies was acquired by the British conglomerate WPP Group, London, in 1989 (see www.hillandknowlton.com).

Long viewed as an ethical and respected leader of public relations counseling, Hill's role in helping the major tobacco companies form the Tobacco Industry Research Committee (TIRC) threatens his legacy. On his recommendation, the presidents of the major tobacco companies agreed to fund the TIRC, with Hill fighting the tobacco wars on behalf of the cigarette industry until he retired from H&K in 1962. Throughout his professional life, however, Hill saw himself as a man of integrity and principle, committing his views to paper:

> Should an existing client company adopt policies which the counsel believes are not in the public interest, he would advise against such policies—and, if he has integrity, be prepared to resign the account in case the client persisted.[58]

When asked directly about his role in the formation of the TIRC and in tobacco public relations, in 1966 Hill responded, "I decline to comment on this matter on the basis that this is an active, highly sensitive account," and he did not cover H&K's tobacco account in his 1963 memoir, *The Making of a Public Relations Man.*[59] Long after Hill's death, however, there is little doubt about his role in creating a public relations front for the tobacco industry:

> Though John Hill had long since passed from such earthly battles, the fact remains that he was the guiding force in the formation of the Tobacco Industry Research Committee and later the Tobacco Institute. Thus, Hill must bear responsibility for that "brilliantly conceived and executed plan" that served the selfish interests of the tobacco industry at the expense of millions of Americans' good health.[60]

Two years before Hill set up shop in Cleveland, **Edward D. Howard II** had also organized a public relations agency there that celebrated its 80th anniversary in 2005. Edward Howard and Company is Ohio's oldest public relations firm and the nation's longest surviving independently owned firm. It is now a member of the Pinnacle Worldwide network of independent public relations firms.

Arthur W. Page.   Among the pioneers shaping today's practice, Arthur W. Page stands at the summit. Page built three successful business careers, yet found time to contribute his talent to many public service endeavors. He was a writer and editor of *World's Work Magazine* and other periodicals of Doubleday, Page and Company from 1905 until 1927. Then he accepted Walter Gifford's offer to succeed James D. Ellsworth as vice president of American Telephone and Telegraph Co.

Arthur Page

At the outset Page made it clear that he would accept only on the conditions that he was not to serve as a publicity man, that he would have a voice in policy, and that the company's performance would be the determinant of its public reputation. Page's philosophy is summed up in this statement:

> All business in a democratic country begins with public permission and exists by public approval. If that be true, it follows that business should be cheerfully willing to tell the public what its policies are, what it is doing, and what it hopes to do. This seems practically a duty.[61]

Although he continued nominally as vice president of AT&T during World War II, he devoted most of his time to the war effort. As Page biographer Noel Griese reported, surely Page's most widely distributed news release, written for President Harry S. Truman, went out on Monday, August 6, 1945:

> Sixteen hours ago an American airplane dropped one bomb on Hiroshima, an important Japanese Army base. That bomb had more power than 20,000 tons of TNT. It had more than two thousand times the blast power of the British "Grand Slam" which is the largest bomb ever yet used in the history of warfare.
>
> The Japanese began the war from the air at Pearl Harbor. They have been repaid manyfold….It is an atomic bomb. It is a harnessing of the basic power of the universe. The force from which the sun draws its powers has been loosed against those who brought war to the Far East.[62]

After the war, Page stayed on at AT&T to mentor his replacement. Page retired January 1, 1947, after integrating public relations concepts and practices into the Bell System. From then until his death in 1960 at age 77, he served as a consultant to many large corporations and gave much of his time to the service of government, higher education, and other causes. However, it was Page's work for AT&T that left his lasting imprint on public relations. His precepts and principles not only endure in the companies that used to be part of AT&T (broken up in 1984 by court order to foster competition), but also are renewed and promoted by the Arthur W. Page Society. (Page's principles are listed in Chapter 5.)

Paul Garrett

Paul Garrett.   Although General Motors had started using institutional advertising in 1923, it did not set up its own public relations department until 1931. GM president and management innovator Alfred P. Sloan Jr. brought in Paul Garrett, another influential pioneer, to head the department. Garrett was the second corporate public relations practitioner to hold the office of vice president. He and AT&T's Page were among the first to use the new science of public opinion polling as the basis for planning and evaluating public relations programs. At GM Garrett built an innovative corporate program, which was widely copied by other corporations. He retired from GM in 1957 and was retained to counsel the then-new Xerox Corporation.[63]

Alice Beeman

Alice L. Beeman.   It was also during this period that a sense of identification and professionalism began to emerge in this new craft. For example, the Association of American College News Bureaus had been organized in April 1917, but had lapsed into inactivity during the World War I. It came alive again in the 1920s.

At the 1925 convention, the organization took on new strength, reflecting the growth of the practice in higher education. Symbolic of its growth in ensuing years, the organization's name was changed in 1930 to the American College Publicity Association, in 1964 to the American College Public Relations Association, and in 1974—after a merger with the American Alumni Council—to the Council for the Advancement and Support of Education (CASE). This merger reflected a shift in emphasis in college public relations from publicity to development and fund-raising.

CASE reinvented itself under the leadership of its first president, Alice L. Beeman. In her new position as president of CASE, Beeman was the first woman to head a national public relations association.

ROOSEVELT ERA AND WORLD WAR II: 1930–1945

Propelled by wartime lessons and a changing America, the practice of public relations moved full speed ahead until the stock market crash in 1929. The ensuing Great Depression marks another milestone. That persistent economic catastrophe and Franklin D. Roosevelt's New Deal prompted development of the practice in many fields.

Louis McHenry Howe.   FDR combined strong leadership with consummate skill to harness the forces of protest into an effective political coalition. He won his battles on front pages and over the radio, a new medium he used with matchless skill. Roosevelt's adroit moves in the public arena can be credited in large part to his public relations mentor, Louis McHenry Howe. The astute, tough-minded Howe served FDR faithfully and effectively from 1912 until Howe's death in 1936.[64]

Events flowing from the Depression and the New Deal brought home to every group the need to build informed public support. New Dealers soon found that this was essential to pave the way for their radical reforms, and government public relations had its greatest expansion under Franklin Roosevelt. School administrators were made to realize the dangers of an uninformed public. The Depression brought a tremendous expansion in social welfare needs and agencies, whose administrators also came to realize the need for better public understanding. Military leaders, looking apprehensively at the buildup of the Nazi and Fascist war machines, began to promote support for more adequate armed forces. Colleges and universities, caught in the web of financial woes, turned more and more to public relations to raise funds.

Business leaders increasingly used public relations specialists to counter Roosevelt's biting criticisms and his legislative reforms. There was a marked trend away from occasional and defensive efforts and toward more positive and continuous programs administered by newly established departments. A growing labor movement, too, found that it had problems and needed guidance. Growth was stimulated all along the line by the social and economic upheavals of the Depression.

This period also brought the tool that promised more precise, more scientific measurement and assessment of public opinion. The Roper and Gallup polls, begun in the mid-1930s, won wide respect in the presidential election of 1936. Perceptive practitioners began using this new tool to advise management and to formulate programs. The public opinion poll, with the application of new sampling methods, has steadily improved in reliability and in utility.

Joseph Varney Baker.   In 1934, the first minority-owned firm opened in Philadelphia. Joseph Varney Baker left his position as city editor of the *Philadelphia Tribune* to provide counsel to the Pennsylvania Railroad Company. Baker was the first African American to serve as president of a PRSA chapter and the first to be accredited by PRSA. His firm's list of clients included Chrysler, Gillette, Procter & Gamble, NBC, RCA, and Scott Paper Company. One authority on minorities in public relations concluded that during the 40 years that Baker's firm existed, it "was hired to communicate only with the black consumer market, and the practice has continued to this day."[65]

Clem Whitaker and Leone Baxter.   This era also produced the forerunner of a major segment of today's practice: the political-campaign specialist. In 1933, husband and wife Clem Whitaker and Leone Baxter formed the first agency specializing in political campaigns, headquartered in San Francisco. California, with its heavy reliance on the initiative and referendum and its weak political party organizations, provided fertile ground for the growth of political firms. From 1935 through 1958, the firm managed 80 major campaigns and won all but six. This agency brought a new approach to politics, including the "media blitz" in the final days of the campaign. Today it has countless imitators.

Leone Baxter

Whitaker and Baxter met in 1933 at a Sacramento, California, meeting of supporters who had proposed that the Central Valley Project sell electrical power to public agencies. Not surprisingly, private utilities—led by Pacific Gas & Electric—got a proposition put on the ballot to defeat the proposal. Even with a small budget, the Whitaker–Baxter campaign defeated the referendum funded by powerful corporate interests. *Time* magazine called them "the acknowledged originals in the field of political public relations."[66]

World War II produced more violent changes in the environment, accelerating the development of public relations. Once more the government led the way, demonstrating the power of an organized informational campaign. This time the instrument was the Office of War Information (OWI).

In the opinion of two public relations scholars, the OWI's greatest contributions derived from its work as the predecessor of the U.S. Information Agency (USIA). OWI was the agency that pointed out the danger in not countering distorted ideas about the United States throughout the world.[67]

Military public relations makes up a major segment of modern practice. Prior to the outbreak of World War II, however, it had been given scant support by military leaders. In 1935, General Douglas MacArthur, then Army chief of staff, appointed a young major, Alexander Surles, to head a public relations branch with the "dual job of getting before the public the War Department's anxiety over things to come in Europe and to help newsmen pry stories out of the War Department."[68]

With the advent of war, the "bureau of public relations" staff quickly grew from 3 to 3,000 officers and civilians. Concurrently, the Navy Department moved to expand and strengthen its public relations. The Army Air Corps, under the imaginative leadership of **General H. H. "Hap" Arnold**, a former information officer, quickly recruited a host of skilled public relations and advertising specialists. Their task was to sell air power in an age of trench-minded generals. Even though the armed forces went into the war ill equipped for public relations, they acquitted themselves well. The work was largely a matter of publicity, censorship, and assistance to war correspondents. In the process they trained countless practitioners for this work after the war and built a solid foundation for practice in the postwar boom.

World War II brought paid advertising to the fore as a major tool of public relations, now in its many forms: public relations advertising, public service advertising, issue or advocacy advertising, and institutional advertising. Beginning in 1942, the War Advertising Council worked with industry and the government to make advertising a major tool in getting citizens to produce for the war, to recycle, to ration scarce resources, to buy war bonds, and to serve in the armed forces.

POSTWAR BOOM: 1946–1964

World War II brought new opportunities; new demonstrations of the utility of public relations in motivating war production, military morale, and civilian support; and new techniques and channels of communication. The war also schooled about 75,000 persons in the practice. The uneasy years of conversion from a wartime to a peacetime economy and from an industrial to a postindustrial, service-oriented society accentuated and extended these developments. For example, in the late 1940s, industry was wracked by a series of bitter, prolonged strikes as organized labor fought to redress grievances built up in the no-strike war period and to keep wartime gains in pay. These struggles and increased public criticism of big business placed heavy demands on public relations in business and industry.[69]

Similarly, the postwar baby boom and the enrollment bulge of soldiers returning from World War II brought new and heavy demands on the nation's schools and colleges. Administrators recognized the need for public relations counsel. School districts had to promote one bond issue after another to build additional schools, and the nation's institutions of higher education had to scramble for funds for more teachers and buildings to meet the exploding demand for higher education and research.

Tim Traverse-Healy.   In Europe, a leader emerged that some called the "Edward Bernays of Europe"—a World War II British officer who formed a public relations firm, Traverse-Healy Limited, in 1947. As a Royal Marine Commando attached to Special Forces, Tim Traverse-Healy had parachuted into rural France during the German occupation to work with the French resistance. He and the locals reactivated an abandoned bakery to bake bread, in which they could encase messages to be distributed to resistance forces. After the war, a young Traverse-Healy and his bride converted the bakery into a vacation residence.

Tim Traverse-Healy

During his illustrious career, he counseled major international corporations, lectured around the world, and cofounded both the British Institute of Public Relations and the International Public Relations Association. He was awarded two of England's highest honors—Fellowship of the Royal Society of Arts and Officer of the Order of the British Empire (OBE). The latter is second only to knighthood and was awarded by the Queen of England for "services to the profession of public relations." He was the first public relations practitioner from outside the United States to address the Public Relations Society of America conference (1957 in Philadelphia), and is the only "foreigner" [his word] inducted into the Arthur W. Page Society "Hall of Fame" (1990).[70] His long career as a practitioner included serving clients such as Airbus Industrie, General Motors, Lockheed, Hilton Hotels, National Westminster Bank (1952–1993), AT&T, and Johnson & Johnson. He sold his firm in 1993 and turned his attention to lecturing and writing standards for public relations practice for the European Union.

Daniel J. Edelman.   Many of the major public relations firms that dominate the practice today were established in the postwar years. In Chicago, following World War II service in the U.S. Army Psychological Warfare and Information Control divisions and four years as public relations director of Toni Company (Gillette), former CBS reporter Daniel J. Edelman started his firm in 1952. Within eight years, expansion began with a branch office in New York, followed by openings in Los Angeles, London, Washington, D.C., and Frankfurt, Germany. Edelman Public Relations Worldwide is now the world's largest independent firm (not owned by a communication conglomerate), with more than 1,800 employees in 40 offices worldwide. Edelman's son, Richard, is now CEO, operating out of coheadquarters in New York (with Chicago) (see www.edelman.com).

Daniel Edelman

Harold Burson had operated his own firm for six years before teaming up with advertising executive Bill Marsteller in 1953 to form Burson-Marsteller. Burson worked as a newspaper journalist before serving with combat engineers in Europe during the last two years of World War II. After the war, he covered the Nuremberg Trials for the American Forces Network. Burson served as chairman and CEO of the firm until 1987. By 1983, Burson-Marsteller was the world's largest public relations firm, with more than 2,400 employee in 58 offices in 27 countries. Today, the firm's 47 wholly owned offices and 53 affiliated firms are in 60 countries, making it one of the few truly global firms.[71] Communication conglomerate Young & Rubicam purchased the firm in 1979 and was in turn purchased in 2000 by the even larger British conglomerate, WPP Group. In conjunction with its 50th anniversary in 2003, the firm and a number of Burson's clients funded the Harold Burson Chair in Public Relations at Boston University (see www.bm.com).

Harold Burson

Inez Kaiser

Inez Y. Kaiser.   In Kansas City, Missouri, Inez Yeargan Kaiser established in 1961 the first public relations firm owned by an African-American female to serve national accounts. Inez Kaiser and Associates worked for 7-Up, Sears, Sterling Drug, Sperry Hutchinson, Continental Baking Company, and Pillsbury, among others. During her 33-year business career, Kaiser was the first Black woman to join the Public Relations Society of America and helped form the National Association of Minority Women in Business. Public relations educators in the Association for Education in Journalism and Mass Communication created the Inez Kaiser Award in 1993, providing one-year memberships to minority graduate students pursuing advanced degrees in public relations education.

The following developments highlighted the 1946–1964 boom period:

1. Steady growth in the number of programs in industries, institutions, social agencies, government bureaus, and trade associations. Already-established programs tended to mature and to move beyond publicity.

2. Stabilization in the number of independent counseling firms, especially in the communication hubs of New York, Washington, Chicago, and Los Angeles.

3. A tremendous spurt in the number of books, articles, and journals devoted to the practice and its philosophy, problems, and techniques.

4. Organization of new associations for practitioners and redirection or consolidation of those already established. Many of these are now mature.

5. Growth in the number of college courses and programs specifically designed to prepare practitioners. Academic preparation in public relations led to greater acceptance of young graduates in the job market.

6. Internationalization of the practice and its standards, reflected in the formation of the International Public Relations Association in 1955.

Additional impetus for the growth of professionalism came with the establishment of one strong general organization and the emergence of a number serving specialized fields of practice. Public Relations Society of America was born August 4, 1947, when representatives of the West Coast American Council on Public Relations and the East Coast National Association of Public Relations Counsel met in Chicago. Members of the Washington-based American Public Relations Association voted not to come in at that time but merged in 1961. Dr. Rex F. Harlow was the moving force in bringing about this merger.

PERIOD OF PROTEST AND EMPOWERMENT (1965–1985)

This era put "consumerism," "environmentalism," "peace," "racism," and "sexism" at the top of the public agenda. A new breed of investigative muckrakers and powerful new advocacy groups pushed for social change, new social safety nets, and increased government oversight of business and industry. Through public demonstrations and "Great Society" legislative initiatives, as well as good-faith negotiation, power was redistributed, and organizations became more responsive to public concerns and values. Protecting the environment and securing civil rights became the flagship causes of this era.

Reminiscent of the early part of the twentieth century, "big business" again became the target of protest movements and media criticism. Also repeating that earlier era, books led the charge. For example, many credit Rachel Carson's *Silent Spring* (1962) with beginning the environmental movement.[72] President John F. Kennedy directed his science advisory committee to study the book's well-documented charges that DDT indiscriminately killed all manner of insects and animals when applied to crops as a pesticide, and that DDT had contaminated the entire food chain. The big pesticide manufacturers responded by threatening that without DDT the Dark Ages would return, and that insects and disease would go unchecked. (Surely, this was not public relations' finest hour.) Public apathy changed to public demands to regulate the pesticide industry and to protect the environment.

Legislators' responses were immediate and long lasting. Congress passed the Clean Air Act of 1963, the National Environmental Policy Act of 1969 (making the protection of the environment national policy), and the Water Quality Improvement Act of 1970. The first "Earth Day" was celebrated in April 1970, and the Environmental Protection Agency (EPA) was created in October 1970. Carson had taken on corporate America...and won, setting the stage for an era of protest and change.

General Motors was another target of protest and public scrutiny, opening the door to greater corporate accountability. Ralph Nader gave birth to the consumer movement when he wrote *Unsafe at Any Speed: The Designed-In Dangers of the American Automobile* (1965).[73] Nader charged that the Chevrolet Corvair's suspension system made the car subject to rolling over. GM's legal department responded by investigating Nader's private life. Subsequently, the company's president had to appear before a Senate subcommittee and apologize to Nader for resorting to intimidation. In addition, the company settled lawsuits out of court for invading Nader's privacy and agreed to change the Corvair suspension system. The National Traffic and Motor Vehicle Safety Act that spelled out safety standards on all vehicles passed in 1966. (Congress also mandated safety in the workplace when it passed the Occupational Safety and Health Act [OSHA] in 1970.)

Nader used the cash settlement and his book royalties to establish the Project on Corporate Responsibility, staffed by young lawyers and investigators. Nader became the "consumer crusader" media darling for the fledgling consumer movement. Corporate secrecy and arrogance suffered many setbacks as "Nader's Raiders" continued to press for corporate accountability over the next four decades. One tactic was to ask shareholders to give their vote proxies to Nader so he could challenge corporate policy and board elections.

Saul Alinsky, a self-described "radical," used similar tactics to take power from Corporate America and others in the "establishment." He made his intentions clear in the first paragraphs of his book:

> *The Prince* was written by Machiavelli for the Haves on how to hold power. *Rules for Radicals* is written for the Have-Nots on how to take it away.
>
> In this book we are concerned with how to create mass organizations to seize power and give it to the people....[74]

Even his book title — *Rules for Radicals* — captures the tenor of that era. And he succeeded in creating widespread participation in his movement, as volunteers offered their proxy votes and active participation:

"Enclosed find my proxies. I wonder whether you have heard from anyone else in my suburb? If you have, I would appreciate receiving their names and addresses so that I can call a housemeeting and organize a San Fernando Valley Chapter of Proxies for People." The second letter said, "...we don't know why you should go to the board meetings with our proxies—why can't we go with our proxies, of course all organized and knowing what we want, but we would like to go ourselves." [Emphasis added by Alinsky.][75]

Without a doubt, Dr. Martin Luther King Jr. is the icon of this era of social change and empowerment. His rise to national leadership began in 1955 when he stood up for Rosa Parks, who was arrested for refusing to give up her seat on a Montgomery, Alabama, bus to a white passenger. He gave his famous "I Have a Dream" speech August 28, 1963, to an estimated 250,000 at the Lincoln Memorial in Washington, D.C. Dr. King gave his prophetic last speech, "I've Been to the Mountain Top," in Memphis, Tennessee, the day before he was assassinated on April 4, 1968. He became the martyr and symbol of the civil rights movement that produced, among many other changes, the 1965 Voting Rights Act and the Open Housing Law (1968). In short, Martin Luther King Jr., and the civil rights movement helped define this era of change and empowerment, affecting both internal and external relationships for all organizations.

Successes of the civil rights movement energized the equal rights movement spearheaded by Gloria Steinem, Bella Abzug, Shirley Chisholm, and Betty Friedan. They formed the National Women's Political Caucus in 1971 to help women run for political office. In addition, the organization endorses candidates supportive of women's issues. The organization continues to call for passage of an amendment to the Constitution mandating equal rights for women, first passed by the Congress in 1972 but never ratified by the states. Regardless, women have entered all phases of work—becoming the majority in public relations, for example—because of the doors opened during this era.

Surely the Vietnam War protests were the most divisive of this era, leading to the "generation gap," "hippies," the "sexual revolution," and—ultimately—Watergate and the impeachment of President Richard Nixon. Students staged antiwar protests on campuses nationwide, but none with more disastrous results than the 1970 demonstrations against the U.S. incursion into Cambodia. National Guard troops shot to death four students on the Kent State University (Ohio) campus, and Mississippi State Police killed two students on the campus of Jackson State College. Seven months later, Congress repealed the 1964 Tonkin Gulf Resolution, which had authorized U.S. action in Vietnam. January 27, 1973, the United States, North Vietnam, South Vietnam, and the Viet Cong Provisional Revolutionary Government signed the agreement "Restoring Peace in Vietnam." The genie was out of the bottle, however, as citizen action had changed public policy and removed a president. A popular saying became, "Power to the People," which also captured the essence of this era.

Public relations textbooks written at the end of this era also reflected the change in public relations practice: No longer was the journalist-in-residence model of "telling our story" going to fulfill the new role of public relations in organizations responding to the new balance of power in society. For example, the sixth edition of the book you are reading introduced "adjustment and adaptation" as the basis for contemporary practice (see Chapter 7). Research courses were added to the public relations curriculum on many campuses, and practitioners who engaged in information gathering were invited to join the management decision-making team in many organizations.

Emerging from the era of protest and empowerment, public relations could no longer focus simply on domestic relations. Technology and global commerce required new approaches to communication and international relations.

DIGITAL AGE AND GLOBALIZATION (1986–PRESENT)

In the computer age, information became "0s" and "1s" stored in ever smaller devices and distributed on "floppies"; CDs and DVDs; and copper, fiber optic, or wireless networks. Computers became affordable for home use. DVDs replaced videotapes. The Internet changed everything—introducing e-mail, online searches, and nearly unrestricted access to a powerful and instantaneous distribution system. Access made "self-publishing" a reality, leading to less control over the public information system by traditional media, to greater diversity in points of view, to increased interest in organizational transparency, and to precisely targeted communication with stakeholders.

Of course, we live in this era and it prescribes the concept and practice of public relations described in the chapters of this book. You will play a role in writing this piece of public relations history.

NOTES

[1] The authoritative references on public relations history are by Scott M. Cutlip: *The Unseen Power: Public Relations—A History* (Hillsdale, NJ: Lawrence Erlbaum Associates, 1994), and *Public Relations History: From the 17th to the 20th Century* (Hillsdale, NJ: Lawrence Erlbaum Associates, 1995).

[2] A. L. Basham, *The Wonder That Was India* (London: Sidgwick and Jackson, 1954), 122.

[3] Samuel Eliot Morison, *The Founding of Harvard College* (Cambridge: Harvard University Press, 1935), 303. Also see Hugh T. Lefler, "Promotional Literature of the Southern Colonies," *Journal of Southern History* 33 (1967): 3–25.

[4] Philip Davidson, *Propaganda and the American Revolution, 1763–1783* (Chapel Hill: University of North Carolina Press, 1941), 3.

[5] For the patriots' version of this historical event, see James Bowdoin, Dr. Joseph Warren, and Samuel Pemberton, "Short Narrative of the Horrid Massacre in Boston," in *Tracts of the American Revolution, 1763–1776,* ed. Merrill Jensen (New York: Bobbs Merrill, 1967). Also available at www.bostonmassacre.net/trial/acct-anonymous1.htm.

[6] Merrill Jensen, "The Sovereign States: Their Antagonisms and Rivalries and Some Consequences," in *Sovereign States in an Age of Uncertainty,* 226–50, ed. Ronald Hoffman and Peter J. Albert (Charlottesville: University of Virginia Press, 1981).

[7] David McCullouch, *John Adams* (New York: Simon & Schuster, 2001), 96.

[8] Jason Karpf, "Adams, Paine and Jefferson: A PR Firm," *Public Relations Tactics* (January 2002): 12.

[9] For the Tory side of the propaganda battle, see Carol Berkin and Jonathan Sewall, *Odyssey of an American Loyalist* (New York: Columbia University Press, 1974).

[10] William Baldwin Jr., "Bicentenary of a Classic Campaign," *Public Relations Quarterly* 10 (Spring 1965).

[11] Robert A. Rutland, *The Ordeal of the Constitution: The Antifederalists and the Ratification Struggle of 1787–88* (Boston: Northeastern University Press, 1983), 3.

[12] Broadus Mitchell, *Alexander Hamilton: Youth to Maturity, 1755–1788* (New York: Macmillan, 1957), 422–23.

[13] Allan Nevins, *The Constitution Makers and the Public, 1785–1790* (New York: Foundation for Public Relations Research and Education, 1962), 10. Also in *Public Relations Review* 4, no. 3 (Fall 1978): 5–16.

[14] John Brooks, *Telephone: The First Hundred Years* (New York: Harper and Row, 1976), 270–71.

[15] T. Swann Harding, "Genesis of One 'Government Propaganda Mill,'" *Public Opinion Quarterly* 11 (Summer 1947): 227–35. (A history of public relations in the U.S. Department of Agriculture.)

[16] Cutlip, *Public Relations History*, 68–120. For an extended source about Kendall's work, see Lynn Marshall, "The Authorship of Jackson's Bank Veto Message," *Mississippi Valley Historical Review,* vol. L (December 1963). For an estimate of Kendall's influence, see Arthur M. Schlesinger Jr., *The Age of Jackson* (Boston: Little, Brown, 1945).

[17] Cutlip, *Public Relations History*, 88–105. For earlier accounts of this epic public relations battle, see Bray Hammond, *Banks and Politics in America* (Princeton, NJ: Princeton University Press, 1957).

[18] Cutlip, *Public Relations History*, 100.

[19] Ibid., 101.

[20] Ibid., 171. For accounts of Davy Crockett's buildup, see Dixon Wecter, *The Hero in America: A Chronicle of Hero-Worship* (New York: Charles Scribner's Sons, 1941/1972), 189–193; Michael Lofaro, ed., *Davy Crockett: The Man, the Legend, the Legacy, 1786–1986* (Knoxville: University of Tennessee Press, 1985); and Michael Lofaro and Joe Cummings, eds., *Crockett at Two Hundred: New Perspectives on the Man and the Myth* (Knoxville: University of Tennessee Press, 1989).

[21] Ibid., 175. See also Irving Wallace, *The Fabulous Showman: Life and Times of P. T. Barnum* (New York: Alfred A. Knopf, 1959); and Phineas Taylor Barnum, *The Life of P. T. Barnum Written by Himself* (New York: Redfield, 1855), 154–74.

[22] Richard C. Overton, *Burlington West* (Cambridge, MA: Harvard University Press, 1941), 158–159.

[23] For a concise account, see Leon Wolff, *Lockout* (New York: Harper and Row, 1965).

[24] Merle Curti, *The Growth of American Thought,* 3rd ed. (New York: Harper and Row, 1964), 634.

[25] Cutlip, *Public Relations History,* 208.

[26] Forrest McDonald, *Insull* (Chicago: University of Chicago Press, 1962), 44–45. (Biography of the utility magnate who blazed many public relations trails before he crashed in ruin.)

[27] Cutlip, *Public Relations History,* 203.

[28] Morris Fishbein, "*History of the American Medical Association, 1847–1947* (Philadelphia: W. B. Saunders Company, 1947), 61.

[29] C. C. Regier, *The Era of the Muckrakers* (Chapel Hill: University of North Carolina Press, 1932). For a generous sampling of newspaper articles, see Arthur Weinberg and Lila Weinberg,

eds., *The Muckrakers* (New York: Simon and Schuster, 1961). For a discussion of the most prolific, if lesser known, muckraker, see Robert Miraldi, "Charles Edward Russell: 'Chief of the Muckrakers,'" *Journalism & Mass Communication Monographs* 150 (April 1995).

[30] Vernon Parrington, *Main Currents in American Thought,* vol. 3, (New York: Harcourt Brace Jovanovich, 1930), 404–5. For details on the rise of the mass media, see Edwin Emery, *The Press and America* (Englewood Cliffs, NJ: Prentice Hall, 1972); Theodore Peterson, *Magazines in the Twentieth Century* (Urbana: University of Illinois Press, 1964); and Stephen Fox, *The Mirror Makers* (New York: Morrow, 1984).

[31] For details, see Scott M. Cutlip, "The Nation's First Public Relations Agency," in *The Unseen Power,* 10–26. See also "The Nation's First Public Relations Firm," *Journalism Quarterly* 43 (Summer 1966). (It was, in fact, a publicity agency, not a public relations firm.)

[32] Cutlip, *The Unseen Power,* 11.

[33] Ray Stannard Baker, "Railroads on Trial," *McClure's Magazine* 26 (March 1906): 535–44. The story is also told in Weinberg and Weinberg's, *The Muckrakers.*

[34] Cutlip, *The Unseen Power,* 16.

[35] "Department Press Agents," Hearing before Committee on Rules, House of Representatives, May 21, 1912, 62d Congress, 2d session (Washington, DC: Government Printing Office, 1912), 16. Also see William Kittle, "The Making of Public Opinion," *Arena* 41 (1909): 443–44.

[36] Ibid., 92–103.

[37] Ibid., 32–33.

[38] Gordon A. Moon II, "George F. Parker: A 'Near Miss' as First White House Press Chief," *Journalism Quarterly* 41 (Spring 1964): 183–90.

[39] Cutlip, *The Unseen Power,* 52–53.

[40] Quoted in Sherman Morse, "An Awakening on Wall Street," *American Magazine* 62 (September 1906): 460.

[41] Ivy L. Lee Papers, Princeton University Library. Lee's 1907 correspondence includes a letter from the president of Pennsylvania Railroad to a colleague in Southern Pacific, saying that the time had come to take measures to "place our case before the public."

[42] Ivy L. Lee, *Publicity: Some of the Things It Is and Is Not* (New York: Industries Publishing Company, 1925), 39.

[43] Ibid., 48.

[44] For testimony on this case, see *Investigation of Nazi and Other Propaganda: Public Hearings before a Subcommittee of the Committee on Un-American Activities, Hearing Number 73-NY-7* (Washington, DC: Government Printing Office, 1934); and *Trials of War Criminals before the Nuremberg Military Tribunal,* Volumes 7 and 8, Case Six, *U.S. v. Krauch,* "The I. G. Farben Case" (Washington, DC: Government Printing Office, 1963).

[45] Ray Eldon Hiebert, *Courtier to the Crowd: The Story of Ivy L. Lee and the Development of Public Relations* (Ames: Iowa State University Press, 1966), 310–311.

[46] See Noel L. Griese, "James D. Ellsworth, 1863–1940," *Public Relations Review* 4 (Summer 1978): 22–31.

[47] For more on the development of public relations in higher education, see Scott M. Cutlip, "Advertising Higher Education: The Early Years of College Public Relations," *College and University Journal* 9 (November 1970), part I, and 10 (January 1971), part II.

[48] For a full account of public relations' role in fund-raising, see Scott M. Cutlip, *Fund Raising in the United States: Its Role in America's Philanthropy* (New Brunswick, NJ: Rutgers

University Press, 1965), and Kathleen S. Kelly, *Effective Fund-Raising Management* (Mahwah, NJ: Lawrence Erlbaum Associates, 1997), Part II, "Historical Context of Fund Raising."

[49] James O. Mock and Cedric Larson, *Words That Won the War* (Princeton, NJ: Princeton University Press, 1939), 4.

[50] *The New York Times,* February 1, 1920, p. 9.

[51] Harold D. Lasswell, *Propaganda Techniques in the World War* (New York: Alfred A. Knopf, 1927), 220.

[52] John F. Budd, "Carl Byoir's Contributions to PR Are Worth Noting Despite Its US Demise," *PRWeek*, December 10, 2001, p. 10.

[53] See Cutlip, *The Unseen Power,* 531–588, for detailed descriptions of the growth and tumultuous times of the Carl Byoir & Associates.

[54] Edward L. Bernays, *Biography of an Idea: Memoirs of Public Relations Counsel Edward L. Bernays* (New York: Simon and Schuster, 1965), 288.

[55] Pamel J. Creedon, "Public Relations History Misses 'Her Story,'" *Journalism Educator* 44, no. 3 (Autumn 1989): 26–30.

[56] Doris Fleischman Bernays, *A Wife Is Many Women* (New York: Crown, 1955), 171. As quoted by Creedon in "Public Relations History," p. 28.

[57] Susan Henry, "Dissonant Notes of a Retiring Feminist: Doris E. Fleischman's Later Years," *Journal of Public Relations Research* 10, no. 1 (1998): 1. (In 1955, she identified herself as "Doris Fleischman Bernays" on the title page of her book, *A Wife Is Many Women*—as Henry's description of Fleischman's later life so vividly portrays.)

[58] Hill Papers (December 3, 1958, memo), as quoted in Cutlip, *The Unseen Power,* 518.

[59] Cutlip, *The Unseen Power,* 487–88.

[60] Ibid., 501.

[61] George Griswold Jr., "How AT&T Public Relations Policies Developed," *Public Relations Quarterly* 12 (Fall 1967): 13. (A special issue devoted to AT&T's public relations.)

[62] Noel L. Griese, *Arthur W. Page: Publisher, Public Relations Pioneer, Patriot* (Tucker, GA: Anvil Publishers, Inc., 2001), 229–230. This is *the* definitive biography of Page.

[63] Cutlip, *The Unseen Power,* 527.

[64] For a balanced view of Howe's contributions to FDR's career and his public relations ideas, see Alfred B. Rollins Jr., *Roosevelt and Howe* (New York: Alfred A. Knopf, 1962).

[65] Marilyn Kern-Foxworth, "Minority Entrepreneurs Challenge the Barriers," *Public Relations Journal* 45, no. 8 (August 1989): 19.

[66] Cutlip, *The Unseen Power,* 598.

[67] For a quick study of the OWI, see Robert L. Bishop and LaMar S. Mackay, "Mysterious Silence, Lyrical Scream: Government Information in World War II," *Journalism Monographs* 19 (May 1971), based on their Ph.D. dissertations written at the University of Wisconsin.

[68] Gordon W. Keisser, *The Marine Corps and Defense Unifications 1944–47* (Washington: National Defense University Press, 1982).

[69] "Business Is Still in Trouble," *Fortune* 39 (May 1949) reflects business' postwar public relations problems. For a biting critique of some business efforts to deal with critics, see William H. Whyte, *Is Anybody Listening?* (New York: Simon and Schuster, 1952).

[70] Personal letter to author (Broom), February 1, 2003. For more information about Traverse-Healy and the collection of his writings, go to www.pr-50years.co.uk/index.html

[71] *The Holmes Report: PR Agency Report Card 2004* (New York: The Holmes Group, 2004), 18.

[72] Rachel Carson, *Silent Spring* (Boston: Houghton Mifflin Co., 1962). A 25th anniversary edition of this landmark book was published in 1987.

[73] Ralph Nader, *Unsafe at Any Speed: The Designed-In Dangers of the American Automobile* (New York: Grossman, 1965).

[74] Saul D. Alinsky, *Rules for Radicals: A Pragmatic Primer for Realistic Radicals* (New York: Random House, 1971), 3.

[75] Ibid., 177.

ADDITIONAL SOURCES

Cutlip, Scott M. *The Unseen Power: Public Relations—A History.* Hillsdale, NJ: Lawrence Erlbaum Associates, 1994.

Cutlip, Scott M. *Public Relations History: From the 17th to the 20th Century.* Hillsdale, NJ: Lawrence Erlbaum Associates, 1995.

Kern-Foxworth, Marilyn. "African-American Achievements in Public Relations." *Public Relations Journal* 47, no. 2 (February 1991): 18–19.

Hallahan, Kirk. "Ivy Lee and the Rockefellers' Response to the 1913–1914 Colorado Coal Strike," *Journal of Public Relations Research* 14, no. 4 (2002): 265–315.

Harrison, Shirley, and Kevin Moloney, "Comparing Two Public Relations Pioneers: American Ivy Lee and British John Elliot." *Public Relations Review* 30, no. 2 (2004), 207–215. Authors draw parallels between the careers of Ivy Lee and the first practitioner in Great Britain to have "public relations" in his job title.

Henry, Susan. "Dissonant Notes of a Retiring Feminist: Doris E. Fleischman's Later Years." *Journal of Public Relations Research* 10, no. 1 (1998): 1–33. Also by Henry, see "Anonymous in Her Own Name: Public Relations Pioneer Doris E. Fleischman." *Journalism History* 23, no. 2 (Summer 1997): 51–62.

Hon, Linda Childers. "To Redeem the Soul of America: Public Relations and the Civil Rights Movement." *Journal of Public Relations Research* 9, no. 3 (1997): 163–212.

Lee, Mordecai, "When Congress Tried to Cut Pentagon Public Relations: A Lesson from History, *Public Relations Review* 26, no. 2 (Summer 2002), 131–154.

Olasky, Marvin N. *Corporate Public Relations: A New Historical Perspective.* Hillsdale, NJ: Lawrence Erlbaum Associates, 1987; and "The Development of Corporate Public Relations, 1850–1930." *Journalism Monograph* 102 (April 1987), by the same author. Olasky recasts the historical role of public relations as an attempt by corporations to limit competition.

Pearson, Ron. "Perspectives on Public Relations History." *Public Relations Review* 16, no. 3 (Fall 1990): 27–38.

Pratt, Cornelius B. "The 40-Year Tobacco Wars: Giving Public Relations a Black Eye?" *Public Relations Quarterly* 42, no. 4 (Winter 1997–98): 5–10.

"Public Relations in American History" (special issue). *Public Relations Review* 4 (Fall 1978). Lectures by historians Allan Nevins, Ray Allen Billington, Frank E. Vandiver, George F. G. Stanley, Eric F. Goldman, and Joe B. Frantz.

Raucher, Alan R. "Public Relations in Business: A Business of Public Relations." *Public Relations Review* 16, no. 3 (Fall 1990): 19–26.

5 ETHICS AND PROFESSIONALISM ·

Decision-making when faced with an ethical dilemma is easy: Do the right thing. Always.

—Alexander M. Cutler[1]
Chairman and CEO, Eaton Corporation

If I have done my job well for the right purpose, my life has substance and meaning. If I have done my job poorly or for the wrong purpose, I have squandered my life, however much I have prospered.

—John Kultgen[2]

STUDY GUIDE

After studying Chapter 5, you should be able to

- Discuss the philosophical basis of pubic relations ethics.

- Explain utilitarian and deontological approaches to ethical decision making.

- Identify the major motivations behind concern for professional ethics in public relations practice.

- List and briefly discuss the five positives of socially responsible public relations, as well as the three major negatives attributed to public relations when it is not practiced in the public interest.

- Outline the major arguments for and against licensing and accreditation of practitioners.

- List and describe the major professional organizations serving the field.

- Outline and apply some of the major articles from the Public Relations Society of America Code of Professional Standards.

This chapter was written in collaboration with Professor Shannon A. Bowen, Ph.D., School of Communication, University of Houston. Dr. Bowen earned her doctorate at the University of Maryland. She previously worked as a research analyst for political and corporate clients in Washington, D.C.

Any discussion of the professional status of public relations necessarily begins with ethics. In fact, adherence to a code of professional ethics separates professions from other skilled occupations. Ethical issues take on added importance because professionals with special expertise have unprecedented power in decisions that affect every aspect of society. In the global village, where information and influence reach most parts of the world with amazing speed and ease, professional power and impact do not stop at national or cultural boundaries. Ethics and professionalism are global concerns, with social responsibility no longer simply a local issue.

This chapter explores the ethical and professional foundations of public relations practice. It also chronicles aspects of an occupation adopting the philosophy and trappings of a calling and an emerging profession.

PHILOSOPHICAL FOUNDATIONS OF ETHICS

Good versus evil, or light versus darkness, is an age-old question of perpetual interest. The *Star Wars* movie series is a good example of the universality of the duel between good and evil. The forces of darkness also try to destroy the forces of good in countless other sagas from classical literature to pop culture. But, do these types of questions apply to public relations? No doubt public relations has a negative connotation as an unethical occupation to some.[3] Some critics have gone so far as to argue that public relations is an inherently evil pursuit, equating it with "spin," propaganda, and manipulation.[4]

In fact, it is intrinsically good: To facilitate dialogue, promote understanding and build mutually beneficial relationships are admirable—even **noble**—pursuits. To qualify as such, however, **public relations must be practiced with a commitment to social responsibility and ethics.**

Early public relations leaders Ivy Lee and John W. Hill argued that public relations should act as the "ethical conscience" of the organization.[5] Some today argue that public relations serves the organization best when it acts as an ethical conscience.[6] The legal department usually advises management on what can be done "legally," not necessarily what it should do ethically. If public relations does not fill the role of ethical conscience in an organization, it may be deferred to the legal department by default. For example, at Enron corporate legal counsel oversaw general ethics, but no one monitored the ethics of its finance and accounting practices that led to the company's demise and bankruptcy. To fill the void, some organizations have hired a different kind of "CEO"—a chief ethics officer.

Moral philosophy is the study of what actions are right, or morally defensible, and what actions are wrong, or morally unworthy. Moral philosophers investigate ethical questions by looking for underlying ethical principles and the justification for why they are ethical. These underlying moral principles are the **maxims** that guide behavior. When philosophers discover general or universally applicable moral maxims, ethical decision making becomes much simpler for everyone. For instance, "do not murder" is a generally accepted moral maxim based on the principle of the value of human life.

Philosophers use various methods for determining what these moral maxims or principles are, but most involve using a rational, logical, or analytical decision-making process. Two approaches in moral philosophy are commonly used in ethical decision making: **utilitarianism** and **deontology**. Although they use different approaches, both utilitarianism and deontology help public relations professionals evaluate and counsel on the ethics of organizational decision making.

Utilitarian Philosophy

Utilitarianism takes into account the **utility**—or expected outcome—of a decision in order to decide what is the "right" thing to do. Utilitarianism is based on the consequences or predicted outcomes of a decision. The consequences of a decision are used to measure the moral worth of an action, so ethical principles are defined by consequences or predicted outcomes.

Utilitarianism holds that ethical actions should create the greatest amount of good for the greatest number of people. This type of philosophy emphasizes serving the public good or the majority in society. Introduced by Jeremy Bentham and later refined by his student, John Stuart Mill, utilitarianism tries to maximize the benefit of decisions for the largest number of people and minimize any negative consequences to others.[7]

To determine the morality of an act from a utilitarian perspective, a public relations professional would consider all available decision alternatives in light of which option produces the greatest good for the greatest number of people. The practitioner would pick the alternative that maximizes positive outcomes and minimizes negative outcomes or harm.

Utilitarianism is arguably the most common approach to ethical decision making in business, but it has several problems that limit its usefulness. Utilitarianism can be used to justify or reinforce a status quo, in which the majority is happy but the minority is not, either purposefully or inadvertently. Always giving the majority preference prevents the organization from adapting to a change impetus initiated by publics and other stakeholders. This approach also requires the public relations professional to accurately predict the future consequences of each alternative. However, many consequences are unexpected, creating the potential for severe and costly miscalculations in a utilitarian analysis.

Deontological Philosophy

Deontological ethics focuses on the moral principle involved, rather than basing the morality of the decision on its projected outcomes. This approach is also called "nonconsequentialist" because it maintains that ethics should be guided by duty rather than consequence. Deontology was developed by German philosopher Immanuel Kant (1724–1804) as an attempt to find the underlying universal principles of morality.[8] Deontology is arguably the most exhaustive approach in ethics and is defined as "the ethical theory taking duty as the basis of morality."[9] In deontology, the ethical nature of an action does not depend on its outcome because predicting the exact outcome is beyond human capability or control.

Deontology is demonstrated in the statement, "Do the right thing." How do we know what the right thing **is** in a complex situation? Deontology holds that our moral duty indicates the right course of action. How we determine where that duty lies—and, therefore what is ethically correct—is clarified by the decision test of deontology known as the **categorical imperative.** It advises: "Act only on that maxim through which you can at the same time will that it should become a universal law."[10]

The categorical imperative applies universally in that it asks the decision maker to consider the decision a universal law that should be used in all similar situations.

After considering what all other rational people might do and putting oneself in all positions around the issue, the option is deemed ethical if it still appears to be the right thing to do. Thus, **the concept of universal duty represents what all rational people would agree is ethical from any perspective on the issue.**

Two aspects of the categorical imperative measure a person's **intention** and maintaining **dignity** and **respect** of others. By intention, Kant refers to the underlying will involved in making the decision. Motivations such as selfishness or doing what is best for the decision maker are not moral, according to this philosophy. Deontology argues that "good will" is the only true moral decision-making guide, because all other motivations can be corrupted.[11]

An example of a deontological decision is the classic Tylenol case discussed in Exhibit 1.3, in which Johnson & Johnson decided to pull all Tylenol from the market in the United States based on product sabotage in Chicago. This recall was extremely expensive to the organization, but Larry Foster and top public relations practitioners believed it was the right thing to do, regardless of the cost to the company or lost market share. Their first concern was protecting the public, a moral principle valuing human life over all other consequences. In this example, the intention of the company was indeed a good will, that the dignity and respect of publics was maintained, and that the decision could be universally applied to all others in similar situations. According to Bill Nielsen, the most-senior public relations executive at Johnson & Johnson headquarters, "The first thing we consider is doing the right thing. Yes, consequences are present, but we do the right thing and then handle the consequences of that later."[12]

Benefits of Deontology

Using the deontological approach in ethical situations means that decisions are made based on what is right or wrong, not who benefits the most[13] (see Figure 5.1). This statement describes the inherent fairness and universal nature of deontology. It allows a communicator to consider the perspectives of multiple stakeholders and to understand their values and the moral principles they hold. It takes organizational bias out of the decision-making process and allows public relations to advise the dominant coalition on the right course of action based on moral principle, rather than cost, self-interest, or expedience.

This type of decision making is likely to keep an organization in balance with the desires of its stakeholder publics. As Marilyn Carlson Nelson, Chairman and CEO of Carlson Companies, put it: "In the end, doing the right thing will always triumph. It has always been so."[14] Another chairman and CEO, Fred Hassan of Schering Plough Corporation, agreed: "By doing the right thing when it comes to business integrity, you will also be doing the right thing to grow your business for the long term."[15]

Yet another benefit of using a deontological approach in public relations is that it is responsive to changing trends or issues via the open communication of systems theory. This type of philosophy allows the organization to react to change pressures from the environment regardless of how many members a public has or who is in the majority. This framework consistently allows the minority to have just as much impact on an issue as the majority: an important consideration for activist groups and demographic minorities alike.

Enacting moral duty is a higher calling than simply advocating an organization's position and allows the public relations professional to truly **act as the ethical conscience** of the organization.[16] **The public relations executive evaluates the ethics of**

FIGURE 5.1

ETHICAL DECISION-
MAKING TRIANGLE

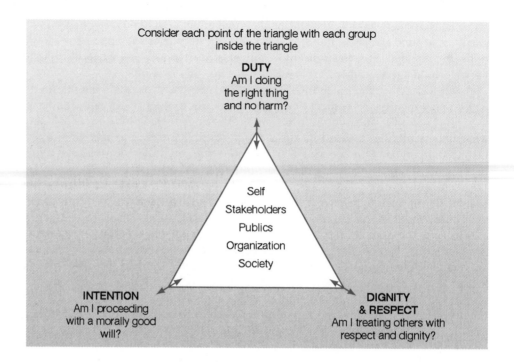

options independent of what the organization desires, so that the role of ethics counsel to top management is valued as distinct, expert input for strategic decision making.

ETHICAL FOUNDATIONS OF PROFESSIONALISM

You do not have to be a cynic to question the ethical foundations of some established professions. News reports tell of a physician who carved his initials into a woman's stomach after performing a caesarian section. Others tell of insurance fraud, unnecessary medical tests, or risky but unnecessary surgery. Lawyers are known for filing absurd claims to harass, intimidate, or frustrate the judicial process. Dentists, pharmacists, accountants, and other professional occupations also have their share of scandal.

Absent rigorous policing of such charlatans erodes the public confidence. Ideally, professional societies or associations engage in self-policing to deter malfeasance, to enforce the collective morality, and to ensure that professionals will engage in what one writer calls "right conduct."[17] Surely, the primary goal is to protect the clients of professional services. At the same time, however, self-policing in the professions protects the professional franchise and maintains public trust and support for professional privilege.

Professional Ethics

Ethical conduct suggests that actions are consistent with moral norms in a society. In professions, the application of moral values in practice is referred to as "applied ethics."[18] Established professions translate widely shared ideas of right conduct into codes of ethics. These statements of applied ethics guide professional practice and provide the basis for enforcement and sanctions. For instance, an attorney convicted of perjury or witness tampering can be disbarred and no longer be allowed to practice law.

Why this concern for professional ethics and enforcement of codes of conduct? The answers are both simple and complex. The simple answer is to protect those who entrust their well-being to the professional. The more complex answer also includes concerns about protecting the profession itself: professional privilege, status, and collegiality.

The Imperative of Trust

Clients' relationships with professionals differ from their relationships with other providers of skills and services. For example, if you go to a hospital emergency room, you will most likely have some degree of confidence that the physicians and nurses are qualified and capable and, furthermore, that it is their ethical duty to perform with your best interests in mind. It is unlikely that you will delay their performance while you check their transcripts to make sure they took the appropriate courses and passed all their exams. Contrast your relationship with these doctors and nurses with the one you establish with a mechanic when your car needs repair service.

The difference centers on the nature of **fiduciary relationships**. When you seek the services of a professional, you put yourself—not just your things—at risk. Your well-being is subject to the judgment and actions of the professional. Professional privilege maintains confidentiality when you must reveal aspects of your person and behavior that normally remain private. In other words, you trust the professional with information and access that often are withheld from even your closest friends and family. Often, you actually entrust yourself and your possessions to the professional. That is, you enter a **fiduciary relationship**, meaning the professional holds you, and possibly your possessions, in trust and is obliged to act in your best interest. This obligation differentiates the professional from other occupations.[19]

Professional Privilege

Professionals traditionally hold privileged positions in society because of the value and trust inherent in fiduciary relationships. Additionally, professionals do work that is seen as especially valuable, in part because of the preparation and practice needed to develop the required knowledge and skills. Not only must professionals invest a great deal of time and effort to acquire their knowledge and skills, but they must also commit themselves to uphold the profession by honoring its obligations and values. For example, the Hippocratic oath, written in 400 B.C., obligates physicians to work for the benefit, not harm, of patients.

When professionals violate fiduciary relationships or otherwise exploit clients, or when they perform substandard practice, they threaten not only their client's welfare but also that of their entire profession. Professional privilege rests on the foundation of public trust and confidence in both the professional's expertise and right conduct.

To protect both clients and their own privileged positions in society, professions establish codes of ethics and standards of practice. These codes often have the weight of law and the power of state sanctions. The argument for codes and rigorous enforcement rests on the belief that professional work involves special and valuable knowledge and skill essential to the public good and is so complex that only those deemed qualified may engage in practice.[20]

Social Responsibility

Professions must also fulfill expectations and moral obligations at the level of society. Commitment to serve society applies to both individual practitioners and the profession collectively. It means that right conduct takes into account the welfare of the larger society as the professional helps clients solve problems. It also means that associations of professionals exercise collective power as moral agents for the betterment of society. To fulfill their social responsibilities, professionals are expected to do more than provide knowledge and skilled services; they are "held responsible for improving the institutions administering those services."[21]

Ultimately, public relations is judged by its impact on society. Public relations' value to society is enhanced when (1) it promotes the free, ethical competition of ideas, information, and education in the marketplace of public opinion; (2) it reveals the sources and goals of participants in the debate; and (3) it enforces high standards of conduct. Value to society is diminished when (1) it suppresses or otherwise limits competition of ideas, (2) it hides or ascribes to others the true sources of public relations efforts, and (3) it leaves unchallenged incompetent or unethical practice.

Positives.   The major positives of socially responsible public relations include the following.

1. Public relations improves professional practice by codifying and enforcing ethical conduct and standards of performance.
2. Public relations improves the conduct of organizations by stressing the need for public approval.
3. Public relations serves the public interest by making all points of view articulate in the public forum.
4. Public relations serves our segmented, scattered society by using communication and mediation to replace misinformation with information, discord with rapport.
5. Public relations fulfills its social responsibility to promote human welfare by helping social systems adapt to changing needs and environments.

Much good can be credited to ethical public relations practice, and opportunities for serving the public interest abound. Public relations' benefits are apparent in the billions of dollars raised to construct buildings, endow professorships, and provide scholarships in universities; in campaigns to eradicate disease and substance abuse, reduce poverty, improve nutrition, and house the homeless; in the lessening of ethnic, racial, and religious discrimination and conflict; in responsive economic enterprises providing profit for investors, jobs for employees, and goods and services for consumers; and in greater understanding of global problems and relations. The potential good inherent in ethical, effective public relations is limitless. So is the potential for dysfunction.

Negatives.   Three major negatives can be attributed to the practice.

1. Public relations gains advantages for and promotes special interests, sometimes at the cost of the public well-being.
2. Publicity clutters already choked channels of communication with the debris of pseudoevents and phony phrases that confuse or influence rather than clarify.
3. Public relations sometimes corrodes our channels of communication with cynicism and credibility gaps.

Too often the thrust of public relations is to obfuscate and obscure rather than to clarify complex public issues. Robert Heilbroner recognized public relations as a social force and charged it with a major part "in the general debasement of communications from which we suffer." He said,

> No one can quarrel with the essential function that public relations fills as a purveyor of genuine ideas and information. No one denies that many public relations men, working for corporations as well as for colleges or causes, honestly communicate things which are worth communication. Nor can anyone absolve public relations for loading the communications channels with noise. We read the news and suspect that behind it lies the "news release." We encounter the reputation and ascribe it to publicity. Worst of all, we no longer credit good behavior with good motives, but cheapen it to the level of "good public relations."[22]

This social aspect of right conduct reminds us that both individual practitioners and the profession as a whole are entrusted with the welfare of larger society as a condition on how they serve clients. This aspect of ethics is referred to as the profession's "**social responsibility**." When choosing such work and life, one also takes on the social responsibility of the profession, as well as its knowledge, skills, trust, and privileges.

In summary, to qualify as a profession, practitioners—both individually and collectively—must operate as moral agents in society. Ethical professional practice requires placing public service and social responsibility over personal gains, as well as the ability to engage in a rational analysis of ethical dilemmas.

CRITERIA OF A PROFESSION

As in other "professional" occupations, many in public relations work to earn status as members of a true profession. Attempts to achieve professional status might be considered selfish by some, but the results of increased professionalism benefits society as a whole. Professionalization institutionalizes the best practices and establishes standards of quality that serve the public interest. Professionalization has, by and large, brought us better health care; safer highways and bridges; better houses; faster cars and airplanes; safer air travel; and higher standards in business, banking, and accounting. Add to this list more competent public relations counsel.

Assessing the progress of contemporary practice toward achieving professional status requires criteria. Of course, **the imperative of ethical practice is paramount**. Other indicators of professional status include:

1. Specialized educational preparation to acquire unique knowledge and skills, based on a body of theory developed through research

2. Recognition by the community of a unique and essential service

3. Autonomy in practice and acceptance of personal responsibility by practitioners

4. Codes of ethics and standards of performance enforced by a self-governing association of colleagues

In summary, for public relations to achieve professional status, there must be specialized educational programs, a body of knowledge, community recognition, individual accountability, and commitment to abide by established codes that protect the public interest and spell out social responsibility.

PROFESSIONAL EDUCATION

As a leading public relations practitioner told students at Ball State University, "Public relations will never reach the status of a profession as long as people can get into the field and prosper without having completed a fairly rigorous course of study in the field."[23] Established professions require extended periods of training to learn the knowledge and skills needed to practice, plus the completion of qualifying or board exams; generally the more rigorous the training and the more complex the knowledge, the higher the professional status.

Because preparation is standardized and demanding, those entering professions go through similar initiations to the values and expectations of practice. Their common socialization experience not only standardizes the practice but also encourages commitment to lifelong careers and strong bonds with colleagues. Because of the commitment, time, and effort invested in acquiring the knowledge and skill base, professionals value achievement in the intellectual aspects of their fields.[24]

Degree Programs

Edward L. Bernays, who had just written *Crystallizing Public Opinion*, offered the first university-level public relations course in 1923. Bernays taught the one-semester-credit course for two years in the journalism department of New York University's School of Commerce, Accounts, and Finance. In the United States, instruction in public relations quickly grew. By 1946, 30 colleges offered 47 courses.[25] In 1956 the Public Relations Society of America (PRSA) made the first comprehensive survey of public relations education and found that the number of colleges offering courses had tripled in a decade.[26] Another survey financed by PRSA in 1970 identified 303 institutions offering one or more courses and increasing scholarly research activity.[27] The 1981 Commission on Public Relations Education estimated that 10,000 students were taking public relations courses at some 300 institutions.[28] Now, there are respected public relations programs at most major universities in countries around the globe.

The most recent Commission on Public Relations Education recommended that undergraduate public relations programs contain the following core content areas of study.

1. *Theory, Origin, Principles, and Professional Practice of Public Relations . . .* nature and role of public relations, the history of public relations, the societal forces affecting the profession and its practice and theories of public relations.

2. *Public Relations Ethics and Law* . . . codes of ethics and practice in public relations and in other professions; specific legal issues such as privacy, defamation, copyright, product liability, and financial disclosure; legal and regulatory compliance and credibility.

3. *Public Relations Research, Measurement, and Performance Evaluation* . . . quantitative and qualitative research designs, processes, and techniques including public opinion polling and survey research; fact-finding and applied research; observation and performance measurement; social, communication, and employee audits; issue tracking; focus groups and interviews; use of external research services and consultants; media clipping and analysis; and historical research.

4. *Public Relations Planning and Management* . . . techniques and models related to setting long- and short- term goals and objectives, designing strategies and tactics, segmenting audiences, analyzing problems and opportunities, communicating with top management, developing budgets.

5. *Public Relations Writing and Production* . . . communication theory; concepts and models for both mass, interpersonal, employee, and internal communication; organizational communication and dynamics; persuasion and propaganda; controlled versus uncontrolled communication; and feedback systems.[29]

The Commission on Public Relations Education advised that these key courses be supported by a public relations internship and coursework focusing on tactical implementation, such as a writing or campaigns class. Finally, they also recommended directed electives in an area of "supporting coursework" in another discipline. The Commission recommended business management and marketing, sociology, public administration, political science, and international business courses.[30]

Continuing Education

Professions require continuing education to keep practitioners current in theory and skills. PRSA and International Association of Business Communicators (IABC) now require or encourage members to earn continuing education units (CEUs) through professional development seminars and workshops.

Requiring practitioners to maintain current expertise and skills, and to perform public service, moves the field even closer to the more established professions. For example, all accredited (APR) members of PRSA must earn points from continuing education, professional development, and public service to maintain their accredited status. Continuing education also demonstrates commitment to the lifetime of learning needed to provide clients current and competent service, part of any profession's implicit contract with society.

RESEARCH AND THE BODY OF KNOWLEDGE

Professional higher education introduces aspiring practitioners to the body of theory, research, and skills on which the profession is based. Continuing education then keeps practitioners up to date on research developments that expand the body of knowledge. Not everyone, however, accepts the concept of a body of knowledge and the value of basic research. Few practitioners subscribe to or read the field's research journals, as many believe experience is enough to guide their activity.

A sure sign of advancement toward professional status, however, is the increasing demand for research and critical examination of the conventional wisdom guiding the practice. Public relations problems in business and industry, for example, are every bit as tough and complicated as the problems faced by engineering, finance, production, or distribution. Practitioners must approach them as methodically and as thoroughly prepared as engineers, economists, and other managers approach their own. Such a scientific approach requires understanding based on a body of knowledge developed through extensive research. Hence, the oft said, "Nothing is more practical than a good theory."

Support for Research

Because professions draw on a specialized body of knowledge developed through research, practitioners are obligated to support the advancement of professional knowledge. To that end, PRSA established the Foundation for Public Relations Research and Education in 1956 to advance professionalism in public relations by funding research, disseminating scholarly writings, and promoting professional education.

During the 1980s, however, the foundation drifted from its original mission and began to exert its independence from PRSA. Directors funded failed attempts to introduce public relations education in business schools and pushed to broaden the appeal of *Public Relations Review* beyond the scholarly research audience. Completing the separation from PRSA in 1989, the foundation changed its name to the Institute for Public Relations (IPR). The IPR bills itself as the only independent foundation in public relations focused on research and education.

The IPR, based at the University of Florida, funds public relations research projects, publishes important books for the field, educates various groups about the responsibilities of public relations, recognizes outstanding scholarship, and awards undergraduate and graduate scholarships. Its annual Pathfinder Award recognizes outstanding programs of research that contribute to the body of knowledge. The annual master's thesis award and graduate research grants encourage advanced public relations studies. The Institute's annual Ketchum Public Relations–funded "SMART" (Scientific Measurement And Research Techniques) grant supports a graduate student's research and includes a paid eight-week internship in Ketchum's New York office.

During the past two decades, the IABC Research Foundation became the major funding agency for public relations research. Estimated to total more than $400,000, its "Excellence in Public Relations and Communication Management" project explored the function's contributions to the bottom line and identified factors contributing to organizational success. Professor James Grunig at the University of Maryland led a team of researchers from the United States and the United Kingdom that produced comprehensive reviews of theory and research and also collected data from more than 200 organizations in the United States, Canada, and the United Kingdom.[31]

The Literature

The literature serving the field reflects the gap between the immediate information needs of practitioners and the theory-building research conducted by scholars. For example, the content of PRSA's *Public Relations Tactics* and IABC's *Communi-*

cation World primarily reflect practitioners' interest in day-to-day problems and techniques related to designing and implementing programs and what one practitioner called "news you can use." The independent *Public Relations Quarterly* features commentaries and scholarly analyses, book reviews, and regular columnists of interest to practitioners. PRSA's slick *Public Relations Strategist* quarterly addresses issues and trends of interest to public relations professionals and—according to the magazine's promotional literature—their peers, meaning "the chief executive officer, marketing managers, and financial and human resources executives."

On the other hand, the scholarly journals—*Public Relations Review* and *Journal of Public Relations Research*—report research on the social context of public relations, factors of effectiveness, and theory development related to the practice. The scholarly literature also mirrors classic concerns of other emerging professions: preoccupation and introspection during the search for collective identity, justification, and recognition.[32]

The University of Wisconsin Press published the first comprehensive bibliography of public relations books and periodical literature in 1957. This first bibliography of the field was compiled by Scott M. Cutlip and was funded by a grant from the then Foundation for Public Relations Research and Education. The second edition, published in 1965, carried nearly 6,000 entries of books and articles relevant to the practice. The third edition in 1974 added 4,000 titles to the growing body of literature. The fourth issue of *Public Relations Review* in 1975 began that journal's series of updated bibliographies.[33] The first such bibliography produced in conjunction with the PRSA Body of Knowledge Project appeared in the spring 1988 issue of *Public Relations Review*.[34] Dramatic increases in the number of scholarly books and journals relevant to public relations practice indicate a growing knowledge base for study and practice and make annual attempts to catalog all new entries more difficult (see Exhibit 5.1).

A majority of public relations analyses and research reports do not get published and widely disseminated. Most research conducted by public relations departments and firms is considered **proprietary** and is therefore not shared beyond the sponsoring organization. Often such research addresses specific issues and publics or tests particular communication strategies and tactics and does not draw on or contribute to the body of theory.

LICENSING AND ACCREDITATION

Pioneer counselor Edward L. Bernays was among the first to advocate licensing of public relations practitioners. In 1953 he argued, "In the entire history of professions, licensing standards and criteria and finally codes of ethics in public conduct have been necessary . . . to exclude those who are not properly qualified."[35] The indefatigable Bernays was still thumping the same drum more than 50 years later: "We must get the two words, public relations, defined by law with licensing and registration of practitioners, as is the case with lawyers, medical doctors and other professionals. Today the term 'public relations' is in the public domain and anyone— many without training, education, or ethical behavior—is welcome to use it to describe what he or she professes to do."[36] Yet practitioners in the United States remain divided on the feasibility and desirability of licensing.

EXHIBIT 5.1

PUBLICATIONS

Scholarly Journals

Journal of Public Relations Research, Lawrence Erlbaum Associates, Inc., 10 Industrial Avenue, Mahwah, NJ 07430 (Ed.: Linda Aldoory, Department of Communication, University of Maryland, College Park, MD 20742-7635)

Public Relations Review, Elsevier Science, UK (Ed.: Ray E. Hiebert, 38091 Beach Rd., Box 180, Colton's Point, MD 20626-0180)

Management Communication Quarterly, Sage Publications, 2455 Teller Rd., Thousand Oaks, CA 91320 (Ed.: Charles Conrad, Department of Communication, Texas A&M University, College Station, TX 77843-4234)

Other scholarly journals with content related to public relations

Journal of Applied Communication Research
Journal of Business Ethics
Journal of Communication Management
Journalism and Mass Communication Quarterly
Public Opinion Quarterly

Professional Periodicals

Communications World, International Association of Business Communicators, One Hallidie Plaza, Suite 600, San Francisco, CA 94102 (nine issues annually)

International Public Relations Review, International Public Relations Association, CP 2100, CH-1211, Geneva 2, Switzerland (quarterly)

Journal of Employee Communication Management, Ragan Communications, 316 N. Michigan Avenue, Chicago, IL 60601 (six issues annually).

O'Dwyer's PR Services Report, J. R. O'Dwyer Company, Inc., 271 Madison Avenue, New York, NY 10016 (monthly)

Public Relations Strategist, Public Relations Society of America, 33 Irving Place, New York, NY 10003 (quarterly)

Public Relations Quarterly, 44 West Market Street, Rhinebeck, NY 12572

PR Week, PR Publications Ltd., 220 Fifth Avenue, New York, NY 10001

Newsletters

Jack O'Dwyer's Newsletter, The J. R. O'Dwyer Co., Inc., 271 Madison Avenue, New York, NY 10016

PR News, Phillips Publishing, Inc., 7811 Montrose Road, Potomac, MD 20854

The Ragan Report, Ragan Communications, 316 N. Michigan Avenue, Chicago, IL 60601

Legal Considerations

The issue of occupational licensure—the permission granted by the state or government to engage in a specific occupation—generates many questions and issues of concern for practitioners around the world. In the Unites States, licensing raises three basic constitutional issues: (1) the right of freedom of expression, (2) the right of the states to regulate occupations, and (3) the right of individuals to pursue occupations without unjustified state interference. Licensure must be justified on the grounds that it is crucial to the well-being and preservation of society.

In the United States, legal objections are raised in the debate over licensing. One is the problem of demonstrating a compelling state interest; another is safeguarding the practitioner's freedom of expression. The right of the states to regulate occupations is based on the Tenth Amendment, which reserves for states the powers not specifically delegated to federal government. The First Amendment protects freedom of speech and allows public relations practitioners free voice in public debate. Therefore, the two broad reasons generally given for public relations licensure—protection of society and professionalization of practitioners—must be considered carefully in the light of "compelling state interest."

The argument for a compelling need to regulate public relations is weak in the eyes of the courts. Although public relations—like any occupation—has the potential for abuse, its actions may be no more dangerous to society as a whole than would be those exercised directly by the organization for whom the practitioner might act. And although public relations practice may be controversial in some instances, the courts have argued in cases such as *Adams v. Tanner*, 244 U.S. 590 (1917), and *Baker v. Daly*, 15 F. Supp.2d 881, that controversy is not sufficient cause to regulate. In fact, U.S. courts tend to rule in favor of public relations and media efforts to foster "vigorous public debate" and to protect the "watchdog of government." The argument that licensing would protect society is directly refuted in law. The U.S. courts have consistently found that even abusive communication merits protection under the First Amendment. Other nations, such as Australia, Germany, the Netherlands, and England, also tend to encourage free and open debate in the media as a means of societal expression.

The second argument for licensure—that it would professionalize the practice— also gets short shrift in the law. It may be a powerful professional argument, but it has no legal basis. In no case have the courts suggested that because licensing would be beneficial, it would be justifiable. Licensing cannot be imposed simply for the benefit of those in an occupational group, either to raise standards or to fence out competition.

Advocates counter that licensing would be voluntary, thereby avoiding conflicts with the constitutionally protected rights. Likewise, organizations cannot be forced to hire only licensed practitioners. Instead, state licensing would limit only the use of the title "**licensed** public relations practitioner" label, not restrict the right of free expression. Advocates also point out that employers and clients would soon learn the value of hiring licensed professionals. On the whole, it appears that licensure will not soon provide a means of elevating and standardizing the preparation, ethics, and competence of practitioners.

Accreditation

In the absence of state licensing, PRSA, IABC, and several state and specialized associations have programs to certify practitioners. The "Universal Accreditation Board," led by PRSA, includes members from nine other participating organizations, whose members may sit for the accreditation exam just as PRSA members. Such accreditation programs typically require a written examination and an oral defense before a panel of qualified peers. Beginning in 1991, PRSA began an accreditation maintenance program, requiring accredited members to remain active in continuing education and public service. To retain their "Accredited Public Relations" designation (or "APR" printed after their names), accredited members must earn 10 points every three years through education, professional development, and public service activities. PRSA lifted the maintenance requirement in 1996 for all members who earned their APR prior to 1991. IABC's accreditation program—Accredited Business Communicator ("ABC")—requires a portfolio presentation in addition to written and oral examinations. According to IABC literature, " 'ABC' after your name is a mark of professional achievement and commitment" that indicates that a practitioner has moved "from craft levels to communication management levels."

Advocates of accreditation have proposed consolidation of the many accreditation programs under a single certification program. The Universal Accreditation Board was a step toward that goal. A single, well-publicized, and strongly enforced accreditation program backed by strong ethics codes would be a significant advance toward professional status. Current practice, however, continues to be guided by weak voluntary codes and splintered efforts by different associations and societies. This situation weakens claims of professionalism and high ethical standards.

PROFESSIONAL ORGANIZATIONS

The growth of professional associations reflects the serious efforts being made by many practitioners to surround the function with status and to advance its competence. Although these associations include only a small portion of all those working in the public relations field, they exert considerable influence through their publications, conferences, seminars, awards programs, and advocacy for the practice. These organizations are international, national, regional, and specialized by area of practice—such as practitioners in health care, agriculture, or financial relations.

International Professional Organizations

The growth of public relations on a global scale makes it possible to have international professional societies devoted to public relations education, research, and professional standards. Groups of scholars such as the International Communication Association also have divisions devoted to public relations research and teaching among their ranks. Practitioners have organized two international societies.

International Association of Business Communicators (IABC)   Progress toward increased professionalism and higher standards in public relations advanced with the emergence of the IABC as a strong organization. Founded in 1970 when the Association of Industrial Editors and the International Council of Industrial Editors merged, IABC grew from 3,500 members to more than 13,000 members today in 60 countries (www.iabc.com). The IABC headquarters is in San Francisco.

To advance the competence and ethics of this field, IABC created a professional development guide for practitioners to help them identify the skills and knowledge necessary for attaining career goals and an ethics review committee to enforce a code of ethics. The code of ethics (see Exhibit 5.2) emphasizes that the principles of professional communication—legal, ethical, and in good taste—apply worldwide.

IABC's Gold Quill and EXCEL awards programs set standards for and recognize excellence in communication program design and implementation. Its *Communication World* magazine, published nine times a year, serves as a news source on emerging issues and a reference on communication trends, theory, and practice. IABC's belief that communication should be a management function is supported with a program to reach key educators. IABC also formed a foundation in 1982 to support education and research. Its primary activities during the 1990s included publishing reports from the "Excellence in Public Relations and Communication Management" and "Velvet Ghetto" studies. IABC recognizes leadership in the field and continues to commission public relations research, such as the "Business Communication Ethics" project.

International Public Relations Association (IPRA)   When IPRA was formed in London in 1955, it had only 15 members in five countries. Membership now totals 1,000

EXHIBIT 5.2

INTERNATIONAL ASSOCIATION OF BUSINESS COMMUNICATORS CODE OF ETHICS

Preface

Because hundreds of thousands of business communicators worldwide engage in activities that affect the lives of millions of people, and because this power carries with it significant social responsibilities, the International Association of Business Communicators developed the Code of Ethics for Professional Communicators. The Code is based on three different yet interrelated principles of professional communication that apply throughout the world.

These principles assume that just societies are governed by a profound respect for human rights and the rule of law; that ethics, the criteria for determining what is right and wrong, can be agreed upon by members of an organization; and, that understanding matters of taste requires sensitivity to cultural norms.

These principles are essential:

- Professional communication is legal.
- Professional communication is ethical.
- Professional communication is in good taste.

Recognizing these principles, members of IABC will

- engage in communication that is not only legal but also ethical and sensitive to cultural values and beliefs;
- engage in truthful, accurate and fair communication that facilitates respect and mutual understanding; and,
- adhere to the following articles of the IABC Code of Ethics for Professional Communicators.

Because conditions in the world are constantly changing, members of IABC will work to improve their individual competence and to increase the body of knowledge in the field with research and education.

Articles

1. Professional communicators uphold the credibility and dignity of their profession by practicing honest, candid and timely communication and by fostering the free flow of essential information in accord with the public interest.

2. Professional communicators disseminate accurate information and promptly correct any erroneous communication for which they may be responsible.

3. Professional communicators understand and support the principles of free speech, freedom of assembly, and access to an open marketplace of ideas; and, act accordingly.

4. Professional communicators are sensitive to cultural values and beliefs and engage in fair and balanced communication activities that foster and encourage mutual understanding.

5. Professional communicators refrain from taking part in any undertaking which the communicator considers to be unethical.

6. Professional communicators obey laws and public policies governing their professional activities and are sensitive to the spirit of all laws and regulations and, should any law or public policy be violated, for whatever reason, act promptly to correct the situation.

7. Professional communicators give credit for unique expressions borrowed from others and identify the sources and purposes of all information disseminated to the public.

8. Professional communicators protect confidential information and, at the same time, comply with all legal requirements for the disclosure of information affecting the welfare of others.

9. Professional communicators do not use confidential information gained as a result of professional activities for personal benefit and do not represent conflicting or competing interests without written consent of those involved.

10. Professional communicators do not accept undisclosed gifts or payments for professional services from anyone other than a client or employer.

11. Professional communicators do not guarantee results that are beyond the power of the practitioner to deliver.

12. Professional communicators are honest not only with others but also, and most importantly, with themselves as individuals; for a professional communicator seeks the truth and speaks that truth first to the self.

Courtesy International Association of Business Communicators. From www.iabc.com (October 2004).

in 77 countries, with headquarters in Geneva, Switzerland (www.ipra.org). IPRA is formally recognized by the United Nations, and its members serve as consultants to the UN Economic and Social Council. In 1965 it adopted the Code of Athens, based on the UN Declaration of Human Rights. To commemorate IPRA's 25th anniversary in 1980, the French Post Office Authority issued the first and only stamp dedicated to public relations.

IPRA promotes professional recognition, high standards, and ethics among practitioners working in international aspects of public relations. In addition, it supports professional development and recognition in parts of the world where public relations is just developing and helps establish new national associations. IPRA meets twice each year, annually recognizes "outstanding contribution to better world understanding," publishes *International Public Relations Review* quarterly, and issues "Gold Papers" on major issues of interest to the global public relations community.

National Professional Organizations

Outside the United States, there are more than 100 national and regional associations of public relations practitioners in more than 70 countries, and the total is increasing as public relations gains recognition around the world. Examples include the Public Relations Institute of Australia (established in 1960), Brazil's Federal Council of Public Relations Professionals (1969), the French Public Relations Federation (1971), the German Society of Public Relations (1958), the Public Relations Society of India (1958), and the Nigerian Institute of Public Relations (1963). Following is more information on a few national public relations societies.

Public Relations Society of America (PRSA)   The largest professional organization is the Public Relations Society of America, with approximately 20,000 members in 116 chapters (www.prsa.org). Headquartered in New York City, PRSA traces its origins to three older associations established to bring together practitioners of this growing vocation. Formed in 1947, PRSA fosters the exchange of ideas through its publications and meetings, promotes a sense of professionalism, provides opportunities for continuing education, and encourages ethical behavior and high standards of practice.

PRSA is organized into smaller "sections" of common interest as a means of dealing more effectively with the problems of public relations specialties. There are 18 sections: Association, Corporate, Counselors Academy, Counselors of Higher Education, Educators Academy, Employee Communications, Environment, Financial Communications, Food and Beverage, Health Academy, Independent Practitioners, International, Military and National Security, Multicultural Communications, Public Affairs and Government, Strategic Social Responsibility, Technology, and Travel and Tourism. Some sections and positions in the organization require PRSA accreditation (APR) for membership.

Following the split with the Foundation (now the Institute) for Public Relations Research and Education in 1989, PRSA established another foundation to support research, to fund scholarships, and to publish materials. Its major projects have been establishing the Body of Knowledge Project and establishing a series of awards and scholarships to encourage research and professionalism in public relations.

French Stamp

Canadian Public Relations Society (CPRS)   Founded in 1948, the same year as PRSA, CPRS has almost 2,000 members in 15 chapters (www.cprs.ca). One-third of the members are accredited. CPRS publishes a quarterly newsletter, *Communiqué*, and holds an annual conference. Headquartered in Ottawa, Ontario, CPRS closely parallels PRSA in philosophy and programming.

Institute of Public Relations (United Kingdom) (IPR)   Also founded in 1948, IPR has regional and sectoral groups (by type of practice) with more than 7,500 members—two-thirds based outside London (www.ipr.org.uk). It is the largest public relations professional association in Europe. Long a leader in establishing and enforcing codes of professional and ethical conduct and in encouraging academic preparation and professional development within the profession, IPR publishes *Profile* six times a year and sponsors the annual "PRIDE" awards program. It is a member of the Confederation Europeene des Relations Publiques.

Public Relations Consultants Association (United Kingdom) (PRCA)   The Public Relations Consultants Association, an association of "consultancies"—called "firms" in the United States—was formed in 1969 to promote professional standards in consultancy practice, to act as a clearinghouse for clients seeking counseling in public relations, and to represent members' interests. Only its 160 member consultancies may use the title "registered public relations consultants" (www.iccopr.com). In addition to publishing consultancy costs and other research, the association works closely with IPR in promoting the profession and in establishing standards of practice. For example, in 1998 PRCA introduced mandatory standards for member firms. The association's charter, definitions, guidelines, codes, and arbitration and disciplinary procedures formed the basis for those adopted by the European Community nations. It also was a founding member of the International Communications Consultancy Organization, which has 850 consultancy members in 24 countries.

PRCA guidelines for member consultancies suggest that all staff members pledge compliance with the association's charter requirements. Furthermore, the guidelines call for a clause requiring compliance in all employment contracts. (www.prca.org.uk).

Specialized, Regional, and Local Associations

The growing memberships of several specialized national organizations attest to the field's growing sense of common interests, developing esprit de corps, and professionalism. Almost every type of industry has an organization for its communicators, and many are organized by geographic location or demographic commonalities. For example, the Hispanic Public Relations Association has a membership of more than 150 in the Los Angeles area.

Here are some examples of specialized associations in public relations:

Religious Public Relations Council	Founded 1929
National School Public Relations Association	1935
Florida Public Relations Association	1938
Agricultural Relations Council	1953
Baptist Public Relations Association	1954
National Society of Fund Raising Executives	1960
National Investor Relations Institute	1969

EXHIBIT 5.3

PUBLIC RELATIONS INSTITUTE OF AUSTRALIA

*Robert Masters, FPRIA
President, Public Relations
Institute of Australia, and
Director, Robert Masters &
Associates Pty Ltd, Melbourne*

The Public Relations Institute of Australia is the major body representing public relations professionals throughout the nation. With more than 3,000 members, the Institute not only enhances the status and education of its members, but also accredits public relations courses in Australian universities taken by people pursuing careers in the profession.

Today there are more than 16 universities offering bachelor's degrees in public relations or communication courses accredited by the PRIA. PRIA also accredits courses offered in masters or doctorate degree programs.

Every four years PRIA reviews courses and programs to ensure the courses are relevant to industry and the development of the profession that has seen Public Relations emerge as one of the major sought-after professions in Australia.

Like all professional bodies the Institute recognizes the strong need to bind all those practicing the profession by a code of practice that enables the profession to continue to grow with high ethical standards. It is estimated that the PRIA represents only one-third of people practicing public relations in Australia.

With this in mind, the Institute has embarked on a major membership drive to increase membership to more than 6,000 within five years. This growth rate is being fostered by each of the six State Councils of the PRIA and the two Territory Councils undertaking a wide range of activities to meet the needs of the membership.

These include inviting international visitor lectures; cosponsoring functions with other professional societies in marketing, financial, health, sports and research; conducting briefings for key federal and state government advisers and departments; funding industry surveys and education scholarships; as well as providing continuing professional education courses to keep members current in the practice.

Black Public Relations Society	1973
Council for Advancement and Support of Education (CASE)	1975
Issue Management Council	1982
Hispanic Public Relations Association	1984

In addition, a number of "exclusive" professional groups have developed over the years, with varying degrees of impact in shaping the practice. These include the Wise Men, begun in 1938 by John W. Hill, Pendleton Dudley, and T. J. Ross; Public Relations Seminar, started in 1951 as an outgrowth of the National Conference of Business Public Relations Executives; and Pride and Alarm, founded in 1957 in New York. Exclusivity for the in-group is their hallmark, and these groups generally hold their meetings in private. Some are small, informal, and area-specific, like the Houston group—Corporate Relations Roundtable. Others are large, formalized, and national or international.

The newest by-invitation-only group is the Arthur W. Page Society, formed in 1983 when deregulation splintered AT&T's public relations unit. The group's literature offers the vision statement (www.awpagesociety.com):

> The Arthur W. Page Society is committed to the belief that public relations as a function of executive management is central to the success of the corporation. The membership of the Society will embrace those individuals who epitomize the highest standards of public relations practice, as exemplified by the Page Principles. [See Exhibit 5.4.]

Elite groups such as the Arthur W. Page Society attempt to provide leadership, continuity, and continued growth for the public relations function. They often encourage the role of the public relations practitioner as the ethical conscience of an organization, help mentor young public relations managers, and advance the role of public relations in management.

Student Organizations

Development of the Public Relations Student Society of America (PRSSA) under the auspices of PRSA has strengthened education and recruitment into the field in the United States. PRSSA's first chapter was chartered in 1968. Currently, PRSSA has chapters on 248 campuses with almost 8,000 members (www.prssa.org). PRSSA's purpose is "to cultivate a favorable and mutually advantageous relationship between students and professional public relations practitioners." To ease graduating PRSSA students' transition into the field, PRSA established a preassociate membership with reduced fees.

IABC also sponsors student chapters on about 45 college campuses in 12 countries (www.iabc.com/student). Although IABC's student organization is smaller than PRSSA, it has the benefit of being international. IABC students also hold

---

EXHIBIT 5.4

ARTHUR W. PAGE PRINCIPLES

Tell the truth
Let the public know what's happening and provide an accurate picture of the company's character, ideals and practices.

Prove it with action
Public perception of an organization is determined 90 percent by doing and 10 percent by talking.

Listen to the customer
To serve the company well, understand what the public wants and needs. Keep top decision-makers and other employees informed about public reaction to company products, policies and practices.

Manage for tomorrow
Anticipate public reaction and eliminate practices that create difficulties. Generate goodwill.

Conduct public relations as if the whole company depends on it
Corporate relations is a management function. No corporate strategy should be implemented without considering its impact on the public. The public relations professional is a policymaker capable of handling a wide range of corporate communications activities.

Remain calm, patient and good-humored
Lay the groundwork for public relations miracles with consistent, calm and reasoned attention to information and contacts. When a crisis arises, remember that cool heads communicate best.

Courtesy Arthur W. Page Society

membership in professional IABC chapters. Territorial disputes emerged when one university's student public relations club tried to affiliate with both PRSSA and IABC. PRSSA's rule forbidding dual affiliation again illustrates the "territorial" disputes and competition for members among the many professional associations and societies governing public relations.

Students worldwide are forming similar affiliates of their country's professional societies. In Russia, for example, more than 400 public relations majors at 67 universities met in Moscow in December 2003 to form the Russian Public Relations Student Association (RASSO), the student division of the Russian Public Relations Association (RASO).[37]

CODES OF ETHICS

In addition to a self-governing organization, a basic requirement for professions is adherence to a set of professional norms, usually referred to as codes of ethics. As acceptance of professionalism and a sense of cohesiveness have developed, there has been increasing concern for standards of professional responsibility. Many practitioners are making an earnest effort to act morally and to advise their organization or clients as an ethical conscience of the company. Others see codes of ethics as obstacles to be avoided, window dressing, or nice-sounding puffery.[38]

Attempts to advance the ethics in this field are reflected in the number of codes of professional standards for public relations practice. In the United States, the principal code is that of the Public Relations Society of America. PRSA's first Code of Professional Standards was adopted in 1954 and revised in 1959, 1963, 1977, 1983, 1988, and 2000 (see Exhibit 5.5).

PRSA members agree to conduct their professional lives in accordance with the code of ethics. Compliance is enforced in confidential proceedings, following complaints of code violations by a PRSA member, by a nonmember, or through media exposure. An eleven-member national Board of Ethics and Professional Standards investigates complaints and makes recommendations on whether or not to bar individuals from membership or to expel members found in violation of the code.

Enforcement by PRSA's Board of Ethics and Professional Standards has been uneven over the years. Few cases get referred to the ethics panel. Most cases that are referred are dismissed because of lack of evidence, settled to the satisfaction of all parties, or dropped because the charged member died or simply resigned. One of the quirks in the code is that it applies only to members.

IABC has a similar approach to its code of ethics for communicators, but has historically not pursued enforcement. Rather than playing an enforcement role, IABC's Ethics Committee encourages professional development activities related to ethics and offers counsel to individual members on how to deal ethically with specific situations. Widespread dissemination of the code in several languages promotes compliance (see Exhibit 5.4). If a governmental agency or judicial body finds a member guilty of a serious offense, however, the IABC executive board is authorized to employ procedures spelled out in the bylaws to terminate membership.

Adoption of a code of ethics does not automatically bring morality to a calling. Generally, having a code reflects a sincere desire to raise standards of ethical practice and to provide criteria to guide and judge individual behavior. But a code without commitment, training, and enforcement means little in practice. Demonstrating

EXHIBIT 5.5

PRSA MEMBER CODE OF ETHICS GUIDELINES

Free Flow of Information

- Preserve the integrity of the process of communication.
- Be honest and accurate in all communications.
- Act promptly to correct erroneous communications for which the practitioner is responsible
- Preserve the free flow of unprejudiced information when giving or receiving gifts by ensuring that gifts are nominal, legal, and infrequent.

Competition

- Follow ethical hiring practices designed to respect the free and open competition without deliberately undermining a competitor.
- Preserve intellectual property rights in the marketplace.

Disclosure of Information

- Be honest and accurate in all communications.
- Act promptly to correct erroneous communications for which the practitioner is responsible.
- Investigate the truthfulness and accuracy of information released on behalf of those represented.
- Reveal the sponsors for causes and interests represented.
- Disclose financial interests (such as stock ownership) in a client's organization.
- Avoid deceptive practices

Safeguard Confidences

- Safeguard the confidences and privacy rights of present, former, and prospective clients and employees.
- Protect privileged, confidential, or insider information gained from a client or organization.

- Immediately advise an appropriate authority if a member discovers that confidential information is being divulged by an employee of a client company or organization.

Conflicts of Interest

- Act in the best interests of the client or employer, even subordinating the member's personal interests.
- Avoid actions and circumstances that may appear to compromise good business judgment or create a conflict between personal and professional interests.
- Disclose promptly any existing or potential conflict of interest to affected clients or organizations.
- Encourage clients and customers to determine if a conflict exists after notifying all affected parties.

Enhancing the Profession

- Acknowledge that there is an obligation to protect and enhance the profession.
- Keep informed and educated about practices in the profession to ensure ethical conduct.
- Actively pursue personal professional development
- Decline representation of clients or organizations that urge or require actions contrary to this Code.
- Accurately define what public relations activities can accomplish.
- Counsel subordinates in proper decision making.
- Require that subordinates adhere to the ethical requirements of the Code.
- Report ethical violations, whether committed by PRSA members or not, to the appropriate authority.

Courtesy Public Relations Society of America.

their commitment to ethical practice, some public relations firms—Epley Associates, Inc.; Ketchum Public Relations; and Manning, Selvage & Lee—require new employees to sign an agreement that obligates them to practice according to the PRSA code, even if they are not themselves members of PRSA. Such agreements are similar to the PRSA Member Code of Ethics Pledge, which all members must sign:

I pledge:

To conduct myself professionally, with truth, accuracy, fairness and responsibility to the public; to improve my individual competence and advance the knowledge and proficiency of the profession through continuing research and education; and to adhere to the articles of the Member Code of Ethics for the practice of public relations as adopted by the governing Assembly of the Public Relations Society of America.

I understand and accept that there is a consequence for misconduct, up to and including membership revocation.[39]

A Canadian counselor pointed out that "Unfortunately, these codes have little real value unless they are accepted in turn by the employers of practitioners and applied to the conduct of the business itself."[40] Longtime leader and crusader for higher ethics in public relations Frank Wylie admonished, "We shouldn't allow ourselves to accept the lowest common denominator of behavior—the negative and retrogressive 'it won't really hurt anyone' philosophy. We must aspire to a better level of ethics, and we must persevere to achieve that goal."[41]

Another common pitfall is the idea, "If it isn't illegal, then it must be all right." This mistaken logic abrogates the moral duty of public relations practitioners to attorneys.[42] Public relations practice is fraught with ethical dilemmas, and practitioners must be prepared to evaluate them using the professional codes of ethics. (See Exhibit 5.6 for examples.)

In public relations scholarship, the debate about codes of ethics is ongoing. Some scholars see codes as unenforceable and voluntary, whereas others see them as necessary baselines for the practice. Public relations ethicists argue that the

EXHIBIT 5.6

PUBLIC RELATIONS ETHICS: SITUATIONS FOR DISCUSSION

Refer to the IABC Code of Ethics in Exhibit 5.2 and the PRSA guidelines in Exhibit 5.4 to resolve the following situations.

Situation 1: Your firm is one of several under consideration by a prospective client planning to introduce a new service. The company anticipates severe opposition from certain groups and politicians. You are given confidential information as to the service and the company's plans for you to use while developing your firm's proposal. The company awards the contract to a competing firm. Can you disclose the information to the company's opposition?

Situation 2: Your firm publishes a newsletter directed to brokerage houses. A corporate executive—one of your clients—asks you to help make the company better known among stockbrokers. You publish a highly optimistic forecast of the company's business prospects, leaving out some information about problems. You also fail to indicate your firm's relationship with the company. Were you under any obligation to disclose this relationship? Should you print a correction that includes all the information you have about the company?

Situation 3: Your employer directs you to set up a supposedly independent citizens' organization to demonstrate support for a new real estate development that requires planning commission approval. The new organization will be financed secretly by your company and a group of contractors who will participate in building the homes. Is there anything wrong with establishing this organization?

Situation 4: Your employer asks you to give a series of talks in communities served by your company. You are to discuss the new plant being built and its operations. You visit the plant before giving the speech prepared by your immediate supervisor. During the tour you learn that several claims in the speech are not true. Can you give the speech as originally written?

Based on an article written by the late Donald B. McCammond, APR, while he served as chairman of PRSA's Board of Ethics and Professional Standards. "Ethics: The Right Choice," *Public Relations Journal* 43, no. 2 (February 1987): 8–10. Used with permission of *Public Relations Journal*.

PRSA code is unenforceable, full of contradictions, and neither professional nor useful to practitioners.[43] Even though codes of ethics are held up as evidence of professional status, enforcement poses little threat or is easily subverted when the subject of enforcement simply drops his or her membership.

Some argue that codes of ethics only "preach to the choir" and do not help where they are actually needed: with ethics training and moral reasoning or moral development.[44] Others argue that codes institutionalize consistent guidelines for public relations practice around the world.[45] Whether a code is used or not often matters less than **who is responsible for making ethical decisions**. One ethicist concluded: "The bottom-line of ethical decision making in our field will continue to rest in the laps of individual practitioners."[46]

WINNING ACCEPTANCE AND STATURE

Even after the considerable progress recorded since the mid-1900s, public relations still falls short of public acceptance as a true profession. The field lacks standardized educational requirements, mandatory certification or licensing, full-fledged devotion to serving the public interest, public acceptance of its social utility, and effective self-regulation. There is a growing consensus on a standardized curriculum for public relations in higher education, but there are no educational requirements for entry into the practice.

As a result, the field continues to be plagued with press agents and publicists parading as strategic counselors and those who are "good with people" but have no knowledge of public relations theory or research.[47] Moreover, the field still tends to attract some practitioners with an asymmetrical bias who are more interested in manipulating opinions than in building true relationships with stakeholders. There is ample evidence that the function is not fully and widely understood, and confusion exists even among its practitioners and students.[48] In sum, the field still attracts many who cannot qualify **morally,** through a commitment to ethical practice, or **functionally,** through knowledge and expertise gained in specialized education. Fortunately, the ranks of those who meet these requirements are growing rapidly.

Ethics and professionalism go hand in hand. One without the other falls short of the ideal: Ethics without competence is meaningless; competence without ethics is directionless—and even dangerous. European scholar Hans-Martin Sass makes the point clearly:

> Ethics and expertise belong together; only together do they constitute true professionalism and provide a morally acceptable foundation for professional fiduciary services. The client . . . expects experienced expertise in making good technical and good moral judgments.[49]

Whether public relations qualifies as a profession is a less important question than the **extent** to which its practitioners use their unique positions as boundary spanners and environmental scanners within the system to engage in dialogue with publics and management. The information and feedback provided by groups in the organization's environment can and should be incorporated into strategic decision making. This can only happen if the public relations counsel is **included in strategic management, valued as a source of information and advice, and seen as a rigorously professional and ethical counselor.**

EXHIBIT 5.7

PUBLIC RELATIONS IN CHINA: GROWTH AND POTENTIAL

Ming Anxiang, Director and Professor, Department of Communication Studies, Institute of Journalism & Communication, Chinese Academy of Social Sciences, Beijing; and Executive Vice-Chairman, Public Relations Society of China

Since the turn of the century, China's emerging public relations industry has grown dramatically and gained in maturity, sophistication, and professionalism. This progress follows some ups and downs, as well as confusion over the concept and practice during the 1980s and 1990s.

Surveys of the profession in China's major mainland cities—including Beijing, Shanghai, and Guangzhou, but excluding Hong Kong and Macao—show 33 percent annual growth in public relations billings. The rapid growth reflects increased annual billings in China by international public relations firms such as Weber Shandwick Worldwide, Burson-Marsteller, Ogilvy Public Relations Worldwide, and Hill & Knowlton, as well as increased billings by emerging local firms.

From Ancient Practice to Imported Modern Concept

Many Chinese scholars consider public relations to be a common and international phenomenon of human behavior that has existed and been practiced in China since ancient times. On the other hand, Chinese public relations scholars agree that the modern concept and practice of public relations in China was imported mainly from the United States. The practice was introduced by public relations departments in international hotels such as Hilton and Sheraton in Guangzhou and Beijing after China opened to the outside world in the early 1980s.

In 1984, I lead a research group to study concepts and theories of Western public relations and to investigate how it was being practiced in foreign and local corporations in China's mainland. In November 1986, the other researchers and I wrote the first Chinese book about public relations, using "the bible of public relations" in the United States—*Effective Public Relations*—as our number-one reference book. The book was published and well received among Chinese readers. Since then, hundreds of books about public relations have been published in China, including the Chinese edition of *Effective Public Relations*.

In 1987 and 1991, the two most important Chinese public relations organizations were established—first, the Public Relations Society of China (PRSC) and then the China International Public Relations Association (CIPRA). Most Chinese provinces and major cities directly under the Central Government now have their own public relations organizations.

From Confusion of Concepts to Professionalism

In the early stage of public relations' development in China, many corporate managers, public relations practitioners, and even some teachers—not to mention ordinary people—confused public relations with advertising and marketing. Others defined it using the negative aspects of Chinese traditional *guanxi*—vulgar private connections. Today, however, there is growing recognition that media coverage, effective events execution, strategic planning, corporate positioning, issues management, and crisis communication are important elements in China's public relations education and practice.

At the beginning of the twenty-first century, PRSC and CIPRA worked with the then-Ministry of Labor and Personnel (now Ministry of Labor and Social Security) to authenticate public relations as one of the formal professional careers in China. Since then, the first textbooks have been published, professional education and training programs established, professional titles authorized, and certificates issued to qualified junior- and middle-level public relations practitioners.

From Bidding for the 2008 Olympics to Expanding International Markets

Beijing's protracted and successful bidding process for the 2008 Olympic Games was the first time that Chinese central and municipal governments consciously and successfully employed modern public relations in the competition to host international events. Several Chinese and international public relations organizations and consultants collaborated throughout the process. The application of modern public relations strategy was an important factor in the final success in securing the 2008 Olympics. Beijing's success was followed by, among others, Shanghai's hosting of the Asia Pacific Economic Cooperation conference in 2002 and its successful 2003 bid to host Expo 2010.

When China joined the World Trade Organization (WTO) in 2001, many Chinese corporations faced new competition with major international conglomerates with world-famous brands. Global competition pushed emerging Chinese corporations and entrepreneurs to learn and employ modern public relations practices. Many consider China to be Asia's greatest potential growth market for professional public relations practice.

TOWARD A PROMISING FUTURE

A century ago a handful of pioneers staked claim to what we call public relations. Moves to professionalize the practice and to accept the nobility of serving the public interest continue to strengthen educational programs, build the body of knowledge, toughen admission requirements, and raise the standards of ethics and acceptable behavior. Consequently, public relations continues to progress professionally and will provide opportunities to achieve professional status to those with the necessary moral commitment, knowledge, and skills. Practitioners committed to high standards of ethics and professionalism will distinguish public relations practice from other skilled occupations and make it a calling serving the public interest.

NOTES

[1] Alexander M. Cutler, "Doing Business Right," in *Building Trust—Leading CEOs Speak Out: How They Create It, Strengthen It, Sustain It* (New York: The Arthur W. Page Society, 2004), 70.

[2] John Kultgen, *Ethics and Professionalism* (Philadelphia: University of Pennsylvania Press, 1988), 371.

[3] John Stauber and Sheldon Rampton, *Toxic Sludge Is Good for You: Lies, Damn Lies, and the Public Relations Industry* (Monroe, ME: Common Courage Press, 1995).

[4] Robert L. Heath and Shannon A. Bowen, "The Public Relations Philosophy of John W. Hill: Bricks in the Foundation of Issues Management," *Journal of Public Affairs,* 2 (2002): 230–46.

[5] Shannon A. Bowen and Robert L. Heath, "Issues Management, Systems, and Rhetoric: Exploring the Distinction between Ethical and Legal Guidelines at Enron," *Journal of Public Affairs* (forthcoming).

[6] Michael Ryan and David L. Martinson, "Journalists and Public Relations Practitioners: Why the Antagonism?" *Journalism Quarterly* 62 (1988), 131–40.

[7] Jeremy Bentham, *The Principles of Morals and Legislation* (Amherst, NY: Prometheus, 1988, original publication 1780); John Stuart Mill, *Utilitarianism* (New York: The Liberal Arts Press, 1957, original publication 1861).

[8] Immanuel Kant, *Groundwork of the Metaphysic of Morals.* (H. J. Paton translation). New York: Harper & Row (1964). (Original work published 1785.)

[9] Antony Flew, *A Dictionary of Philosophy*, 2nd ed. (New York: St. Martin's Press, 1979).

[10] Kant, *Groundwork of the Metaphysic of Morals.*

[11] Ibid.

[12] Bill Nielsen, personal communication, Dec. 3, 1999.

[13] For more detailed discussion of this model, see Shannon A. Bowen, "A Practical Model for Ethical Decision Making in Issues Management and Public Relations," *Journal of Public Relations Research 17* (2005).

[14] Marilyn Carlson Nelson, "The Long View" in *Building Trust*, ibid., 312.

[15] Fred Hassan, "Business Integrity" in *Building Trust*, ibid., 29.

[16] Michael Ryan and David L. Martinson, " The P.R. Officer as Corporate Conscience. *Public Relations Quarterly* 28, no. 2 (1983), 20–23; and Shannon A. Bowen, "A Theory of Ethical Issues Management: Contributions of Kantian Deontology to Public Relations' Ethics and Decision Making" (unpublished doctoral dissertation, University of Maryland, 2000).

[17] R. M. Veatch, "The Danger of Virtue," *Journal of Medicine and Philosophy* 13 (1988): 445–46.

[18] Baruch Brody, *Ethics and Its Applications* (New York: Harcourt Brace Jovanovich, 1983).

[19] Robert Sokolowski, "The Fiduciary Relationship and the Nature of Professions," in *Ethics, Trust, and the Professions: Philosophical and Cultural Aspects*, ed. Edmund D. Pellegrino, Robert M. Veatch, and John P. Langan, 23–43 (Washington, DC: Georgetown University Press, 1991).

[20] For more detailed discussion of the bases for professional privilege, see Eliot Freidson, "Nourishing Professionalism," in *Ethics, Trust, and the Professions*, ed. Edmund D. Pellegrino, Robert M. Veatch, and John P. Langan, 193–220 (Washington, DC: Georgetown University Press, 1991).

[21] John Kultgen, *Ethics and Professionalism* (Philadelphia: University of Pennsylvania Press, 1988), 248.

[22] Robert Heilbroner, "Public Relations: The Invisible Sell," in Reo M. Christenson and Robert O. McWilliams, *Voice of the People,* 2d ed., 485 (New York: McGraw-Hill, 1967).

[23] David Ferguson, "A Practitioner Looks at Public Relations Education," 1987 Vern C. Schranz Distinguished Lecture in Public Relations (Ball State University, Muncie, IN).

[24] Freidson, "Nourishing Professionalism."

[25] Hale Nelson, "Training for Public Relations," *Public Relations Journal* 12, no. 9 (September 1956).

[26] Ray Eldon Hiebert, *Trends in Public Relations Education, 1964–1970* (New York: Foundation for Public Relations Research and Education, 1970). Also see "PR in Classroom," *Public Relations Journal* 26 (September 1970).

[27] Kenneth O. Smith, "Report of the 1981 Commission on Public Relations Education," *Public Relations Review* 8 (Summer, 1982): 66–68.

[28] William P. Ehling and Betsy Plank, *Design for Undergraduate Public Relations Education* (Chicago: Commission on Undergraduate Public Relations Education, 1987).

[29] Dean Kruckeberg and John Paluszek, "Report of the Commission on Public Relations Education." *A port of entry: Public relations education for the 21st century.* (October, 1999): 21.

[30] Ibid., 22.

[31] The IABC Excellence study research team included Professor David M. Dozier, San Diego State University; Professor William P. Ehling, Syracuse University; Professor James E. Grunig, Professor Larissa A. Grunig, University of Maryland; and public relations consultants Fred C. Repper (deceased), and Jon White, Bedford, UK. Books reporting the project results include James E. Grunig, ed., *Excellence in Public Relations and Communication Management: Contributions to Effective Organizations* (Hillsdale, NJ: Lawrence Erlbaum Associates, 1992); David M. Dozier, *Manager's Guide to Excellence in Public Relations and Communication Management* (Mahwah, NJ: Lawrence Erlbaum Associates, 1995); and Larissa A. Grunig, James E. Grunig, and David M. Dozier, *Excellent Public Relations and Effective Organizations: A Study of Communication Management in Three Countries* (Mahwah, NJ: Lawrence Erlbaum Associates, 2002).

[32] Glen M. Broom, Mark S. Cox, Elizabeth A. Krueger, and Carol M. Liebler, "The Gap between Professional and Research Agendas in Public Relations Journals," *Public Relations Research Annual* 1 (1989): 141–54.

[33] Scott M. Cutlip, *A Public Relations Bibliography* (Madison: University of Wisconsin Press, 1957, 1965); Robert L. Bishop, *Public Relations: A Comprehensive Bibliography* (Ann Arbor: University of Michigan Press, 1974); and Bishop's two updates published in *Public Relations Review* 1, no. 4 (Winter Supplement 1975–1976), and 3, no. 2 (Summer 1977).

[34] Hiebert, *Trends in Public Relations Education.* Also see "PR in Classroom," *Public Relations Journal* 26 (September 1970).

[35] Edward L. Bernays, "Should Public Relations Counsel Be Licensed?" *Printers Ink* (December 25, 1953).

[36] Edward L. Bernays, "The Case for Licensing PR Practitioners," *Public Relations Quarterly* 28 (Spring 1983): 32.

[37] "Russian PR Students Establish Association," *PR Tactics* (March 2004): 30.

[38] Bowen and Heath, "Issues Management, Systems, and Rhetoric."

[39] Public Relations Society of America, *The Blue Book* (New York: PRSA, 2004), B19.

[40] Leonard Knott, *Plain Talk about Public Relations* (Toronto: McClelland and Stewart, 1961), 3. Written by one who pioneered and shaped the practice in Canada.

[41] Frank Wylie, "Professional Ethics and Other Misconceptions." Address before the Publicity Club of Chicago, April 20, 1977.

[42] Bowen and Heath, "Issues Management, Systems, and Rhetoric."

[43] Michael Parkinson, "The PRSA Code of Professional Standards and Member Code of Ethics: Why They Are Neither Professional nor Ethical," *Public Relations Quarterly* 46, no. 3 (2001): 27–31; and Donald K. Wright, "Enforcement Dilemma: Voluntary Nature of Public Relations Codes," *Public Relations Review* 19, no. 1 (1993): 13–20.

[44] Larissa A. Grunig, "Toward the Philosophy of Public Relations," in *Rhetorical and Critical Approaches to Public Relations*, ed. Elizabeth. L. Toth and Robert L. Heath (Hillsdale, NJ: Lawrence Erlbaum Associates, 1992), 65–91; Shannon A. Bowen, "Organizational Factors Encouraging Ethical Decision Making: An Exploration into the Case of an Exemplar," *Journal of Business Ethics* 53, no. 4 (2004): 311–24.

[45] Kathy R. Fitzpatrick, "The Role of Public Relations in the Institutionalization of Ethics," *Public Relations Review* 22, no. 3 (1996): 249–58; and Dean Kruckeberg, "Universal Ethics Code: Both Possible and Feasible," *Public Relations Review* 19, no. 1 (1993): 21–31.

[46] Donald K. Wright, "Ethics Research in Public Relations: An Overview," *Public Relations Review* 15, no. 2 (Summer 1989): 4.

[47] Shannon A. Bowen, "I Thought It Would Be More Glamorous: Preconceptions and Misconceptions of Public Relations among Students in the Principles Course," *Public Relations Review* 29 (2003): 199–214.

[48] Christopher Spicer, "Images of PR in the Print Media," *Journal of Public Relations Research* 5, no. 1 (1993): 47–61.

[49] Hans-Martin Sass, "Professional Organizations and Professional Ethics: A European View," in *Ethics, Trust, and the Professions*, ed. Edmund D. Pellegrino, Robert M. Veatch, and John P. Langan, 270–71 (Washington, DC: Georgetown University Press, 1991).

ADDITIONAL SOURCES

Baker, Lee. *The Credibility Factor: Putting Ethics to Work in Public Relations.* Homewood, IL: Business One Irwin, 1993.

Brown, Marvin T. *The ethical process: An approach to disagreements and controversial issues,* 3rd ed. Upper Saddle River, NJ: Prentice Hall, 2003.

Building Trust—Leading CEOs Speak Out: How They Create It, Strengthen It, Sustain It. New York: The Arthur W. Page Society, 2004.

Curtin, Patricia A., and Lois A. Boynton. (2001). "Ethics in Public Relations: Theory and Practice." In *Handbook of Public Relations*, edited by Robert L. Heath, 411–22. Thousand Oaks, CA: Sage, 2001.

De George, Richard T. *Business Ethics*, 5th ed. Englewood Cliffs, NJ: Prentice Hall, 1999. An excellent and accessible introduction to business ethics.

Donaldson, Thomas and Patricia Werhane. *Ethical Issues in Business*, 6th ed. Upper Saddle River, NJ: Prentice Hall, 1999. Authors outline truth, virtue, global and multinational ethics, justice, diversity, and the role of corporations and their moral mission.

Gower, Karla K. *Legal and Ethical Restraints on Public Relations.* Prospect Heights, IL: Waveland Press, 2003. A practical guide to common situations.

Huang, Yi-Hui. "Should a public relations code of ethics be enforced?" *Journal of Business Ethics* 31, no. 3 (2001): 259–70.

Petersen, Barbara K. "Logic, Licensing and Public Relations." *Communication Law and Policy* 1 (1996): 139–76.

Sallot, Lynne M., Glen T. Cameron, and Ruth Ann Weaver Lariscy. "Professional Standards in Public Relations: A Survey of Educators." *Public Relations Review* 23, no. 3 (Fall 1997): 197–216.

Seeger, Matthew W. *Ethics and Organizational Communication.* Cresskill, NJ: Hampton Press, 1997. Organizational ethics arranged topically by chapter.

Wright, Donald K., ed. "Special Issue: Ethics in Public Relations." *Public Relations Review* 15, no. 2 (Summer 1989).

6 LEGAL CONSIDERATIONS

It is the purpose of the First Amendment to preserve an uninhibited marketplace of ideas in which truth will ultimately prevail.

—Justice Byron White

STUDY GUIDE

After studying Chapter 6, you should be able to

- Summarize the basic structure of law in the United States and its relevance to the practice of public relations.

- Outline the major principles of First Amendment adjudication by the U.S. Supreme Court, applying the hierarchy of speech protection relevant to the speech, press, assembly, and petition provisions.

- Describe permissible federal regulation of First Amendment protected expression in key areas of public relations practice—election communication, lobbying, communication between labor and management, and financial public relations/investor relations.

- Outline constitutional protection and permissible federal regulation of those segments of intellectual property law most relevant to public relations work—copyright and trademark law.

- Define and explain the major provisions of libel law and privacy law relevant to public relations work.

This chapter was written in collaboration with Professor Barbara K. Petersen, Ph.D., University of South Florida, Tampa. Professor Petersen is a First Amendment scholar who worked in public relations, public information, and broadcasting for more than 13 years before beginning her career in higher education.

Did ads for Michael Moore's political documentary *Fahrenheit 911* showing President Bush in unflattering circumstances violate federal campaign finance laws?[1] Did photographs by a Utah artist depicting Barbie® dolls in quirky positions intended to question gender and political ideals infringe upon Mattel's legal rights under copyright and trademark laws?[2] Could workers on strike against the management of their company be found guilty under libel law if they call those who cross their picket lines "traitors?"[3] Would an unauthorized video of a daredevil circus performer's entire act, which lasts only 15 seconds, violate the performer's "right of publicity?"[4]

Public relations practitioners do not operate in a societal vacuum. Situations like those just mentioned are examples of what occurs regularly in today's complex society, and each of them has some connection to public relations work. Accordingly, practitioners need to know how to evaluate such situations if they want to succeed in their jobs. This may come as a surprise to those who subscribe to the common misconceptions that law is incomprehensible to those who are not lawyers, and that law is only narrowly applicable or relevant to public relations.

Clearly, this chapter alone cannot provide everything a practitioner needs to know. Instead, it presents a summary of major legal issues affecting public relations work. It is important to remember, however, that public relations practitioners *do not practice law*, but knowledge of the law will help them work with their organizations' legal staff in situations that require collaboration.

■

WHAT IS LAW?

To place legal issues in context, it is first necessary to understand the distinction between "law" and "ethics." Fundamentally, **law** is that system of rules that governs a particular society. Thus, in the United States it has long been accepted that such actions as murder, assault, and theft are wrong, and that the people expect their government to enforce strict sanctions against those who violate the societal norm. On the other hand, **ethics** involves the decisions people make in their personal and professional lives. Individuals establish ethical norms for their own behaviors, some of which involve voluntary adherence to norms established by a particular professional group (e.g., PRSA). That is why it is so important to first have a strong foundation in the law, and why this brief introduction to legal principles is presented.

The origin of law and its application differ from nation to nation. In the U.S. government structure, both the **executive and legislative branches make law**, whereas the **judicial branch interprets law** to ensure that it complies with existing statutes and ultimately, the U.S. Constitution. The U.S. legal structure includes (a) federal laws—made by the president and the Congress, along with *regulations* produced by federal government agencies—as well as (b) state laws enacted by governors, legislatures, and administrative agencies in each of the 50 states. Law is hierarchical, meaning that "the law" at a higher classification will supersede what is classified lower in the hierarchy. The U.S. Constitution, the fundamental source of all law in the U.S., provides a minimum set of rights to which any state constitution may add for its residents.

To illustrate the relationship between federal and state law, Exhibit 6.1 presents the sources of law in the U.S. organized in the hierarchy of their authority over one another. Knowing where a particular law originates as well as what other type of law can supersede it will help practitioners better evaluate the impact of any single part

EXHIBIT 6.1

LAW SOURCES HIERARCHY

Constitution[a]

Federal
U.S. Constitution
(Predominantly First Amendment for communication law)

State/Local
State Constitution

Statutes[b]

Federal
U.S. Congress

State/Local
State Legislature, City Council, County Commission

Administrative Rules[c]

Federal
Federal agencies
(e.g., Securities & Exchange Commission)

State/Local
State agencies
(e.g., State Elections Commission)

Executive Actions[d]

Federal
President

State/Local
Governor, Mayor, County Executive

Common Law[e]

Decisions that rise from local, through regional, then to national courts

Initiated in a federal or state trial court

Appealed to a State appeals court and/or then to one of 13 Federal Courts of Appeal

Interpretation by U.S. Supreme Court sets national precedent

Law of Equity[f]

Decisions by judges based on a fundamental notion of fairness

E.g., Promissory estoppel (keeping promises)

---

[a]*Constitutional law* represents the basic legal charters of the federal and state governments, spelling out basic legal principles, rights, and authorities. The federal constitution is the final arbiter of constitutional law, because no law in conflict with the U.S. Constitution can be enforced by the government.

[b]*Statutory law* is that body of statutes and ordinances written and passed by legislative bodies at the federal, state, and local levels, including everything from acts of Congress to city ordinances.

[c]*Administrative law* includes rules and decisions of the numerous governmental agencies established by statute to write and enforce administrative rules in regulated areas and activities, such as communication (Federal Communication Commission), advertising and trade (Federal Trade Commission), public trading of stocks (Securities and Exchange Commission), and communication between labor and management (National Labor Relations Board).

[d]*Executive Actions* are made by the top elected government official at the federal level (President), state level (Governor), city level (Mayor), and so forth.

[e]*Common law* in the United States derives from the accumulation of court rulings over time and is based on English common law. There is no federal common law, however, because each state has its own judicial traditions that are subject to change as conditions and values change. The U.S. Supreme Court sets national precedent.

[f]*Law of Equity* is a part of common law, but there are no jury decisions, only rulings by judges.

---

of the law on public relations work. For the most part, all legal principles discussed in this chapter cite U.S. Supreme Court decisions as their authority because those rulings apply to the nation as a whole.

Federal and state courts are separated into criminal courts—to review laws against actions that harm "the state" (society in general) such as murder and theft—and civil courts, to resolve disputes between private individuals such as defamation and privacy invasion. Most legal decisions affecting public relations work occur in civil court.

PUBLIC RELATIONS AND THE FIRST AMENDMENT

Congress shall make no law respecting an establishment of religion, or prohibiting the free exercise thereof; or abridging the freedom of speech; or of the press; or the right of the people peaceably to assemble, and to petition the Government for a redress of grievances.

The power of the First Amendment to the U.S. Constitution is uniquely American. Adopted in 1791, it was not until early in the twentieth century that U.S. Supreme Court decisions began to reveal its power.[5]

The First Amendment prevents government restriction of five separate rights—religion, speech, presses, assembly, and petition. The Constitutional separation of church and state protects practitioners who work to "propagate the faith," so the other four clauses are at the core of public relations activities.

- "Speech" rights include protection of "ideological" (containing ideas) expression; "symbolic" (communication without words) expression; the right to "hear"; and the right to remain silent.
- "Press" rights refer to dissemination of information; they belong to all citizens, not just the media.
- "Assembly" rights allow people to gather together for any purpose connected with government policies or ideas.
- "Petition" rights allow people to question their government representatives without fear of reprisal.

There is no such category as "public relations speech" in the lexicon of the courts or First Amendment scholars. But that does not mean that the U. S. Supreme Court has no knowledge of the field. In fact, Petersen and Lang's content analysis of U.S. Supreme Court decisions from 1766 through 1999 concluded that "over the years, the justices have had a much better understanding of the public relations practice than has the typical citizen;"[6] that there is a strong association of public relations with the highly protected speech used in lobbying the government for redress of grievances;[7] and that the justices know the similarities as well as differences between public relations and advertising.[8] Petersen and Lang found that

The strong First Amendment connection with public relations tactics such as publicity campaigns….Even when the justices pointed out publicity practices they deemed unethical, they still emphasized the fact that constitutionally, such practices are protected alongside other contentious exchanges in the marketplace of ideas.[9]

Public relations practitioners who know when to invoke their clients' rights under the First Amendment to the U.S. Constitution, and when to caution clients that certain speech activities can be limited by the government, will not only better serve their clients but also provide higher quality public relations counsel. The First Amendment is not absolute, however. The majority of U.S. Supreme Court justices have always agreed that there are times when speech needs to be balanced with other personal or social values. Yet, persons or corporations whose ideological expression defames, invades privacy, or disturbs the peace of others may only be sanctioned *after* they have spoken/written, because prior restraints on expression are presumptively unconstitutional.[10]

Knowing why as well as how the government can regulate First Amendment freedoms will help public relations practitioners evaluate both their words and their actions in media relations, product advertising, financial public relations, and corporate reputation communication.

PUBLIC RELATIONS ACCESS TO MASS MEDIA

Public relations practitioners have a symbiotic relationship with journalists.[11] To achieve "free publicity" for their work, practitioners need access to the news media to disseminate the ideas, information, or causes of organizations and clients they represent. Journalists rely on information in press releases for articles about newsworthy events in their communities. However, First Amendment protection of press rights means that journalists can choose whether or not they will use a particular press release, or interview a particular person, or print letters to the editor. Even commercial speech gets this type of First Amendment protection, meaning mass media companies have the choice to publish or not publish a particular category of advertisements.

A new legal twist on the journalist/public relations practitioner relationship came about in the early 1990s because of a U.S. Supreme Court decision about the way journalists treat their sources of information. Drawing on a previously obscure part of the law, that journalists must keep the promises they make to their sources; in this case, it was a public relations political consultant. If the source suffers harm because the promise was not kept, judges will apply principles of fundamental fairness to hold the journalists accountable. This was obviously not good news for journalists, but it presents a potential boon to public relations practitioners and others who are misquoted or misunderstood by the media and suffer some personal harm to their reputations.

Print Media

Public relations practitioners need to know that First Amendment protection of press freedom means that no citizen has a guaranteed right to require the print media to publish specific information. In 1974, the U.S. Supreme Court declared unconstitutional a Florida statute requiring a newspaper to give a candidate for public office free space to reply to criticism.[12] The Court said the state government should not be allowed to compel a newspaper to print something that its editors would not have chosen, because this would interfere with the editorial control that First Amendment press freedom protects.[13]

Broadcast Media

In an apparent contradiction of First Amendment principles, U.S. broadcast media have been subject to government regulation since their inception, providing several opportunities for public relations practitioners to gain access to this medium.

It is important to note that "broadcasting" means only **over-the-air signals** that are capable of being received by a television or radio with the use of a simple antenna, and are thus accessible to people who do not have cable or satellite service. Federal government regulation of the technological aspects of broadcasting began early in the twentieth century under the jurisdiction of the Secretary of Commerce and Labor,[14] with the original justification for government oversight borrowed from the Interstate Commerce Commission—public interest, convenience, and necessity.[15] That standard continues today under the control of the Federal Communications Commission (FCC).

The FCC was created by the **Communications Act of 1934**, which gave the agency the power to make and enforce programming policies for broadcasting and issue, renew, or deny licenses to individual station operators. An early challenge to the FCC's power to regulate program content, on the grounds that this violated the First Amendment, was rejected by the U.S. Supreme Court, which ruled, "… the right of free speech does not include … the right to use the facilities of radio without a license."[16]

The basic justification for regulating broadcast content that the Supreme Court has accepted over the years is based on the 1934 congressional assertion that the U.S. airwaves are owned by the public and are a scarce resource that needs to be protected. Accordingly, those who receive licenses to use this limited resource must be trustees for all those who do not get to operate a broadcast station.

Cable Systems

Cable technology was developed in the late 1940s and applied to broadcasting by Community Antenna Television Systems (CATVs), whose primary purpose was to improve a community's reception of available, but hard to receive over-the-air broadcast signals. The CATVs were not licensed by the FCC, but instead were awarded state and local government franchises to serve a particular geographic location. There was no specific cable legislation at that time, and the FCC had statutory authority to only regulate broadcasting, the U.S. Supreme Court ruled that cable regulation was necessary to ensure "fair, efficient, and equitable" broadcasting service, and that the FCC had the authority to do so because the Communications Act of 1934 required the Commission to take action "reasonably ancillary" (connected) to its responsibility to regulate broadcasting.[17] Ultimately, the courts made it clear that cable operators have more First Amendment rights than do broadcasters, though cable still falls far short of the constitutional freedom of expression rights granted the print media.[18]

In 1984, Congress enacted the Cable Communication Policy Act giving the FCC jurisdictional authority over cable, deregulating rates and program choices, and providing benefits for cities and counties regarding franchise fees. This Act also required cable applicants to set aside channels on its systems for public, educational, and governmental access. These public access channels also provide valuable tools for public relations practitioners who need to reach particular publics directly through a mass medium, such as giving citizens opportunities to observe City Council meetings and other local government activities.

The Internet

The 1997 Supreme Court decision *Reno v. American Civil Liberties Union* made it clear that speech on the Internet was fully protected by the First Amendment.[19] The decision overturned the Communications Decency Act (CDA) of 1996, in which Congress tried to regulate indecency on the Internet by forbidding the operation of certain Web sites. The Court found that the law to contain unconstitutional content regulation was both vague and overbroad. The justices ultimately decided that the Internet was more like the traditional public forum, mentioned earlier in this chapter, concluding, "As the most participatory form of mass speech yet developed, the Internet deserves the highest protection from government intrusion."[20] This gives public relations practitioners "free rein" to use the Internet to send unmediated communication to various constituencies.

The Children's Internet Protection Act (CIPA) of 2000 requires public schools and libraries that receive some federal money for Internet use to install "technology prevention measures," meaning filters, on computers used by those 17 or younger to block material that is obscene, or is child pornography, or is "harmful to minors." The Supreme Court upheld this legislation regulating Internet speech as constitutional. Libraries that do not comply risk losing their share of federal funding for computers in libraries.

ACCESS TO GOVERNMENT INFORMATION AND MEETINGS

Access to government-controlled information is important to every citizen because the legal presumption in a democracy is that such accounts belong to the people, not the government. Thus, to encourage open government and an informed electorate, the federal government and all 50 states have statutes governing open records and meetings.

The structure of laws at the state level is similar to that of the federal statutes, but the extent of access varies considerably from state to state. Accordingly, this section will discuss only the U.S. federal laws, and public relations practitioners must study on their own the access laws of the particular state or nation in which they do business. A compilation of access laws for all 50 states is available online through the Marion Brechner Citizen Access Project (http//www.citizenaccess.org).

It might surprise some that the heaviest users of open access laws are not journalists. Various estimates over the years of *who* requests government records the most agree that it is business, with approximately one-half of all requests each year. Journalist requests make up only about one-quarter of the requests, with the remaining one-quarter made by the general citizenry. Indeed, the U.S. Supreme Court has ruled in several decisions that the media's right of access to government sources of information is only as extensive with that of the public.[21] Most important is the fact that the U.S. Supreme Court has ruled there is no First Amendment or other federal constitutional right of access to government-controlled information.[22]

Public relations practitioners in government organizations must be fully informed about both federal and state open access legislation because they are responsible for responding appropriately to requests for access to information and meetings relevant to their particular agencies. Practitioners must also make sure that the officials with whom they work are aware of their obligations under both federal and state laws. In fact, government public information officers are often called upon to resolve the conflict between a government agency's desire to work in relative secrecy and journalists' demands for full disclosure of government information.

The federal **Freedom of Information Act (FOIA) of 1966** was a bipartisan effort in the U.S. Congress to promote full disclosure from the executive branch of government. It applies to "any executive department, military department, government corporation, government controlled corporation or other establishment in the executive branch of the federal government…, or any independent regulatory agency." The Act applies only to records, meaning *tangible* items of information such as documents, but not to *intangible* information, meaning agency employees are not required to answer any questions. The **1996 Electronic Freedom of Information Act** added access to digital information (e.g., computer databases) held by those federal government agencies subject to the FOIA.

The federal FOIA specifies nine categories of exemptions from disclosure, giving government employees discretion to decide if they should provide access to items in these categories. Exemption categories are different from specific statutes that say a particular agency must not disclose a particular item. Government employees are given no discretionary power with statutes—they must follow the statutory language exactly when it mandates that entire documents be withheld, or when it provides precise criteria for determining what parts should be withheld.

The nine categories of exemptions are national security, agency rules and procedures, statutory exemptions, confidential business information, agency memoranda, personnel or medical, law enforcement investigations, banking reports, and information about oil and gas wells.[23]

CORPORATE POLITICAL EXPRESSION

First Amendment protection is considered to be an individual right in our democracy. However, a more complex question of great importance to public relations practitioners is whether the organizations they represent also have constitutional rights for "political speech." A "corporation" is an artificial construction in the law that simulates a person, thus providing an organization legal standing in the courts. Historically, U.S. Supreme Court decisions have afforded corporations *some* of the same legal rights as individuals, but courts have also upheld many restrictions on corporate legal rights. The same is true in First Amendment jurisprudence. Corporations regularly engage in First Amendment protected "commercial speech" (i.e., advertising), but as noted previously, such speech is protected at a lower level than is "political speech." On the other hand, First Amendment protection for "*corporate political speech*" is a separate matter.

In the precedent-setting decision defining corporate political speech rights, *First National Bank of Boston v. Bellotti*, the Supreme Court ruled that the First Amendment protects "political speech" regardless of who (individual or corporation) is speaking.[24] The case in question involved a Massachusetts statute prohibiting corporations from trying to influence a ballot item that did not relate directly to their businesses. First National Bank and four other companies wanted to buy advertising to oppose a referendum on establishing a state personal income tax.

In striking down the statute, the U.S. Supreme Court said that the inherent worth of speech that informs the public "does not depend upon the identity of its source, whether corporation, association, union, or individual."[25] The justices dismissed the argument that corporations were too powerful to be allowed participation in the marketplace of ideas. There is no evidence, they said, "that the relative voice of corporations has been overwhelming or even significant in influencing referenda in Massachusetts, or that there has been any threat to the confidence of the citizenry in government."[26]

However, the Court did not say that corporate political speech rights were equal to individual rights. Rather, the Court said the proper question is not whether corporations have First Amendment rights but whether the state statute abridges free expression. The Court struck down the statute because it prohibited political expression that "was at the heart of the First Amendment's protection." An advertisement expressing a view on a tax referendum, said the justices, "is the type of speech indispensable to decision making in a democracy, and this is no less true because the speech comes from a corporation rather than an individual."[27] The Court's ruling opened the door for corporations to participate in a wide variety of political affairs. This involves public relations practitioners directly, because they research and influence organizational communication.

Two other important Supreme Court decisions regarding corporate speech rights dealt with energy utility companies that were subject to state regulations, and the matters in dispute were traditional public relations activities. For example, in 1980, the Court struck down a New York Public Service Commission ruling that barred regulated utilities from including messages about public issues in a customer's monthly bill mailing. Consolidated Edison Company had included in its bills a pamphlet advocating nuclear power as the best alternative for large-scale energy generation, but opponents of nuclear power did not want a government-regulated utility to participate in this political debate. The Court ruled that Consolidated Edison could publish its perspective on the issue precisely because its customers should have access to a variety of viewpoints on this controversial topic.[28]

Three years later across the country in California, a special-interest group called The Utility Reform Network (TURN), which opposed large-scale energy generation, wanted to include its opinions and fund-raising appeals in monthly billing notices sent out by Pacific Gas & Electric Company to its customers. The High Court ruled that the company did not need to disseminate speech with which it did not agree. In other words, as it does for individuals, the First Amendment also protects the right of corporations to *not* speak.[29]

Even though the Supreme Court has recognized some speech rights for corporations, many instances remain in which such rights are restricted by government regulations that have been justified by the long-standing fear of the potential corrupting influence of business. Such regulations mean the government has demonstrated a **compelling interest** to regulate corporate political speech. Four major areas of federal legislation limiting corporate speech that are relevant to public relations include political elections, lobbying, labor organization communication with management, and securities trading. See Exhibit 6.2 for regulations concerning political election contributions.

As Exhibit 6.2 shows, the three main provisions of the BCRA were "soft money" prohibitions (money donated to political parties for "party building" purposes), increases in contribution limits, and limits on "electioneering communications" (commercials that support or oppose a candidate without explicitly urging that candidate's election or defeat).

LOBBYING

Because of the fear that lobbyists for groups could corrupt the lawmaking process, Congress passed several laws regulating lobbyists' attempts to influence legislation and regulations directly. Because lobbying has been one of the fastest growing specialties in public relations practice, these regulations are important to practitioners.

Lobbyists for organizations were first required to disclose their activities under Title III, the **Federal Regulation of Lobbying Act of 1946**.[30] Lobbyists were required to register with Congress, file quarterly financial statements detailing their lobbying expenses and sources of income, and report any articles or editorials the lobbyist had caused to be published to influence legislation. In 1953 and 1954 decisions, the U.S. Supreme Court narrowed the law so that it applied only to people and organizations

EXHIBIT 6.2

CAMPAIGN FINANCE REFORM

Bipartisan Campaign Reform Act (BCRA) of 2002 ("McCain-Feingold") [in effect since November 6, 2002]

- **Soft Money Prohibition ["soft money" donated to political parties for "party building" purposes]**

  Corporations and labor unions may not *contribute* or make *expenditures* on behalf of the national political party committees or Leadership PACs (set up by federal candidates and officeholders as nonprofit organizations raising funds for the campaigns of those particular federal candidates or officeholders).

  Only individuals and federal PACs, subject to federal limits, may *contribute* to the national parties and Leadership PACs, though state parties may continue to give $25,000 under federal hard dollar limits to the national parties.

  Corporations and labor unions may still *contribute* to state and local organizations as permitted under state law, although these organizations are limited in how they can use money raised outside the federal limits.

  Members of Congress may no longer solicit funds for *soft money* accounts, including for their own Leadership PACs and for state and local parties.

  Members of Congress may raise no more than $20,000 per individual donor for *voter registration and get-out-the-vote (GOTV) efforts* by 501(c) (general nonprofit) and Section 527 (nonprofit political) organizations, but they may continue to solicit funds for a nonprofit organization's *non*-political activities.

- **Post-BCRA Contribution Limits**

  An individual may *contribute* no more than $2,000 per election (the primary and general count separately) to any one federal candidate (twice the previous limit).

  The contribution limit to a federal candidate may be increased to $3,000 per election if the candidate's opponent spends a specified amount of his or her personal funds on the race.

An individual may *contribute* no more than $5,000 per calendar year to any one federal PAC (no change).

An individual may *contribute* no more than $25,000 per calendar year to a national political party committee.

An individual may *contribute* no more than $10,000/ calendar year to the federal account of a state political party.

During the two-year election cycle, an individual may *contribute* no more than $95,000, *of which*

No more than $37,500 may be contributed to federal candidates, and

No more than $57,500 may be contributed to national political parties and federal PACs, *of which* no more than $37,500 may be contributed to federal PACs, state/local party committees.

Contribution limits to candidates and national party committees are indexed for inflation while contributions limits to PACs are not.

- **Limits on "Electioneering Communications" ("issue ads") [commercials that support or oppose a candidate without explicitly urging that candidate's election or defeat]**

  Radio or television advertising that refers to a *federal candidate* and is made within 60 days of a general election and within 30 days of a primary is an "electioneering communication."

  Corporations, trade associations, and labor unions may only run "electioneering communications" through their PACs, using hard money contributions.

  Any entity making "electioneering communications" must file a *disclosure report* with the FEC listing those who *gave* more than $1,000 for the communication and those who *received* more than $200 relative to the advertisement.

whose main purpose was to influence legislation through "direct communication with members of Congress on pending or proposed federal legislation."[31] Concerns continued, however, that the lobbying legislation was inadequate to control all instances of potential corruption.

To more effectively regulate lobbying and protect public confidence in government, Congress enacted the **Lobbying Disclosure Act of 1995**, with updated definitions, disclosure requirements, and restrictions.[32]

A *lobbyist* is someone employed or retained by a client who makes more than one contact on behalf of that client and spends at least 20 percent of her/his time during a six-month period providing that service to the client.

A *lobbying firm* is an entity that has at least one person who was hired to represent someone other than her/his employer. The term also applies to self-employed individuals who represent other people or entities.

A *lobbying contact* is defined as a communication, either oral or written, on behalf of a client to a covered executive or legislative branch official regarding legislation, rules, regulations, grants, loans, permits, programs, or the nomination of anyone subject to Senate confirmation.[33]

Lobbying includes direct pressure on members of Congress through an "artificially stimulated letter writing campaign."[34] But lobbying does not include general public relations campaigns, sometimes called "grassroots lobbying," that attempt to "saturate thinking of the community" about public issues.[35] Nor does it include testimony before a committee of Congress (because such testimony is invited by the legislators), or magazines and newspapers that in the ordinary course of business publish news items and editorials urging the passage or defeat of legislation.[36]

Lobbyists and lobbying firms must register with the Secretary of the Senate and the Clerk of the House and must report names, addresses, places of business, and phone numbers of their own business, their clients, and anyone else who contributes more than $10,000 in a six-month period to lobbying activities conducted by the registrant. In addition, all registrants must file reports twice a year, providing "good faith estimates" of the amounts paid by clients or spent on lobbying.[37] Lobbying laws also apply to nonprofit charitable, educational, and other tax-exempt organizations. Nonprofit organizations that engage in lobbying are prohibited from receiving federal grants, awards, contracts, and loans.

The law allows nonprofit charitable, educational, and other tax-exempt organizations to simply file a copy of their IRS Form 990, which reports lobbying expenditures, rather than requiring them to file a separate report. Nonprofit organizations that engage in lobbying are prohibited from receiving federal grants, awards, contracts, and loans.[38] The act exempts public officials, the working press, and those who provide testimony before congressional committees. It also excludes those whose total work for a client consists of less than 20 percent of the activities qualifying as lobbying.

"Grassroots lobbying" is part of an organization's First Amendment right to express itself on public issues. It is distinguished from the type of lobbying that requires registration with the government by the fact that it is not "direct" contact with government officials. Instead, successful lobbyists typically use public relations campaign techniques to sway public opinion to activate constituents and, thereby, increase pressure on legislators and government agencies.

All public relations practitioners working for "foreign principals" must register under the **Foreign Agents Registration Act of 1938** (FARA), whether or not they lobby U.S. government officials.[39] The law requires all persons who work as agents of foreign governments, companies, or political parties to register within 10 days with the U.S. Attorney General. Congress passed FARA because members believed "the spotlight of pitiless publicity will serve as a deterrent to the spread of pernicious propaganda. We feel that our people are entitled to know the sources of any such efforts, and the person or persons or agencies carrying on such work in the United States."[40]

The Lobbying Disclosure Act of 1995 also applies to the Foreign Agents Registration Act. The law defines a "foreign agent" as anyone in the United States who works as a "public relations counsel, publicity agent, information service employee, or political consultant," acting "at the order, request, or under the direction or control" of a "foreign principal," which could be a government, political party, business, or other organization.[41] Information materials produced by foreign agents are defined as any communication designed to influence the American public about political interests or policies of a foreign government; to influence U.S. foreign policy; to promote racial, religious, or social tensions; or to advocate the forceful overthrow of other Western Hemisphere countries.[42] Foreign agents must label lobbying materials as "political propaganda" being distributed by a registered foreign agent. They also must provide copies to the U.S. Attorney General.

LABOR RELATIONS

Public relations specialists whose work involves communication between unions and management must comply with the provisions of the **National Labor Relations Act of 1935** (Wagner Act) and the **Labor Management Relations Act of 1947** (Taft-Hartley Act). The 1935 statute created the independent, federal National Labor Relations Board (NLRB) to administer laws governing relations between unions and employers in the private sector. These prohibit both unions and management from engaging in unfair labor practices, primarily by forbidding coercive expression during political elections and also by forbidding management from interfering with labor's right to organize and to bargain collectively once a union is established.

Representative Elections

In 1941, the U.S. Supreme Court ruled that an employer could not be barred "from expressing its view on labor policies." The employer, the Court said, is free "to take any side it may choose" on a controversial labor issue as long as the employer does not restrain or coerce his employees.[43] This ruling has major implications for public relations work in internal communication.

Management does not engage in an unfair labor practice if it communicates to employees through speeches, talks, and letters to tell workers about the strike history of the union, the likely dues and assessments, and the merits of working for a company without a union. But management cannot threaten to fire or punish employees because of union activities, make promises of special benefits to influence votes, spy on union meetings, or call employees separately to discuss the union. Management also cannot urge employees individually to vote against the union.

Collective Bargaining

The Labor Management Relations Act of 1947 also requires companies and unions to enter negotiations with open minds and with a willingness to reach an agreement.

If management is unwilling to meet or is unreasonably firm in its offers, or if unions engage in unfair labor practices, public relations practitioners will need to practice crisis communication.

Practitioners find updated explanations of NLRB policies by regularly visiting the agency's Web site (http://www.nlrb.gov), where the "News Room" publishes fact sheets, press releases, and case summaries of the Board's actions.

REGULATIONS OF PUBLICLY OWNED COMPANIES

Public relations specialists whose work involves communication by publicly owned companies must comply with the **Securities Act of 1933** and the **Securities Exchange Act of 1934**, which were enacted in response to the great stock market crash of 1929. The 1933 act restricts corporate communication before and during the period that new securities offerings are being registered.[44] The Securities and Exchange Commission Act of 1934, which regulates trading of securities after their initial distribution, requires periodic reporting about a company.[45] The 1934 statute also created the independent, federal **Securities and Exchange Commission (SEC)** to enforce the newly passed securities laws, to promote stability in the markets, and most important of all, to protect investors. The **Investment Company Act of 1940** and the **Investment Advisers Act of 1940** regulate investment companies and advisers.[46] In addition, practitioners in this field are subject to the disclosure rules of the stock exchange that lists their company's stock.

Financial public relations, sometimes called "investor relations," requires public practitioners to also have in-depth knowledge of corporate finance, accounting, and law.[47] Under the SEC's "integrated disclosure system," corporations in which members of the public own shares must continuously provide information that affects the understanding of stockholders and investors about the financial position and prospectus of a company. Accordingly, practitioners must issue press releases, draft speeches, and write quarterly and annual reports to achieve the "adequate and accurate information" required under federal law. Public relations practitioners keep current with changes in securities regulations by regularly visiting the SEC's Web site (http://www.sec.gov).

Disclosure requirements take two forms—that mandated by statute, and that required to avoid fraud. Both the Securities Act of 1933 and the Securities and Exchange Act of 1934 mandate disclosure by "senior officials" of a corporation, defined as "any director, executive officer, investor relations or public relations officer, or other person with similar functions."[48]

The 1933 Securities Act requires filings with the Securities and Exchange Commission when securities are offered to the public. The law requires that companies provide "material information" about new security offerings so that investors can make purchasing decisions based on facts. Information is considered "material" if the information is likely to have a significant effect on securities prices, or if it is likely to be considered important by a reasonable investor when making decisions to buy, hold, or sell shares. The Securities Act also requires a company to register its stock with the Securities and Exchange Commission and to provide detailed information about its financial history and prospects. Furthermore, it prohibits a company from offering to sell or to buy a security before the security is registered with the SEC.

The Private Securities Litigation Reform Act of 1995 made several reforms to the Securities Act of 1933 and the Securities Exchange Act of 1934, primarily in restricting such abusive litigation practices as routine filing of class action lawsuits against public companies following sharp drops in stock prices and abuse of the discovery process by plaintiffs' attorneys to extort settlements from publicly traded companies that might be willing to settle simply to avoid costly litigation.[49] Additionally, the Act created a new "Safe Harbor for Forward-Looking Statements" to encourage dissemination of information without fear of litigation. Companies may be protected from liability for predictions about earnings and performance as long as such forecasts are tempered by "meaningful" cautionary statements telling investors why the projections might fail to come true.[50]

The Securities Exchange Act of 1934 mandates disclosure to ensure that investors have accurate information during the trading of securities. Section 13 of the Act requires companies registered with the SEC to file quarterly, annual, and other reports with the SEC.

In addition to writing annual reports, public relations professionals are likely to have an important role in issuing proxy materials and organizing the company's annual meetings. Proxies are the statements companies must provide to tell shareholders when and where the annual meeting will be held and what business will be conducted. Stockholders who cannot attend the meeting can vote their shares by proxy—giving specific directions in writing about how their votes are to be cast. The financial relations practitioner may have a hand in writing management policy proposals, publishing them in the proxy statements, and organizing and conducting the annual meeting at which proposals will be voted upon. During proxy fights, in which a group of shareholders tries to sway votes to oppose management, the public relations practitioner may help choose issues, plan appeals to stockholders, and buy editorial advertising to promote management's positions.

Practitioners also participate in the "continuous disclosure" required by the securities laws and the rules of the stock exchanges. Companies must provide "current reports" within 15 days of any material change in the company such as shifts in the control of the company, acquisition or disposition of assets, bankruptcy or receivership, changes in the company's certifying accountants and financial statements, and resignations of directors.

Simply issuing a press release may not be sufficient to fulfill the disclosure requirements. The American Stock Exchange disclosure policies, for example, require a company, "at a minimum" to release announcements of material information simultaneously to the national business and financial news wire services, the national news wire services, the *New York Times,* the *Wall Street Journal, Moody's Investors Service,* and *Standard & Poor's Corporation.* Appropriate disclosure procedure depends on the size of a company and the dispersion of its stockholders, but the basic principle remains the same—public statements must be truthful.

Securities regulations also prohibit fraud in securities trading.[51] In order for there to be fraud in the buying and selling of securities, it is usually necessary to show that insiders are using nonpublic information to help them trade securities profitably or that insiders are "tipping" friends and clients with information that gives them an unfair advantage over the average investor. "Insiders" barred from tipping or trading on information not available to the public include corporate executives, public relations personnel, outside accountants, lawyers, outside public relations counsel, and other professionals with access to corporate plans.

COPYRIGHT AND TRADEMARK LAW

Legal protection for "intellectual property," so called because it refers to rights in intangible products of the mind or intellect, is found in the U.S. Constitution.[52] The two parts of this body of law most relevant for public relations work are copyright law and trademark law, both of which apply to creative works regardless of the medium in which they are expressed (print, broadcast, Internet).

Copyright

Copyright protection has the multiple goals of providing economic incentive for creative people to produce original work and for publishers to distribute those works, and also to preserve the public interest by guaranteeing that the right to use the works without restrictions will eventually be passed to all people.

The statutory definition of copyright is that it subsists in "original works of authorship fixed in any tangible medium of expression...from which they can be perceived, reproduced, or otherwise communicated."[53] In this definition, "original" does not necessarily mean unique, novel, or even "good," because copyright is not about the work's inherent intellectual worth but rather, about the means or manner in which the work is presented or expressed—the wording or visual representation, for example. "Fixed in tangible medium of expression" means that the work is sufficiently permanent or stable to permit it to be perceived, reproduced, or otherwise communicated for a significant duration of time. This eliminates from copyright protection such transient creative works as skywriting.

Public ownership of creative material exists—that is, it is in the "public domain"—when a copyright has expired, when an author has never claimed copyright, and when the materials involved were produced by government employees on government-paid time.[54]

The eight categories of works that can be copyrighted are literary works (includes databases, computer programs); musical works; dramatic works, pantomimes and choreographic works; pictorial, graphic, and sculptural works (i.e., artwork, which is the largest category); motion pictures and other audiovisual works; sound recordings; and architectural works (i.e., blueprints) created after 1990. People cannot copyright such useful items as tables and chairs, or formats and layouts, because they are considered too unoriginal. Copyright protects expression, but not the idea of creating the expression or the facts contained in the expression. For example, photographers can copyright the unique elements that make up their particular picture of a beautiful mountain, but they can't copyright the idea of taking the picture.

Copyright law requires public relations practitioners to check the copyright date of each work to determine which copyright act applies and to then calculate from that date when the work will pass into the "public domain," when it can be used without restriction (see Table 6.1).

Contrary to popular belief, neither registration nor publication is required for a copyright to be valid. A copyright exists automatically the moment a work is created and copyright notice is placed on the work. The copyright notice must have three elements: (a) the word "Copyright," or the abbreviation "Copr.," or the copyright symbol ©; (b) the year of first publication; and (c) the name of the copyright owner. An example of a correct copyright notice is "© 2004 by Jane Q. Citizen." However, formal registration is necessary for a copyright owner to bring suit for infringement,

TABLE 6.1

TERM OF COPYRIGHT OWNERSHIP

	Personal Authors	Corporate Authors, Works for Hire, and Anonymous Authors
1909 Copyright Act (original protection given 1909–1976)	75 years from date of copyright	75 years from date of copyright
1976 Copyright Act (original protection given 1977–present)	Lifetime + 70 years	95 years after first publication **or** 120 years from creation, whichever occurs first
Visual Art created after 1990	Lifetime of artist only	Not applicable

but that formal registration can be made after the infringement has occurred.[55]

Copyright ownership is a valuable intellectual commodity because it involves five powerful rights:

1. *Reproduction Rights*—the power to copy a work.
2. *Distribution Rights*—the power to distribute copies of a work (e.g., through publishing, selling, renting, loaning).
3. *Adaptation Rights*—the power to authorize derivative works (e.g., making a movie from a novel).
4. *Performance Rights*—the power to collect royalties each time a work is used publicly (e.g., reciting a poem, performing a play).
5. *Display Rights*—the power to earn money from a work being exhibited (e.g., art work displayed at a gallery opening).

Generally, copyright belongs to the "author" of the work. However, when an author publishes a book, at least some of the rights of ownership transfer to the publisher, who purchases the rights to reproduce and distribute the book. Depending on the terms of a publisher's contract, an author might be able to negotiate to retain some copyright rights, for example, adaptation rights.

Who owns the copyright when an individual completes a "work for hire" is a complex issue. The Copyright Act includes two different definitions of this term.[56] In the first, the phrase refers to works made by an employee as part of his/her employment, in which case copyright ownership belongs to the employer. The second definition refers to "a work specially ordered or commissioned," such as that produced by freelance writers, and who owns the copyright depends upon whether the person creating the work is considered an "employee" of the organization that commissioned the work or an "independent contractor."

In a 1989 decision, the U.S. Supreme Court set the guidelines for something to be considered a freelancer's work product, rather than the intellectual property of the employer.[57] Essentially, if an independent contractor wants to keep control of the copyright for something produced as a "work for hire," the person must have a written agreement signed by all parties specifying this ownership.

Infringement of copyright involves a violation of one or more of copyright "rights" of an owner. Legally, the copyright owner must show proof of three elements—originality of the work, probable access by the infringer, and substantial similarity of the unauthorized work to the original.[58]

Trademarks

The Lanham Act of 1946 and its amendments protect **trademarks**—words, names, and symbols used by companies to identify and distinguish their goods or services from those of another. A trademark can be a product brand name such as Kleenex. A **trade name**, on the other hand, identifies the commercial name of the producer. Thus, Kimberly-Clark Corporation, a trade name, manufactures Kleenex™ tissues, a trademark. A **service mark** differs from a trademark only in that it identifies a source of services, rather than a source of goods. For example, *ServiceMaster* is a registered name for a company that provides cleaning services.

Trademark rights are created through adoption and use of the mark on goods in trade. Trademark rights are protected under common law, but registration of a trademark with the U.S. Patent and Trademark Office creates presumptions of ownership that are important should infringement be claimed. Application for trademark registration can be filed before or after the mark is used in commerce, but usually after a commercial research firm has confirmed that no other party has registered the name, phrase, or logo intended as a trademark.

The formal trademark application process includes filing a written application form with a drawing of the trademark, paying the filing fee, and providing three examples of how the trademark is being used. The ® symbol or the phrase "Registered in U.S. Patent and Trademark Office" indicates a completed trademark registration. Often, the "TM" subscript is used when the registration is pending for a mark identifying a product, whereas "SM" is used to identify a service mark. The completed trademark registration lasts for 10 years, with 10-year renewals granted for as long as the mark is used in commerce.

Trademark enforcement is limited to situations that have a likelihood of confusion or deception or a probability that the public will be misled because of the use of confusingly similar marks. Also subject to enforcement are situations where the use of a trademark would tarnish or dilute its value. For example, the Coca-Cola Company formally objected to associations of its soft drinks with the abbreviation "coke" meaning cocaine.[59]

Owners of trademarks frequently run advertisements in such specialty publications as *Editor and Publisher* reminding journalists and public relations practitioners to use trademarks as adjectives, not as nouns or verbs, and to use capital letters when referring to their products. For example, people may use a Xerox photocopier, or simply a photocopying machine, but they do not "Xerox" a document. These policing efforts are designed to avoid losing exclusive use of a trademark by allowing it to fall into common usage as a generic word. This is what happened to the previously trademarked words *linoleum, trampoline, kerosene, yo-yo, lanolin, cornflakes, dry ice, nylon,* and *high octane.*

Penalties for infringement are specified in the federal trademark law. In a successful infringement suit, the trademark owner is allowed to recover *treble damages.* This means the persons who infringed the trademark must pay the owner three times the infringer's profits from using the mark or three times any damages sustained by the legal owner, *whichever is greater*, plus reasonable attorney's fees to cover the costs of the trademark action. Furthermore, whatever materials have been created using the infringed trademark "shall be delivered up and destroyed."[60]

TORT LAW: LIBEL AND PRIVACY INVASION

In civil law, a tort is anything considered legally wrong that one party does to harm another, such as defaming someone's reputation or invading someone's privacy. If a legal remedy is sought for that wrong, the party committing the offense becomes the "defendant" who is sued for monetary damages by the person who was harmed, or the "plaintiff." If the plaintiff is successful in the lawsuit, the defendant can be ordered by the court to compensate the plaintiff for loss or injury ("compensatory" or "general damages") and/or to reimburse the plaintiff for actual monetary losses ("special damages"). Under certain circumstances, the court may also order payments designed solely to punish the defendant ("punitive damages").

Public relations practitioners need to understand tort law because they could become either plaintiffs or defendants in civil lawsuits. Practitioners responsible for writing news releases, speeches, corporate reports, newsletters, brochures, and other communications need to be constantly aware that pictures and statements could defame someone or invade someone's privacy. On the other hand, practitioners could just as easily be plaintiffs in a civil suit if their own reputations are wrongfully damaged or their legitimate expectations of privacy are invaded.

Because tort law varies among the states, it is imperative for practitioners to know and understand the applicability of state law regarding libel or privacy lawsuits in their states. To begin that process, practitioners can make use of a free legal information service on the Internet at http://www.findlaw.com.

Libel

This section and the next discuss issues regarding libel and privacy lawsuits, as well as First Amendment defenses in any such suits, because these matters will be applicable in every state in the United States. At the onset, it is significant to know that **libel law is about the dissemination of false information**, whereas **privacy law involves true information**. Importantly, the legal terms used to classify the status of plaintiffs and tort actions have the same use in both bodies of law.

Libel is a legal action designed to compensate someone whose reputation or standing in the community has been wrongfully damaged, essentially the definition of **defamation**. Technically, libel is written defamation, whereas slander is spoken definition, but that distinction became blurred after the advent of broadcasting. Accordingly, this section will use the term *libel* generically to discuss both types of legal actions.

Any individual, business, nonprofit organization (e.g., church), or unincorporated association (e.g., labor union) has the right to sue for libel. Government institutions cannot bring suit for criticism of their official conduct because it is a fundamental First Amendment right of citizens to criticize government action, but public officials may sue as individuals when they think their reputations have been subjected to defamatory statements that cause injury or actual damage. Because defamation is a matter of personal reputation, individuals cannot sue on behalf of relatives or friends, and large groups of people cannot sue for damage to the group as a whole.[61]

Suing may not be the wisest course, however. Corporations and executives considering suits against critics whom they believe have defamed them must consider the public relations ramifications of their suits in the court of public opinion as well as their chances of winning in a court of law. Moreover, public practitioners must remind thin-skinned executives that the First Amendment protects caustic and even false comments that can arise from public discussion of controversial issues.

In all libel actions, the **plaintiff** (i.e., the person or institution whose reputation has been wrongfully harmed) has the **burden of proof** (responsibility) that libel exists. This means plaintiffs must demonstrate in court proceedings that they have evidence for all the elements of the libel suit according to a particular state's laws, or the courts will not allow the lawsuit to go forward. Though specific requirements for bringing a libel suit may differ among the states, there are key elements that are the same nationwide.

- *Defamation* is at the core of a libel lawsuit. It is defined as an intentional false communication…that injures another's reputation or good name.[62] It is often referred to as a false statement of "fact" (something that can be proven true or false), as opposed to an "opinion" or a mere supposition (what a person thinks or believes that cannot be proved or disproved). It is up to the jury in a libel action to decide if the language in the particular circumstances of the case actually defamed the plaintiff.[63]

- *Publication* of defamatory communication means there must be a witness to the matter. For a nonmedia defendant (i.e., a public relations practitioner), only one person is necessary other than the plaintiff and defendant to see or hear the defamatory communication. For mass media defendants (i.e., newspaper, TV station), the publication burden is presumed to be met. Publication can occur in public relations brochures, newsletters, fiction, yard signs, interoffice memos, conversations, interviews, business letters, e-mail, and Web sites. Any individual who repeats the libelous statement can also be sued.

- *Identification* of the plaintiff in the defamatory communication is required in a libel lawsuit. Plaintiffs must prove that the defamatory language is "of or concerning" them, and that at least one reader/viewer/listener could identify them. Many libel cases involve naming the wrong person because of careless reporting or writing by the defendant. People can also be identified without actually being named (e.g., providing a job description).

- *Retraction* requested by the plaintiff is required in most states before any legal action can commence. Generally, the plaintiff must serve written notice to the defendant that communication contains the specific statements alleged to be defamatory. There is no obligation for the defendant to publish a retraction, but many state laws will reduce certain damage awards if retraction occurs.

- *Fault* is the most complex and most misunderstood element of a plaintiff's burden of proof in libel law. "Fault" is defined as "negligence; an error or defect of judgment or of conduct; any deviation from prudence, duty, or rectitude; any shortcoming, or neglect of care or performance resulting from inattention, inca- pacity, or perversity...."[64] For purposes of the present discussion, fault can be considered to be some sort of "mistake." The degree of fault (how serious was the mistake) that must be proved depends on who is suing whom, as well as what is the content of the alleged defamation.

Before 1964, all that was required in state libel laws was whether the plaintiff could provide evidence of defamation, identification, and publication. There was no real defense available to persons being sued, and there were no different standards of proof based on who was the plaintiff or the defendant or what was the con- tentious issue. However, a 1964 landmark U.S. Supreme Court decision, *New York Times v. Sullivan*,[65] was the first of several High Court decisions that added First Amendment standards to libel law nationwide, so that when the plaintiff is a public official, criticism of official government action is not stifled.[66] The resulting catego- rization applies to both libel and privacy actions nationwide.

- *Public Official.* As defined by the Supreme Court these are government employ- ees who have, or appear to the public to have, substantial responsibility for or decision making control in governmental affairs.[67] Not all public employees are public officials, but only those who hold positions that invite greater public scruti- ny (*e.g.*, city tax assessor, county medical examiner, public university president).

- *Public Figure.* As defined by the Supreme Court in *Gertz v. Welch*,[68] these are people who invite attention and comment and thus voluntarily expose themselves to an increased risk of public scrutiny and possibly, to defamatory falsehoods.

- *Private Figures.* Also defined by the Supreme Court in *Gertz v. Welch*, private persons are more vulnerable to injury, and can thus suffer more irreparable damage to their reputations. The *standard of proof required* for the lawsuit to go forward is set, because the Supreme Court ruled that public officials and public figures should have a higher standard than private persons.

- *Actual Malice.* In the *New York Times* decision, the Court ruled that the consti- tution guarantees require a federal rule that prohibits a **public official** from recovering damages for a defamatory falsehood relating to his official conduct unless he proves that the statement was made with "actual malice." That means the false statement is made with knowledge that it was false or with reckless dis- regard to its truthfulness. In subsequent decisions, the Court ruled that this should also be the standard of proof for public figures.

- *Negligence.* In most states, the standard of proof for private figures is the failure to act as a reasonable person would in similar circumstances. Examples include the failure to verify statements, or to misinterpret court records.

In all libel actions, the **defendant** (i.e., the person or institution being sued) has a number of legal defenses available to counter a libel lawsuit.

- *Summary judgment.* If a defendant believes that a plaintiff does not have suffi- cient evidence to meet a libel action's burden of proof, she/he can ask the judge at any point in the proceedings to issue "summary judgment" in favor of the defendant.

- *Statute of limitations.* There is only a limited amount of time in which a plaintiff can bring a lawsuit for libel, as established by each state's libel statute.
- *Truth.* It is really quite difficult to have sufficient evidence for a defendant to prove in court that statements published about the plaintiff are **literally** true. Perhaps the defendant's witnesses refuse to testify, or perhaps either the witnesses or the defendant do not seem credible to the jury.
- *Privilege.* In tort law, **privilege** is defined as "the ability to act contrary to another individual's legal right without that individual having legal redress for the consequences of that act."[69] By definition, therefore, actions that are classified as privileged cannot be libelous. Two types of privilege are classified in libel law.
- *Opinion Defenses.* The definition of libel includes the requirement that there be a false statement of **fact**, with fact defined as something that is provably true or false. Pure opinion by definition is an expression of belief or judgment, not an assertion of fact. Traditionally, courts protected opinion from successful libel lawsuits because the punishment of opinion involves the punishment of ideas, and this is at the heart of First Amendment protection for speech and press freedom.

The standard of fault necessary for the plaintiff to prove to receive compensatory damages varies from state to state, with the average libel award close to $1 million. However, about 75 percent of jury awards nationwide end up being reduced or thrown out when the trial court's decision is appealed. Accordingly, public relations practitioners should pay close attention to appeals of court decisions in libel actions in their states to best understand how to model their own activities.

Privacy

As noted in the previous discussion, the legal terminology in lawsuits involving libel and invasion of privacy is similar, especially regarding definitions in the libel plaintiff's burden of proof regarding the "fault" component and "damages" to be awarded. Privacy tort law, however, involves invasion of personal privacy, rather than the so-called "constitutional right of privacy" that is at issue in such laws as those requiring motorcyclists to wear protective helmets. Both tort law and the constitutional right of privacy, however, protect an individual's "right to be left alone." In this regard, public relations practitioners have increasing responsibilities to safeguard the privacy of their clients as well as that of other employees in their organizations.

Legal scholars divide the law of privacy into four different torts, each of which is "an interference with the right of the plaintiff… 'to be let alone.'"[70]

1. **Intrusion** upon the plaintiff's seclusion or solitude, or into her/his private affairs.
2. **Public disclosure** of embarrassing private facts about the plaintiff.
3. Publicity that places the plaintiff in a **false light** in the public eye.
4. **Appropriation** of the plaintiff's name or likeness for the advantage of the defendant.

In privacy legal actions, the defendant has a number of legal defenses available to counter an invasion of privacy lawsuit. These legal tactics are primarily used by media defendants, though they are also relevant for situations in which public relations practitioners are the defendants.

The U.S. Supreme Court has acknowledged that the publication of some private information is protected by the First Amendment. The Court has allowed publication of most truthful information that was lawfully obtained from official government records or court proceedings.[71] Common law provides broad protection for publication of newsworthy information, and that **newsworthiness outweighs privacy interests in stories of public interest involving public officials or public figures participating in public proceedings**. The newsworthiness defense also overrides the privacy interests of private individuals—the key is not the status of a person as a public or private figure, but rather, the status of an event as being newsworthy.

Public relations practitioners typically get **formal consent** for anything that is not obviously newsworthy, and especially for disclosing very private facts. The necessary components of such formal consent are that it be written, that it states the names of all parties to the agreement, that it states the scope and duration of the terms of the agreement, and that it provides for consideration or payment.[72] Practitioners must make sure the appropriate person signs the consent form, keeping in mind that minors and mentally disabled persons cannot give legal consent.

OTHER LEGAL ISSUES

Litigation Public Relations

The increased recognition of the impact of public opinion on organizations involved in legal controversies spawned the development of a specialty practice area in public relations called "litigation public relations." Those practicing litigation public relations help organizations address important interests that extend beyond legal concerns. For example, a company might be concerned about the effect of litigation on its shareholders and the price of its stock, on its employees and the company's effort to recruit, on its customers and the sale of its products, and on its relationships with industry partners such as distributors and suppliers and others. In short, because the damage caused outside the courtroom can be greater than that incurred in resolving the legal issues, it is in a company's best interest to seek both legal and public relations counsel.

Whether practitioners are knowledgeable or not, legal considerations often define, limit, and regulate modern public relations practice. That is not likely to change anytime soon. As a result, most large communication businesses—public relations firms, advertising agencies, and news media—have specialized lawyers on staff or law firms on retainer.

Contract Law

Legal issues also guide the business practices of public relations professionals. Contract law in particular calls for frequent specialized legal counsel. For example, when an advertising agency successfully sued when more than half the employees left with most of the agency's business in 1954, employment contracts began to routinely contain "noncompete" clauses. The principle established was that employees cannot use their employer's time and facilities to develop their own separate business. For example, Manning, Selvage & Lee sued three former executives in the Atlanta office—Glen Jackson, Boling Spalding, and Joseph Ledlie—who quit to start their own firm, Jackson Spalding Ledlie. The two firms settled out of court.[73]

In the majority of cases, however, the courts have not upheld noncompete clauses in employment contracts, favoring employees over their former employers seeking damages. Most contractual noncompete agreements apparently fail to meet one or more of three tests. First, they must be reasonable, being no broader than necessary to protect the legitimate business interests of the employer without placing undue restriction on an employee's ability to earn a living. Second, they must be supported by some monetary consideration, such as the offer of employment, raise, promotion, or continuing employment. Third, they must protect only the employer's legitimate business interests, such as unique products and services, trade secrets, and goodwill. Attempts to eliminate competition or other purposes not related to the three tests have led courts to not uphold noncompete clauses.[74]

POSTSCRIPT

It is important to remember that **public relations practitioners do not practice law**. However, sound knowledge of the law will help practitioners work in partnership with legal personnel so that lawyers do not try to do public relations work without the practitioner's involvement.

NOTES

[1] NO, according to the Federal Election Commission (FEC), which dismissed a complaint by Citizens United, a conservative advocacy group, that the ads were "electioneering communication" and thus subject to government regulation. The Reporters Committee for Freedom of the Press. "Group alleges 'Fahrenheit 9/11' ads flout federal election laws." *News Media Update.* 25 June 2004. (http://www.rcfp.org/news/2004/0625fahren.html) (29 July 2004). The Reporters Committee for Freedom of the Press. "FEC dismisses Fahrenheit 9/11" complaint." *News Media Update.* 10 August 2004. (http://www.rcfp.org/news/2004/0625fahren.html) (11 August 2004) The larger issue, however, is that the First Amendment prohibits government interference with artistic expression such as that found in Moore's satiric political documentary.

[2] NO. Tom Forsythe, a Utah artist, used the dolls for parody and to comment on the notion of impossible beauty. Such speech is protected by the First Amendment. After five years of legal battles, a federal court ordered Mattel to pay Forsythe nearly $2 million in legal fees. The Reporters Committee for Freedom of the Press. "Judge OKs legal fees for artist critiquing Barbie." *News Media Update.* 29 June 2004. (http://www.rcfp.org/news/2004/0629mattel.html) (29 July 2004).

[3] NO. Colorful language such as this example is frequently introduced into heated arguments about labor matters. Judges would decide that no reasonable person could believe that the epithet "traitor" really meant that a person has betrayed her/his country. *National Association of Letter Carriers v. Austin*, 418 U.S. 264 (1974)

[4] YES. It is never acceptable under copyright law to duplicate an entire creative product, no matter how small that product might be. News organizations must also comply with copyright law, which means the photographer needed to first obtain formal permission from the performer before taking his film. *Zacchini v. Scripps Howard*, 433 U.S. 562 (1977).

[5] SEE, e.g., the opposing positions taken by Justice Oliver Wendell Holmes regarding the kind of speech that would constitute a "clear and present danger" to the nation, and therefore would not be protected by the First Amendment, as presented in two U.S. Supreme Court decisions regarding alleged violations by dissidents of the Espionage Act of 1917 and its 1918 Amendment. *Schenk v. U.S.*, 249 U.S. 47 (1919), and *Abrams v. U.S.*, 250 U.S. 616 (1919).

[6] Barbara K. Petersen and Allison R. Lang. "A 200-year Analysis of U.S. Supreme Court Interpretations of Public Relations." A paper presented to the Law Division of the Association for Education in Journalism and Mass Communications (AEJMC) Southeast Colloquium, Chapel Hill, NC, March 16–18, 2000. At 49.

[7] Ibid. at 50.

[8] Ibid. at 60.

[9] Ibid. at 49.

[10] The precedent is *Near v. Minnesota*, 283 U.S. 697 (1931), which declared unconstitutional a Minnesota law requiring newspapers to be reviewed by judges before publication to ensure they did not contain harmful expression.

[11] In a recent study of how journalists view their relationships with public relations practitioners, the respondents estimated that 44 percent of the content of the U.S. news media is subsidized by practitioners. Lynne M. Sallot and Elizabeth A. Johnson, "War and Peace Between Journalists and Public Relations Practitioners: Working Together to Set, Frame and Build the Public Agenda 1991–2003." A paper presented to the Public Relations Division of the Association for Education in Journalism and Mass Communications (AEJMC), Annual Convention, Toronto, Canada, August 4–7, 2004.

[12] *Miami Herald Publishing Co. v. Tornillo*, 418 U.S. 241 (1974).

[13] Ibid. at 256.

[14] Wireless Ship Act of 1910, Radio Act of 1912, and Federal Radio Act of 1927.

[15] *Black's Law,* s.v. "public interest" and s.v. "public convenience and necessity." *Public interest* is "something in which the public, the community at large, has some pecuniary interests, or some interest by their legal rights or liabilities are affected." *Public convenience and necessity* is the common criterion used in public utility matters when a board or agency is faced with a petition for action at the request of the utility.

[16] *NBC v. FCC*, 319 U.S. 190, (1943).

[17] *U.S. v. Southwestern Cable Co.,* 392 U.S. 157 (1968).

[18] SEE, e.g., *Wilkinson v. Jones*, 800 F.2d 989, *aff'd without opinion*, 480 U.S. 926 (1987), in which the federal courts declared the Utah Cable TV Programming Decency Act an overbroad restriction of cable system operators' First Amendment rights to choose programming. Likewise, provisions in the Cable TV Consumer Protection & Competition Act of 1992 to ban "indecency" on cable were found to violate the First Amendment (*Denver Area Educational Telecommunications Consortium, Inc. v. FCC*, 518 U.S. 727, 1996). Indecency is not the same as obscenity, which was declared outside the protection of the First Amendment in *Miller v. California*, 413 U.S. 15 (1973). Instead, the FCC

defined indecency as something that depicts or describes sexual or excretory activities or organs in a patently offensive manner and that is offensive to the contemporary community standards for the broadcasting medium. The U.S. Supreme Court supported the FCC's ban on indecency on broadcasting in *FCC v. Pacifica Foundation*, 438 U.S. 726 (1978) because the agency believed broadcasting is a uniquely pervasive presence in the lives of all Americans, even in the privacy of the home, and because "broadcasting is uniquely accessible to children, even those too young to read." In *Wilkinson*, the Court ruled the opposite was true for cable.

[19] 521 U.S. 844 (1997).

[20] Ibid. at 863.

[21] *Saxbe v. Washington Post Co.,* 417 U.S. 843 (1974); *Houchins v. KQED*, 438 U.S. 1 (1978); *Pell v. Procunier*, 417 U.S. 817 (1984).

[22] *Branzburg v. Hayes,* 408 U.S. 665 (1972).

[23] The U.S. Supreme Court reviewed FOIA's exemptions and found them constitutional since federal agencies are *not required* to withhold documents, though they *may* do so under their own discretion. *Chrysler Corp. v. Brown*, 441 U.S. 281 (1979)

[24] *First National Bank of Boston v. Bellotti,* 435 U.S. 765 (1978).

[25] Ibid. at 777.

[26] Ibid. at 789–90.

[27] Ibid. at 776–777.

[28] *Consolidated Edison Co. of New York v. Public Service Commission of New York*, 447 U.S. 530, 535 (1980).

[29] *Pacific Gas & Electric Co. v. Public Utilities Commission of California*, 475 U.S. 1 (1986).

[30] 2 U.S.C. sec. 261 et seq. (1988).

[31] *U.S. v. Harris*, 347 U.S. 612, 620 (1954).

[32] The Senate passed S1060, 98-0, July 25, 1995. The House passed HR2564, 421-0, then cleared S1060, Nov. 29, 1995. President Clinton signed S1060 into law (PL 104-65), Dec. 19, 1995.

[33] "Lawmakers Enact Lobbying Reforms," Congressional Quarterly 1995 Almanac: 104th Congress (Washington, DC: Congressional Quarterly, 1996), sec. 1, 40.

[34] *U.S. v. Harris*, 347 U.S. 612, 620 (1954).

[35] *U.S. v. Rumely*, 345 U.S. 41, 47 (1953). However, if a powerful corporation uses a public relations campaign to do damage to another, it may run afoul of antitrust laws. In *Eastern Railroad Presidents Conference v. Noerr* (365 U.S. 127, 1961), the U.S. Supreme Court ruled that antitrust laws, which prohibit anticompetitive restraints of trade, do not bar corporations from joining with public relations counsel in a "no-holds-barred" public relations campaign to affect legislation. The Court said railroads could try through public opinion to kill legislation favored by truckers. However, the Court said there may be situations where a publicity campaign, "ostensibly directed toward influencing governmental action, is a mere sham to cover…an attempt to interfere directly with the business relationships of a competitor" (365 U.S. 127, 144, (1961).

[36] 2 U.S.C. sec. 267 (1988).

[37] "Lawmakers Enact Lobbying Reforms," Congressional Quarterly 1995 Almanac: 104 Congress (Washington, DC: Congressional Quarterly, 1996), sec. 1, 40.

[38] For example, the law precludes the most powerful lobbying organization in Washington, DC—the American Association of Retired Persons (AARP)—from receiving such government largess because it lobbies the federal government on Social Security, Medicare, taxes, and other issues important to its members.

[39] 22 U.S.C. sec 611 et seq. (1988). See original Act at 52 U.S. Statutes at Large, pp. 631–33, or PL 583, 8 June 1938.

[40] Congressman Emanuel Celler summarized legislators' motivations for passing FARA in 83 Cong. Rec. 7, 8022 (1938).

[41] 22 U.S.C. sec. 611 (c)(1)(iii) (1988).

[42] 22 U.S.C. secs. 611, 614 (1988).

[43] *National Labor Relations Board v. Virginia Electric & Power Co.,* 314 U.S. 469, 477 (1941).

[44] 15 U.S.C. sec. 77a et seq. (1988).

[45] 15 U.S.C. sec. 78a et seq. (1988).

[46] 15 U.S.C. sec. 80a-1 et seq. (1988) and 15 U.S.C. sec. 80b-1 et seq. (1988).

[47] See Barbara K. Petersen and Hugh J. Martin, "CEO Perceptions of Investor Relations as a Public Relations Function: An Exploratory Study." *Journal of Public Relations Research* 8(3) 1996, 173–209. CEO respondents in the study reported here did not perceive public relations knowledge as relevant for conducting effective investor relations programs, but instead, preferred to have them supervised and conducted by financial affairs executives and departments.

[48] 17 CFR 243.101(f).

[49] Private Securities Litigation Reform Act of 1995, Pub. L. No. 104-67, 109 Stat. 737 (1995).

[50] See Mary S. Diemer, "Reforms Change Landscape of Securities Litigation," *Litigation News 21,* no. 3 (March 1996): 1, 4.

[51] *Black's,* s.v. "fraud." Anything calculated to deceive, whether by a single act or combination, or by suppression of truth, or suggestion of what is false, whether it be by direct falsehood or innuendo, by speech or silence, word of mouth, or look or gesture. …"Bad faith" and "fraud" are synonymous, and also synonyms of dishonesty, infidelity, faithlessness, perfidy, unfairness, etc.

[52] U.S. Constitution, Article I, Section 8.

[53] 17 U.S.C., Sec. 102.

[54] 17 U.S.C., Sec. 101, 105.

[55] *Salinger v. Random House, Inc.,* 811 F.2d 90 (2d Cir. 1987), *cert. denied,* 484 U.S. 890 (1987). The author J. D. Salinger did not register his copyright of unpublished letters until after he became aware that they were scheduled to be published in a forthcoming book.

[56] *Supra note* 123.

[57] *Community for Creative Non-Violence v. Reid,* 476 U.S. 693 (1989).

[58] 17 U.S.C., Sec. 506(a). Plagiarism and photocopying are two ways to show substantial similarity.

[59] In *Coca-Cola Co. v. Gemini Rising, Inc.*, 346 F. Supp. 1183 (E.D.N.Y. 1972), a federal court stopped a company from selling posters that were printed in the colors and type of script used by Coca Cola to identify its drinks, but that instead urged people to "enjoy cocaine."

[60] 15 U.S.C.S. Sec. 1117 (2004).

[61] According to the *Restatement (Second) of Torts,* 560, "liability exists when the group is so small that the matter can reasonably be understood to refer to an individual or the circumstances reasonably lead to the conclusion that there is a particular reference to one person."

[62] *Black's,* s.v. "defamation."

[63] *Restatement (Second) of Torts,* Sec. 559, 563, 614.

[64] *Black's,* s.v. "fault."

[65] *New York Times v. Sullivan*, 376 U.S. 255 (1964).

[66] In *New York Times* (Ibid at 270), the Court said that the United States has "a profound national commitment to the principle that debate on public issues should be uninhibited, robust, and wide-open, and that it may well include vehement, caustic, and sometimes unpleasantly sharp attacks on government and public officials."

[67] 383 U.S. 75 (1966).

[68] 418 U.S. 323 (1974).

[69] *Black's,* s.v. "privilege."

[70] William L. Prosser, *48 Calif. L. Rev.* 383 (1960)

[71] *Cox Broadcasting Corp. v. Cohn,* 420 U.S. 469 (1975).

[72] Traditionally, participants in public relations photographs or films are given a token "consideration" such as a one dollar bill.

[73] "MS&L, JSL of Atlanta Settle Lawsuit," *Jack O'Dwyer's Newsletter 30*, no. 13 (March 26, 1997): 7.

[74] "Are Non-Compete Clauses Enforceable?" *Public Relations Tactics 4*, no. 12 (December 1997): 10.

ADDITIONAL SOURCES

Black's Law Dictionary® (8th ed). Garner, Byran A., ed. St. Paul, MN: West Publishing Co., 2004.

Fitzpatrick, Kathy R. "Public Relations and the Law: A Survey of Practitioners." *Public Relations Review, 22, no. 1* (Spring 1996): 1–8.

Fitzpatrick, Kathy R., and Maureen Shubow Rubin. "Public Relations vs. Legal Strategies in Organizational Crisis Decisions." *Public Relations Review, 21, no. 1* (Spring 1995): 21–33.

Gower, Karla K. *Legal and Ethical Restraints on Public Relations*. Prospect Heights, IL: Waveland Press, 2003.

Middleton, Kent R., William E. Lee, and Bill F. Chamberlin. *The Law of Public Communication* (6th ed.). Boston: Allyn & Bacon, 2004.

Petersen, Barbara K. "Logic, Licensing, and Public Relations." *Communication Law and Policy 1, no. 1* (1996): 139–176.

Roschwalb, Susanne A., and Richard A Stach. *Litigation Public Relations: Courting Public Opinion.* Littleton, CO: Fred B. Rothman, 1995. Judges, lawyers, and public relations specialists present cases to illustrate such public relations involvement as strategy, publicity, and media relations during legal processes.

Wren, Christopher G., and Jill Robinson Wren, *The Legal Research Manual: A Game Plan for Legal Research and Analysis*. Madison, WI: Legal Education Pub., 1999. A user-friendly instruction guide to help the beginner conduct legal research.

Zelezny, John D. *Communications Law: Liberties, Restraints, and Modern Media* (4th ed.). Belmont, CA: Wadsworth, 2004.

7 THEORETICAL UNDERPINNINGS: ADJUSTMENT AND ADAPTATION

Our organizations are living systems, existing in a turbulent environment that constantly tests their abilities to survive…the forces of fierce global competition, dizzying technological advances, vacillating economies, and highly sophisticated and demanding customers.

–Carol Kinsey Goman[1]

STUDY GUIDE

After studying Chapter 7, you should be able to

- Define a system and explain how systems theory is useful for explaining how adjustment and adaptation are essential to public relations.

- Explain the differences between open and closed systems, using notions of reactive and proactive public relations.

- Define major concepts from systems theory, including homeostasis, static and dynamic states, morphogenesis, negative and positive feedback, and cybernetics.

- Diagram, label, and explain the open systems model of public relations.

This chapter presents a theoretical model for public relations. Such a framework is necessary for understanding, organizing, and integrating the many activities and purposes of public relations. In addition, the professionalization of the field requires a body of knowledge grounded in theory.

As defined in Chapter 1, **public relations** deals with the relationships that organizations build and maintain with publics. These relationships are subjected to political, social, economic, and technological change pressures in an ever-changing environment. Careful assessment of these forces is essential if organizations are to steer a safe, steady course through uncharted territory in the increasingly global community. Why are Sears and Nordstrom strong organizations and Wards department stores and Woolworth's 400 five-and-dime stores gone from the scene? To paraphrase Darwin, it is not the powerful organizations that will survive in the new millennium, it is those able to adjust and adapt to a changing world.

———————— ■ ————————

THE ECOLOGICAL APPROACH

This was the first public relations book to suggest using a social systems perspective when in 1952 it introduced the concept of **ecology** to public relations. Borrowed from the life sciences, the term helped students and practitioners understand that public relations deals with the **interdependence** of organizations and others in their environments. Viewed in this perspective, public relations' essential role is to help organizations adjust and adapt to changes in their environments.

Organizations depend on their environments for many things: charters to operate, personnel, funds to operate and grow, freedom to pursue missions, and too many others to list. To prosper and endure, all organizations must (1) accept the public responsibility imposed by an increasingly interdependent society; (2) communicate, despite multiplying barriers, with publics that are often distant and diverse; and (3) achieve integration into the communities that they were created to serve. The first point represents the **source of public relations thinking in management**. The second point explains the growth of public relations as a **specialized staff function**. The third point states the **goal** of both management and the specialized practice.

In short, the job of public relations is to help organizations adjust and adapt to their environments. Public relations counselors monitor public opinion, social change, political movements, cultural shifts, technological developments, and even the natural environment. They then interpret these environmental factors and work with management to develop strategic plans of organizational change and responsiveness.

Years ago Alvin Toffler foresaw a more dynamic environment emerging from what he called the "technology-driven Information Age." He said the changes would include "new family styles; changed ways of working, loving, and living; a new economy; new political conflicts; and beyond all this an altered consciousness as well."[2] The revolution in information and communication is not so much about technology as it is the social consequences of the new communication systems, according to communication scholar Frederick Williams: "Never before in history have so many people had so much information at their fingertips."[3]

Public relations specialists must anticipate and monitor such changes in an organization's environment and help interpret them to management. The successful public relations counselor constantly surveys the environment, always trying to extend vision farther beyond the horizon and trying to increase both the size and the resolution of the picture of present and future realities. In essence, such attempts to see clearly and to anticipate are designed to give the organization time to plan, an opportunity to be **proactive** rather than simply **reactive** to environmental changes.

Specific changes and forces at play must be identified, studied, and understood for particular situations and organizational settings. At the same time, however, overriding basic changes drive other change pressures and produce consequences for all organizations, such as the tragic events of September 11, 2001, and the continuing war on terrorism.

TRACKING THE TRENDS

This discussion of major trends and changes is far from complete, but it indicates how major forces affect organizations. It simply is not possible to build an omnibus list that would cover all situations. Instead, the role of public relations is to track and analyze the specific trends and forces at play in particular situations.

For example, how will the growing animal rights movement affect an organization's ability to accomplish its mission? The *Los Angeles Times Magazine* reported that the Maryland-based animal rights group People for the Ethical Treatment of Animals (PETA) "has grown from humble origins to an 800-pound gorilla…the largest organization of its kind in the country, claiming more than 350,000 members."[4] Cosmetics manufacturers, medical research laboratories, meat packers, and even federal government agencies have had to factor the views of this new activist force into their decision making.

The animal rights movement forced Avon, Estée Lauder, Benetton, and Tonka Toy Company, among others, to stop testing products on rabbits, guinea pigs, and other animals. It forced the National Institutes of Health to close a research clinic that used animals in research and the Pentagon to halt wound tests on animals. A slaughterhouse in Texas was ordered shut after PETA pressure. PETA is also winning the battle for public opinion, as an overwhelming majority support animal rights and think it should be illegal to kill animals for fur or use animals in cosmetics research.

Consider the issue of education reform: As more and more Americans enter the job market without basic writing, math, and problem-solving skills, American industry slips further behind in the competitive global marketplace. At the same time, parents must cope with ever-increasing costs for postsecondary education. RJR Nabisco Corporation (now split into separate tobacco and food companies) matches employees' annual contributions to a tax-deferred educational savings plan. RJR Nabisco contributes up to $4,000 toward the costs of college, everything from a two-year college to an Ivy League university. Many other companies have "adopted" schools to help promote improvement in the educational system. Others have started their own basic education programs in an attempt to equip employees with basic job skills. Few organizations escape problems brought on by the education crisis, the changing family, new technology, or global competition.

A SYSTEMS PERSPECTIVE

System is a set of interacting units that endures through time within an established boundary by responding and adjusting to change pressures from the environment to achieve and maintain goal states.

This discussion of changes and their impact on organizations suggests a systems perspective for public relations. The systems perspective applies because mutually dependent relationships are established and maintained between organizations and their publics.

The concepts of adjustment and adaptation, as well as our definition of public relations, employ concepts and propositions from systems theory. For example, a university is part of a system composed of alumni, donors, neighbors, employers, high school counselors and teachers, and other universities in the area, to name but a few of the many publics. Even the simplest definition of a system—a set of interdependent parts—illustrates this perspective. However, a **system** is best defined more elaborately **as a set of interacting units that endures through time within an**

EXHIBIT 7.1

TRACKING TRENDS AND ISSUES

Picture yourself as the captain of the Starship Enterprise.

You want to be sure that you have a radar system that can accurately anticipate fast-moving meteors and the location of nearby planets to avoid impending disasters.

While moving through space at warp speeds, you don't want to wait until these obstacles are in sight to adjust your course and keep the ship out of danger.

The same is true about an organization—your organization—facing a meteor shower of issues in today's rapidly changing environment.

As issues affecting your organization arise, it is best to have a radar system in place that will help management anticipate trends and issues likely to affect your organization and its publics, rather than waiting until it's too late to do anything except react defensively.

If you are in public relations, you must start being more systematic in the tracking and management of issues. If you don't, someone else in your organization will. It's a prerequisite for organizational survival.

Even the Starship Enterprise would find it difficult to navigate through the turbulent issues environment most organizations face today.

_____

Quote from Kerry Tucker, Chairman, Nuffer, Smith, Tucker, Inc., San Diego, CA. Used with permission.

established boundary by responding and adjusting to change pressures from the environment to achieve and maintain goal states.

In the case of public relations, the set of interacting units includes the organization and the publics with which it has or will have relations. They are somehow mutually affected or involved. Unlike physical and biological systems, however, social systems are not especially dependent on the physical closeness of component parts. Rather, specification of organization–public interactions defines systems. In other words, an organization–publics system consists of an organization and the people involved with and affected by the organization. Whereas the organizational component in the system is relatively easy to define, publics are abstractions defined by the public relations manager applying the systems approach. In fact, different publics, and therefore a different system boundary, must be defined for each situation or problem.

This principle of systems theory can be illustrated by comparing a university's publics when the goal is recruiting students as opposed to when the goal is raising money for a new computing center for the business school. The student recruitment campaign might include college-bound high school students, their parents, high school counselors, students currently enrolled at the university, and alumni. Because the university tends to attract students from a particular region or segments of the population, program planners would have to identify the geographic and socio-graphic territory to be covered in the recruitment effort. In effect, each of these decisions defines the components and boundary of the system for the student recruitment program.

The capital campaign for the new computing center at the same university, on the other hand, calls for a different definition of the organization–publics system. Program planners would determine what groups or entities are most interested in such a facility or most likely to benefit from its presence on campus. Surely the local business community would include potential donors. In cities far from the campus, corporate foundations that have historically funded innovative educational programs would be included as prospective contributors. More specifically, computer hardware and software companies that hire computer scientists would be identified as a third public for this campaign. Not all alumni are likely contributors, but those who have succeeded in professions calling for computing skills could be selected from the alumni list to make up a fourth public.

In both situations, definitions of the publics include those with whom the organization must establish and maintain enduring and mutually beneficial relationships. Most relationships, however, extend well beyond the period of such specific campaigns. Therefore, even though relationships must be defined specifically for each situation and program goal, they also must be viewed in the larger context of the university's overall public relations program.

Public relations efforts, then, are part of an organization's **purposive** and, therefore, **managed** behavior to achieve goals. For example, a fire that destroys a museum certainly has an impact on the museum's relationships with donors and others. Such an unplanned event, however, clearly is not part of the public relations program. On the other hand, the fund-raising campaign, groundbreaking ceremony, and grand opening gala are public relations responses to the situation created by the fire. These events are intended to establish or maintain relationships necessary for rebuilding the museum.

In some cases, goals can be achieved by simply maintaining existing relationships in the face of changing conditions. More likely, however, organizations must continually adjust their relationships with publics in response to an ever-changing social milieu. Because organization–publics systems exist in changing environments, they must be capable of adapting their goals and relationships to accommodate change pressures from their complex and dynamic settings. A classic case of adjustment and adaptation is the redirection of March of Dimes fund-raising and research to birth defects after the polio vaccine eliminated the disease for which the organization–publics system was originally created.

Environmental Change Pressures

Systems theorists typically define the environment as anything that generates change pressures—information, energy, and matter inputs—on a system. Environmental inputs to organization–publics systems take many forms. For example, news reports about abuses by top executives at United Way—lavish lifestyles, high salaries, consulting fees paid to associates, limousine and luxury hotel expenses, and even Concorde flights to Europe—certainly affected the charity's relationships with donors and local United Way chapters. And the impact was not limited to United Way, as all charities braced for a donor backlash, greater public scrutiny, and even government investigations of high salaries and generous benefits packages of nonprofit organizations executives. Soon after the United Way case made headlines in the nation's news media, the biweekly *Chronicle of Philanthropy* reported that more than one-fourth of the nation's largest 117 charities paid top executives $200,000 or more annually. Years later, the issue of charity executives' pay made headline news: "Officials at AIDS Charities under Fire over $100,000-Plus Salaries."[5]

Changes in educational levels and values of those entering the local workforce affect relationships between a local manufacturing company and labor unions, community groups, local government, and other employers in the area. Shifts in university students' majors—from history to business, for example—put stress on the rather rigidly structured faculty and resources at a university. Changes in the university in turn affect relationships with its various publics: prospective students, current students, faculty, alumni, trustees, donors, legislators, and prospective employers of graduating students. Relationships with other institutions of higher education will change as the universities compete for history majors and refer business students to each other's campuses.

Even "an insignificant leak" of radioactive water in a power utility's nuclear-generating reactor puts stress on a utility's relationships with regulators, antinuclear citizen groups, and the financial community. Or recall the media coverage of protest groups picketing tuna-canning companies because their fishing practices killed dolphins. Almost immediately sales slumped, government scrutiny increased, children and parents alike erroneously accused the companies of killing "Flipper" for profit, and protest stickers were attached to the product on grocery store shelves. Socially conscious investors sold tuna stock as prices plummeted.

These examples illustrate that change pressures on organization–publics systems come from many types of environmental sources. In turn, organization–publics relationships change in response to these environmental pressures. If they do not change, old relationships become dysfunctional because the organization acts and reacts in ways inappropriate to the new circumstances. If they are unmanaged and nonpurposive in their responses to environmental changes, systems tend to degenerate to maximum disorder, what systems theorists call "entropy." In social systems, this means that coordinated behavior to attain mutually beneficial goals is no longer possible. In effect, systems break up. Public relations is charged with keeping organizational relationships in tune with the mutual interests and goals of organizations and their publics.

Subsystems and Suprasystems

To this point, a system has been defined as including the organization and its publics. Similarly, the organization is itself composed of a set of interacting units. From this perspective, the organization can also be viewed as a system. Because organizations exist in dynamic social settings, they must modify internal processes and restructure themselves in response to changing environments. In the absence of such adjustment and adaptation, organizations—just like any other social system—become out of step with the world around them. As counselors to line management, the public relations staff is charged with keeping the organization sensitive to environmental changes, anticipating as well as reacting to change pressures.

Likewise, the organization–publics system can be part of a larger set of interacting units, thus viewed as a component of a higher-order social system. For example, a local United Way–publics system is but one component of the community's charitable social service system. It is also only one subsystem in the national system of affiliates, which in turn is but one component of the nation's charitable social service system. Eventually, of course, one could project this series of ever-larger systems to the highest level on earth, the world. Many public relations specialists work at the level of the private enterprise system, health-care system, educational system, or international development system, to name but a few examples of regional, national, and international systems.

The systems perspective, then, suggests that the level and definition of the system must be appropriate to the concern or the problem situation. A component—

a subsystem—in one system may be itself analyzed as a system in another context. Likewise, a system defined as such for one purpose may be but a component or sub-system in a higher-order suprasystem when the reason for the analysis changes.

For example, when reorganizing the local United Way's internal structure and programming, the organization is viewed as the system and the publics are viewed as parts of the environment. When the United Way scandal made the headlines, how-ever, for some purposes each of the 2,100 local United Way organizations and their publics became local systems within an even larger environmental context. Like-wise, the national United Way of America, made up of national headquarters and all 2,100 local units, can be viewed as but one component in the national or interna-tional charity system. And the charities taken as a group are but one component in the larger set of tax-exempt, nonprofit organizations some have referred to as the "third sector" of the economy.

The United Way scandal illustrates the latter level of systems analysis, as news of national United Way President William Aramony's high salary and extravagant lifestyle produced change pressures on all tax-exempt charitable, religious, and edu-cational groups and foundations. Individual donors called for more accountability and greater scrutiny of what charities do, as did the National Committee for Responsive Philanthropy. A congressional subcommittee called for more Internal Revenue Service staff members to monitor the more than one million tax-exempt organizations. (The one million total does not include almost 350,000 churches and other national groups such as 4-H, Boy Scouts, Girl Scouts, and Boys and Girls Clubs!) Television evangelists, national foundations, universities, and even local charities all felt the heat of media attention and increased public scrutiny.

Systems theorist James G. Miller uses the concept of higher-order systems to define a system's environment:

> The immediate environment is the suprasystem minus the system itself. The entire environment includes this plus the suprasystem and systems at all higher levels which contain it. In order to survive, the system must interact with and adjust to its environ-ment, the other parts of the suprasystem. These processes alter both the system and its environment. It is not surprising that characteristically living systems adapt to their envi-ronment and, in return, mold it. The result is that, after some period of interaction, each in some sense becomes a mirror of the other.[6]

Organizations as Systems

Miller says "living systems" engage in exchanges with their environments, producing changes in both the systems and their environments. Such imagery of exchange processes, structural change, and adaptation captures the essence of the public rela-tions function in organizations. Specifically, public relations is part of what organiza-tion theorists call the adaptive subsystem, as distinct from the **production**, **supportive-disposal**, **maintenance**, and **managerial subsystems**.[7] The latter—the managerial subsystem—is defined as "direction, adjudication, and control" of the other subsystems.

Adaptive subsystems vary in their sensitivity to their environments, just as do the public relations functions within organizations. Some organizations actively monitor their social environments and make adjustments based on what is learned. An example is a church that begins offering single-parent counseling and social events in response to the growing number of households headed by divorced and single parents. On the other hand, given public concerns about health-care costs and excessive corporate profits, how sensitive was the pharmaceutical company that charged 100 times more for a drug when it was used to treat human cancer than when the same drug was sold as an antiparasitic agent in farm animals?

The amount of resources, time, and effort an organization devotes to monitoring its environment is determined by

1. The degree of conflict or competition with the external environment, typically related to the extent of involvement with and dependence on government

2. The degree of dependence on internal support and unity

3. The degree to which internal operations and the external environment are believed to be rationalized, that is, characterized by predictable uniformities and therefore subject to planned influence, and affecting all of these

4. The size and structure of the organization, its heterogeneity of membership and diversity of goals, its centralization of authority[8]

Organizational adjustment and adaptation to new conditions depend in part on how open organizations are to their environments. Differences in how sensitive organizations are to their environments provide a useful basis for further systems analysis of the public relations function.

OPEN AND CLOSED SYSTEMS

All systems—mechanical, organic, and social—can be classified in terms of the nature and amount of interchange with their environments. The continuum ranges from closed systems on one extreme to open systems on the other. **Closed systems** have impermeable boundaries, so they cannot exchange matter, energy, or information with their environments. **Open systems**, on the other hand, exchange inputs and outputs through boundaries that are permeable. Of course, social systems cannot be completely closed or totally open, so they are either **relatively open** or **relatively closed**. The distinction is important.

The extent to which systems are closed is an indication of their insensitivity to their environments. Closed systems do not take in new matter, energy, or information. In short, closed systems do not adapt to external change and eventually disintegrate. On the other hand, open systems are responsive to environmental changes. Survival and growth of open systems depend on interchange with their environment. The most successful organizations are "especially adroit at continually responding to change of any sort in their environments."[9]

Open systems adjust and adapt to counteract or accommodate environmental variations. Inputs from the environment can be reactions to a system's own outputs or the result of changes independent of system outputs. In either case, inputs have an impact on system goal states, those conditions the system holds as "ideal" or "desired." Inputs can cause deviations from these system goal states. When that happens, feedback within a system causes adjustments in both system **structure** (what the system is) and **processes** (what the system does). The adjustments are intended to reduce, maintain, or increase the deviations. The output of adjustments can be directed internally, externally, or both. Internal outputs change or maintain goal states. External outputs change or maintain environmental conditions. Which type of output should public relations stress? That depends, for "there is no property of an organization that is good in any absolute sense; all are relative to some given environment, or to some given set of threats and disturbances, or to some given set of problems."[10] And does it mean that an open system will adjust effectively? Not necessarily, for "there is maladjustment as well as adjustment; the function concept only poses the question of adequacy but does not settle it beforehand."[11] (Figure 7.1 represents the cyclical nature of an open system's interchange with its environment, assessment and reassessment, and adjustment and adaptation essential to the system maintenance and change.)

The ultimate goal of systems, of course, is survival. But because they exist in changing environments, open systems must continually adjust to maintain states of equilibrium or balance. The conditions necessary for survival are represented as the "goal states" in the model. Paradoxically, open systems must continually change to remain the same, an enduring set of interacting units. To differentiate the **dynamic** states of relatively open systems from the **static** states of relatively closed systems, systems theorists refer to the changeable goal states as **homeostasis**. This term is used "to avoid the static connotations of equilibrium and to bring out the dynamic, processual, potential-maintaining properties of basically unstable … systems."[12] The person credited with coining the term homeostasis said it "does not imply something set and immobile, as stagnation," but rather "a condition which may vary."[13]

Homeostasis, then, refers to goal states that, although **relatively stable**, are subject to change as a result of system inputs. For example, your academic department attempts to maintain a certain student population, but that goal may change if the state reduces the university's budget. The student census goal could be increased if new resources were added, such as a newly endowed lectureship made possible by wealthy alumni. Yet another term is needed, however, to describe other changes characteristic of open systems that adjust and adapt to environmental inputs.

Whereas homeostasis represents the maintenance of dynamic system goal states, **morphogenesis** refers to changes in the structure and process element in the

FIGURE 7.1

OPEN SYSTEMS MODEL

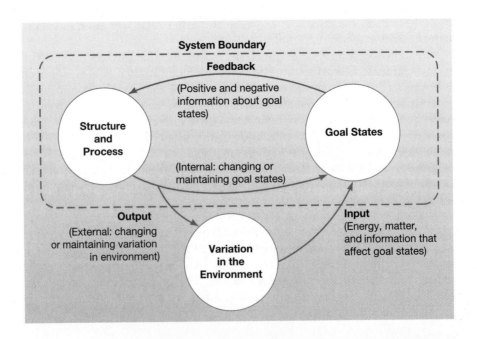

open systems model in Figure 7.1. For example, press and public criticism of how the state fair is being managed prompts the board of directors to appoint a new administrator and to reorganize the business office. In addition, the board revises procedures for awarding contracts. Notice that the structure and processes may change even if the goal states do not, and vice versa. What changes and to what extent depends on the nature of the feedback in the system. According to Littlejohn,

> Feedback can be classified as positive or negative, depending on the way the system responds to it. *Negative feedback* is an error message indicating deviation, and the system adjusts by reducing or counteracting the deviation. Negative feedback is important for balance because it maintains a steady state.
>
> A system can also respond by amplifying or maintaining deviation, in which case the feedback is *positive*. This kind of interaction is important to morphogenesis, or system growth such as learning… [T]he response to negative feedback is "cut back, slow down, discontinue." Response to positive feedback is "increase, maintain, keep going."[14]

Systems, then, can adjust and adapt their goals, structures, or processes, depending on the kind and amount of feedback. Open systems not only generate different types of feedback as a result of system inputs, but they also exhibit more flexibility in adjusting to inputs. Choices among alternative adaptive strategies are made on the basis of which ones are most effective in helping the system maintain or achieve system goals in the context of environmental change pressures. As one systems theorist put it, "All systems are adaptive, and the real question is what they are adaptive to and to what extent."[15]

CYBERNETICS IN OPEN SYSTEMS

Study of this input–output self-regulation process in systems is referred to as **cybernetics**. Buckley's general cybernetic model (Figure 7.2) portrays what tends to occur or would occur ("were it not for complicating factors") in goal-seeking systems. The model contains five elements: (1) goals established in a control center; (2) outputs related to the goals, which have impact on the state of the system and its environment; (3) feedback to the control center on the effects of the output;

FIGURE 7.2

CYBERNETIC CONTROL MODEL

From Walter Buckley, *Sociology and Modern Systems Theory* ©1973, p. 173. Reprinted with permission from Prentice Hall Inc., Englewood Cliffs, NJ.

(4) a comparison of the new system state with the goal state; and (5) control center determination of the need for corrective output.[16]

Cybernetic control systems used for navigation on space shuttles, airplanes, and ships are good examples. Early in the twentieth century, sailors called the first such navigational system "iron mike." This relatively simple cybernetic system contained a course-setting device, a course indicator to signal discrepancies from the set course, and a mechanism for activating the rudder to make course corrections. Compare that with the sophisticated cybernetic control system on the most advanced and largest sailing ship, the 617-foot *Wind Surf*:

> A hard gust of wind generates pressure on the sails. The extent of that increase in pressure is measured, and the computer instructs the sheets, which are attached to the clews of the sails, to slacken off—spilling the incremental wind and thereby easing the tension. Simultaneously, the computer instructs the windward seawater ballast to ingest more water, while the leeward ballast chamber rushes to empty its supply of water. It is most terribly important to do all of this before the ship lists over more than two degrees, that being, [on *Wind Surf*] the limit of official toleration. If the ship were to heel more than two degrees, passengers might notice that they were under sail, and that isn't really the idea, on the world's largest sailboat. So that everything described above happens within approximately three seconds.[17]

Even a thermostat-furnace system can be described as a cybernetic system. Just as does *Wind Surf*, this system responds (corrective actions) to deviations from the goal state (the temperature set in the thermostat). Its responses, however, include either production or cessation of heat only: turning the furnace on or off. Similarly, relatively simple organisms have limited options for dealing with variations in their environments. For example, the cuttlefish (Figure 7.3)—a squidlike marine mollusk—indiscriminately squirts an inky fluid when it encounters something in its surroundings.

FIGURE 7.3

CUTTLEFISH

Photograph courtesy Gerhard Saueracker, Perth, Western Australia.

Organizations, much like the *Wind Surf*, have so many sophisticated options available for dealing with environmental change that they make turning on the heat and squirting ink seem primitive. Or do they? Some public relations programs are routinized to the point that, regardless of the problem and without regard to environmental conditions, the response is to get out a press release "telling our story." In other words, the response is both predetermined and applied indiscriminately from situation to situation. Maybe the cuttlefish's strategy for squirting ink at problems is not unique to that species!

Simple mechanical cybernetic systems and living organisms typically do not change structurally except when pushed to the limit of system tolerance. For example, even though the cuttlefish makes cosmetic changes to blend in with its environment, structural change is not an option when it confronts threats in its surroundings. Social systems and complex cybernetic systems such as those used in "smart buildings," on the other hand, have the capacity to use cybernetic self-regulation to make relatively major structural changes. Such changes help the system to adapt to new environmental conditions or to modify outputs to change or neutralize the sources of change pressure. This interchange between systems and their environments is characteristic of open systems and makes morphogenesis—purposive changes in structure and process—possible. In short, open systems have the capacity to adjust and adapt to constantly changing environments.

Another quality of open systems becomes apparent when social systems are compared with mechanical systems and many living organisms. Simple, relatively closed systems react to outside events only if the input—change pressure—is sufficient to penetrate the system boundary. Complex, relatively open systems monitor—and in some cases actively probe—their environments to detect and predict changing conditions. In other words, sophisticated open systems **anticipate** changes in their environments and initiate corrective actions designed to counteract or neutralize the changes before they become major problems.

Public relations exhibits a similar range of closed versus open approaches. When public relations practitioners get together, they often use the terms *reactive* and *proactive* to describe programs. Reactive programs employ relatively closed systems approaches to program planning and management. Like the cuttlefish squirting ink, a reactive public relations program activates only when disturbed. For example, *Forbes* magazine suggested that Weyerhaeuser's management philosophy "minimizes outside pressures for performance on management." The magazine went on to say, "The company is structured in ways that once made sense but no longer do." According to *Forbes*, the longtime chairman's (the founder's great-grandson) "reaction to criticism was to shrug it off," hiring from the outside "was nearly taboo," and "change moves at a glacial pace in this company." Completing the picture of a relatively closed systems approach, the magazine reported that company representatives "declined to talk with *Forbes* for this story, citing among other things a negative story that ran 13 years ago. Like an elephant, Weyerhaeuser never forgets. Like an elephant, it is also hard to turn around."[18]

Similarly, apparently Amarillo city officials and the Texas beef industry were operating in the reactive mode of relatively closed systems when they dealt with Oprah Winfrey, the nation's top-rated talk show host. Oprah taped her show in Amarillo while defending herself in court against charges that she had defamed beef during a program about mad cow disease. Texas cattlemen and the Texas Beef Group sued. Chamber of Commerce leaders decided not to welcome Oprah and forbade Chamber employees to attend tapings of the program. Oprah won in the court of law and in the court of public opinion, increasing her position as one of the most popular talk show hosts on television. City officials missed an opportunity to put the city in a good light when they refused to cooperate with Oprah's staff and did not provide information about Amarillo and its attractions. Typical of such closed systems' responses, the mayor was quoted afterward as saying, "I didn't realize the depth and breadth of Oprah's popularity."[19]

Exhibiting the telltale signs of a closed system, the beef industry responded with similar denial and "ink squirting" when confronted with the clear evidence that "mad cow disease" had been found in a cow slaughtered in the United States. Industry groups resisted calls for increased inspection and screening of cattle being slaughtered for human consumption and for an end to adding parts of slaughtered animals to cattle feed. The routine, defensive tactics and resistance to structural change represent a system slow to adjust to environmental change.

Proactive programs, in contrast, use their early-warning "radar" to gather information, to make adjustments, and to generate internal and external output to prevent or avoid problems. In contrast to the beef industry, pistachio growers in California responded as an open, self-correcting system when increased levels of mold were found in their product. The California Pistachio Commission—representing growers—asked the Agriculture Department to lower allowable levels of mold and to increase inspections.

Digital Research's announcement that it would no longer merely issue a steady stream of press releases is another example of an organization changing from a closed systems approach to public relations to a more open systems model. Instead of indiscriminately squirting ink like a cuttlefish, the computer software company adopted a proactive open systems approach. To that end Digital Research not only retained a public relations firm but also added the firm's head to its board of directors. The first step in the new approach was a series of strategic planning sessions—a proactive response.

FIGURE 7.4

REACTIVE PUBLIC RELATIONS

Courtesy Doug Marlette, The *Charlotte Observer*.

Similarly, even a power utility, long thought of as the corporate equivalent of an elephant, can behave as a proactive open system. For example, while other utilities were fighting acid rain regulations and legislation, Minneapolis-based Northern States Power Company had already factored pollution control and reduction into operations. "Their policy is to exceed every environmental requirement that's placed on them," according to a Minnesota pollution-control agency program chief. Northern States, for example, to comply with new emission regulations, started buying low-sulfur Western coal years before it needed to. By doing so it locked in prices and transportation costs well into the twenty-first century. Meanwhile, other Midwest utilities continued to burn the cheaper, high-sulfur Midwestern and Eastern coals. As a result, these coal-burning utilities now pay premium prices for the cleaner-burning Western coal. Northern States also installed scrubbers to clean sulfur from smoke and gases emerging from its furnaces in the early 1970s and has improved their efficiency since then. Utilities that waited until the 1980s and 1990s paid more than five times as much for scrubbers. The company's president and chief executive took the long view: "You have to be environmentally responsible to have a hope for success or longevity."[20]

OPEN SYSTEMS MODEL OF PUBLIC RELATIONS

Output of a steady stream of press releases and other traditional reactive public relations responses is suggestive of closed systems thinking. This all-too-common approach to the function is apparently based on two assumptions: (1) that the purpose of public relations is limited to effecting changes in the environment, and more mistakenly, (2) that organizations have the power to change their environments, thereby eliminating the need to change themselves. Does this kind of thinking remind you of the cuttlefish and thermostat–furnace system? On the other hand, an open systems approach casts public relations in the role of bringing about changes in both environments and organizations as a result of environmental inputs.

Bell and Bell refer to the first approach to public relations as functionary and the second as **functional**. In their view, the **functionary** role is similar to a closed systems approach:

> Public relations functionaries attempt to preserve and promote a favorable image of the organization in the community on the hypothesis that if the organization is "liked" the public will continue to absorb the organization's outputs. Such functionaries are only concerned with supplying information about the organization to the environment and not with supplying information to the organization about the environment. Because functionaries do not supply feedback information, they do not function in decision-making or even in advisory roles in relation to environmental concerns. Therefore, *they have little to say about **what** is said; they are mainly concerned with **how** things are said.*[21]

In this approach to public relations, the emphasis is on maintaining the status quo within the organization while effecting change in the organization's publics. The goal of building and maintaining relations between the organization and its publics is to bring the publics into line with the organization's plans.

In contrast, a functional view of public relations calls for an open systems approach, changing both the organization and the environment. Relations between the organization and its publics are maintained or changed on the basis of reciprocal output–feedback adjustment. In the functional approach:

EXHIBIT 7.2

ADJUSTMENT AND ADAPTATION—"MA BELL" STYLE

Before government and media turned their attention toward Microsoft's alleged domination of the software industry, maybe no organizational change received as much attention as did the court-ordered divestiture of the Bell System. On January 1, 1984, the then-107-year-old American Telephone and Telegraph split into eight separate companies: AT&T and seven regional companies. The old AT&T had been the world's largest company, secure in its position as a virtual monopoly and employer of almost a million "telephone people." It began with the famous words of Alexander Graham Bell, "Mr. Watson, come here. I want to see you." Its transformation stands as an extreme example of system adjustment and adaptation to a changed environment.

Even during the long court fight against divestiture, AT&T was planning a new structure to respond to the new legal, social, economic, and technological environments. AT&T's chairman had decided that the fight would have gone on for years with little hope of avoiding the inevitable breakup. When it happened, advertisements announced, "We've been working to make the biggest change in our lives a small change in yours."

The response should have been anticipated: Theodore N. Vail, twice chairman of AT&T—1878 to 1887 and 1907 to 1920—pioneered in making the corporation responsive to its social setting. He did not fight public regulation and hired James D. Ellsworth to begin a public relations program that responded to public interests. Arthur W. Page succeeded Ellsworth. Page's philosophy of public relations and corporate social responsibility endures (see Exhibit 5.4).

By the early 1990s, AT&T and the seven regional companies had broadened their missions and product lines well beyond what was once thought of as "the telephone company." They manufactured computers and other communication equipment, expanded their publishing businesses, diversified their communication services, and became leaders in the generation and transmission of information. Cable television companies, other manufacturers, publishers, and other telephone companies faced not one, but eight competitors. By the late 1990s, mergers had reduced the number of regional "integrated telcos" to five, and AT&T had once again divested, spinning off its Bell Laboratories to form a new company—Lucent Technologies—and spinning off former cash register manufacturer NCR as a computer company. AT&T also began building high-speed fiber-optic voice and data transmission networks, and even reentered the local telephone service business in 1999 by linking its operations with Time Warner's millions of cable television lines.

In short, AT&T transformed itself into a powerful player in a new digital, wireless, and multimedia environment. It is no longer "The Telephone Company" or "Ma Bell." The old AT&T adjusted and adapted.

It was not an easy transition, however. Longtime AT&T consultant Chester Burger recalls that in the early 1980s there were 1,700 full-time public relations specialists on AT&T's payroll with a total budget of about $170 million. Much of the public relations effort was to defend the company's historic monopoly in providing telephone service and the equipment that could be connected to the system. Burger concludes, however, that (1) public relations strategy can't overcome broad social factors, (2) it is easy to convince yourself that corporate self-interest coincides with the public interest, and (3) technology is changing the world.

Simply put, AT&T either had to change or it would have followed other corporate dinosaurs into extinction.

Source: Chester Burger, APR, Fellow PRSA, "Last Word: When Public Relations Fails," *The Public Relations Strategist* 3, no. 3 (Fall 1997): 56.

[Public relations] has the potential to act in an advisory capacity and to have impact on decision-making. This potential in turn leads to some control over its own domain in times of crisis and, as a sensing device, public relations can be effective in preventing many potential crisis situations. Management properly remains the "large wheel" but the small wheel that is public relations may occasionally be capable of influencing the larger one. If observations of external and internal environments indicate that a policy or practice is detrimental to the best interests of the organization (and, increasingly, society) management can be encouraged to adjust.[22]

The functionary approach casts public relations practitioners in the technician role discussed in Chapter 2. In this limited role, they monitor the environment (if at all) to make communication output more effective, not to make changes within the organization. In organizations in which public relations operates in the functional mode, on the other hand, practitioners become part of top management, "the dominant coalition."

> Practitioners with the knowledge, training, and experience to practice a two-way model of public relations are more likely to be included in the organization's dominant coalition. They also are more likely to have power in that coalition rather than to serve it in an advisory role. When public relations managers have power in the dominant coalition, they can influence organizational ideology and the choice of publics in the environment for which strategic public relations programs are planned. At that point, public relations practitioners can fulfill a communication counseling and management role—and truly practice the profession defined for them in public relations textbooks but seldom fulfilled in the real world.[23]

In effect, public relations practiced in the closed systems (functionary) model attempts to maintain the status quo within organizations while directing change efforts at the environment. When public relations is part of organizations' strategic attempts to adjust and adapt to their dynamic environments, the practice reflects the open systems (functional) model.

The open systems approach radically changes the practice from how it is widely practiced. Whereas the more common functionary version attempts to exercise control over environmental forces, the open systems model suggests adjustment and adaptation as the more realistic and appropriate responses. Most definitions of organizational environment suggest that it includes factors outside organizational boundaries and often outside organizations' control. An organization's **specific environment** includes those "constituencies that can positively or negatively influence the organization's effectiveness. It is unique to each organization and it changes with conditions."[24]

The open systems model uses "two-way symmetric" approaches, meaning that communication is two way and that information exchange causes changes on both sides of organization–public relationships. The difference between one-way and two-way communication led the Grunigs to propose yet another way to describe closed and open systems public relations: craft public relations versus professional public relations.

> Practitioners of craft public relations seem to believe that their job consists solely of the application of communication techniques and as an end in itself. To them, the purpose of public relations simply is to get publicity or information into the media or other channels of communication. Practitioners of professional public relations, in contrast, rely on a body of knowledge as well as technique and see public relations as having a strategic purpose for an organization: to manage conflict and build relationships with strategic publics that limit the autonomy of the organization.[25]

Both approaches emphasize the primary role of communication in social systems. As Buckley put it, "the interrelations characterizing higher levels (of systems) come to depend more and more on the transmission of **information**—a principle fundamental to modern complex system analysis."[26]

Applying the open systems approach to public relations first and foremost calls for purposeful sensing of the environment to anticipate and detect changes that affect organizational relationships with publics. Following an open systems approach, public relations must be selectively sensitive to specifically defined publics that are mutually affected or involved by organizational policies, procedures, and actions. The open systems model of public relations calls for research skills to monitor publics and other environmental forces, as well as forces within organizations.

Open systems public relations also has the capacity to initiate corrective actions within organizations and direct programs to affect knowledge, predisposition, and behavior of both internal and external publics. The outcomes sought are maintenance or achievement of goals that reflect the mutual interests of organizations and their publics. Those found in conflict with mutual interests are changed or eliminated, **before** they become issues or problems. Proactive corrective action may be the major and most useful aspect of the open systems model of public relations. Steps taken in advance reduce both the amount of effort required and the trauma associated with crisis-oriented reactive public relations.

Thus, organizations employing open systems public relations maintain their relationships by adjusting and adapting themselves and their publics to everchanging social, political, and economic environments. (Figure 7.5 illustrates the open systems model applied to public relations.)

As early as 1923, in one of the earliest public relations books, *Crystallizing Public Opinion*, Edward L. Bernays wrote about the role of the "public relations counsel" in a democratic society. Expressing a model of public relations similar to our open systems approach, he said that the public relations counsel recognizes changes in the organization's social setting and advises clients or employers how the organization should change itself and respond so as to establish a "common meeting ground." Not many years later, Harwood Childs said that the function of public relations is to "reconcile or adjust in the public interest" those aspects of organizations that have social significance. This concept of public relations, based on the open systems theoretical model, serves as the basis for the many activities under the banner of public relations and spells out its essential role in organizations and society.

In the final analysis, public relations practitioners are applied social and behavioral scientists working as part of a strategic plan. According to employee communication expert Paul Sanchez at Watson Wyatt Communication Consulting Practice, a public relations plan "also tilts the balance toward proactive communication, thus avoiding wasted time on purely reactive communication that does not support strategic goals."[27]

FIGURE 7.5

OPEN SYSTEMS MODEL OF PUBLIC RELATIONS

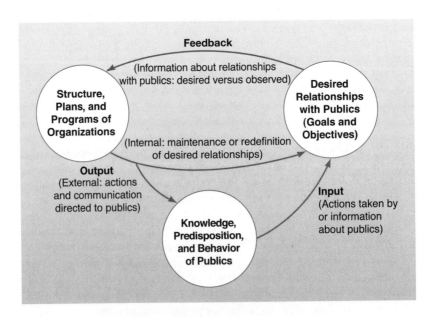

EXHIBIT 7.3

GOOD THEORY DRIVES BEST PRACTICE

*James Everett, Ph.D.,
Associate Professor
School of Advertising, Marketing
and Public Relations
Queensland University of
Technology
Brisbane, Australia*

The importance of a good theory is that it guides our thinking, informs our practice, and sets imperatives for refining our understanding. The adjustment and adaptation model of public relations is in many ways a centrifugal force in public relations because it fulfills these obligations to thinking and practice, but equally, points toward how to do both better.

While some see theory as a barrier to effective action, in fact it is a necessary, if usually tacit, precursor to such action. In this context, the adjustment and adaptation model refines our understanding of the significance and functional role of public relations in organizations by moving the boundaries of practice beyond prescriptive, journalistic output toward a new horizon of responsibilities linked to management decision making. In this role, the boundary-spanning nature of public relations creates a core operational activity that serves as a "mind in the middle" to provide critical monitoring and knowledge management functions through which the organization interprets its environment and creates sustainable relationships with stakeholders.

The adjustment and adaptation model, first built in this text two decades ago, anticipated the contemporary turn in sociology and the management disciplines to organizational ecology for describing the relationship of organizations to their social environments. Today, the insight offered by those early

statements of public relations as an applied discipline set within organizational ecology remains one of the essential challenges for building our discipline in the twenty-first century.

In applied social sciences like public relations, good theory also helps provide an understanding of the teaching and learning requirements that eventually become what philosopher T. S. Kuhn called the discipline's "textbook tradition." Here the adjustment and adaptation model clearly differentiates the education and training of students and practitioners from the discipline's journalistic past. The model establishes the tenet that the quality of communication between an organization and stakeholder publics is a necessary but insufficient requirement of good practice.

Perhaps more fundamentally, the model stipulates that good practice must include the capacity to monitor and interpret the organization's social environment. Under these terms, contemporary public relations education should emphasize construction of a professional "portfolio" that, in addition to writing skills, includes skills related to measurement, analysis, and predicative modelling. The implications of the adjustment and adaptation model are that such skills are critical to practitioners who are called on to describe, explain, and influence the nature of such realities as public opinion in the organization's social environment and cultural elements within the organization that are inertial barriers to adaptation.

Additionally, practitioners who must defend program strategy and related budgets do so by the capacity to measure the effects of public relations programs on target publics. Such skill sets require commitments to lifelong learning by practitioners whose work is inextricably linked to the challenging problems of social influence, organizational legitimacy, and collective behavior. Those problems ensure not only the viability of our discipline in the twenty-first century, but also the value of its central theoretical model.

Working on behalf of their organizations and in the public interest, public relations professionals are **agents** and **managers of change**, both inside and outside their organizations. They plan and facilitate organizational and social adjustment and adaptation using primarily communication, the topic of the next chapter.

NOTES

[1] Carol Kinsey Goman, "Energizing a Restructured Work Force," *Communication World* 14, no. 3 (February 1997): 55–57.

[2] Alvin Toffler, *The Third Wave* (New York: Bantam Books, 1980), paperback, 9. See also Toffler's *Future Shock*.

[3] Frederick Williams, *The New Communications*, 3d ed. (Belmont, CA: Wadsworth Publishing Company, 1992), 340.

[4] Howard Rosenberg, "Fighting Tooth and Claw: Ingrid Newkirk's Combative Style and Headline-Grabbing Stunts Have Shaken Up the Animal-Rights Movement," *Los Angeles Times Magazine*, March 22, 1992, p. 18.

[5] Jonathan D. Salant, Associated Press story published in the *San Diego Union-Tribune*, May 7, 1998, p. A–11.

[6] James G. Miller, *Living Systems* (New York: McGraw-Hill Book Company, 1978), 29–30.

[7] For more complete explications of these subsystems, see landmark books by Chris Argyris, *Integrating the Individual and the Organization* (New York: John Wiley and Sons, 1964), and Daniel Katz and Robert L. Kahn, *The Social Psychology of Organizations* (New York: John Wiley and Sons, 1966), 39–47.

[8] Harold L. Wilensky, *Organizational Intelligence: Knowledge and Policy in Government and Industry* (New York: Basic Books, 1967), 10.

[9] Thomas J. Peters and Robert H. Waterman Jr., *In Search of Excellence* (New York: Harper and Row, 1982), 12.

[10] R. Ashby, "Principles of the Self-Organizing System," in *Principles of Self-Organization*, ed. H. Von Foerster and G. W. Zopf (New York: Pergamon Press, 1962), 266.

[11] Siegfried F. Nadel, *Foundations of Social Anthropology* (London: Cohen and West, 1951), 375.

[12] Walter Buckley, *Sociology and Modern Systems Theory* (Englewood Cliffs, NJ: Prentice Hall, 1967), 14.

[13] Walter B. Cannon, *The Wisdom of the Body* (New York: W. W. Norton and Company, 1939), 24.

[14] Stephen W. Littlejohn, *Theories of Human Communication*, 7th ed. (Belmont, CA: Wadsworth/Thompson Learning, 2002), 45. Chapter 3 presents a good summary of systems concepts and their application to communication. The most complete reference on systems theory is Miller's previously cited 1,100-page *Living Systems*. More readable and probably most cited is Ludwig von Bertalanffy, *General Systems Theory: Foundations, Development, Applications*, rev. ed. (New York: George Braziller, 1968).

[15] Lotfi A. Zadeh, as quoted by George J. Klir, *Facets of Systems Science* (New York: Plenum Press, 1991), 143.

[16] Buckley, *Sociology and Modern Systems Theory*, 172–76. Cybernetic theory of self-regulating systems was first detailed in Norbert Wiener's *Cybernetics* (Cambridge, MA: MIT Press, 1948) and revised in a 1961 second edition (New York: John Wiley and Sons).

[17] William F. Buckley Jr., "Haut Boat," *Forbes FYI* (March 16, 1992), 88 and 90. The ship was renamed *Wind Surf* in 2000 (from *Club Med 1*).

[18] John H. Taylor, "Rip Van Weyerhaeuser," *Forbes* 148, no. 10 (October 28, 1992): 38–40. The story reported changes in top management, structure, and incentive programs to make the company more responsive and profitable.

[19] Billy Layne Smith, "When Oprah's Cattle Battle Came to Amarillo," *Public Relations Tactics* 5, no. 4 (April 1998): 1, 9, and 27.

[20] Steve Weiner, "Profit without Pollution," *Forbes* 139, no. 11 (May 18, 1987): 46.

[21] Sue H. Bell and Eugene C. Bell, "Public Relations: Functional or Functionary?" *Public Relations Review* 2, no. 2 (Summer 1976): 51–52.

[22] Ibid., 53.

[23] James E. Grunig and Larissa Schneider Grunig, "Toward a Theory of the Public Relations Behavior of Organizations: Review of a Program of Research," *Public Relations Research Annual* 1 (1989): 60.

[24] Stephen P. Robbins, *Organization Theory: Structure, Design, and Applications*, 3rd ed. (Englewood Cliffs, NJ: Prentice Hall, 1990), 207.

[25] James E. Grunig and Larissa A. Grunig, chapter 11, "Models of Public Relations and Communication," in *Excellence in Public Relations and Communication Management*, ed. James E. Grunig (Hillsdale, NJ: Lawrence Erlbaum Associates, 1992), 312.

[26] Buckley, *Sociology and Modern Systems Theory*, 47.

[27] Paul Sanchez, "Agents for Change," *Communication World* 14, no. 3 (February 1997): 53.

ADDITIONAL SOURCES

Adams, Tyrone L., and Norman E. Clark. *The Internet: Effective Online Communication.* New York: Thomson Wadsworth, 2001.

Cadwallader, Mervyn L. "The Cybernetic Analysis of Change in Complex Social Organizations." In *Communication and Culture: Readings In the Codes of Human Interaction*, edited by Alfred G. Smith, 396–401. New York: Holt, Rinehart and Winston, 1966.

Cancel, Amanda E., Glen T. Cameron, Lynne M. Sallot, and Michael A. Mitrook. "It Depends: A Contingency Theory of Accommodation in Public Relations." *Journal of Public Relations Research* 9, no. 1 (1997): 31–63. Presents a theory of sources of variance in the degree of accommodation in public relations practice, in contrast to Grunig's normative two-way symmetrical model.

Churchman, C. West. *The Systems Approach.* New York: Dell Publishing Co., 1979. Applies systems approach to management and decision making.

Dozier, David M., with Larissa A. Grunig and James E. Grunig. *Manager's Guide to Excellence in Public Relations and Communication Management.* Mahwah, NJ: Lawrence Erlbaum Associates, 1995. Deals with power and change in organizations, building linkages to and working with top management, and qualities of public relations excellence.

Grunig, Larissa A., James E. Grunig, and David M. Dozier, *Excellent Public Relations and Effective Organizations: A Study of Communication Management in Three Countries* (Mahwah, NJ: Lawrence Erlbaum Associates, 2002). Provides evidence supporting systems approach to public relations "excellence."

Hage, Jerald. *Theories of Organizations: Form, Process, and Transformation.* New York: John Wiley and Sons (Wiley-Interscience), 1980. Classic work on organizations as adaptive systems.

Heath, Robert L., and Douglas D. Abel. "Proactive Response to Citizen Risk Concerns: Increasing Citizens' Knowledge of Emergency Response Practices." *Journal of Public Relations Research* 8, no. 3 (1996): 151–71.

Knoke, William. *Bold New World: The Essential Road Map to the Twenty-First Century.* New York: Kodansha America, 1996). Investment banker's optimistic views about how social, political, and technological changes will change assumptions about place, time, space, organizations, relationships, government, and work.

Kotter, John P. *Leading Change*. Boston: Harvard Business School Press, 1996. Outlines eight-step process for organizational change, as well as the obstacles communicators and managers must overcome in change efforts.

Kuhn, Alfred J. *Organizational Cybernetics and Business Policy: System Design for Performance Control*. University Park: Pennsylvania State University Press, 1986. Presents a seven-phase model for applying systems theory to the design and management of complex business organizations. Uses General Motors as a case study.

Monge, Peter R. "Systems Theory and Research in the Study of Organizational Communication: The Correspondence Problem." *Human Communication Research* 8 (Spring 1982): 245–61.

Rapoport, Anatol. *General Systems Theory: Essential Concepts and Applications*. Tunbridge Wells, UK: Abacus, 1985.

8 COMMUNICATION AND PUBLIC OPINION

No human capability has been more fundamental to the development of civilization than the ability to collect, share, and apply knowledge. Civilization has been possible only through the process of human communication.

—Frederick Williams[1]

STUDY GUIDE

After studying Chapter 8, you should be able to:

- Outline the tasks of public relations communications in the crowded message environment.

- Define communication as a two-way process taking place within intrapersonal, interpersonal, and social contexts.

- Diagram the communication model, and label and briefly discuss its elements.

- Describe the main theories of mass media effects that underpin public relations communication.

- List and briefly discuss the effects of public relations communication.

- Identify and discuss the five dimensions of public opinion.

- Define an attitude and an opinion and distinguish between them.

- Diagram and explain the model of individual orientation and the model of coorientation.

- Define the four states of coorientational consensus.

The force of public opinion has steadily gained strength around the world as mass communication has become a global phenomenon. Governments and institutions formerly somewhat isolated from the glare of media attention and public scrutiny now see their actions or inaction reported via international news media. For example, international pressure was marshaled against Afghanistan after media reports confirmed the existence of terrorist training camps and support of terrorist movements.

Other issues, however, fail to catch the attention of busy, distracted, and media-saturated publics. For example, the war in western Sudan failed to capture much attention, even while the country's militia employed a "scorched earth policy," committed genocidal atrocities, and turned their backs on crimes against humanity.[2] More than a million Sudanese refuges fled as the crisis worsened, many crossing the border to Chad for protection. This chapter provides a theoretical framework for understanding why certain communications are more or less effective than others.

Practically instantaneous global media coverage is possible today, making mass communication a rapidly changing and far-reaching phenomenon. Satellite signals and the Internet carry images of bombed buildings, starving children, and terrorist beheadings, causing a convergence of attention on events around the world. Who can forget the image of a lone student blocking a column of military tanks in Beijing's Tiananmen Square? Nor could the world audience ignore video of the destruction of Saddam Hussein statures after the fall of Baghdad. Media have expanded the "world outside" and increased the number of "pictures in our heads," to borrow from Walter Lippmann.[3] The media themselves have multiplied to the point that competition for audience attention has never been greater. The nature of "news" itself has changed, as competitive mass media outlets pursue even-more unique, distant, novel, interesting, and sensational information.

THE BATTLE FOR ATTENTION

In the United States alone, book publishers issue more than 60,000 new titles each year. During the same period, a typical U.S. child watches television for 1,023 hours, including about 40,000 television commercials. By age 18, the typical person has seen 16,000 television murders.[4] There are at least 150,000 magazines and periodicals in the United States, 13,476 radio stations, almost 12,000 daily and weekly newspapers, about 1,300 television stations, ubiquitous signage and billboard advertising, Internet pop-ups, and new media technologies too numerous to count.[5] Each competes for audience attention. Estimating how many messages each of us is exposed to each day by all these media has become a complex game of probabilities. No doubt each of us is exposed to hundreds, even thousands, of messages each day.

You chose to read this section of *Effective Public Relations*, but more likely during the rest of the day you are exposed to many more messages, most of which you do not seek out. You probably screen out many because you have little or no interest in the content. You skip some because you do not have time to pay attention. You miss others simply because you are preoccupied with something else and "tune out." In short, your attention is the object of fierce competition. The contenders are endless varieties of advertisers, news media, and entertainment media. To defend against the onslaught of attention seekers, you may become choosy, even resistant. As a result of this onslaught of messages and information overload, few messages get your attention. Even fewer have an impact. No wonder one communication scholar refers to "the obstinate audience."[6]

Public relations communications compete in this crowded message environment. The first task is to get the **attention** of target publics. The second is to stimulate *interest* in message content. The third is to build a **desire** and **intention** to act on the message.

And the fourth is to direct the **action** of those who behave consistent with the message. Unfortunately, the communication process is not as simple as many apparently believe.

DISSEMINATION VERSUS COMMUNICATION

The myth of communication suggests that sending a message is the same as communicating a message. In essence, dissemination is confused with **communication.** This confusion is apparent in public relations when practitioners offer media placements (clippings and broadcast logs) as evidence that communication has occurred. These practitioners probably subscribe to the communication model introduced by information scientists Shannon and Weaver, based on their work for Bell Telephone Laboratories in the late 1940s.[7]

Shannon and Weaver's model consists of an information source, message or signal, channel, and receiver or destination. Not surprisingly, because of their telephone perspective, the communication process produces relatively few and simple problems. **Technical** problems arise when the signal or channel limits or distorts the message being transmitted from the source to the sender. **Semantic** problems occur when the receiver's perception of the message and meaning are not the same as those intended by the sender. **Influence** problems indicate that the sender's message did not produce the desired result on the part of the receiver. As Weaver wrote,

> The questions to be studied in a communication system have to do with the amount of information, the capacity of the communication channel, the coding process that may be used to change a message into a signal and the effects of noise.[8]

But as public relations practitioners will tell you, communication with target publics is much more complicated than this set of questions suggests. As the late Wilbur Schramm pointed out, communication is complicated by people:

> Communication (*human* communication, at least) is *something people do*. It has no life of its own. There is no magic about it except what people in the communication relationship put into it. There is no meaning in a message except what the people put into it. When one studies communication, therefore, one studies people—relating to each other and to their groups, organizations, and societies, influencing each other, being influenced, informing and being informed, teaching and being taught, entertaining and being entertained—by means of certain signs which exist separately from either of them. To understand the human communication process one must understand how people relate to each other.[9]

This is no simple task. In fact, Schramm's concept of communication requires a two-way-process model in which sender and receiver operate within the contexts of their respective frames of reference, their relationship, and the social situation.

As Figure 8.1 illustrates, **communication is a reciprocal process of exchanging signals to inform, persuade, or instruct, based on shared meanings and conditioned by the communicators' relationship and the social context.**

The process of **informing** involves four steps: (1) attracting attention to the communication, (2) achieving acceptance of the message, (3) having it interpreted as intended, and (4) getting the message stored for later use. The more demanding process of **instruction** adds a fifth step: stimulating active learning and practice. The

> **Communication is a reciprocal process of exchanging signals to inform, persuade, or instruct, based on shared meanings and conditioned by the communicators' relationship and the social context.**

FIGURE 8.1

COMMUNICATION PROCESS MODEL

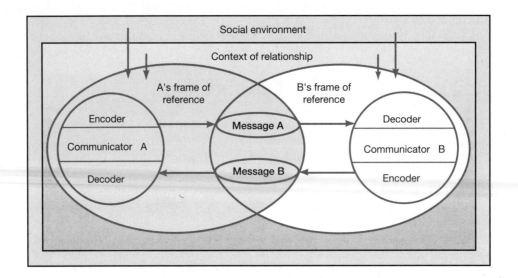

process of **persuasion** goes beyond active learning to a sixth step—accepting change: yielding to the wishes or point of view of the sender. Clearly, barriers to achieving the outcomes of informing, instruction, and persuasion increase with the addition of the fifth and sixth steps in the processes.[10]

ELEMENTS OF THE COMMUNICATION MODEL

Early communication researchers studied the individual elements in the communication process model to determine the effect of each on the effectiveness of the process. Most studies dealt with persuasion as the desired outcome, but more recent studies have expanded the range of effects studied.

The Sender

Characteristics of message sources affect receivers' initial acceptance of the message but have little effect on long-term message impact. Hovland and his colleagues called this long-term source impact the "sleeper effect."[11] For example, according to the theory of source credibility and attractiveness, safe-sex messages promoting prevention of HIV infection among college students are more readily accepted as believable when presented by highly credible sources, such as a recognized medical authority, than when presented by peers.

More recent research suggests both short-term and long-term source impact. Source credibility amplifies the value of information, according to one scholar. The theory suggests that the perceived status, reliability, and expertness of the source add weight to messages. Multiplying the three source characteristics by each other yields the weight factor of the source in the communication process.[12]

Researchers have concluded that although source characteristics affect the communication process, their impact varies from situation to situation, from topic to topic, and from time to time. At a minimum, however, source characteristics affect receivers' initial receptivity to messages.

The Message

Message characteristics surely have an impact in the communication process, but many communication scholars agree that "meaning is in people, not words." This observation leads naturally to the conclusion that different people receiving the same message may interpret it differently, attribute different meanings to it, and react to it in different ways. All the same, message characteristics can have powerful effects, even if they do not conform to simple and direct cause-and-effect explanations. As suggested by the notion of the obstinate audience, message effects are mediated by receivers, thereby frustrating the search for rules that apply in all communication situations.

Early persuasion research on message characteristics produced few such rules, but did provide guidance still used in public relations today. For instance, if you wish to persuade, should the message contain only one side of the issue, or should it address both sides of an argument? Research findings generally support the following recommendations:

1. If receivers oppose your position, present arguments on both sides of the issue.
2. If receivers already agree with your position, your message will have greater impact—probably reinforcement—if you present only arguments consistent with the receivers' views.
3. If receivers are well educated, include both sides of the argument.
4. If you use messages containing both sides of the argument, do not leave out relevant arguments on the opposing side, or receivers who notice the omission will grow suspicious of your presentation.[13]
5. If receivers are likely to be exposed later to persuasive messages countering your position, use two-sided messages to "inoculate" the audience to build resistance to the later messages.[14]

Research on message effects suggests that gaining compliance is a complicated process, however. If the message source has little power or control to exercise over the receiver, then persuasion becomes the primary strategy. If, on the other hand, the sender has power or control, then instruction or direction becomes the relevant strategy. Researchers list four major approaches to gaining compliance through communication:

1. *Sanction strategies* use rewards and punishments controlled by the sender, the receiver, or the result of the situation.
2. *Altruism strategies* call upon the receiver to comply so as to help or come to the aid of the sender or some third party represented by the sender.
3. *Argument strategies* employ (a) **direct requests**, in which the sender does not give the receiver the rationale or motivation for the request; (b) **explanations**, in which the sender gives the receiver one or more reasons for complying; and (c) **hints**, in which the sender sets up the situation or suggests circumstances from which the receiver draws the desired conclusion and compliance.
4. *Circumvention* strategies misrepresent the situation, give false rationales, or promise rewards and punishments not within the sender's power to deliver.[15]

Research on the impact of message characteristics supports the general conclusion from the previous section: Message impact is mediated or conditioned by receivers. For example, the classic study of order of presentation—"primacy" versus "recency"—demonstrated that the first part of the message has the greatest effect on receivers with low initial interest. The last part of the message has the greatest effect on those with high initial interest.[16]

Another line of message research initiated by Hovland and his associates at Yale deals with the use of fear to achieve compliance. After conducting an experiment using messages about dental hygiene, Janis and Feshbach concluded that low-fear messages produce more compliance than do high-fear messages. High-fear messages apparently produce defensive reactions in the receiver that led to distortion, denial, or rejection of the message.[17] Some recent research on fear appeals, however, suggests a much more complicated relationship in which several factors influence the relationship between fear messages and subsequent compliance.

For example, high-fear messages about the dangers of smoking and of venereal disease, when combined with believable recommendations, produce high scores on intended compliance. Three factors affect the impact of fear messages: (1) the seriousness or harmfulness of the subject, (2) the likelihood or probability of the feared event, and (3) the efficacy of the recommended course of action. Apparently receivers evaluate fear-producing messages on these three characteristics before making a decision to adopt recommended courses of action. Researchers refer to this decision process as "protection motivation."[18]

You can see many highly effective fear-based messages today around public health issues. For example, the Truth campaign against smoking uses fear appeals based on scientific evidence in a minor-friendly, animated format.[19] In the final analysis, however, many characteristics of the source, receiver, and communication situation mediate the impact of messages on receivers. One writer concluded,

> When main-effect findings demonstrated relationships between the selected variable and some measure of attitude/behavior change, additional variables such as source characteristics, power, and receiver variables were investigated.[20]

The Medium or Channel

New technologies for delivering messages challenge conventional wisdom. For example, in many organizations, e-mail has changed communication within organizations and even across national boundaries. For example, meetings take place in a variety of virtual or digital formats, changing the nature of the interaction but providing benefits in cost and convenience.

Communication scholars and practitioners historically have considered face-to-face interpersonal communication the most direct, powerful, and preferred method for exchanging information. In contrast with mass communication, interpersonal communication involves as few as two communicators (typically in close proximity), uses many senses, and provides immediate feedback. This description of the interpersonal communication situation, however, does not take into account the possibility that mass media messages may be directed to only a few in a very specific public. Likewise, physical proximity can be less important than the nature of the relationship between communicators, what one scholar calls the "intimacy-transcends-distance phenomenon." What begins as impersonal communication when people initially exchange messages can become interpersonal communication as the communicators develop a relationship.[21]

Extending time and distance, however, often requires using message delivery systems other than in-person presentations. In much of contemporary society, face-to-face contacts give way to mediated transmissions. Spoken words give way to written communication. Individually addressed letters give way to printed messages. Printed publications give way to broadcast words and pictures. Broadcast messages give way to networks of computers carrying digital signals translated into all manner of information. Choosing the right *medium* (singular) or *media* (plural) requires an understanding of media and media effects.

The Receivers

Communication models—and public relations programs—often mistakenly consider the audience passive recipients at the end of a message transmission process. This tradition continues even though research evidence and constant references to "two-way" suggest a different model and role for the audience.

In early mass communication studies, however, mass society audiences were viewed as vulnerable to messages and media manipulated by those in control. Critics saw people as alienated and isolated from the kind of strong social and psychological forces found in traditional societies, as a consequence of industrialization, urbanization, and modernization. However, the evidence gathered on audience effects suggests a more active receiver. The Yale persuasion experiments demonstrated that receivers are not uniformly influenced by messages designed to change attitudes. For example, receivers who value group membership are relatively unaffected by messages espousing positions counter to those of the group. Those who are persistently aggressive toward others tend to be resistant to persuasive messages. On the other hand, receivers with low self-esteem and feelings of social inadequacy are influenced more by persuasive messages than are people with high self-esteem and feelings of indifference toward others.[22] These differences in impact place a great responsibility on the communicator to target messages to specific and well-defined publics.

In short, the notion of a monolithic and passive mass audience does not describe reality. A more accurate description suggests selected active receivers processing messages designed for the few, not the masses:

> Since audiences are known to be evasive at best and recalcitrant at worst, efforts are directed at targeting messages for different audience segments and promoting audience involvement wherever possible.[23]

Context of the Relationship

Communication occurs within the context of the communicators' relationship. The range of such relationships includes close and intimate relationships as well as formal, competitive, and conflictual interpersonal relationships in a variety of settings. The point, of course, is that the **relationship** itself affects much about the communication process.

All relational communication reflects four basic dimensions: (1) emotional arousal, composure, and formality; (2) intimacy and similarity; (3) immediacy or liking; and (4) dominance–submission.[24] For example, your supervisor announces changes in scheduled work hours for student assistants without consulting with the students (the first dimension just listed) by posting the new schedule on the office bulletin board (the second dimension). The notice also expresses the supervisor's hope that the new schedule does not inconvenience any of the assistants (the third dimension) but indicates that the supervisor has the power to establish work schedules (the fourth dimension).

Not surprisingly, nonverbal behaviors play important roles in relational communication. **Proximity** communicates intimacy, attraction, trust, caring, dominance, persuasiveness, and aggressiveness. **Smiling** communicates emotional arousal, composure, formality, intimacy, and liking. **Touching** suggests intimacy. **Eye contact** intensifies the other nonverbal behaviors.[25] Obviously, these interpretations of nonverbal behaviors do not take cultural differences into account. For example, in Navajo and some Asian cultures, eye contact can be interpreted as a sign of disrespect or challenge. In some cultures, touching in public is taboo.

Whether verbal or nonverbal, communication in relationships helps the parties make predictions about others in the relationship. Communication reduces uncertainty about the probable outcomes of future exchanges and provides a basis for the continuing relationship. Understanding the communication process, however, requires not only an understanding of the relationship between the communicators but also the larger social context within which communication occurs.

The Social Environment

Communication affects and is affected by the social setting. Thus, communication occurs as a structured process within evolving systems of related components and activities. Social systems include families, groups, organizations, and all kinds of collectivities that are at the same time both producers and products of communication.

For example, when people think they can achieve something through joint action that they cannot accomplish individually, they form groups. Communication in groups depends on the nature of the group (primary versus secondary, formal versus informal, task-oriented versus experiential), characteristics of group members, group size, group structure, group cohesiveness, and group purpose.[26]

Successful group decision making requires accomplishing four tasks: (1) developing an adequate and accurate assessment of the problem, (2) developing a shared and complete understanding of the goal and the criteria for success, (3) agreeing on the positive outcomes of decisions, and (4) agreeing on the negative outcomes of decisions. Decision-making effectiveness, therefore, depends on the extent to which members' communication helps achieve these group functions.[27]

Organizations impose additional layers of complexity and constraints on communication. Forces at play in the larger society affect how all communicators—individuals, groups, and organizations—approach their publics, shape the content of their messages, define communication goals, and condition audience responses. Recall our ongoing connection to systems theory: All elements of a system are interdependent and mutually influenced by forces in their environment. In short, communication—when it occurs—results from a complex reciprocal process in which communicators try to inform, persuade, or negotiate within the contexts of their relationships and the larger social setting.

COMMUNICATION EFFECTS

Communication effects have long been the object of concern and study. The range of effects runs the gamut from early concerns about "all-powerful" media to "no effects." Hypothesized unlimited effects of movies on helpless children motivated the Payne Fund studies of the 1920s. Maybe critics simply feared too much. After ambitious public persuasion and political campaigns in the 1940s and 1950s produced disappointing results, many concluded that mass communication has almost no impact. Maybe the campaign planners simply asked too much of mass communication. More recent evidence supports theories in which mass communication effects occur under specified conditions. Apparently, the answer depends on what question you ask.

Creating Perceptions of the World around Us

Early theorists cast mass communication in the role of telling us about events, things, people, and places we could not experience directly ourselves. Walter Lippmann said it best when he wrote about "the world outside and the pictures in our heads." He described a "triangular relationship" between the scene of action (interpreted to include people, places, actions, and the entire range of possible phenomena), perceptions of that scene, and responses based on the perceptions. The last side of the triangle is complete when the responses have impact on the original scene of action. Mass media fit in the model between the scene of action and audience perceptions (see Figure 8.2).[28]

Lippmann pointed out that most of us cannot or do not have direct access to much of the world; it is "out of reach, out of sight, out of mind." The mass media help us create a "trustworthy picture" of the world that is beyond our reach and direct experience. His notions of media impact on public perceptions not only set the stage for studying mass communication effects but also arguably established the conceptual basis for much of what later became public relations.

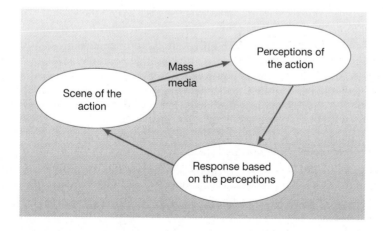

FIGURE 8.2

MASS MEDIA IN PUBLIC OPINION FORMATION

Source: Based on "triangular relationship" in Walter Lippmann, *Public Opinion* (New York: Harcourt, Brace and Company, 1927), pp. 16–17.

Setting the Agenda

The "agenda-setting" theory of mass communication effects builds on Lippmann's notion of media impact by distinguishing between *what we think about* and *what we think*. The difference is that the former includes what we know about (cognition) whereas the latter refers to our opinions and feelings (predisposition). Agenda setting suggests that mass media can have substantial and important impact on the cognitive level without affecting predisposition.[29] But it should be clear that even if media are limited to this one effect, setting the agenda is not a trivial consequence.

For example, early explorations of agenda setting by the press during presidential elections found that relative media emphasis on issues has a cumulative effect on the electorate. The same issues, with the same relative emphasis as that given by the media, make up the voters' agenda. In other words, the issues considered least to most important by voters reflect patterns of media coverage rather than a particular political agenda. Furthermore, the relative number of people concerned about issues parallels the relative media emphasis of those issues. Media and public agendas were most similar during the early stages of the campaign and for those issues least likely to be within peoples' direct experience.[30]

Imagine the potential consequences of media agenda setting. First of all, media coverage can elevate the public standing of issues, people, organizations, institutions, and so forth. Second, changes in the amount of media attention can lead to changes in public priorities. Third, the more concerned people are about something, the more they tend to learn about it, the stronger their opinions are of it, and the more they tend to take action on it. (Notice, however, that the agenda-setting theory does not predict what information they will seek, which way their opinions will change, or what types of actions they will take.) Fourth, media coverage can affect the agenda priorities of some specific and important publics, such as legislators, regulators, and other policy makers.

In summary, mass communication can affect public opinion by raising the salience of issues and positions taken by people and groups in the news.[31] Furthermore, like Lippmann's theory of media effects, the agenda-setting theory contributes to the conceptual foundation for public relations mass communication.

For public relations practitioners, getting an issue onto the media agenda can be a good thing (i.e., when you want to raise awareness of an issue) or a bad thing (e.g., when something embarrassing, dangerous, or illegal happens at your organization). Being aware of the power of media agenda setting is a key to the strategic management of public relations communication. Public relations can contribute tremendously to the effectiveness of the organization when it carefully and strategically considers its own issues in regard to the media agenda. Oftentimes, public relations saves an organization money and resources by resolving a problem before it gets onto the media agenda. In other instances, getting an issue onto the media agenda is a crucial part of press agentry and a valuable method of creating symmetrical dialogue on an issue.

Two concepts in agenda-setting theory and research are especially useful in public relations:

1. *Issue salience* determines the **prominence** and **penetration** the issue has with the audience, or how well it **resonates** with each public. People care the most about issues that are close to their own interests. Researchers found that frequency of discussion was the single largest predictor of issue salience. Interpersonal communication enhanced the agenda-setting effect of the media or interfered with the agenda-setting effect when the interpersonal discussion conflicts with media content.[32]

2. *Cognitive priming* describes the **personal experience** or **connection** someone has with an issue. Researchers thought that a person with little or no personal experience on an issue must rely on the media for information. Scholars initially expected to find that the media had weak or no agenda-setting effect on issues with which people had personal experience. Quite to the contrary, they found support for the cognitive priming hypothesis, which states that previous or personal exposure to an issue **stimulates** interest in that issue's media coverage, thus **enhancing** the agenda-setting effects.[33]

Researchers McCombs and Shaw reformulated and expanded agenda-setting theory, stating, "**Media not only tell us what to think about, but how to think about it, and, consequently, what to think**."[34] Indeed, this new theory of mediated, powerful effects provides a promising theoretical framework for application in the practice of public relations.

Diffusing Information and Innovation

Beyond setting the issue agenda, research in a variety of settings shows that mass communication facilitates social interaction and change. Sources may come from different social, economic, and educational backgrounds but are accessible through the media. The media, then, provide information from sources that would otherwise not be available through interpersonal networks in which "like talks to like." Once people get information from the media, however, they enter conversations armed with useful new information. What we learn from the mass media often determines what we talk about with others, providing the common ground needed to begin conversation: "Did you see in this morning's paper that …?" or "Can you believe Jay Leno already announced his retirement?" In effect, mass media provide information to those who seek it and supply information needed for subsequent interpersonal communication, thereby diffusing information to others.[35]

Diffusion of information and innovation theory explains this process. Characteristics of innovation—or new ideas—as well as characteristics of the adopters influence the adoption process. Ideas or innovations are more readily adopted if they are (1) more advantageous than the current situation, (2) compatible with previous experience and other aspects of the situation, (3) simple, (4) easily tried, and (5) observable with readily apparent outcomes. "Innovators" are the first to adopt new ideas, followed by "early adopters," "early majority," "late majority," and "laggards." Characteristics of the individuals in each of the categories vary with the nature of change being adopted and the context.[36]

Diffusion and adoption processes illustrate the impact that mass communication has on interpersonal communication and networks. More important, they show how mass and interpersonal communication interact in social systems and in social change.

Defining Social Support

"Spiral of silence" theory suggests a phenomenon commonly referred to as "the silent majority." Individuals who think their opinion conflicts with the opinions of most other people tend to remain silent on an issue. Carried to an extreme, even if a majority actually agree but do not individually recognize social support, their silence and inactivity can lead to the erroneous conclusion that not many people support a particular view. On the other hand, individuals who think that many others share

FIGURE 8.3

SOCIOCULTURAL MODEL OF PERSUASION

Source: Melvin L. DeFleur and Sandra J. Ball-Rokeach, Theories of Mass Communication, 4th ed. (New York: Longman, 1982), p. 225.

their view, or that the number of people who agree is growing rapidly are more likely to express their views. Under these conditions, a vocal minority that sees itself on the winning side can appear to represent a widely shared perspective. In either case, as Lippmann pointed out more than 50 years before the spiral of silence theory, people "respond as powerfully to fictions as they do to realities, and ... in many cases they help to create the very fictions to which they respond."[37]

In essence, public opinion arises as individuals collectively discern support for their views through personal interaction and by attending to the mass media. Individuals observe and assess their social environments, estimating the distributions of opinions, evaluating the strength and chances of success for each, and determining the social sanctions and costs associated with each. The spiral begins when individuals choose to remain silent or decide to express their views. It continues as others observe the presence or absence of support for their own views. It gains apparent legitimacy when increasing numbers of individuals translate their observations into either public silence or expression. It is reinforced when the media cover the views being displayed most forcefully and most frequently and do not make an effort to determine the actual distribution of views.

Media coverage can reflect, enforce, or challenge the spiral of silence effect on public opinion. But understanding the dynamics of individuals' collective observations of their social environments and public opinion translates rather directly into public relations practice. Examples include public information campaigns designed to break the spirals of silence associated with domestic violence, sexual harassment, and stalking, to list only a few. In each instance, and for many other public issues, mass communication plays a key role in redefining socially accepted expression and behavior.

As illustrated in Figure 8.3, mass media messages can provide individuals pictures of their social environment, of whether there is social approval or disapproval of their views or actions. This "sociocultural model" of communication effects suggests that "messages presented via the mass media may provide the appearance of consensus regarding orientation and action with respect to a given object or goal of persuasion."[38]

PUBLICS AND THEIR OPINIONS

Nineteenth-century writer and first editor of *Atlantic Monthly* James Russell Lowell said, "The pressure of public opinion is like the atmosphere. You can't see it, but all the same it is sixteen pounds to the square inch." Lowell's words have even more relevance now. Public opinion has never been more powerful, more fragmented, more volatile, and more exploited and manipulated. For example, researchers studying U.S. presidential campaign coverage found ample evidence of "a powerful relationship between news media coverage and public opinion in presidential elections."[39]

Public opinion polls have long guided politics, government programs, entertainment programming, and even corporate decision making. In short, much as Lowell suggested, public opinion is an always-present, dynamic force. It is part of public relations' mission to help organizations recognize, understand, and deal with this powerful influence in their environments.

This is not an easy task, however. As the former vice president of AT&T said:

> Public opinion is not necessarily logical; it is amorphous, ambivalent, contradictory, volatile. Consequently, those of us who would hope to influence public opinion can only expect that our efforts, over time, may nudge the consensus toward some reasonable perception of the issues.[40]

Organizations of all types must deal with *real* and *perceived* public opinion as they establish and maintain relationships with their many internal and external publics. But organizations are the actors; public opinion is simply the "energizer" of their actions.

> (Public opinion) is … an expression of social energy that integrates individual actors into social groupings in ways that affect the polity. This understanding takes the concept of public opinion out of metaphysics and … avoids reducing it to a set of discrete individualized observations that cannot account for its composite sociopolitical significance.[41]

Definition of Public Opinion

The common notion of public opinion holds that it is simply the aggregation of individual views on some issue. This "individual agreement" approach to defining public opinion, however, misses the point that it is **public**. Individual cognition may or may not represent the **consensus**, or "thinking together," that more fully represents the kinds of opinions that form and are formed by public discussion among those sharing a "sense of commonness."

Thus, public opinion represents more than the collected views held by a particular category of individuals at one point in time. Public opinion is not adequately defined as simply a *state* of individual cognition. Instead, it reflects a dynamic *process* in which ideas are "expressed, adjusted, and compromised en route to collective determination of a course of action."[42] Public opinion is found among publics, or groups of communicating people who have some common interest. They collectively hold a view of an issue, why it is a cause for concern, and what can or should be done in the situation. The process is, unquestionably, ongoing.

In practice, however, both researchers and public relations practitioners take "snapshots" of public opinion, essentially freezing the process at one point in time so as to describe it and compare it with opinion at other times. Their surveys too often measure only direction and intensity, ignoring other important dimensions.

Direction of opinion indicates the evaluative quality of a predisposition, telling us the "positive-negative-neutral," "for-against-undecided," or "pro-con-it-depends" evaluation of publics. In its simplest form, direction is a yes–no answer to a survey question. Media frequently report public opinion survey results as simply the percentages for or against some issue, proposition, or candidate. For example, stories reporting poll results, popularity, margin, and other indicators of the direction of public opinion about the candidates dominated coverage of the 1996 U.S. presidential campaign, comprising 38 percent of all stories.[43] (Character stories were second at 18 percent.) Direction clearly represents the most basic and most frequently used measure of public opinion.

Intensity measures show how strongly people feel about their opinions, whatever the direction. For example, pollsters ask registered voters to indicate "on a scale of 1 to 10" how strongly they felt about a wide range of issues related to the election. Likewise, surveys often ask respondents to indicate whether they "strongly disagree / disagree / neutral / agree / strongly agree" with a statement. This question format is a common means of measuring both direction and intensity of feelings. Intensity measures provide an initial estimate of the relative strength of predisposition. Intensity and direction are often reported to indicate not only how people feel about issues, but also how deeply they hold the feelings. For instance, the issue of abortion commonly polarizes publics based on the intensity of their beliefs.

Stability refers to how long respondents have held or will hold the same direction and intensity of feelings. Measures of stability require observations taken at two or more points in time. Think of this dimension as something like the charts that track stock prices or temperature patterns over time. In effect, the stability measure provides evidence of how reactive public opinion is to events or other information.

Informational support refers to how much knowledge people hold about the object of opinion. For example, voters who have little information about candidates tend to focus on who they see as being involved or associated with a candidate and how they think the candidate would affect them personally. Better-informed voters, in contrast, "are more likely to ignore consideration of the specific groups involved in favor of a more general interpretation of the issue."[44]

Other researchers studying a mayoral election found that those more informed about issues hold stronger opinions about the issues, but the direction of the opinions is not easily predicted. Furthermore, those with more knowledge and strong opinions are more likely to vote and to contact local officials.[45]

Absence of "information mass" behind an opinion on relatively nonpartisan issues may indicate that the direction and intensity are susceptible to change. For example, if Monsanto finds that public opinion against field testing of genetically engineered plants is not well informed, the company could mount a public information campaign designed to educate community members about the risks and benefits involved, taking care to frame the messages in the context of who is affected and involved (including the consensus views of community leaders), as well as how the field tests will affect those in the community—potential risks (if any) and benefits.

Social support measures provide evidence of the extent to which people think their opinions are shared by others in their social milieu. The persuasion model in Figure 8.3 (page 206) indicates the power of perceptions of social approval or disapproval. Pollsters probing this dimension of public opinion ask respondents to report their impressions of what significant others think about an issue or to estimate the distribution of public opinion on the issue under study. In effect, measures of social support show how people define the nature of the consensus on issues.

The social context of opinion may be simply the tendency to think that other people are more influenced by media or events than ourselves. Researchers have found "third-person effects"—people tend to underestimate media impact on themselves and overestimate impact on others. Such effects could have consequences in how public policy is determined (protecting those perceived to be vulnerable others), or how political campaigns are conducted (influencing easily persuaded voters). "So the third-person effect may have a number of behavioral implications, even though it is basically a perceptual phenomenon."[46]

Think of both informational and social support as giving predisposition weight and inertia. If, for example, people with a strong opinion on an issue hold a lot of information—pro and con—about that issue and see their particular position as being widely shared, then the direction and expression of the opinion are not likely to change. Just as the direction of a bowling ball is little affected by the air movement created by an air conditioner, opinions with much informational and social support have great mass and are not susceptible to easy or quick change. On the other hand, even strongly held opinions can change if they are not backed by information and perceived social support. They can change direction as frequently and rapidly as a hurricane!

Describing and understanding public opinion requires greater measurement sensitivity and depth than the simple yes–no questions often used in telephone polling. Public opinion reflects a dynamic process of interpersonal and media communication on issues among groups of people who have the capacity to act in similar ways. "Thinking together" often leads to "acting together," the real reason for understanding public opinion.

Publics

First of all, **practitioners of public relations must discard notions about "the general public."** Sociographic and demographic variables, such as age, education, and income, naturally segment society into very large groups. Add to that the many different ethnic, racial, religious, geographic, political, occupational, social, and special-interest groupings and the result is that the concept of a general or mass public holds little, if any, value in public relations. Rather, effective programs communicate and build relationships with **specifically defined "target publics"** or **"strategic publics."** Without such specific definitions and detailed information about intended audiences of messages, how do program planners measure public opinion, establish program objectives, develop meaningful message and action strategies, select media to deliver messages selectively and effectively, and determine whether the program worked?

Philosopher and educator John Dewey defined a public as an active social unit consisting of all those affected who recognize a common problem for which they can seek common solutions. He wrote that publics are formed by "recognition of evil consequence brought about a common interest." Without communication, however, it "will remain shadowy and formless, seeking spasmodically for itself, but seizing and holding its shadow rather than its substance."[47]

Grunig expands Dewey's concept by outlining three factors that move **latent publics** to become communicating **active publics** through Grunig's situational theory of publics:

1. *Problem recognition* represents the extent to which people are aware that something is missing or amiss in a situation, thereby knowing that they need information.

2. *Constraint recognition* represents the extent to which people see themselves limited by external factors, versus seeing that they can do something about the

situation. If people think they can make a difference or have an effect on the problem situation, they will seek information to make plans for action.

3. *Level of involvement* represents the extent to which people see themselves being involved and affected by a situation. In other words, the more they see themselves connected to a situation, the more likely they will communicate about it.[48]

These three variables are measured against how active or passive the communication behavior of a public is. Active communication behavior is called **information seeking** because people in that group are likely to seek information on the issue. Passive communication behavior is called **information processing** because a passive audience may or may not attend to a message.

After testing his "situational theory of publics" on a variety of environmental issues, Grunig concludes that environmental publics defined according to their communication behavioral similarities are not the same as those identified by demographic attributes or attitudes.[49] He consistently finds four types of publics:

1. *All-issue publics* are active on all issues.
2. *Apathetic publics* are inattentive and inactive on all issues.
3. *Single-issue publics* are active on one or a limited number of related issues. (Such publics include "pro-life," environmental, and animal rights groups.)
4. *Hot-issue publics* are active after media expose almost everyone, and the issue becomes the topic of widespread social conversation. (Firestone's latest tire recall created publics after attracting extensive media attention.)[50]

As suggested by Grunig's situational theory of publics, messages must be individually tailored to fit the information needs of different publics, based on how active or passive their communication behavior is and what are issues of importance to them. Useful definitions of publics go beyond demographics or "psychographics" to include relevant indicators of common recognition of mutual interests and situational variables that tie certain individuals, but not others, to specific situations or issues. In other words, publics result from specific issues or situations, not shared cross-situational traits. Dewey said,

> [When] a church, a trade union, a business corporation, or an educational institution conducts itself so as to affect large numbers outside of itself, those who are affected form a public which endeavors to act through suitable structures, and thus to organize itself for oversight and regulation.[51]

Specific issues and situations determine each public's composition, size, and range of responses. For example, an organization's philanthropic donation to support construction of a controversial abstract sculpture in a park can activate many individuals to respond in a variety of ways. Some, if not most, of those who see themselves affected by the organization's charity probably have no direct contact with the organization making the donation and do not live near the park. On the other hand, if the same organization proposes a complex restructuring of its long-term debt, then probably only a few top executives who fear being presented early retirements, financial analysts, and institutional investors may respond to the proposed changes.

From the perspective of the publics that come into existence in the two situations, a wider range of publics and a greater number of people are moved to react in a variety of ways by the charitable contribution than by the restructuring proposal. It is conceivable, however, that the long-term "evil consequences" of financial restructuring will have a much greater impact on the community than will the existence of a piece of public art. For specific issues, specific publics arise that have differing information needs, values, and priorities than other publics of the same organization. For this reason, public relations practitioners target specific messages to strategic publics; they know that the public receiving the information will care about the issue and attend to the message.

INDIVIDUAL ORIENTATIONS AND COORIENTATION

The different publics and reactions stimulated by the two situations in the previous scenarios suggest both individual and shared orientations. Individual orientations, however, do not become public opinion until they are shared—or perceived to be shared—by others. The realization, rightly or wrongly, that an individual's views of a situation are similar to those held by others evokes a sense of identification among individuals and the perception of a common interest. In other words, individual orientations include perceptions of issues or objects in one's environment, as well as perceptions of significant others' views of those same issues or objects. When two or more individuals' orientations include the same issues or objects and each other, they are in a state of "coorientation."

Orientation

Individuals hold opinions of varying degrees of relevance and intensity. Individuals assign value to objects in their environment on the basis of both their previous history with the objects and their assessment of the objects in the current context (see Figure 8.4). The former value is **salience**, or the feelings about an object derived from an individual's experiences and reinforcements from previous situations.

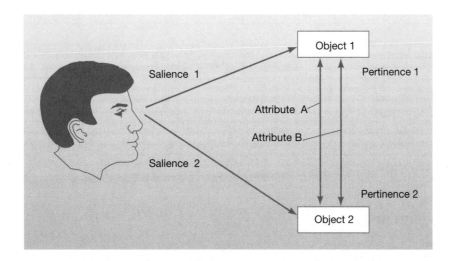

FIGURE 8.4

MODEL OF INDIVIDUAL ORIENTATION

Source: Adapted from Richard F. Carter, "Communication and Affective Relations." *Journalism Quarterly* 42, no. 2 (Spring) 1965, p. 204.

Salience refers to what the individual brings to a situation as a result of history. The second source of value is **pertinence**, which refers to the relative value of an object on the basis of object-by-object comparisons on the basis of some attribute or attributes. Pertinence value can vary depending on which attribute is used to make the comparison or what other objects are used in the comparison.[52] In other words, salience indicates how individuals feel about an object, independent of the situation, whereas pertinence depends on how the individual defines the situation. To describe and understand an individual's opinion about some object, then, you have to measure both salience and pertinence. The distinction helps clarify the relationship between attitudes and opinions.

An **attitude** is the cross-situational predisposition or preference with respect to an object. Attitudes predispose individuals to respond in certain ways toward objects from one situation to another, based on a lifetime of accumulating and evaluating information and experiences. Crespi substitutes "attitudinal system" when referring to what others call "attitude." He defines attitude systems as comprising of four components:

1. Evaluative frames of reference (values and interests)
2. Cognition (knowledge and beliefs)
3. Affection (feelings). Because many use the term *attitude* as referring only or primarily to the affective mode, whereas others use attitude more generally, an added benefit of adopting this nomenclature is that it avoids confusing the affective response mode with the entire system.
4. Conation (behavioral intentions)[53]

On the other hand, an opinion is the judgment expressed about an object in a particular situation or given a specific set of circumstances. Opinions tend to reflect an individual's related attitudes but also take into account aspects of the current situation.

Scholars have generally distinguished between attitudes and opinions in two ways:

> First, opinions are generally considered to be verbal, or otherwise overt responses to a specific stimulus (an issue), while attitudes are more basic global tendencies to respond favorably or unfavorably to a general class of stimuli. While opinions are largely situational, attitudes are more enduring with a person across situations. Second, opinions are considered to be more cognitive and somewhat less affective in their makeup....An attitude is an immediate, intuitive orientation while an opinion is a thought-out, reasoned choice between alternatives for action in a social matrix.[54]

The notion that opinions are expressed makes them important to the formation and study of public opinion. On the other hand, unexpressed intrapersonal predisposition does not affect *public* opinion formation. Not until attitudes are expressed through opinions in discussion or other public communication do they have an impact on the processes of forming and changing public opinion. That opinions are public expressions establishes public opinion as a social phenomenon.

Coorientation

The social or interpersonal concept of public opinion requires two or more individuals oriented to and communicating about an object of mutual interest. In other words, they are "cooriented" to something in common and to each other.

The coorientational model in Figure 8.5 illustrates the **intrapersonal** and **interpersonal** elements of communication relationships.[55] First, the intrapersonal construct of **congruency** describes the extent to which your own views match your estimate of another's views on the same issue. Some refer to this variable as "perceived agreement." On the basis of this estimate, you formulate strategies for dealing with the other person or for spontaneously responding in interactions.

The extent to which you accurately estimate another's views determines the appropriateness of your actions. Each of us recalls instances in which we misjudged another person's position on some issue of mutual interest and responded to them inappropriately until we learned what the person really thought about the issue. **Accuracy**, then, represents the extent to which your estimate matches the other person's actual views. Because it requires a comparison of observations taken from two different people, accuracy represents an interpersonal construct.

The other interpersonal constructs include **agreement** and **understanding**. Agreement represents the extent to which two or more persons share **similar evaluations** of an issue of mutual interest. Understanding measures the **similarities in the definitions** of two or more persons. In terms used in the individual orientation paradigm, agreement compares saliences, whereas understanding compares pertinences.

Coorientational Consensus

By including many individuals simultaneously oriented to issues of mutual concern and interest, the interpersonal coorientational model is extended to large social groupings.

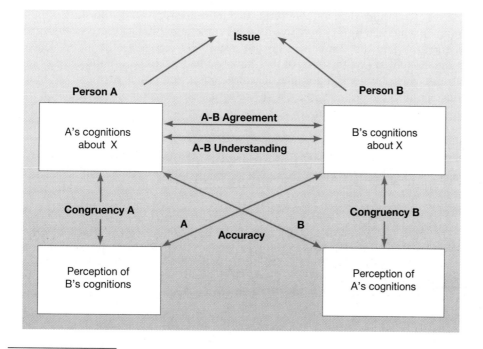

FIGURE 8.5

MODEL OF COORIENTATION

Source: Adapted from Jack M. McLeod and Steven H. Chaffee, "Interpersonal Approaches to Communication Research," in *Interpersonal Perception and Communication,* ed. Steven J. Chaffee and Jack M. McLeod, special edition of *American Behavioral Scientist,* 16, no. 4 (March–April 1973), pp. 483–88.

A coorientational concept of public opinion in communities and society provides an alternative to the usual psychological approaches to describing states of consensus.

First, the coorientational approach does not use the traditional "individual agreement" approach to describing public opinion, that is, an aggregation of individual orientations to some issue or topic. Instead, the coorientational approach casts public opinion as the product of both individual perceptions on an issue and their perceptions of what significant others think about the same issue.

Social scientists long ago recognized the need to take into account **perceptions of agreement** in addition to **actual agreement**. Scheff, for one, argued that perceptions of agreement can be independent of actual agreement and that perceptions of agreement more likely affect public behavior than does actual agreement. In fact, it is often the case that those involved in issues of public debate do not know the state of actual agreement, operating instead on their perceptions of agreement.[56]

Conceiving public opinion—or consensus—in this way makes it a complex social phenomenon that can be described using coorientational concepts. For example, the state of **monolithic consensus** represents high levels of actual agreement accurately recognized as such by those involved. **Dissensus** exists when high levels of actual disagreement are accurately perceived as such (see Table 8.1).

Public opinion based on inaccurate perceptions of agreement is more troublesome in relationships. Unlike actual agreement or disagreement, however, inaccurate perceptions are at least subject to change as a result of effective communication. For example, after extended interaction, two or more persons may simply agree to disagree. At least they each know where the other stands on the issue. The same cannot be said about situations based on inaccurate perceptions of each other's views.

False consensus exists when there is actual disagreement but the majority of those involved think they agree. **Pluralistic ignorance** represents the state of public opinion in which a majority perceive little agreement, but in fact there is widespread agreement. When those involved do not accurately recognize the state of actual agreement, they act on the basis of their inaccurate perceptions. In the cases of false consensus and pluralistic ignorance, their responses and public expressions (that is, public opinion) are not consistent with the actual distribution of individual orientations on issues of common interest. Accurate perceptions of others' views, however, are surely the most likely outcome of public communication and the greatest motivation for maintaining communication in society and in relationships.

What may appear as logical in the context of this discussion, however, apparently is not widely recognized by those who commission or practice public relations.

TABLE 8.1 TYPES OF COORIENTATIONAL CONSENSUS		**Perceives That Majority Also Agrees on Issue**	**Perceives That Majority Does not Agree on Issue**
	Majority actually agrees on issue	Monolithic Consensus	Pluralistic Ignorance
	Majority does not agree on issue	False Consensus	Dissensus

Source: Adapted from Thomas J. Scheff, "Toward a Sociological Model of Consensus," *American Sociological Review,* 32, no. 1 (February 1967), p. 39.

Instead of trying to increase the accuracy of cross perceptions in social relationships, most communication efforts attempt to influence levels of agreement or to "engineer consent." But actual agreement can exist independent of perceptions of agreement, leading to Scheff's more useful definition of coorientational public opinion:

> Complete consensus on an issue exists in a group [read "public"] when there is an infinite series of reciprocating understandings between the members of the group [read "public"] concerning the issue. I know that you know that I know, and so on.[57] (Words in brackets added.)

In the context of public relations, the coorientational approach to consensus and relationships is also useful for describing the nature of organization–public relationships.

Coorientational Relationships

The coorientational approach helps identify three public relations problems that call for rather straightforward communication strategies:

1. An organization and a public hold different definitions of an issue. They simply are not talking about the same thing when they engage in communication about "the issue." They are talking about different issues.

2. The organization's perceptions of a public's views of an issue (evaluations "and" or "or" definitions) do not match the public's actual views. Organizational management makes decisions about a public based on inaccurate estimates of the public's views. Not surprisingly, the relationship suffers when members of that public are subjected to the organization's actions and communications.

3. Members of a public hold inaccurate perceptions of an organization's positions on an issue of mutual concern. Public responses to the organization's management, its products, its actions and procedures, and so forth are based on inaccurate estimates of management policy and values.

Note that in all cases, the nature of the organization–public relationship is threatened by differing definitions and inaccurate perceptions, not by disagreement over the issue itself. None of the situations calls for communication designed to change the level of agreement–disagreement on the issue. Communication that helps create shared definitions and increase accuracy improves the relationship and makes each side's dealings with the other more appropriate (see Figure 8.6).

For example, even though the Army Corps of Engineers communicated the advantages of a proposed flood-control project to the various publics who would be affected, they apparently did not do the same for the project's disadvantages. Convinced that the various publics supported the project, the Corps scheduled what was to be the final public hearing for project approval. Project planners were surprised by the suspicions, concerns, objections, and uncertainties expressed at the hearing. The project was delayed for the additional meetings and negotiations needed to improve accuracy in both the Corps's and publics' perceptions of the project and each other's views.[58] Had the Corps initially used the coorientational approach to assess public opinion of the project, they might have identified their relationship problems and taken steps to avoid the costly delays.

FIGURE 8.6

COORIENTATIONAL
MODEL OF
ORGANIZATION–
PUBLIC RELATIONS

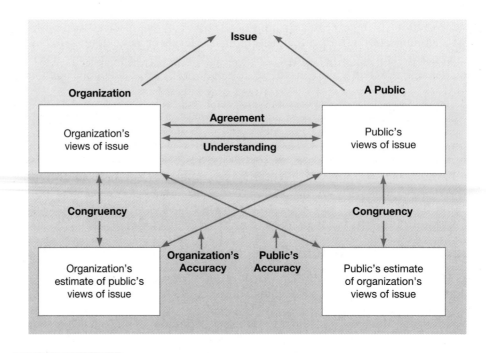

Source: Adapted from Jack M. McLeod and Steven H. Chaffee, "Interpersonal Approaches to Communication Research," in *Interpersonal Perception and Communication,* ed. Steven J. Chaffee and Jack M. McLeod, special edition of *American Behavioral Scientist,* 16, no. 4 (March–April 1973), pp. 483–88.

As this example illustrates, the coorientational approach serves three major purposes in public relations planning. First, coorientational measures provide the information needed to identify and describe problems in organization–public relationships. Rather than defining problems in ways that limit strategies to those designed to increase agreement by changing public perceptions, this approach calls for an assessment of all parties' views in order to understand relationships.

Second, coorientational measures provide useful guidance for planning appropriate messages and responses to correct organization–public relationship problems. Coorientational assessments of relationships can lead to atypical, yet efficient, solutions. For example, imagine that the analysis shows that management has an inaccurate perception of a public's views on an issue and as a result is proposing what will be an inappropriate action or response. Simply reporting the public's actual views on the issue to management may be the only corrective action needed.

Third, repeated use of coorientational measures indicates how the relationship changes as a result of the communication and other corrective actions. In other words, agreement, understanding, congruency, and accuracy serve as outcome criteria for assessing the impact of public relations efforts on organization–public relationships.[59]

In conclusion, public relations establishes and maintains relationships between organizations and their publics by—but not limited to—facilitating two-way communication. The communication, however, may have less impact on the extent to which parties agree or disagree than on the accuracy of their cross-perceptions of each other's views. In the final analysis, Lippmann's "pictures in our heads" of the "world outside" include our estimates of what others think. These perceptions of social reality lead to the formation of active publics and condition actions toward others, both other individuals and other organizations. Researchers studying how people interact with their computer, television, and new media arrived at the same conclusion: "What *seems* to be true is often more influential than what really is true.... *Perceptions* are far more influential than reality defined more objectively."[60] As Lippmann said, "That is why until we know what others think they know, we cannot truly understand their acts."[61]

Communication, then, not only moves information from one party in a relationship to another but also defines the relationships and social environment within which we all function: as citizens, employees, managers, and policy makers. Not surprisingly, the media of communication—the topic of the next two chapters—play essential roles in shaping both issues and their social contexts. Mass media make possible the thinking together that shapes and represents the states of consensus in complex organizations, in communities, and in the larger global society.

NOTES

[1] Frederick Williams, *The New Communications*, 3d ed. (Belmont, CA: Wadsworth Publishing Company, 1992), 9.

[2] Retrieved from www.AfricaFocus.org/docs04/sudo4o5a.php

[3] Walter Lippmann, *Public Opinion* (New York: Harcourt, Brace and Company, 1922), 3 and 4.

[4] Retrieved from www.tv-turnoff.org/factsheets.htm

[5] Retrieved from www.publist.com; www.mediauk.com/article/9761; personal communication with Rebecca Fisher of the FCC, Washington, D.C.

[6] Paul F. Lazarsfeld, Bernard Berelson, and Hazel Gaudet, *The People's Choice: How the Voter Makes Up His Mind in a Presidential Campaign*, 3d ed. (New York: Columbia University Press, 1968), 151.

[7] Warren Weaver, "The Mathematics of Communication," in *Communication and Culture: Reading in the Codes of Human Interaction*, ed. Alfred G. Smith (New York: Holt, Rinehart and Winston, 1966), 17. Reprinted from *Scientific American*, 181 (1949): 11–15. Original theory published in Claude E. Shannon and Warren Weaver, *The Mathematical Theory of Communication* (Urbana: University of Illinois Press, 1949).

[8] Ibid., 17.

[9] Wilbur Schramm, "The Nature of Communication Between Humans," in *The Process and Effects of Mass Communication*, rev. ed., ed. Wilbur Schramm and Donald F. Roberts (Urbana: University of Illinois Press, 1971), 17.

[10] Ibid., 38–47.

[11] Carl I. Hovland, Irving L. Janis, and Harold H. Kelley, *Communication and Persuasion* (New Haven: Yale University Press, 1953). The World War II "Yale studies" provided the foundation for persuasion theory still used for designing both persuasion effects research and public communication campaigns.

[12] Norman H. Anderson, "Integration Theory and Attitude Change," *Psychological Review* 78, no. 3 (May 1971): 171–206.

[13] Adapted from Carl I. Hovland, Arthur A. Lumsdaine, and Fred D. Sheffield, "The Effect of Presenting 'One Side' versus 'Both Sides' in Changing Opinions on a Controversial Subject," in *Experiments on Mass Communication*, 201–27 (Princeton: Princeton University Press, 1949). Also in Schramm and Roberts, *The Process and Effects of Mass Communication*, 467–84.

[14] Arthur A. Lumsdaine and Irving L. Janis, "Resistance to 'Counterpropaganda' Produced by One-Sided and Two-Sided 'Propaganda' Presentations," *Public Opinion Quarterly* 17, no. 3 (1953): 311–18. See also William J. McGuire, "Persuasion, Resistance, and Attitude Change," in *Handbook of Communication*, ed. Ithiel de Sola Pool and others, 216–52 (Skokie, IL: Rand McNally, 1973).

[15] Adapted from Richard L. Wiseman and William Schenck-Hamlin, "A Multidimensional Scaling Validation of an Inductively Derived Set of Compliance-Gaining Strategies," *Communication Monographs* 48, no. 4 (December 1981): 257–58.

[16] Carl I. Hovland, ed., *The Order of Presentation in Persuasion* (New Haven: Yale University Press, 1957). Reports series of experiments from the Yale studies of message effects in persuasion. The order of presentation, however, turned out to be a relatively minor factor in the communication process, inspiring little research over the years.

[17] Reported in Hovland, Janis, and Kelley, *Communication and Persuasion*.

[18] Ronald W. Rogers, "A Protection Motivation Theory of Fear Appeals and Attitude Change," *Journal of Psychology* 91 (September 1975): 93–114. See also Rogers and C. R. Mewborn, "Fear Appeals and Attitude Change: Effects of a Threat's Noxiousness, Probability of Occurrence, and the Efficacy of Coping Responses," *Journal of Personality and Social Psychology* 34, no. 1 (July 1976): 54–61.

[19] Retrieved from www.thetruth.com

[20] Michael Burgoon, "Messages and Persuasive Effects," in *Message Effects in Communication Science: Sage Annual Reviews of Communication Research* 17, ed. James J. Bradac (Newbury Park, CA: Sage Publications, 1989), 157.

[21] See Gerald R. Miller, "Interpersonal Communication," chapter 5 in *Human Communication: Theory and Research*, ed. Gordon L. Dahnke and Glen W. Clatterbuck, 91–122 (Belmont, CA: Wadsworth Publishing Company, 1990), for a review of interpersonal communication.

[22] Summary of "Developing Frameworks for Studying Mass Communication," chapter 1 in Lowery and DeFleur, *Milestones in Mass Communication Research*, 1–29.

[23] Brenda Dervin, "Audience as Listener and Learner, Teacher and Confidante: The Sense-Making Approach," in *Public Communication Campaigns*, 2d ed., ed. Ronald E. Rice and Charles K. Atkin (Newbury Park, CA: Sage Publications, 1989), 69.

[24] See Chapter 7, "The Relationship," in Stephen W. Littlejohn and Karen A. Foss. *Theories of Human Communication*, 8th ed. (Belmont, CA: Thomson Wadsworth, 2005), 186–212, for detailed discusion of theory about communication relationships.

[25] Ibid.

[26] Marvin E. Shaw and Dennis S. Gouran, "Group Dynamics and Communication," in *Human Communication: Theory and Research*, ed. Gordon L. Dahnke and Glen W. Clatterbuck, 123–55 (Belmont, CA: Wadsworth Publishing Company, 1990).

[27] Randy Y. Hirokawa, "Group Communication and Decision Making Performance: A Continued Test of the Functional Perspective," *Human Communication Research* 14, no. 4 (Summer 1988): 487–515.

[28] Walter Lippmann, "The World Outside and the Pictures in Our Heads," chapter 1, *Public Opinion* (New York: Harcourt, Brace and Company, 1922). Reprinted in *The Process and Effects of Mass Communication*, rev. ed., edited by Schramm and Roberts, 265–86.

[29] Maxwell E. McCombs and Donald L. Shaw, "The Agenda-Setting Function of Mass Media," *Public Opinion Quarterly* 36, no. 2 (Summer 1972): 176–87. First of many reports of media agenda-setting effects on a variety of issues in a variety of settings.

[30] Maxwell McCombs, Edna Einsiedel, and David Weaver, *Contemporary Public Opinion: Issues and the News* (Hillsdale, NJ: Lawrence Erlbaum Associates, 1991), 12–17.

[31] Ibid., 17–21.

[32] Wayne Wanta and Y. C. Wu, "Interpersonal communication and the agenda-setting process," *Journalism Quarterly* 69, no. 4 (1992): 847–855.

[33] David Demers, "Issue obtrusiveness and the agenda-setting effects of national network news," *Communication Research* 16, no. 6, (1989): 793–812.

[34] Maxwell E. McCombs and Donald L. Shaw, "The evolution of agenda-setting research: Twenty-five years in the marketplace of ideas," *Journal of Communication* 43, no. 2 (1993): 65.

[35] Steven H. Chaffee, "The Interpersonal Context of Mass Communication," in Current Perspectives in Mass Communication Research, vol. 1, ed. F. Gerald Kline and Phillip J. Tichenor, 95–120 (Beverly Hills, CA: Sage Publications, 1972).

[36] Everett M. Rogers, "Communication and Social Change," in *Human Communication*, ed. Dahnke and Clatterbuck, 259–71.

[37] Elizabeth Noelle-Neumann, "The Spiral of Silence: A Theory of Public Opinion," *Journal of Communication* 24, (1974): 24–51. Later published in book form, *The Spiral of Silence: Public Opinion—Our Social Skin* (Chicago: University of Chicago Press, 1984).

[38] Lippmann, *Public Opinion*, 14.

[39] Melvin L. DeFleur and Sandra J. Ball-Rokeach, *Theories of Mass Communication*, 4th ed. (New York: Longman, 1982), 226.

[40] Edward M. Block, "How Public Opinion Is Formed," *Public Relations Review* 3, no. 3 (Fall 1977): 15.

[41] Irving Crespi, *The Public Opinion Process: How the People Speak* (Mahwah, NJ: Lawrence Erlbaum Associates, 1997): 10.

[42] Vincent Price and Donald F. Roberts, "Public Opinion Processes," in *Handbook of Communication Science*, ed. Berger and Chaffee, 784.

[43] David Domke, David P. Fan, Michael Fibison, Dhavan V. Shah, Steven S. Smith, and Mark D. Watts, "News Media, Candidates and Issues, and Public Opinion in the 1996 Presidential Campaign," *Journalism & Mass Communication Quarterly* 74, no. 4 (Winter 1997): 733.

[44] Dennis Chong, "Creating Common Frames of Reference on Political Issues," Chapter 8 in *Political Persuasion and Attitude Change*, ed. Diana C. Mutz, Paul M. Sniderman, and Richard A Brody (Ann Arbor: University of Michigan Press, 1996): 199.

[45] Dan Drew and David Weaver, "Media Attention, Media Exposure, and Media Effects," *Journalism Quarterly* 67, no. 4 (Winter 1990): 740–48.

[46] Vincent Price, Li-Ning Huang, and David Tewksbury, "Third-Person Effects of News Coverage: Orientations toward Media," *Journalism & Mass Communication Quarterly* 74, no. 3 (Autumn 1997): 525.

[47] John Dewey, *The Public and Its Problems* (New York: Henry Holt and Company, 1927), 15–17.

[48] James E. Grunig and Fred C. Repper, "Strategic Management, Publics, and Issues," in *Excellence in Public Relations and Communication Management*, ed. James E. Grunig (Hillsdale, NJ: Lawrence Erlbaum Associates, 1992), 135–37.

[49] See also James E. Grunig, "Communication Behaviors and Attitudes of Environmental Publics: Two Studies," *Journalism Monographs* 81 (March 1983): 40–41.

[50] Grunig and Repper, "Strategic Management, Publics, and Issues," 139.

[51] Dewey, *The Public and Its Problems*, 28–29.

[52] Concepts and paradigm of individual orientation adapted from Richard F. Carter, "Communication and Affective Relations," *Journalism Quarterly* 42, no. 2 (Spring 1965): 203–12.

[53] Crespi, *The Public Opinion Process*, 19.

[54] Price and Roberts, "Public Opinion Processes," 787.

[55] Model and coorientational concepts from Jack M. McLeod and Steven H. Chaffee, "Interpersonal Approaches to Communication Research," in *Interpersonal Perception and Communication*, edited by Steven H. Chaffee and Jack M. McLeod, special edition of *American Behavioral Scientist* 16, no. 4 (March–April 1973): 483–88.

[56] Thomas J. Scheff, "Toward a Sociological Model of Consensus," *American Sociological Review* 32, no. 1 (February 1967): 32–46.

[57] Ibid., 37.

[58] Keith R. Stamm and John E. Bowes, "Communicating During an Environmental Decision," *Journal of Environmental Education* 3, no. 3 (Spring 1972): 49–56.

[59] Glen M. Broom, "Coorientational Measurement of Public Issues," *Public Relations Review* 3, no. 4 (Winter 1977): 110–19. See also Glen M. Broom and David M. Dozier, *Using Research in Public Relations* (Englewood Cliffs, NJ: Prentice Hall, 1990): 36–39.

[60] Byron Reeves and Clifford Nass, *The Media Equation* (Cambridge, UK: Cambridge University Press, 1996): 253.

[61] Lippmann, *Public Opinion*, 13.

ADDITIONAL SOURCES

Ewen, Stuart. *PR! A Social History of Spin.* New York: Basic Books, Division of HarperCollins, 1997. Almost 500 pages outlining a critical view of how public relations evolved from the work and thoughts of Edward Bernays and Walter Lippmann.

Glasser, Theodore L., and Charles T. Salmon, eds. *Public Opinion and the Communication of Consent.* New York: Guilford Press, 1995. Assembles 17 chapters written by 30 leading scholars on the nature, contexts, processes, and impact of public opinion.

Jeffres, Leo W. *Mass Media Effects*, 2nd. ed. Prospect Heights, IL: Waveland Press, 1997. Summarizes and updates literature on media effects previously published as two books.

Knapp, Mark L., and Anita L. Vangelisti. *Interpersonal Communication and Human Relationships.* Boston: Allyn & Bacon, 1992. Summary of literature and theory related to dialogue, interaction rituals, relationships, and other aspects of relational communication.

Littlejohn, Stephen W., and Karen A. Foss. *Theories of Human Communication*, 8th ed. Belmont, CA: Thomson Wadsworth, 2005.

O'Keefe, Garrett, Dennis P. Rosenbaum, Paul J. Lavrakas, Kathaleen Reid, and Renee A. Botta. *Taking a Bite Out of Crime: The Impact of the National Citizens' Crime Prevention Campaign.* Thousand Oaks, CA: Sage Publications, 1996. Tracks impact of campaign from its beginning in 1979, presenting findings of effectiveness of print, radio, and television media campaign.

Mutz, Diana C., and Joe Soss. "Reading Public Opinion: The Influence of News Coverage on Perceptions of Public Sentiment," *Public Opinion Quarterly* 61 (1997): 431–51.

Richard M. Perloff. *The Dynamics of Persuasion*. Mahwah, NJ: Lawrence Erlbaum Associates, 2003. Comprehensive introduction to persuasive communication and attitude change.

Reese, Stephen D., Oscar H. Gandy, Jr., and A. E. Grant. *Framing Public Life: Perspectives on Media and our Understanding of the Social World*. Mahwah, NJ: Lawrence Erlbaum Associates, 2001. A compendium of research on mass media framing.

Van Ginneken, Jaap. *Collective Behavior and Public Opinion*. Mahwah, NJ: Lawrence Erlbaum Associates, 2003. Outlines new thinking on the dynamics of public opinion.

Wanta, Wayne. *The Public and the National Agenda: How People Learn about Important Issues.* Mahwah, NJ: Lawrence Erlbaum Associates, 1997. Examines agenda-setting effects by examining demographic, psychological, and behavioral influences. Provides exhaustive list of agenda-setting references.

9 INTERNAL RELATIONS AND EMPLOYEE COMMUNICATION

In order to have a winner, the team must have a feeling of unity; every player must put the team first—ahead of personal glory.

–Paul "Bear" Bryant[1]

STUDY GUIDE

After studying Chapter 9, you should be able to:

- Define internal and employee communication as a part of the public relations function, using the basic elements of the definition of public relations.

- Argue convincingly for the importance of the internal relations function.

- Discuss the impact of organizational culture on internal communication.

- Explain the differences between participative and authoritarian organizational cultures, and how each affects internal communication.

- Explain the major goals of employee communications.

- Discuss some of the major challenges intrinsic to internal relations.

- Describe many media used for communicating with internal publics.

- Outline basic guidelines for building good internal relations and working with various internal publics.

Public relations deals with the relationships among organizations and all types of various publics on whom its success or failure depends. You probably think of public relations as communicating with external publics. However, the internal publics—employees—are any organization's most important publics.

This chapter was written in collaboration with Professor Shannon A. Bowen, Ph.D., School of Communication, University of Houston. Dr. Bowen earned her doctorate at the University of Maryland. She previously worked as a research analyst for political and corporate clients in Washington, D.C.

This chapter discusses how public relations contributes to effective communication *within* an organization, also referred to as "internal relations." Communication inside an organization is arguably even more important than external communication, because the organization has to function effectively toward its goals in order to survive. Internal relations means building and maintaining relationships with all the publics inside an organization, including production line workers, managers and supervisors, administrative staff, and facilities and maintenance support, to name but a few. For example, the CEO of the automotive giant General Motors (GM) identified internal communication as a "top three priority" because it is so vital to organizational success.[2]

What follows is a review of theory and practice in internal relations, applying organizational culture theory to what you already know about public relations. The first part of this chapter discusses why organizational communication and culture are important concepts for internal relations. The second part provides a theoretical framework for understanding the internal communication processes in an organization. The third section addresses some of the problems and challenges faced in internal relations. The chapter concludes with a brief review of the media commonly used by public relations practitioners in conducting internal relations.

IMPORTANCE OF INTERNAL RELATIONS

An organization's most important relationships are those with employees at all levels. The terms *internal publics* and *employee publics* refer to both managers and the people being supervised. These publics represent an organization's greatest resource—its people. According to Alvie Smith, former director of corporate communications at General Motors, two factors are changing internal communication with employees and enhancing management's respect for this part of the public relations function:

1. *The value of understanding, teamwork, and commitment by employees in achieving bottom-line results.* These positive aspects of worker behavior are strongly influenced by effective, way-of-life interactive communications throughout the organization.

2. *The need to build a strong manager communication network, one that makes every supervisor at every level accountable for communicating effectively with his or her employees.* This needs to be more than just job-related information and should include key business and public issues affecting the total organization.[3] [Emphasis added.]

Organizations miss out on a sizable share of their human resource potential because they do not put a high priority on effective, two-way communication—the foundation for management–employee relations and overall job performance. Smith calls the consequence "slothing on the job":

> The ugly truth is that employee disloyalty and lack of commitment to organizational goals may be costing American businesses more than $50 billion a year... the cost of absenteeism, labor grievances, production interruptions, poor quality, repair and warranty expenses. Perhaps most costly of all is inaction by employees who withhold their best efforts and ideas; who cruise along with just passable performance.[4]

The coordination and mediation necessary for dealing with employees today put the public relations staff, with its communication knowledge and skills, square in the middle of managing internal relationships. For example, former Delta Air Lines chairman and CEO Ronald W. Allen, who rose through the ranks by running departments such as human resources and training, saw his primary job as cultivating a motivated and loyal workforce.[5]

Day-to-day working relationships involve a great deal of contact, but effective employee communication develops in a climate of trust and honesty.[6] Ideally, working relationships are characterized by at least seven conditions:

1. Confidence and trust between employer and employees
2. Honest, candid information flowing freely up, down, and sideways in the organization
3. Satisfying status and participation for each person
4. Continuity of work without strife
5. Healthy or safe surroundings
6. Success for the enterprise
7. Optimism about the future

The chief executive must establish this culture and endorse it as formal policy. Even with such support from the top, however, many barriers stand in the way of free-flowing, two-way communication in organizations.

Opinion Research Corporation has tracked employee opinions of organizational internal communication since 1950. Large majorities consistently give their organizations favorable scores on credibility, but less than half say their organizations do a good job of "letting them know what is going on," or **downward communication** (management to employee). Less than half also give high marks to their organization's willingness to "listen to their views," or **upward communication** (employee to management).

Similar surveys conducted by consulting firm Towers Perrin found the grapevine second only to immediate supervisors as employees' most frequent source of organizational information. Nine out of ten surveyed, however, rated their immediate supervisor as the "preferred source" of information, often noting a preference for face-to-face communication, and ranked the grapevine as the least-preferred source (see Figure 9.1).

A Watson Wyatt Company survey of corporate readers of its employee communication newsletter identified "help employees understand business direction–mission" as the number-one objective of employee communication programs. Employee publications, bulletin boards, group meetings, policy handbooks, and memos are the most frequently used media for management communication directed to employees. Face-to-face communication with an "open-door policy" is the primary medium for encouraging **upward, two-way communication** and for building good working relationships with employees.

Balancing the needs for employee satisfaction with the success of the enterprise is but one aspect of the continuous adjustment and reconciliation in employer–employee relationships—especially in multicultural settings (see Exhibit 9.1). **As a part of the larger public relations function, however, the goal of internal relations is to establish and maintain mutually beneficial relationships between an organization and the employees on whom its success or failure depends.**

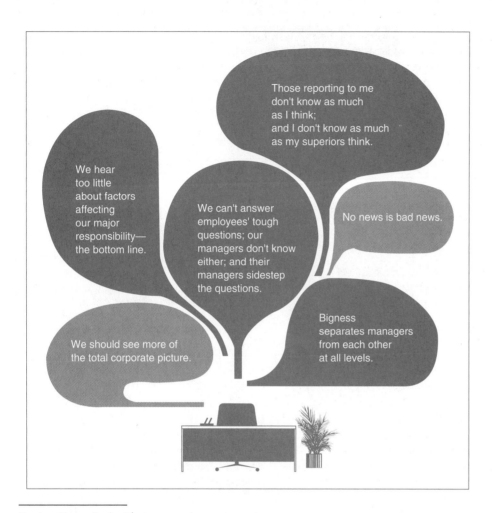

FIGURE 9.1

MANAGERS: THE MISSING LINK

Courtesy Towers Perrin, Atlanta.

ORGANIZATIONAL CULTURE

Understanding the internal communication of any organization requires one to consider the culture of that organization. Some who study organizational culture define it as the shared meanings and assumptions of group members.[7] Others focus on culture as a common values system or the behavioral norms in the organization.[8] Organizational culture is an important consideration because it has a significant impact on the model of public relations an organization practices and on the internal communications that follow.

Organizational culture is defined as follows:

Organizational culture is the sum total of shared values, symbols, meanings, beliefs, assumptions, and expectations that organize and integrate a group of people who work together.[9]

The culture of an organization is often what defines it as different from other organizations, and—if managed properly—can be a valuable asset in building cohesion

EXHIBIT 9.1

CO-ACCULTURATION IN MULTINATIONAL ORGANIZATIONS

Suman Lee, Ph.D.,
Assistant Professor
Greenlee School of Journalism
and Communication
Iowa State University

Doing business in the new global economy has created new kinds of organizations—multinational/multicultural organizations. It is now commonplace for multinational companies to include two or more cultures under a single corporate umbrella. In the multinational corporate setting, managers and workers are cultural strangers; each group with its own patterns of cognitive, affective, and behavioral structures and processes. Because of such cultural differences, multinational companies face unique challenges, and sometimes more serious manager–worker relationship problems, than do companies operating in their home settings.

For example, there can be problems in training new employees and in communication between managers and workers. Misconceptions led by cultural differences can interfere with the integration of new workers and cause higher turnover. In this regard, success or failure of a multinational company cannot be explained by economic factors alone. Effective communication and mutually beneficial relationships between cultural groups, especially manager–worker relationships, also serve as significant indicators of successful operation of multinational companies in the global economy.

Co-acculturation is a theoretical model for examining relationships between managers and workers in a multicultural, multinational organization. **Co-acculturation** can be defined as ***simultaneous orientation toward each other and toward aspects of each other's culture.***

Co-acculturation combines and extends concepts derived from acculturation theory and the concept of coorientational consensus. Co-acculturation is not one individual's or one group's acculturation to a fixed and given host culture, such as when immigrants and international students "acculturate" to a host-country's culture. Rather, it represents ***mutual and relational acculturation*** between two or more cultural groups.

For example, Samsung Tijuana Park is a manufacturing plant in Mexico with expatriated Korean managers and resi-

dent Mexican workers. In this situation, both Koreans and Mexicans simultaneously acculturate to each other's cultures. Relationships in the co-acculturation paradigm require three measures: agreement, congruency, and accuracy.

Co-acculturation agreement is the comparison of one cultural group's view with the views held by the other group toward the same behavioral artifacts of culture. It represents the degree to which the cultural groups share the similar evaluations of the cultural artifacts. Therefore, co-acculturation agreement indicates the degree of cultural similarity between groups. **Co-acculturation congruency** is the comparison of one's own view on cultural aspects with his or her estimates of the other cultural group's view on the same dimensions. **Co-acculturation accuracy** is the degree to which members of different cultural groups estimate the other group's perceptions correctly. Improving co-acculturation agreement, congruency, and accuracy is a common goal for public relations programs.

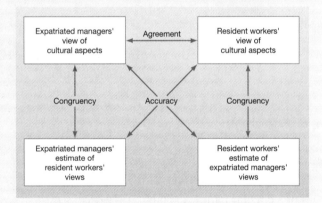

Co-acculturation theory has potential practical applications. Co-acculturation synthesizing acculturation theory and coorientational model has heuristic value not only in multinational organizations, but also in organizations undergoing merger or acquisition, as well as other organizations that employ from different cultural groups.

To some extent, public relations practitioners function as cultural messengers within and outside an organization. As globalization makes work settings much more culturally diverse, it will become the bigger challenge for public relations practitioners to facilitate communication within an organization. Co-acculturation provides a paradigm for understanding this challenge.

and teamwork inside the organization, resulting in organizational effectiveness—reaching its goals. Organizational culture defines the values and norms used by decision makers in an organization. Worldviews and organizational culture define the range of responses available in any given issue situation. Although it is often unspoken, organizational culture is a powerful influence on how behavior is defined in the organization, including who has power and how they use power.

Culture and Power

Power is the ability to affect the outcomes of decisions in an organization.[10] Power can be directed toward achieving organizational goals. **Formal power** is officially vested in officers and departments. It represents the authority to carry out responsibilities, such as the broad power of top executives and the more limited power of the legal department. In contrast, informal power is exercised by people who have the ability to influence others to act in accordance with their wishes, not through an official directive but by having "pull" in an organization. Some argue that this type of power is "illegitimate" because it often relies on manipulation. The idea behind power is that someone has the ability to cause something to be accomplished.

The dominant coalition holds the most power in an organization. This group includes the top decision makers—generally five to eight senior executives. Although many members of the dominant coalition hold formal power through their office—such as a CEO, or COO—a person holding informal power may also be included in the dominant coalition. Such is the case with major donors, figureheads, or influential members of a board of directors who have influence over decisions.

Power-control theory holds that the dominant coalition determines an organization's goals and how business is conducted. The dominant coalition tends to hold similar ideas and agree on desirable organizational outcomes. For example, Enron CEO Ken Lay claimed not to know of the fraudulent accounting practices of his Chief Financial Officer, Andrew Fastow. But, either way, Lay knew of Enron's exceptionally aggressive strategy of innovation, creating new markets and market dominance. Members of the dominant coalition at Enron were ideologically in sync, even if they were allegedly not operationally in sync.[11]

Public relations scholars argue that the relationship between power and culture is of a circular nature, explaining, "People in power develop the culture of an organization and organizational culture influences *who* gains power."[12]

Dominant Coalition's Impact on Public Relations

Power comes to the public relations function in an organization when the members of the dominant coalition value it as a vital management function, rather than relegate it to simply a technical role implementing the communication strategy decided by others.[13] If public relations has a "seat at the table" of the dominant coalition, then public relations plays a greater role in determining and achieving organizational outcomes.[14]

When viewed by the dominant coalition as a vital management function, public relations professionals have input into the strategic decision making of an organization and can see that the opinions of publics are taken into account when determining organizational strategy. This role adds value to the organization because, if the opinions of publics are included in the organization's decision making, those decisions are likely to be more balanced in terms of what publics expect from the organization. Therefore, the decisions are more enduring and cause fewer negative reactions because the views of publics were factored into the decisions.

Fulfilling this strategic role, however, requires that public relations professionals have skills in strategic management not typically associated with many practitioners. As the Excellence Project researchers concluded,

> These strategic functions are evaluation research, environmental scanning, and research to segment publics. In short, the data suggest that communication managers are more likely to be technical supervisors than strategic managers.[15]

Worldview and Organizational Culture

"Worldview" means the basic value and belief system prevalent in an organization. It is generally the worldview of the dominant coalition that, in turn, shapes the worldview of the organization as a whole through internal communication. There are two primary types of worldviews—symmetrical and asymmetrical.[16]

An asymmetrical worldview is one in which an organization's goal is to get what it wants without having to change the way it does business internally. This worldview focuses almost exclusively on the goals of the organization, and the culture is to resist change. In an asymmetrical worldview, power in decision making tends to remain on the side of the organization and is not shared with publics. The asymmetrical worldview is common in competitive business environments.

A symmetrical worldview incorporates the ideas of negotiation, conflict resolution, and compromise in an organization's operating procedures. The organization is not only self-oriented, but also oriented on satisfying the interests of strategic publics. Therefore, desires and goals are set in a shared fashion by incorporating some of what the publics want. Change occurs on both sides of the relationship—a give-and-take on behalf of both organization and its publics. Change may not always be balanced in every instance, but both the organization and its publics are open to adopting or adapting to the views of the other through dialogue and negotiation. Power is, to varying degrees, shared between organization and publics in the symmetrical worldview, with each having the opportunity to have input into a decision. The symmetrical worldview can be found in all types of organizations, but occurs most frequently in businesses or industries that are heavily regulated by government.

Symmetrical and asymmetrical worldviews produce different organizational cultures—authoritarian and participative. These two organizational cultures have direct and indirect effects on the nature and flow of internal communication in the organization.

Authoritarian Organizational Culture.   An authoritarian organizational culture arises from an asymmetrical worldview. In this type of culture, communication processes are **structured and formalized** within a decision-making hierarchy. Military organizations typically are examples of authoritarian organizational cultures.

In authoritarian organizational cultures, decisions are made at the top levels of the organization and implemented by those at lower levels. Decision making is **centralized** at the highest level of the organization, and input is typically not sought from middle- and lower-level employees. An authoritarian organizational culture usually stresses **individual accountability** for an area of limited scope, and organizational departments are independent, rather than interdependent. Authoritarian cultures are often based on the idea of a "mechanistic" or "mechanical" organizational structure, in which tasks are routinized and there is a high **division of labor**. For example, at Amazon.com, one employee is responsible for sealing and labeling boxes as they roll off the stocking line, while another employee stacks the boxes in the warehouse where they wait to be shipped. **There is little role for dialogue or feedback in an authoritarian organizational culture, because the input of employees is not seen as vital in management**.[17,18]

Communication in authoritarian cultures, therefore, takes on the form of disseminating the ideas and goals decided by upper management to various internal employee publics, such as midlevel and lower-level management, administrative and support staff, supervisors, skilled laborers, and unskilled laborers. This means that communication is generally one sided—or asymmetrical—in that management directs employees, but little communication flows from employees back to management. Efficiency is valued over innovation in many authoritarian cultures due to the emphasis on uniform output of a product or standardized provision of a service.

Authoritarian cultures tend to resist change. Input from publics is viewed as a threat to authority rather than as an opportunity for change. These organizations also resist sharing power with "outsiders." Even internal publics face recalcitrant management in an authoritarian culture, leading to high employee turnover and lower levels of job satisfaction than reported in other types of organizational cultures.

Participative Organizational Culture. Participative organizational cultures are based on a symmetrical worldview that values **dialogue** and two-sided input. **Teamwork** is valued, and emphasis is placed on the **collective rather than the individual**, meaning that the organization and employees share goals. A participative organizational culture values innovation and seeks input from employees and other stakeholder groups to ensure a thorough analysis of decisions and policy. Organizational departments are often integrated or multifunctional and stress open communication across different departments.[19]

A participative organizational culture values information and seeks input from internal publics. Symmetrical feedback and upward communication allow employees and those at lower levels of an organization to have a voice in management decision making. Feedback is encouraged and sought. This type of culture is organic, as opposed to mechanistic, as parts of the team work together in an environment that encourages and rewards **innovation**.

An example of using a participative organizational culture took place in a global pharmaceutical company early in the fight against AIDS. The company developed an experimental AIDS drug that could only be produced in a very limited quantity due to the virus synthesis involved, but the drug would extend the life of those to whom it was provided. The company realized that it needed help in deciding how to allocate the drug in order to avoid accusations of favoritism, so it asked AIDS activist groups for advice on distribution. After many meetings between the pharmaceutical company leaders and the leaders of AIDS activist groups, a lottery format was decided on as the fairest way of determining which AIDS patients could be treated with the pioneering drug. The life-extending properties of that drug proved to be a major breakthrough in the management of AIDS.[20] As this case illustrates, feedback from publics is a vital component that a participative organizational culture encourages.

In participative organizational cultures, decisions are made in a decentralized manner—across varying levels of the organization—and implemented by those who hold responsibility over a specific area. **Innovative ideas can come from any level of the organization,** from the manufacturing line to top management, and thus feedback at all levels of the organization is sought and valued. One effect of a participative organizational culture is increased teamwork and higher value placed on employees at all levels.

Consequently, participative organizations reach shared goals much more quickly and efficiently than do organizations with poorly defined or divergent goals. As Theus explained: "Organizational culture is a significant pillar upon which communication efficacy rests."[21] In conclusion, **symmetrical internal relations and communication result in a greater overall organizational effectiveness.**

INTERNAL RELATIONS CHALLENGES

Internal relations involves more than communicating with employee publics in isolation. For example, complying with government regulations can cover everything from toxic waste disposal to employee working hours: U.S. Department of Labor laws require organizations to hang mandatory posters in the workplace that list federal, state, and OSHA standards. These posters, which are usually displayed on bulletin boards or near time clocks or lockers, include topics such as minimum wage, safety standards, hand washing, and wearing protective equipment.

FIGURE 9.2

ROW BOATS CARTOON

Courtesy Harold Smith, Asheville, NC.

Safety and Compliance

Every organization must comply with the governing standards of the country in which it operates, even if the organization operates locations in many nations. The different standards for each country must be followed, or the organization can face severe penalties and fines from regulators. Internal relations specialists work hard at making sure the standards of each country are known and communicated internally in a global organization with locations around the world. Saying "that isn't the way things are done in our home country" holds no weight with foreign governments, and their regulations can vary tremendously from an organization's "standard operating procedure" at home. Every country has the equivalent of taxes, labor laws that govern workers, operational laws that govern workplace safety, and environmental laws concerning waste and transportation of materials. These laws are in addition to what the organization must also handle externally, such as import and export regulations, competition, and other civil and criminal laws.

Internal relations staff also educate employees about compliance with government regulations. Employees need to understand the rules under which they are required to operate in order to maximize their own safety. One primary responsibility of the internal relations function is to communicate Occupational Safety and Health Administration (OSHA) worker safety standards required by the government. OSHA governs everything from requiring hard hats in construction areas to the quality of air in office buildings. For example, OSHA regulates work conditions and safety of those handling the printing chemicals used to produce this book.

The Environmental Protection Agency (EPA) is another U.S. government agency that regulates disposal and transportation of goods, especially those deemed hazardous in nature, such as petroleum products, industrial chemicals such as DMSO or benzene, or pesticides. Many hazardous chemicals are used in manufacturing, so they must be produced at a chemical plant, are transported to the manufacturing site, and are eventually discarded after use. For example, textile dying and manufacturing plants often have large, concrete "settling ponds" in which used dyestuff is treated to decompose over time into biodegradable sediment. Or, Dow Chemical uses benzene, a highly poisonous solvent if airborne, and must maintain sensitive benzene monitors and alarms throughout its facility in case of accidental leaks. The EPA regulates sites such as these, and many others, for environmental safety compliance.

So, in many organizations, another important task of internal relations provides communication support to ensure that environmental regulations and worker safety standards are maintained. Responsible internal communication about these issues can be a matter of life and death and can help prevent the accidents and violations that damage organizational reputations.

Labor Relations

One of the most significant tasks of internal relations is interacting with hourly employees, some of whom belong to labor unions. The relationship with laborers is a vital relationship on which the success or failure of the organization literally depends. This relationship cannot—and should not—be taken for granted. Maintenance of the relationship with labor constitutes a large part of an internal relations specialist's work, especially in organizations with a "unionized shop."

There is an inherent and undeniable tension between the roles of management and labor. This tension is the basis for many schools of thought in sociology and economics, in which labor and management are seen as adversaries locked in an eternal battle between the "haves" and the "have nots." Out of this socioeconomic theory arises the tension that exists in everyday relations with labor. There is a core value that labor enacts work and management controls work. Controlling resource allocations—money and number of jobs—is a main function of management, but workers would also like a voice in this process, and that is where internal relations comes into play.

Relationships with unionized workers and their unions must be attended to continually, and internal relations specialists facilitate and help maintain those relationships. Some assume that human resources (HR) is in charge of this organizational function, but the role of HR typically is limited to hiring, firing, training, and benefits. If a union is thinking of striking, it is the public relations function in management (usually the internal relations specialist) who first learns of the discontent. This "early warning system" is an exceptionally valuable part of two-way symmetrical internal relations. It is also the responsibility of internal relations to communicate about matters of dissention and try to find ways to resolve labor–management relationship problems. Although unions often draw much attention, the savvy internal relations manager accords just as much time and attention to communicating with nonunionized labor. (See Chapter 6 for legal considerations in labor–management communication.)

Organizational Change: Mergers, Acquisitions, and Layoffs

Internal communication specialists have important strategic responsibilities during organizational change. Communication during periods of change and uncertainty is more than just "hand-holding," as it plays an important role in helping employees cope with uncertainty and adjust to change (see Exhibit 9.2).

In situations such as a merger or acquisition, internal publics of all levels immediately have a need for communication about the future of their position in the organization. These situations tend to produce anxiety, especially for those not involved in the discussions and decisions that led to organizational change. The role of internal relations should be to guide the merger or acquisition communication with internal publics in a forthright and expedient manner, dealing with questions and uncertainties in an honest manner. Often, if employees know that a decision is still under consideration, their anxiety will be less than if they know nothing at all. Again, "We are still working that out" is a better answer than "No comment."

Public relations consultant Jim McBride also notes the importance of providing information to employee publics: "Knowledge enables them to feel more 'connected' to the organization; so that what happens to the organization, happens to them."[22] Publics with a high level of involvement in the organization will have a greater need for information in times of uncertainty than in normal times, and internal relations should respond immediately and proactively. For example, a sharp drop in stock prices can cause both employees and investors to become concerned and to want accurate information rapidly. This information must be truthful.

In the Enron case, top executives were selling their own stock while assuring employees that the company was not losing value. This is an abhorrent example of allowing circumstances to dominate truth—rather than allowing truth to decide circumstances. It is the responsibility of the internal relations manager to be honest

EXHIBIT 9.2

COMMUNICATING ORGANIZATIONAL CHANGE

David B. McKinney, APR, ABC
Public Affairs Manager
Shell Chemical Company,
Deer Park, Texas

Employees who learn from the local TV news that their company has just been acquired or the plant where they make widgets is shutting down have a right to be upset. After all, who has a greater personal and emotional stake in an organization than those who actually work there?

A line from a popular song proclaims: "The winds of change are always blowing." Today's business environment is characterized by frequent and unexpected change, with few certainties as to the future of the organization or individual jobs. At the same time, the abundance of and reliance on electronic communications, particularly e-mail and the intranet, is creating an information overload for all levels of employees.

Ironically, information breakdowns often occur when *effective* internal communication is the most critical: during workplace change or uncertainty such as layoffs, mergers, product recalls, and scandals. Addressing employee concerns, distraction and resistance requires attention to *content* (*what* is being communicated), and understanding the role of available *tools* or *mediums* (*how, where,* and *when* information is delivered). Additional challenges include how quickly management should respond; how much information should be given; and how employee support is gained and maintained. Objectives should be to keep up staff morale, boost staff's enthusiasm and interest in their jobs, and show what is being done to help those who lose their jobs.

Shell International Ltd. takes a three-phase approach to communicating change: Phase 1 has to do with "unfreezing" or acknowledging the passing of the old and celebration of the new. Phase 2 addresses "changing" or cognitive restructuring, which is timing critical (denial/resistance/explo-

ration/commitment). Phase 3 is "refreezing" or commitment—reward, training, and validation. Understanding these phases can remove fear and uncertainty, limit rumors, and restore a sense of control.

Every step of the way, internal communication must support business objectives, generate internal community spirit to raise and maintain morale, and be honest and open. Employees should be given the information they want and need, as well as being told what management wants to say. **During workplace change or uncertainty, employees want to know what it means for them**: do they have a job, where will they work, why are the changes happening and how will it improve the business? The focus should be on face-to-face communication because it is, by far, the most effective. Other methods, such as e-mail, newsletters, and the intranet, can be used to raise awareness and share information, saving face-to-face discussion for debate, clarifying understanding, and private feedback—not for information dumping.

Internal communication is often overshadowed in the context of overall communication efforts. Attention typically is targeted toward external relations with media, investors, government agencies, the community, and other stakeholders. However, organizational change or uncertainty requires a communication plan that is sensitive to employees and acknowledges their potential impact as communication ambassadors for the organization as they interact with families, neighbors, and others in the community. Armed with factual information, informed employees are less likely to be discontent or engage in rumors and speculation—usually negative—caused by lack of, bad, or no "official" information.

As the song reminds us, the winds of change are always blowing. Effective, conscientious management ensures that when change occurs, the information winds blow to and from employees, facilitating two-way dialogue early, often, and in a credible, open manner.

Courtesy David B. McKinney and Shell International Ltd.

and forthcoming with information to internal publics, even when it means pushing recalcitrant top management to do the right thing.

During reorganization and layoffs, responsible organizations respond by helping employees to the greatest extent that it can. For instance, when a manufacturing site is to move, the company could pay to relocate employees to the new location or provide them with job search assistance and retraining. This is how Johnson & Johnson responded when the company sold a surgical scrubs facility that had employed many mentally challenged persons in garment folding and packing. The company worked with the buyer to make sure that this community outreach initiative was continued and then helped place some of the displaced workers in other Johnson & Johnson facilities.

COMMUNICATING INTERNALLY

There are many ways to communicate with internal publics, limited only by the imagination of public relations professionals.[23] Advancing technology has changed the way communication is produced, distributed, displayed, and stored. The digital age makes communication faster than ever before with even "internal" messages capable of being global in a matter of mere seconds. Internal relations specialists have to deal with expanding technology changing the way employee communication takes place. Internal communication is spoken, electronic, visual, and written, as discussed in sections that follow.

Vision Statements

Vision statements provide an overview of future organizational goals in the broadest sense. Although mission statements are better known, vision statements are the starting point for developing a more specific organizational mission. The terms *mission statement* and *vision statement* are closely related; however, there are basic differences between the two concepts.

The vision statement represents a future goal that outlines general priorities for where the organization is headed. An effective vision statement answers the basic questions: "Why does this organization exist?" and "What would we like to accomplish?" A shared vision is an integral part of the culture of an organization and is communicated through internal relations. If employees share a common vision and clearly defined goals, the organization can make more strategic and effective decisions than they can without a clear vision. **A vision statement spells out a target for strategy and the future goal of an organization.**

Vision statements are important tools of internal relations, particularly for helping manage reactions to changes in the environment. A well-planned vision statement gives employees an idea of what the organization will strive for in the future, the values it holds, and the areas of the business that will be of most strategic importance—ranging from strategies as diverse as research and development of new products to maintaining market share or developing relationships with new distributors.

A vision statement is usually created at the highest level of the organization by the CEO or other members of the dominant coalition. One danger here is that creating a vision statement in the top level of the organization alone misses the opportunity to engage internal publics in the discussion of organizational mission. Employees often report that feelings of pride, ownership, and responsibility are fostered when many participants work together at creating a vision statement.[24] Participating in the process can create a "shared vision" of the organization's future throughout the organization.

Mission Statements

The mission statement answers the question: "How are we different from our competitors?" They convey goals, organizational structure and strategy, legitimacy, values, participation and ownership among employees, leadership, responsibility to the community, ethical priorities, and commitment to publics and stakeholders. Although mission statements and vision statements are similar, mission statements are more specific and operational than are vision statements. **The mission statement helps employees set priorities and goals, so that all members of the organization are committed to achieving the mission specified in the statement.**

Mission statements encourage members in an organization to focus on its strengths by emphasizing areas and attributes in which it has success. The focus fostered by a compelling mission statement can provide a competitive advantage. It does so by allowing members of the organization to remain "on strategy," both in conducting their responsibilities and in allocating resources. Without a clearly defined mission statement, an organization might make decisions that are well intentioned, but that do not emphasize the unique competitive strengths of the organization. By building on what it does well, an organization reinvests resources in the areas where it is strongest and thus become less dependent on the areas in which it is weaker, giving it an overall competitive advantage.

An organization whose mission focuses on providing the highest quality product would have a different strategic mission than an organization focused on creating the most innovative products, or another that offers the most inexpensive merchandise. For example, Kia Motors' mission statement is "Provide high quality, high value vehicles at prices well below the competition…" (www.Kia.com). Kia's internal communication emphasizes value and pricing. On the other hand, Mercedes Benz' mission statement states: "Mercedes has been the name of the world's most innovative car brands for more than 100 years now. Mercedes Benz is the most successful premium brand [due to] its technical perfection, quality standards, innovative impact…" (www.mercedesbenz.com/). Mercedes Benz emphasizes technical perfection and innovation, whereas Kia emphasizes quality and economy. Each mission statement spells out to employees what the organization values and rewards.

There is little standardization of content and style among mission statements, but top-performing organizations almost always subscribe to exemplary statements of vision and mission.[25] In short, a clear vision for the future and a thoroughly articulated mission are vital to organizational success.

Policy Documents

Organizational policy and procedures are communicated through various channels to employees. Most organizations have an employee handbook telling how to implement policies and procedures in common situations. For example, many organizations have a policy regarding employee nondisclosure of confidential or privileged information. Manuals often specify the internal policies and the governmental laws that regulate the organization, such as antitrust laws and rules to prevent insider trading of stocks.

Policy manuals are generally exhaustive documents in book or electronic form that specify rights, responsibilities, and bureaucratic channels for procedures. A policy manual might include the procedure for reporting a sexual harassment situation or other problematic issue for employees, as well as routine procedures for requesting a promotion or personal use of office computers. A major drawback of this medium is that most policy manuals are little used because of their sheer length and complex content. For example, the Faculty Handbook for the University of Houston is an Adobe™ pdf document of more than 300 pages. Because of the presentation's detail and complexity, many employees refer to the policy manual only as a last resort. However, policy manuals can be effective tools of internal communication if they are well written, concise, interesting, and organized.

Another common policy document is a **code of ethics** or an **ethics statement**. A code of ethics, by definition, provides a guide to organizational values, priorities, standards, and policy as viewed by senior management. The ethics statement spells out in clear terms the ethical parameters used by the organization in evaluating decision options. A well-written code of ethics provides more concrete guidance and priorities than does a vision or mission statement, but it is much briefer than a policy manual. Codes of ethics, also known as ethics statements, credos, principles, beliefs, values, or standards, are officially adopted and formalized statements that the organization adopts as its guide for ethical decision making. Johnson & Johnson's credo is an outstanding example of an ethics statement (www.jnj.com/our_company_/our_credo).

At Johnson & Johnson's New Jersey headquarters, the ethics statement dominates the lobby, engraved in hard, immobile granite. The choice of "writing the credo in stone" was deliberate, in order to communicate that the values and identity of this organization were not mobile, changing things, but foundations firmly inscribed in the heart of the company. The credo holding a prominent place in organizational culture clearly helped Johnson & Johnson survive the organizational Tylenol poisonings crisis.

Training Materials

Training materials help socialize new employees into the culture of the organization. The socialization process is a means of learning the values, standards, and norms of the organization, as well as what is expected in relation to job responsibilities. An employee is enculturated when he or she internalizes the values of the organization and begins to identify him or herself as part of the organization. **Socializing and enculturating new employees are important aspects of internal relations.**

New employee **orientation** at every level of the organization, from labor to executive management, can cover topics in the policy manual, benefits, and related procedures.

For example, one global corporation provided a weeklong training seminar for all CEOs and COOs of its Middle Eastern and Asian subsidiaries. The seminar included sessions on ethics, issues management, corporate responsibility, crisis management, consumer product sales and marketing, teamwork and high-pressure decision making, and media spokesperson training. Even aggressive "reporters" interviewed the CEOs and COOs, subjecting them to hostile questions and bright camera lights in simulated press conferences.

Training provides internal relations staff an opportunity to help the human resources department to socialize and to enculturate employees at all levels of the organization. Assuming that all employees who join the organization hold similar values and the same rigorous approach to business decision making is not a realistic expectation.[26] Rather, employees need to be taught what is expected of them and the standards and methods to be used in that evaluation. Doing so builds more consistent organizational decision making, which can make maintaining relationships with publics easier. Providing rigorous training and setting clear expectations for employees also allows them to proceed in their responsibilities with the confidence that the organization will stand behind them when they act in accordance with its values.

INTERNAL MEDIA

Communication in an organization occurs in both verbal and written forms. All of these communications and the media they use are the responsibility of internal relations.

Employee Publications

Even with the new communication technology, printed publications remain the primary media for internal communication in most organizations. Imagine the competition for attention these publications must overcome when they reach the homes of employees and their families. The usual goals of such publications include

1. Keeping employees informed of the organization's strategy and goals
2. Providing employees the information they need to perform their assignments well
3. Encouraging employees to maintain and enhance the organization's standards for and commitment to quality improvement, increased efficiency, improved service, and greater social responsibility
4. Recognizing employees' achievements and successes
5. Creating an opportunity for two-way communication to generate employee feedback, questions, and concerns

Each publication, each issue, each printed word is part of a coordinated employee communication program designed to achieve these and other goals set in response to particular organizational settings and situations. Because of their impact, permanence, and reference value, printed words remain the workhorses of employee communication.

An organizational publication can take the form of a simple newsletter, a Web site, an intranet, a regularly distributed e-mail, a newspaper, a magazine, or a "magapaper" that combines the format of a newspaper with the style of a magazine. Many are high-quality, four-color publications (see Figure 9.3).

All organizational publications have these characteristics in common: They satisfy the organizational need to go on record with its positions and to communicate information essential for achieving organizational objectives; they permit the organization to deliver messages to specific target publics; and they let the organization communicate in its own words, in its own way, without interruption or alteration. In short, they give the organization a means of **controlled** communication.

The organizational publication is versatile. It can be edited to serve the narrow interests of its sponsor. It can be edited to shed light on issues important to employees and other publics. Most often it combines editorial content that both espouses the sponsor's point of view and addresses concerns of targeted publics. (Without the

FIGURE 9.3

DYSTAR EMPLOYEE
PUBLICATIONS

Courtesy DyStar, Frankfurt, Germany.

latter, of course, it would die for lack of readers outside the inner circle of top management.)

Organizational publications are directed to many publics, but the most common use is in employee communication. Practitioners responding to surveys usually rate employees as a primary audience for organizational publications. The major advantage of publications is their ability to deliver specific and detailed information to narrowly defined target publics who have an interest in the issues being discussed. As a result, many organizations have several employee publications, each designed to meet the information needs of different employee publics. For example, because about half of Callaway Vineyards' employees speak Spanish, it prints its employee publication in both English and Spanish. Ciba Geigy Canada Ltd. publishes its employee publications in both English and French. The front cover and pages to the center staple are in one language; flip the publication, and the back cover becomes the front cover for the half published in the other language.

Many organizations construct their publications as **two-way** communication — inviting questions, seeking input and comments, and conducting surveys, then reporting the results (see Figure 9.4). This requires the full cooperation of top management because of the time required to respond to questions and the expense of conducting surveys. Two-way communication also demands a climate of trust. Employees are often reluctant to submit questions or write for publication, so that sometimes comments are solicited anonymously. Nonetheless, internal publications provide an excellent mechanism for feedback and responsive communication. Comment cards provide a greater sense of anonymity to employees than do Web sites or intranet systems with feedback forms, as those people who want to comment anonymously sometimes fear that electronic communication will be traced back to them.

Newsletters

Printed newsletters remain the "workhorse" of employee communication, even in the computer and intranet age. They are the most common form of periodical publication. Because of readily available and inexpensive desktop publishing technology, newsletters are relatively easy, fast, and inexpensive to produce. As a result, most organizations rely on newsletters to communicate news in a timely and targeted fashion. According to Paul Swift, managing editor of the *Newsletter on Newsletters*:

> Newsletters are a medium that is here to stay … and grow.…There is more value being put on targeting communication with the corporate world and between associations and their members, as opposed to mass media. They [newsletters] are good for getting a specific message to a targeted audience in a specific context. Narrowcasting—what newsletters are, as opposed to broadcasting—is growing coincidentally with the desktop revolution.[27]

Merck & Co. distributes a daily newsletter at its corporate headquarters in New Jersey. The newsletter updates employees on what is happening in other departments, stock prices, management initiatives, philanthropic and social events, special seminars for employees and so on. The daily newsletter supplements a monthly magazine that is a glossy, full-color publication, sent to more than 90,000 employees worldwide. Merck further facilitates good internal relations with publics at its headquarters by providing many on-site conveniences for employee use, such as a bank, convenience store, post office, dry cleaner, physician, DVD rental, and a complete athletic facility. Merck also holds special events on Fridays, such as having arts-and-crafts vendors bring their wares on-site for employees to browse or purchase. Inventive ideas such as these serve to increase employee morale, build teamwork, and facilitate internal dialogue.

Letters

Even with the dominance of e-mail, traditional letters remain the backbone of internal organizational communication. They are perceived as more formal, directed, personal, and costly than e-mail, and therefore generate more attention on the part

FIGURE 9.4

EMPLOYEE "SPEAK OUT!" FORM

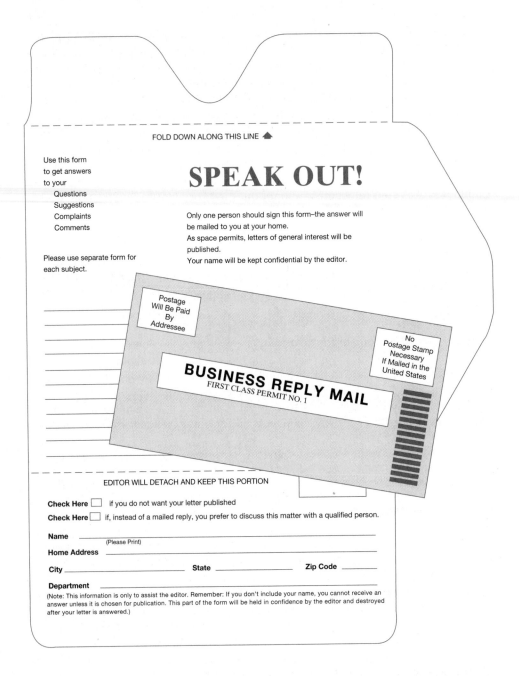

FOLD DOWN ALONG THIS LINE 🔺

Use this form
to get answers
to your
    Questions
    Suggestions
    Complaints
    Comments

Please use separate form for
each subject.

SPEAK OUT!

Only one person should sign this form–the answer will
be mailed to you at your home.
As space permits, letters of general interest will be
published.
Your name will be kept confidential by the editor.

Postage
Will Be Paid
By
Addressee

No
Postage Stamp
Necessary
If Mailed in the
United States

BUSINESS REPLY MAIL
FIRST CLASS PERMIT NO. 1

EDITOR WILL DETACH AND KEEP THIS PORTION

Check Here ☐ if you do not want your letter published

Check Here ☐ if, instead of a mailed reply, you prefer to discuss this matter with a qualified person.

Name _____
       (Please Print)

Home Address _____

City _____ **State** _____ **Zip Code** _____

Department _____

(Note: This information is only to assist the editor. Remember: If you don't include your name, you cannot receive an
answer unless it is chosen for publication. This part of the form will be held in confidence by the editor and destroyed
after your letter is answered.)

of the recipient. Word processing software or "direct-mail" companies can generate
individualized letters, used increasingly to establish direct, speedy communication
with employees and other specific publics, such as union members or retirees. They
offer an opportunity for the chief executive and other managers to communicate
with employees and their families in a personalized and strategically tailored manner. Among their advantages are economy, a direct and individualized approach, an
impressive appearance, impact, and speed.

Depending on the need, organization officials direct letters to community opinion leaders, to members of selected professions such as medicine or education, to legislators, suppliers, retailers, or media executives and reporters. These letters have the obvious advantage of individualized addresses and salutations, in addition to specifically targeted statements in the body of the letter. The importance of effective letters that evoke pleased reactions, not irritation or confusion, is obvious. Yet many organizations continue in the rut of cold, stilted, hackneyed letters that do more to confuse and obscure than to clarify.

The normal flow of letters, e-mails, and memos constitutes an important and influential means of helping create an organizational culture and for providing consistent reinforcement of messages and identity around these communications.

Inserts and Enclosures

Anyone who has received bills from utilities or oil companies knows about inserts and enclosures. A common form of insert is the "payroll stuffer" that goes into paycheck envelopes or direct deposit receipts. The insert is a valuable medium for appealing to natural constituencies for support and for important notices and news. Examples include calls for employees or stockholders to write legislators in support of an organization's stand on a public policy issue or notification of changes in benefits or procedures.

One obvious advantage of the insert is that the message goes to a strategically targeted public who is predisposed to be interested in the message. Readership and receptivity can be high. Another advantage is economy. A small, lightweight printed insert need not add to postage.

Published Speeches, Position Papers, and "Backgrounders"

Expressing an organization's position by electronically posting CEO speeches and position statements on an organizational Web site is a common method of communicating with external publics. It is an effective way to provide information to internal publics. Making such documents available on the Web site or intranet gives employees easy access to quotes and position statements and helps them follow developments and to more effectively represent the organization's positions in their communities. Reprinting CEO speeches or news articles in their entirety provides access to employees to the ideas of the CEO that they will probably not have on a personal basis.

Position papers and backgrounders also help employees understand new assignments quickly and might prevent them from exploring previously tried approaches to problems on the issue if they are familiar with the history of the situation. The downside of this information is that generally only publics with a need for information will seek it out. Information seekers benefit from such information, but internal relations must also encourage other employees to visit the publications archive.

Another method of extending the reach of limited-circulation materials is reprinting publications. With permission from the original publications, favorable publicity, analyses of important issues, and other relevant media coverage of interest to an organization's stakeholder publics can be reprinted and distributed. This adds control to what would otherwise be uncontrolled media coverage. Reprints can be added to the organizational archive for employees to continue referring to as necessary.

Bulletin Boards and Electronic Notices

The use of bulletin boards is widespread and here to stay. If there were no other reason, laws requiring the posting of an ever-increasing number of notices (OSHA and Homeland Security notices, for example) would preserve this medium. Bulletin boards represent both physical spaces that display traditional notices as well as electronic notices. Bulletin boards offer a good public place to corroborate information with brief messages. They provide quick access for making announcements and countering rumors from both internal and external sources.

In order to be effective, bulletin boards need to have regular attention and to be updated often. Seeing the same notice again and again becomes an annoyance and soon leads to inattention. The same category applies to **notices, posters,** and **placards** on walls or columns in work areas. The themes of such postings are usually safety, health, housekeeping, productivity, and security. Keep in mind that many of these items are required by regulations, and the specific mandated wording leaves little room for creativity. Employees get used to these items as part of the environment and often pay little attention to them. Therefore, other forms of internal communication are often needed to supplement bulletin boards and notices in a creative manner to remind employees of the message or to heighten awareness.

Intranet postings are for internal use, as only employees can access the system. The intranet can contain an e-mail system, electronic employee publications, policy manuals, electronic bulletin boards, and many sources of shared information such as project data. Having information available as an electronic document, such as a procedures manual, allows employees to search the document using key terms.

Using an intranet makes employees more productive because information can be located quickly and shared easily. Approximately three-fourths of American businesses use an intranet system because:

1. It gives you the ability to disseminate information widely and rapidly.

2. An intranet empowers employees by providing them with ready access to the information they need.

3. It overcomes geography, so that people in distant locations can work together on projects. Communication is likely to be more frequent and more two-way in a work group that uses an intranet.[28]

Senior Vice President of IBM Jon Iwata said that in recent restructuring, "We figured out that what employees want is one intranet where everything is logically integrated. They don't want to hop around 8,000 sites; they want to stay in one place and have everything come to them. That requires all kinds of collaboration inside the company." He estimated that its intranet saved the organization $2 billion cost of operation savings in a few years of use.[29]

Intranets also create concern in internal relations. The advent of "spyware," or software that monitors everything a PC does, raises the issue of privacy. Many versions of snooping software can be installed on a machine without the knowledge of the user, and some can even be placed and activated on the computer surreptitiously via e-mail.[30] Employees might feel less empowered, and mistrusted, if their every move on the computer is monitored, although this approach can prevent policy infractions such as the use of scandalous Web sites. However the ethical and legal issues of computer surveillance are handled, internal publics should be involved in and aware of the decision.

A second problem for an intranet system is that hackers could sabotage, disrupt, or steal information by electronically breaking into the site. Web sites can be hijacked internally by employee hackers or accessed externally to redirect those trying to enter a legitimate site. In the case of Westpac Banking Corporation, for example, the Australian organization's Web site was hijacked through an Internet service provider in the United States. Even though customer banking information remained secure, the breach shook primarily customer confidence in the bank's security. For these reasons, security of intranet and Internet sites are major concerns. Potential threats should be communicated about immediately.

FACE-TO-FACE COMMUNICATION AND THE "GRAPEVINE"

The heart of communication inside an organization is verbal communication. Research findings show that employees prefer direct communication from their superiors over e-mail, memo, voice mail, or any other form. Studies also show that the most memorable and effective type of message delivery for employees is traditional face-to-face communication. Verbal communication has a significant impact on organizational culture and deserves attention, even though it is often an informal medium.[31]

The grapevine is neither a formal nor a controlled medium, but **word of mouth** is often the quickest means for communicating information. The grapevine is a potent line of communication, but is also dangerous because the information it carries is often unreliable or "enhanced." And e-mail makes the grapevine work with the speed of electrons on copper wire or the speed of light over the fiber optic network!

Sometimes the grapevine is actually harmful, or threatens to be. Rumors of downsizing and layoff, of a hostile takeover by a competitor, of friction among officials, of sexual harassment charges, or of bad blood between factions can cause dissention within the organization with the speed of a wildfire. Rumors can travel far beyond the organization, becoming more and more distorted as it spreads. Hints of trouble tend to breed trouble whenever there is a chip on somebody's shoulder.

The public relations staff usually stays tuned in to the grapevine. When trouble brews, they squelch the gossip by releasing the full facts. Too often, however, the grapevine is the source of misinformation. **The lesson for the public relations practitioner is that the grapevine will fill the information gaps left by an inadequate internal communication program.** The informal, uncontrolled channels take over when the formal, controlled channels do not meet the need and demand for information.

HOTLINES

Hotlines and toll-free phone numbers are not just used to communicate with external publics anymore. They are also used to allow employees to call with concerns or even as an anonymous whistle-blower source to report fraud. Anonymous e-mail systems are also used as "tip-off" hotlines in which employees can report wrongdoing for further investigation without the stigma of being named the "whistle-blower."

For example, in the United States, section 301(4)(B) of the Sarbanes Oxley Act requires publicly held (i.e., stock issuing) organizations to have an anonymous system that allows for reporting "questionable" accounting and management practices. As a result, companies that act as third-party call centers have become popular because they guarantee source anonymity and have a consistent method of interviewing callers and documenting claims for further investigation. For a good example, visit www.tnwinc.com, a company that says it provides whistle-blower service to one-third of the largest American businesses.

Hotlines should not be limited to whistle-blower alerts, however. They can also be helpful for identifying trends within the organization that are problematic and need resolution before they rise to the level of an issue or crisis. The concerns reported on a hotline can range from work schedule conflicts with picking up children before the day care closes, to exposing someone padding an expense account report to accusations of sexual harassment.

Hotlines are also used in internal relations for disseminating basic information. For example, Johnson & Johnson employees use a toll-free hotline to dial for emergency or weather information, such as closing due to ice or heavy snow. This information is also sent to radio stations, but the hotline provides employees a convenient and expedient source of organizational information.

Adding a hotline number exclusively for employees or adding a "push a certain number" menu option to an existing employee toll-free number are economical ways to provide information and for giving information and for giving employees an opportunity to give feedback. Such a two-way symmetrical communication outlet that should not be overlooked as a valuable source of feedback from internal publics.

MEETINGS AND TELECONFERENCES

Meetings bring people together, providing both opportunities to speak and opportunities to listen, a method of two-way communication. Work group meetings, quality control circles, and participative management sessions are examples of small, task-oriented meetings. Face-to-face meetings are expensive in time away from routine tasks and often include travel expenses. However, meetings are economical in the long run because of both the ideas they produce and their team-building effects. Employees prefer face-to-face communication on many topics—from organizational goals to financial and competitor information.[32]

Just as with other communication strategies, a meeting requires specific objectives, careful planning and staging, and skillful direction. Exchange of viewpoints can be open but controlled so that the meeting does not drag or get diverted from its purpose. Effectiveness depends on the conveyor's ability to lead and articulate. For some meetings, specially trained group-process facilitators serve this vital role, while participants delve into important content issues. One school of thought is that important meetings involving people of different levels trying to resolve conflicts, to address crises, or to make critical decisions should be guided by a process facilitator so that power, content, and process are not vested in one person—the boss.

For large gatherings, particularly those bringing together the entire employee force or important external publics, the public relations staff is called on to help plan the meeting. Annual meetings, for example, require a great deal of preparation for top executives and commitment from shareholders expecting a return on their time investment. Preparation for such large meetings is complex and extensive, so much so that many organizations contract with specialized firms to provide meeting-management services.

To accomplish group decisions, many organizations use the latest satellite, telecommunication, and computer technologies to bring ideas and people together. One approach is to give members gathered around a table their own individual key-pads connected to a single computer.

Some major global corporations have created state-of-the-art electronic meeting systems capable of connecting people around the world instantaneously to work together on a single problem. For example, IBM installed 20 "TeamFocus electronic meeting rooms" with personal computers and multimedia capabilities on a global network. Whether installed in a single room or designed as a multimedia global network, these new electronic "group decision support systems" are replacing traditional meetings when time or budget constraints do not allow for travel. Electronic communication, such as the use of intranet systems, often takes the place of face-to-face communication.[33] However, traditional, face-to-face meetings are still highly valued and a preferred means of communication by employees, especially when their input on an issue is sought.

The primary reason for using teleconferencing is to reach people at many locations all at the same time with the same message. During the Tylenol poisoning crisis, for example, Johnson & Johnson used teleconferencing to hold national press conferences in 30 cities to answer reporters' questions and to keep the media updated on developments. In the several decades since that crisis, teleconferencing technology has expanded to include both Internet and satellite teleconferencing. Internet technology, in particular, has expanded the range of possibilities for meetings and speeches. For example, key speakers unable to take time to travel to participate in person can address the meeting via teleconferencing. Or simultaneous sessions in several cities can be linked electronically with speakers shown on large-screen television equipment. The savings in travel time and costs, meeting facilities, and boarding of participants can more than offset the costs of technology.

For example, both PRSA and IABC regularly hold educational teleconference (or video-conference) seminars for members. A typical teleconference by IABC reaches about 1,200 members in 22 cities. There are many uses for this technology, and the level of two-way interactivity allowed depends on the technology used. For example, the National Safety Council held a meeting for almost 2,000 participants in 45 U.S. cities. Part of the program consisted of a question-and-answer period in which participants engaged in two-way communication with the speakers.

VIDEO AND FILM PRESENTATIONS

Sponsored videos and films are produced by or commissioned by an organization for sales, training, or public relations purposes. The intent is not to reap direct, immediate monetary return at the box office, but rather to develop favorable impressions, reactions, and behavior in viewing audiences.

A classic case demonstrates the potential impact and audience for film and video—Allstate Insurance Company's short subject, *Ridin' the Edge*. Allstate campaigned vigorously to make air bags standard safety equipment on new cars, whereas some auto manufacturers resisted. A crash scene in the Hollywood movie *Moving Violation* called for a stunt driver to crash into a concrete wall at 33 miles per hour. Allstate provided air bag–equipped cars from their test fleet and technical advice in exchange for the right to use the scene footage in *Ridin' the Edge*. The film short was shown more than 125,000 times during the first four years and seen by more than 46 million people. Follow-up research on opinions toward air bags indicated that 27 percent more viewers approved of air bags than nonviewers. Only 2 percent of viewers disapproved of air bags, compared with 9 percent for nonviewers.[34]

The film was shown on commercial, public, and cable television; as a short in theaters; and to all types of groups and classes. Many police academies, driver education instructors, and insurance class teachers still use the film. Allstate's film surely helped keep air bags on the public agenda despite the then-strong resistance by automobile manufacturers.

Of course, the Internet is also used to disseminate video productions to publics. For example, BMW created "mini" films commissioning some of Hollywood's top directors to produce video just for Internet distribution. The video reached target publics and audiences. Web-monitoring software totaled how many "hits" were made, helping BMW select the most effective messages to communicate with target publics.

Motion pictures and video offer the following communication strengths:

1. They combine the impact of sight, sound, drama and movement, color, and music.
2. They present ideas involving motion that cannot be described effectively by print or audio means.
3. They attract sustained and exclusive attention to a message for the length of the showing.
4. They make explicit the time factor in any operation or series of events
5. They provide a believable record of events.
6. They show processes that cannot ordinarily be seen by the naked eye.
7. They bring the past and the distant to the viewer.
8. They enlarge, reduce, or simplify objects, as well as illustrate abstractions through the use of photography, cartoons, and graphics.
9. Above all, they let the viewers see with their own eyes: seeing is believing.

Digital video-editing technology and nonlinear video-editing software have added speed and economy to video production. Organizations use audio and video production because they have complete control of their messages. Organizations frequently use digital video technology, as it has become more affordable. These changes allow for higher-quality products for small businesses and nonprofits in most budgets. Some video-production classes or public relations campaigns classes even include filming and producing a public service announcement (PSA) for a nonprofit organization as class fieldwork. Public relations work in the public interest is often donated by firms, and is known as **pro bono** (free) work. For example, all communication related to the *Discovery Place Science Museum* in Charlotte, North Carolina, was produced pro bono service by the public relations department of a local multiservice agency.

DISPLAYS

In almost every factory, headquarters, or hospital there is a reception room, show-room, cafeteria, or lounge. Almost every industry has a common location that is useful for displaying information about the organization. For example, every college has the equivalent of an Old Main, student union, or "main quad" on campus. Every branch of the military and government has sites for displays and exhibits to perpetuate its memories, receive guests, and show its progress, as illustrated in Figure 9.5. Exhibits serve to perpetuate **organizational memory** about **shared history** and a **sense of identity** among internal publics and also serve to educate external publics about the organization.

Permanent installations at theme parks, zoos, museums, airports, and other public attractions have become major public relations tools. Corporate displays now serve as both entertainment and information attractions at the major Walt Disney centers in Florida and California, as well as Sea Worlds in Florida, Ohio, and California. The University of Illinois College of Agricultural, Consumer and Environmental Sciences provides educational exhibits for Chicago's Lincoln Park Farm-in-the-Zoo as a way to reach urban residents with information about agriculture, consumer issues, and the environment.

For anyone who has ever taken a plant tour or visited a major fair, the content of such exhibits needs little explanation. Displays must be conceived as part of the total public relations program designed to reach target publics, both internal and external. Displays include the following public relations uses:

1. Create or maintain an identity of the organization, emphasizing its successes
2. Show the depth and breadth of the organization's operations
3. Reinforce organizational culture and generate a team spirit
4. Recruit personnel
5. Remind visitors of what the organization values

FIGURE 9.5

"FAT MAN" AND "LITTLE BOY" EXHIBIT, BRADBURY SCIENCE MUSEUM, LOS ALAMOS NATIONAL LABORATORY, NEW MEXICO

For example, the lobby display at Johnson & Johnson's corporate headquarters includes a broad display of the organization's products—including interesting historical products from the nineteenth century—and features the founders and the organization's credo.

This chapter did not cover all the internal media available to practitioners. The intent here was to introduce the major media and employee communication channels used in internal relations. **Controlled media** are the primary media for communicating with internal publics. The composition and concentration of internal publics makes them relatively easy to reach with controlled media such as employee publications, training videos, and the intranet. Because external publics are often large and dispersed, sometimes making controlled media impractical, uncontrolled media and other communication targeted at external publics are topics in the next chapter.

NOTES

[1] Paul Bear Bryant, *Great Quotes from Great Leaders* (Lombard, IL: Celebrating Excellence Publishing, 1990), 119.

[2] Jonah Bloom, "Internal Communications is Key Ingredient to Growing Starbucks Worldwide," *P.R. Week* (September 16, 2002): 8.

[3] Alvie L. Smith in letter to authors, March 28, 1993.

[4] Alvie L. Smith, "Getting Managers Off Their Butts and into the Communication Game," *Communication World* 9, no. 1 (January 1992): 35.

[5] Linda Grant, "The Ascent of Delta," *Los Angeles Times Magazine* (June 16, 1991): 17–19, 32–33.

[6] Paul Holmes. "Employers Must Be Up Front with Employees, Who Are Well Equipped to Cut through the Spin," *P.R. Week* (January 19, 2004): 9.

[7] Eric M. Eisenberg and Patricia Riley, "Organizational Culture" in *The New Handbook of Organizational Communication,* ed. Fred M. Jablin and Linda L. Putnam (Thousand Oaks, CA: Sage, 2001), 291–322.

[8] Geert Hofstede, *Culture's Consequences: International Differences in Work Related Values* (Newbury Park, CA: Sage, 1980).

[9] Larissa A. Grunig, James E. Grunig, and David M. Dozier, *Excellent Public Relations and Effective Organizations: A Study of Communication Management in Three Countries* (Mahwah, NJ: Lawrence Erlbaum Associates, 2002), 482.

[10] Henry Mintzberg, *Power in and around Organizations*, (Englewood Cliffs, NJ: Prentice Hall, 1983).

[11] Shannon A. Bowen and Robert L. Heath "Issues Management, Systems, and Rhetoric: Exploring the Distinction between Ethical and Legal Guidelines at Enron," *Journal of Public Affairs* (in press).

[12] James E. Grunig and Larissa A. Grunig, "Models of Public Relations and Communication," in *Excellence in Public Relations and Communication Management*, ed. James E. Grunig (Hillsdale, NJ: Lawrence Erlbaum Associates, 1992), 299.

[13] Ibid.

[14] Larissa A. Grunig, James E. Grunig, and David M. Dozier, *Excellent Public Relations and Effective Organizations: A Study of Communication Management in Three Countries* (Mahwah, NJ: Lawrence Erlbaum Associates, 2002), 535.

[15] Ibid., 61.

[16] James E. Grunig and Jon White, "The Effect of Worldviews on Public Relations Theory and Practice" in *Excellence in Public Relations and Communication Management*, ed. James E. Grunig (Hillsdale, NJ: Lawrence Erlbaum Associates, 1992), 31–64.

[17] Krishnamurthy Sriramesh, James E. Grunig, and Jody Buffington, "Corporate Culture and Public Relations," in *Excellence in Public Relations and Communication Management*, ed. James E. Grunig (Hillsdale, NJ: Lawrence Erlbaum Associates, 1992), 577–595.

[18] Stephen P. Robbins, *Organization Theory: Structure, Design, and Applications*, 3rd ed. (Englewood Cliffs, NJ: Prentice Hall, 1990).

[19] David M. Dozier, with Larrisa A. Grunig, and James E. Grunig. *Manager's Guide to Excellence in Public Relations and Communication Management* (Mahwah, NJ: Lawrence Erlbaum Associates, 1995), 15.

[20] Shannon A. Bowen, *A Theory of Ethical Issues Management: Contributions of Kantian Deontology to Public Relations' Ethics and Decision Making,* (Unpublished Doctoral Dissertation, University of Maryland, College Park, MD, 2000).

[21] Kathryn Theus, "Organizational Ideology, Structure, and Communication Efficacy: A Causal Analysis," in *Public Relations Research Annual* (Vol. 3) ed. James E. Grunig and Larissa A. Grunig (Hillsdale, NJ: Lawrence Erlbaum Associates, 1991), 147.

[22] Jim McBride, "Enhance Employee Commitment by Improving Knowledge of Organizational Goals," *San Diego Daily Transcript*, (Fri., April 12, 2002).

[23] Shannon A. Bowen and Robert L. Heath "Issues Management, Systems, and Rhetoric: Exploring the Distinction between Ethical and Legal Guidelines at Enron."

[24] Robert L. Heath, *Management of Corporate Communication: From Interpersonal Contacts to External Affairs*, (Hillsdale, NJ: Lawrence Erlbaum Associates, 1994).

[25] Patrick E. Murphy, *Eighty Exemplary Ethics Statements*, (Notre Dame, IN: University of Notre Dame Press, 1998).

[26] Shannon A. Bowen, "Elite Executives in Issues Management: The Role of Ethical Paradigms in Decision Making," *Journal of Public Affairs* 2, no. 4 (2002): 270–283.

[27] *pr reporter* 35, no. 50 (December 21, 1992), 1, 3.

[28] Intranets Revolutionize How Companies Operate and Communicate, *Ragan's Intranet Report* 10, no. 10 (1996): 1–8, 1.

[29] "Interview with Jon Iwata: Employee Comms Vital to How IBM's Work Gets Done," *P.R. Week* (May 17, 2004), 7.

[30] John Schwartz, "Snoop Software Is Generating Privacy Concerns," *New York Times* (October 10, 2003), C1.

[31] Angela D. Sinickas, "Intranets, anyone?" *Communication World* (January February, 2004): 30–34.

[32] Ibid., 31.

[33] Ibid., 33.

[34] Don Costa, "Winning with a Short Subject Film," *Public Relations Journal* 38, no. 9 (September 1982), 24–26.

ADDITIONAL SOURCES

Daft, Richard L. *Organization Theory and Design,* 5th ed. Minneapolis, MN: West Publishing Co., 1995. Discusses internal organizational effectiveness from a business management perspective.

Grunig, James E. "Symmetrical Systems of Internal Communication." In *Excellence in Public Relations and Communication Management*, edited by James E. Grunig, 531–75. Hillsdale, NJ: Lawrence Erlbaum Associates, 1992. Develops model of internal communication as a symmetrical, information sharing system.

Grunig, Larissa A., James E. Grunig, and David M. Dozier. *Excellent Public Relations and Effective Organizations: A Study of Communication Management in Three Countries.* Mahwah, NJ: Lawrence Erlbaum Associates, 2002. Chapter 11 reports findings on organizational culture, gender and diversity, knowledge, CEO value, and organizational structure.

Heath, Robert L. *Management of Corporate Communication: From Interpersonal Contacts to External Affairs.* Hillsdale, NJ: Lawrence Erlbaum Associates, 1994. Links public relations and organizational communication theory.

Hickson, Mark III, and Don W. Stacks. *Organizational Communication in the Personal Context.* Needham Heights, MA: Allyn & Bacon, 1998. Outlines role of communication in organization, tracing the function from the employee's perspective "from interview to retirement."

Johnson, Melissa A. "Public Relations and Technology: Practitioner Perspectives." *Journal of Public Relations Research* 9, no. 3 (1997): 213–36. Reports study of how new communication technologies affect public relations roles and work.

10 EXTERNAL MEDIA AND MEDIA RELATIONS

Every newspaper when it reaches the reader is the result of a whole series of selections as to what items shall be printed, in what position they shall be printed, how much space each shall occupy, what emphasis each shall have. There are no objective standards here. There are conventions.[1]

—Walter Lippmann, 1922

The Internet gives you the power to end-run reporters, editors, and even complete news organizations when you really need to communicate directly with important audiences.[2]

—Shirley Fulton and Al Guyant, 2002

STUDY GUIDE

After studying Chapter 10, you should be able to

- Outline how technology has changed external communication practice and media.

- Discuss the major controlled and uncontrolled media used for communicating with external publics.

- Define the relationship between practitioners and journalists as being mutually dependent and mutually beneficial, but sometimes as adversarial.

- Outline basic guidelines for building good media relations and working with the press.

Practitioners of public relations use printed words, spoken words, images, and combinations of all these communication forms. They use both controlled media and uncontrolled media to communicate with their organizations' many publics. *Controlled* media include those in which practitioners have the say over what is said, how it is said, when it is said, and—to some extent—to whom it is said. *Uncontrolled* media are those over which practitioners have no direct role in decisions about media content. Instead, media gatekeepers decide if it is reported, what is reported, how it is reported, when it is reported, and to whom it is reported.

Technology has changed our notions about media, especially the concept of mass media. As one scholar concluded years ago, "The net effect of all these technologies will be to make channels, and the kinds of content they carry, differentially available to the public."[3] Notions about mass, undifferentiated passive audiences are also outdated as *interactive* media replace conventional one-way channels.

Each advance in communication technology results in more individualized communications, such as customized textbooks and music CDs. Sophisticated software programs linked to databases and high-speed printers generate thousands of letters addressed to individuals with information specific to each. For example, after making a donation to a charity's annual fund drive, you likely will receive an individualized thank-you letter. The capability to individualize direct mail and e-mail changes the media mix in many programs targeting important stakeholder publics.

Some meeting and convention planners incorporate interactive audience response systems to get immediate input and feedback on program topics and presentations. Movie producers use real-time audience response systems to pretest story lines and outcomes, replacing passive movie viewing followed by questionnaires. Online polls make even newspapers, magazines, radio, and television quasi two-way media. Broadband and DSL networks create veritable information freeways that have changed communication, commerce, and social relationships at all levels. In short, new media and communication technology have changed the media–audience experience.

What follows is a snapshot of the major media used in public relations. The first part of this chapter summarizes some of the new media developments that are changing communication at an unprecedented rate. In fact, no textbook can keep up with the almost daily changes in the media landscape. The second part of the chapter examines the media used primarily for—but not limited to—reaching large and dispersed publics. The chapter concludes with a discussion of media relations, one of public relations' primary assignments.

NEW MEDIA, NEW CHALLENGES

The Internet represents the most ubiquitous leading edge of the communication revolution. The digital world has changed communication within organizations and between organizations and their various publics. In public relations, to paraphrase the words of a song, it's the information superhighway or no way.

New-media experts John Pavlik and Shawn McIntosh call the sea change in media "convergence":

> …The coming together of computing, telecommunications, and media in a digital environment. Convergence and the changes it is bringing are fundamentally changing many aspects of mass media and communication.[4]

Advancing technology has changed the way communication is produced, distributed, displayed, and stored. And although many recognize that new media technology changes how public relations is practiced, the rapidity of change illustrates how practitioners are scrambling to adjust. Consequently, the Institute for Public Relations and WORLDCOM Public Relations Group commissioned a study of the Internet's impact on public relations. Although the findings may not impress college students today, they document a major change in the practice at the beginning of the twenty-first century. The conclusions include the following.

- There was virtually unanimous agreement (98%) when the public relations professionals were asked if recent advances in technology such as e-mail and the Internet have had an impact on how they do their jobs.
- A huge majority (91%) believe they now stay in touch with more people in their business and professional environments than they did before e-mail arrived. Only 7 percent disagree with this statement.
- Most (90%) agreed the ability to transmit instantaneous written communication via e-mail and to access real-time information via the Internet has quickened the pace of decision making in news journalism.
- The average public relations professional surveyed in this study spends between 15 and 19 hours online each week, and goes online 5.8 days during an average week. …One-third (33%) say they are online seven days each week.
- Subjects were also asked whether they would prefer a daily newspaper, Internet-connected computer, radio, telephone, or television if they were stranded alone somewhere for an extended period of time and could have access to only one of those media. Results show 69 percent choose the Internet-connected computer….[5]

This study also raised the possibility of another major change in how public relations operates vis-à-vis the media:

> In fact, one of the greatest advantages of the Internet as a public relations medium is the reality it has…to provide direct and immediate access to specific target audiences, thus bypassing journalists and traditional news media.[6]

The change is even more profound, however. The basic encoding of messages has changed from analog to digital, what Nicholas Negroponte calls the transition from "atoms" to "bits."[7] The change from atoms to digits, which led to convergence, changed the nature of communication. In the "analog" era, publishers disseminated information to audiences who had limited ways to communicate with each other or with the source. In contrast,

> Audiences in the age of convergence can communicate via e-mail, online forums, and other interactive media more easily and quickly with those who create and publish mass communication content. In addition, they can also create mass communication content themselves and reach far larger audiences for much lower costs than they could have with traditional media.[8]

For example, weblogs, or "blogs," began as simply personal electronic journals posted on the Internet. Bloggers could "publish" their observations, opinion, and interpretations. By the time the Democrats met in Boston and the Republicans in New York for their national conventions in 2004, some well-established bloggers worked as "credentialed media" alongside reporters from the traditional news organizations. As one blogger predicted: "The 2004 conventions will be remembered as the conventions of the blog; just like the 1952 Republican convention was the convention of the television, and the 1924 conventions were the conventions of the radio."[9]

But of course, bloggers did not have to attend the conventions in order to become publishers of news and opinion about the issues, speakers, and candidates. For those in virtual communities of like-thinking participants, blogs have become the sources of choice in the interconnected and digitalized cyberspace. Public relations practitioners are increasingly turning to these new media players to reach Web-savvy publics, both by trying to attract blog coverage and by creating their own blogs as part of a communication strategy.

Relatively easy, cheap, and fast access to the Internet has also changed politics in other countries as well. Maybe the most dramatic demonstration of the impact of communication technology occurred in Korea, the world's most wired nation: In the 2002 presidential election, exit polls showed that the candidate most popular with young voters, Roh Moo Hyun, was losing. What happened next surely was a first in the application of convergence:

> His supporters hit the chat rooms to drum up support. Within minutes more than 800,000 e-mails were sent to mobiles to urge supporters to go out and vote. Traditionally apathetic voters surged to the polls and, by 2 p.m., Roh took the lead and went on to win the election. A man with little support from either the mainstream media or the nation's conglomerates sashayed into office on an Internet on-ramp.[10]

New Internet-based communication methods have changed the media landscape in organization-public communication. The World Wide Web has the potential to communicate with a mass, global audience. On one hand, it is the power to instantly send messages to specific target publics, as well as receive messages from them, 24 hours a day and seven days a week that makes the Internet so central to public relations communication. Rapidly advancing technology requires new knowledge and skill sets in a "cyberworld" without borders and with an insatiable appetite for access, exchange, news, and information.

The practitioner who heads Fleishman-Hillard's worldwide interactive practices summarized the new context of public relations communication:

> In the digital world, text, voice, photographs, video and animation flow along a single bit-stream of information that consumers process in a 360-degree manner. A casual look at Web sites of major U.S. newspapers today shows the degree to which one-dimensional newsprint has morphed into three-dimensional, multilevel content.[11]

Trying to document developments in new media technology produces information with the shelf life of lettuce. By the time this chapter is published, no doubt some of the examples may be passé. However, the overriding conclusion is obvious: Rapidly evolving technology and blurring distinctions among media converging in the digital world will send shock waves of change in how media are used to communicate **with** stakeholder publics. The key for public relations is that the new technology promotes **interactive communication**, the essence of building and maintaining relationships. Nevertheless, traditional media still have roles to play—the topics of the sections that follow.

TRADITIONAL MEDIA, NEW USES

Traditional mass media have long provided economical, effective methods of communicating with large and widely dispersed publics. Consequently, work in public relations requires understanding of and skills in using newspapers, magazines, trade publications, AM and FM radio, television, cable, books, and so on. To handle this part of the job, practitioners must understand the role of information, the various media and their production requirements, and the values of the gatekeepers who control access.

Practitioners also need to understand that media are constrained by their mechanical requirements, their values, their rules, and—for many—the necessity of "delivering" an audience to advertisers. Today's communicators are confronted with a paradox: Multiplying channels of communication permit a sharper focus of messages, but greatly escalate competition for audience attention.

Mass media reach into nearly every home and workplace, showering citizens with far more messages than they can absorb. General and specialized media appear to represent an easily used means of disseminating ideas and information to publics, but this can be delusive. Just because these media distribute messages and have audiences, that does not mean that the messages are received, accepted, or acted upon.

Additionally, the public media have a relatively fixed capacity; newspapers and magazines have a limited number of columns for editorial matter, and there are only 24 hours in a broadcast day. Hence, any one of these media cannot possibly convey all the news and information available. Receivers also have limited time and attention to give to the millions of messages. In a media world crammed with messages, only a tiny fraction gets past the door and into the home. Even fewer get attention. Fewer yet have impact.

Nonetheless, institutionalized power is largely exercised through control of the means and content of mass communication. Mass media constitute the key components in a nation's public-information system, a system in which public relations practitioners play an increasingly important role. Competition for access to media is spirited and is becoming more so. Consequently, practitioners must adjust their communication strategy to rapidly changing media and audiences.

Newspapers

Newspapers remain the workhorse of the public information system. When people think of publicity, they almost instinctively think of the newspaper. For good reason, because newspaper coverage remains the foundation of most information programs.

Daily, weekend, Sunday, weekly, semiweekly, ethnic, labor, religious, scholastic, and foreign language newspapers are most frequently read by the most literate people. For most influential citizens, reading the newspaper is as much a daily habit as are eating and sleeping. As a result, the influence of the world's great newspapers is also great. Journalism scholar and educator John C. Merrill refers to these as the "internationally elite newspapers":

> Such papers—mainly dailies—are read by the world's intellectuals, political and opinion leaders, and cosmopolitan, concerned citizens of various countries. They are directed at a fairly homogeneous audience globally and have a greater interest in international relations and the arts and humanities than the general run of mass-appeal papers. They are well-informed, articulate papers that thoughtful people the world over take seriously.[12]

U.S. papers on Merrill's list of elite dailies include the *New York Times*, *Los Angeles Times*, *Washington Post*, and *Christian Science Monitor*. His European list includes *Le Monde* in France, *Neue Zürcher Zeitung* in Switzerland, *El País* in Spain, *Daily Telegraph* in England, and *Svenska Dagbladet* in Sweden. Asia's elite dailies include Japan's *Asahi Shimbun* and *Mainichi Shimbun*, and India's *Times of India* and *Statesman*. According to Merrill, "The elite papers recognize that they will not reach many people, but they seek to have an impact that no other medium does on the serious, intellectual, opinion-leading segment of the world community."[13] On the other hand, *USA Today* and *The Wall Street Journal* reach both large U.S. and international audiences, with 2.6 and 2.1 million subscribers, respectively.[14]

Newspapers are a moving force in society. As the late Supreme Court Justice Felix Frankfurter once said: "To an extent far beyond the public's own realization, public opinion is shaped by the kind, the volume, and the quality of the news columns." Nor should editorial endorsement be totally discounted. For example, when last-minute challenges threatened to bring to a halt the "Block E" downtown revitalization project in Minneapolis, public relations firm Carmichael Lynch Spong helped place an opinion piece written with the city mayor in the *Star Tribune*, the major daily in Minnesota. Within days, the paper's editorial staff wrote a similarly supportive editorial. The project proceeded without serious opposition and delay.

Newspaper scholars have suggested that the power of the press comes from its dissemination of information and its impact on public interest in important issues (see Chapter 8 for discussion of the agenda-setting function). Although no longer the primary news medium for the majority, newspapers remain a powerful force in shaping the public agenda and influencing the outcome of debate. In short, individuals seeking in-depth political content turn to newspapers.[15]

From the early part of the twentieth century until World War II, when newspapers were the prime source of news and entertainment, the number of daily newspapers has declined. The number began to stabilize in the 1950s and remained about the same through the mid-1970s. For example, there were 1,772 daily papers in 1950, with only 16 fewer, 1,756, in 1975. Today, however, the number has dropped to only 1,457 dailies because of mergers and discontinued editions.[16]

Newspaper circulation in the United States peaked in 1993 at almost 63 million. Recent circulation figures have dropped below 59 million, but the number of readers per copy is 2.3. On Sundays, circulation is 59 million, and the number of readers per copy is more than 2.4.[17] There are 102 daily newspapers in Canada, with a total circulation of 5 million. In both countries, the major change was from evening editions to morning editions. Whereas in 1980, only about one out of five daily newspapers had morning editions, now more than half are morning papers.[18]

Although the number of dailies continues to decline, the average circulation for surviving papers increases, and newspaper reading remains fairly stable despite increased media competition. Figures compiled by the Newspaper Association of America show that approximately 59 percent of all adults read a daily newspaper and 67 percent read Sunday papers. However, only 13 percent of 18- to 24-year-olds read a newspaper daily. On the other hand, more than 43 percent of all readers had attended college or had college degrees. Newspapers tend to attract disproportionately white readers, however, as 84 percent are white.[19]

A study of newspaper readers in Brazil identified five types: **Instrumental readers** use newspapers to get information they think will be useful for daily living. Reading is purely an information-seeking activity to understand what is happening and why it is happening. **Opinion makers** use newspapers to get advice and guidance for forming and validating opinion. Newspapers help them make up their minds on issues and provide insight on what others are thinking. **Pleasure readers** use newspaper reading as an enjoyable habit. They see newspapers as a source of enjoyment and reading as an end in itself, not as a means for accomplishing some other purpose. **Ego boosters** use newspapers as a source of information for impressing others. They read to enhance their self-image and status with others. **Scanners** use newspapers for many and varied reasons, but there is no single motivation or pattern strong enough to suggest they belong in one of the other four types.[20]

The number and circulation of weekly and other newspapers papers published less than four times each week has rebounded in recent years. There are 6,700 "weeklies" with a circulation of more than 50 million.[21] Most weeklies emphasize **local** news about government, nonprofit organizations, schools, sports, business developments, and personal news. Likewise, births, weddings, anniversaries, and obituaries are big news. As many will tell you, they read the obituaries first. Public relations practitioners, walled in by skyscrapers and stuck in traffic jams or crowded mass transit, should not forget the people in rural, small-town, and suburban settings or the newspapers that help shape their opinions. In fact, many executives (with public relations assistance) write "specials to..." for the opinion–editorial pages of these papers to express views on issues relevant to local operations and the organization's interests beyond the local setting.

The Sunday paper generally gets a more intensive and leisurely reading. It tends to emphasize feature material—stories without a time element—with stories often more like those in a magazine than in a daily paper. In addition, practitioners should not overlook the national Sunday supplement magazines and local weekend magazines published by large-city newspapers. For example, 345 newspapers include *Parade Magazine* every Sunday, with a circulation of 36 million and almost 75 million readers. The second-largest Sunday supplement is *USA Weekend*, which has a circulation of more than 22 million.[22]

Newspaper space allocated to news has decreased in recent years, at least relative to the increased glut of information pouring into newsrooms. Typically newspapers devote about 50 percent of their space to editorial matter, some as little as 25 percent. The rest is advertising (averaging 46 percent) and unpaid public service (4 percent). Local news makes up the largest proportion of editorial content—about 75 percent of all news published.

The **strengths** of newspapers are many. No other medium offers comparable audience size and breadth day in and day out or the range and depth of content. Most newspapers are produced in local communities and are indigenous to those communities. They have a firsthand intimacy with their local publics. The local YMCA can reach its community publics through its local newspaper. The state health department can reach its publics through the state's daily and weekly newspapers. A commercial concern with regional distribution can reach its publics using a regional selection of newspapers. Similarly, a national organization can reach many national audiences with newspapers. In short, the local connections give newspapers a perceived credibility that is hard to match.

Technology has changed not only the content of newspapers, but also their organizational structures and how they process news and information. Newspapers have their own Web sites and links to consumer companies. Increasing numbers of readers access newspapers through the Internet. (See Exhibit 10.1 about how the *Los Angeles Times* operates in the age of convergence.)

Wire Services and News Syndicates

News wire services economically and effectively distribute human-interest stories and spot news to state, regional, national, or international media. Publicity with a local angle can be directed to individual media where the information is relevant. For timely stories not limited to a locale, placing them on the wires increases the likelihood of immediate

EXHIBIT 10.1

YOUR FATHER'S NEWSPAPER AND A WHOLE LOT MORE

Carol Perruso
Former President, LATimes.com
Los Angeles Times

Although an ink-on-paper product delivered every 24 hours is still the norm for daily newspapers, and regularly scheduled news shows are the staple of broadcast and cable news, journalists and publishers now realize that the traditional news cycle and format don't meet all of their readers' or viewers' needs.

Readers and viewers consume news at all times of the day and night, whether from an all-news station, a news Web site, a cell phone, or a WiFi connection on their laptops. And much news content—enterprise reporting and analysis, features, reviews, recipes and graphics—has a shelf life considerably longer than 24 hours. For example, a series on HMOs or a map showing earthquake faults or a personal investment column may be most useful at a later date—when the reader or viewer is choosing a new health care plan, buying a house, or deciding on an IRA. So news organizations must be able to produce news 24/7 and make their archives always available.

News format isn't restricted by type of news outlet anymore either. Newspaper Web sites include video and audio, and the Web sites for broadcast/cable news organizations now offer viewers tons of text.

Another development that is altering the way people consume news is Google. Not just a search engine anymore, Google is now a major news outlet. Every day, without human editors, news.google.com displays stories from 4,500 news organizations ranging from ABC, Reuters, and the *Los Angeles Times* to the *New Zealand Herald* or the *Minot Daily News*. Computer algorithms "decide" the top stories. This news judgment is not perfect, but the result is a respectable news product.

The Web has also changed reporting. Information that once had to come from a public relations person (who might

be unavailable on deadline) can now be found on an organization's Web site. Information put online for one use can find itself being repurposed by clever reporters. For example, when NBA Lakers star Kobe Bryant was arrested on suspicion of sexual assault, a Southern California reporter said he was able to download room layouts from the Web site of the resort where the incident took place. He also found the name of the limousine company that served the resort and thereby was able interview limo drivers who might have transported Bryant or his accuser.

How are all these changes affecting how public relations practitioners do their jobs?

- They must be able to respond more quickly to a breaking event.
- The phone numbers and e-mail addresses of Web site editors should be in their Rolodexes and PDAs along with those of reporters.
- News releases should be written with the expectation that they will be archived on their client's Web site.
- Tracking the coverage that they help generate means knowing where it ran on the Web as well as in print and on the air—and how long it stays online. Old information can prove embarrassing at a later date.
- Reporters may want digital copies of press releases and supporting documents so that they can be put on Web.

Digital media will continue to change how we communicate and consume information. Blogs, customizable news feeds, instant text messaging and dynamically generated pages of Web content are just some of the ways that many people consume information today. Digital media will continue to evolve. That doesn't change the fundamental mission of a news organization. It is still to gather and edit the news. It probably won't change the fundamental mission of the public relations practitioner either. But the "physical" product that journalists and PR people produce—to the extent that it still exists in an analog form—is vastly different, as are the deadlines on which they are produced.

and widespread coverage. Being carried by a wire service also increases the acceptability of the practitioner's copy. A well-written wire story can reach newspaper readers, radio listeners, and TV viewers across the nation or around the world. Transmitting millions of words and pictures daily, wire services are influential beyond calculation. Access to these networks is through the nearest bureau or "stringer" correspondent.

Each of the two major wire services in the United States operates international, national, regional, state, and local bureaus. In addition to their newspaper subscribers, both serve online and broadcast customers with news copy and audio feeds. Both sell their news reporting services and products to media worldwide.

Associated Press, founded in 1848 and headquartered in New York City, has 3,700 employees working in 242 bureaus with almost 17,000 media subscribers in 121 countries. "AP"—as it is better known—is a cooperative owned by member newspapers. Subscribers in the United States include almost 1,700 daily and weekly newspapers, 5,000 radio and television stations, and 1,000 AP Radio Network affiliates. Internationally, AP serves 8,500 subscribers. In addition, AP markets its news services to non-media clients. Beginning in early 1993, AP began transmitting publicity photos for a fee, putting it in direct competition with the publicity wire services. (See www.ap.org.)

Privately owned United Press International (UPI) is headquartered in Washington, D.C. It was formed in 1958 by the merger of United Press (founded in 1907 by newspaper magnate E. W. Scripps) and William Randolph Hearst's International News Service. UPI operates under the principles that it provides an independent coverage of world news, and that any newspaper or news organization could purchase the new product. UPI also provides worldwide service, with offices in Hong Kong, London, Santiago, Seoul, and Tokyo. (See www.upi.com.)

Newspapers also subscribe to news services from *New York Times*, *Washington Post*, *Los Angeles Times*, Knight-Ridder, and newspaper syndicates such as King Features Syndicate, National Newspaper Syndicate, News America Syndicate, United Features Syndicate, and Newspaper Enterprises Syndicate.

Internationally, Reuters (United Kingdom), Agence France-Presse (France), New China News Agency (People's Republic of China), and Kyoto (Japan) are a few of the major news services providing news and features for not only newspapers but also radio, television, magazines, and private subscribers. These are large organizations with reporters, editors, and other staff in most major capitals and market centers.

Much like the news wire services, commercial public relations wires provide news from organizations and public relations firms. Practitioners use these distribution services to speed time-critical press releases simultaneously into newsrooms worldwide.

PR Newswire (PRN) introduced electronic distribution of news releases in New York City in 1954. Other PR wires copied the concept. The idea quickly evolved into national systems in the United States, Canada, and England, followed by worldwide news-release distribution systems. Although they differ greatly in size, all these services operate in essentially the same way: charging clients to electronically transmit print, audio, and video new releases to the media and other organizations, with fees based on the extent and type of distribution ordered. For example, PRN can deliver a publicity release by satellite, landline, and Internet to more than 22,000 media outlets worldwide. Media receive these news services at no charge. (See www.prnewswire.com.)

Because they offer fast, simultaneous transmission to the media, practitioners use these wires to send news ranging from major corporate developments and earnings reports, sporting events, and obituaries to invitations to press conferences. They are especially useful in times of emergency. For example, a baby food manufacturer had to urgently distribute a product recall to many media outlets quickly and simultaneously when glass shards were found in one shipment of food products.

Another large portion of print and electronic media content is supplied by the feature, photo, and specialized news syndicates. As in the case of the wire services, placement of a feature or a picture with a syndicate ensures wide, economical distribution and increases the acceptability of material. Most syndicates also distribute columns and comics. For example, United Feature Syndicate distributes columns and commentaries, editorial cartoons, and comic strips. Offerings include Scott Adams's popular "Dilbert," the late Charles Schulz's "Peanuts," and Greg Evans's "Luann." Syndicates charge fees based on each client's circulation or audience size.

As in the case of paid publicity wires, there are also feature services that supply newspapers and periodicals with client-sponsored material without charge. Clients pay the bill. Typical is Derus Media, Chicago, which distributes a monthly script and visual service to radio and television outlets. It also distributes news releases to media reaching Hispanic audiences. Another such service is North American Precis Syndicate, Inc. (NAPS), with offices in New York, Washington, Atlanta, Chicago, and Los Angeles. In its *Featurettes/News To Use*, NAPS distributes consumer news for 750 companies and organizations to more than 7,000 to dailies, weeklies, monthlies, and shoppers.

Magazines

More than 17,000 (some estimate more than 20,000) magazines and specialized publications published in the United States offer effective specialized channels of communication to narrowly defined audiences. Variations in content and audience appeal are almost limitless and ever changing. In 2003 alone, hopeful publishers launched 440 new magazines, but typically only one in 10 is successful.[23] Some do not make it to the first issue. Others fail after the first year or two, disappointing enthusiastic publishers who had visions of attracting both subscribers and advertisers.

One author claims that the first magazines was "America's only national medium," referring to the *Saturday Evening Post*, first published in 1821. Long before, Benjamin Franklin published *General Magazine* in February 1741. Technically, Andrew Bradford's *American Magazine* was the first American magazine, because it appeared in print three days before Franklin's magazine. Historians generally agree, however, that Franklin originated the concept of a magazine.[24]

Magazines provide an array and variety of communication media to reach audiences who share common interests. Circulation giants such as *Modern Maturity*, *Reader's Digest*, *TV Guide*, *National Geographic*, *Better Homes and Gardens*, *Time*, *Newsweek*, *U.S. News & World Report*, *Cosmopolitan*, *Sports Illustrated*, and *Good Housekeeping* reach large national audiences. More narrowly targeted magazines include *Ms.*, *Rolling Stone*, *PC World*, *Wired*, and *Architectural Digest*. Trade and business magazine include *Hoard's Dairyman*, *Women's Wear Daily*, *Business Week*, *Fortune*, and *Forbes*. The sports-recreation-hobby magazines category includes *World Tennis*, *Video Review*, *Popular Photography*, *Snowboarding*, and *Ski* magazine. Clearly, magazines enable communicators to target specific messages to specific audiences.

The changing magazine market—from general to specialized publications—reflects the nation's changing interests and lifestyles. There is a magazine or periodical catering to almost every interest, vocation, and hobby. Advances in offset printing and computerized production have stimulated circulation and advertising revenues by giving advertisers options for buying targeted portions of the total circulation. Regional advertising in such national magazines as *Time* and *Newsweek*, for example, allows advertisers to advertise to a market within a market, even local markets.

Thousands of business and professional publications serve the specialized needs of professional groups, trade associations, and business and industry. These publications generally use prepared news releases if the content serves their readers' economic or professional needs. Each of these publications caters to a carefully defined audience, usually representing the membership lists of the organization publishing the magazine. Examples include PRSA's the *Strategist*, IABC's *Communication World*, and the American Medical Association's *American Medical News*. In addition to collecting subscription fees built into membership fees, many of these publications carry advertising for products and services specific to readers' occupations or professional practices.

Magazines offer several advantages: Opinion leaders read magazines. Magazines provide more durable information than newspapers. Magazine readers have the opportunity to read, reread, discuss, and debate the information gleaned from this source. Readers with special interests turn to magazines for in-depth treatment of topics, such as when older citizens report that magazines are second only to health care specialists as a source for health information. Magazines shape opinions, create preferences for fashions and products, influence house designs and decoration, help set standards for professions and businesses, and enlist political support.

Practitioners study magazines' topics, styles, policies, trends, formats, and so forth, and then apply this knowledge by slanting news and features to specific magazines. They generally do not submit unsolicited material, however. Rather, they work on a tip or query basis when they have something that would have reader appeal. They submit story outlines or feature suggestions. If one is accepted, a practitioner works with the magazine's staff or freelance writers to develop the story. The practitioner's job is to sell ideas to editors and then to cooperate with writers and photographers, who build the ideas into articles.

Magazine publicity placement is almost essential for organizations seeking to influence national or specialized audiences. Yet many practitioners fail in their efforts to get such publicity because they do not understand the lead time of national magazines and the stiff competition for space. The competition comes from the magazine's own editors and staff writers, frequent contributors, and freelance writers who write regularly for national magazines.

Practitioners sometimes overlook working with freelancers. Freelance writers who regularly sell to national magazines are interested in a story about an institution, a person, or an event that possesses at least one of these three qualities: (1) national importance or significance; (2) elements of struggle, conflict, contest, or drama; or (3) anecdotal enrichment and entertainment value. In other words, give the story to a freelance writer. The experienced freelancer known to the magazine gets a check from the magazine and the practitioner gets a publicity placement in a magazine.

Radio

Once thought to be fading because of television and cable, radio today serves a useful and pervasive role in our public information system. Radio offers a wide range of publicity possibilities. It is a mobile medium suited to a mobile people. (Newspaper people like to point out that their medium is also "mobile," and batteries are not required.) It reaches the bedroom and breakfast table in the morning; rides to and from work in the car; goes along to the beach, to the woods, and on fishing trips; and lulls us to sleep at night—a flexibility no other medium can match.

Radio listening remains relatively constant at almost three hours a day, or about 21 hours each week. Almost half listen in cars (46 percent), with the next largest segment listening at home (36 percent). Every day, 75 percent of those 12 years old and older listen to radio, and more than 95 percent listen during each week—reaching a weekly listening audience of more than 223 million. Many begin and end their days listening to radio, with the "New/Talk/Information" (all news, all sports, news and talk, and all talk) format the most popular choice. For example, this format attracts a 16.5 percent share of the total audience, and 41 percent of listeners 65+ years old chose this format.[25]

The Federal Communication Commission (FCC) lists 13,476 licensed radio stations in the United States, of which 2,471 are public "education" FM stations. There are 4,781 AM stations and 6,224 FM stations.[26] In the early 1970s, AM stations attracted three-fourths of the audience. By the early 1990s, more than three-fourths of the total radio listening audience tuned to FM stations. The AM dial is so crowded that nearly half the AM stations ("daytimers") have to shut down 15 minutes after sunset to avoid interfering with others' signals. FM also gained listeners because of its high-quality, static-free stereo sound, which coincided with the development of noise-free recordings. Subscription satellite radio is the fastest-growing option, because it is usually free of advertisements and offers an array of format choices.

Public relations practitioners use radio news releases and audio feeds sent to stations through networks such as the CNNRadio (www.cnn.com), North American Network (Bethesda, MD, www.radiospace.com/about.htm), and News Broadcast Network (New York City, www.newsbroadcastnetwork.com). Distribution is over the Internet or telephone lines to stations targeted by region and format. CNNRadio, for example, distributes to 2,000 affiliated stations worldwide 24 hours a day with four minutes of news on the hour, two-minute updates 30 minutes later, and one-minute news cutaways. To increase local station airings, some audio news services also provide interviews or sound bites that stations then localize.

Even though it is a "mass" medium, radio possesses the qualities of a direct, personal touch, because it uses the spoken word, for the most part, to convey its message. Broadcast pioneer Arthur Godfrey understood this intimate quality when he decided that other radio speakers were reading to, not talking with their audiences. He decided that he would always have a mental image of talking to only one person on the other side of the microphone.

Indeed, radio is a person-to-person medium that flourishes on conversation. Call-in talk shows now set the public agenda and provide a forum for public debate on many local and national issues. The potential impact is great. For example, radio talk-show hosts killed a proposed congressional pay raise and certainly played a role in the Bush–Kerry presidential campaign. Rush Limbaugh has a national radio audience of dedicated listeners. To counter the long dominance of right-leaning radio talk shows, left-leaning talk shows featuring the likes of Al Franken took to the airwaves in the 2004 presidential campaign.

Almost every major city has its own radio all-talk shows that capitalize on local conflict, sensational topics, and legitimate public debate of important issues. Increased emphasis on the discussion format opens up many possibilities for practitioners. Popular talk shows and telephone interviews focusing on controversial issues have an almost insatiable appetite for guests with a message—however controversial it may be.

Public service time seldom is prime listening time, but it is not without value. Since the Federal Communications Commission relaxed its public service requirements for broadcasters, many stations have reduced the number of public service and other nonrevenue programs they broadcast. Yet most stations provide some free time to nonprofit agencies as part of the station's community relations program. In non–prime time the competition for airtime is less intense than during the more desirable—and salable—drive time and other high-listenership hours. That is not to say, however, that an effective program cannot attract and hold listeners even in prime time.

An effective way is to provide radio (and television) *public service announcements* (PSAs)—10 seconds, 30 seconds, or 60 seconds in length. A PSA is any announcement that promotes programs and services of government and voluntary agencies, for which no payment is made to the station. Stations set their own standards, but most use well-prepared PSAs. And they can be effective. For example, the Ad Council produces and distributes PSAs promoting use of seat belts, booster seats, and baby seats, no doubt saving many lives. Local, regional, and state groups promote recycling, storm water pollution prevention, and litter reduction ("Don't Mess with Texas").

Television

The communication phenomenon of the twentieth century was television. No other medium matches television's ability to provide a window on the world. What other medium could transmit live coverage from the international space station as an astronaut and cosmonaut make repairs outside the craft? How could any other medium convey the sights, sounds, and feelings of war like the embedded journalists did during the Iraq war? And most vivid of all, what other medium could convey the horror of the airliners crashing into the World Trade Center towers?

A medium that uses the printed word, spoken word, pictures in motion, color, music, animation, and sound effects—all blended into one message—possesses immeasurable potency. It offers a vast range of possibilities for telling a story, from a terse, 60-second video on a TV newscast, to a half-hour or one-hour documentary film, to 24-hour coverage of a crisis such as the World Trade Center terrorist attacks, to a miniseries extended over several evenings or weeks. Satellites transmit news from any place on the globe, making the powerful, pervasive impact of television a worldwide phenomenon. Television took the lead from newspapers in 1963 as the primary source of news in the United States.

In the United States, 1,750 TV stations broadcast almost around the clock to nearly every household. Literally hundreds of cable channels give viewers more options than they can carefully consider.[27] The average time spent with television approaches the length of a typical workday. Children spend more time watching TV than with their teachers in classrooms. They grow up using the remote control to explore a seemingly endless array of program services such as Disney, Discovery, Black Entertainment TV, TNT, HBO, CNN, and C-SPAN, to name but a few. As former FCC chairman Newton Minow said, viewers' choices have "skyrocketed":

> If you are a sports fan, a news junkie, a stock market follower, a rock music devotee, a person who speaks Spanish, a nostalgic old-movie buff, a congressional-hearing observer, a weather watcher—you now have your own choice. The FCC objective in the early '60s to expand choice has been fulfilled—beyond all expectations.[28]

This is our most intimate mass medium, yet it can attract half the population to watch Janet Jackson "perform" her infamous "wardrobe malfunction" during the 2004 Super Bowl halftime. Television rears our young, serves as the prime source of news and entertainment for most Americans, and provides a powerful soapbox from which citizens' protests can be communicated to the nation and the world. This medium has greatly altered national election campaigns and diminished the role of the political parties.

Researchers in Germany, for example, found that TV newscasts not only caused changes in awareness of problems, but also had consequences on voting intentions.[29] National and international wire services and global TV news networks have created a truly global forum. Events made large by TV shape public opinion worldwide.

Television greatly heightens citizen awareness of the conduct of public institutions. It also creates a sense of frustration for citizens, who witness much that they cannot control—be it the collapse of the World Trade Center towers, Coast Guard cutters intercepting boats overloaded with Haitian refugees, bloated stomachs of starving children and refugees in Sudan, pro-life protesters blockading the entrance to a health-care clinic, the wretched life of homeless families, or developers scraping hillsides flat to build more look-alike houses.

TV brings these and many more pictures of the world into our homes. As Newton Minow concluded, "The most important educational institution in America is television. More people learn more each day, each year, each lifetime from television than from any other source."[30]

Heavy reliance on TV news as a primary source of news disturbs thoughtful observers who know that the limits of time and dominance of dramatic pictures inevitably oversimplify and distort the news. For example, evening network shows, watched by millions of people each night, must tell the story of the world in 4,000 words or less, the equivalent of four columns in a standard-sized newspaper. A "major" story gets 58 seconds. Before retiring from the *MacNeil-Lehrer News Hour* on PBS (now the *News Hour*), Robert MacNeil bluntly admitted,

> In most of the stories television cares to cover there is always the "right bit," the most violent, the most bloody, the most pathetic, the most tragic, the most wonderful, the most awful moment. Getting the effective "bit" is what television news is all about.[31]

The wide range of news stories and time pressures in television news, coupled with today's news values and technology, produces a compound of fiction and fact in terse fragments to viewers around the world. Adam Clayton Powell III says major TV networks have entered agreements with video news services around the world to get news once covered by their own foreign bureaus, "capturing images on videotape and distributing them within seconds to dozens or even hundreds of newsrooms around the country and around the world for immediate use."[32]

Local television stations also contract with news services and independent journalists in other cities worldwide for news feeds reported under the banner of the local station. Not only is the source of the news ambiguous, or even misleading, but also so may be the journalistic integrity of the "news." This is especially evident when the "news" is about the trials and tribulations of the remaining "survivors," or about the stars *de jour* in the latest "reality" series.

Television documentaries also blur the line between entertainment and objective journalism:

> The documentary's claims to offer unprejudiced rendering of objective reality were strained by a number of factors associated with the story-telling conventions of popular television, including considerations of plot, character, pursuit of an affective response from audiences, and conscious competition with entertaining programming…. Editing and camera techniques also suggested the malleable nature of the medium. Indeed, these techniques helped to generate debate over what is commonly referred to in the industry as "actuality," that is, material captured by photographic or audio equipment which "documents" the analysis of the producer.[33]

Practitioners "pitch" story ideas to TV producers. Producers then decide if an author's new book is reviewed, if the author is interviewed, or if a personality appears on network shows such as NBC's *Today* and *Tonight with Jay Leno*, or on syndicated shows such as *Oprah, Live with Regis and Kelly, Montel Williams,* and *Ellen DeGeneres* (or similar local programs). The most common technique for placing a message on television, however, is providing video for news or documentary programs in the form of a video news release (VNR).

TV Guide blew the whistle on VNRs used in newscasts without viewers being informed that the video was provided by an outside source. The magazine referred to the video press releases as "fake news," suggesting that VNRs blur the line between news and commercials.[34] Others have expressed concern that VNRs can be aired without first having passed journalistic standards for verifying accuracy, can be shown without identifying the source, can be used to manipulate media content in favor of the VNR source, and can violate generally accepted ethical principles in public relations and journalism.[35] In fact, however, local television news directors are pressed to fill ever-larger "news holes" with smaller staffs and budgets. Consequently, local news operations are increasingly dependent on public relations sources, although they are loath to admit that reality.

Responding to such concerns, a special committee of the Public Relations Service Council established a "Code of Good Practice for Video New Releases" (see Exhibit 10.2). Bob Kimmel of News Broadcast Network (New York City VNR producer) lists techniques to increase the chances that stations will use a VNR:

1. Don't mix natural sound with voice-over narration.
2. Don't overuse stills as a substitute for action video.
3. Don't place titles of "supers" on the video news segment itself. Provide the information separately so stations can insert titles in their regular fonts and styles.
4. Don't use fancy special effects and repetitive dissolves not ordinarily used in news packages.
5. Don't commercialize the VNR with blatant product or service presentations.
6. Don't put your own reporter on the screen.
7. Don't produce a VNR unless you have a news story or a timely feature of general interest.[36]

EXHIBIT 10.2

CODE OF GOOD PRACTICE FOR VIDEO NEWS RELEASES

1. The objective of VNR is to present information, pictures, and sound that TV journalists can use and rely on for quality, accuracy, and perspective.

2. Information contained in a VNR, to the extent possible, must be accurate and verifiable. Intentionally false of misleading information must be avoided.

3. A VNR must be clearly identified on the video's opening slate and any advisory material and scripts that precede or accompany tape distribution.

4. The sponsoring company, organization, or individual must also be clearly identified on the video slate.

5. The name and phone number of a responsible party must be provided on the video for journalists to contact.

6. Persons interviewed in the VNR must be accurately identified by name, title, and affiliation on the video.

Used with permission of Public Relations Service Council.

"At one time, VNRs were assailed by TV journalists because they too closely resembled advertisements. VNRs are under attack today, video experts say, because they deliver what they promise: news!"[37]

More frequently, satellite transmission makes it possible to instantaneously distribute public relations messages. The SMT has replaced the time-consuming and expensive city hopping that was formerly part of political campaigns, crisis communication programs (see Tylenol Exhibit 1.3), movie openings, product launches, and breaking news.

> Turn on any morning news show and you see anchors interviewing doctors, writers, entertainers, CEOs and other experts. Most of the time the interviews are via satellite from locations other than the anchors' TV stations....In the course of two or three hours, a typical SMT can cover 12 to 20 stations.[38]

SMTs work best when local stations cannot produce the same story themselves, when the story fits morning programming before being bumped by breaking news, and when the story calls for top management appearances on the global television medium.

Cable and Satellite Television

The growth of cable and satellite television with its 500-channel-capacity and high-definition capabilities has profoundly altered the nation's communication and viewing patterns. Cable was born in 1948, when the first community-antenna television (CATV) system was built in a small Pennsylvania community that suffered from poor television reception. It was Cable News Network's (CNN) live coverage of the 1986 Challenger disaster; the round-the-clock coverage of the 1991 Gulf War and 2003 Iraq War; and 24-hour coverage of the September 11, 2001, World Trade Center and Pentagon attacks, however, that made cable news a major player in the global information system. CNN coverage was so complete that several network affiliates and many independent stations carried CNN reports.

As new technology expands the channel-carrying capacity and converts systems to on-demand programming, cable and satellite TV may become only part of the packages of services carried. Cable companies offer interactive services such as shopping, banking, information databases, local and long-distance telephone services, and emergency alert connections to police and fire departments.

Fiber-optic and asymmetric digital subscriber line (DSL) networks link viewers 24 hours a day directly to central computers to retrieve and send information. Just as futurists had predicted, the line between television, telephone, other media, and home computers has blurred as both information and entertainment services are delivered to homes over wire and wireless systems. Convergence is reality.

WORKING WITH THE MEDIA

Knowing about the media—knowing how to work with each medium, produce content for each, meet the deadlines of each, adhere to specific style requirements, and address each medium's audience—is a major part of many practitioners' jobs. Practitioners must build and maintain relationships of mutual respect and trust with

EXHIBIT 10.3

GENERAL MOTORS VERSUS NBC NEWS

Alvie L. Smith, APR
Director of Corporate
Communications (retired)
General Motors Corporation

The Situation

In November 1992, a 16-minute segment entitled "Waiting to Explode" on the television news magazine *Dateline NBC* focused on what it called the unsafe design of GM full-sized pickups built from 1973 through 1987. The show included a one-minute segment of "unscientific" demonstration crashes conducted by the Institute for Safety Analysis (ISA) in which one truck catches fire after being struck in the side by a car.

Seventeen million viewers saw apparent visual support for interviews with safety experts who claimed that the trucks were vulnerable to fires and explosions because of fuel tank design and placement.

The television segment also included interviews with the parents of a 17-year-old who was killed when his pickup was broadsided by a car driven by a drunk driver. GM officially complained to NBC that the show was "grossly unfair, misleading, and irresponsible."

In February 1993, the jury found GM "negligent" and awarded the parents $105.2 million. GM appealed, claiming that the 70-miles-per-hour impact into the cab, not the fire, killed the truck driver.

Although NBC and ISA claimed that the test vehicles had been destroyed after the demonstration crashes, GM investigators found them and got court approval to study the vehicles to recreate the demonstrations and results.

GM's Response

In a February 8, 1993, press conference in Detroit, GM's chief counsel presented a well-researched refutation of the *Dateline NBC* segment. GM locations throughout the world and North American dealers received the press conference via satellite. Hundreds of videotapes of the press conference were distributed. While displaying the crash truck fuel tank and slow-motion sequences of the crash, GM's counsel pointed out major deceptions in the report and test crash:

1. NBC did not tell viewers that incendiary rocket devices were taped under the trucks and timed to go off on impact to ignite any spilled gasoline.

2. The fuel tank had been "topped off" before the test and fitted with a nonstandard cap that allowed gasoline to escape as the incendiary device was fired.

3. There was no puncture of the gas tank, as had been claimed in the NBC report.

4. Impact speed in the demonstration were significantly higher than those NBC reported: one at 39 miles per hour, not 30, and the other at least 47, not 40.

GM filed a lawsuit against NBC and ISA for defaming its reputation. This was the first such action in GM's history.

NBC's Response

NBC carried highlights of GM's charges in its February 8 newscast, but NBC News President Michael Gartner defended the segment. On February 10, however, *Dateline NBC* coanchors Jane Pauley and Stone Phillips read a lengthy retraction negotiated by NBC and GM that day. NBC did not contest any of GM's accusations. "NBC deeply regrets using the one-minute crash segment," Phillips said. "We apologize to our viewers and to GM."

Results

GM accepted NBC's apology and dropped the lawsuit, with the provision that NBC pay GM's research expenses, about $2 million. Quick acceptance of NBC's apology and dropping legal action took the matter out of the media spotlight. In March 1993, Gartner resigned from *NBC News* and three other executives were fired. A group of independent lawyers hired by NBC had scathing criticism for the show's producers. NBC announced it would reorganize its procedures to ensure future accuracy and fairness. *Detroit Free Press* columnist Steven Brill wrote: "NBC's candid apology was a pivotal event in the annals of journalism—a refreshing reversal of the usual arrogance and stonewalling and hiding behind a justifiably permissive law."

media gatekeepers. These relationships, although mutually beneficial, remain adversarial at their core, because journalists and practitioners are not in the same business and often do not have the same communication goals.

The Person in the Middle

To be effective in the go-between and mediating roles, practitioners must have the confidence of both their organization's management and the media. This is not an easy job. CEOs and other line managers are naturally suspicious of the media, just as journalists are by nature questioning and somewhat untrusting of those they put in the spotlight. Practitioners and others in organizations complain: "Why does the press always sensationalize things?" "Journalists never get things right." "I didn't say that!" "They take things out of context or twist things to fit their story." For example, the Queen of England's late father, King George VI, collected newspaper clippings in a scrapbook titled, "Things my daughters never did."[39] And that was before the days of *Star* and *National Enquirer*!

Journalists counter: "That organization never tells the truth!" "We don't get to talk with the person who has the real story and real news." "What we get is PR fluff." "You get the feeling they're trying to hide something." "Spacegrabbers!"

This is not breaking news. The conflict between journalists and public relations practitioners has a long history of contradiction:

> Journalists wanted information to be easily available, yet resented the men and women who made it available. By the mid twentieth century, journalists were dependent upon PR practitioners for a large percentage of the stories appearing in newspapers. But admitting their dependence would shatter cherished ideals. Journalists were proud of their ability to uncover stories, verify details, and expose sham. Thus, they were unlikely to admit their dependence, lack of skepticism, failure to verify, and failure to expose every sham.[40]

As one business columnist wrote, "I hate PR people." He went on to "confess" a "journalistic sin": "In this issue, there are three (smallish) examples of PR pitches that worked on me. See if you can find them." One public relations practitioner took the challenge, finding that five of his own pitches had apparently worked: "For the record, I placed five articles in that magazine. I like pointing that out to him."[41] One wonders how many other practitioners could have found stories that they had pitched in the same issue.

The adversarial—sometimes even hostile—feelings that exist between practitioners and journalists often spill over into public debate. Herbert Schmertz, Mobil Corporation vice president of public affairs in the 1980s, criticized journalists and media performance by providing what he called "constructive, responsible criticism."[42] Mobil periodically used its advocacy advertising to criticize the media (see Figure 10.1), to which Schmertz credits substantial progress in improving print coverage of his corporation and business in general. He saved his harshest criticism for television news and:

> The questionable values that afflict TV journalism—the slavery to ratings...the pandering to the lowest common denominator...the emotional presentation to entice a larger audience...the subversion of news values to entertainment values...the ruthless compression of facts to fit preordained timetables.[43]

Mobil Corporation's Advertisement on "The Myth of Open Airwaves."

FIGURE 10.1

MYTH OF THE OPEN AIRWAVES

4. The myth of the open airwaves

There is a simple, yet overwhelming, difference between the print media and television journalism. Newspapers and magazines offer regular access to their pages to those who wish to rebut what has been printed. The major television networks do not.

Access to television is supposed to be governed largely by the Federal Communications Commission's Fairness Doctrine. That doctrine owes its existence to the theory that the airwaves are a scarce resource and must therefore be allocated among potential users. The doctrine requires owners of broadcast licenses "...to encourage and implement the broadcast of all sides of controversial public issues..." and to play "...a conscious and positive role in bringing about the balanced presentation of the opposing viewpoints." In theory, the Fairness Doctrine doesn't preclude anything. In reality, the networks have turned it into a doctrine of unfairness.

Under a mandate to present all sides of a public issue, the networks confine debate through controls imposed by their own news departments. Through their news staffs, the networks exercise total control over the agenda of issues, and who may speak to the public. Unfortunately, the result of this network control, with no system or forum for rebuttal, has resulted in a narrow and selective discussion of major public issues—and the systematic exclusion or distortion of many viewpoints.

Mobil has often been denied the opportunity to rebut inaccurate television news broadcasts. Frequently, the broadcasts appeared at times when critical energy legislation was under debate in Congress—legislation regarding oil company divestiture, natural gas deregulation, oil decontrol, and the "windfall profit" tax. At such times, the networks' systematic exclusion of ideas and information impaired the public's ability to rationally decide fundamental policy issues.

Other companies have experienced similar frustrations in their attempts to gain adequate airtime to rebut erroneous television newscasts. Kaiser Aluminum & Chemical Corporation had to threaten a slander suit and had to ask the FCC to order ABC to give it time to respond to charges made on a 1980 *20/20* segment, before ABC finally gave the company the opportunity for an unedited reply. It took more than a year, however, before the rebuttal was aired on prime-time TV.

In response to a 1979 CBS *60 Minutes* broadcast, Illinois Power Company produced its own tape to point out the network's distortions. Called "60 Minutes/Our Reply," the power company's rebuttal exposed the bias of the broadcast by including CBS film footage not included in the original segment. The program has been widely shown to various groups across the country, but it has not been aired on television.

The networks not only block rebuttals, they refuse to air advertisements on "controversial" issues, and have rejected Mobil advocacy commercials since 1974—despite evidence that public support for issue advertising is strong. (Network policies would preclude the very message you are currently reading.) A 1980 survey by the Opinion Research Corporation found that 85 percent of the American public think corporations should be allowed to present their views on controversial matters in television commercials. And most independent stations and network affiliates have opened their doors to advocacy advertising, without creating the chaos the networks profess to fear.

As the Supreme Court affirmed in its 1978 *Bellotti* decision: "The press does not have a monopoly on either the First Amendment or the ability to enlighten."

Mobil®

Courtesy Mobil Corporation.

Schmertz was not alone in his criticism. Unhappy with television coverage of the B-2 bomber and the plane's price tag, veterans' organizations and the defense industry counterattacked:

> By its very nature, television news suffers from a variety of limitations and constraints. The process by which television editors, producers, and reporters compile, summarize, and synthesize complicated issues often leads to misrepresentations or outright distortions of the news....
>
> Network television shies away from complicated events, focusing instead on simplicity. Entertainment. Images....
>
> Absent an image, television journalists do not seem capable of presenting the news. Even with an image, broadcast journalism is less serious, and oftentimes less responsible, than print journalism.[44]

General Motors counterattacked when an NBC News reporter staged accidents and fires involving GM's full-sized pickups manufactured from 1973 through 1987. The report aired on "Dateline NBC" under the title "Waiting to Explode." Exhibit 10.3 summarizes this case in which the NBC admitted fault and apologized to viewers and to GM.

Others share the acrimony. When Meg Greenfield was *Washington Post* editorial page editor, she issued a memo barring practitioners entry to editorial offices: "We don't want any of that damned crowd around here." Subsequently, *Post* executive editor Ben Bradlee extended the ban, forbidding reporters to talk to public relations sources, a directive quickly ignored because reporters depend on public relations sources.[45]

After studying public relations "information subsidies" provided to news media, Judy VanSlyke Turk concluded:

> In journalistic folklore there is a distrust, or mistrust, of public relations practitioners as biased "flacks" engaged in puffery and manipulations of information, and indeed public relations practitioners themselves are indoctrinated to expect that attitude of distrust from journalists.[46]

In practice, practitioners and journalists operate in a mutually dependent and mutually beneficial relationship, sometimes as adversaries and sometimes as colleagues cooperating in each of their own self-interests. Not as frequently, but occasionally, the news media are manipulated by the practitioner, who may have more resources, as well as control access to news sources. With at least equal frequency, news media frustrate practitioners in their attempts to get information to publics.

In short, there is a dynamic tension in the relationship between practitioners and journalists that is "firmly embedded in journalistic culture."[47] Often, however, neither employers nor journalists understand the practitioner's liaison role in establishing and maintaining media relations.

Guidelines for Good Media Relations

The underlying conflict of interests and missions necessarily makes the practitioner–journalist relationship adversarial. The practitioner advancing a particular cause or organization stands in stark contrast to the journalist's drive to dig up news through good reporting and journalistic initiative. Given the experience of at least a century, the adversarial relationship appears to serve the public interest and the needs of the public information system.

The sound approach for organizations and practitioners is to view media relations as an investment. Accuracy and fairness in press coverage does not result from reporters' work alone. Ultimately, the relationship between practitioners and journalists has an impact on the quality of new coverage about organizations.[48] Those relationships can best be achieved when practitioners follow a few basic rules: (1) shoot squarely, (2) give service, (3) do not beg or carp, (4) do not ask for kills, and (5) do not flood the media.

1. *Shoot squarely.* It is not just politically correct to counsel "honesty is the best policy" in dealing with the press; it is good business and good common sense. Jerry Dalton Jr., past PRSA national president, says the practitioner's most important asset in dealing with the media is credibility: "It must be earned, usually over a period of time. It means simply that a reporter can trust [the practitioner] totally, and vice versa. It means never lying. If you can't, for some legitimate reason, speak the truth, then say nothing."[49]

   Journalists point out that good and bad news tend to even out over time, so if practitioners are honest with bad news, then they are more likely to be trusted with good news. As one writer summarized the point: "Stick with journalists in the bad times as well as good. …Any company smart enough to make their [journalists] job easier will reap the benefits in the long run."[50]

   Another fundamental principle is that a practitioner cannot favor one news outlet at the expense of others. The safest rule is that spot news should go out to all relevant media as fast as possible, letting the media determine the cycle in which it breaks. Less time-sensitive feature material should be alternated evenly among the competitors. As a corollary, practitioners must protect journalistic initiative. For example, if a reporter gets a tip and asks for information, the story belongs to that journalist. The same information should not be given to other outlets unless they come after it. This is a policy with which no reporter can justly quarrel, because each of them would demand the same protection for their scoops.

2. *Give service.* The quickest, surest way to gain the cooperation of journalists is to provide them with newsworthy, interesting, and timely stories and pictures that they want, when they want them, and in a form they can readily use. Author Carole Howard suggests, "Be a reporter's reporter. When asked for information, do not hesitate to ask enough questions so you have a full understanding of the story the reporter is working on."[51]

   Journalists work with fixed and sometimes tight deadlines. Practitioners who hope to place stories in the news media must know and adhere to media lead times. Again, Howard advises:

   > Learn the regular and late-breaking deadlines of all the media that normally cover your organization. A reporter's life is controlled by very short deadlines, especially in the broadcast and Internet media, and you must meet the reporter's deadline or your information is useless.[52]

   Journalists also count on and cooperate with the practitioner who willingly responds to a midnight call for a photo and biographical sketch of an executive who just died. News, a highly perishable commodity, occurs around the clock, as do news deadlines in the global media environment. Therefore, some practitioners are on call around the clock. Howard suggests keeping key materials at home, for as Dalton points out, "News doesn't wait—for anyone or anything."

3. *Do not beg or carp.* Nothing irritates journalists and their editors and news directors more than the practitioner who begs to have stories used or complains about story treatment. Journalists have finely developed senses of journalistic objectivity and news value. If information is not sufficiently newsworthy on its own merits to attract their interest, no amount of begging and carping can change the quality of that information. Some practitioners (or their interns!) call journalists to ask, "Did you receive my release?" One online editor succinctly states how most journalists react to such follow-calls: "Assume that whatever it was you sent, we got it. If you don't hear back from us, we're not interested."[53]

   Nothing, however, is more offensive to a journalist than a practitioner who tries to pressure the editorial staff to use a story, change a story treatment, or kill a story by holding hostage the organization's advertising business. That kind of pressure does not work when up against journalistic integrity and will surely lead to resentment or to an immediate public response.

   Threats to "pull our advertising" can lead to banner headlines or lead stories on the evening news, pitting the media against a corporate bully. The rule of thumb is that advertising belongs in the advertising department, and news—good and bad—is for journalists to report in news columns and newscasts. Journalists refer to the "fire wall" between the two. Even though Reuters does not accept advertising, the international wire service's "Trust Principles" statement summarizes this journalistic value in no uncertain terms: "The integrity, independence and freedom from bias of Reuters shall at all times be fully preserved." In other words—to paraphrase a popular Texas slogan—"Don't mess with Reuters," or the editorial side of other respected news media.

4. *Do not ask for "kills."* Practitioners have no right to ask the press to suppress or kill a story. It seldom works, is unprofessional, and brings only ill will. To journalists, this is a crude insult and an abuse of the First Amendment. It is asking journalists to betray their public trust. The best way to keep unfavorable stories out of the press is to prevent situations that produce such stories.

   At the same time, there are occasions when it is perfectly legitimate to request a delay in publication or to explain to the press any part of the story that might be damaging to the public interest. For example, hospital public relations staff cannot release the names and condition of accident or crime victims before the next of kin have been notified or without permission of the patient or family. Likewise the Departments of Defense and Homeland Security do not release, or may legitimately request media to delay releasing, information potentially compromising to military operations or threatening to public safety. Then again, in the latter cases, some will remind us of what California U.S. Senator Hiram Johnson said in 1917: "The first casualty when war comes is truth."[54] That is why public relations specialists in those organizations establish and maintain relationships of trust with their media counterparts.

   However, if the press reports an inaccurate or misleading story, ask for a correction. Many news media, in the interest of their own public relations, have adopted policies of publishing or broadcasting corrections, albeit often in an inconspicuous manner. At the same time, practitioners also should ask that the erroneous information be corrected in the computer database—what used to be called the "morgue" or library—so the information does not get repeated in subsequent stories.

Some organizations provide updated background information about the organization, its finances, its products or services, or executives to media so it will be in the file when stories break. For example, the Pharmaceutical Manufacturers' Association sends a file of information to news outlets with this note: "If your files on the prescription drug industry don't include the information in this folder, your files may be incomplete." Many organizations send annual fact books to the media (see Figure 10.2). Most make such information accessible on the organization's Web site with links to the "News Room," "Press Room," or similar label.[55]

5. *Do not flood the media.* Study and experience teach the boundaries of newsworthiness, and common sense dictates respect for them. If a financial editor receives information appropriate for the sports or real estate editor, the financial editor loses respect for the practitioner who engages in blanketing the media with releases. The best advice includes the following: (1) stick to what journalists will consider news, (2) keep media mailing lists current, and (3) send to only one—the most appropriate—journalist at each news medium.

To document how much his reporters and editors have to cull each day, Paul Steiger, then the *Wall Street Journal*'s New York managing editor, asked the 17 domestic bureau managers to save for one day all news materials they received. They collected press releases, public relations wire stories, faxes, and letters, but not news sent over the Internet. The stack of boxes and bins in Steiger's office was more than 2 feet high and 10 feet long.[56] A similar avalanche of public relations materials reaches newsrooms around the globe. Not all of it will get through the careful scrutiny of media gatekeepers, and they quickly learn which sources provide information with real news value.

Guidelines for Working with the Press

Former CBS news reporter and long-time counselor Chester Burger says the press "is often unfair, unreasonable, and simply wrong. But even if it isn't our friend, it is the best friend the nation has, and we should be thankful for it."[57] Based on notions of a free and independent press, as well as principles of sound public relations practice, seasoned practitioners offer the following guidelines for working with the press:

1. *Talk from the viewpoint of the public's interest, not the organization's.* The soft-drink bottler who launches a campaign to collect and recycle bottles can frankly admit that it does not want to irritate the public by having its product litter the landscape.

2. *Make the news easy to read and use.* Use a short, punchy headline to attract attention and give potential users an indication of the topic. Do not use jargon, unfamiliar acronyms, or technical terms. Personal pronouns, names, and quotations make your copy easier to read and more interesting. Put the name, address, and phone number of the news source and contact at the top of releases.

3. *If you do not want some statement quoted, do not make it.* Spokespersons should avoid talking "off the record," because such statements may well wind up published without the source identified. Some news organizations forbid reporters to accept such information. Moreover, it is absolutely too late to qualify something as off the record after you make a statement to a reporter.

FIGURE 10.2

UCLA MEDIA GUIDE

UCLA Media Guide

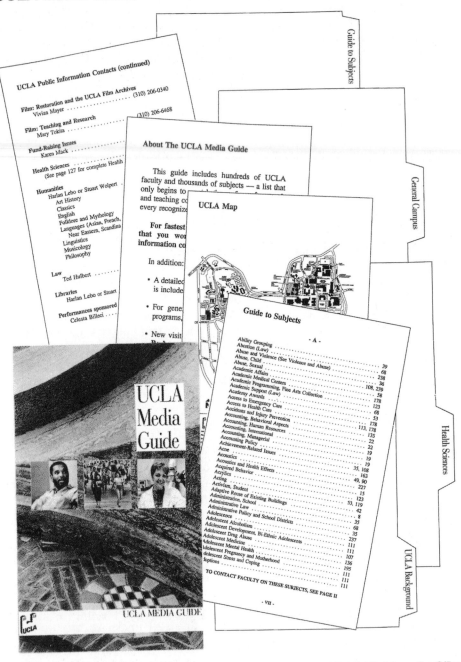

Courtesy UCLA Public Information Office.

4. *State the most important fact at the beginning.* A manager's logical presentation may first list the facts that led to a decision, but news reporters want the decision. The first-level response to a reporter's question is a short summary of your position or newsworthy announcement. The second-level response includes a concrete example or evidence to back up your first statement. If the reporter persists, return to the first-level summary statement.

5. *Do not argue with a reporter or lose your cool.* Understand that journalists seek an interesting story and will go to great lengths to get the story. To paraphrase an old public relations maxim, do not argue with people who buy printers ink by the barrel or with people who own the transmitter or cable system; these people have the final say.

6. *If a question contains offensive language or simply words you do not like, do not repeat them even to deny them.* Along the line of having final say, reporters also can select quotes, portions of quotes, or even single words for the final story. Reporters often use the gambit of putting words into subject's mouths, such as, "Do you mean …?" or "Is what you are really saying …?" For example, ABC-TV's Sam Donaldson is well known for his ability to goad subjects into saying headline-making statements using this technique.

7. *If the reporter asks a direct question, give an equally direct answer.* Feeling pressure to say something more than what is called for by a question is a common error. If the appropriate answer is "yes" or "no," give the correct response and say no more. Some reporters will remain silent after getting an answer in hopes that the subject will volunteer more information. Assume that the camera is on at all times; otherwise the unguarded comment will be the sound bite on the evening news! Media adviser Roger Ailes's rule of thumb is that the tougher the question, the shorter the answer should be.

8. *If spokespersons do not know the answer to a question, they should simply say, "I don't know, but I'll get the answer for you."* This is a commitment to follow through by providing the information as quickly as possible. Better yet, prepare for the interview by anticipating what questions will be asked, by developing succinct answers, and by rehearsing with someone playing the role of the reporter.

9. *Tell the truth, even if it hurts.* Do not think for a moment that bad news will go away or that the media will miss it. Treat it as you would any other story: Prepare as if it were good news and take it to the media. Not only does that mean that you will keep some control over the story and how it is covered, but it also means that you are not on the defensive, making yourself vulnerable to charges of trying to hide the facts or of having been exposed by the media. This may be the most difficult position to sell to those in top management, who often see the practitioner's job as keeping bad news out of the media.

10. *Do not call a press conference unless you have what reporters consider news.* When is a news conference justified? Seldom. In fact, call a news conference only when there is no other means to get an important breaking story to the media in a timely fashion. Examples include important controversial matters such as labor–management disputes and settlements, important political announcements, and major policy changes affecting large numbers of people. The determining factor is the need to give reporters an opportunity to ask questions and pursue the story rather than simply issuing a statement or making an announcement. Complex matters that require backgrounding and

detailed explanation, such as a technological breakthrough, may justify a press conference. Simple, straightforward, or noncontroversial announcements rarely justify the expense and effort of media coverage. And finally, if you do call a press conference, follow the suggestions outlined in steps 1 through 9.[58]

These suggestions can help practitioners build and maintain good relations with journalists in the news media. Because of the crucial gatekeeper role played by reporters and editors in print, broadcast and online media, practitioners have little choice but to earn and keep the respect of journalists. At the same time, although the public has a right to public information, there are limits. Some information is confidential, and some information cannot be disclosed because of individual privacy or because of the proprietary nature of the information in a competitive business environment. Knowing how to keep control of the agenda when dealing with the press is part of the media training required for all those acting as spokespersons and manager of media relations.

In the final analysis, however, the practitioner–journalist relationship is an adversarial relationship. After being accused of doing something immoral by teaching people how to deal with the press, Roger Ailes told a journalism seminar:

> We always advise our clients to tell the truth. But the thing that disturbs me most is that you are here in journalism school learning how to ask the questions, yet you would deny a person the right to learn how to answer those questions.[59]

Part of the motivation for giving managers media training is that the top executives in many organizations are public figures without training or experience in dealing with this aspect of their public life. Some suggest that CEOs are obliged to deal with the media and to face the public when their organizations make important

FIGURE 10.3

NAVY PRESS CONFERENCE

Courtesy U.S. Navy.

decisions or are involved in crises that have impact beyond the organization. This obligation applies equally to leaders in corporations, nonprofit agencies, health and health-care organizations, educational institutions, government, and all other organizations concerned about their relationships with publics.

Because a free press plays a central role in our free society, this is the era of the media-savvy top executive. Media training designed to help executives deal directly with the press is a responsibility of the public relations department and an essential investment in building and maintaining good media relations.

NOTES

[1] Walter Lippmann, *Public Opinion* (New York: Harcourt, Brace and Company, 1922), 354.

[2] Shirley Fulton and Al Guyant, *Beat the Press* (Salt Lake City, UT: American Book Business Press, 2002), 215.

[3] James G. Webster, "Audience Behavior in the Media Environment," *Journal of Communication* 36, no. 3 (Summer 1986): 83.

[4] John V. Pavlik and Shawn McIntosh, *Converging Media: An Introduction to Mass Communication* (Boston: Pearson–Allyn & Bacon, 2004), 19.

[5] Donald K. Wright (Principal Investigator), "The Magic Communication Machine: Examining the Internet's Impact on Public Relations, Journalism, and the Public" (Gainesville, FL: The Institute for Public Relations, 2001), 37–39. (Online at http://www.instituteforpr.com/internet_-_new_technology.phtm.)

[6] Ibid., 36.

[7] Nicholas Negroponte, *Being Digital* (New York: Vintage Books, 1995), 11–20.

[8] Pavlik and McIntosh, *Converging Media*, 22.

[9] Blogger Patrick Belton, as quoted by Alan Elsner, "Bloggers Make Debut at Democratic Convention," Reuters (July 26, 2004). http://www.reuters.com/newsArticle.jhtml?type=internetNews&storyID=5777817.

[10] Benjamin Fulford, "Korea's Weird Wired World, *Forbes,* July 21, 2003, 92–93.

[11] David Wickenden, "High-Tech Trends That Will Matter to PR Executives," *Public Relations Strategist* 9, No. 2 (Summer 2003): 24.

[12] John C. Merrill, "Global Elite: A Newspaper Community of Reason," in "World Media," special issue of *Gannett Center Journal* 4, no. 4 (Fall 1990): 93.

[13] Ibid., 101.

[14] "The Top 150 Daily Newspapers," Audit Bureau of Circulations, Schaumburg, IL (July 26, 2004), http://www.accessabc.com/reader/top100.htm.

[15] Stacey Frank Kanihan and Steven H. Chaffee, "Situational Influence of Political Involvement on Information Seeking: A Field Experiment." Paper presented to the Annual Convention of the Association for Education in Journalism and Mass Communication, Anaheim, CA, August 1996, p. 28.

[16] "Facts About Newspapers 2003" (Vienna, VA: Newspaper Association of America, 2004), 14, http://www.naa.org/org/info/facts03/index.html.

[17] Ibid., and p. 4.

[18] Ibid., 12, 13.

[19] Ibid.

[20] A. Carlos Ruotolo, "A Typology of Newspaper Readers," *Journalism Quarterly* 65, no. 1 (Spring 1988): 126–30.

[21] "Facts About Newspapers 2003," 13, http://www.naa.org/org/info/facts03/index.html.

[22] Meredith Corporation (online), http://www.Meredith.com'default.sph/pr_user.class"FNC=ViewRelease_Aextemplate_thml_884.

[23] "The Magazine Handbook 2004/05" (New York: Magazine Publishers of America, 2004), 7. (See http://www.magazine.org.)

[24] Shirley Biagi, *Media/Impact: An Introduction to Mass Media*, 4th ed. (Belmont, CA: Wadsworth Publishing Company, 1999), 66–67.

[25] "Radio Marketing Guide & Fact Book for Advertisers: 2003–2004 Edition" (New York: Radio Advertising Bureau, 2003), http://www.rab.com/station/marketing_guide/RMGFB2004.pdf.

[26] Federal Communications Commission, "Broadcast Station Totals as of March 31, 2004," http://www.fcc.gov/mb/audio/totals/beo40331.html.

[27] Ibid.

[28] Newton N. Minow, "How Vast the Wasteland Now?" Address given at the Gannett Foundation Media Center (Now Freedom Forum Center for Media Studies), Columbia University, New York City, May 9, 1991 (30th anniversary of Minow's "Vast Wasteland" speech to the National Association of Broadcasters).

[29] Hans-Bernd Brosius and Hans Mathias Kepplinger, "Beyond Agenda-Setting: The Influence of Partisanship and Television Reporting on the Electorate's Voting Intentions," *Journalism Quarterly* 69, no. 4 (Winter 1992): 893–901.

[30] Minow, "How Vast the Wasteland Now?"

[31] Robert MacNeil, *The Right Place at the Right Time* (Boston: Little, Brown, 1982), 129.

[32] Adam Clayton Powell, III, "The Global TV News Hour," in "World Media" issue of *Gannett Center Journal* 4, no. 4 (Fall 1990): 119.

[33] Michael Curtain, "Packaging Reality: The Influence of Fictional Forms on the Early Development of Television Documentary," *Journalism Monographs* 137 (February 1993): 19.

[34] David Lieberman, "Fake News," *TV Guide* 40, no. 8 (February 22, 1992), 10–14, 16, and 26.

[35] K. Tim Wulfemeyer and Lowell Frazier, "The Ethics of Video News Releases: A Qualitative Analysis," *Journal of Mass Media Ethics* 7, no. 3 (1992): 151–68.

[36] "Ten Tips on How to Get Your VNR Aired," *Communication World* 9, no. 9 (September 1992): 10.

[37] Adam Shell, "VNRs: In the News," *Public Relations Journal* 48, no. 12 (December 1992): 21.

[38] Monica Jennings, "Creating SMTs that Deliver, *Public Relations Tactics* (July 2003), 16.

[39] Donald Trelford, "50 Years of Covering the Queen," *IPI Global Journalist* 8, no. 3 (Third Quarter, 2002): 17–19. Magazine published by the International Press Institute, University of Missouri, Columbia.

[40] Denise E. DeLorme and Fred Fedler, "Journalists' Hostility toward Public Relations: An Historical Analysis," *Public Relations Review* 29, no. 2 (June 2003), 113.

[41] "WBF Openly Expresses Its Love-Hate Relationship with Pitches," *PRWeek*, April 29, 2002, 12.

[42] "Inquiry: Press Can't Have the Right to Lie," *USA Today*, November 4, 1983, 11A.

[43] Herbert Schmertz, "The Press and Morality." Remarks to Guild Hall Discussion Series, East Hampton, NY, July 12, 1983.

[44] Stephen Aubin, "The B-2 and Network News: A Case Study in Media Distortion." Report published by the Aerospace Education Foundation (an affiliate of the Air Force Association), Arlington, VA, January 1991, p. 1.

[45] "Flack Attack: The *Post* Spurns P.R. 'Wolves,'" *Time*, May 10, 1982, p. 101; and Carl Cannon, "The Great Flack Flap," *Washington Journalism Review* 4 (September 1982): 35.

[46] Judy VanSlyke Turk, "Information Subsidies and Media Content: A Study of Public Relations Influence on the News," *Journalism Monographs* 100 (December 1986): 26–27.

[47] Michael Ryan and David L. Martinson, "Journalists and Public Relations Practitioners: Why the Antagonism?" *Journalism Quarterly* 65, no. 1 (Spring 1988): 139.

[48] Mark S. Cox, "Media Relations and the Content of Business News" (Master of Science in Mass Communication thesis, San Diego State University, May 1983).

[49] H. J. Dalton Jr., personal letter and enclosure—"50 Basic Thoughts on Good News Media Relations" (undated presentation to Veterans Administration public affairs training seminar).

[50] Douglas Quenqua, "Stick with Journalists in the Bad Times As Well As Good, *PRWeek*, April 29, 2002, 9.

[51] Carole M. Howard, "Working with Reporters: Mastering the Fundamentals to Build Long-Term Relationships," *Public Relations Quarterly* 49, no. 1 (Spring 2004): 37.

[52] Ibid., 36–37.

[53] "Have You Read My Release?" *PRWeek*, September 17, 2001, 21.

[54] Coy Callison, "Media Relations and the Internet: How *Fortune* Company Web Sites Assist Journalists in News Gathering," *Public Relations Review* 29, no. 1 (March 2003): 33.

[55] Paul McMasters, "Journalists Aren't Winning Their Gulf War," *The Quill* 79, no. 2 (March 1991): 8. Also online at http://www.brainyquote.com/quotes/quotes/h/hiramjohns108417.html.

[56] "News Is Stacked Up at Wall St. Journal," *Jack O'Dwyer's Newsletter*, August 26, 1992, p. 4.

[57] Chester Burger, "Phony Communication Is Worse Than None at All." Arthur W. Page Society Hall of Fame induction speech, Amelia Island, FL, September 23, 1992.

[58] Adapted from Roger Ailes (with Jon Kraushar), *You Are the Message: Secrets of the Master Communicators* (Homewood, IL: Dow Jones-Irwin, 1988); Chester Burger, "How to Meet the Press," *Harvard Business Review*, July–August 1975; Christel K. Beard and H. J. Dalton Jr., "The Power of Positive Press," *Sales and Marketing Management*, January 1991: 37–43; Dalton, "50 Basic Thoughts on Good News Media Relations"; and Howard, "Working with Reporters."

[59] Ailes, *You Are the Message*, 165.

ADDITIONAL SOURCES

Diggs-Brown, Barbara, and Jodi L. Glou. *The PR Styleguide: Formats for Public Relations Practice.* Belmont, CA: Thomson Wadsworth, 2004.

Cottle, Simon, ed. *News, Public Relations, and Power.* London: Sage Publications, 2003. Outlines how nongovernmental groups (NGOs) use the Internet and new media technology to even up the media battle with governments and corporations.

Fulton, Shirley, and Al Guyant. *Beat the Press.* Salt Lake City, UT: American Book Business Press, 2002. Outlines strategy and tactics for dealing with the media.

Howard, Carole M., and Wilma K. Mathews. *On Deadline: Managing Media Relations*, 3rd ed. Prospect Heights, IL: Waveland Press, 2000. Summarizes how to deal with reporters, prepare spokespersons, and other aspects of effective media relations.

Shoemaker, Pamela J., and Stephen D. Reese. *Mediating the Message: Theories of Influences on Mass Media Content.* New York: Longman, 1991. Reviews research on the various influences on media content, including the impact of media professionals, media routines, organizational factors, outside sources, and ideological perspectives.

"The State of the News Media 2004." The Project for Excellence in Journalism, http://www.stateofthenewsmedia.org/index.asp.

Weaver, David H., and G. Cleveland Wilhoit, *The American Journalist in the 1990s: U.S. News People at the End of an Era.* Mahwah, NJ: Lawrence Erlbaum Associates, 1996.

Willis, Jim. *Journalism: State of the Art.* New York: Praeger Publishers, 1990. Synthesizes scholarly research on journalists, their work settings, their ethics, their relationships with news sources, and their decision-making processes.

STEP ONE: DEFINING PUBLIC RELATIONS PROBLEMS

The old "flying by the seat of the pants" approach to solving public relations problems is over.

—Edward J. Robinson

STUDY GUIDE

After studying Chapter 11, you should be able to

- Outline the four-step problem-solving process as it applies to public relations.

- Define research, identify its major purpose as reducing uncertainty in decision making, and discuss why it is essential in public relations program management.

- Describe the attributes of a useful problem statement.

- Differentiate between informal ("exploratory") and formal methods of research, giving examples of both.

Dr. Edward Robinson wrote the obituary for the "seat-of-the-pants" approach to doing public relations in 1969. He saw the public relations practitioner as "an applied social and behavioral scientist" using "research to help in the problem-solving process." He may have been a bit premature in his assessment, however, when he wrote this in the first public relations research book. Intuitive, individualistic approaches to problem solving often still guide the practice in many settings, even though, as Robinson wrote, research is "the most powerful tool available to the applied practitioner."[1]

The open systems approach discussed in Chapter 7 combines rational problem solving and proactive strategic planning. From its origins as the art of reacting to outside

---

Chapters 11–14 were updated in collaboration with Professor Bey-Ling Sha, Ph.D., APR, School of Communication, San Diego State University. Before joining the SDSU faculty, Professor Sha taught at the University of Maryland—College Park and at the American University of Paris, served as a public affairs specialist with the U.S. Census Bureau and provided counsel in communication research and strategy for Microsoft Corp., and Perrier-Vittel, among other clients.

threats, public relations has evolved into an applied science. No longer do hunches, gut feelings, and personal experiences, alone or in combination, serve as an adequate basis for public relations programs. And rarely do top managers or clients accept on faith alone a practitioner's recommendations or simple assertions that a program was successful.

---- ■ ----

MANAGEMENT PROCESS

In its most advanced form, public relations is a scientifically managed part of an organization's problem-solving and change processes. Practitioners of this type of public relations use theory and the best available evidence in a four-step problem-solving process:

1. *Defining the problem (or opportunity).* This first step involves probing and monitoring knowledge, opinions, attitudes, and behaviors of those concerned with and affected by the acts and policies of an organization. In essence, this is an organization's intelligence function. It provides the foundation for all the other steps in the problem-solving process by determining, "What's happening now?"

2. *Planning and programming.* Information gathered in the first step is used to make decisions about program publics, objectives, action and communication strategies, tactics, and goals. This involves factoring the findings from the first step into the policies and programs of the organization. This second step in the process answers, "Based on what we have learned about the situation, what should we change or do, and say?"

3. *Taking action and communicating.* The third step involves implementing the program of action and communication designed to achieve the specific objectives for each of the publics to accomplish the program goal. The questions in this step are, "Who should do and say it, and when, where, and how?"

4. *Evaluating the program.* The final step in the process involves assessing the preparation, implementation, and results of the program. Adjustments are made while the program is being implemented, based on evaluation feedback on how it is or is not working. Programs are continued or stopped after learning, "How are we doing, or how did we do?"

Each step is as important as the others, but the process begins with gathering intelligence to diagnose the problem. Information and understanding developed in the first step motivate and guide subsequent steps in the process. In practice, of course, diagnosis, planning, implementation, and evaluation cannot be so neatly compartmentalized, because the process is continuous and cyclical and is applied in a dynamic setting. Figure 11.1 illustrates the continuous, overlapping, and cyclical nature of public relations problem solving.

How an oil company's public relations staff managed a problem situation some years ago illustrates the four-step process. The company decided to close one of its sales divisions as part of a reorganization to increase efficiency. This meant that 600 employees would have to move or find new jobs, the community where the division was located would suffer economic loss, customers of the sales division would be

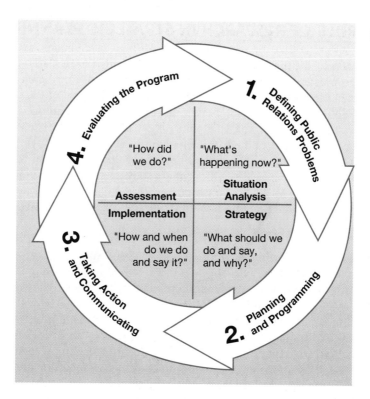

FIGURE 11.1

FOUR-STEP PUBLIC RELATIONS PROCESS

concerned about getting equally good service under the new setup, and investors would be curious about the meaning of the move.

The first task was to marshal all the facts through research so that the move could be explained and justified in terms of those concerned. The next step was to plan the announcement. Timing was important. The news had to be broken swiftly, before rumors started, released simultaneously to all those affected, and communicated in such a way as to explain satisfactorily the necessity and wisdom of the change.

Materials included a procedure memorandum to guide the staff, a presentation script for meetings, letters to several different groups of employees, letters to all dealers, a news release, a statement on banking arrangements for community banks, a general office letter, and plans for meetings. The news was released in a coordinated program of meetings, letters, and media coverage. Finally, evaluation focused on the department's original assessment of the problem situation, the techniques used, and the reactions of those affected, with an eye to improving procedures. The lessons learned were put to good use a few years later when the company closed a plant in another location, demonstrating how systematic research and evaluation improves the practice over time.

Obviously, this is an oversimplified presentation of what actually happened. The process includes many smaller steps within each of the four major steps represented in the model. These will be outlined in greater detail in this and the next three chapters. In this chapter we will concentrate on the research and fact-finding methods necessary for beginning the strategic planning process.

ROLE OF RESEARCH IN STRATEGIC PLANNING

Monitoring the social environment is not only the first step in the process; it is also the most difficult one. One is reminded of the fable of the elephant and the six blind men of Indostan: Each encounters only a single part of the beast and describes the elephant based on that limited information. For example, the one who grabs the trunk concludes, "The Elephant is very like a snake!" The one who feels the knee says, "'Tis clear enough the Elephant is very like a tree!" This process continues, with each experiencing only a portion of the elephant. In the end, each was partly right and mostly wrong about the nature of the beast but argued "loud and long" based on his respective encounter with the elephant.[2] Without researching a problem situation, practitioners run the risk of acting like the six blind men from Indostan.

Surveys of practitioners routinely show that research training tops the list of needed professional continuing education. Surveys also show that practitioners often say that they do not do more research because they lack funds and have too little time. A better explanation of why so little research is used in public relations, however, is a combination of (1) not understanding how to do and use research and (2) many employers' and clients' views that research is not necessary. While in college, few practitioners studied research methods or anticipated that research would be part of their professional work. Once they began professional practice, they felt little pressure from employers and clients, who often did not demand or fund research. As one corporate public relations executive responded in a Ketchum Public Relations survey, "The problem is not with research methodology, but with the inability—or perhaps laziness—of PR professionals who prefer to fly by the seats of their pants."[3]

For years, executives and practitioners alike bought the popular myth that public relations deals with intangibles that cannot be measured. David Rockland, Ketchum's global research director, says, "What I hear all the time is, 'You can't measure that. You can't test that. Let's just go with our gut.'"[4] With each passing day it becomes increasingly difficult to sell that position to results-oriented management (many with MBA degrees) accustomed to making decisions based on evidence and objective analysis. A practitioner in a nonprofit organization attributes "the decline of PR … to the lack of monitoring and substantive evaluation of results. That's why PR is seen by CEOs as 'fluff.'"[5]

Without research, practitioners are limited to asserting that they know the situation and can recommend a solution. With research and analysis, they can present and advocate proposals supported by evidence and theory. In this context, research is the systematic gathering of information to describe and understand situations and to check out assumptions about publics and public relations consequences. It is the scientific alternative to tenacity, authority, and intuition. Its main purpose is to reduce uncertainty in decision making. Even though it cannot answer all the questions or sway all decisions, methodical, systematic research is the foundation of effective public relations.

RESEARCH ATTITUDE

Computers and management information specialists have greatly increased organizations' abilities to gather, process, transfer, and interpret information. The increase in MBA-prepared, information-conscious middle and upper managers intensifies the pressure on public relations for accountability. In short, a research orientation is necessary for those practicing public relations in the information age. An early researcher who helped build the automotive industry, C. F. Kettering, once described this attitude toward research in these words:

> Research is a high-hat word that scares a lot of people. It need not. It is rather simple. Essentially, it is nothing but a state of mind—a friendly, welcoming attitude toward change. Going out to look for change, instead of waiting for it to come. Research … is an effort to do things better and not be caught asleep at the switch. The research state of mind can apply to anything. Personal affairs or any kind of business, big or little. It is the problem-solving mind as contrasted with the let-well-enough-alone mind. It is the composer mind, instead of the fiddler mind; it is the "tomorrow" mind instead of the "yesterday" mind.[6]

Research is no longer a specialized activity delegated to "chi-square types" tucked away in the bowels of an organization. As Rossi and Freeman put it, "It is also a political and management activity, an input into the complex mosaic from which policy decisions and allocations emerge for the planning, design, implementation, and continuation of programs."[7]

Modern managers are a fact-minded lot; they want figures. In many organizations, these executives tend to be isolated from problems by cadres of specialists and subordinates. When the public relations aspect of organizational problems must be brought home to them, the research-based approach is most effective. As other parts of organizations such as marketing, finance, and personnel have adapted a research-based approach, so must public relations. In fact, research findings suggest a strong linkage between doing research and earning one of the few seats at the management strategy table. Studies of practitioners show that participation in management increases when practitioners do research.[8]

LISTENING AS SYSTEMATIC RESEARCH

The International Listening Association defines "listening" as "the process of receiving, constructing meaning from, and responding to spoken and/or nonverbal messages." Effective public relations starts with listening, which requires openness and systematic effort. Too often, what purports to be communication is simply opposing ideas passing each other in different one-way channels, for example, in a management-versus-labor bargaining situation with each side merely wanting to score points, not listening to the other's views. As Wilbur Schramm explained, "Feedback is a powerful tool. When it does not exist or is delayed or feeble … then the situation engenders doubt and concern in the communicator, and frustration and sometimes hostility in the audience."[9] Also using his words, "Feedback tells the communicator how his message is being received."[10]

Listening is not an easy task. Channels from the worker out in the plant or from the alumnus in Seattle must be created and kept open. Failure to listen often leads to purposeless "communications" on issues that do not exist to publics that are not there. Unless you know the orientation, predisposition, and language of your audience—learned through empathetic listening—you are not likely to communicate effectively. Research is simply one method of structuring systematic listening into the communication process (see Exhibit 11.1).

EXHIBIT 11.1

WALTER BARLOW ON RESEARCH AS LISTENING

*Walter G. Barlow, President
Research Strategies
Corporation*

At the end of a meeting with the CEO of a large corporation some years ago, he asked me, "Son, tell me, just what kind of 'racket' are you in?"

I replied, "Well, if you will let me ask a few questions, I think I can demonstrate what I do, but I warn you, the questions might cause you to throw me out of this office."

"Go ahead," he said.

"Well, how much of your business day would you say is spent in communication of some sort—having a conversation like this, attending meetings and conferences, reading reports, calling on the phone, and all the rest?"

He thought for a moment and replied, "You have pretty much described how I spend all of my time. I'm either communicating in some way, preparing for it, or seriously thinking about it."

That warmed me up a bit, because I felt safe to proceed. "Well, you have just told me that your time, valued at about $800,000 in salary last year, is spent in the *process* of communication. Now, tell me, in this communication, do you do all the talking?"

He smiled right away, "Of course not!"

"Would you say you spend, say, 40 percent of your communicating time in listening, or taking in information in some way?"

"That would probably be about right. I know I talk a lot, but I do listen too."

"Suppose I had asked the top fifty executives in your company the same question, do you think I would have gotten agreement on at least 40 percent?"

Again, he replied immediately, "I damned well hope you would."

"Now, we have established something else, and that is that you allocate around $320,000 of your base salary to the process of listening, and if I multiplied that 40 percent times the salaries of the fifty others, we would have a figure in the millions."

He was now totally absorbed in the interchange. "Yes, I see. I had never thought of it that way."

Here I had a chance to move in with the clincher: "Well, I happen to know that your advertising budget is in the neighborhood of $35 million, and if we added in all the other corporate 'talking,' we would certainly come up with a figure over $100 million." I had his total attention now.

"And just how much does your corporation spend in listening? Is it any wonder that from time to time you must feel that nobody really understands you?"

I did not get an answer to the question, because the point had been made: whatever listening was going on had to be a tiny fraction of the talking, a situation he would never have brooked in his personal corporate life.

"Well, corporations like yours can't listen like you're doing now. The only way we have found yet to do that is through scientifically planned research. It can reflect back to you how people are reacting to the corporate talking you do in so many ways."

"And that is the racket I am in: helping corporations close the loop and listen to their constituencies."

Courtesy Walter G. Barlow, President, Research Strategies Corporation, Princeton, NJ.

An able listener of another time, Abraham Lincoln, knew the importance of listening. Twice a week, Lincoln set aside a time for conversations with ordinary folk: housewives, farmers, merchants, and pension seekers. He listened patiently to what they had to say, no matter how humble their circumstances or how trivial their business. A military aide once protested to the president that he was wasting valuable time on these unimportant people. Lincoln rebuked him, saying, "I tell you, Major … that I call these receptions my public opinion bath … the effect, as a whole is renovating and invigorating."[11] Today the White House has sophisticated and elaborate methods for monitoring constituent opinion: daily analyses of media and mail content, sophisticated telephone voice mail tabulations of calls, as well as regular polling of public opinion.

Prudence dictates the systematic listening to an organization's publics through scientific research. Yet many organizations fail to utilize this public relations tool fully. In some, two-way communication is seen as organized back talk and a potential threat, rather than an essential tool of modern management. More likely, systematic listening to obtain reliable feedback is limited because it takes effort and skill. The amount of information input, however, determines the extent to which an organization operates as an open rather than a closed system in dealing with problems.

DEFINING PUBLIC RELATIONS PROBLEMS

In closed systems, of course, problems are allowed to define themselves, often as crises. The public relations effort then necessarily reverts into "firefighting" rather than "fire prevention." Examples include spending millions of dollars to counter proposals made by dissident stockholders; paying millions of dollars for advertising time and space to apologize for past actions and to announce corrective measures; and suffering costly construction delays because active citizen groups resorted to legal action to stop proposed, yet unexplained, projects.

Such situations have long histories, and sometimes neither side recalls what caused the blowup. Heading off such blowups is part of the task. The earlier a complaint is caught, the easier it is to handle. Continuous fact-finding uncovers many problems while they are still small enough to permit corrective action and communication before becoming major public issues. The same attentive listening catches rumors before they become widespread and part of the public's perceptions of the organization.

Problem definition begins with someone making a value judgment that something is either wrong, could soon be, or could be better. Implicit is the notion that organizational goals provide the criteria for making such judgments. Goal states serve as the basis for deciding if and when a real or potential problem exists. Once a judgment is made, however, the process becomes an objective, systematic research task designed to describe in detail the dimensions of the problem, the factors contributing to or alleviating the problem, and the publics involved in or affected by the situation. In short, research is used to determine "What's happening now?"

Problem Statement

A useful problem statement summarizes what was learned about the problem situation: **(1) It is written in the present tense, describing the current situation. (2) It describes the situation in specific and measurable terms, detailing most of or all of the following:**

What is the source of concern?

Where is this a problem?

When is it a problem?

Who is involved or affected?

How are they involved or affected?

Why is this a concern to the organization and its publics?

(3) A problem statement does not imply solutions or place blame. If it did, program strategies would be predetermined and limited, much like the cuttlefish's limited options for responding to its environment. The classic example of a problem statement that has an implied solution is the overused, "What we have here is a communication problem." Communication is part of the solution, not the problem!

The real problem could be that only 5 percent of new graduates join the alumni association during the first year following graduation, compared with 21 percent of all graduates, resulting in lost contact and reduced support for the university. Or in the case of a fund-raising effort for a new youth center, the problem could be stated as, the building fund is $200,000 short of the amount needed to complete and equip the new gymnasium by the planned June 1 opening. If you had worked for one of the major oil companies several years ago, you might have been concerned about the "divestiture problem": A plurality (47 percent) of Americans agree with proposals to break up each of the major oil companies into four separate and competing operating companies, thus encouraging some in Congress to vote in favor of divestiture legislation. Notice that each of these problem statements contains concrete measures of the problem situation based on objective research and documentation. Notice also that solutions are not implied, meaning that no particular strategy is suggested in any of the problem statements. In other words, communication may be part of the solution, but it is not stated as part of the problem. Finally, notice that the three examples describe the current situation—"What's happening now?"—not the future.

Situation Analysis

A problem statement represents a concise description of the situation, often written in a sentence or short paragraph. In contrast, a situation analysis is the unabridged collection of all that is known about the situation, its history, forces operating on it, and those involved or affected internally and externally. A situation analysis contains all the background information needed to expand upon and to illustrate in detail the meaning of a problem statement. In the process of analyzing the situation, one is able to clearly and specifically define and refine the problem statement. Typically, the definition process begins with a tentative problem statement, followed by investigation of the situation, which leads to refining the problem definition, and so on. The situation analysis results in what some practitioners call their "fact book," often in the form of information assembled in three-ring binders or files.

The section on **internal factors** deals with organizational policies, procedures, and actions related to the problem situation. Rather than direct all the attention to the publics and other external factors, a situation analysis begins with a thorough and searching review of perceptions and actions of key actors in the organization, structures and processes of organizational units relevant to the problem, and the history of the organization's involvement.

The internal situation analysis also includes a "communication audit"—a systematic documentation of an organization's communication efforts for the purpose of understanding how it communicates with its publics. One practitioner describes the communication audit as follows:

> A complete analysis of an organization's communications—internal and/or external designed to "take a picture" of communication needs, policies, practices, and capabilities, and to uncover necessary data to allow top management to make informed, economical decisions about future objectives of the organization's communication.[12]

Consistent with the open systems model, practitioners do an audit to learn in detail how, what, and to whom they communicate. An audit provides decision makers a clear picture of what is currently done and a basis for deciding what changes need to be made.

Another essential part of the internal portion of a situation analysis is a constantly updated organizational almanac. This file not only serves as an essential organizational background reference when working on specific problems but also provides ideas and information for speeches, pamphlets, special reports, exhibits, and media requests. Most organizations do not have librarians or historians, so public relations departments often handle queries that cannot be answered by others. Journalists expect and need quick answers. Ready access to complete and accurate information on an organization, its history, performance, and managers can give the public relations department a start on crises or rumors in the making.

After helping to develop an understanding of the organizational side of the problem situation, an analysis focuses on the **external factors**, both positive and negative. The starting point may be a systematic review of the history of the problem situation outside the organization. A situation analysis also calls for detailed study of who is currently involved or affected and how. Much of what is done under the banner of public relations research includes gathering information about **stakeholders**: what they know, how they feel, and what they do that is related to the problem.

"Stakeholder analysis" is the process of identifying who is involved and who is affected in a situation. Stakeholders are **people**—in the imagery of system theory—who are part of the same system as an organization. They are in interdependent relationships with an organization, meaning that what they know, feel, and do has impact on the organization and vice versa. In the interest of building and maintaining mutually beneficial relationships, organizations undertake periodic stakeholder analyses to monitor how organizational policies, procedures, decisions, actions, and goals affect others. The different stakeholder groups can be ranked or rated according to the extent to which each is interdependent with an organization in a particular problem situation. Notice that not all those identified as stakeholders necessarily become publics for a program designed to address a particular problem (more on defining publics in the next chapter).[13]

How could you set objectives for each of the publics if you do not know what they currently know, what their opinions are, and how they behave? How could you develop action and communication strategies without a detailed understanding of and empathy for the target publics? At least four additional questions must be answered through research:

1. How much do people use information in the problem situation? Communication is effective only if receivers see a need for information. The situation analysis research must determine to what extent different people actually feel a need for and use information related to a given problem situation.

2. What kinds of information do people use or seek? Whereas "why" questions make up 20 to 35 percent of the questions people typically ask in situations,

these are the ones least likely to be answered successfully in communication programs. Programs that respond to audience needs rather than the interests of the source are based on knowledge of what information different people want.

3. **How do people use information?** Information is rarely an end in itself, because people use information in many different ways. Receivers see information as useful if they think that it relates to a specific action, topic, or plan they consider important. Rarely are they helped simply because they received general information.

4. **What predicts information use?** Demographics or other cross-situational characteristics often do not predict how people use information. Rather, where receivers are in the decision-making process relevant to a problem, or how they see themselves in the situation, determines whether or not they will use the information. In other words, you must know how different individuals see themselves involved in or affected by the situation.[14]

The importance of situation-specific understanding of stakeholders is also evident in Van Leuven's theory of message and media selection: "(1) the user selects media and messages for his or her own rational-appearing and personally relevant purposes; (2) the user will attach his or her own personal meanings to a selected message; (3) the user's behavior reflects anticipated future communication satisfaction as well as a history of prior motivation, intentionality, and reinforcement."[15]

Researching the stakeholders before planning program strategies tests the accuracy of assumptions about who they are, what they know, how they feel about the situation, how they are involved or affected, what information they see as important, how they use it, and even how they get information. With that information in hand—and only then—can program planners write objectives for each public and develop strategies to achieve them.

Systematic definition and study of the stakeholders is needed also to determine an order of priority. Rarely does a practitioner have the staff or money to mount programs directed to all stakeholders. Priorities must be assigned based on which of them are most central to the particular problem at hand, not in response to internal or external pressures unrelated to the problem situation.

Increased understanding of the stakeholders helps determine their information needs and uses; thus, this understanding helps practitioners develop the appropriate message content. Researching their communication patterns and media preferences helps practitioners select the most effective and efficient media strategy for delivering those messages.

Only after the situation has been completely analyzed can practitioners set realistic program goals. Lacking complete and accurate information, practitioners can be guilty of overpromises and underdelivery. Without a complete understanding of the problem situation, practitioners run the risk of developing programs that do not address the major causes of the problem. No amount of public relations communication can change bad performance into good performance or socially irresponsible action into responsible behavior. Neither can it compensate for lack of integrity or persuade publics that an unfair or self-serving policy is fair and unselfish. Overenthusiastic selling of the public relations function often results from incomplete comprehension of the problem situation and leads to the appearance of program failure.

Researching the situation gives practitioners and their employers and clients the timely, complete, and accurate information they need to understand the problem, which serves as a basis for decision making. (Exhibit 11.2 lists topics covered in a situation analysis.) Research is simply an attempt to reduce uncertainty, or as one executive put it, "to help really see what's there to be seen."

Detailed analyses of the internal and external factors in the problem situation provide practitioners with the information they need to assess organizational strengths (S) and weaknesses (W) and to identify the opportunities (O) and threats (T) in the external environment. In practice, practitioners refer to this approach to summarizing the situation analysis as "SWOT" or "TOWS" analysis. Several strategic implications logically flow from this analytic framework:

EXHIBIT 11.2

CONTENT OF SITUATION ANALYSIS

I. Internal Factors

1. Statements of the organization's mission, charter, bylaws, history, and structure

2. Lists, biographies, and photos of key officers, board members, managers, and so forth

3. Descriptions and histories of programs, products, services, and so forth

4. Statistics about resources, budget, staffing, sales, profits, stockholders, and so forth

5. Policy statements and procedures related to the problem situation

6. Position statements (quotations) by key executives regarding the problem situation

7. Description of how the organization currently handles the problem situation

8. Descriptions and lists of the organization's internal stakeholders

9. Lists of organizational media (two-way) for communicating with internal groups

II. External Factors

1. Clippings from newspaper, magazine, trade publication, newsletter, and online coverage of the organization and the problem situation

2. Reports, transcripts, and tapes of radio, television, and cable coverage

3. Content analyses of media coverage and Internet sources

4. Lists of media, journalists, columnists, talk-show hosts, freelance writers, online bloggers, Web sites, and producers who report news and features about the organization and issues related to the problem situation

5. Lists of and background information on individuals and groups who share the organization's concerns, interests, and positions on the problem situation (including their controlled internal and external media outlets)

6. Lists of and background information on individuals and groups who oppose the organization's concerns, interests, and positions on the problem situation (including their controlled internal and external media outlets)

7. Results of surveys and public opinion polls related to the organization and the problem situation

8. Schedules of special events, observances, and other important dates related to the organization and the problem situation

9. Lists of government agencies, legislators, and other officials with regulatory and legislative power affecting the organization and the problem situation

10. Copies of relevant regulations, legislation, pending bills, referenda, government publications, and hearing reports

11. Copies of published research on topics related to the problem situation

12. Lists of important reference books, records, and directories, as well as their locations in the organization

1. *SO* strategies build on organizational strengths to take advantage of opportunities in the external environment.
2. *ST* strategies also build on organizational strengths to counter threats in the external environment.
3. *WO* strategies attempt to minimize organizational weaknesses to take advantage of external opportunities.
4. *WT* strategies attempt to minimize both organizational weaknesses and environmental threats.[16]

Another analytic technique for summarizing the findings of a situation analysis is "force-field analysis," based on the theories of Kurt Lewin, which originated in the 1950s. Before researching the situation, practitioners and others on the management team brainstorm the negative forces contributing to or causing the problem, as well as the positive forces alleviating or solving the problem. The research on the internal and external forces helps determine the extent to which each contributes positively or negatively to the problem situation. Just as with SWOT analysis, the results of a force-field analysis lead to strategic decisions designed to minimize or neutralize the impact of negative forces and to maximize or enhance the contributions from positive forces.[17]

RESEARCH PROCESS

The central roles of research in modern public relations, addressed further in Chapter 14, are demonstrated here. Sometimes practitioners do the research themselves. Other times practitioners hire research specialists or research firms to design the research, gather the information, or analyze the data. In either approach, practitioners must know the research process and concepts. Simply put, you cannot satisfactorily explain to someone else something you do not understand yourself. Ann H. Barkelew, senior vice president and general manager of Fleishman-Hillard's Minneapolis office, says, "You cannot practice public relations today—successfully or effectively—without research."[18]

Scientists have developed a generally accepted approach to research. The process begins with a clear statement of the problem under investigation. Some choose to phrase the problem in the form of a question. Others pose hypothetical relationships between observable phenomena for testing and theory building. The next step is to develop the research design, the plan for making the observations related to the research problem. Is a survey needed? An experiment? Or will the observations be taken from published census reports? This is followed by the specific methods for gathering, analyzing, and interpreting data.[19]

Whereas two research projects are seldom the same in the specifics of how they are implemented, they share a common goal of increasing our understanding of situations and society. The approach and methods chosen for a particular project will depend on the problem being addressed, the skills and preferences of the researcher, the available resources, and the constraints imposed by others or as a result of the situation. Informal and formal research methods differ primarily in their sample selection and sample size, as well as the generalizability of the findings they produce.

INFORMAL OR "EXPLORATORY" METHODS

Informal methods still dominate public relations research, even though highly developed social scientific methods are available. Informal methods can be useful, however, if practitioners recognize their weaknesses and purposes. The major problem—samples of unknown representativeness—results from how samples are selected. The issue is the extent to which the results from samples represent anybody other than the few from whom information was gathered. For example, the results may represent only the opinions of a vocal minority rather than the majority.

If viewed as good methods for *detecting* and *exploring* problem situations and for pretesting research and program strategies, then informal methods serve valuable purposes. If the results are used as the basis for program planning and evaluation as if the findings were representative of target publics, then these methods are misused. "Exploratory" best represents the probing nature of informal methods.

The following sections describe some of the informal methods used in public relations.

Personal Contacts

In 1893 Lord Bryce said, "The best way in which the tendencies at work in any community can be best discovered and estimated is by moving freely about among all sorts and conditions of men." Politicians have been doing this for a long time. Skill in sizing up people's awareness, opinions, and attitudes has long been and always will be a prime qualification of public relations professionals.

For example, when management requested an employee communication campaign against drug abuse, a corporate practitioner, posing as a patient, checked into a drug treatment center and spent three days acquiring firsthand knowledge about drugs, their use, and their potential effects on employees. Others have worked in wheelchairs to gain perspective on what it is like to go for coffee breaks, use the bathroom, or complete other tasks in facilities not designed for easy access. Trade shows, community and professional meetings, or other occasions that attract stakeholders provide opportunities for practitioners to listen carefully and gain understanding.

Feedback from periodic personal visits can be encouraged, extended, and amplified in many ways. For example, when the late Los Angeles Mayor Thomas Bradley first took office, he opened his door to local citizens one day a month. They were given a chance to talk to the mayor about poor sewer facilities, increases in school vandalism, or whatever was on their minds. The mayor of Utica, New York, went a step further. To encourage people to drop in and air their complaints, he took his door off its hinges and put up a sign over his couch that read, "The Town's Living Room." The president of Delta Airlines maintains an open-door policy for employees.

A more structured use of personal contacts is exemplified by the annual shareholder meetings held each year by publicly owned corporations. For example, managers in one company visited shareholders in their homes after business hours. Each year management personnel in various locations personally talked with shareholders about the company's business. In another aggressive approach to getting feedback, a state highway department used a travel trailer as a mobile information center to collect citizens' views on proposed highway projects. The trailer provided an atmosphere for candid one-on-one discussions with highway personnel and gave people who are reluctant to speak in public meetings an opportunity to air their views.

Key Informants

Practitioners commonly talk with key informants, a variation on personal contacts. This approach involves selecting and interviewing knowledgeable leaders and experts. The interview typically takes the form of an open-ended discussion in which selected individuals are encouraged to talk about the problem or issue in their own terms. Because in-depth interviews with key informants take so long to complete and require such careful content analysis, the technique is limited to a relatively small number of respondents.

Many practitioners regularly consult influential people such as authors, editors, reporters, ministers, labor leaders, professors, civic leaders, bankers, and special-interest group leaders. Some have consulted bartenders and taxi drivers. The basis for selecting key informants is their perceived knowledge of an issue and their ability to represent others' views. The major limitation, of course, is that because they were selected purposely because they are seen to have special knowledge and leadership roles, by definition they do not reflect current views of followers. In-depth interviews with key informants often yield early warning signals on important issues.

Focus Groups and Community Forums

It is only a short step from personal contacts and key informants to asking groups for ideas and feedback. The range of groups runs from open town meetings, such as those used by the Clinton administration, to the highly structured and videotaped focus group, a technique commonly used in both public relations and consumer marketing research. A focus group involves about 8 to 12 people, who discuss a topic, led by a moderator. For example, Twentieth Century Fox conducted focus groups in 1977 to see how audiences felt about a movie that director George Lucas wanted to call *Star Wars*.[20] An effective moderator who is an able interviewer and facilitator of the group process is key to the success of this approach.

Practitioners use focus groups and community forums to explore how people will react to proposals and to gather information useful for developing questionnaires to be used in more formal research methods. Unexpected insights are gained from the sometimes-spirited dialogue among participants. Researchers call such information "serendipitous findings," but unanticipated reactions may be the best reason for using these informal research methods. It is better to learn such things before going to the field with a full-blown survey or program test.

For example, the United Soybean Board (USB) developed a fruitful variation of the community forum when it held a series of town hall meetings for soybean producers. An influential producer was asked to invite neighbors to hear presentations and to comment on how the organization was spending producers' funds contributed through a mandatory checkoff on soybean sales. Producers hosted a total of 375 meetings in 28 states, providing USB useful feedback on its program and producers' interests. Similarly, the Chicago Welfare Council staged a "listen-in" for community leaders to get guidance and reactions for program planning.

Government agencies have long used this exploratory strategy to solicit information and participation. The Forest Service, the Army Corps of Engineers, and the Environmental Protection Agency regularly conduct public meetings and hearings to get information and reactions to various project and program proposals. One of the lessons learned from their experiences is that community input must be sought early and often to keep agencies responsive to citizen interests. One communication scholar has investigated government officials' "rules of thumb" for holding successful public meetings, which include things to do before, during, and after the meeting.[21] Focus groups represent a more structured approach. Typically, focus groups include 6 to 12 carefully selected representatives from a target public. They are asked to discuss a specific issue or program proposal in depth. Sessions are videotaped, and the recordings carefully analyzed to catch the smallest detail in participants' comments. For example, one organization conducted focus-group research to learn what middle school teachers want in curriculum materials provided by outside sources. One authority says the major strength of focus groups is the open, spontaneous, and detailed discussions they generate, even among people who did not know each other before the session began.[22] They can be planned, conducted, and analyzed in a matter of days, providing insights and understanding that can be factored into program planning.

Even when members of a group are carefully selected, as with information gained from personal contacts, the results cannot be used to make inferences to a larger population or public. Because the group is small, selection is usually not truly random, and the group-discussion context introduces an artificial setting, the results are not representative—in a scientific sense—of a public or the publics from which the participants were selected. As with other informal methods, focus groups are typically small groups of unknown representativeness.

Moderators also can have an effect on what and how the group discusses. Those viewing the session filter what is said through their own subjective perceptions and interpretations. It is simply not appropriate to suggest that findings from this approach can be used in place of data gathered from scientifically selected samples. The major functions are to identify and explore issues for further study in formal surveys and to pretest program strategies before full-blown field testing.

Advisory Committees and Boards

A standing committee, panel, or board can sometimes be more useful than a single group session, particularly for long-running programs and issues. In some instances such a group can serve as a continuous feedback mechanism for detecting possible changes in public opinion on issues, even before they would show up in polls and surveys. There is a price, however, for using advisory committees and boards. Their advice must be given earnest consideration, or this method will backfire. Members quickly sense when they are being used for cosmetic purposes or being showcased to demonstrate concern for community input. Appoint such a committee or board only when the major motivation is to solicit input and guidance on a regular basis, and be prepared to act on the input.

Nonprofit organizations use this approach to tap the professional public relations community for both expertise and services. Almost every chapter of the United Way, the Arthritis Foundation, Easter Seals, and similar organizations has a public relations advisory committee. Committee service is one way public relations practitioners fulfill their public service obligation as professionals.

Other organizations, for-profit and nonprofit alike, use advisory committees and boards. For example, your city's children's hospital, chamber of commerce, and police department probably use this method of gathering information. The insurance industry created advisory committees and complaint bureaus to facilitate policyholder feedback in response to the consumer movement. An accounting firm set up a public review board to provide an outside perspective on operations. A board of education set up a 24-member community advisory committee to give the board a better sense of community attitudes and needs. The New York Stock Exchange created an advisory committee of 15 senior corporate officers to facilitate communication with the corporations listed on the exchange. The American Frozen Food Institute formed an advisory board on frozen goods made up of food editors and home economics instructors. Advisory committees and boards provide valuable information and guidance, but they cannot substitute for formal approaches to determining the distribution of opinions and reactions among target publics. They provide effective forums for increasing interaction, participation, and in-depth probing of issues. In other words, they are exploratory techniques used to supplement more formal methods.

Ombudsman or Ombuds Officer

The ombuds officer in an organization is someone who listens to the concerns of internal organizational publics. This person may also review organizational policies and mediate disputes between the organization and its employees. The term *ombudsman* originated when the Swedish government established the first such position in 1713. Growing dissatisfaction with ever-longer lines of communication to increasingly isolated managers and bureaucrats has brought about widespread adoption of this informal information-gathering method in government agencies. In countless corporations the ombudsman concept has proved useful in providing feedback and ideas for solving problems while they are still manageable.

Two kinds of ombudsmen are used. One, true to the roots of the original, investigates and solves problems. The second, who at best parries problems, often is there to protect the bureaucracy and to create the illusion of a responsive organization. The former has independent authority to take action on complaints; the latter facilitates communication and seeks authority from others to implement remedies.[23]

The ombudsman's role and scope of its authority vary widely. Dow Chemical Company once established an "ombudswoman" to help promote the advancement of women in the company. At Bronx Community College the ombudsman, appointed by the president, acts as a conduit for student complaints but has no authority to make full-scale investigations. At the University of Nebraska–Lincoln, on the other hand, the ombudsman sees the job as "reporting to nobody and responsible to everyone." The U.S. Navy started its family ombudsman program in 1809 and sees the ombudsman's role as one of cutting governmental red tape and acting as liaison between interested parties and the Navy offices. The ombudsman "investigates organizational problems and makes recommendations for remedial action to improve the quality of administration and redress individual grievances." A large New York hospital employs, as do many hospitals, a "patient representative" to serve as an advocate of patients "to help them and their families find satisfactory solutions to problems." ARCO has an ombudsman to mediate problems dealers cannot get resolved through usual channels: "In a sense, I'm the court of last resort, so this office manages to resolve nearly all disputes."

In each of these settings, the ombudsman provides an effective means for facilitating greater management awareness of public reactions and views. If sincerely used and competently staffed, the ombudsman position can be an important means of obtaining organizational feedback, as well as for helping people get solutions for their problems and answers to their questions. But because this method relies on people who seek out the opportunity to make their feelings and complaints known—a self-selected sample—it also is an exploratory, informal approach to gathering information. Although it *can help identify and detect potential problems*, information gathered by an ombudsman may not accurately describe the frequency or distribution of problems or concerns among the larger group, particularly among less assertive members.

Call-In Telephone Lines

Toll-free 800 numbers are commonly used to obtain instant feedback and to monitor the concerns and interests of various publics. Johnson & Johnson tracked telephone calls during the consumer panic associated with the seven deaths caused by cyanide-laced Extra-Strength Tylenol capsules. Similarly, Procter & Gamble (P&G) monitored more than 100,000 calls on its 800 number when a rumor was circulating that P&G promoted Satanism. The calls not only gave the companies opportunities to respond to concerned consumers but also provided constantly updated information on public concerns and reactions.

Companies also recognize the public relations value of giving consumers and customers access to the corporation and of answering questions directly. By doing so, consumer and customer hot lines provide companies feedback on their products, services, facilities, and employees. For example, General Electric's customer-service Answer Center gets more than 6,000 calls a day. Whirlpool Corporation, among the first in the 1960s to provide a customer call-in service in response to growing customer dissatisfaction, found that about 70 percent of its "Cool Line" service calls were from customers who wanted information on repairs.

Some organizations use this method to field questions from employees; some hospitals use it to provide information and take complaints from patients and their families; other health-care centers use toll-free numbers both to provide help and to determine the extent of health problems; and many government agencies use them to help citizens find their way through the bureaucratic maze. For example, the Internal Revenue Service Form 1040 publication lists toll-free 800 numbers for every state, the District of Columbia, and Puerto Rico. Taxpayers can ask IRS representatives how to complete tax forms or other tax questions. By dialing 1-800-TAX-FORM, taxpayers may order IRS forms. Both services help the IRS track taxpayer interests and needs.

To be effective, a call-in service must be used with sincerity. For example, the U.S. Bureau of Mines, acting in the wake of several major mine disasters, announced with great fanfare that it was installing hot-line telephones at the entrance of every coal mine so that miners could alert the bureau if they found unsafe conditions. The bureau promised "instant action" on the reports. A few months later a reporter for the *Wall Street Journal* found that the bureau had not monitored the recorded calls for almost two months. The newspaper reported that bureau employees "had forgotten about the machine."

Nonprofit organizations also use analyses of telephone calls to track stakeholder concerns. For example, the American Red Cross analyzed more than 1,700 calls about AIDS to determine information needs and which messages to target to different publics. In addition, program planners learned that many people did not understand some of the words used in AIDS educational messages. Based on their analyses of the telephone calls, program planners learned not only what questions needed to be answered but also what words to use and avoid when answering.[24]

A pejorative description of radio talk shows, however, serves as a reminder of the danger in putting too much stock in analyses of telephone calls: SLOP, which stands for a self-selected listener opinion poll. Surely analyses of telephone calls can provide early evidence for detecting potential problems and public opinions. The caution, however, is that detecting problems and opinions cannot substitute for describing the frequency of problems or the distribution of opinions in an organizations' publics.

Mail Analysis

Another economical way of collecting information is periodic analysis of incoming mail. Stakeholders' correspondence reveals areas of favor and disfavor and information needs. Letter writers, however, tend to be critical rather than commendatory. Letters may serve as early warnings of ill will or problem relationships, but they do not reflect a cross section of public opinion or even the views of a particular public.

President John F. Kennedy borrowed a leaf from Franklin D. Roosevelt's book on keeping in touch with constituents. Kennedy directed that every 50th letter coming to the White House be brought to him. Periodic mail samples helped both these leaders bridge the moat surrounding the White House. Other chief executives in organizations of all kinds use daily or weekly reports on the mail to read the pulse of citizens' concerns and opinions. Many organizations file brief summaries of letters to track public concerns.

At its peak, Ford Motor Company's "We Listen Better" campaign brought in 18,000 letters a week from Ford owners. Letters were answered personally, not with form letters, which required a large investment in money and human resources. Comments, suggestions, and criticisms were carefully coded and keyed into a computer file. Printouts of the running tallies provided Ford executives useful information, even though the data came from a self-selected sample.

Similarly, the U.S. Census Bureau analyzed more than 12,000 e-mails from concerned residents about various issues related to the 2000 census. This analysis gave the agency a better idea of the census-related questions that people had, so that preparations could be made for the next census to address these concerns proactively.

The exploratory nature of mail analysis provides information useful for detecting concerns and problems before they become widespread. Those who feel so strongly about something that they take time to write letters or e-mails may not be representative of entire publics, but they may be the first of many to follow. In this role, those who write letters join those who call 800 numbers as early-warning signals of situations that need attention and may indicate a need for formal research.

Online Sources

New communication technology creates opportunities for friend and foe to talk about each other, as well as about organizations, causes, and events. Prudent public relations practitioners now also monitor what is being said about their organizations online. Rumors on the Internet have the potential to influence labor negotiations, attract regulatory attention, drive stock prices up or down, and increase or decrease sales. Among those accessing messages on the Internet, an organization's reputation can be damaged, its brand franchise can suffer, and its hard-earned goodwill can be diminished.

Jackson and Stoakes referred to the Internet's "dark side, where the spread of false and misleading information can cause serious injury to an unprepared target." They recommend that public relations practitioners monitor the Internet to prevent a "cybercrisis" because "rumors that originate on the Internet often make their way into print and broadcast media before a company even knows they exist."[25] Some search engines that are particularly useful for scanning what is being said on the World Wide Web include www.google.com, www.yahoo.com, www.altavista.com, and www.askjeeves.com.

Again, such searches are informal methods for detecting what is being said on the Internet; they cannot produce profiles of public opinion. And that may be the most important point: monitoring online sources can help practitioners tap into the rapidly expanding channels of interactive communication and to intervene in the virtual conversation.

Field Reports

Many organizations have district agents, field representatives, or recruiters who live in and travel the territories served. These agents should be trained to listen and observe and be given an easy, regular means of reporting their observations. In this way they can serve as the eyes and ears of an organization.

Studies of organizational intelligence and communication demonstrate, however, that such representatives tend to gild the lily and to report what they think will set well with their bosses. This is particularly true if field staff know that their reports will pass through a gauntlet of superiors, the same people who hold power over their futures in the organization.

For example, to assess the impact of a company's "progress week," management asked sales representatives to evaluate the program. Forty percent ventured no opinion. About half of those who did respond said the week's promotion had produced more favorable opinions of the company. A formal survey later found that only about one in 10 of the target population was inclined to be more favorable in their opinion of the company. After comparing the field reports with the survey results, it was clear that only 12 of the 42 grassroots observers accurately assessed the results of the promotion. The comparison serves as a reminder that all subjective reports such as field reports must be used with caution. Like the other informal methods, field reports serve best as an early warning to detect situations that may call for more thorough investigation.

FORMAL METHODS

The purpose of both informal and formal methods is to gather accurate and useful information. Formal methods are designed to gather data from scientifically representative samples. Formal methods help answer questions about situations that simply cannot be answered adequately using informal approaches.

The danger is that practitioner–researchers can become more concerned about the methods used than the purpose of the study. As one writer put it, "In science as in love, concentration on technique is quite likely to lead to impotence." Those who get bogged down in research techniques at the expense of usefulness often spend time and resources to produce volumes of data that sit unused on shelves.

Formal methods are useful, however, only if the research question and objectives are clearly determined *before* the research design is selected (see Exhibit 11.3). Done correctly, each formal approach can yield information that describes phenomena and situations within established ranges of accuracy and tolerance for error. These approaches also make it possible to use inferential statistics, the process of using data from representative samples to estimate characteristics of populations. In other words, systematic formal methods make it possible for practitioners to make accurate statements about publics based on evidence drawn from scientifically representative samples.

Successful public relations managers know about formal research methods and statistics. Public relations education at many universities now includes a research methods course as part of the curriculum. Continuing education programs for practitioners typically include offerings on how to use research in program planning, management, and evaluation. The following sections introduce some of the methods and issues in conducting formal research.

EXHIBIT 11.3

CHECKLIST FOR STARTING A RESEARCH PROJECT

1. How will the results obtained from the research be used? This may seem like an obvious question, but it is often easy, particularly in time of crisis, to jump into a research project without a plan for using the results.

2. What is the specific population (public) being studied, and how should the sample be chosen? In some studies, determining the population in question can constitute one of the more difficult aspects. Wise sample selection can minimize project costs and maximize the accuracy of results.

3. What type of research technique is most appropriate in this instance? Do not automatically assume that a survey is best. Perhaps a focus group or secondary research will yield better results.

4. If a survey is to be used, what sort of field methodology will be most efficient? There are three primary choices here: mail, telephone, and in-person interviews. The practitioner should be familiar with the pros and cons of each.

5. Are closed-ended questions, open-ended questions, or a combination of the two recommended? The response to the first question above will have a major effect on the types of questions used.

6. What is the experience level of the research firm being considered, and what are the backgrounds of its personnel? It is especially important to inquire into the firm's experience with the particular type of research being contemplated. Do not be afraid to ask for references.

7. How will the data be analyzed and the results reported? This is very important! Many practitioners have assumed that they were purchasing complete reports, only to be handed stacks of computer runs as the final product.

8. How soon will the results be provided? The luxury of proper planning, when available, can prevent a research project from becoming an unnecessarily costly undertaking.

9. How much will it cost? Professional research is expensive. It is wise to obtain written proposals from three firms. At the same time, many problems can be prevented by insisting that the proposals address each of these nine questions.

Secondary Analysis and Online Databases

Doing research does not always call for gathering data yourself. Secondary analysis reuses data gathered by someone else, often for other purposes.[26]

Numerous governmental and commercial organizations conduct national, regional, and local surveys. Some of these surveys track issues and trends. For example, the U.S. Census Bureau has a long history of developing standardized definitions, sampling techniques, sophisticated methods, and publications of findings. Within government, specialized departments have large research staffs tracking major developments and trends in agriculture, health, labor, business, the economy, and education, to name but a few of the areas under constant study.

Since the 1930s, major commercial polling firms such as those formed by A. C. Nielsen, George Gallup, Elmo Roper, and Louis Harris have made their names synonymous with measures of public opinion. Almost every major city has similar research firms tracking local public opinion trends and conducting marketing research. Major newspapers, television stations, and other news organizations regularly conduct their own surveys and report their results. The results of these surveys often can be segmented on the basis of geography, demographics, and other attributes relevant to public relations problem situations.

Sometimes overlooked are the survey research centers maintained by almost all major universities. Research conducted with public funds is often published and available for the asking. Most public agencies can provide listings of data sets and publications. For much less than the cost of conducting a survey, additional analyses of available data often can be done to help answer questions not asked in the original analysis.

Special-interest publications and scholarly journals regularly publish research data. A great deal of research is conducted to answer questions previously answered by competent researchers and reviewed by knowledgeable editorial boards. Online searches now make it easy and cost effective to search research literature for studies done on specific topics. It makes little sense to design and conduct research until after exploring the possibility that someone else has already done the work and published the results.

The most frequently used research approach to information gathering in public relations, however, is researching online databases. Some of the most-used databases include Lexis-Nexis, Dun and Bradstreet, Dow Jones News/Retrieval, NewsNet, Data Times, Wise Wire, News Sites, and Burrelle's Broadcast Database (all are brand names). Practitioners use these services to access and search through news and technical publications, business information services, market research, financial reports, government records, and broadcast transcripts. For example, the New York public relations firm Chacma, Inc., conducted database searches for economic and political facts on foreign governments and clients dating back 10 to 12 years. Online feeds of international news wires allowed the firm to track developments abroad, with summary printouts available each morning.[27]

Some online database companies customize services to meet the specific needs of subscribers. For example, to track the over-the-counter cold remedy field, the manager of information services at Ketchum Public Relations in New York subscribed to Dow Jones's customized service to get relevant information faxed to her office as soon as it goes online. NewsNet and Lexis-Nexis will set up special files for subscribers, making it easy for customers to access information without the usual cost of a conventional search of the entire database.[28]

Content Analysis

Content analysis is the application of systematic procedures for objectively determining what is being reported in the media.[29] Press clippings and broadcast monitor reports, all available from commercial services, have long been used as the bases for content analyses. They indicate only what is being printed or broadcast, *not* what is read or heard. And they *do not* measure whether or not the audiences learned or believed message content. For example, a content analysis of newspaper clippings provides a useful measure of what messages are being placed in the media, but it does not indicate readership or impact.

Analyzing the editorials and letters to the editor may yield little more than the views of the editor and publisher. The range of letters sent is seldom represented by those chosen for publication.[30] And the editorial page does not represent public opinion, as is made abundantly clear when candidates receiving newspaper endorsements do not win elections. As agenda-setting researchers caution, media are better at telling us what to think about than they are at telling us what to think.[31]

As John Naisbitt demonstrated in his popular books on trends, however, content analysis can provide valuable insights into what is likely to be on the public agenda in the future. Recognizing the role of the media in reporting and influencing trends, in 1968 Naisbitt began publishing a quarterly newsletter, *Trend Report*, based on content analyses of 206 metropolitan newspapers. Now the national and regional newsletters report content analyses of more than 6,000 newspapers. Based in Washington, D.C., but no longer owned by Naisbitt, these newsletters give corporate and government subscribers an early warning system for forecasting social and economic conditions, often long before they are apparent to most observers.

Increasingly, public relations firms are helping their clients anticipate issues by either subscribing to issues-tracking services or by doing their own media content analyses. It is important to note, however, that these media content analyses employ a more systematic, formal method than the usual informal approaches used for monitoring the media. The key differences are the representativeness of the content selected for analysis and the objectivity used in measuring and coding the content.

Surveys

Surveys are systematic queries of subsets of the population under study. Surveys are administered in many ways, including by mail, in person, via telephone, and online. The adequacy of the administration method depends on the sampling procedures used, what questions are asked, and how the questions are asked.

Advantages of mailed questionnaires—the most traditional method—include considerable savings of time and money, convenience for respondents because they determine when to answer the questions, greater assurance of anonymity, standardized wording, no interviewer bias, access to respondents not readily reached in person by interviewers, and opportunity for respondents to take time to gather information needed to complete the questionnaire. According to one professional, another advantage to using surveys for information gathering is that "quantitative data is (sic) viewed as accurate."[32]

The biggest **disadvantages** of mail surveys are that researchers have no control over who responds and that low response rates are typical. Whereas the original mailing list may have been a randomly selected and representative sample, unless all respond there is no assurance of an unbiased sample. Even a 90 percent response rate could be inadequate if those not responding represent a significant and uniform segment of the population being studied. Remember that elections are often won by fractions of a percent. There is no basis for the conventional wisdom that a 50 percent return is adequate. The unanswered question remains, which half of the sample did or did not respond?

Other disadvantages include lack of control over the conditions under which the questionnaire is completed, no assurance that the intended respondent completed the questionnaire, lack of flexibility in how questions are asked if the respondent does not understand what is being asked, and difficulties in getting and maintaining current mailing lists.

A variation of the mailed questionnaire takes the form of a page included in publications or distributed with other materials. Whereas the cost of a separate mailing is saved, all the advantages and disadvantages of the mailed questionnaire apply and in some cases are magnified.

In-person, face-to-face administration of surveys gives researchers higher response rates compared to mail surveys, greater flexibility in dealing with the respondents, more control over conditions under which the questions are asked, increased control over the order and completeness of questioning, and opportunity to observe and record reactions not covered by the questionnaire. However, disadvantages include relatively greater research costs, the tendency of respondents to answer certain questions differently in the face of an interviewer, greater inconvenience imposed on respondents, less anonymity for respondents, increased difficulty in contacting those selected in the sample, and respondents' negative reactions resulting from misuse of survey approaches by salespersons and other solicitors posing as researchers. Furthermore, during both in-person and telephone survey administrations, the interviewers themselves can influence the information gathered, so interviewer training is an essential element of these approaches.

Telephone interviews offer a faster and more cost-effective way to complete interview studies while providing somewhat greater anonymity to respondents. However, one major challenge for telephone-administered surveys is sample selection: more than 95 percent of households have telephones, but not all are listed in directories. Computer-assisted random digit dialing (RDD) has helped solve the sampling problem caused by incomplete directory listings. But even with the most sophisticated software, sampling phone numbers produces only about two working phone numbers for every three numbers dialed. The reasons for the relatively low—and dropping—rate of working phone numbers among those dialed are modems, faxes, and second and third lines. New area codes make frequent changes in the dialing software necessary, and special area codes for cell phones add to the challenge of finding respondents without inconveniencing them. So although the numbers selected for calls may be representative, answering machines and refusal rates have made it more difficult to obtain representative samples and have driven up telephone surveying costs.[33]

For example, the research firm Survey Sampling, Inc., estimates that researchers must call five phone numbers to complete one interview in Chicago and three calls to complete one interview in Cincinnati. Moreover, although 36 percent of adults have refused to participate in a research study, they said inconvenience was the major reason for refusing. Notably, more people than ever are participating in surveys. Forty-two percent of all adults have participated in some type of survey. Even 84 percent of those who had refused to cooperate in one survey said that they had participated in another survey.[34]

One common variation in the telephone survey is computer-assisted telephone interviews (CATI). In this method of survey administration, researchers enter respondents' answers directly into a computer system, which directs the flow of these complex surveys by skipping questions or asking supplemental ones depending on how respondents answer various "filter" questions. Another variation on the telephone survey is the IVR—interactive voice response—survey in which respondents call a number and complete the questionnaire at their convenience, responding verbally to questions asked by a computer, which in turn codes responses by recognizing key terms in participants' answers.

Finally, the online administration of surveys is viewed by some researchers as the inevitable wave of the future. These methods may include graphics-based questionnaires that respondents access through a special URL and complete by clicking on various multiple-choice options, text-based questionnaires that are sent and completed via e-mail, or a combination in which an e-mailed note invites respondents to access a particular URL for participation in the survey. Advantages of the online administration of surveys include greater convenience for the respondent, as well as greater efficiency for the researcher, who can rely on computer systems to translate the data automatically into numeric form, rather than hand-coding each response.

However, one challenge for online survey administration lies in obtaining adequate sampling frames, or lists of e-mail addresses from which researchers can select their samples. Another challenge is low response rates, usually resulting from the junk mail filtering services provide on most e-mail accounts. The Council for Marketing and Opinion Research has even proposed a new method of calculating online response rates that would account for nonrespondents who never even see the initial request to participate in a survey.

Usually single surveys are conducted on *cross-section samples* of a population or public at a single point in time. If the study is designed to learn how people change over time or to track a process, however, a longitudinal study, either as a **panel study** or **trend study**, is the better approach. In panel studies the same respondents are interviewed several times during the study, are asked to complete a series of questionnaires on a fixed schedule, or are required to maintain a diary during the study period. For example, the "Baccalaureate and Beyond" study conducted by the National Center for Education Statistics surveyed the same group of bachelor's degree recipients over a period of 10 years. Two problems common to panel studies are that respondents drop out over the course of the project ("panel mortality") and that respondents become more attentive to the issues being examined because of the repeated contact with researchers ("sensitization"). A trend study uses different samples drawn from the same population to track change over time. Because different people are in the samples, however, not being able to attribute changes to particular types of people is the cost of solving panel mortality and sensitization problems.

In summary, formal research methods follow the rules of science, use representative samples, and employ other systematic procedures for making the observations, taking the measurements, and analyzing the data. Like other skills based on specialized knowledge, doing formal research requires study and practice. Done correctly, however, formal research helps practitioners describe reality accurately. Research findings, combined with experience and judgment, provide the foundation for defining public relations problems and for designing programs to address those problems. In other words, research builds the information foundation necessary for effective public relations practice and management.

This chapter highlights only some of the approaches for gathering the informal and formal information needed to understand and define public relations problem situations. Whereas research is often viewed as a necessary step for evaluating program impact, it is equally necessary in the initial step of the problem-solving process—defining the problem situation. Not only does research provide the information necessary for understanding the problem, but also this "benchmark" description serves as the basis for monitoring and evaluating program effectiveness. How do you plan the program if you do not know what you are dealing with? How do you determine how the program is working if you do not know where you started?

Practitioners know that research initiates, monitors, and concludes the problem-solving process. It is the essential ingredient that makes public relations a management function as well as a managed function.

NOTES

[1] Edward J. Robinson, *Public Relations Research and Survey Research: Achieving Organizational Goals in a Communication Context* (New York: Appleton-Century-Crofts, 1969). The first book devoted to using social science survey research methods in public relations.

[2] From the fable, "The Blind Men and the Elephant," by John Godfrey Saxe (1816–1887), quoted by Henry Mintzberg, "Strategy Formation: Schools of Thought," in *Perspectives on Strategic Management*, ed. James W. Fredrickson, 105–6 (New York: Harper Business Division of Harper & Row, 1990).

[3] Quoted in Walter K. Lindenmann, "Research, Evaluation, and Measurement: A National Perspective," *Public Relations Review* 16, no. 2 (Summer 1990): 14.

[4] Quoted in Sherri Deatherage Green. "Strategy by Numbers: Up-Front Research Doesn't Yet Have a Permanent Place in PR," *PRWeek* (August 4, 2003): 15.

[5] Lindenmann, Ibid.

[6] C. F. Kettering, "More Music Please, Composers," *Saturday Evening Post* 211, no. 32 (1938).

[7] Peter H. Rossi and Howard E. Freeman, *Evaluation: A Systematic Approach*, 4th ed. (Newbury Park, CA: Sage Publications, 1989), 27.

[8] David M. Dozier, "The Innovation of Research in Public Relations Practice: Review of a Program of Studies," *Public Relations Research Annual* 2 (1990): 3–28. See also Jon White and David M. Dozier, "Public Relations and Management Decision Making," in *Excellence in Public Relations and Communication Management*, ed. James E. Grunig, 91–108 (Hillsdale, NJ: Lawrence Erlbaum Associates, 1992).

[9] Wilbur Schramm, *Men, Messages, and Media: A Look at Human Communication* (New York: Harper and Row, 1973), 51.

[10] Wilbur Schramm, "The Nature of Communication between Humans," in *The Process and Effects of Mass Communication*, rev. ed., ed. Wilbur Schramm and Donald F. Roberts, 26 (Urbana: University of Illinois Press, 1971).

[11] Carl Sandburg, *Abraham Lincoln: The War Years II* (New York: Harcourt, Brace and World, 1939): 236–37.

[12] Joseph A. Kopec, "The Communication Audit," *Public Relations Journal* 38, no. 5 (May 1982): 24.

[13] For more on the distinction between "stakeholders" and "publics," see James E. Grunig and Fred C. Repper, "Strategic Management, Publics, and Issues," in *Excellence in Public Relations*, 127–46.

[14] Adapted from Brenda Dervin, "Audience as Listener and Learner, Teacher and Confidante: The Sense Making Approach," in *Public Communication Campaigns*, 2nd ed., ed. Ronald E. Rice and Charles K. Atkin, 67–86 (Newbury Park, CA: Sage Publications, 1989).

[15] Jim Van Leuven, "Expectancy Theory in Media and Message Selection," *Communication Research* 8, no. 4 (October 1981): 431.

[16] Heinz Weihrich, "The TOWS Matrix: A Tool for Situational Analysis," in *Strategic Planning: Models and Analytical Techniques*, ed. Robert G. Dyson, 17–36 (Chichester, UK: John Wiley and Sons, 1990).

[17] Kerry Tucker and Doris Derelian, *Public Relations Writing: A Planned Approach for Creating Results* (Englewood Cliffs, NJ: Prentice Hall, 1989), 41–46.

[18] Glen M. Broom and David M. Dozier, *Using Research in Public Relations: Applications to Program Management* (Englewood Cliffs, NJ: Prentice Hall, 1990), 20.

[19] For more detailed discussion of research methods, see Broom and Dozier, *Using Research in Public Relations*.

[20] "Flashbacks: Name That Gold Mine," *Forbes* (June 10, 2002): 60.

[21] Katherine A McComas. "Theory and practice of public meetings," *Communication Theory* 11, no. 1 (February 2001): 36–55.

[22] Larissa A. Grunig, "Using Focus Group Research in Public Relations," *Public Relations Review* 16, no. 2 (Summer 1990): 36–37.

[23] For an account of the origins and uses of the ombudsman concept, see Donald C. Rowat, ed., *The Ombudsman: Citizen's Defender*, 2nd ed. (London: George Allen and Unwin, 1968).

[24] Meryl Davids, "Panic Prevention," *Public Relations Journal* 43, no. 3 (March 1987): 21.

[25] Amy Jackson and Unity Stoakes, "Internet Vigilance: Monitoring Public Opinion Online," *Public Relations Tactics*, November 1997, p. 12.

[26] David W. Stewart and Michael A. Kamins, *Secondary Research: Information Sources and Methods*, 2nd ed. (Newbury Park, CA: Sage Publications, 1993). Discusses how to locate information from various sources, including government agencies, online information search services, and CD-ROM delivery systems.

[27] O'Dwyer's FARA Report 1, no. 2 (March 1991): 5. (Monthly newsletter reporting developments under the Foreign Agents Registration Act.)

[28] John Masterton, "Discovering Databases: On-Line Services Put Research at Practitioner's Fingertips," *Public Relations Journal* 48, no. 11 (November 1992): 12–19, 27.

[29] For more detailed descriptions of content analysis procedures, see Robert P. Weber, *Basic Content Analysis* (Beverly Hills, CA: Sage Publications, 1985); and Guido H. Stempel III, "Content Analysis," in *Research Methods in Mass Communication*, ed. Guido H. Stempel III and Bruce H. Westley, 119–31 (Englewood Cliffs, NJ: Prentice Hall, 1981).

[30] David L. Grey and Trevor R. Brown, "Letters to the Editor: Hazy Reflections of Public Opinion," *Journalism Quarterly* 47 (Autumn 1970): 450–56, 471.

[31] For a good summary of two decades of agenda-setting research, see the special issue of *Journalism Quarterly* 69, no. 4 (Winter 1992); and Maxwell McCombs, Edna Einseidel, and David Weaver, "The Agenda-Setting Role of Mass Communication," chapter 2 of

Contemporary Public Opinion: Issues and the News (Hillsdale, NJ: Lawrence Erlbaum Associates, 1991), 11–21.

[32] Margaret Grisdela. "Create Surveys That Get the Press Calling," *Public Relations Tactics* (April 2003): 11.

[33] Terrence Coen, "Improve Phoneroom Efficiency," *The Frame*, November 1997, p. 1. (Quarterly newsletter published by Survey Sampling, Inc., Fairfield, CT.)

[34] Pat Lewis, "Cooperation Rates, the Ups and the Downs," *The Frame* 14, no. 1 (1991): 2.

ADDITIONAL SOURCES

Broom, Glen M., and David M. Dozier. *Using Research in Public Relations: Applications to Program Management*. Englewood Cliffs, NJ: Prentice Hall, 1990.

Fink, Arlene. *How to Analyze Survey Data* (The Survey Kit, Vol. 8) and *How to Report on Surveys* (The Survey Kit, Vol. 9). Thousand Oaks, CA: Sage Publications, 1995.

Fowler, Floyd J. Jr. *Survey Research Methods*, 2nd ed. Newbury Park, CA: Sage Publications, 1993. Covers essentials of survey research and adapts it to personal computers for data entry and analysis.

Greenbaum, Thomas L. *The Handbook for Focus Group Research*, 2nd ed. Thousand Oaks, CA: Sage Publications, 1997. Author summarizes 20 years of experience in focus group research.

Hyman, Herbert H. *Secondary Analysis of Sample Surveys: Principles, Procedures, and Potentialities*. New York: John Wiley and Sons, 1972. Considered the classic reference on doing secondary analyses.

Lavrakas, Paul J. *Telephone Survey Methods*, 2nd ed. Newbury Park, CA: Sage Publications, 1993. Outlines the use of new technology for conducting telephone research, sampling techniques, supervising interviewers, and securing cooperation of respondents.

Miller, Delbert C. *Handbook of Research Design and Social Measurement*, 6th ed. Thousand Oaks, CA: Sage Publications, 2002. This may be the most complete manual on social science research methods. Most valuable are the guides to doing research and presentations of selected scales and indices.

Stacks, Don W. *Primer of Public Relations Research*. New York: The Guilford Press, 2002. A welcome addition to the growing body of literature on research in the practice.

Williams, Frederick. *Reasoning with Statistics*, 4th ed. New York: Holt, Rinehart and Winston, 1991. Uses communication examples to introduce statistics.

12

STEP TWO: PLANNING AND PROGRAMMING

Strategy is a driving force in any business or organization. It's the intellectual force that helps organize, prioritize and energize what they do. No strategy; no energy. No strategy; no direction. No strategy; no momentum. No strategy; no impact.

—Jim Lukaszewski[1]

STUDY GUIDE

After studying Chapter 12, you should be able to

- Define **strategic thinking** and **strategy**, and explain how they apply to **strategic public relations management.**

- Describe the application of management by objectives (MBO) to public relations planning and management.

- Outline the major steps in the planning and programming process.

- List and describe the major approaches to defining publics.

- Discuss the characteristics of useful program objectives and write examples.

- Describe and give examples of the three major categories of disasters and crises that practitioners must anticipate and plan for.

Once the public relations problem or opportunity has been defined through research and analysis, practitioners must devise a strategy for coping with the problem or for capitalizing on the opportunity. This is planning and programming—making the basic strategic decisions about what will be done in what order in response to or in anticipation of a problem or opportunity. The effectiveness of the tactics used in the next step of the process—taking action and communicating (Chapter 13)—depends on the sound planning done in this, the second step. Yet many practitioners do not take the time necessary to give planning more than a glancing blow; they do "pseudoplanning."[2] Like the cuttlefish squirting ink, inadequate planning leads to routine responses whose origins and motivations are lost in history. Such reaction-based programs may or may not be appropriate in the present context.

———————— ■ ————————

STRATEGIC THINKING

Strategic thinking involves predicting or establishing a desired future goal state, determining what forces will help and hinder movement toward the goal, and formulating a plan for achieving the desired state. But as President Dwight D. Eisenhower is quoted as having said when he commanded U.S. forces during World War II in Europe: "The plan is nothing. Planning is everything!" When planning a program, an organization is, in effect, making tomorrow's decisions today. Skimping on the strategic planning step in the public relations process results in programs that may reinforce controversy rather than resolve it, waste money on audiences that are not there, or facilitate misunderstanding and confusion instead of understanding and clarification.

Many difficult public relations problems were born of yesterday's spur-of-the-moment decisions. For example, the American Heart Association's short-lived "seal-of-approval" program for food products was canceled under heavy pressure from the U.S. Department of Agriculture and other interested parties. Surely the PGA Tour regretted its announcement that disabled tour pro Casey Martin could not use a golf cart. The IRS regretted and retracted its announcement that fans who caught Mark McGwire's record-setting home run balls would have to pay a large "gift tax." Another example is the public relations disaster that resulted when Nestlé marketed in developing nations an infant-formula substitute for breastfeeding. The company apparently did not take into account that the formula would be mixed with water unsafe for babies. Exxon's handling of the tanker *Valdez* oil spill cleanup in Prince William Sound on the Alaskan coast provides yet another case study of inadequate planning and programming for such a disaster. One writer described Exxon's response in an article titled "Exxon *Valdez*: How to Spend Billions and Still Get a Black Eye."[3]

In all these cases, program planners apparently made strategic decisions based on inadequate situation analyses or without fully considering possible unintended consequences of their program tactics. In effect, programs represent strategic interventions for which both planners and their organizations are held responsible.

Public Relations as Part of Strategic Thinking

A definition of strategy captures the essence of strategic thinking and management expectations:

> Strategy can be defined as the determination of the basic long-term goals and objectives of an enterprise, and the adoption of courses of action and the allocation of resources necessary for carrying out these goals.[4]

Corporate-level strategy provides the overall goal and direction within which an organization's divisions operate. Business-level strategy establishes the goals and directions for each division, each operating unit, or, in diversified organizations, each business. In a **planning mode**, strategy takes the form of a systematic plan and guidelines for achieving corporate- and business-level strategies. In an **evolutionary mode**, strategies develop over time, representing a pattern of decisions that respond to opportunities and threats in the environment. Whereas the planning mode has been the preferred model, the evolutionary mode is increasingly accepted as the more appropriate approach for dealing with rapidly changing organizations and environments.[5] As such, plans that spell out the goals and strategy—including the public relations components—become dynamic documents that reflect the open systems approach discussed in Chapter 7.

Reliance on research findings as the basis for strategic planning to achieve effective public relations varies widely. Walter Lindenmann, former senior vice president and director of research at Ketchum Public Relations in New York, surveyed practitioners to learn how many use research as the basis for program planning. Seventy-five percent of all those surveyed reported that they "occasionally" or "frequently" do research specifically for the purpose of planning. Counselors were most likely to use research, 89 percent, whereas practitioners in nonprofit settings were least likely, 68 percent.[6]

Another study concludes that practitioners' use of strategic thinking and program evaluation are correlated with the number of social science, statistics, and computer courses taken by practitioners. Seat-of-the-pants approaches are not correlated with taking social science or statistics courses and are negatively correlated with coursework in using computers. Furthermore, the more practitioners engage in various types of research, the more likely they are to approach their work as managers and to be involved in management decision making.[7] As one practitioner put it, "If you don't have information to take to the table, then you don't get invited to the table [management meetings]."

Management Expectations

In many organizations, top management limits public relations participation in management decision making. "Many public relations people fantasize their roles in strategic planning, but few are really involved in any meaningful fashion," according to a principal of a major public relations firm.[8] Responding to management expectations requires practitioners to think outside the boundaries of public relations by analyzing and understanding the needs and concerns of operating units. In short, line managers expect public relations efforts to help achieve organizational goals, or in the words of some managers, "affect the bottom line."

Longtime AT&T public relations executive Ed Block outlined a CEO's expectations of the chief public relations officer:

> In this role, I need someone with an exquisite public relations "gut" combined with a comprehensive knowledge of the business and its external and internal environment. I want someone who is in touch with the "soul" of the business, someone who shares my vision and understands my sensibilities. I don't need a "handler" or a gate keeper. I need someone whose counsel, over time, will influence my thinking in broad terms, not someone who hectors me on every piddling issue that crosses my desk. I also want someone whose counsel is sought out by others in top management because it is timely and thoughtful and helpful—not because it comes from someone who has special access to me.[9]

In the information age of instant computer communication and online databases, the days of playing hunches and simply replaying the past as the primary basis for planning are history. Others in the organization may make strategic decisions based on financial, legal, or technical considerations and data. It is the responsibility of the public relations practitioner to anticipate the impact of those decisions on various stakeholder groups. In the words of another telephone company executive, "We lead an issues management group that functions as an early warning sentinel for the corporation." He credits the environmental scanning and "up-front counseling" for public relations' companywide acceptance in the strategic planning process. "Or to put it another way," he concludes, "we help plan the parade, not just carry the shovels afterward!"[10]

AT&T's CEO and chairman, Robert E. Allen, made the same point, "I need PR people at my side not in my wake."[11]

Prudent long-range planning, anticipating conceivable developments, is more likely to result in the following:

1. An integrated program in which the total effort results in definite accomplishments toward specific goals.
2. Increased management participation and support.
3. A program emphasis that is positive rather than defensive.
4. Careful deliberation on choice of themes, timing, and tactics.

Even though the values of planning are evident and widely acknowledged, there is too little emphasis on this step in public relations. The following appear to be the main obstacles:

1. Failure of employers and clients to include the practitioner in deliberations that lead to policies and programs; a failure often born of lack of confidence in the public relations officer or counselor.
2. Absence of clearly agreed-upon objectives for implementing the public relations program.
3. Inadequate time because of the pressures of meeting daily problems.
4. Frustrations and delays that practitioners encounter in getting internal clearance and in coordinating with other departments.

Despite the problems, in the final analysis management expects public relations to help manage threats from the environment, to enhance the organization's competitive edge (usually in the form of marketing support), and—most important—to protect an organization's most important assets, its good name and reputation. "Buildings depreciate, patents expire, but, properly managed, a company's name and reputation grow in value every year."[12]

Often the health of the bottom line depends on the health of an organization's reputation. An organization's market share, its ability to attract and retain valuable employees, its attractiveness to prospective donors and members, its autonomy and freedom to carry out its missions, and even its stock price are affected by its reputation among various stakeholders. Management expects the public relations unit to manage the organization's reputation and good standing with the same strategic thinking that goes into managing other assets.

Counselor Davis Young says there is no quick and easy way to build an organization's reputation:

If you want people to regard your organization highly, that must be a priority to which you allocate both time and money, one for which you plan and budget as you would for any aspect of your business. . . . It may take years to build a reputation but only a moment to destroy one. . . . A reputation is a priceless asset to be protected and managed at all times.[13]

STRATEGIC MANAGEMENT

Strategic management represents the open systems approach to public relations rather than the closed systems, reactive approach. One counselor defines strategic management as "a process that enables any organization—company, association, nonprofit or government agency—to identify its long-term opportunities and threats, mobilize its assets to address them and carry out a successful implementation strategy."[14]

Strategic planning in public relations involves making decisions about program goals and objectives, identifying key publics, setting policies or rules to guide selection of strategies, and determining strategies. There must be a close linkage between the overall program goal, the objectives established for each of the publics, and the strategies selected. The key point is that strategies are selected to achieve a particular outcome (as stated in a goal or objective). On the other hand, if you don't care where you end up, any route will get you there.

Public relations practitioners work with other managers to develop strategic program plans. Although each program calls for specifically tailored and unique elements, the overall approach is similar from plan to plan. The planning and programming process typically includes the following steps:

1. *Defining roles and missions.* Determining the nature and scope of the work to be performed.
2. *Determining key results areas.* Determining where to invest time, energy, and talent.
3. *Identifying and specifying indicators of effectiveness.* Determining measurable factors on which objectives may be set.
4. *Selecting and setting objectives.* Determining results to be achieved.
5. *Preparing action plans.* Determining how to achieve specific objectives.
   A. *Programming.* Establishing a sequence of actions to follow in reaching objectives.
   B. *Scheduling.* Establishing time requirements for objectives and action steps.
   C. *Budgeting.* Determining and assigning the resources required to reach objectives.
   D. *Fixing accountability.* Determining who will see to the accomplishment of objectives and action steps.
   E. *Reviewing and reconciling.* Testing and revising a tentative plan, as needed, prior to commitment to action.
6. *Establishing controls.* Ensuring the effective accomplishment of objectives.
7. *Communicating.* Determining the organizational communications necessary for achieving understanding and commitment in the previous six steps.

8. *Implementing.* Securing agreement among all key people regarding who and what needs to be committed to the effort, what approach will work best, who needs to be involved, and what action steps need to be taken immediately.[15]

Mission Statements

The four-step public relations process outlined in Chapters 11 through 14 is based on the assumption that the organization has clearly defined its overall mission and goals and that public relations is part of the plan to achieve them.

Most organizations have a written statement of goals and objectives, both long range and immediate. The purpose is to state succinctly why an organization exists, such as Merck Pharmaceuticals', "We are in the business of preserving and improving human life." Mission statements typically make public commitments of citizenship obligations and social responsibility. They often give the organization's attitude in dealing with its employees, members, clients, neighbors, and donors. They may state the organization's posture on government regulation or environmental issues, explain how it measures its own progress, and so on. In short, they are idealistic and inspirational statements designed to give those in the organization a sense of purpose and direction (see Exhibit 12.1).

Mission statements without management commitment and support, however, become simply cosmetic additions to brochures, reports, and speeches. The challenge is to instill a sense of mission, values, and behavior standards throughout an organization. Each organization has to define its own unique mission, matching its strategy and values, and creating its own culture.[16]

Whether these documents are kept private for competitive or security reasons or are open statements of mission, standards of conduct, or specific purposes, public relations staff are privy to them. In organizations where no such statements have been set down, there is an urgent need for the top public relations officer to propose one.

Mission statements of organizational goals, obligations, values, and social responsibility serve two important purposes in public relations: First, they commit the whole organization to accountability, and that means visibility or communication of some sort. Second, the attitudes expressed provide a framework in which public relations can devise its goals and objectives, build its budgets, direct its talents, devise its programs, and assess its impact.

The mission statement for the public relations function builds on the organization's mission statement. Typically the mission of public relations is to help the organization achieve its mission by doing the following:

1. Collecting and analyzing information on the changing knowledge, opinions, and behaviors of key publics and stakeholder groups.
2. Serving as the central source of information about an organization and as the official channel of communication between an organization and its publics.
3. Communicating significant information, opinions, and interpretations to keep an organization's publics and other stakeholders aware of organizational policies and actions.
4. Coordinating activities that affect an organization's relationships with its publics and other stakeholder groups.

To the extent that these activities and an organization's mission are connected to measurable goals and objectives, then public relations is part of management. To

EXHIBIT 12.1

MISSION STATEMENTS

Weyerhaeuser Company (Tacoma, Washington)

Our Vision. The Best Forest Products Company in the World.

Our Strategies. We shall achieve our vision by: Making Total Quality the Weyerhaeuser way of doing business. Relentless pursuit of full customer satisfaction. Empowering Weyerhaeuser people. Leading the industry in forest management and manufacturing excellence. Producing superior returns for our shareholders.

Our Values. Customers: We listen to our customers and improve our products and services to meet their present and future needs. **People:** Our success depends upon high-performing people working together in a safe and healthy workplace where diversity, development and teamwork are valued and recognized. **Accountability:** We expect superior performance and are accountable for our actions and results. Our leaders set clear goals and expectations, are supportive, and provide and seek frequent feedback. **Citizenship:** We support the communities where we do business, hold ourselves to the highest standards of ethical conduct and environmental responsibility, and communicate openly with Weyerhaeuser people and the public. **Financial Responsibility:** We are prudent and effective in the use of the resources entrusted to us.

New York Stock Exchange

Mission Statement. Support the capital-raising and asset-management process by providing the highest quality and most cost-effective, self-regulated marketplace for the trading of financial instruments; promote confidence in and understanding of that process; and serve as a forum for discussion of relevant national and international policy issues.

Johnson & Johnson

Our Credo. We believe our first responsibility is to the doctors, nurses and patients, to mothers and fathers and all others who use our products and services. In meeting their needs everything we do must be of high quality. We must constantly strive to reduce our costs in order to maintain reasonable prices. Customers' orders must be serviced promptly and accurately. Our suppliers and distributors must have an opportunity to make a fair profit.

We are responsible to our employees, the men and women who work with us throughout the world. Everyone must be considered as an individual. We must respect their dignity and recognize their merit. They must have a sense of security in their jobs. Compensation must be fair and adequate, and working conditions clean, orderly and safe. We must be mindful of ways to help our employees fulfill their family responsibilities. Employees must feel free to make suggestions and complaints. There must be equal opportunity for employment, development and advancement for those qualified. We must provide competent management, and their actions must be just and ethical.

We are responsible to the communities in which we live and work and to the world community as well. We must be good citizens—support good works and charities and bear our fair share of taxes. We must encourage civic improvements and better health and education. We must maintain in good order the property we are privileged to use, protecting the environment and natural resources.

Our final responsibility is to our stockholders. Business must make a sound profit. We must experiment with new ideas. Research must be carried on, innovative programs developed and mistakes paid for. New equipment must be purchased, new facilities provided and new products launched. Reserves must be created to provide for adverse times. When we operate according to these principles, the stockholders should realize a fair return.

Used with permission. Courtesy Weyerhaeuser Company, New York Stock Exchange, and Johnson & Johnson.

attain organizational maturity, the public relations function must be mainstreamed in every sense, not a sideshow, and have management agreement of a clear-cut charter, or mission.

Management by Objectives

As executives have become sophisticated in the ways of public relations, they have become more demanding. Most organizations operate on the basis of management by objectives (MBO) or, as others term it, management by objectives and results (MOR). Simply put, MBO systematically applies effective management techniques to running an organization. It specifies the outcomes (consequences, results, impact) to be achieved, thereby establishing the criteria for selecting strategies, monitoring performance and progress, and evaluating program effectiveness.

As now applied, MBO operates at two levels of outcomes: goals and objectives. Goals are summative statements that spell out the overall outcomes of a program. Such a program may involve many different parts of an organization as well as many different strategies. Goals state what the coordinated effort is intended to accomplish and by when it will be accomplished. Goals establish what will be accomplished if the objectives set for each of the publics are achieved.

Objectives represent the specific knowledge, opinion, and behavioral outcomes to be achieved for each well-defined target public, what some call "key results." The outcome criteria take the form of measurable program effects to be achieved by specified dates. In practice, objectives do the following:

1. Give focus and direction for developing program strategies and tactics.
2. Provide guidance and motivation to those implementing the program.
3. Spell out the criteria for monitoring progress and for assessing impact.

An organization's overall goals provide the outcome criteria for unit and individual goals, including those for the public relations department. Just as an organization has a written MBO plan, so should public relations have a long-range MBO plan on paper. A separate document should give guidance within the department. Just as managers or general officers are periodically subject to performance review by a superior officer, so is the public relations manager. If line departments and other staff functions hold annual conferences to reenergize the staff, so should public relations. Most important, however, public relations must operate within and as part of an organization's overall MBO plan, must be held accountable in the same way as other functions, and must show how public relations contributes to the achievement of the organization's mission and goals.

Strategy and Tactics

The terms *strategy* and *tactics* are often confused. Borrowed from the military, strategy involves the crucial decisions of a war or campaign, such as whether to rely on missiles or aerial bombardment. Strategy represents the overall game plan. Tactics are decisions made during the course of battle. Tactics represent on-the-spot decisions necessitated because of developments as the strategic plan is implemented. In effect, tactics are the decisions or actions taken to make the strategy fit the reality and contingencies of the field of battle.

In public relations practice, however, strategy typically refers to the overall concept, approach, or general plan for the program designed to achieve a goal. Tactics refer to the operational level: the actual events, media, and methods used to implement the strategy. For example, the Wisconsin Milk Marketing Board's (WMMB) successful program to pass a referendum illustrates the difference between strategies and tactics.

WMMB wanted to win dairy producers' support for increasing, from 5 to 10 cents per hundredweight of milk produced, the amount directed to state and regional promotions of dairy products. Congress mandated that dairy farmers nationwide contribute 15 cents for each hundredweight of milk they sell to do research and to promote the sale of dairy products. Of the mandatory checkoff, five cents goes to the National Dairy Promotion and Research Board, and five cents goes to state or regional organizations. Dairy farmers then choose which organization gets the other five cents, often called the "middle nickel." WMMB wanted Wisconsin producers to direct the discretionary five cents to the state organization.

Program strategies included reinforcing the producers' belief in the need to build markets for Wisconsin dairy products; demonstrating WMMB's successes in marketing, research, and education; and enlisting influential third-party endorsements to reach targeted groups of producers. Tactics included check stuffers, newsletters, informational meetings, an 800-telephone number information service, the annual report, and exhibit booths at Farm Progress Days and the World Dairy Expo. The effect of these strategies and tactics was that 93 percent of the producers who cast ballots in the referendum voted in favor of directing the middle nickel to WMMB.

Reasons for Planning

Preparing a plan does not guarantee success, but it greatly enhances its chances. Strategic planning, however, is not universally accepted as part of public relations practice. The excuses practitioners give for not planning are similar to those offered by other managers:

1. *"We don't have time."* Practitioners who feel that they are already overloaded with work offer this excuse. Of course, they are missing the point that those with a plan typically make better use of their time, thus making time spent planning a wise investment.

2. *"Why plan when things are changing so fast?"* Plans get modified in light of changing circumstances; they are not cast in concrete. Having a plan, however, provides the baseline from which modifications can be made with full awareness that changes in strategy and direction are occurring. In fact, the more turbulent the environment, the greater the need to chart the changing course to the desired result, to have a plan.

3. *"We get paid for results, not for planning."* Public relations practitioners tend to be oriented more to activities than to strategic planning. A dollar spent on research and planning is often viewed as a dollar not available for implementing program activities. This orientation generally leads to counting activities rather than results that count. In fact, practitioners are paid for results that happen according to a plan.

4. *"We're doing O.K. without a plan."* Short-term success can change to failure if conditions change. For example, it is easy to see how an injury to a football team's star quarterback can change an entire football season. Such was the case in a business setting when the founder and CEO of a new and successful computer company died in an automobile accident the very day the company's stock went public. The stock offer was withdrawn until new management was in place. A few weeks later the company stock was again offered but commanded a substantially lower price. Soon thereafter, Eagle Computer went out of business. Part of planning involves building in strategies for handling contingencies such as industrial accidents and other operational crises; top management decisions that attract media and public scrutiny; changes in management and other key personnel; and charges by government agencies, consumer groups, unions, or whistle-blowers.[17]

Planning is for the purpose of making something happen or preventing it from happening, for the purpose of exploiting a situation or remedying one. Public relations practice is engaged more often in trying to create a viewpoint or a happening than trying to prevent one and trying to take advantage of an opportunity more often than trying to remedy an undesired situation. There remain, however, many situations and occasions when remedial public relations measures are required because preventive measures were not taken or were taken but failed.

Public relations calls for long-term planning and programming in many areas, such as public policy and social problems, but crises often give birth to public relations planning. Preventive public relations is tied most often to long-term planning. Remedial public relations actions tend to be of short duration and have minimal time for planning. The immediate need quite often is to pick up the pieces of a negative situation or to exploit a positive one. The latter works best if done within the framework of a long-term plan that includes strategies for such contingencies.

WRITING THE PROGRAM

Writing the program is a challenge. When the program meshes with organizational goals, the employer knows that the public relations practitioner understands what management is trying to do and is part of the management team. Counselor Jim Lukaszewski paraphrases the CEO's position: "Please spare me from another amateur corporate strategist—the person who doesn't have a clue about how the company operates, my goals or our critical strategic needs; but who yaps at me every day and calls it strategy."[18]

The task of writing an overall program or a proposal would rarely fall on a new member of a staff. It is important, however, that all members understand how proposals and presentations evolve. By seeing how all the parts come together, all members are better able to perform their own segment or specialty when programs are implemented. Plans and programs are generally infused with enthusiasm. That helps get approval by employers and clients. But overenthusiasm carries with it the serious danger of overpromising: "This employee communication program has everything necessary to eliminate the turnover problem." Those are dangerous words. Suppose the program falls short, reducing employee turnover by "only" 50 percent? Ordinarily such a reduction might be considered an acceptable performance, but evaluated against the unrealistic earlier statement, it might be considered not up to the level promised.

Program Plan

A public relations plan starts with the organization's mission statement. It proceeds from the specific role assigned to it in the form of a public relations mission. It engages in whatever fact-finding is indicated, as discussed in Chapter 11. An orderly investigative process involves the following four aspects of a situation analysis:

1. *A searching look backward.* There is no organization, no problem, no opportunity without a history. Learning that history is the first step. In a newly created entity, who founded it? For what purpose? Is it time for an anniversary event,

an institutional museum, a biography of the founder? Can public relations help? Background information is also essential if public relations is brought into an entity to deal with a pressing problem. What is the background of the problem? What has happened that has caused public relations to be involved in a new or different way? Public relations problems, too, have a history.

2. *A wide look around.* Where there has been no ongoing monitoring of public opinion toward the organization, that is the next step. How do employees feel about the conditions of their employment, their leadership? How do the neighbors feel about the presence and conduct of the organization? Is there a breakdown in understanding between the organization and any of its constituent publics? Is there a resentment simmering somewhere? In a crunch, on whom could the organization depend? In that crunch, what groups would delight in the troubles or embarrassment of the organization?

3. *A deep look inside.* Every organization has a character and a personality. Both tend to be reflections of those who control the organization by their ownership, management, votes, membership, or tenure or in some other way. Character can be discovered by examining the policies set down and by determining if day-to-day actions square with the words. Personality is evident in the style of administration: centralized authority or generous delegation, openness and candor or secretiveness and suspicion. It is portrayed by contemporary or traditional decor and equipment, open or closed doors on executive offices, symbols of stature, approachability of officials, and whether communication is formalized, as by memo, or casual, as by phone. The practitioner needs to know what makes the organization tick and whether it ticks with convictions, values, and standards that the practitioner can share and honestly promote.

4. *A long, long look ahead.* Is the mission of the organization realistically attainable? Can public relations planning and programming fit in? Can they make a practical contribution? Will this organization be around in 10 years? Will it be larger and more solidly entrenched, or will it be engaged in a slow retreat toward oblivion? What are the pros and cons? What are the forces that will affect the organization's chances for success or failure? Are the game and the outcome worth getting involved?

Implementing these steps has been greatly enhanced by advances in technology and resources. Online databases, for example, as well as increasingly sophisticated issue-tracking techniques and services enable practitioners to meet executives' demands for data as a basis for planning. These data are used to build the foundation of the program: the problem statement and situation analysis (discussed in Chapter 11) and the program goal. The final plan (or proposal) typically includes the ten components outlined in Exhibit 12.2.

Role of Working Theory

A program plan represents someone's working theory of what has to be done to achieve a desired outcome. In the words and form of a theoretical statement, "If we implement these actions and communications, then we will achieve these outcomes with our publics, which should lead to accomplishing the program goal." Theory also determines the selection of tactics. Someone's working theory guides how a special event is designed, how a newsletter or press release is worded, and how a

EXHIBIT 12.2

PUBLIC RELATIONS STRATEGIC PLANNING PROCESS

Four-Step Process	Strategic Planning Steps and Program Outline
A. Defining the Problem (Chapter 11)	**1.** The Problem, Concern, or Opportunity "What's happening now?" **2.** Situation Analysis (Internal and External) "What positive and negative forces are operating? "Who is involved and/or affected?" "How are they involved and/or affected?"
B. Planning and Programming (Chapter 12)	**3.** Program Goal "What is the desired solution?" **4.** Target Publics "Who—internal and external—must the program respond to, reach, and affect?" **5.** Objectives "What must be achieved with each public to accomplish the program goal?"
C. Taking Action and Communicating (Chapter 13)	**6.** Action Strategies "What changes must be made to achieve the outcomes stated in the objectives?" **7.** Communication Strategies "What message content must be communicated to achieve the outcomes stated in the objectives?" "What media best deliver that content to the target publics?" **8.** Program Implementation Plans "Who will be responsible for implementing each of the action and communication tactics?" "What is the sequence of events and the schedule?" "How much will the program cost?"
D. Evaluating the Program (Chapter 14)	**9.** Evaluation Plans "How will the outcomes specified in the program goal and objectives be measured?" **10.** Feedback and Program Adjustment "How will the results of the evaluations be reported to program managers and used to make program changes?"

community function is conducted. The theory that guides how each tactic is executed represents the practitioner's idea of what will cause a desired result. So when people say a program is "all theory," they are right!

The role of theory is obvious, although not always made explicit, at every step of the planning process. Otherwise how would decisions be made? For example, theory clearly guides the process when writing program objectives and determining the strategies to achieve them. Assume that the goal of an employee communication program is to reduce the number of employees seriously injured or killed while driving to and from work and while driving on the job. The situation analysis background research shows that traffic accidents are the leading cause of workplace fatalities and cost U.S. employers almost $55 billion annually. The federal Department of Transportation estimates that 2,000 people die each year in work-related crashes, or 40 percent of all workplace deaths. Investigation within the organization shows that a surprisingly large percentage of employees do not wear seat belts while driving or when a passenger. Program planners decide to develop a program to increase seat belt use among employees. (Clearly, their theory is that increased seat belt use will lead to a reduction in serious injuries and deaths.)

The situation analysis research also shows, however, that delivery drivers are the ones most frequently injured or killed in accidents, and that the accidents occur during work hours. Program planners decide that to have the greatest impact on solving the problem and achieving the program goal, the program should target delivery drivers and car parking-lot attendants. Planners then outline what each of the two publics must learn from the program, what opinions each must hold after the program, and what each must do to reach the goal of increased seat belt use: another complex theoretical model of what the program must achieve. Their working theory follows the "learn-feel-do" causal sequence that guides most public communication programs:

Information Gain ⇒ Opinion Change ⇒ Behavioral Change

The working theory is made explicit when stated in the form of objectives for the two target publics. After the objectives are written, planners then turn to developing strategies and tactics to cause the sequence of outcomes specified by the objectives. If during implementation or after the program, the expected (theorized) outcomes are not being achieved, then program planners must decide whether their theory was flawed or whether the program implementation was flawed.

It is indeed the wise practitioner who keeps track of the conditions under which theorized cause-and-effect relationships appear to work and when those assumptions about the linkages between program activities and program effects do not occur. For example, did the third-party endorsements used in the Wisconsin Milk Marketing Board referendum campaign actually make a difference in the number of votes cast in favor of the middle nickel checkoff? If so, maybe the strategy can be generalized to other programs. If not, are dairy producers unique and more resistant to such endorsements?

In summary, working theory drives every program decision, whether the assumptions about the causal relationships behind the decisions are made explicit or not. Practitioners are continually devising and testing their working theories. Those who can bridge the gap between theory and practice are the ones most likely to achieve management positions in the twenty-first century.[19]

Defining Target Publics

First of all, practitioners define publics; they are abstractions imposed by program planners. Planners must reify publics so as to develop the objectives, strategies, and tactics necessary for implementing a program. Reification is treating an abstraction as if it exists as a concrete or material entity. The "general public" is the grandest and least useful reification of all; there simply is no such thing. Given unlimited resources, practitioners could avoid the need to reify by targeting individuals. Useful and practical definitions of publics, however, necessarily represent some degree of reification.

The usual demographic and cross-situational approaches to defining publics typically provide minimal useful guidance for developing program strategy. Simply listing general categories of potential stakeholder groups gives those planning and implementing a program little information about how people in each of the categories uniquely contribute to or are affected by the problem situation and organization.

Stakeholder categories such as employees, stockholders, alumni, consumers, community groups, government, and so forth, each may contain what public relations scholar James Grunig calls "nonpublics, latent publics, aware publics, and active publics."[20] *Nonpublics* are people who do not face a problem or situation in which they are mutually involved with or affected by either an organization or other people. Their level of involvement is so low that they have no impact on the organization, and the organization has no recognizable impact on them. **Latent publics** include people who are simply unaware of their connections to others and an organization with respect to some issue or other problem situation. **Aware publics** are those people who recognize that they are somehow affected by or involved in a problem situation shared by others but have not communicated about it with others. When they begin to communicate and organize to do something about the situation, they become **active publics**.

Useful definitions describe program publics on the basis of how people are involved in or affected by the problem situation or issue, who they are, where they live, what relevant organizations they belong to, what they do that is relevant to the situation, and so forth. The definitions derive from the particular situation for which a public relations intervention is being planned.

For example, suppose that a university has the goal of increasing the number of incoming freshmen for the next academic year. The target publics for the program might include staff members in the admissions and academic advising offices (internal publics), high school students and others who have written or called academic departments requesting information about particular majors, high school seniors with grade point averages of at least 3.0 in high schools within 100 miles of the university, parents of targeted student publics, and high school guidance counselors in those same schools. When a local newspaper accuses two starting football players at the same university of receiving bogus academic credit for summer work experience, however, the public relations office will define different target publics for the university's response. It is obvious that different people, with different kinds of connections to the university, are involved in and affected by the potential crisis in the university's football program.

Following are approaches used alone and in combination to define target publics from among the various stakeholder groups:

1. *Geographics*—natural or political boundaries—indicate where to find people but give little useful insight about important differences within the boundaries. This approach is useful for selecting media outlets and allocating program resources according to population density. ZIP codes, telephone area codes, city limits, county lines, voting districts, and so forth are examples of the geographic approach to defining publics.

2. *Demographics*—gender, income, age, marital status, education—are the most frequently used individual characteristics but provide little understanding of why or how people are involved or affected. Demographics and geographics help practitioners make the first cut, but without additional information about how people are involved or affected by an issue, problem, or situation, they usually give little guidance to developing strategy and tactics.

3. *Psychographics*—psychological and lifestyle characteristics (cross-situational)—widely used under the name "VALS," segment adults on the basis of "psychological maturity." Knowing about lifestyle and values is useful, but typically only when combined with other attributes that tie the segments to something related to a particular situation.

4. *Covert power*—behind-the-scenes political or economic power—describes people at the top of a power pyramid who operate across situations. They exert power over others on a wide range of issues but often not in ways easily observed. Identifying these people requires a combination of careful observation over time, interviews with others in the problem situation, analyses of documents that record or track the exercise of covert power, or any combination of the three.

5. *Position* uses the positions held by individuals, not attributes of the individuals themselves, to identify target publics. People are identified as important in a particular situation because of the roles they play in positions of influence in those situations. The positions they hold make them important players in the efforts to achieve program goals and objectives.

6. *Reputation* identifies "knowledgeables" or "influentials" based on others' perceptions of these individuals. These publics are referred to as "opinion leaders" or "influencers," but they are defined as such by people in the situation of interest and are not to be confused by the cross-situational covert power group or defined as opinion leaders by the observer using some cross-situational definition.

7. *Membership* uses appearance on an organizational roster, list, or affiliation as the attribute relevant to a particular situation. For example, membership in a professional association or special-interest group signals a person's involvement in a situation, not the individual attributes of the member. Usually members receive controlled media from the organization with whom they are affiliated.

8. *Role in the decision process* calls for observing the decision-making process to learn who plays what roles in influencing decisions in a particular situation. This approach helps identify the most active among the active publics, those who really make decisions, take action, and communicate. Again, knowing their individual attributes can be less important than knowing how they behave in the process that leads to decisions related to the issue or problem of interest.

In short, remember that defining publics by superficial characteristics alone is insufficient. The key to defining publics strategically is to identify how people are involved and affected in the situation for which the program intervention is being developed, which requires greater information-gathering efforts than simply labeling groups of people who appear to have something in common. Program planners can develop specific and responsive program objectives and strategies if they know what different people know about an issue or situation, how they feel about it, and what they do that is either contributing to it or reacting to it. This understanding of what they know, how they feel, and what they do, combined with who and where they are, provides the basis for writing useful program objectives for each target public.

Writing Program Objectives

Objectives spell out the key results that must be achieved with each public to reach the program goal. In practice, objectives

1. Give focus and direction to those developing program strategy and tactics.
2. Provide guidance and motivation to those charged with implementing the program.
3. Spell out the outcome criteria to be used for monitoring and evaluating the program.

All too often, however, public relations program objectives either describe the tactic, or means, rather than the consequences, or ends, to be achieved. For example, "To mail out 12 monthly issues of . . ." and "To inform people about . . ." both describe activities, not results. Objectives should outline the intended impact of the 12 issues and of the effort to inform.

Objectives also make concrete the working theory behind the program, usually in the "learn-feel-do" causal sequence. Program objectives for each public specify the desired outcomes and in what sequence, by what dates, and in what magnitude they are needed to achieve the overall program goal (see Exhibit 12.3). The more specific the objectives, the more precise is everything that follows. Following are examples of useful program objectives for the three levels of outcomes:

1. *Knowledge outcome:* By July 1, to increase the number of local homeowners from 13 percent to 27 percent who know that wildland fires destroyed 2,500 homes during the past three fire seasons.
2. *Predisposition (opinion or attitude) outcome:* To increase neighboring property owners' confidence in our ability to conduct field tests safely from a mean confidence rating of 2.7 to 3.5 by January 15.
3. *Behavioral outcome:* To increase the percentage of employees who use seat belts when driving on the job from the current 51 percent to at least 70 percent within 30 days after the program begins.

These examples illustrate the elements and form of useful program objectives:

1. Begin with "to" followed by a verb describing the direction to the intended outcome. There are three possibilities: "to increase," "to decrease," and "to maintain."

EXHIBIT 12.3

SAMPLE PROGRAM GOAL AND OBJECTIVES

Program Goal

To reduce the number of delivery drivers seriously injured or killed while driving on the job from a five-year average of five per year to no more than two in the next fiscal year.

Objectives for Delivery Drivers

1. To increase, within 6 weeks after starting the program, the percentage of drivers from 8 percent to at least 90 percent who are aware that in a typical year four company delivery drivers are seriously injured and one is killed while driving on the job.

2. To increase, within 2 months after starting the program, the percentage of drivers from 5 percent to at least 80 percent who know that 55 percent of all fatalities and 65 percent of all injuries from vehicle crashes could be prevented if seat belts were used properly.

3. To increase, within 2 months after starting the program, driver's awareness to at least 85 percent that 95 percent of all city employees, police, and emergency vehicle drivers use shoulder restraints and seat belts any time they drive on the same city streets.

4. To reduce, within 3 months after starting the program, the number of drivers from 67 percent to less than 25 percent who feel that using seat belts while driving adds to delivery time and extends the time needed to complete routes.

5. To decrease, by the end of the third month after the program begins, the number of drivers from 70 percent to less than 35 percent who "agree" or "strongly agree" with the statement that their own safe driving prevents serious driving accidents to the point that seat belts are not necessary.

6. To increase the percentage of drivers who use seat belts from the current 51 percent to at least 70 percent within 3 months after the program begins, to at least 80 percent within 5 months, and to at least 90 percent by the end of the first year.

7. After the 90 percent level of use is achieved, to maintain that level of seat belt use among all permanent and all temporary replacement drivers.

2. Specify the outcome to be achieved. Again, there are three possible categories of what is to be maintained or changed: what people are aware of, know, or understand (knowledge outcomes); how people feel (predisposition outcomes); and what people do (behavioral outcomes). Each objective should spell out a single, specific outcome.

3. State the magnitude of change or level to be maintained in measurable terms. To provide useful and verifiable outcome criteria, objectives must be stated in quantifiable terms. Surely the levels must be realistic and consistent with the resources available to those implementing the program. Experience and judgment, plus evidence from the situation analysis research, provide the bases for setting the levels of outcomes to be achieved. Without benchmark data, judgment dominates when setting the outcome levels.

4. Set the target date for when the outcome is to be achieved. Dates stated in the objectives follow the working theory of the sequence of what has to happen. Typically, outcomes must be achieved in order, with one necessary before another. Each successive outcome is a logical consequence of the previous outcomes. Dates also provide guidance for those developing strategies and tactics, even down to deciding when to schedule communications and events.

Objectives should be in writing, with copies available to each person working on the program. Objectives become the primary basis for developing and implementing program strategy and tactics. Objectives should be discussed frequently, because they provide the guidance for planning, managing, and evaluating program elements and the overall program. As the topic of staff discussions, objectives keep the program on track. As conditions change, program planners change the objectives to reflect the evolving program environment.

Without objectives, programs drift according to the whims and desires of clients and employers and the intuitions and preferences of practitioners. People in power choose program strategy and tactics because they like them, not because they are logically related to intended outcomes. Practitioners select strategy and tactics because of habit, because of comfort based on previous experience, or because they worked last time. In effect, objectives provide a road map, derived from the working theory, to the desired goal.

PLANNING FOR PROGRAM IMPLEMENTATION

Plans, if they are to be carried out effectively, must be monitored at each step of the way. Preparation and follow-up support are necessary to ensure a return on the investment made in planning and programming. Anticipation and follow-through on plans are just as important in the practice of public relations as in sports.

Writing Planning Scenarios

Writing planning scenarios is the art of forecasting and describing the range of possible future states. Scenarios provide either longitudinal or cross-sectional summative statements about the future for the purpose of planning. Forecasters working in the Rand Corporation in the 1950s were the first to refer to "scenario writing" when describing their more qualitative approach to forecasting the future. The process differs from more traditional quantitative forecasting in that planners develop a number of plausible predictions of the future rather than relying on a single projection as the bases for charting strategy.[21]

The origins of scenario writing are more qualitative than quantitative. In fact, the pioneer of the technique said that the most important parts of the process are "simply to think about the problem" and to engage in "systematic conjecture."[22] The goal is to help clients anticipate more than one possible future state and plan for events that may have no history on which to build.

Futurists generally agree that the range of useful scenarios is two to four, but that the ideal number is three. And although the labels may vary, they represent high-, low-, and middle-ground future states, with the middle-ground scenario often viewed as the one most likely to occur. Some experienced planners, however, argue that to avoid the appearance of assigning probabilities, scenarios should be titled according to some major theme or major attribute. Still others suggest "optimistic, surprise-free, and pessimistic" labels, again without suggesting probabilities. These planners point out that futurists cannot predict an uncertain future with certainty, so they cannot attach probabilities to scenarios.[23] Catastrophic events, political revolutions, and other dramatic and unanticipated changes in the social, political, economic, and technological environments demonstrate that scenarios represent possibilities. In contrast, the vision of hindsight reported in case studies gives the appearance of predictability; but note that case studies describe the past, not the future, and for that reason are sometimes referred to as "lessons learned" documents.

The danger of labeling one scenario as "most likely" or "probable" is that program planners tend to develop strategy for only that one possible future state, thereby defeating the purpose of having developed scenarios. After all, the purpose of writing scenarios is to construct descriptions of possible future states so that contingency planning can help prepare for the range of possibilities. The greater the future uncertainty, the greater the need for planning scenarios. Predictions based on historical data, traditional forecasting models, and trend analyses may not meet the needs of public relations planners who must be prepared for the unexpected. This is not to say that one would be wise to abandon traditional quantitative methods, however.

Anticipating Disasters and Crises

A common type of planning scenario involves anticipating the worst things that could possibly happen to an organization; this is crisis planning. According to one practitioner, an effective corporate crisis communications plan is essential because "[I]t's only a matter of time before all companies experience an organizational or product crisis that could threaten their performance—or their very future."[24]

Scholars of organizational communication have identified multiple stages in the life cycle of an issue: nonexistent, potential, dormant, imminent, current, and critical.[25] Crises by definition are issues confronting the organization that have reached the critical stage.

Whereas public relations practitioners typically cannot predict a specific disaster or crisis, they can anticipate that the unexpected will occur. It is the "unexpected" nature of events that creates a crisis situation: "An organizational crisis is a low-probability, high-impact event that threatens the viability of the organization and is characterized by ambiguity of cause, effect, and means of resolution, as well as by a belief that decisions must be made swiftly."[26]

First, though, practitioners must determine the types of crises, because the response depends in part on the type and duration of possible scenarios. Many types of classification schemes exist for grouping similar types of crises. A scholar of crisis management categorized eight types of crises caused by either management failures or environmental forces: natural, technological, confrontation, malevolence, skewed management values, deception, management misconduct, and business and economic.[27] Somewhat in jest, some use the "banana index" to describe crises: **green**—new and emerging issues and problem situations; **yellow**—current and ripe; and **brown**—old and moldy. A serious attempt to define crises also uses time as the critical variable:

1. *Immediate crises*—the most dreaded type—happen so suddenly and unexpectedly that there is little or no time for research and planning. Examples include a plane crash, product tampering, death of a key officer, fire, earthquake, bomb scare, and workplace shooting by a disgruntled former employee. These call for working out in advance a consensus among top management for a general plan on how to react to such crises to avoid confusion, conflict, and delay.

2. *Emerging crises* allow more time for research and planning, but they may erupt suddenly after brewing for long periods. Examples include employee dissatisfaction and low morale, sexual harassment in the workplace, substance abuse on the job, and overcharges on government contracts. The challenge is to convince top management to take corrective action before the crisis reaches the critical stage.

3. *Sustained crises* are those that persist for months or even years despite the best efforts of management. Rumors or speculation get reported in the media or circulated by word of mouth, outside the control of public relations. No amount of denial or countering seems to stop the rumor or purge the news database, meaning that reporters working on a new story will see the old story and may repeat the misinformation. Examples include persistent rumors of eminent downsizing, suggestions that Procter & Gamble's logo contains Satanic symbolism (this paragraph is an example of how such rumors get repeated to new audiences!), and the charges of promiscuity that plagued President Bill Clinton throughout his two terms in office.[28]

Practitioners who prepare for the worst are anticipating and responding to the needs of top management. For example, in the insurance industry, a string of catastrophic losses—earthquakes, fires, floods, hurricanes, and tornadoes—and the politicization of insurance issues helped establish the role of public relations in planning and management. In an industry in which disasters and crises are part of the business, senior managers regard public relations as essential to maintaining the industry's public franchise.[29]

Most organizations know how to deal with operational crises internally. It is the "unplanned visibility" following such crises, however, that can turn them into events that threaten reputation, credibility, and market position.[30] A quick public response is critical because, as a former vice president for CNN says, "If you don't respond quickly to what happens, you create a vacuum. And everyone else—the news media, your competitors—is going to step into that vacuum and tell your story the way they want to tell it, not the way you want it to be told."[31]

An example of how a slow response can harm the organization is the way the Catholic Church took a long time to address the issue of child sexual abuse by its priests. Because the organizational leadership was slow to acknowledge the problem and take timely steps to address it, the church lost the trust and financial support of many of its members.[32]

Common mistakes in handling crises include the following:

1. *Hesitation*—which leads to public perception of confusion, callousness, incompetence, or lack of preparation.

2. *Obfuscation*—which leads to the perception of dishonesty and insensitivity.

3. *Retaliation*—which increases tension and intensifies emotion rather than reducing them.

4. *Prevarication* or *equivocation*—which creates the biggest problem, because nothing substitutes for truth.

5. *Pontification*—which creates vulnerability by taking a high-handed approach without really dealing with the issue at hand.

6. *Confrontation*—which provides others visibility by keeping the issue alive, giving them a platform, and giving them more to respond to.

7. *Litigation*—which guarantees even greater visibility and may eliminate more reasonable solutions.[33]

The key to anticipating and avoiding crises is assessing what can go wrong, what can affect people or the environment, and what will create visibility. In other words, crisis prevention means implementing an open systems approach to public relations so that the function can engage in environmental scanning to identify potential issues before they develop into critical ones or crises. Guidelines for preparing for public relations crises include the following.

1. Identify things that can go wrong and become highly visible; assess vulnerabilities throughout the organization.

2. Assign priorities based on which vulnerabilities are most urgent and most likely.

3. Draft questions, answers, and resolutions for each potential crisis scenario.

4. Focus on the two most important tasks—what to do and what to say—during the first critical hours following a crisis.

   A. Guidelines for "what to do" may include a telephone call tree showing the order in which key decision makers need to be informed.

   B. Guidelines for "what to say" may include "Q&As" that list questions likely to be asked by reporters and other publics, as well as the appropriate answers to these questions, and "standby statements" that are stock organizational positions regarding possible scenarios, with situation-specific information left blank to be filled in once the crisis occurs.

5. Develop a strategy to contain and counteract, not react and respond.[34]

The value of having such a plan was demonstrated by a fire on the then-new $200-million luxury liner Crystal Harmony. The Los Angeles–based ship's captain called by radio phone to report that a fire in the ship's auxiliary engine room had disabled the ship. There were no deaths or injuries among the 920 guests and 540 crew members, but the ship was dead in the water. Public relations director Darlene Papalini turned to the company's 61-page "Crisis Communication Manual." It covered five types of emergency scenarios: (1) trade: labor strike or delayed sailing; (2) business page: "bad press," unfavorable financial news, or sale of a company; (3) shipboard: natural catastrophes, such as a hurricane or accidents such as a ship running aground; (4) media: a bomb threat, fire, or threat of sinking; and (5) international: terrorist or other attack. Each executive member of the crisis management team had a copy of the manual at home as well as a copy at the office.

The crisis was successfully handled with passengers, media, port agents, employees, vendors, and suppliers in part because such a crisis had been anticipated as a possible scenario and plans had been put on paper. According to Papalini, "We certainly do not want to go through such a thing again, but we were most pleased that people understood the plan and followed it; it worked."[35]

Successful handling of this and other crises requires an ability to anticipate possible emergencies and vulnerabilities, skills in planning strategy for responding to possible emergency scenarios, recognition of the early stages of crises, and the capacity to respond immediately as part of a systematic crisis management planning process (see Exhibit 12.4).

Establishing an Information Center

Many organizations have discovered the dangers of rumors and the need to provide authentic information. When a crisis arises, it suddenly becomes apparent that some seemingly unimportant facets of an operation have been overlooked and must be given hurried attention. Inevitably one such area of weakness is the availability of information. A knee-jerk response usually results in a jerry-built rumor center that operates through the crisis period, then fades away without serious thought until the next crisis comes.

EXHIBIT 12.4

CHECKLIST FOR CRISIS COMMUNICATION

Do the Following:

✓ Get out your prepared crisis plan, call together the crisis management steering committee, call in experts to help analyze and explain the crisis, and open the lines of communication.

✓ Notify top management and refer them to the crisis plan. Give them the task of making impact projections in preparation for inquiries from employees, government agencies, and the media.

✓ Channel all inquiries to the designated spokesperson, who was selected and trained in advance as part of the crisis planning preparation. Notify receptionists, operators, secretaries, and others to direct all inquiries to the designated spokesperson without giving their own versions or opinions.

✓ Set up a news center for media and begin providing information as quickly as it becomes available. Provide information background packets, telephones, computers and printers, fax machines, and a place for television interviews away from the crisis scene.

✓ Be open and tell the full story. If you do not, someone else will and you will lose control as journalists turn to other sources and outside experts to fill in gaps in the story.

✓ Demonstrate the organization's concern for what is happening and for the people who are involved and affected. At the same time, explain what the organization is doing or planning to do to solve the problem.

✓ Have someone on call 24 hours a day and stay with the story as long as the media are interested.

✓ Reconvene the crisis management team afterward to summarize what happened, to review and evaluate how the plan worked, and to recommend improvements in the crisis plan.

On the Other Hand:

✓ Do not speculate publicly about what you do not know to be fact. And do not respond to reporters' questions designed to solicit speculation.

✓ Do not minimize the problem or try to underplay a serious situation. The press will find out the truth soon enough.

✓ Do not let the story dribble out bit by bit. Each new disclosure becomes a potential headline or lead story.

✓ Do not release information about people if it will violate their privacy or if it blames them for anything.

✓ Do not say "no comment" or make off-the-record comments. If you cannot say something on the record, then explain why and tell reporters when they can expect the information. If information is simply not available, say so and assure reporters that you will get it to them as soon as you can.

✓ Do not play favorites among the media or the reporters. Respect reporters' work by not undercutting their scoops and enterprise.

✓ Do not try to capitalize on media attention and interest by trying to promote the organization, cause, products, or services. Do not do what will be perceived as a self-serving pitch while in the crisis spotlight.

Adapted from Claudia Reinhardt, "Workshop: How to Handle a Crisis," *Public Relations Journal* 43, no. 11 (November 1987): 43–44. Used with permission of *Public Relations Journal*.

There are three major points to remember in planning for an information center. First, the center must be recognized for what it is: a place where information moves from the institution directly to an organization's publics. It is not a media operation. To saddle an organization's media relations office with an added responsibility of answering questions from other publics reduces the effectiveness of both functions. Media and public information centers must be closely coordinated, but where the organization can afford it, they must be separate entities, each directed toward its own specific function.

Second, the center should be in two parts. Rumor centers are almost exclusively telephone operations. Of course, there must be an answering service or information center. So one group deals directly with the publics, taking questions and providing answers. If that group does not have the information, they promise to have it within a certain period of time. The second group, however, is a coordinating agency—the point of contact between the information center and the institution's staff and agencies. The coordinating agency goes to the institution's staff for information and checks material with the highest level of the administration for accuracy, coordinates it with the media relations office, and relays it to the center for use. Hence, all information flows through the coordinating agency, where it can be accounted for and logged. In addition to raw information—the factual material used to answer direct and simple questions—the coordinating agency should have qualified people available to speak on policy or to conduct philosophical discussions of current issues. As the sole source of material for the information center, this agency controls the center and what is being said to the various publics. Although not an official spokesperson, it does provide for a "one-voice" response to the institution's problems in a crisis situation.

Third, and perhaps the most important, any such center must have credibility established long before any crisis; it must be the accepted source of accurate information. This cannot be accomplished during the period of crisis alone. The flow of credible information must be established during routine times. The function must become an accepted part of the institution on a full-time, continuing basis, identical in crisis or routine situations. It must also, over an extended period, encourage both internal and external publics to use it with faith and confidence. This amounts to more than establishing a reputation for truth; it involves education.

Internally, all agencies of the institution must be made aware that such a system exists and must be encouraged to use it to make information for which they are responsible available. At the same time, employees at every level in the organization must be advised to direct all calls to the information center. One crisis management specialist warns,

> The most damaging information or story points will come from individuals who work with us or who have worked for us; from documents or studies that should never have been written or done; from hand-written notes in the margins of otherwise innocuous documents; or from dumb, colorful statements or phrases a spokesperson just couldn't resist saying.[36]

Such an information or fact center, operating normally over a long period of time, sets the pattern within an institution for quickly and efficiently moving information. If the institution is tuned to such an operation in routine times, the transition is far less shattering in troubled times. When all the pieces of the crisis management plan work, some crises are avoided or preempted, and others are managed in ways that minimize damage. Pearson and Clair outline a broader definition of success, however:

Effective crisis management involves minimizing potential risk before a triggering event. In response to a triggering event, effective crisis management involves improvising and interacting by key stakeholders so that individual and collective sense making, shared meaning, and roles are reconstructed. Following a triggering event, effective crisis management entails individual and organizational readjustment of basic assumptions, as well as behavioral and emotional responses aimed at recovery and readjustment.[37]

The difficulties of dealing with one type of crisis—a pernicious rumor—are illustrated by giant Procter & Gamble's handling of a wild rumor. "Word was" that P&G was in "league with Satan" and giving part of the corporation's money to the "church of Satan." Supposed evidence for such claims was Procter & Gamble's logo, which had evolved over more than a century, showing the man in the moon and stars. To deal with this rumor, the company went to the media, the pulpit, and the courts to stop the wild charges emanating from religious fanatics. But in April 1985, Procter & Gamble gave up the fight and announced that it would remove the logo from its products. In 1991, Procter & Gamble modernized its logo for the first time since 1930 but did not use it on products or in advertising for several years thereafter.

Old

New

Budgeting

There is as much art and artistry in public relations budgeting as there is science. Available literature on the subject is sparse. Few practitioners study accounting and finance as part of their professional education. Canadian practitioners rated budgeting as their weakest skill, with 60 percent reporting that they had never received financial training.[38] Other surveys of practitioners reveal that they typically use their computers for word processing and desktop publishing but not to manage financial data. Yet about 40 percent of them manage budgets of $1 million or more.[39]

No doubt practitioners in other countries suffer from the same deficiency in their professional preparation. At professional seminars, the most frequently mentioned guideline seems to be, "Always ask for more than you need." Of course the deliberate, habitual padding of budget requests is not peculiar to public relations. It has become part of the system but cannot be recommended as responsible management.

In established departments, budgets generally relate to one of four control factors. One is the total income or funds available to the enterprise, the second is the "competitive necessity," the third is the overall task or goal set for the organization, and the fourth is the profit or surplus over expenses.

When **total income** or **funds available** is the basis, as in marketing or fundraising activities, public relations is generally allocated a percentage. The percentage relates to the organization's total operating budget, to gross sales, to funds raised, or to funds allocated from taxes. When **competitive necessity** is the criterion, the amount spent by a similar charity or a competing organization is matched or exceeded. This method is very risky. The *task* or *goal* basis usually provides for public relations to have a share of the funding set aside to achieve the desired end result. For example, to achieve a fund-raising goal, a museum might increase the percentage of the operating budget allocated to "development" activities. The final approach—based on how much money is "left over"—usually sets a fluctuating figure that can go up or down, depending on "the point at which we break even," or in a nonprofit operation, "the point at which we cover all expenses." Not only is it difficult to plan and staff under this option, but it also reinforces the impression that public relations is something you do only if you have money to spend after covering the essentials.

Budgeting is rarely a one-person job. Each specialist is called on to estimate and itemize variable costs that will be incurred to implement the public relations plan during the next budget year. Variable costs are those associated with projects and activities, such as printing, rent for special events facilities, speakers' fees, photographers, advertising, travel, and entertainment. The department head, or someone designated, adds the estimated variable costs to the unit's fixed costs, including such expenses as salaries and benefits, overhead for office space, phone, service, equipment leases, supplies, subscriptions, and service contracts. The next executive up the line evaluates the budgets from the departments for which he or she is responsible, negotiates and adjusts the budget requests to fit the total available or needed, and finally either approves or forwards the budgets to the next level for approval (see Figure 12.1).

The following three guidelines may be helpful.

1. *Know the cost of what you propose to buy.* If you plan to do a special mailing, find out the exact costs for photography and artwork, printing and folding, mailing lists, labeling and sorting, delivery, postage, and everything else needed to complete the job. Do not guess, because you will have to live within the budget that gets approved and deliver what was promised.

2. *Communicate the budget in terms of what it costs to achieve specific results.* The details of actual variable and fixed costs used to develop the budget may not be of interest to management or to a client. Managers who must approve the budget typically want to know how much it will cost to achieve goals and objectives. They look to you to manage the process in a cost-effective fashion.

3. *Use the power of your computer to manage the program.* Develop a master spreadsheet, as well as spreadsheets for individual projects. By tracking each project and linking each to the master spreadsheet, you can estimate cash-flow requirements in advance and monitor expenditures against cost estimates.

Too often, budgets are put aside after they are approved and are not used as management tools. Used in conjunction with other elements of program planning, however, budgets provide guidance for scheduling staff resources, contracting for services, tracking project costs, and establishing accountability. Individual staff members, as well as the entire unit, should refer to the budget when assessing performance against expectations.

Budgets often play an important part in shaping and maintaining the relationship between the public relations staff and their clients and top management. In the final analysis, practitioners must have realistic budgets, must use them to direct staff efforts, must review them frequently with clients and top management, and must be able to link costs to performance and outcomes.

Pretesting Program Elements

Once the strategic plan is formulated, it should be tried on a pilot basis. Marketers have been doing this for decades. Only recently has pretesting a plan of action and communication become somewhat routine in public relations.

Many qualitative and quantitative tools are available for pretesting efforts: interviews with opinion leaders, focus groups, controlled laboratory tests, and field tests in pilot communities. Careful pretests of strategy, tactics, and program materi-

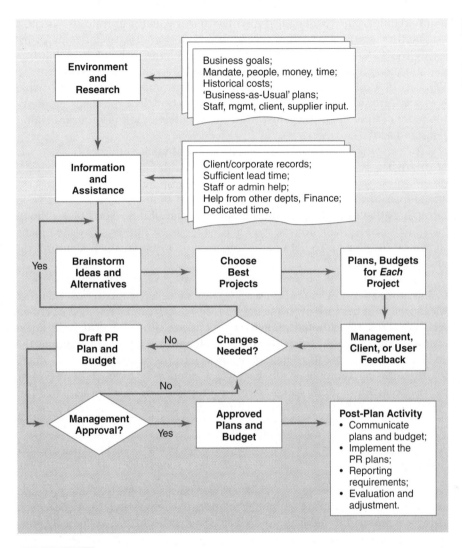

FIGURE 12.1

PUBLIC RELATIONS BUDGETING AND PLANNING PROCESS

Source: Bob Delaney, APR, SIRIS Consulting, Mississauga, Ontario. Used with permission.

als provide estimates of how they will work, provide comparisons of alternatives to determine which works best, and detect possible backlash effects of unanticipated, unfavorable results.

Backlash effects can be avoided by conducting a response analysis. This means using a sample audience to observe immediate reaction to specific communication content. As an example, the Occupational Safety and Health Administration (OSHA) would have been spared much embarrassment had it pretested its 16-page booklet, "Safety with Beef Cattle." A pretest would have eliminated such nonsense warnings as, "Be careful not to step into the manure pits," "If your ladder is broken, do not climb it," and "Beams that are too low can hurt you."

Message pretesting also can help increase the understandability of the information for its intended audience. The symbolism chosen for a public relations document may represent perfect clarity to its creator but be both uninteresting and unintelligible to the reader. Or the symbol may be inappropriate, as when Caterpillar Tractor Company sent 10,000 calendars to its Saudi Arabia dealer, Zahid Tractor. When government inspectors opened the shipment they found that the calendar contained a picture of a village in Iceland showing a church with two crosses. Workers blotted out the crosses with heavy black markers because Christian symbols are forbidden in the devoutly Islamic nation. The blotches created 10,000 reminders of the need to pretest even the smallest detail in program communications and activities.

A few years ago an experimental program of health education was undertaken in an isolated Peruvian community high in the Andes. As part of the program, a film on the transmission of typhus by lice, featuring graphic close-up shots, was prepared and shown to the villagers. It became apparent that the message was not getting through. A survey of the people who had seen the film revealed that although they had many lice in their homes, they had never been bothered by the "giant" kind shown on the screen. To get results, appeals and symbols must be appropriate and understood.

A cautionary note on pretesting must be inserted. The stream of public opinion rushes along swiftly. An idea that worked well in a pretest might prove a fiasco upon widespread use because of a time lag. Seasons change and with them so change people's concerns, recreational pursuits, and so forth. Overpowering and unexpected events can quickly alter the public opinion climate overnight; for example, the United Way of America national headquarters scandal dramatically changed the climate for fund-raising campaigns run by local United Way organizations. When using pretest results as a guide to communication programs, practitioners need to be as certain as possible that program conditions are similar to those that existed during the pretest and that pretest subjects are representative of the program target publics.

Selling the Plan

Research, analysis, precedents, and experience must be converted into program forms acceptable to those who are not public relations executives and to clients. Some are not sensitively attuned to public opinion. Some are cost oriented, or publicly gun shy, or both. Some do not commit comfortably to speculative expenditures with no guarantee of return. Some are nervous about issuing information to news media. Goals and objectives not tied directly to sales or profits are ephemeral to many. The more specific the institutional goals, the more specific and effective the public relations plan can be.

Selling the program proposal puts the practitioner's persuasive and technical communication skills to the test. It calls for effective writing, persuasive speaking, skillful use of presentation audiovisual materials, and careful reading of those around the conference table. But effective selling begins with an effective program proposal.

After a program has been approved at the policy level, it becomes necessary to familiarize colleagues with what is to follow. Otherwise, these important collaborators may wind up uninformed, like an outside counselor who is not allowed to participate in the planning. Then, they would not be able to do their part. They would not be in a position to solicit support from the people under their supervision.

Some generally accepted tenets related to introducing others to the public relations program merit noting. Explain the basic problems in terms of the harm that can be done if they are left unattended. Then, explain the immediate remedial measures in relation to long-term plans. Use similar case examples, precedents, and survey results to substantiate the plan. Eliminate personal opinion except as it applies to special knowledge of related cases. Relate the program to the climate in which the organization operates and that it hopes to enjoy in the future. Stress that the activities will have a desirable ultimate effect on public opinion. Keep explanations short and to the point. Be decisive and have conviction in the plan, qualities highly respected by administrators.

Staff orientation and indoctrination are best handled through informal sessions in which people can air their views and talk things out. Often, meetings are arranged in which the practitioner presents the program and then throws the meeting open to discussion. When this is done, a summary should be supplied afterward to all participants in the discussion. It can take the form of meeting minutes, a program timetable, a roster of projects, or a report explaining the plans. It is important for future relationships that the programming agreed upon be a matter of record. Getting the plan on paper tends to make the planning and programming steps real and tangible for those charged with implementing the program. After all, "excellent strategists must have the executional capability to implement the strategy. . . . You can't divorce the two [strategy and implementation]."[40]

NOTES

[1] Jim Lukaszewski, "Let's Get Serious about Strategy," *strategy* I (Supplement to *pr reporter* newsletter), March 2, 1998, p. 1.

[2] David M. Dozier and Larissa A. Grunig, "The Organization of the Public Relations Function," in *Excellence in Public Relations and Communication Management*, ed. James E. Grunig, 412–13 (Hillsdale, NJ: Lawrence Erlbaum Associates, 1992).

[3] William J. Small, "Exxon Valdez: How to Spend Billions and Still Get a Black Eye," *Public Relations Review* 17, no. 1 (Spring 1991): 9–25.

[4] Stephen P. Robbins, *Organization Theory: Structure, Design, and Applications*, 3rd ed. (Englewood Cliffs, NJ: Prentice Hall, 1990), 121.

[5] Ibid., 121–23.

[6] Walter K. Lindenmann, "Research, Evaluation, and Measurement: A National Perspective," *Public Relations Review* 16, no. 2 (Summer 1990): 8.

[7] David M. Dozier, "The Innovation of Research in Public Relations Practice: Review of a Program of Studies," *Public Relations Annual* 2 (1990): 15–21.

[8] Robert W. Kinkead and Dena Winokur, "How Public Relations Professionals Help CEOs Make the Right Moves," *Public Relations Journal* 48, no. 10 (October 1992): 19.

[9] Ed Block, "Expectations of PR: A Colloquy," *Arthur W. Page Society Newsletter* 7, no. 2 (June 1991): 4.

[10] David M. Bicofsky of New York Telephone Company, quoted in Kinkead and Winokur, "How Public Relations Professionals Help CEOs," 23.

[11] Quoted in Dena Winokur and Robert W. Kinkead, "How Public Relations Fits into Corporate Strategy," *Public Relations Journal* 49, no. 5 (May 1993): 21.

[12] Kinkead and Winokur, "How Public Relations Professionals Help CEOs," 21.

[13] Davis Young, *Building Your Company's Good Name* (New York: American Management Association, 1996): 12.

[14] Paul S. Forbes, "Applying Strategic Management to Public Relations," *Public Relations Journal* 48, no. 3 (March 1992): 32.

[15] Adapted from George L. Morrisey, *Management by Objectives and Results for Business and Industry*, 2nd ed. (Reading, MA: Addison-Wesley Publishing, 1982), 107, 216–20.

[16] Andrew Campbell, "The Power of Mission: Aligning Strategy and Culture," *Planning Review* 20, no. 5 (September–October 1992): 10–12, 63.

[17] Adapted from Patrick J. Below, George L. Morrisey, and Betty L. Acomb, *The Executive Guide to Strategic Planning* (San Francisco: Jossey-Bass Publishers, 1987), 17–19; and Robert B. Irvine, "The Crisis Outlook for '92 and Beyond," *Public Relations Journal* 48, no. 10 (October 1992): 8, 34.

[18] Lukaszewski, "Let's Get Serious about Strategy," 2–3.

[19] Winokur and Kinkead, "How Public Relations Fits into Corporate Strategy," 23.

[20] James E. Grunig and Fred C. Repper, "Strategic Management, Publics and Issues," in *Excellence in Public Relations and Communication Management*, ed. James Grunig (Hillsdale, NJ: Lawrence Erlbaum Associates, 1992), 127.

[21] Steven P. Schnaars, "How to Develop and Use Scenarios," in *Strategic Planning: Models and Analytical Techniques*, ed. Robert G. Dyson, 153–67 (Chichester, UK: John Wiley and Sons, 1990).

[22] Herman Kahn, *The Japanese Challenge* (New York: Thomas Y. Crowell, 1979), 5, as quoted in Schnaars, "How to Develop and Use Scenarios," 160.

[23] Schnaars, "How to Develop and Use Scenarios," 158–65.

[24] Andy Bowen, "Crisis Procedures That Stand the Test of Time," *PR Tactics* (August 2001): 16.

[25] Richard E. Crable and Steven L. Vibbert, *Public Relations as Communication Management* (Edina, MN: Bellwether Press, 1986).

[26] Christine M. Pearson and Judith A. Clair, "Reframing Crisis Management," *Academy of Management Review* 23, no. 2 (January 1998): 60.

[27] Otto Lerbinger, *The Crisis Manager: Facing Risk and Responsibility* (Hillsdale, NJ: Lawrence Erlbaum Associates, 1997), Part II.

[28] Adapted from Claudia Reinhardt, "Workshop: How to Handle a Crisis," *Public Relations Journal* 43, no. 11 (November 1987): 43–44.

[29] Robert J. Gore, "In a High-Profile, Crisis-Laden Business, Insurance CEOs Rely on Public Relations," *Public Relations Journal* 49, no. 5 (May 1993): 21.

[30] James E. Lukaszewski, "How to Handle a Public Relations Crisis," *World Executive's Digest* 12, no. 6 (June 1991): 68.

[31] David Bernkopf, quoted in Jeff Siegel, "Damage Control: How Prepared Are You for an Unforseen Disaster?" *Southwest Airlines Spirit* (October 2003): 52.

[32] James Burnett, "Crisis and the Cross," *PRWeek* (April 22, 2002): 17.

[33] Adapted from Lukaszewski, "How to Handle a Public Relations Crisis," 68–69.

[34] Ibid.

[35] Norman Sklarewitz, "Cruise Company Handles Crisis by the Book," *Public Relations Journal* 47, no. 5 (May 1991): 34–36.

[36] Lukaszewski, "A Primer on the News Magazine Shows," *Executive Action* (January/February/March 1997). Quote from The Lukaszewski Group Inc. newsletter. Used with permission.

[37] Pearson and Clair, "Reframing Crisis Management," p. 66.

[38] Bob Delaney and Michael Lewis, "Planning and Budgeting for Public Relations Professionals." Paper presented to the 1990 Annual Conference of the Canadian Public Relations Society, June 1990.

[39] Profile 1997 (San Francisco: International Association of Business Communicators, 1997): V–6.

[40] Jack Bergen, Quoted in Alan Crawford, "Selling Strategic: Strategic PR is All the Rage. What is it and Why is it Happening?" *PRWEEK* (July 9, 2001):19.

ADDITIONAL SOURCES

Dozier, David M., with Larissa A. Grunig and James E. Grunig. *Manager's Guide to Excellence in Public Relations and Communication Management*. Mahwah, NJ: Lawrence Erlbaum Associates, 1995.

Fearn-Banks, Kathleen. *Crisis Communications: A Casebook Approach*. Mahwah, NJ: Lawrence Erlbaum Associates, 1996. Presents case studies of how problems can turn into crises, then catastrophes, if not managed effectively.

Lerbinger, Otto. *The Crisis Manager: Facing Risk and Responsibility*. Mahwah, NJ: Lawrence Erlbaum Associates, 1997. Builds case for central role of communication in the management of crises.

Lukaszewski, James E. "Establishing Individual and Corporate Crisis Communication Standards: The Principles and Protocols." *Public Relations Quarterly* 42, no. 3 (Fall 1997): 7–14. Summarizes lessons learned by crisis communication management expert.

McElreath, Mark P. *Managing Systematic and Ethical Public Relations Campaigns*, 2nd ed. Dubuque, IA: Brown & Benchmark Publishers, 1996. Outlines "how-to" steps of researching, planning, implementing, and evaluation of public relations campaigns.

Rice, Ronald E., and Charles K. Atkin, eds. *Public Information Campaigns*, 2nd ed. Newbury Park, CA: Sage Publications, 1989. Useful reference for students and practitioners with interests in government and politics, and public health.

Smith, Ronald D. *Strategic Planning for Public Relations*, 2nd ed. Mahwah, NJ: Lawrence Erlbaum Associates, 2005. Detailed, step-by-step application of planning process to implementing public relations program.

Schwarts, Peter. *The Art of the Long View*. New York: Currency Doubleday, 1996. Originally published in 1991, this remains the definitive guide for scenario building, and the author remains one of the leading strategists.

13

STEP THREE: TAKING ACTION AND COMMUNICATING

Words are merely words, and they can be purely cosmetic if they aren't backed by convictions, actions and policies.[1]

—Harold Burson

The third step of the management process moves the public relations program into implementation. This stage applies to the fact-finding and strategic planning of the first two steps. Once a problem has been defined and a solution worked out, the next steps are *action* and *communication*.

---■---

ACTION AND COMMUNICATION

Public relations has matured into the role of helping organizations decide not only **what to say**, but **what to do**, according to Harold Burson. In its infancy and into the

1960s, public relations simply crafted and distributed the message handed down from management. Reflecting their view of public relations, management asked, "How do I say it?" In response to the social changes of the 1960s, organizations and their CEOs were increasingly held accountable on such issues as public and employee safety, equal opportunity, and the environment. In addition to how to say something, management asked public relations, "What shall I say?" Beginning in the 1980s, however, public relations entered a third stage; in addition to asking communication questions, management now asked, "What do I do?"[2]

Burson attributes this new role to unavoidable and increasingly detailed public scrutiny of what organizations do and say. This scrutiny has intensified in the wake of numerous corporate scandals in recent years, such as Enron, Tyco, WorldCom, and ImClone. Public response is also quick because of almost instantaneous worldwide communication. Modern communication technology closes the loop between message and behavior to the point that they are almost one and the same: What an organization does can be reported as quickly as what the organization says. As a result, all organizations need public relations more than ever, first to help determine what to do, and then to work out what to say and how to say it.[3]

THE ACTION COMPONENT OF STRATEGY

In the words of an old adage, "Actions speak louder than words." Yet many people in management, and unfortunately even some in public relations, believe the myth that communication alone can solve most public relations problems. Typically, however, public relations problems result from something done, not something said. The exception is when the "something said" becomes an event itself, such as when someone in authority or in a prominent position makes a sexist remark, racial slur, or other bigoted comment. For example, in December 2002, then-incoming Senate Majority Leader Trent Lott (R-Miss.) resigned from his leadership position after a poor choice of words at a colleague's birthday party resulted in public perception that he was a racist. Even more problematic is when such a comment appears in official organizational communications.

Acting Responsively and Responsibly

It stands to reason that if something that was done caused the problem, then something must be done to solve the problem. In other words, corrective action is necessary to eliminate the original source of the problem. An example of the need for corrective action is the university that had difficulties attracting freshmen. Investigators discovered that the word was out, "Don't go to State, freshmen can't get classes." Sure enough, freshmen had the lowest priority for registering for classes. Only after the university gave freshmen registration priority did the number of first-year students increase significantly.

Another example is the "wild horse problem." The Bureau of Land Management (BLM) runs the Department of the Interior's mandated program to manage the wild horse and wild burro populations on federal lands. Protected under the Wild Horse and Burro Act of 1971, the wild herds grew too large for the range and invaded the grazing land leased to ranchers. The BLM rounded up horses and burros and made them available through the successful "Adopt-a-Horse" program. Because not all horses and burros are desirable to potential adopters, who pay a $125 adoption fee, the BLM waived adoption fees for ranchers who took large numbers of the surplus animals.

Animal-protection protesters charged the BLM with condoning the slaughter of wild horses, "our national heritage," by giving them to ranchers. They alleged that the ranchers shipped the animals directly to slaughterhouses, making a handsome profit in the process. BLM officials disavowed any role in the commercial slaughter of wild horses and burros for pet food but questioned the wisdom of spending millions of dollars each year to board surplus captured horses at a time when government programs for the poor were being cut. Still the angry protests continued. No amount of communication strategy appeared to ease the problem. When BLM officials recognized that their fee-waiver program was a major contributing factor, the program was canceled. Moreover, the agency changed policy with respect to ownership—ranchers would not take title of adopted horses and burros for one year. For that year, even though the rancher was responsible for care and feeding, the animals remained public property. Again, actions spoke louder than words.

The classic case study of responsive and responsible public relations actions, however, remains Johnson & Johnson's handling of the Tylenol crisis (review Exhibit 1.3).

Coordinating Action and Communication

The Tylenol poisoning crisis also illustrates the need for coordinated action and communication: Late in 1982, McNeil Consumer Products, a subsidiary of Johnson & Johnson, was suddenly confronted with a crisis when seven persons on Chicago's West Side died mysteriously Authorities determined that they had died from cyanide poison that had been inserted in Tylenol capsules. The news spread rapidly over television and the news wires. Panic among consumers, hospitals, doctors, and pharmacists ensued nationwide. The crisis called for an immediate action response supported by communication. The following are the **action components** of the company's response:

1. Stop production of Tylenol capsules and halt promotional advertising.
2. Establish liaison with the Chicago police, the FBI, and the Food and Drug Administration.
3. Recall all Tylenol capsules: 31 million bottles with a retail value of more than $100 million dollars.
4. Design and produce tamper-resistant packaging.
5. Return Tylenol capsules—in new packaging—to the market with a stepped-up marketing effort to assure users of the product's safety.

Communication strategy supports the action program (Exhibit 13.1): (1) to inform internal and external target publics of the action; (2) to persuade those publics to support and accept the action; and possibly (3) to instruct publics in skills needed to translate intention into action. The following highlights summarize the communication components of Johnson & Johnson's strategy:

1. *Publics:* Consumers, pharmacists, management and staff of food chains, hospital administrators and staff, doctors, the Food and Drug Administration contacts, FBI contacts, medical press, and general press.

EXHIBIT 13.1

COORDINATING ACTION AND COMMUNICATION

Few corporate management decisions are as difficult as a decision to relocate a company's headquarters. When Southern Railway System and its parent company, Norfolk Southern Corporation, made such a decision, several publics were affected by the decision. The reasons for the move and its ramifications had to be explained as effectively and quickly as possible.

Southern Railway had been headquartered in Washington, DC, since its founding in 1894. Although Atlanta had always been the operational center of the Southern system, the company's top management and up to 700 key officers and support staff were headquartered in Washington.

Southern Railway and Norfolk and Western Railway consolidated under joint ownership of the newly formed Norfolk Southern Corporation. In the first state of the new partnership, the holding company was established at Norfolk, Virginia; the executive and operating headquarters of the Northern and Western were retained at Roanoke, Virginia; and Southern retained its executive offices in Washington and its operational headquarters in Atlanta.

As implementation of the merger plans unfolded, management determined that the maximum efficiency of operations could be achieved by consolidating Southern's executive and operating headquarters. Atlanta, as the operating heart of this 13-state, 10,000-mile railroad, was the logical site. Thus, the decision was made to close the Washington office and to relocate the personnel either to Norfolk or to Atlanta.

Except for a relatively few personnel who would remain in Washington, all employees would be involved in the relocation, so hundreds of employees and their families would be affected. The first priority of management, then, was to inform employees of the move officially, before they read about it in the paper.

Once the decision to move was final, department heads in the headquarters building were briefed on the decision and then told to advise the personnel in their departments immediately. Everyone used a general letter signed by the president of the parent company as the authoritative source for information about the move. They were told the reasons for the move, were advised that new offices would be constructed in Atlanta to accommodate them, were told that they would be given adequate time to plan an orderly relocation, and were informed that the company offered an extremely generous relocation assistance program.

On the obvious assumption that word of the decision would soon spread, the decision was made to inform key news media in both Washington and Atlanta. The wisdom in this approach, in contrast to saying nothing and then having to handle a "leak" situation, was borne out by universally favorable coverage of the relocation. Not a single negative word appeared in news or editorial coverage.

As word of the pending move spread through the media and other channels, favorable results continued. Southern's public relations department responded to numerous requests for information on the company's traditional relationship with Atlanta and Washington, details on who would move to Atlanta and when, and related questions. All inquiries were answered promptly and thoroughly.

Further evidence of the effectiveness of communicating the move came at a major conference of government, transportation, and business leaders in Atlanta. The mayor of Atlanta gave a resounding official welcome to Southern and told Southern's president, before television cameras and media representatives from around the country, that Atlanta would do everything it could to make the move comfortable and mutually profitable.

"This transition undoubtedly could have been made without a word being uttered," one company public relations officer noted. "But we discovered once again, as we have so many times in the past, that the results are much more positive when you 'talk about it now' rather than have to 'defend it later.'"

2. *Message strategy:* Intensive effort to gather facts on production of the lot of capsules in the Chicago market. Full cooperation with the Food and Drug Administration. Assurance to alarmed inquirers of the company's determination to solve the mystery and to ensure the purity of its products.

3. *Media strategy:* Full, candid cooperation with the media to get facts to the public as quickly as possible, including the use of a 30-city press conference conducted via television satellite. Centralized release of all information. Appearance of Johnson & Johnson chairman on television, including *60 Minutes*.

Although communication is important, it is not enough—as one practitioner put it, "You simply can't communicate your way out of a situation you've behaved your way into."[4] In these cases, the organization's communication efforts must be supported by action.

Action as an Open Systems Response

Public relations action is "socially responsible acts taken by public relations departments or other parts of the organization with your counsel."[5] Action strategy typically includes changes in an organization's policies, procedures, products, services, and behavior. These changes are designed to achieve program objectives and organizational goals, while at the same time responding to the needs and well-being of an organization's publics. In short, corrective actions serve the **mutual interests** of an organization and its publics.

Action strategy results from knowing how an organization's policies, procedures, actions, and other outputs contribute to public relations problems. As pointed out in the situation analysis section of Chapter 11, a thorough understanding of the problem situation is essential for designing the action strategy. For example, when the Atlanta Bureau of Police Services (ABPS) tackled the problem of not enough police for public safety and security, it began by studying its own recruiting and training program. Before developing any external recruitment communications, ABPS changed how it operated its recruiting program. First, ABPS expanded the search area from the metropolitan Atlanta area to all Georgia. Second, it staffed an office specifically to handle recruiting. Third, ABPS equipped the office with the computer equipment necessary for expediting applications. These internal changes and the accompanying communication campaign resulted in more than 1,800 applicants and a net gain of 80 new officers on the force in one year. Previous attempts at statewide recruiting without the other changes in structure and processing had not reversed the attrition problem.

Action strategy concentrates on adjustment and adaptation **within** the organization. An opportunity to implement such changes, however, requires that both top management and practitioners define public relations as something much more than publicity and persuasive communication. As Harold Burson pointed out, in its mature form, public relations helps relationships determine what is done as well as what and how something is said. The case of Sybron Chemical Inc. provides yet another illustration.

Sixty neighbors of the Birmingham, New Jersey, manufacturer of water purification resins were evacuated following the accidental release of a noxious chemical. A month later, two plant workers were seriously burned during a process accident. These accidents and the resulting publicity only heightened public concerns about odors from the plant, plant safety, and the lack of information about plant operations. Neighbors and a U.S. senator called for new state and federal controls. Some in the community demanded that the plant be closed.[6]

With public relations counsel, Sybron devised a strategy to "take immediate, effective and credible action regarding each of the concerns identified by neighbors, local officials and state regulatory officials." The company also decided to break with past practice and begin regularly communicating both what was happening and the results of corrective actions. Action strategies included hiring an independent engineering firm to solve odor and chemical-handling safety problems and to upgrade plant facilities. Communication strategy included forming the Sybron

Neighborhood Involvement Council to promote face-to-face communication; issuing a quarterly newspaper, *Sybron Community Update*; holding the first Sybron open house and plant tour; and installing a computerized 24-hour phone system (PINS Hotline) that calls neighbors' homes if there is a problem and allows neighbors to call any time of day for updated information (see Figure 13.1).[7]

A follow-up survey of neighbors indicated that 90 percent felt more secure about Sybron as a neighbor and almost all believed that the company had improved communication with its neighbors. A report describes the award-winning program as "the story of how a new commitment to corrective action and communications resulted in a complete turn-around, in just seven months, with state regulators praising Sybron's actions as a model for the entire chemical industry."[8]

"Sybron is certainly a textbook example of how a company can turn neighborhood fear and anger into trust and credibility," according to Christine Foschetti, account executive at Sybron's public relations firm, Holt and Ross, Inc. Sybron's management first had to mount an action strategy that included significant odor-reduction efforts and substantial environmental improvements. According to Foschetti, "Without these two very important elements, the company's public outreach program would have been doomed to fail."[9]

Action strategy puts into practice what Chapter 7 refers to as the open systems model, or what James Grunig calls "two-way symmetrical" public relations.[10] The first assumption basic to this approach is that change is as likely within the organization as it is on the part of the organization's publics. Another assumption of this

FIGURE 13.1

SYBRON CHEMICALS' COMMUNITY HOTLINE

Courtesy Environmental Affairs Institute, Edison, NJ.

approach is that changes result in win–win outcomes, meaning that both sides in an organization–public relationship can benefit. A third assumption that drives action strategy is suggested by the quote in Chapter 7, "Clean up your act, not just your image." If public relations is to have an impact in shaping the mutually beneficial relationships necessary for organizational survival and success, it must participate in developing the action strategy and in coordinating this strategy with the communication efforts that follow.

COMMUNICATION COMPONENT OF STRATEGY

Action strategy necessarily makes up the main thrust of a program but represents the part of the public relations iceberg that might not show above the surface. Communication, typically the more visible component, serves as the program catalyst to interpret and support the action strategy. Chapter 8 outlines relevant communication theory and concepts that serve as the foundation for this section. What follow are fundamentals and principles for applying the theory to the practice.

Framing the Message

The first principle of framing message content for the communication effort is to know the client's or employer's position and the problem situation intimately. The second principle is to know the needs, interests, and concerns of the target publics. In the words of one practitioner, "Get smart and put yourself in the other party's shoes."[11]

Attempting to establish any single set of surefire rules for framing message content would be disappointing, if not futile. Such rules might appear perfect in principle yet be rendered ineffectual by an unseen characteristic of the audience; for example, a religious belief that bans certain foods. The timing could be bad. A carefully timed announcement of a new stock offering by an oil company was smothered in the news by revelations that the organization had used corporate funds for political campaigns in the United States and for bribes abroad. The audience could harbor an unspoken prejudice, such as confronts a Democrat campaigning in a Republican precinct. The wording of the message could be such that it does not square with the images in the heads of the audience, or perhaps the audience is not in a listening mood. Regardless of the specific barrier, standardized programming can generate results that are frustrating or futile.

Effective communication must be designed for the situation, time, place, and audience. It means careful selection of media and technique. For example, the annual spring migration of college students to Florida's beaches poses health problems for that state, among them the spread of venereal diseases. One year the Florida Health Department gave Frisbees™ carrying messages on how to recognize and prevent venereal diseases to students as they swarmed the Florida beaches. This is targeted communication. So is the campaign against teenagers drinking and driving in Tucson, Arizona: "Driving Drunk Will Put Your Lights Out"—a message framed in the imagery and language of the target public.

Advances in technology and specialized media have created a wealth of possibilities for serving the needs of special audiences. Practitioners would be well advised to think in terms of smaller and more circumscribed patterns of communication as they seek to modify or mobilize opinions. No communication or action, simply because it worked once before in a given situation, can be carted about like a trunk full of old clothes and fitted to a new situation. With rare exceptions, the clothes will not fit the second wearer. If nothing else, they will be out of style.

All public relations problems, however, do have people as a common denominator and require communication to bring the people and their viewpoints closer together. This applies whether the programming calls for news releases, institutional advertising, meetings, or any other tool of contact. Continuity is required in communication. So is repetition of a consistent message in simple form, careful selection of time, place, and method, and a variety of media that converge on the audience from several avenues.

Public relations, with its powerful and varied means of selectively disseminating targeted information, suffers from an overcapacity. Simon and Garfunkel sang in "The Sounds of Silence" that our problem is people talking without speaking, people hearing without listening. Likewise, practitioners must define audiences with great precision and must use different strategies and techniques to accomplish different goals. For example, different concerns and different levels of intensity about an issue call for different message strategy.

The following time-tested techniques help reduce the discrepancy between the communicator's position and the audience's attitudes.

1. Use the media most closely identified with the audience's position.
2. Use a communications source that enjoys high credibility for the audience **on the topic of communication**.
3. Play down the differences between the positions of the communicator and those of the audience.
4. Seek identification in vocabulary and anecdote with the audience **in an area removed from the issue**.
5. Establish the communicator's position as being the majority opinion, defining the majority from the audience itself.
6. Bring the audience's group identifications into play when those identifications will help develop a positive response. The converse is also true.
7. Modify the message to fit the organization's need.[12]

Besides framing their message for the target public, public relations practitioners must also frame their messages for the media. According to some estimates, 9 out of 10 news releases get discarded.[13] Practitioners can increase their chances of getting the attention of journalists by carefully adhering to the *Associated Press Stylebook* and using multimedia tools in the presentation of their messages.[14] Most importantly, framing the message for the media and media gatekeepers requires attention to news value. Traditional criteria applied by gatekeepers, who see their role as acting on behalf of media audiences, include the following.

1. *Impact*—the number of people affected, the seriousness of the consequence, the directness of cause and effect, and the immediacy of the effect. This criterion applies not only to news but also to other information.
2. *Proximity*—the distance between the audience and the problem or issue of concern. This criterion simply suggests that local connections or news angles increase news value.

3. *Timeliness*—perishability. Like bread, news gets stale. This criterion also explains why journalists and media compete to be first with the news but why print media cannot compete with broadcast media on timeliness. As a result, print media may be more interested in why and how than in when, although daily newspapers remain concerned with the timeliness of information.

4. *Prominence*—recognizable and well known. Almost by definition, celebrity and celebrities are of interest to large numbers of people; they are newsworthy. Prominence means that journalists and their audiences are interested in the private lives of public organizations and figures.

5. *Novelty*—the unusual, bizarre, deviant, and offbeat. Some even define news as deviation from the normal. Journalists and editors know that people are attracted by and interested in what is new, unique, and unexpected.

6. *Conflict*—strikes, fights, disputes, wars, crime, politics, and sports. All too often, conflict is the major ingredient in news, not only because of its appeal to journalists but also because of media pandering to public interest in the sensational and uncertain. Conflict situations often have issues that are not clearly defined, uncertainty about what is right or wrong, and oversimplified versions of winners and losers.[15]

Defining news may not be that simple, however. Some contend that news is anything that affects the lives and interests or stimulates the concern and curiosity of a significant number of people. In the final analysis, the distinction between hard news and soft news changes to accommodate audience interests in an ever-expanding range of topics, including science, culture, environment, social change, and education, to name but a few. Day-to-day news selection by gatekeepers, however, may result more from routine, deadline pressures, mechanical requirements, and their perceptions of what other journalists are saying and doing.[16]

Public relations practitioners must frame their messages to make them **newsworthy**, by whatever standard (hence the requirement to know the media and media gatekeepers). Messages also must be **understandable**—uncomplicated, free of jargon, and simple to grasp. They must be topical or local to take advantage of audience interest in information that is both timely and close to home. Most important, however, is that the message must be **immediately actionable**. In the same way that the action strategy must be mutually beneficial, so must messages. The content should be framed in such a way that the information answers questions, responds to audience interests and concerns, and empowers members of the audience to act on their interests and concerns (see Figure 13.2, Trades Hall, Melbourne, Australia). The actionable quality deserves special attention.

Journalists systematically tend to shy away from including "mobilizing information" in their news stories. This is the information about identification, location, and instruction or direction that audience members would need to act on their predisposition. One could speculate that journalists might feel that providing such information would be a departure from their perceived role of objective news reporters. When they include mobilizing information in stories about charities, other community drives, and crises, journalists may see this either as a forgivable departure, given the positive context, or as acceptable professional behavior.[17]

Another useful approach to framing the message is to use the "30-3-30" formula devised by the late author-scholar Clay Schoenfeld.[18] The first number means

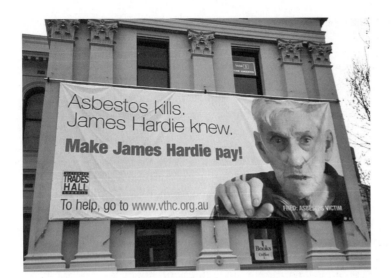

FIGURE 13.2

MESSAGE FRAMING: "MAKE JAMES HARDIE PAY!"

that many in the audience will give you no more than 30 seconds to get your audience's attention, meaning that your key points must be strong, positive, and dominantly displayed. The second number indicates that some will give you up to three minutes, meaning that you can count on bold lines, subheads, illustrations, photo captions, and even highlighted summary statements to carry the message. Thirty-minute audience members will spend the time necessary to get message content, even though the details are reported in small type. Maybe a 3-30-3 formula should replace Schoenfeld's optimistic 30-3-30 formula when framing most public relations messages.

Finally, framing the message strategy requires attention to four fundamental facts.

1. The audience consists of people. These people live, work, worship, and play in the framework of social institutions in cities, in suburbs, in villages, or on farms. Consequently, each person is subject to many influences, of which the communicator's message is typically only one small source of influence.

2. People tend to read, watch, or listen to communications that present points of view with which they are sympathetic or in which they have a personal stake. For example, communication scholarship has shown that people who are Republican tend to pay more attention to television ads featuring Republican candidates, whereas Democrats tend to pay more attention to ads featuring Democratic candidates.

3. Media create their separate communities. For example, those who read *Soldier of Fortune* and *The National Enquirer* are not likely to read *Scientific American* and *Architectural Digest*. Similarly, online chat rooms are a high-tech example of communities created by specialized media.

4. Media have a wide variety of effects on individual and collective knowledge, predisposition, and behavior, not all of which are readily measurable. Careful framing must take into account both the intended and unintended effects of message content.

Semantics

Semantics is the science of what words mean. Language is constantly changing, with new words appearing (such as *faxed*) and words dropping from use (such as *groovy*). The meanings of words can change (such as *politically correct*). Others take on so many meanings that they become almost meaningless (such as *bottom line* and *strategic planning*, according to some in public relations!).

Here we have space only to acknowledge the importance of semantics in public relations. Do not be misled, however; the subject really deserves and gets a great deal of attention from men and women in public relations. For in communicating and interpreting, practitioners live by words and make their living by them. For example, Edward Bernays referred to the "semantic tyranny" represented by the title of what is widely recognized as one of history's greatest special events, "Light's Golden Jubilee," the celebration of the 50th anniversary of Thomas Edison's invention of the incandescent lightbulb. There is no escape for communicators from what T. S. Eliot described as "the intolerable wrestle with words and meanings." Practitioners must seek mastery of word meanings and nuances.

When communicating with diverse audiences, the challenge is further complicated by the need to translate English-language words with accuracy, yet with a careful eye toward semantics in the end-language. For example, during Census 2000, the U.S. Census Bureau wanted to encourage Hispanics to complete and return their census forms. The English-language tagline was "This is your future. Don't leave it blank." In the initial Spanish-language translation, "blank" became "blanco," which some Hispanic community leaders felt implied that failure to complete the ethnicity question on the census form would lead to Hispanics getting counted as non-Hispanic Whites. Thus, the Census Bureau decided to go with the tagline "Es nuestro futuro. Hagase contar."—"This is our future. Make it count."—for its Spanish-language campaign.

In this midst of the wrestle with words—in any language—is the public relations practitioner. Studying the words that leap out of people's mouths, stare up from newspapers, and smile out from a television tube, the practitioner is expected to react and then to be able to tell what those words mean—not what they say, but what they really mean. Then the public relations specialist is expected to combine words and actions that will correct misunderstandings, educate where there is a lack of knowledge, and, in general, clear up confusion.

Practitioners are constantly making decisions about word meanings, so the basic importance of semantics must not be overlooked. Deciding what the refusal of people to work should be called represents a decision in semantics. Is it a strike, a work stoppage, or an outrage against the people? Cutbacks are referred to as "downsizing" or "rightsizing." Procter & Gamble called its notification that the company was about to cut 13,000 jobs and close 30 factories "the global initiative announcement." Weapons of mass destruction are called "peacekeepers," military invasions are referred to as "police actions," and new taxes are camouflaged as "revenue enhancements." Clearly, there is no one-to-one ratio between a word and its meaning. The same signs and word symbols have different meanings for different people.

In addition, they have two different kinds of meaning: **denotative** and **connotative**. Denotative meaning is the common dictionary meaning, generally accepted by most people with the same language and culture. Connotative meaning is the emotional or evaluative meaning we read into words because of our experience and background. For example, all people will agree that *dog* **denotes** a four-legged, usually furry, canine animal. For most people, *dog* **connotes** a friendly, faithful pet and usually awakens nostalgic memories about a childhood pet. To others, however, the word **connotes** a dangerous animal or the cause of dander that causes a severe allergic reaction. Another example is the word *bullfight*. North and South Americans fully agree on what the term denotes, but its connotative meaning differs sharply north and south of the United States–Mexico border.

Our political language has become an integral part of events and helps shape their meaning. The campaign for national prohibition made *saloon* a dirty word, so today, those who drink do so in *taverns* and *lounges*. Incidentally, the Drys were too wise to campaign for "prohibition," a harsh word; they advocated "temperance." Another great coup in semantics was scored in coining the term *life insurance* to describe what could be called more properly *death insurance*, but the latter would be harder to sell. A ten-strike in semantics has been the successful effort of bowling promoters to change *bowling alleys* to *bowling lanes* and *bowling centers*. *Educational television* became *public television*, which has a more popular ring for fund-raising. Semantic manipulation is an old art.

Words can excite and inflame. For example, there is evidence that a mistake in translating a message sent by the Japanese government near the end of World War II may have triggered the bombing of Hiroshima and thus ushered in atomic warfare. The word *mokusatsu*, used by Japan in response to the U.S. surrender ultimatum, was translated as *ignore* instead of its correct meaning, "withhold comment until a decision has been made." And some years ago, semantic difficulties caused a crisis between the United States and Panama: Panamanians interpreted the English verb *negotiate* as a commitment to negotiate a new treaty, the meaning of the Spanish verb *negociar*. The U.S. State Department intended it simply in its noncommittal sense of "to discuss."

Words often become code words to convey an unspoken but unmistakable meaning; for instance, "right to life," "law and order," "reverse discrimination," and "ethnic purity of neighborhoods." Even the meaning of commonplace words cannot be taken for granted. For example, one of the authors used the word *fallacy* on an exam, only to find that many students did not know what the word meant.

Public relations people must be able to select and transmit for various audiences words that will be received as kinfolk. Think of the harm that has been done, the confusion created, by legal language. The same is true for the language of doctors, educators, the military, and government. Each has a special jargon not readily understandable to others: legalese, educationese, militarese, and governmentese. And besides jargon there are slang, dialects, slogans, and exaggerations. Practitioners must work with their counterparts in the press, radio, and television and on the platform to help straighten things out for their publics.

Poet Anne Sexton cautioned, "Words, like eggs, must be handled with care; once broken, they are beyond repair." Practitioners must have a flair for picturesque, memorable terms, and a feeling for words.

Symbols

Communication involves more than semantics; in large measure it uses **symbols** and **stereotypes**. The symbol offers a dramatic and direct means of persuasive communication with large numbers of people over long lines of communication. Symbols have been used since the dawn of history to compress and convey complex messages to the multitudes. The Star of David and the Cross of Christ remind us of this. Most people need the shorthand of symbols to deal with whatever is abstract, diffuse, or difficult.

Years ago, Lippmann explained the need met by symbols and stereotypes as "introducing (1) **definiteness** and **distinction** and (2) **consistency** or **stability** of meaning into what otherwise is vague and wavering. . . . We tend to perceive that which we have picked out in the form stereotyped for us by our culture."[19] Here is a current example of Lippmann's point: "Pro-life" is a powerful symbol because it condenses an enormous amount of meaning, information, and experience.

The value and use of a venerated symbol is seen in the British monarchy. The greatly diminished British Commonwealth of Nations today is a free association of independent nations shakily held together, not by legal ties, but by the symbol of the Queen of England. She symbolizes the traditional loyalties, the common interests, the traditional institutional forms held more or less in common, and the family ties.

Symbols play an important role in the public relations and fund-raising programs of health and welfare agencies. Probably the best-known symbol of the kind is the Red Cross, from which that agency takes its name. The Red Cross originated in Switzerland and created its symbol by reversing the white cross and red background of the Swiss flag. The upright sword of the American Cancer Society, chosen in a nationwide poster contest, was created to portray its crusading spirit. Another crusade, that of the National Tuberculosis Association, is symbolized by the Cross of Lorraine, which dates back to the Crusades.

One of the most effective symbols ever created is that of Smokey Bear, used by the U.S. Forest Service, the Association of State Foresters, and the Advertising Council to promote forest-fire prevention. The idea originated in 1944 with a group of foresters and advertising specialists concerned about the need to protect our forests. After experimenting with drawings of deer, squirrels, and other small animals to carry fire-prevention messages, they had the idea of using a bear. A bear—with its humanlike posture, its way of handling itself, and its universal appeal to young and old—seemed ideal to build into a persuasive symbol (see Figure 13.3).

The Smokey Bear symbol changed over the years, as did the appeals used in the public service announcements. More than five decades of public awareness campaigns have produced almost universal awareness of Smokey Bear, with 98 percent aided recall in some parts of the country. Surveys typically show that about 95 percent of adults and 85 percent of children recognize Smokey's message, "Only *you* can prevent forest fires." But even though the symbol enjoys widespread recognition, many of the young urban children exposed to Smokey Bear in school programs do not know what to do to prevent forest fires. The bear, however, remains a credible symbol of forest-fire prevention.[20]

Increasingly, for-profit and nonprofit organizations emphasize symbols (designs and logos) to create a public image and instant recognition or to capitalize on widespread public awareness and acceptance. A current example of the latter is the symbol for recycling, which marketers and organizations use to demonstrate their concern for the environment. In fact, another new term—*green*—has entered the language to describe communication and an action strategy shaped to demonstrate sensitivity and commitment to protecting the environment.

Surely symbols should be distinct, different, and in character for the institutions using them. However, a changing public climate governed by new and different values can make symbols obsolete or offensive. For example, new public sensitivity for the rights and feelings of minority groups has forced Syracuse University, St. John's University, and Stanford University to abandon American Indian symbols and names for their athletic teams. The University of Illinois and Florida State University face increasing pressure to drop their long-standing Indian symbols and mas-

Smokey Bear

FIGURE 13.3

SMOKEY BEAR

cots—clearly, the universities and the tribes hold different views of the use of Native American symbols.[21]

Barriers and Stereotypes

Barriers to understanding and to the clarity of messages exist in the communicator and the audience alike. As Lippmann noted, each person lives in the protective shelter of a cocoon of his or her own spinning. This cocoon insulates the individual from the incessant communication babble that is steadily increasing in intensity. There are social barriers, age barriers, language or vocabulary barriers, and political and economic barriers. There is also the race barrier; the barriers and distortions that block communication are seen starkly in the gulf between racial and ethnic groups in the multicultural American society. There is peer pressure exerted within groups, where "reality" is shared and interpreted. There is also the often-overlooked barrier of the audience's ability or willingness to absorb messages. Finally, there is the constant roar of competition for people's attention in the noisy public arena. Barriers are not the only complications in communication, however.

People have impressions about everything that touches their consciousness. All people live in a world of their own symbols. Public figures, for example, during their lifetimes and afterward, are known partly through a personality created by images fixed in the public imagination. Astronauts, politicians, rock stars, and sports heroes are good examples. Their families and associates know them as people entirely different from their public personalities. People who live on one side of town tend to know people on the other side of town, as well as those in remote cities, in a half-fictional, half-imagined way. The only feeling that people can have about an event they do not experience or a person they do not know is by their own mental image of the event or person, developed from fragmentary, secondary sources.

In communication, nothing raises more problems than the reality that most mass media audiences have limited access to the facts. With limited access, and with some information tending to confuse as much as it clarifies, people rely heavily on *stereotypes*. Specific and significant impressions become generalities. As Lippmann pointed out, the "pictures in our head" derive mainly from what we see and hear in the mass media. Certainly our impressions of the war on terrorism, nuclear tests in India, and riots in Jakarta (Indonesia), as well as our stereotypes of the people in each situation, came from cable and network television, newsmagazines, newspapers, and radio.

Readers looking at a magazine cover picture entitled "Criminal" may pick out two or three sharply defined features. Perhaps they select a low forehead, a squinting eye, a scarred face, or a mouth that curls at the corner. From then on, the impression may be so deeply rooted that readers feel sure that they know the "criminal type" whenever they see it. They can classify everyone, including friends, as to whether or not they are criminal types. Indeed, people have classifications into which they can fit almost everyone they see or hear about.

Such distorted stereotypes pose public relations problems. For example, a newly elected president of the California State Bar announced that she would make addressing negative and distorted public stereotypes of lawyers her highest priority. Unfortunately for lawyers everywhere, however, cartoonists took advantage of her announcement by exploiting stereotypes in a new rash of cartoons portraying lawyers as snakes, vultures, wolves, sharks, and so forth. The media help create new stereotypes by reducing complex people, groups, countries, and situations to their simplest and most general—sometimes distorted—attributes.

Lippmann emphasized the sacrosanct regard that people have for stereotypes as "the core of our personal tradition, the defense of our position in society."

> They may not be a complete picture of the world, but they are a picture of a possible world to which we are adapted. In that world people and things have their well-known places, and do certain expected things. We feel at home there. We fit in. We are members. We know the way around. . . . The stereotypes are, therefore, highly charged with the feelings that are attached to them. They are the fortress of our tradition, and behind its defenses we can continue to feel ourselves safe in the position we occupy.[22]

Stereotypes, then, serve as a defense mechanism against having to exert the effort required to learn about and understand the uniqueness and details of each person, group, and situation. They also form a moral code from which personal standards of behavior are derived. Practitioners must learn to recognize the influence and the presence of symbols and stereotypes in what appear to be the contradictions and contrariness of public opinion. Symbols are used to counter symbols, and stereotypes are used to counter stereotypes.

There is yet another side to stereotypes, however. In the context of a multicultural society, media are trying to be more sensitive and respectful of differences based on age, gender, sexual orientation, race, body shape, and ethnicity. Some criticize efforts to purge the language of stereotypes as yielding to the "politically correct language" movement. They say the movement is headed by the kind of "thought police" George Orwell warned us about. Others see eliminating words and phrases that are pejorative stereotypes as a way to promote acceptance of diversity and to make media content more inclusive and less offensive.[23] As one writer put it, "[t]argeting a multicultural audience takes more than a dictionary—it takes tact, understanding, and relevance."[24]

To avoid having the words themselves become a public relations problem, practitioners must be sensitive to word choice. A good reference on words to avoid is the *Dictionary of Cautionary Words and Phrases*, published by the University of Missouri, which includes a checklist of offensive words and stereotypes.[25] Some other organizations, such as the Asian American Journalists Association, publish compendia of connotative meanings of words, both positive and negative.[26] In the final analysis, language changes carried to extremes can debase the language by substituting euphemisms for accurate and meaningful descriptions. Responding to every charge of "oppression" without care can take away from the real effort to rid language of sexist, racist, and other insensitive stereotypes. Paradoxically, "political correctness" has taken on many different connotations to many different people in many different contexts, robbing the term itself of real meaning.

Putting It All Together in a Campaign

The difficulty of public information campaigns can be clearly seen in the battle to save us from polluted air, polluted water, and chemically dangerous foods. America's pioneer ecologist, Aldo Leopold, thought in his early years that "if the public were told how much harm ensues from unwise land-use, it would mend its ways." In his twilight years, he knew that this conclusion was based on three mistaken assumptions: that the public is listening or can be made to listen; that the public responds, or can be made to respond, to fear of harm; and that ways can be mended without any important change in the public itself.[27]

In an often-quoted article, Hyman and Sheatsley codified the major reasons why many information campaigns fail. They include the following:

1. There exists a hard core of chronic "know-nothings." These people are difficult to reach, no matter what the level or nature of the information.

2. Interested people acquire the most information. Motivation is essential to learning or assimilating knowledge, yet there are large groups in the population who admit that they have little or no interest in public issues.

3. People seek information that is compatible with their prior attitudes and avoid exposure to that which is not compatible.

4. People interpret the same information differently. Selective perception and interpretation of content follows exposure: Persons perceive, absorb, and remember content differently.

5. Information does not necessarily change attitudes. Changes in views or behavior following exposure to a message may be differentially affected by the individual's initial predisposition.[28]

Another researcher, Harold Mendelsohn, countered with an analysis of why information campaigns can succeed.

What little empirical experience we have accumulated from the past suggests that public information campaigns have relatively high success potentials:

1. If they are planned around the assumption that most of the publics to which they will be addressed will be either only mildly interested or not at all interested in what is communicated.

2. If middle-range goals which can be reasonably achieved as a consequence of exposure are set as specific objectives. Frequently it is equally important either to set up or to utilize environmental support systems to help sheer information giving become effective in influencing behavior.

3. If, after middle-range objectives are set, careful consideration is given to delineating specific targets in terms of their demographic and psychological attributes, their lifestyle, value and belief systems, and mass media habits. Here, it is important not only to determine the scope of prior indifference, but to uncover its roots as well.[29]

That public information campaigns can succeed has been demonstrated by numerous campaigns against smoking in public places, the highly successful effort by Mothers Against Drunk Driving (MADD), the "Back to Sleep" campaign by the National Institute of Child Health and Human Development, and American Cancer Society efforts promoting cancer detection and prevention, to name but a few. The jury is still out on campaigns to prevent HIV infections, to reduce drug abuse, and to promote social tolerance.

Disseminating the Message

Gaining acceptance of an idea or an innovation is more than simply beaming it to an audience through a mass medium or internal publication. To illuminate, communication must be aimed with the precision of a laser beam, not cast in all directions in the manner of a lightbulb. Even after many years of research, there is still not definitive evidence of a single model of how ideas are disseminated among people. Elmo Roper, after nearly 30 years of opinion research, formulated a hypothesis that has some value as a guide. His concentric-circle theory says that ideas penetrate to the whole public very slowly through a process similar to osmosis. Histories of public campaigns substantiate this. They move out in concentric circles from great thinkers to great disciples to great disseminators to lesser disseminators to the politically active to the politically inert. This hypothesis assumes that American society can be stratified as indicated and emphasizes the importance of using opinion leaders in the public relations process.

The rate of flow in the transmission and acceptance of ideas, however, is governed by many factors other than the characteristics of the people involved. These include Lippmann's "barriers to communication" and George Gallup's "regulators of absorption rate" illustrated in Figure 13.4.

The communication step in the public relations process often requires influencing knowledge, opinions, and actions among sizable and distant groups. The accelerating rate at which innovations are being invented, developed, and spread makes it vital that communicators be able to transfer information to those who need it. Examples include gaining public acceptance of using sunscreen lotions to protect against skin cancer; overcoming fear of technology, such as programming a DVD player or paying bills online; and getting high-risk publics to get blood pressure checkups. And the rate of adopting new technology is accelerating: "(In 1997) 100 million people logged onto the Internet, up from 40 million the year before. That is faster than the phone, TV, and radio were adopted. When President Clinton took office [in 1992] there were only 50 web sites. Now [in 1998] 65,000 are being added . . . every hour."[30]

Diffusion refers to this process by which new ideas and practices are spread to members of a social system. The U.S. Department of Agriculture has been working at this task longer than most. It learned from experience that getting new ideas

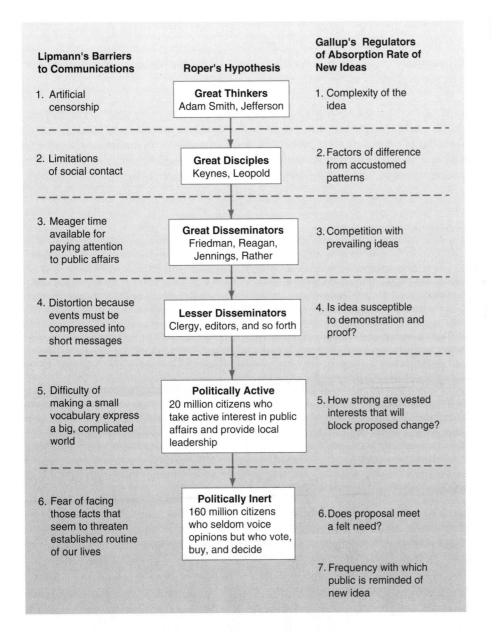

FIGURE 13.4

COMMUNICATION BARRIERS AND DISSEMINATION

Lipmann's Barriers to Communications

1. Artificial censorship

2. Limitations of social contact

3. Meager time available for paying attention to public affairs

4. Distortion because events must be compressed into short messages

5. Difficulty of making a small vocabulary express a big, complicated world

6. Fear of facing those facts that seem to threaten established routine of our lives

Roper's Hypothesis

Great Thinkers
Adam Smith, Jefferson

Great Disciples
Keynes, Leopold

Great Disseminators
Friedman, Reagan, Jennings, Rather

Lesser Disseminators
Clergy, editors, and so forth

Politically Active
20 million citizens who take active interest in public affairs and provide local leadership

Politically Inert
160 million citizens who seldom voice opinions but who vote, buy, and decide

Gallup's Regulators of Absorption Rate of New Ideas

1. Complexity of the idea

2. Factors of difference from accustomed patterns

3. Competition with prevailing ideas

4. Is idea susceptible to demonstration and proof?

5. How strong are vested interests that will block proposed change?

6. Does proposal meet a felt need?

7. Frequency with which public is reminded of new idea

accepted involves more than simply discovering a new grain and publicizing it. It took 13 years to gain widespread adoption of hybrid seed corn on America's farms, for example. Out of their long experience and evaluation research, agricultural sociologists have concluded that acceptance goes through five stages:

1. *Knowledge.* People learn about an innovation and some gain understanding of what it is.
2. *Persuasion.* Potential adopters develop interest in the innovation. They seek more information and consider its general merits.
3. *Decision.* Potential adopters decide to adopt or reject the innovation after weighing its merits for their own situation.
4. *Implementation.* Those willing to try the innovation actually apply it to their situation, usually on a small scale. They are interested in the practice, techniques, and conditions for application.
5. *Confirmation.* Adoption is either reinforced or the decision to adopt is reversed based on the evaluation.[31]

Mass media have their greatest impact and usefulness in creating awareness in the knowledge stage. For farmers, at least, the mass media become less and less influential as the acceptance process advances toward confirmation of the adoption. Interpersonal influence increases with each step. This diffusion model, developed through extensive research among rural families, was supported in subsequent studies in other settings. Chaffee suggests that there are several reasons for this pattern of diffusion:

> The media are comparatively rich in news content, whereas personal associates are likely to have had relevant "consumer" experience. Further, since consumption is partly a matter of defining one's social "self," other persons would be able to offer normative social guides to appropriate consumption patterns that the media cannot. Finally, some matters may not be dealt with by the media in sufficient depth or detail to satisfy personal information needs.[32]

The research conclusions demonstrate that communicating a new idea or practice is a long, tedious task. Different communication tactics are effective at different points and in different ways. The influence of influentials and opinion leaders is great in many situations. It is important for the communicator to know what media and techniques to use at different stages and how to mobilize these influences effectively. In summary, however, effective communication is expensive in research, preparation, attention, and implementation. The cost is higher than is commonly supposed.

Reconsidering the Process

The three elements common to all communication efforts are the source or sender, the message, and the destination or receiver. A communication breakdown can involve one or more of these three elements. Effective communication requires efficiency on the part of all three. The communicator must have **adequate information**. The communicator must have **credibility** in the eyes of the receiver. The communicator must be able to transmit information in codes the receiver can **comprehend**. The communicator must use a **channel** that will carry the message to the receiver.

The message must be within the receiver's **capacity to comprehend** and be **relevant** to the receiver's interests or needs. Finally, the message must motivate the receiver's self-interest and cause a **response**.

Wise communicators see receivers not as passive subjects but as selective users of information for their own purposes. Too many public relations programs do not gauge the individual's role in the process. Public relations educator and scholar Doug Newsom says that practitioners should not use "the term 'audiences,' because it implies 'recipients' of messages instead of participants in communication."[33]

Words are symbols. There are words that serve as symbols for real objects—*table, chair*—thing words. There are words that are symbols of abstract ideas—such as *freedom, love*—nothing words. Children are taught, for example, that a furry little animal with long ears and a short, fuzzy tail is a "rabbit." Once the word and the little animal are associated, the word will always evoke the image of that creature. Word symbols for real objects are readily understood and agreed upon. This is not so with symbols for abstractions. Abstractions such as *pro-choice* or *pro-life* have no simple or universally accepted referents in the real world of objects. It is difficult for people to agree on an image of *free trade* when they cannot see, touch, hear, taste, or smell it. This difficulty goes right to the heart of the communication problem.

To communicate effectively, the sender's words and symbols must mean the same thing to the receiver that they do to the sender. The word *communication* is derived from the Latin *communis*, meaning "common." So *communication* means establishing a sense of commonness. A sender can encode a message and a receiver decode it only in terms of their own experience and knowledge. But if there has been no common experience, then communication becomes virtually impossible. This explains a layperson's inability to understand an Einstein. It explains why—despite the tremendous flow of words to and from China—Americans and Chinese still have little understanding of each other.

Common knowledge and experience provide the connections. The greater the overlap in common interest and common experience, the easier it is to communicate. Many barriers impede achieving this overlap of commonness, but commonness in communication is essential to link people and purpose together in any cooperative system.

Public relations communication provides the climate for an action's acceptance and implementation, but it is only one element. For example, successful public campaigns against smoking, unsafe sex, drinking and driving, drug use, and careless use of fire in forests must be accompanied by action strategy that changes the problem situation and provides enforcement and social support.

IMPLEMENTING THE STRATEGY

The purpose of this chapter was to introduce some of the major considerations and principles of implementing public relations programs. However, entire books devoted to the topic cannot adequately cover the range of issues and practices related to putting the program in place. The chapter concludes with the venerable seven Cs of public relations communication:

1. *Credibility.* Communication starts with a climate of belief. This climate is built by performance on the part of the institution, reflecting an earnest desire to

serve stakeholders and publics. Receivers must have confidence in the sender and high regard for the source's competence on the subject.

2. *Context.* A communications program must square with the realities of its environment. Mass media only supplement the words and deeds of daily living. The context must provide for participation and playback. It must confirm, not contradict, the message. Effective communication requires a supportive social environment, one largely set by the news media.

3. *Content.* The message must have meaning for receivers, and it must be compatible with their value system. It must have relevance to the receivers' situation. In general, people select those items of information that promise them the greatest rewards. The content determines the audience.

4. *Clarity.* The message must be put in simple terms. Words must mean the same to the receivers as to the sender. Complex issues must be compressed into themes, slogans, or stereotypes that have simplicity and clarity. The farther a message has to travel, the simpler it must be. An organization must speak with one voice, not many voices.

5. *Continuity and consistency.* Communication is an unending process. It requires repetition to achieve penetration. Repetition—with variation—contributes to both learning and persuasion. The story must be consistent.

6. *Channels.* Established channels of communication should be used, channels that receivers use and respect. Creating new ones can be difficult, time consuming, and expensive. Different channels have different effects and serve effectively in different stages of the diffusion process. Selective channels are called for in reaching target publics. People associate different values with the many channels of communication.

7. *Capability of the audience.* Communication must take into account the capability of the audience. Communications are most effective when they require the least effort on the part of receivers. This involves factors of availability, habits, reading ability, and prior knowledge.

Communication and action are not the ends, but only the means to ends. The ends of public relations are the outcomes spelled out in program goals and objectives. Assessing the effectiveness of program strategy—the fourth step—is the topic of the next chapter.

NOTES

[1] Speech to Raymond Simon Institute for Public Relations, Utica College, Syracuse University, March 5, 1987.

[2] Harold Burson, "Beyond 'PR': Redefining the Role of Public Relations," 29th Annual Distinguished Lecture of the Institute for Public Relations Research and Education, Inc., New York, October 2, 1990.

[3] Ibid.

[4] Don Etling, Senior Vice President, Fleishman-Hillard, quoted in Craig McGuire, "From the Top Down: A Sturdy Reputation Program Requires Buy-in From All Parts of a Corporation," *PRWeek* (January 19, 2004): 17.

[5] Norman R. Nager and T. Harrell Allen, *Public Relations Management by Objectives* (Lanham, MD: University Press of America, 1984), 241–42. (Originally published by Longman.)

[6] Caron Chess, Michal Tamuz, Alex Saville, and Michael Greenberg, "Reducing Uncertainty and Increasing Credibility: The Case of Sybron Chemicals Inc.," *Industrial Crisis Quarterly* 6, no. 1 (1992): 55–70.

[7] PINS Hotline is the registered trademark for the Prompt Inquiry and Notification System of the Environmental Affairs Institute, Inc., Edison, NJ.

[8] Public Relations Society of America, "1990 Silver Anvil Winners: Index and Summaries," New York, 1990, 1–2.

[9] Christine S. Foschetti, Edison, NJ, correspondence to the authors, July 15, 1993.

[10] James E. Grunig, "Communication, Public Relations, and Effective Organizations: An Overview of the Book," in *Excellence in Public Relations and Communication Management*, ed. James E. Grunig (Hillsdale, NJ: Lawrence Erlbaum Associates, 1992), 18–19.

[11] A. C. Croft, "Delayed Action Allows Informed Response," *Public Relations Journal* 48, no. 5 (May 1992): 31.

[12] Eugene F. Lane, "Applied Behavioral Science," *Public Relations Journal* 23, no. 7 (July 1967): 6.

[13] Randy Hines and Joe Basso, "Do Editors a Favor: Use '*The Associated Press Stylebook*'," *PR Tactics* (February 2003): 16.

[14] Ibid.; Sara Calabro, "Get the Smarts: Using Multimedia Releases," *PRWeek* (November 3, 2003): 26.

[15] Adapted from Brian S. Brooks, George Kennedy, Daryl R. Moen, and Don Ranly, *News Reporting and Writing*, 3rd ed. (New York: St. Martin's Press, 1988).

[16] Pamela J. Shoemaker, *Gatekeeping: Communication Concepts* 3 (Newbury Park, CA: Sage Publications, 1991), 50–52.

[17] James B. Lemert and Marguerite Gemson Ashman, "Extent of Mobilizing Information in Opinion and News Magazines," *Journalism Quarterly* 60, no. 4 (Winter 1983): 657–62.

[18] Clay Schoenfeld, "Thirty Seconds to Live," *Writer's Market*, February 1977, p. 29.

[19] Walter Lippmann, *Public Opinion* (New York: Harcourt, Brace and Company, 1922), 81.

[20] Smokey's history is summarized in *Public Communication Campaigns*, 2nd ed., edited by Ronald E. Rice and Charles K. Atkin (Newbury Park, CA: Sage Publications, 1989), 215–18.

[21] Jason Edward Black, "The 'Mascotting' of Native America: Construction, Commodity, and Assimilation," *American Indian Quarterly* 26:4 (2002): 605–622.

[22] Lippmann, *Public Opinion*, 95–96.

[23] Natasha Spring, "Freedom of Speech vs. Politically Correct Language," *Communication World* 9, no. 5 (April 1992): 34–38.

[24] Julia Hood, "Good Translations," *PRWeek* (August 18, 2003): 13.

[25] This useful reference was compiled by the 1989 Multicultural Management Program Fellows at the University of Missouri School of Journalism. It lists derogatory and offensive terms, as well as preferred substitutes.

[26] "All-American: How to Cover Asian America," Asian American Journalists Association (San Francisco: 2000).

[27] For the story of Leopold's career as an innovator and environmentalist, see Susan Flader, *Thinking Like a Mountain* (Columbia: University of Missouri Press, 1974).

[28] Herbert H. Hyman and Paul B. Sheatsley, "Some Reasons Why Information Campaigns Fail," *Public Opinion Quarterly* 11 (1947): 412–23.

[29] Harold Mendelsohn, "Why Information Campaigns Can Succeed," *Public Opinion Quarterly* 37 (Spring 1973): 50–61.

[30] William M. Daley, Secretary, U.S. Department of Commerce, Washington, DC, April 15, 1998, as quoted in *Collective Destiny* 2, no. 2 (April 1998): 1. *Collective Destiny* is a publication of the Japan–U.S. Telecommunications Research Institute, San Diego State University.

[31] Everett M. Rogers, *Diffusion of Innovations*, 3rd ed. (New York: Free Press, 1983).

[32] Steven H. Chaffee, "The Interpersonal Context of Communication," in *Current Perspectives in Mass Communication Research*, ed. F. Gerald Kline and Phillip J. Tichenor (Beverly Hills, CA: Sage Publications, 1972), 103.

[33] Doug Newsom, Texas Christian University, as quoted in *pr reporter* 36, no. 17 (April 26, 1993): 4.

ADDITIONAL SOURCES

Bivins, Thomas. *Public Relations Writing: The Essentials of Style and Format*, 5th ed. New York: McGraw-Hill, 2004. One of several good how-to books on preparing public relations and publicity materials—writing—based on a strategic plan.

Carstarphen, Meta G. and Richard A. Wells. *Writing PR: A Multimedia Approach*. Boston: Pearson, 2004

Holtz, Shel. *Public Relations on the Net*, 2nd ed. New York: American Management Association, 2002. Looks at the impact of new technologies on communication with various stakeholders.

Hunt, Todd, and James E. Grunig. *Public Relations Techniques*. Fort Worth, TX: Harcourt Brace College Publishers, 1994. Adapts authors' theory and principles of managing public relations to program implementation.

Newsom, Doug, and Jim Haynes. *Public Relations Writing: Form and Style*, 7th ed. Belmont, CA: Wadsworth Publishing Company, 2004. Instructs how to prepare and present information in the wide variety of public relations media.

Thompson, William. *Targeting the Message: A Receiver-Centered Process for Public Relations Writing*. New York: Longman, 1996. Presents an audience-centered approach to communicating information as an alternative to the too-frequent role as "press agents for our bosses' egos."

Wilcox, Dennis L., and Patrick Jackson. *Public Relations Writing and Media Techniques*, 4th ed. New York: Longman, 2000. Addresses a wide range of public relations writing assignments, including advertising, special events, conferences, meetings, and audiovisual presentations.

14 STEP FOUR: EVALUATING THE PROGRAM

When you can measure what you are speaking about, and express it in numbers, you know something about it. But when you cannot measure it, when you cannot express it in numbers, your knowledge is of a meager and unsatisfactory kind.

—Lord Kelvin[1]

In an organizational environment characterized by downsizing and zero-based budgeting, public relations no longer can convincingly argue that the function is justified without evidence of measurable results.

—Linda Childers Hon[2]

STUDY GUIDE

After studying Chapter 14, you should be able to

- Define evaluation research.

- Discuss how research is used to evaluate the **preparation, implementation,** and **impact** phases of public relations programs.

- Outline the recommended steps for conducting evaluation research.

- Outline the criteria used in evaluating the preparation, implementation, and impact phases of public relations programs.

- Use the "benchmarks model" to depict the roles of formative and summative evaluation research in public relations programs.

No topic dominates the practice as does program evaluation—the final step in the process. But not all practitioners "walk the talk," because systematic measurement of program effectiveness lags behind practitioner interest in program evaluation. In the words of Ketchum Public Relations Worldwide's former research director, Walter K. Lindenmann,

By the start of the next century, many of us are convinced that this whole area of endeavor known as PR measurement and evaluation will be widely understood and accepted in our field, rather than being treated as something of a novelty, which has been the case up to now.[3]

Increasingly practitioners are being asked to document measurable results and returns that are commensurate with program costs. Public relations, like other staff and line functions, is being evaluated by how much it contributes to advancing the organization's mission and achieving organizational goals. Executives in all types of organizations, from the largest corporations to the smallest nonprofit groups, ask for evidence of program *impact*—particularly when budgets are reviewed, when new budgets are negotiated, or when organizations are downsized to be more competitive.

THE PUSH FOR MEASURABLE RESULTS

A "results orientation" of top management accounts for much of the increased use of computers to track program progress and of evaluation research to measure impact. Many executives look at unsupported claims with suspicion. As CEO of Biz360, Mon Tsang, put it, "It's almost inconceivable to invest money in a significant program like communications without understanding the results."[4]

More sophisticated use of measurable outcome criteria in public relations objectives (see the "Management by Objectives" section of Chapter 12) also makes it possible to measure program impact. Fewer and fewer practitioners get by with the claim that program impact cannot be measured: "It's intangible." The following exchange captures the essence of the problem in taking the position that public relations results are not measurable.

"Why not?"

"They're intangible. You can't actually see the results of public relations."

"Why should I pay you for something that can't be detected—what you call 'intangible results'?"

"Because public relations is different and can't be held to the same performance standards as other departments."

"Well, O.K. Here's your money."

"Where? I don't see any money."

"Of course not. It can't be detected—it's what you call 'intangible.'"

Surely knowledge outcomes, predisposition changes, and behavior can be measured. So what excuse justifies not knowing if the action and communication strategies are making progress toward achieving program objectives? What justifies not documenting how the program worked? What justifies not being able to say whether or not the problem has been solved?

Concurrent with increased interest in evaluation is rapid development of supportive literature. For example, Sage Publications has become the leading publisher of books and journals devoted to the general field of evaluation research. The 1990s began with the publication of two books devoted to using research in public relations programs.[5] *Public Relations Review* devoted entire issues to the topic.[6] Both the *Review* and *Journal of Public Relations Research* periodically publish scholarly articles related to evaluation research. The February 1993 issue of *Public Relations Journal* featured articles on measuring the impact of public relations. Its replacement, *Public Relations Tactics*, as well as *Communication World* and *Public Relations Quarterly*, regularly publish research and evaluation how-to features for practitioners. So lack of available published guidance is not a defense for not using research.

This body of literature serves as the basis for evaluation research courses now taught at many universities and included in a growing number of public relations curricula. As noted in Chapter 5, the Commission on Undergraduate Public Relations Education identified research for planning and evaluation as one of five areas of study in the core curriculum. Among senior practitioners, however, there are many who did not study research methods and even some who question whether research and evaluation are necessary.

Nevertheless, an increasing number of public relations firms build evaluation research into the services they offer clients, either using their own staff, those of a research subsidiary, or those of a contractor. The latter development is called "outsourcing" (the 1990s euphemism for contracting with outside vendors and suppliers) for research services. In fact, most public relations firms do not staff a telephone survey center or keep data-entry specialists on payroll, choosing instead to contract with outside research firms to do most of their data gathering and compilation.

The trend is to contract with specialized research companies providing formative and summative evaluation research services. Miami-based Strategy Research and San Diego–based Market Development Inc. (MDI) illustrate why public relations firms turn to specialized research companies. These are the two largest research companies specializing in Hispanic population research. A staff of full-time MDI professionals and part-time bilingual telephone interviewers conduct the quarterly Hispanic Poll for 1,250 clients and other users; the quarterly Hispanic Teen Poll, based on a sample of 750 teens in Los Angeles, Miami, Houston, New York, and San Antonio; and the semiannual MDI Mexico Poll, which reports findings from 750 in-home interviews conducted in Mexico City, Guadalajara, and Monterrey. Similar research companies develop databases and expertise in specialized niches based on ethnicity, occupation, geography, demographics, or other categories of interest to clients. Farm Research Institute, based in Urbana, Illinois, for example, provides research results for agricultural companies, associations, agencies, and firms.

Some clients, some line managers, and even some public relations practitioners still do not budget for research or see research as an integral part of the process. A recent study of practitioners found that only 53 percent of respondents budgeted for public relations measurement programs, and 57 percent of those surveyed used only informal methods to measure the effectiveness of their work.[7] It seems that too many practitioners are content with the "warm fuzzy feeling they get from counting their media clips," according to many who work in public relations. "If they feel it's working, they don't want to spend the money to get the data," says another. The trend is clear, however, as more are budgeting for research "because top management is asking them to be more accountable," according to Lindenmann. He thinks that there will be more research and evaluation because "students of public relations will see measurement and evaluation techniques built into their curriculums."[8]

An encouraging trend is that research is increasingly vital to firms seeking new business accounts. The ability to document baseline data and subsequent results gives firms a competitive edge. In short, good research is fundamental, not an extra. As practitioner Gary Barton, Monsanto Company (St. Louis), put it,

> In general, public relations people are being asked more and more by either their management or their clients to justify the expenditures for a project or the program. For example, after spending $200,000 or whatever for a program, they ask, "Did that change people's minds? Do they think differently now? Are they more aware of the company?" In other words, did it accomplish the objectives you said you were going to accomplish? That is the evaluative use of research at the end of the program. Without research, it is much harder to show results.[9]

EVALUATION RESEARCH PROCESS

The process of evaluating program planning, implementation, and impact is called "evaluation research," although "measurement" has become an industry buzzword.[10] Rossi and Freeman use the terms "evaluation research" and "evaluation" interchangeably to represent "the systematic application of social research procedures for assessing the conceptualization, design, implementation, and utility of social intervention programs."[11] They outline the basic questions in evaluation as follows:

Program conceptualization and design

What is the extent and distribution of the target problem and/or, population?

Is the program designed in conformity with intended goals; is there a coherent rationale underlying it; and have chances of successful delivery been maximized?

What are projected or existing costs, and what is their relation to benefits and effectiveness?

Monitoring and accountability of program implementation

Is the program reaching the specified target population or target area?

Are the intervention efforts being conducted as specified in the program design?

Assessment of program utility: impact and efficiency

Is the program effective in achieving its intended goals?

Can the results of the program be explained by some alternative process that does not include the program?

Is the program having some effects that were not intended?

What are the costs to deliver services and benefits to program participants?

Is the program an efficient use of resources, compared with alternative uses of the resources?[12]

Evaluation research is used to learn what happened and why, not to prove or do something. For example, one organization set up an evaluation project for the sole purpose of justifying the firing of its senior communication officer. In other cases, evaluation research is done to delay or justify decisions or to persuade someone to support or not support something. The major distinction is that true evaluation research is done to gather information objectively, whereas **symbolic** uses are to support positions already held or decisions already made.[13]

Program managers use such "pseudoresearch" for three reasons:

1. *Organizational politics:* Research is used solely to gain power, justify decisions, or serve as a scapegoat.

2. *Service promotion:* Pseudoresearch is undertaken to impress clients or prospects that the sponsor is sophisticated, modern, or sincere.

3. *Personal satisfaction:* Research is done as an ego-bolstering activity to keep up with fads or to demonstrate acquired skills.[14]

In the long haul, these spurious efforts are self-defeating.

Figure 14.1 illustrates the basic steps in the evaluation process, outlined in the following 10 steps:

1. *Establish agreement on the uses and purposes of the evaluation.* Without such agreement, research often produces volumes of unused and often useless data. Commit to paper the problem, concern, or question that motivates the research effort. Next, detail how research findings will be used. Such statements are doubly important when outside research specialists are hired to avoid buying "canned" or "off-the-shelf" services.

2. *Secure organizational commitment to evaluation* and make research basic to the program. Evaluation cannot be tacked on as an afterthought. Build research into the entire process, with sufficient resources to make it central to the problem definition, planning and programming, implementation, and evaluation steps.

3. *Develop consensus on using evaluation research within the department.* Even practitioners not eager to trade in their notions of public relations as intangible must be part of the effort. They have to accept the concept of evaluation research long enough to give the process time to work and must feel secure that research will not replace completely the lessons and insight gained from experience.

4. *Write program objectives in observable and measurable terms.* Without measurable outcomes specified in the program objectives, evaluation research cannot be designed to evaluate program impact. If an objective cannot be evaluated, it is not useful. The evaluation imperative forces clarity and precision in the planning process, particularly when writing specific objectives for each of the target publics.

5. *Select the most appropriate criteria.* Objectives spell out intended outcomes. If increasing awareness of an organization's support of local charities is stated in an objective, for example, then column inches and favorable mentions in the media are inappropriate measures of the knowledge outcomes sought. Identify what changes in knowledge, opinions, attitudes, and behaviors are specified in the objectives before gathering evidence. The same applies when the program seeks to maintain existing levels of desired states. (Review the "Writing Program Objectives" section of Chapter 12.)

6. *Determine the best way to gather evidence.* Surveys are not always the best way to find out about program impact. Sometimes organizational records contain

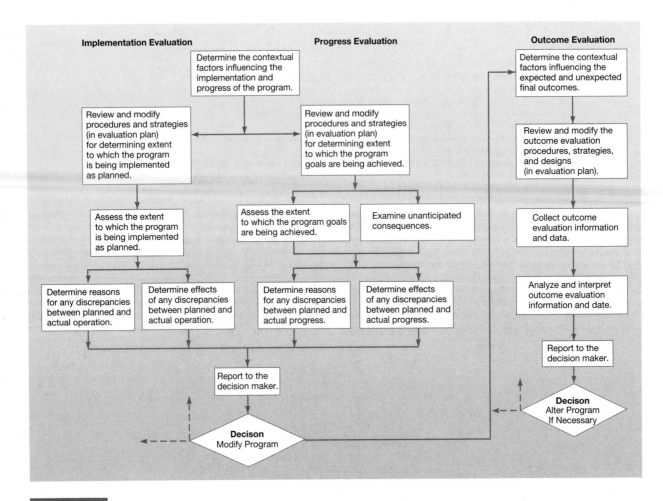

Implementation Evaluation

Progress Evaluation

Outcome Evaluation

FIGURE 14.1

EVALUATION PROCESS

Adapted from UCLA Study
of Evaluation Model

the evidence needed. In other cases, a field experiment or case study may be the only way to test and evaluate a program. There is no single right way to gather data for evaluations. The method used depends on (1) the questions and purposes motivating the evaluation; (2) the outcome criteria specified in the objectives; and (3) the cost of research resulting from the complexity of the program, setting, or both.

7. *Keep complete program records.* Program strategies and materials are real-world expressions of practitioners' working theories of cause and effect. Complete documentation helps identify what worked and what did not work. Records help reduce the impact of selective perception and personal bias when reconstructing the interventions and events that contributed to program success or failure.

8. *Use evaluation findings to manage the program.* Each cycle of the program process can be more effective than the preceding cycle if the results of evaluation are used to make adjustments. Problem statements and situation analyses should be more detailed and precise with the addition of new evidence from the evaluation. Revised goals and objectives should reflect what was learned. Action and communication strategies can be continued, fine-tuned, or discarded on the basis of knowledge of what did and what did not work.

9. *Report evaluation results to management.* Develop a procedure for regularly reporting to line and staff managers. Documented results and adjustments based on evidence illustrate that public relations is being managed to contribute to achieving organizational goals. Evaluation reports also help demonstrate the essentiality of the function.

10. *Add to professional knowledge.* Scientific management of public relations leads to greater understanding of the process and its effects. Most program evaluations tend to be organization- and time-specific, but some findings are cross-situational. For example, findings about how many employees learned about a proposed reorganization from an article may be relevant only to that one article and organization. On the other hand, learning that employees want more information about organizational plans not only provides guidance for future issues of a particular newsletter but also may apply in other organizations. Sharing the knowledge gained from relevant research distinguishes the professional practice from the aggregate of technical crafts practiced under the public relations rubric.

The evaluation process is not new; the need has long been recognized. To illustrate, here is what an early publicity specialist, Evart G. Routzahn, told the 1920 National Conference of Social Work:

> After the returns are all in—when the last meeting has been held, the final distribution of printed matter made, and all activities of the immediate effort have been recorded as history—is the time to put yourself and your methods through the third degree . . . with prayerful solicitude that you will be able to untangle the lessons to be applied to the next project.[15]

His counsel has only recently been fully accepted—if not always applied—in public relations, even though its merit has long been obvious.

LEVELS OF PROGRAM EVALUATION

Evaluation means different things to different practitioners. To some it is the "best annual report" award plaque, a letter from the boss or client complimenting the writing and photographs in a new brochure, IABC's Gold Quill Award for publication design, or a PRSA Silver Anvil trophy for a community relations program. To some it is clippings from newspapers around the world. To others the only meaningful evaluations are scientific measures of increased awareness, or changed opinions, attitudes, and behaviors. To those concerned about public policy or social problems, only evidence of economic, political, or social change satisfies their requirements for program evaluation. In fact, these all represent different levels of a complete program evaluation: **preparation**, **implementation**, and **impact**.

Figure 14.2 shows the stages and levels of program evaluation. The sequence represents typically **necessary**, but not **sufficient**, program elements leading to problem resolution and social change. The most common error in program evaluation is substituting measures from one level for those at another level. This is most clearly illustrated when practitioners use the number of news releases sent, brochures distributed, or meetings held (implementation efforts) to document alleged program effectiveness (impact). Or if asked to document program impact, they substitute

FIGURE 14.2

STAGES AND LEVELS
FOR EVALUATING
PUBLIC RELATIONS
PROGRAMS

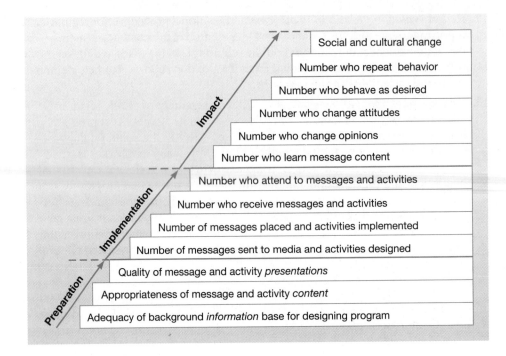

publicity placements, in the form of column inches or airtime, for the changes in target publics' knowledge, predisposition, and behavior spelled out in program objectives. Evaluation researchers refer to this as the "substitution game." Somewhat analogously, to create an illusion, magicians talk of "misdirecting" audience attention from what is really happening.

Each stage in program evaluation contributes to increased understanding and adds information for assessing effectiveness. **Preparation evaluation** assesses the quality and adequacy of information gathering and strategic planning. **Implementation evaluation** documents the adequacy of the tactics and effort. **Impact evaluation** provides feedback on the consequences of the program. No evaluation is complete without addressing criteria at each level.

Preparation Criteria and Methods

During a program, practitioners periodically find that vital information was missing from the original situation analysis. Done systematically and recorded, this assessment represents an evaluation of the **adequacy of the background information** used for planning the program. Were key publics missed in the original determination of stakeholder groups? What assumptions about the publics proved to be in error? Did journalists request information that was not readily available in the background packet or fact book? What last-minute crises called for additional research and organization of information? Had all the key actors in the situation been identified? In effect, this part of the evaluation assesses the adequacy of the information-gathering and intelligence steps in the preparation phase of the process.

The second step in evaluation addresses the **organization and appropriateness of program and message strategy and tactics**. Critical review of what was said and what was done with the advantage of hindsight gives guidance for future program efforts, but only if done with the motivation of constructive criticism. In politics, for example, campaign planners study their candidate's statements in speeches and televised debates in light of media reactions and voter responses in follow-up polls. Did program message content match the problems, objectives, and media? Were communications accurate, timely, and appropriate for the intended publics? Were there adverse reactions to messages or actions? Did the events, corrective actions, and other activities support the program effort? Was enough done? Did the communications capitalize on and complement the action components of the program? Were staff and budget adequate for the task? This phase of the evaluation calls for a review of how well the program matched the demands of the situation.

Content analyses of materials produced, speeches and other presentations, press clippings, and broadcasts also provide evidence for evaluating how closely program efforts match the plan. Practitioners use the results of content analyses of media placements to make changes in how the program is being implemented, as well as for reassessing planned strategy and tactics (preparation). Public relations and research firms are able to customize content analyses of what is published or aired about clients or issues.

In addition to the usual media names and types, cities, amount of coverage, and nature of coverage, online databases such as those offered by Factiva, Lexis-Nexis, and Dialog News Edge make it possible to identify the sources quoted in stories, key message points in the content, the names of journalists or writers, content devoted to other organizations or opposing points of view, and what other subjects the media are reporting. According to Lindenmann, "When we do content analyses for our clients, we build 36 to 40 variables into the computer program."[16] Computer analysis makes it possible to cross-tabulate content by geographic areas, by types of treatment, by audience characteristics, and even by reporters and writers.

Quality of message and other program elements constitutes the final step of preparation evaluation. The awards programs of many professional societies and groups employ criteria from this step. Often the "best" annual report, the "most effective" overall program, and even the "outstanding" professional are picked on the basis of style, format, and presentation of program materials. Best graphic design, best use of photographs, or best multimedia presentation are but three of dozens of categories in which awards are given on the basis of production values and judgments of presentation merit. These are the attributes that communication techniques courses and professional workshops emphasize. This step in program evaluation considers the quality of professional performance in light of conventional wisdom and consensus among practitioners as to what is good and bad technique. Presentation quality is not judged by subjective criteria alone, however.

Readability tests are frequently used to objectively assess message preparation. These tests, however, take into account only the approximate ease with which printed material can be read and comprehended; they do not consider the content, format, organization, and other elements of writing style. These factors, coupled with an understanding that what writers bring to their writing and readers bring to their reading, all shape the reception and impact of printed words. If used with this perspective in mind, readability tests are useful guides for making copy more readable and for increasing comprehension.

Two commonly used methods for measuring readability include the Flesch Formula and the Gunning Formula.

1. *The Flesch Formula.* Dr. Rudolf Flesch's Readability Score provides an indication of reading difficulty and approximate educational level required to read

TABLE 14.1

INTERPRETATION OF FLESCH READABILITY SCORE

Score	Readability	Grade Level
90–100	Very easy	5th
80–90	Easy	6th
70–80	Fairly easy	7th
60–70	Plain English	8th and 9th
50–60	Fairly difficult	10th to 12th
30–50	Difficult	College
0–30	Very difficult	College graduate

Source: Adapted from Rudolph Flesch, *How to Write Plain English: A Book for Lawyers and Consumers* (New York: Harper & Row, 1979), 25–26.

the material. Calculations require at least two 100-word randomly selected samples of text (or an entire short manuscript).[17]

A. Count the sentences, words, and syllables (count numbers, abbreviations, symbols, and hyphenated words as single words).

B. Compute the **average sentence length** by dividing the number of words by the number of sentences.

C. Compute the **average word length** by dividing the number of syllables by the number of words.

D. Use these averages in the **Readability Score Formula**. Multiply average sentence length by 1.015. Multiply average word length by 84.6. Subtract the sum of these two numbers from the baseline value of 206.835.

> **Readability Score** = 206.835 − [(average sentence length × 1.015) + (average word length × 84.6)]

E. Estimate the relative reading difficulty using Table 14.1. According to Flesch, "plain English" scores at least 60, and conversational English scores at least 80.

2. *The Gunning Formula.* Robert Gunning's Fog Index measures reading difficulty based on average sentence length and the percentage of words with three or more syllables.[18] The index is based on the number of whole sentences in at least two samples of text containing 100 words. Divide the number of words in the sentences by the number of whole sentences. Next count the number of words with three or more syllables (but not counting capitalized words; those ending in "es," "er," or "ed"; and those that combine simple words, such as *heretofore*). Enter the counts into the following formula.

> Fog Index = 0.04 × (average number of words per sentence + number of long words per 100 words)

The Fog Index provides an indication of the number of years of education needed to find copy easy to read (see Table 14.2.)

TABLE 14.2

**INTERPRETATION OF
GUNNING FOG INDEX**

Fog Index	Grade Level	
17	College graduate	
16	College senior	
15	College junior	
14	College sophomore	
13	College freshman	
		"Danger line"
12	High school senior	
11	High school junior	
10	High school sophomore	
9	High school freshman	
8	Eighth grader	"Easy-reading range"
7	Seventh grader	
6	Sixth grader	

Source: Adapted from Robert Gunning, *The Technique of Clear Writing,* rev. ed. (New York: McGraw-Hill, 1968), 40.

Irving Fang's Easy Listening Formula (ELF) provides a comparable measure for estimating the "listenability" of broadcast copy, speeches, and other scripts. In fact, scores correlate highly with Flesch scores ($r = 0.96$). Simply calculate the average number of syllables (above one per word) in sentences. Like the Flesch Readability Score, the ELF score represents the approximate grade level required to follow and understand what is being said easily. Fang found that good television news copy averages below 12 on the ELF.[19]

Readability and listenability scores provide only rough indicators of how comprehensible messages are to target publics. Jargon, technical terms, and even dialect may make written material difficult to understand even when the Flesch, Gunning, or Fang indices indicate otherwise. These measures can help writers gauge the extent to which their copy matches audience needs for easy-to-read-and-understand messages. The measures simply give quantitative and objective indicators useful for monitoring one aspect of writing style.

Clearly, evaluation of the preparation phase of the program includes a mix of subjective and objective assessments of (1) the adequacy of the background research, (2) the organization and content of program materials, and (3) the packaging and presentation of program materials. The next phase of evaluation deals with how effectively the program was implemented and how communication messages and materials were disseminated to target publics.

Implementation Criteria and Methods

Public relations evaluations are most often done on the implementation phase. This approach typically involves counting the numbers of publications printed; news releases distributed; stories placed in the media; and readers, viewers, or listeners (potential and actual). The ease with which practitioners can amass large numbers of column inches, broadcast minutes, readers, viewers, attendees, and gross impressions probably accounts for widespread use—and misuse—of evaluations at this level.

Whereas records of program implementation are essential for program evaluation, measures at this level cannot be substituted for program impact. Evaluation researchers warn of substituting "countable activities" or recorded effort for achievement of program objectives. This amounts to using the amount of effort and resources expended (means) in place of measures of intended outcomes (ends). Without complete documentation and evaluation of the implementation phase of the program, however, practitioners cannot track what went right or wrong, and why.

Criteria and some methods for evaluating the communication portions of program implementation follow. Analogous evaluations must be done on the action components to complete the assessment of implementation.

The phase begins with keeping records of distribution—**number of messages distributed**. This step is a straightforward documentation of how many letters, news releases, feature stories, publications, public service announcements, and other communications were produced and distributed. It also includes how many speeches, broadcast appearances, audiovisual presentations, and exhibits were used in the program. In other words, this step calls for documenting all the materials and activities produced and distributed. During the program, such records provide evidence that the program is being implemented as planned. Unsatisfactory results identified in subsequent steps may be traced back to the amount of the program directed to specific publics or to the program placement, the next criterion.

Regardless of how much is produced and distributed, the **number of messages placed in the media** determines whether or not target publics have an opportunity for exposure. Clippings and broadcast logs have long been used to measure how many and what portions of news releases and public service announcements were used by media. Similarly, the number of organizations using a speakers' bureau, audiovisual presentations, and exhibits indicates effectiveness in getting messages placed in the intended channels of communication.

Evaluations at this level sometimes detect fatal flaws in program procedures. Lindenmann reports the case of a client who launched an expensive publicity campaign that produced little use of the materials sent to media. A poll of the media found that the materials were not being used because the right people were not receiving them:

> The press contact list that the client had been using was sorely out of date. . . . Since the individuals to whom the materials were being sent were no longer at the media at which they were addressed, most of the materials were ending up in the garbage.[20]

Even the most effectively written materials have no chance of impact if they are not available to the intended publics.

Clipping and monitoring services such as Bacon's PR and Media Information Systems (Chicago), Burrelles*Luce* Press Clipping Service (Livingston, New Jersey), Vocus, (Lanham, Maryland), and Delahaye Medialink Worldwide (Portsmouth, New Hampshire) track national and international print and broadcast media placements for clients. Similar regional and local services in many areas provide documentation of media placements. Increasingly, though, clipping news stories also involves analyzing media coverage of an organization or an issue; counting the number of clips is no longer enough.[21]

Specialized services track publicity placements in selected trade or special-interest print media, help clients monitor crises or other breaking news with same-day customized clipping services, and verify VNR placements on television news programs. One such service that monitors VNR placements, for example, puts an invisible code onto a client's video and then monitors stations to see if any or all of the VNR is aired. The monitor signal decoder is capable of detecting and recording airtime and date, station, and exact content aired.[22] CyberScan Internet Clipping Service (Los Angeles) is one of several companies tracking "hits" and providing "clips" from the World Wide Web. Delahaye Medialink Worldwide also monitors the Internet for clients. Increasingly, what is being said in the digital world of cyber-space is being measured, catalogued, and reported to clients.

Services vary in how they operate, but the general procedure calls for the client to provide key words and topics to watch for: organization's name, staff names, products or services, and even similar or competing organizations. Typically, the client also sends its monitoring service copies of news releases and broadcast scripts sent to the media. As noted in the second step in "Preparation Criteria and Methods," computerization of media placements and coverage makes possible any number of analyses of the quality and quantity of publicity content resulting from program efforts.

Most local organizations maintain their own clipping files and placement records. Interns and entry-level practitioners often find "clipping the media" in their job descriptions. Rather than being a dreaded chore, however, it should be viewed as an opportunity to systematically study content and style preferences of the various media. Maintaining the clipping files also gives beginning practitioners opportunities to practice media surveillance and to learn about issues relevant to their organizations.

Clippings and similar media placement records have gotten a bad name in public relations because too often they are misrepresented as measures of program impact. Used properly, they are important elements of program implementation evaluation.

The next step is determining how many in the target publics received the messages, that is, **the number of people potentially exposed to program messages**. Care must be taken to separate the **delivered audience** from the **effective audience**. The delivered audience includes all potential readers, viewers, listeners, or those attending. The effective audience represents only those who are in the target publics. Audience size is seldom the major consideration; rather, the makeup of the audience is more important to program evaluation. For example, placement in a prestigious publication not read by the intended target public may make the boss happy but probably contributes little to program success. Practitioners can capitalize on the placement, however, by reprinting the article (with permission) and distributing it themselves to key publics. The expense of such a strategy usually makes placement in appropriate media initially a more cost-efficient practice.

Circulation figures and audience-size data are readily available for most publications and broadcast media. Most newspapers and major magazines belong to the Audit Bureau of Circulations (ABC), which publishes guaranteed circulation figures for member publications. Circulation departments of local newspapers and magazines regularly report the number of paid subscriptions, as well as audience size and characteristics. A. C. Nielsen Company and the Arbitron Company report audience estimates for television stations in more than 200 market areas. Arbitron does most of the ratings research for local and network radio. Local television and radio stations often selectively report audience data in their own promotional materials, forcing practitioners to survey all stations in an area to obtain the complete picture of audience size and demographics.

Traffic Audit Bureau for Media Measurement (TAB) and Simmons Market Research Bureau report audience reach and frequency figures for outdoor advertising, whereas local transportation authorities and commissions provide ridership figures for estimating audience size for transit public service advertising placed inside buses, subways, and trains. Attendance figures for events, meetings, and exhibits are also part of the record used to measure potential exposure to program messages.

Although publicity is not the whole of public relations, it is a large segment of most programs. Astute practitioners have developed tracking systems for evaluating effectiveness in delivering messages to target publics. And nearly every public relations firm has its proprietary method for calculating both the number and the value of news clips.

Calculations of potential audience size produce huge totals that must be interpreted with care. Some evaluation reports boast of literally billions of potential exposures to program messages. Surely few managers and clients are so naive as to think these figures alone indicate program effectiveness. Not unexpectedly, the next question should be, "Of those potentially exposed, how many actually paid attention to the message?"

The number of people who attend to the message, then, constitutes the next criterion in program implementation evaluations. Readership, listenership, and viewership studies measure audience attention to media and messages. Readership studies identify how many read, and what they read, how much they read, as well as who reads and who does not. Studies of broadcast audiences produce similar findings, and researchers and practitioners are developing similar measures of "hits" and other indicators of attention to messages on the Internet.

Readership studies of employee publications are commonplace. Weyerhaeuser Corporate Communications tracks readership of the company-produced *Today* to learn how many employees read each of the stories, their interest in stories, the magazine's readability and appearance, and the perceived balance in how issues are reported. Sometimes readership studies produce surprising results. For example,

FIGURE 14.3

PUBLICITY TRACKING REPORT

Placement Type	DMA Target Audience*	Avg. Size/ Length	Avg. Media Units	Publicity Exposure Units	Avg. Impact Factor	Publicity Value Units
NEWSPAPERS	4,552,000	1/9 page	.93	4,233,000	1.26	5,334,000
MAGAZINES	268,000	1/2 page	1.66	455,000	1.47	656,000
TELEVISION, network	95,000	5:10 min	1.93	183,000	.81	149,000
TELEVISION, local	504,000	6:05 min	2.13	1,073,000	1.81	1,946,000
RADIO, local	200,000	10:00 min	2.60	520,000	1.40	728,000
Totals	**5,619,000**		**1.15**	**6,454,000**	**1.37**	**8,813,000**

Publicity Exposure Norm* – Orlando DMA 5,960,000
Publicity Exposure Index – 6,464/5,960   1.08
Publicity Value Index – 8,813/5,960   1.48–

The Publicity Exposure Index suggests that the campaign's exposure was 1.08 as good as expected on a Normal* (= 1.00) basis.

Courtesy Ketchum Public Relations.

The Publicity Value Index suggests that the impact value of the campaign was 1.48 times as good as expected on a Normal* (= 1.00) basis.

The Publicity Exposure Norms are established by estimating the target audiences, (adults 18-49, weighted 60% male, 40% female) exposure of a "good" hypothetical placement schedule.

© Ketchum Public Relations

when Jim McBride surveyed San Diego Kaiser Permanente hospital and clinic employees, he found that fewer than half read anything in the employee newsletter. Readership was high among those who received the publication, but about half of all employees did not receive the newsletter! His findings prompted changes in the method of distribution, not changes in the content, which received high marks from readers. This case illustrates the necessity of evaluating every step in the program implementation process.

The best-known print advertising readership technique is Daniel Starch's recognition method, as used by Starch INRA Hooper, Inc. Results divide readers into three levels of readership. **Noted readers** simply recall having seen the advertisement. **Associated readers** also remember the name of the advertiser. **Read most** readers say that they read at least 50 percent of the copy and recall enough of the content to support their claim. This method is called "aided recall" because respondents are shown the advertising or other published material and then asked if they recall having read the material. Simmons Market Research Bureau is one of several firms providing magazine and newspaper readership data. Magazine Publishers of America and National Newspaper Publishers Association commission numerous readership studies to track audience characteristics and reading habits.

Radio and television audience research employs four primary methods:

1. *Diary.* The diary method requires some member (or members) of the household to keep a written record or log of listening or viewing. Recent research findings indicate that this method has a built-in bias, because those who agree to participate may differ significantly from nonrespondents.[23]

2. *Meter.* The meter method electronically records individual set tuning by frequency or channel and time of day. The information is sent over telephone lines to a central computer. This is the method used by both Nielsen and Arbitron in major cities for the "overnight" ratings reported for major television programs. A major problem with this method is that the meter cannot always reliably detect who (if anyone, or how many people) is watching or listening.

3. *People meter.* Audience measurement companies use sophisticated meters in an attempt to solve the missing-information problem of audimeters and television meters. Each person in a metered home has his or her button to push when watching television. The meter records who in the household is watching what program and feeds the information over telephone lines to the base computer. The people meter also is used in marketing research to report purchasing behavior and then to correlate purchases with television viewing. Not surprisingly, people tire of having to "punch in" and "punch out" and of entering all the other information requested, such as entering for small children too young to manage the technology that goes with living in a metered home. Another problem is that not all television sets in a home are metered, so the people meter yields incomplete reports of household viewing.

4. *Telephone interview.* The telephone interview method involves calls either during or following a given program to determine audience size and composition. The most common approach is the telephone coincidental survey, meaning that calls are made while the program is running. Answering machines, cell phones, caller-ID technology, and abusive and high-pressure telemarketers causing nonresponses are making it increasingly difficult to obtain representative samples using this technique.[24]

Combinations of these and other methods are used by audience research firms to measure broadcast audiences for clients. Notice, however, that these, and assessments of print media audiences, are discussed under **the implementation** section of the evaluation process, because they provide no evidence of program effects on target publics.

Similarly, a measure of called advertising value equivalency, or "AVE," is popular with some practitioners. This approach supposedly estimates how much money an organization would have had to pay to secure the same space or time in the media. There is no theoretical or empirical basis for making the leap from paid advertising to nonpaid media attention. Yet, because the numbers can be so impressive, many practitioners use this measure of the "return on investment" to build their case for public relations "effectiveness." As the head of research at Ogilvy Public Relations Worldwide, David Michaelson, said, "To claim that advertising equivalency can be determined for PR activities is one of the greatest urban legends of our industry." Even more to the point, Jack Bergen, former president of the Council of PR Firms and now senior vice president of Siemens Corporation, concluded that, "AVE is [a] totally inappropriate measure for what we do."[25]

So, what are appropriate measures of program **impact**? The answer depends on the level of outcomes specified in the program objectives and goal. Note that the methods discussed in this section address only how well the program was **implemented**, not if it caused the intended outcomes—**impact**. Impact is the next level of program evaluation.

Impact Criteria and Methods

As a practitioner once put it, "We must not only seek results, we must be able to measure them." But, according to Katie Delahaye Paine, a pioneer in the field of public relations measurement, even though many organizations already have the data to measure program outcome, they do not: "The motivation is fear—absolute terror of what happens if I'm putting all this effort into stuff and nothing is really happening"[26] Perhaps for this reason, 83 percent of all organizations responding to a survey marked "no formal review" when asked how often they measure the return on investments made in employee communication.[27] The survey report concluded:

> Communication will no longer be effective simply because it looks good and reads well. It will be effective when it influences action of employees to meet the organization's business objectives and we can demonstrate this influence. . . . We'll have to document our goals and collect data proving that we have met those goals. In short, we will have the same bottom-line accountabilities as other organizational functions.[28]

Impact measurement documents the extent to which the outcomes spelled out in objectives for each target public and the overall program goal were achieved. In Chapter 11 the term *benchmark* was used to describe how formative research findings define the problem situation and establish the starting point for the program. **Intermediate** impact assessments monitor progress toward objectives and goals while the program is being implemented. Why wait until the end to find out that the program did not work? Frequent monitoring of progress toward achieving intended outcomes can indicate where changes need to be made. **Summative** impact assessments provide evidence of success or failure in reaching the planned ending point.

The benchmark model in Figure 14.4 illustrates the program evaluation cycle, showing how summative evaluations ($Time_2$) serve as formative evaluations ($Time_1$) for the next program cycle. Here we are limited to discussing only general guidelines and methods for impact assessments, because intended outcomes are unique to each program. Specific criteria for evaluating program effects should be clearly stated in the objectives that guided program preparation and implementation. For impact evaluation, these same criteria identify both the nature and the magnitude of changes in or maintenance of knowledge, predisposition, and behaviors of internal and external publics. These criteria were chosen because they were viewed as essential steps to achieving the overall program goal (working theory). The first impact assessment deals with what people learned from the program.

The number of people who learn message content is clearly the logical follow-up to measures of how many attended to the message. Most programs seek to communicate information to increase knowledge, awareness, and understanding among internal and external target publics. Increasing knowledge is often critical to increasing their interest or motivation, a sequence leading to taking action. What people know about your organization—regardless of where they got the information—affects how they feel and act and, therefore, the organization's relationships with them. What they do not know may be even more critical: As long as explorers believed that the world was flat, they dared not sail too far toward the horizon. Similarly, what people know or do not know about issues and events may influence opinions and behaviors relevant to organization–public relationships.

The key to evaluating what people learned from a program (or concurrent sources) is to measure the same knowledge, awareness, and understanding variables that were measured before the program began. To determine change, comparisons must be made between at least two comparable measures: by repeating the measures on the same or similar people or by making comparable measures in a control group of similar people not exposed to the program. This same principle applies to all assessments of program impact.

For example, a gas and electric utility evaluates an energy conservation information program designed in part to increase knowledge of how much energy is saved with proper insulation. The research design calls for comparing survey results from a sample of homeowners who received the information ("treatment group")

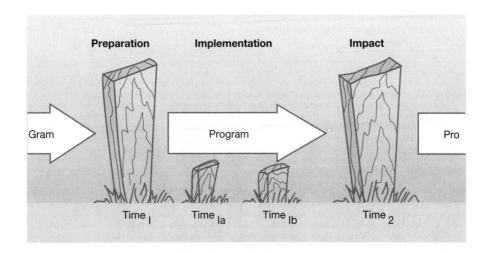

FIGURE 14.4

BENCHMARKS EVALUATION MODEL

with results from a similar survey of homeowners who did not receive the information ("control group"). An employee communication specialist in a manufacturing organization evaluates a program to increase production employees' awareness of safety procedures by comparing precampaign and postcampaign survey results. Similar research designs are used to assess changes in opinions and attitudes.[29]

The gas and electric utility may also want to know **the number of people who change their opinions** about the value of home energy conservation efforts. The manufacturer conducting the safety information program could be interested in increasing employee interest in on-the-job safety. The same surveys used to measure changes in knowledge, awareness, and understanding can be used to determine if the programs had an impact on audience predisposition. Different questions would be required, however, because increased knowledge and opinion change are different outcomes, and one can occur without the other. Similarly, changes in opinions that are specific to a particular issue or situation may or may not reflect changes in more basic underlying attitudes.

The number of people who change their attitudes is a higher-order program impact. Attitudes represent broad, cross-situational predisposition. They are less subject to short-term change. They result from a lifetime of reinforcement and experience, so they typically require time and effort to change. And, what you see expressed in a situation may or may not represent the underlying attitude. For example, just because a homeowner holds the opinion that adding attic insulation will save on energy bills does not necessarily mean that the person qualifies as a conservationist *attitudinally*. Determining whether or not people hold an attitude about energy conservation requires measuring their predisposition across many energy use issues and situations. (Review the "Orientation" section of Chapter 8 for the distinction between opinions and attitudes.)

The number of people who act in the desired fashion—behavioral change—likewise may or may not follow a sequence of knowledge and predisposition changes. Chain-link fences, for example, negate the need for informational and persuasive communications designed to keep all but the most determined people from entering restricted areas. Seldom do public relations programs have such powers, so typically people must be informed and persuaded before behavioral changes occur. Assessments of program impact on behavior include self-reports of behavior through surveys, direct observation of people's actions, and indirect observation through the examination of official records or other "tracks" left by those engaging or not engaging in the behavior.

Surveys sometimes yield unreliable measures of behavior, especially if respondents are asked to report sensitive or socially acceptable actions. Not surprisingly, few employees willingly report that they ignored management policy. Folks tend to claim more viewing of public television programs than detected by other audience measures. Imagine how many students would admit not doing assigned readings on the professor's class survey, or how many taxpayers would mark, "Yes, I cheated on last year's income taxes" on an IRS questionnaire! With validation questions built into the survey, however, many types of behavior can be measured using survey methods.

Examples of direct observation are turnstiles at events, head counts at meetings, tallies of telephone or mail responses, and participant observation. The local Red Cross or blood bank does not need to develop an elaborate measurement technique to determine how many people respond to a call for donations of a rare blood type. Nor does an organization hire a research consultant to learn if protesters stopped picketing in the main lobby. Some public relations research executives have even considered using direct observation in the form of ethnography—observing people in their natural habitats, such as in their homes or at the store—but this method is expensive and hard for clients to understand.[30] Indirect methods for observing behavior include a social service agency's records of client appointments, a museum's maintenance records showing where worn floor tiles are most frequently replaced, and library checkout records. By studying these by-products of behavior, assessments are made about how many people used agency services, which areas or exhibits in the museum are most popular, and how many students checked out assigned public relations reference books. This type of observation technique is called "unobtrusive measures."[31] This approach to assessing impact does not depend on the cooperation of those being observed, and the measurement technique does not contaminate the behavior being observed.

One example of a campaign that apparently resulted in behavior change—as measured by indirect methods—was the National Park Service's "Keep Yosemite Bears Wild," which educated campers about how their own behavior—feeding wild bears—was encouraging these animals to become more aggressive in damaging people's cars and other property in their search for human food. The campaign strategy was "to shift responsibility for the situation to people by persuading visitors to act properly, rather than blaming the bears." As a result of the campaign, implemented from April to October 1999, incidents of property damage at Yosemite National Park fell from about 1,600 in 1998 to 760 in 1999; the examination of property damage records served in this case as an indirect measure of changed human behavior (as well as changed bear behavior!).[32]

In summary, measures of behavior call for a combination of research skills and ingenuity to get valid evidence for the evaluation and to avoid influencing the behavior of those being observed.

Public relations programs are usually designed to increase **the number of people who repeat or sustain the desired behavior**. Counts of the number of people who give up smoking on the day of the Great American Smokeout are not sufficient measures of program success for those wanting to decrease the number of people engaging in this health-threatening habit. As any reformed smoker will attest, success in quitting cannot be determined by checking only once shortly after a quit-smoking program.

Evaluation must include follow-up measures sometimes continuing for months or even years. United Nations family-planning programs are more interested in repeated use of contraceptive methods, not just short-term trials motivated by an educational movie and samples. The same applies to those interested in assessing the impact of safe-sex education programs among at-risk high school and college populations. Evaluating program success in changing long-term behavior calls for an extended period of observation and measurement to document program impact.

At some point in this series of impact levels, the program goal is achieved or the problem solved. Election and referendum results, legislative victories or defeats, and fund balances provide summative indications of the success or failure of political, lobbying, and fund-raising programs, respectively. The program goal spells out the appropriate summative evaluation criteria. It should also be clear that evaluation must extend to this level, because it is possible that some or many of the intermediate impact outcomes may occur without the program goal being achieved.

For example, the goal of an energy conservation program was to reduce total energy consumption. Increased knowledge of cost-saving practices, increased interest in energy conservation, and even changes in energy-use habits do not indicate success or failure in achieving the **overall program goal**. The utility reported program success this way:

> The average cost of all conservation advertising to provide you with information on how to save energy is about 11 cents per month per customer. An analysis conducted on the actual savings realized by customers through conservation indicates that the savings averaged $10 for each $1 spent on conservation advertising.

The utility's suggestion that the conservation advertising caused the savings illustrates a major problem in program evaluation—the tentative nature of cause-and-effect claims. To list but a few alternative explanations for reduced consumption, the drop in energy consumption occurred during a period of escalating energy costs, energy conservation was a topic of many news stories and features in the national and local media, and manufacturers were introducing more energy-efficient appliances. In the uncontrolled environment of most public relations programs, evaluation research only helps answer questions about impact. Definitive answers are elusive, but objectively and systematically gathered evidence certainly beats assertions and strengthens the case for or against claims of program success or failure. (See Figure 14.5 for a similar model of the hierarchy of program evaluation.)

The ultimate summative evaluation of programs and the practice of public relations is their contribution to positive social and cultural change. To complete the

FIGURE 14.5

PYRAMID MODEL OF PR RESEARCH

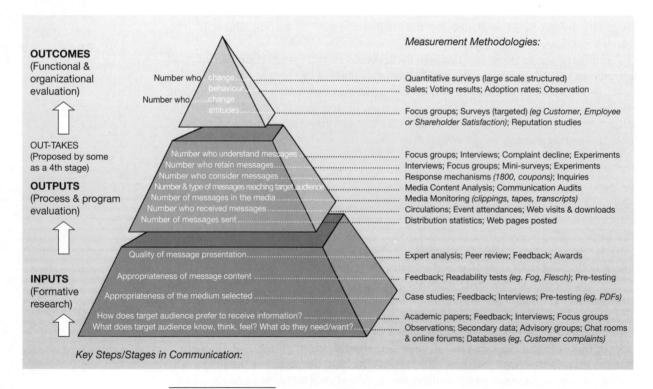

range of impact assessments, we conclude with this step. Evaluation at this level is confounded by the passage of time and the existence of other causal factors and is usually left to scholars in sociology and anthropology. Early programs promoted settlement in the West. Health and nutrition education programs have both reduced infant mortality and extended life. Programs that resolved conflicts and built new relationships maintained the dynamic public consensus necessary for meeting human needs. Those in the calling derive their professional motivation and fulfill their social responsibility by being concerned about the impact of their work on society and culture. Both individual practitioners and the practice of public relations will be judged accordingly by future generations.

INTERPRETING AND USING RESULTS OF EVALUATION

In open systems public relations, evaluations are not limited to measures of external change. Implicit to all the evaluation steps discussed in this chapter is that the evaluation criteria refer to both inside and outside the organization. Complete summative evaluation calls for measuring program impact on publics, the organization, and their shared social and cultural environments. The magnitude and complexity of the task probably explains in part why so little evaluation research is done in the closed systems programs that still dominate the practice.

Demonstrating program effects can be a difficult task. Stanford professor Byron Reeves summarizes the requirements for demonstrating program effects as including the following:

> (1) knowledge of the stimulus material; (2) control of its application; (3) assessment of impact; and (4) understanding of the mechanism or process underlying the effect. In question form: What's having an effect, who's affected, what changes, and when and how does it change?[33]

Evaluation is continuous and central to the process. **Summative research** after the program showing that program effects did or did not occur is of little value. **Formative research** before and during the program provides the information necessary for comparing summative research findings with conditions at the beginning of the program and for making midcourse corrections. Even armed with evidence, however, the practitioner requires care when interpreting and using evaluation results. Three major interpretations are possible when the expected impact is not detected in the evaluations:

1. Even though preparation and implementation were adequate, **the theory behind the program strategy was faulty**. This type of failure is typified by the common notion that "telling our side" will win agreement.

2. If the theory guiding the program was useful, then the absence of impact may be attributed to **program failure: errors made when preparing and/or, implementing the program**.

3. It is also possible that the program succeeded in all respects but that the **evaluation methods did not detect the program impact**. Observations were made on the wrong people, the observations were not valid or used unreliable measures, or the effect was so elusive that it could not be detected using conventional measurement techniques.

In the final analysis, program evaluation involves a great deal of knowledge beyond familiarity with traditional scientific research techniques. Sometimes an in-depth case study in which both qualitative and quantitative data are gathered is the only reasonable approach.[34] The principle in practice is to gather the best available evidence to manage and evaluate public relations programs.

Top management support and acceptance by practitioners are primary among the many structural, process, and organizational factors influencing the utilization of evaluation research in public relations. Following are recommendations for increasing the probability that research will become central to managing public relations.

1. Show how research findings relate to potential users' current concerns, policies, procedures, and practices before discussing long-term applications.

2. Maintain frequent and direct participation of and communication with potential users and other stakeholders throughout the research.

3. Limit reports of research findings to either those with immediate application or those with implications for long-term changes. Save the other type of findings for another report and setting.

4. Report only implications that are logically derived from and supported by the data.

5. Use researchers with established credibility and integrity and avoid using people who might be seen by others as having a vested interest in the results.

6. Use research designs and methods that conform to rigorous scientific standards and technical soundness.

7. Emphasize corroborating information over information that contradicts users' expectations and frames of reference, minimize negative surprises, and avoid early closure on politically sensitive recommendations.

8. Enlist sponsorship of key managers in encouraging serious consideration and use of what was learned from the research.

9. Take the time and effort necessary to persuade potential users to consider and understand the findings and to help them apply what was learned from the research.

10. Conduct the research and use the findings in an ethical and socially responsible manner; respect basic human and civil rights.[35]

Useful program evaluations call for planning from the beginning to the end of their process. Effective program planning and effective program evaluation are inseparable:

> The sins of the program are often visited on the evaluation. When programs are well-conceptualized and developed, with clearly defined goals and consistent methods of work, the lot of evaluation is relatively easy. But when the programs are disorganized, beset with disruptions, ineffectively designed, or poorly managed, the evaluation falls heir to the problems of the setting.[36]

Equally important is viewing research as central to the management of public relations, not seeing it as only the means by which practitioners are held accountable and the worth of their programs is assessed. As the benchmark model suggests, today's evaluation of program impact is tomorrow's baseline for the next program cycle. The late public relations executive Kalman B. Druck vividly made the same point: "I have found that research is too frequently used as an odometer rather than as a speedometer. Research is often used to tell us where we have been, not where we are going."[37]

This chapter concludes on the same point that began these four chapters on the management process: Research initiates, monitors, and concludes the problem-solving process. It is the essential ingredient that makes public relations a management function, as well as a managed function.

NOTES

[1] Lord Kelvin, more correctly, First Baron Kelvin, was the British physicist, mathematician, and inventor William Thompson (1824–1907).

[2] Linda Childers Hon, "What Have You Done for Me Lately: Exploring Effectiveness in Public Relations," *Journal of Public Relations Research*, 9, no. 1 (1997): 1.

[3] Walter K. Lindenmann, "Setting Minimum Standards for Measuring Public Relations Effectiveness," *Public Relations Review* 23, no. 4 (1997): 402.

[4] Quoted in Julia Hood, "The Value of Measurement: What's the ROI on measurement, and who should foot the bill?" *PRWeek* (February 3, 2003): 15.

[5] Glen M. Broom and David M. Dozier, *Using Research in Public Relations: Applications to Program Management* (Englewood Cliffs, NJ: Prentice Hall, 1990), and E. W. Brody and Gerald C. Stone, *Public Relations Research* (New York: Praeger Publishers, 1989).

[6] *Public Relations Review* 16, no. 2 (Summer 1990), devoted entirely to "Using Research to Plan and Evaluate Public Relations"; *Public Relations Review* 10, no. 2 (Summer 1984), featured articles on "Measuring Public Relations Impact"; and *Public Relations Review* 3, no. 4 (Winter 1977), published papers from the 1977 National Conference on Measuring the Effectiveness of Public Relations held at the University of Maryland and sponsored by AT&T.

[7] Sara Calabro, "Comms Measurement Not High Priority, Survey Shows," *PRWeek* (March 24, 2003): 3.

[8] Quoted by Deborah Hauss in "Setting Benchmarks Leads to Effective Programs," *Public Relations Journal* 49, no. 2 (February 1993): 16.

[9] Quoted in Broom and Dozier, *Using Research in Public Relations*, 11.

[10] John Guiniven, "Ask the Professor: Embracing Measurement," *PR Tactics* (August 2004): 6; Jeff Miller, "Media Measurement: It's More Than Looking at ROI," *O'Dwyer's PR Services Report* 18, no. 3 (March 2004): 13; "More Clients, Agencies Find the Value in Measurement," *PRWeek* (May 31, 2004): 7.

[11] Peter H. Rossi and Howard E. Freeman, *Evaluation: A Systematic Approach*, 5th ed. (Newbury Park, CA: Sage Publications, 1993), 5.

[12] Ibid., 34–41. The questions appeared in earlier editions.

[13] Broom and Dozier, *Using Research in Public Relations*, 299.

[14] Stewart A. Smith, "Research and Pseudo-Research in Marketing," *Harvard Business Review* 52, no. 2 (March–April 1974): 73–76.

[15] Routzahn (1869–1939) was a social worker and foundation executive, associate director of the Russell Sage Foundation, 1912–1934. He also was the founding chairman of the Social Work Publicity Council, one of the first professional public relations groups. The quotation is from the 1920 National Conference of Social Work proceedings.

[16] Quoted in Hauss, "Setting Benchmarks Leads to Effective Programs," 15.

[17] Rudolf Flesch, *How to Write Plain English: A Book for Lawyers and Consumers* (New York: Harper & Row, 1979), 23–26.

[18] Robert Gunning, *The Technique of Clear Writing*, rev. ed. (New York: McGraw-Hill, 1968), 38–40.

[19] Irving E. Fang, "The 'Easy Listening Formula,'" *Journal of Broadcasting* 11, no. 1 (Winter 1966–67): 63–68.

[20] Walter K. Lindenmann, "Dealing with the Major Obstacles to Implementing Public Relations Research," *Public Relations Quarterly* 28, no. 3 (Fall 1983): 12–16.

[21] Phil Leggiere, "Analyzing Press Clippings," *PRWeek* (July 16, 2001): 18.

[22] "Hi-Tech VNR Tracking Service Comes of Age," *Public Relations Journal* 47, no. 12 (December 1991): 23, 28.

[23] H. Leslie Steeves and Lloyd R. Bostian, "A Comparison of Cooperation Levels of Diary and Questionnaire Respondents," *Journalism Quarterly* 59, no. 4 (Winter 1982): 610–16.

[24] Will Lester, "Hang-ups Bedevil the Telephone Pollsters," *San Diego Union-Tribune* (November 30, 2002): A11.

[25] "Is Ad Value Equivalency a Credible Measurement of PR's Effectiveness?" *PRWeek* (October 8, 2001): 10.

[26] Cited in Matthew Creamer, "Life Beyond the Clip Book: Measuring Business Outcomes Is Far Easier Than Most Companies Think," *PRWeek* (October 6, 2003): 17.

[27] "The Changing Role of Today's Communicator," *Communication World* 9, no. 6 (May–June 1992): 39.

[28] Ibid., 38.

[29] For more information about research designs for evaluating program impact, see chapter 5, "Designing the Research," in Broom and Dozier, *Using Research in Public Relations*, 89–113.

[30] Sherri Deatherage Green, "A Question of Cost: Ethnography Raises the Research Bar (side box)," *PRWeek* (April 7, 2003): 17.

[31] Eugene J. Webb, Donald T. Campbell, Richard D. Schwartz, and Lee Sechrest, *Unobtrusive Measures: Nonreactive Research in the Social Sciences* (Chicago: Rand McNally, 1966).

[32] Aimee Grove, "Yosemite Puts Lid on Bear Market," *PRWeek* (June 12, 2000): 28.

[33] Byron Reeves, "Now You See Them, Now You Don't: Demonstrating Effects of Communication Programs," *Public Relations Quarterly* 28, no. 3 (Fall 1983): 17.

[34] Robert K. Yin, *Case Study Research: Design and Methods*, rev. ed. (Newbury Park, CA: Sage Publications, 1989).

[35] Broom and Dozier, *Using Research in Public Relations*, 302–13.

[36] Carol H. Weiss, "Between the Cup and the Lip," *Evaluation* 1, no. 1 (1973): 54.

[37] *Arthur W. Page Society Newsletter* 4, no. 1 (April 1988): 4.

ADDITIONAL SOURCES

Broom, Glen M., and David M. Dozier. *Using Research in Public Relations: Applications to Program Management*. Englewood Cliffs, NJ: Prentice Hall, 1990. Still the most comprehensive introduction to using research in public relations, he said immodestly.

Caroll, Tina, and Don W. Stacks. *Bibliography of Public Relations Measurement*. Gainesville, FL: Institute for Public Relations, 2004. Extensive list of measurement-related sources for public relations practitioners and educators of all levels.

Dozier, David M., with Larissa A. Grunig and James E. Grunig. *Manager's Guide to Excellence in Public Relations and Communication Management*. Mahwah, NJ: Lawrence Erlbaum Associates, 1995. User-friendly source for how the "Excellence Project" findings apply to the practice.

Grunig, James E., ed. *Excellence in Public Relations and Communication Management*. Hillsdale, NJ: Lawrence Erlbaum Associates, 1992. See in particular David M. Dozier and Fred C. Repper, "Evaluation of Public Relations Programs: What the Literature Tells Us about Their Effects," pp. 159–84; and William P. Ehling, "Estimating the Value of Public Relations and Communication to an Organization," pp. 617–38.

Hon, Linda C. "Demonstrating Effectiveness in Public Relations: Goals, Objectives and Evaluation," *Journal of Public Relations Research*, 10 (1998): 103–135.

Lindenmann, Walter K., et al. *Guidelines and Standards for Measuring PR Effectiveness*. Gainesville, FL: Institute for Public Relations Research and Education, 1997. Admirable attempt to establish criteria and "ground rules" for measuring and evaluating public relations.

Lindenmann, Walter K. *Public Relations Research for Planning and Evaluation*. Gainesville, FL: Institute for Public Relations, 2003.

Miller, Delbert C. *Handbook of Research Design and Social Measurement*, 5th ed. Newbury Park, CA: Sage Publications, 1991. An encyclopedic presentation of research methods, measurement scales, and references.

Olson, Beth. Media Effects Research for Public Relations Practitioners. In *Handbook of Public Relations*, edited by Robert L. Heath, 269–278. Thousand Oaks, CA : Sage, 2001.

Rossi, Peter H., and Howard E. Freeman. *Evaluation: A Systematic Approach*, 5th ed. Newbury Park, CA: Sage Publications, 1993. Essential reading for those engaged in program evaluation.

Smith, Mary John. Contemporary Communication Research Methods. Belmont, CA: Wadsworth Publishing Company, 1988. Addresses how to do communication research in naturalistic settings, combining traditional empiricism with analytical and critical methods of the arts and humanities.

United Way of America. *Measuring Program Outcomes: A Practical Approach*. Alexandria, VA: United Way of America, 1996. A useful guide that lives up to its title.

Wimmer, Roger D., and Joseph R. Dominick. *Mass Media Research: An Introduction*, 8th ed. Belmont, CA: Wadsworth/Thompson Learning, 2006. Useful research methods reference for understanding and interpreting media research.

15 BUSINESS AND INDUSTRY PUBLIC RELATIONS

All business in a democratic country begins with public permission and exists by public approval.

—Arthur W. Page

STUDY GUIDE

After studying Chapter 15, you should be able to

- Describe the role of public relations in supporting profit-driven corporations.

- Discuss current business issues, such as corporate governance, executive compensation, and corporate social responsibility.

- Explain how the public relations function contributes to corporate well-being in the post-9/11 era of heightened security and increased threats from terrorism.

- Describe the crucial role of public relations in communicating with the financial community.

- Outline the role of philanthropy as a key element in corporate citizenship.

The first half-decade of the new millennium was a roller-coaster ride for corporate America. The twenty-first century arrived amid great optimism for growth, sustained profitability and expansion into many new markets around the world. These new markets were essentially created by the fall of the Soviet Union and the emergence of many new countries, some of them rich in raw materials but with relatively primitive economies.

This chapter was written in collaboration with Professor Richard K. Long, Department of Communications, Brigham Young University, Provo, Utah. Previously he held senior corporate public relations positions with Dow Chemical Company and Weyerhaeuser Company.

These great expectations quickly soured for most American corporations. One factor was the September 11, 2001, attacks on the World Trade Center and the Pentagon. The subsequent hyperfocus on homeland security and terrorism had multiple effects on the business sector.

First, the U.S. economy was already showing signs of weakness, and the infamous "9/11" helped shove the economy into a full-fledged recession. This, in turn, led to the loss of thousands of U.S. jobs as companies downsized to adjust for reduced profits.

A second economic reality was the exporting of thousands of American jobs to Third World countries, where increasing amounts of manufacturing are done for U.S. companies. Wal-Mart Corp., for example, is said to account for 17 percent of the total manufacturing output of the People's Republic of China.

A third factor causing economic uncertainty in American markets is the war on terrorism. In the space of three years, American troops were sent to Afghanistan and Iraq to topple authoritarian governments. Particularly in Iraq, a quick military victory was followed by sustained insurgency that continued to claim American and Iraqi lives, among others. American companies, anxious to participate in the rebuilding of Afghanistan and Iraq, were soon faced with the realities of kidnapped and executed employees, often with grisly details posted on the World Wide Web. This, coupled with terrorist bombings in other nations, is not the stability large corporations seek when looking for new or expanded markets. The resulting conservatism may eventually be measured in billions of dollars of lost opportunities and flat earnings for many large companies.

Finally, the early years of the new millennium were marked with unprecedented corporate misconduct, victimized employees, indicted executives, and massive class-action suits by shareholders against senior management of various corporations. Eventually, news headlines featured jail time for numerous former executives who were part of over-reported profits, understated expenses, and illusory off-shore ventures that had the substance of a pound of fog.

And what of the public relations roles in corporations affected by this collection of disappointing economic news, increased danger in world markets, and unbridled greed in executive suites? As this is written, no public relations executives have been jailed for involvement in bogus financial dealings. The painful, but fair, question is whether public relations officers were kept in the dark or abetted some of the schemes by dutifully writing their news releases and responding to media queries with barely plausible information.

Corporate public relations has only become more complex over the past several decades. Although this has resulted in increased pressures, it has also created marvelous opportunities for the profession to demonstrate its abilities to help companies behave responsibly and solve complex problems.

—————————— ■ ——————————

THE PROFIT MOTIVE

Corporate America deals with a somewhat schizoid public view of what businesses do. On one point, there should be no mystery—corporations exist to make a profit and create value for their shareholders. Although not a mystery, this truism inevitably raises many questions:

- **How** did XYZ Company achieve a 55 percent increase in profits over the previous year?

- What **portion** of those increased earnings went to the shareholders vs. the management team, and how much of the new profitability will be used to improve the company's social responsibility obligations?
- **Why** did XYZ's chief executive receive $15 million in compensation in a year in which the company's earnings dropped by one-third?
- How many **jobs** were eliminated and/or exported to developing countries, and how much did this contribute to increased profits last year?
- Will increased earnings withstand public scrutiny in the aftermath of Enron, Tyco International, ImClone, and other corporate misdeeds?

Beneficiaries of the focus on profits, its stockholders, are the "owners" of the company and can be identified in three distinct categories:

Individuals, sometimes referred to as "mom-and-pop investors," are those who may buy a few shares each month and might own several hundred shares of stock.

Institutional investors own 70 to 80 percent of all the shares in corporations. These are mutual funds, insurance companies, pension plans (CalPERS, which represents employees and retirees of the State of California, owns stocks worth more than $160 billion, making it a substantial force in the companies whose shares it owns), and universities. It is not unusual for a $20 billion corporation to have two-thirds of its shares held by just 80 to 100 institutional investors.

The third category is less publicized than the other two. However, it is crucial for employees of a corporation to find out how much of its stock is held by its own **senior management and board**. A CEO who decides not to exercise stock options in his/her company because of a lack of confidence that the firm will be successful sends a chilling message. And, in a painfully logical manner, why should blue-collar or white-collar employees invest in their company's stock if the top 20 executives do not?

Ownership of stock is one of the cornerstones of American finance. Whether an investor owns shares directly, through a mutual fund or a 401(k) plan, or as part of a company pension plan, stock ownership makes a person part of yet another fundamental economic fact: Corporations create wealth. Properly managed and overseen by an alert board of directors, corporations make profits, thus increasing market value. Stock dividends paid quarterly provide additional rewards for investors, many of whom reinvest those dividends and turn them into additional shares of ownership.

There's nothing wrong with the profit motive. Nor is there anything fundamentally flawed with free enterprise. However, corporations are under greater scrutiny than at any time since the robber baron and arrogant monopoly eras of the late 1800s. Whether public relations practitioners consider this a "problem" or an "opportunity" will determine whether public trust can be maintained (or restored).

PUBLIC RELATIONS IN CORPORATE ORGANIZATIONS

Much has been written about the ideal organizational scheme to make optimum use of the public relations function. Most senior practitioners prefer reporting directly to the chief executive officer. This makes for the most-informed and best-supported PR officer because of the removal of "filters" in the form of organizational layers.

As much as it makes sense to report to the CEO, the reality is that all corporate functions have an argument for the same reporting relationship—human resources, legal, research & development, quality assurance, and others. Even an extraordinarily competent CEO will normally manage perhaps a dozen direct reports, and the heads of the profit sectors, the chief operating officer, and the chief financial officer are certain to be part of that direct staff.

In practice, the senior public relations officer is normally a vice president or a senior vice president reporting to one of the CEO's direct staff members. Titles can be misleading, though. One company might pay more attention to **influence** than to trappings such as job titles. Another might be hierarchy intensive, where several hundred executives will have titles of vice president or higher.

In practice, companies organize in a way that best suits their culture, tradition, market orientation, public profile, and other needs. A very large consumer products company with high name recognition would organize one way, whereas an equally large industrial company with only 200 to 300 key customers would have different needs and organize accordingly.

Experienced public relations professionals cite several factors that are more crucial than the reporting relationship.

- Through networking and organizational savvy, public relations practitioners realize that most decisions made in an organization come about through a **consensus process**. In decisions with some element of controversy, it's a certainty that marketing, manufacturing, the profit centers, legal, investor relations, and other functions will have legitimate stakes in the outcome. Public relations officers who have nurtured relationships with the heads of these departments will find they have more support when key decisions are finalized.

- Some senior public relations professionals allow pride to take precedence over ways to gain maximum influence, even if his/her arguments are carried forward by a boss who is "in the management tent." Though difficult for many to accept, it's a fact that if the practitioner isn't in the inner circle of 8 to 10 executives, he/she will want to report to the strongest available alternative.

- In every organization there are influential people, often with modest job titles, whose advice is highly valued by the CEO. Sometimes called "change agents," these people are extremely tuned into the CEO's agenda and have an intuitive sense of what will (or won't) pass muster at that level. Once a public relations practitioner identifies these important colleagues, he/she must develop working relationships based on trust, sound processes, and insights about the way CEOs think and operate.

For many reasons, public relations officers are loath to report to human resources (HR) or the legal department. HR is seldom a viable alternative, because its focus is primarily **internal**. The HR officer is being pressed by senior management to reduce the cost of employee health care or find ways to control absenteeism and turnover. Public relations frequently provides assistance in these areas but also has a much broader portfolio and is decidedly more **external** in focus.

Public relations practitioners will develop working relationships with the legal department, because litigation has become "America's second national pastime," trailing only baseball. Large companies are sued hundreds, perhaps thousands, of times each year in cases involving product liability, sexual harassment, wrongful termination, racial discrimination, breach of contract, and other issues. The plaintiffs' attorneys usually take the offense and make public allegations about company behavior or practices.

Companies with "green light" lawyers will work closely with public relations to determine what the two functions can do within the legal system to defend the company's good name. "Red light" lawyers, concerned mostly about risk, prefer a "no comment" position on virtually all media queries, mostly because they cannot predict what twists and turns a lawsuit may take.

Much has also been written about reporting to the marketing function. Critics of such arrangements (sometimes with justification) say marketing executives are so narrowly focused on product sales, market share, pricing, and sales promotion that they seldom pay proper attention to the nonmarketing roles that are central to public relations. As in most such disputes, there are practitioners who have had ideal working relationships with marketing vice presidents *and* the freedom to serve their many other clients internally. No doubt, there are others who have seemed to fail in issues management or crisis communication roles because their boss would not allocate resources to anything not directly related to sales and marketing.

CORPORATE SOCIAL RESPONSIBILITY

Corporations have always had obligations to the society in which they operate. Although true, the historical overview found elsewhere in this text has shown that many companies had to be **forced** to meet their obligations.

Historians may debate when social responsibility appeared on corporate radar screens. One view is that the obligations facing firms today probably got their start in the 1960s, as outlined in the "Period of Protests and Empowerment (1965–1985) in Chapter 4.

In addition to the environmental, consumer, and civil rights movements in the 1960s and 1970s, the United States saw its first indicators that civil litigation was going to create hundreds of public issues. Individual and class-action suits were highly publicized, emotional claims were made, and corporations were usually the targets because they had both large assets and a tendency to become stationary targets for the litigators. This litigation frenzy has bankrupted many companies, especially those caught in asbestos-related cases, and caused other companies to shift business and research strategies because of a hostile public climate.

A major challenge for corporations is to understand widely varying definitions of social responsibility. There are fundamental tenets of a corporation's obligations to the society it serves, but where do the expectations end?

Answers may come in the form of federal legislation, judicial rulings, or simply the press of public opinion. At present, there is probably consensus that a publicly traded corporation's social obligations include the following:

1. Provide a stable source of employment, with a visible commitment to **diversity** in hiring, promoting, and compensating workers at all levels.

2. Operate profitably and provide a **reasonable** return on investment to its shareholders.

3. Establish and meet **strategic** objectives that provide for long-term growth and competitiveness.

4. Voluntarily **comply with—or exceed**—government regulations regarding health, safety, and the environment.

5. Set aside a reasonable amount of yearly revenue for **philanthropic** purposes.

6. Maintain comparable operating standards in **every** country where the company does business.

7. Participate actively in **public policy processes** affecting the company, its industry, and other stakeholders who are part of the "public interest."

The challenge is in defining what serves the public interest and meets shareholder demands or government requirements. This is where the board of directors should provide important assistance. Many corporations now have board committees focused on "corporate governance," "public interest," and "stakeholder relations." In most cases, these committees are comprised of nonemployee directors (i.e., they are able to give senior management an outside-in view of public expectations and then ensure programs address those needs).

These decisions are often more complex than meets the eye. For example, a company may comply with current air quality standards at all its manufacturing plants. For an additional investment of $100 million, the company could go 10 percent **beyond** government regulations. Although this may be greeted with enthusiasm by advocacy groups and even neighbors in plant communities, it also means $100 million that cannot be used for other purposes—or go back to the stockholders in a dividend.

Or, a company may be operating an older plant that is marginally profitable. The most obvious economic decision is to close the plant and lay off the employees. But the company may have operated in the particular community for 60 years and have many second- and third-generation employees. In some areas, "the company **is** the town," and vice versa. Once again, social obligations may collide with economic realities and commitments to stockholders.

Many companies have had written operating philosophies for decades. These may be called something like "core values" or, as has been well-documented, Johnson & Johnson's "Credo." After the corporate misconduct binge of 2001–2003, many firms have developed new codes of conduct or guidelines for optimum business behavior.

The vital question, however, is how companies treat **violations** of these codes. Often called an "acid test," the real gut wrenching occurs when a company discovers behavior that is in direct conflict with its code of conduct. What does the organization do? Some options are to immediately cease the noncompliance behavior, fire the employee(s) involved in illegal and/or questionable activities, take tangible steps to demonstrate the seriousness of the code, or—for those with a desire for considerable public criticism and cynicism—do nothing.

The public relations practitioner is, in many cases, the best interpreter of public concerns and reactions. These analyses may come in the form of survey data, newspaper editorial analyses, assessments of news coverage, reaction from Capitol Hill, and, quite often, the internal buzzing sound from employees discussing a new concern or opportunity.

Dozens of corporations have launched meaningful programs that partially contributed to their social obligations. Here are just a few (in alphabetical order).

BP (formerly British Petroleum) is something of an enigma in the oil and gas industry. It moves quickly and decisively, nurtures relationships with organizations other companies would prefer to avoid, and is not afraid to address public perceptions that are negative toward its industry. An example is global warming, which most petroleum companies say is an elusive concept lacking in solid scientific data. BP, on the other hand, seeks opportunities to discuss its impact on the environment, especially with influential "NGOs" (nongovernment organizations) whose agendas focus on global warming, natural resource sustainability, and related issues.

BP's John Browne was the first oil industry CEO to acknowledge its impact on the environment and implement plans to reduce greenhouse gas emissions. The resulting dialogue has shown other results, too. Whereas companies such as Exxon Mobil have been unwilling to make changes without better science, BP has steadily increased its reputation as "the green oil company." BP is also aggressively pursuing a growth strategy that has already acquired U.S.–based Amoco and Atlantic Richfield, passing Exxon Mobil as the second-largest company in the world. Aggressive, yet thoughtful, community relations and public affairs work has clearly contributed its share to that growth.[1]

The Chicago Bulls are a professional sports franchise that demonstrates its commitment to metropolitan Chicago and surrounding areas. The effort serves both the Bulls and their primary publics—current and prospective ticket holders and community organizations that benefit from exposure to successful professional athletes. In the process, the Bulls and the National Basketball Association gain from positive impacts on community members.

The Bulls' multifaceted community effort includes

- A "Read to Achieve" program is active in all NBA cities, but Chicago takes the program further. Each October, Bulls' players start their new season with an event for young students at Chicago's Berto Center. Each month thereafter, the Bulls send players to libraries, schools, and youth centers to promote literacy as a key to success in the adult world.

- Special "Reading Time-Outs" are scheduled during the December holidays, on Martin Luther King Jr.'s birthday in January, and during February's Black History Month.

- The organization builds a new Reading and Learning Center each year at a school, library, youth center, or group home. The Centers are renovated with needed paint, lighting, computers, and other supplies to provide a local area with a quiet, well-equipped area for reading and study.

- In conjunction with the Chicago Public Schools, the Bulls host an annual spring Spelling Bee involving more than 30 schools. Winning foursomes are recognized at a Bulls' halftime ceremony.

- Each year, the Bulls' organization contributes more than 5,000 new books to local libraries, schools, youth centers, and clubs.

- For more than 15 years, the Bulls have sponsored "FestaBulls," dinner auctions that provide fan–player interaction and autograph sessions and raise nearly $150,000 per year for charity.

- Bob Love, a former Bull and three-time NBA All-Star, has served as the franchise's director of community affairs since 1991. He travels the country making some 300 presentations per year to encourage people to overcome their challenges. Love shares his personal experience of a haunting problem with stuttering that lasted from childhood until well into his professional career.

- The franchise's charitable arm, "CharitaBulls," contributed $4.5 million to build a Boys & Girls Club and Family Life Center in the western part of Chicago and named it for the late James Jordan, father of Michael Jordan, the most popular Bulls player in history. Current players contribute their time to the program (see Figure 15.1).

IKEA Corporation (www.ikea.com) is a Sweden-based furniture company that has attracted significant attention for its ability to deal early and decisively with social responsibility issues.

IKEA's first significant encounter with critics came over the issue of child labor in countries where suppliers were employing young children—in one case, Pakistani children, who were chained to their weaving looms. IKEA sent its carpeting business manager to Pakistan to investigate the charges. On arrival, the business manager terminated the supplier's contract and soon thereafter added a paragraph to all the company's supplier contracts prohibiting child labor from involvement with any IKEA product. For good measure, IKEA hired a consulting firm to monitor supplier compliance with the new policy.

IKEA then visited UNICEF, the International Labor Organization and individual unions to seek deeper solutions to the child labor issue. In the next several months, IKEA contributed more than $500,000 to support programs addressing child labor abuses.

The company also surprised industry observers by contributing $2.5 million to a coalition of advocacy groups to fund a global forestry mapping project and agreed with another group to sell no products made of old-growth teak, a Southeast Asian hardwood.

Newsweek had this to say about IKEA's efforts to address public scrutiny:

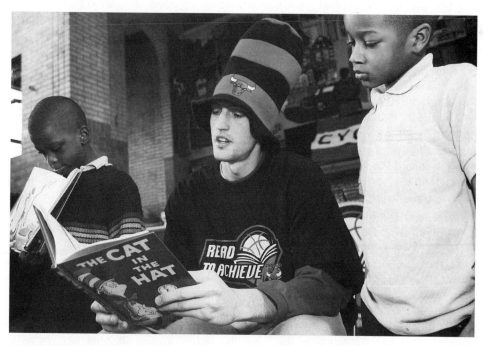

Used with permission. Courtesy Chicago Bulls.

FIGURE 15.1

CHICAGO BULLS AT BOYS & GIRLS CLUBS

> In the end, IKEA's Teflon shield is less a product of luck and Swedishness than of hard work. It was forged in rapid response to crises, hardened by strategic retreat when necessary and covered by a policy of discreet silence—even when IKEA was trying to do the right thing....IKEA has drafted a code of conduct for all 2,000 suppliers governing everything from overtime to recycling techniques. In-house inspectors around the globe will use a 59-item checklist to evaluate suppliers every two years.[2]

McDonald's Corporation defines social responsibility as "striving to do what is right, being a good neighbor in the community and integrating social and environmental priorities into restaurants and relationships with suppliers and business partners." Social responsibility is a key part of the company's heritage and business strategy.

From creating an independent advisory council on animal welfare, to working with suppliers to phase out the use of growth-promoting antibiotics in its dedicated poultry supply, measure environmental performance, and set goals for improvement, McDonald's also aims to be a pioneer in building social responsibility.

And McDonald's also takes responsibility for environmental impacts. Since 1990, the company has worked with suppliers to reduce the amount of material used in its packaging and increase the amount of recycled material in use. Many McDonald's restaurants around the world recycle used cooking oil and wastes such as corrugated paper packaging.

Community involvement is also a cornerstone of the McDonald's business approach, with a philanthropic focus on programs that benefit children. That was the impetus behind the creation of World Children's Day—a fund-raising event that takes place each November in McDonald's restaurants in more than 100 countries. Since its inception in 2002, World Children's Day has raised more than $27 million for Ronald McDonald House Charities® and other nonprofit children's organizations.

Together with individual donors and other corporations, McDonald's, its owner/operators, and its suppliers are key supporters of Ronald McDonald House Charities and its three core programs.

The Ronald McDonald House® program provides a home away from home for the families of seriously ill children being treated at nearby hospitals. Started in 1974 in Philadelphia, the program has grown to nearly 250 Ronald McDonald Houses in 24 countries and has helped more than 10 million families around the world.

Nearly 70 Ronald McDonald Family Rooms™ have been created in hospitals in nine countries to provide a place of respite within the walls of the hospital where the families of critically ill children can rest and relax.

The Ronald McDonald Care Mobile™ program delivers cost-effective medical, dental, and health-education services to children who are uninsured and/or unable to access quality health care. By the end of 2005, the company will have more than 30 Ronald McDonald Care Mobile programs in operation in the United States, Argentina, and New Zealand.

Shell Oil is a major corporation owned primarily by British and Dutch interests, but it does business all over the world. Shell has a high profile in many U.S. communities, and where Shell Oil Company (U.S.) does business, and it seeks to advance major and sustained social responsibility programs.

One of the most visible and successful programs has been the Shell Youth Training Academy (SYTA) that operated primarily in Chicago, Houston, Los Angeles, and Oakland, California, since 1993. This program worked with inner-city youth to prepare them for college and/or the workplace. In the first decade of the program, more than 2,500 high school students graduated from the SYTA program, and more than 90 percent of them were fully employed, in college, or both.

The Oakland phase of SYTA was founded in 1998 in conjunction with the Oakland Unified School District. In 2002, Shell Oil Company was named the Oakland Corporate Citizen of the Year, with U.S. Sen. Barbara Boxer (D-Calif.) presenting the award. Since its inception in 1992, the Oakland program has awarded nearly $1 million in scholarships to graduates of the SYTA program. (The Los Angeles 2004 graduates are shown in Figure 15.2.)

Habitat for Humanity is an excellent example of a nonprofit organization that benefits from the social responsibility efforts of many large and small corporations, as well as community-minded volunteers. The program was founded in 1976 by Millard and Linda Fuller. The couple, who had been very successful in the private sector, had "a vision of a world without homelessness and shacks."

The concept was—and is—to build houses with families in need, sell the houses at cost and without interest, then cycle the mortgage payments back into the program to build more houses. By mid-2004, more than 150,000 homes had been built by families in partnership with one of Habitat's 2,100 active affiliates in 100 countries and all 50 of the United States, the District of Columbia, Guam, and Puerto Rico. Corporations such as Whirlpool Corp., Yale Locks, and Schneider Electric (maker of Square D products) have participated with employee voluntarism, donated equipment and building supplies, and other tactics. Former President Jimmy Carter has also been a very visible supporter of the effort.

The foregoing are just a few of the thousands of initiatives undertaken each year by the corporate world. Some others include a $2 million grant by Hewlett-Packard (Canada) in 2003 to create an endowed research chair in corporate social responsibility at York University's Schulich School of Business; a $500,000 contribution by ChevronTexaco to Harvard University in 2004 for creation of a program to enhance corporate responsibility by addressing crucial global social, economic, and

FIGURE 15.2

SHELL YOUTH TRAINING ACADEMY GRADUATES

Used with permission. Courtesy Shell Oil Company.

environmental issues; and creation of a Strategic Social Responsibility Section within the Public Relations Society of America.

These and countless other examples have some common denominators. The most obvious one is that no matter how much a corporation does in the public interest or how much money they spend on social and community causes, they will remain visible targets of advocacy groups on some basis. McDonald's, for example, has traditionally been regarded as one of the most responsible corporations in America. At the same time, they have been targeted by some groups for allegedly contributing to obesity among their customers. We live in contentious times, and for every good work, there is at least one offsetting critic group. Ultimately public opinion has to decide which arguments are most substantive. And, if it isn't already obvious, a corporation's good works have to be visible and sustained to be of any value, and public relations practitioners have the tremendous opportunity of finding ways to maximize good works and address critics.

CORPORATE PHILANTHROPY

Companies have always wrestled with complex questions about their charitable giving programs: How much should we give? To whom? How closely should our grants be tied to our business purpose? Do we reduce charitable giving in an economic slowdown, even though recipient needs clearly increase? Do we give cash? Equipment? Loaned executive time? All the above?

It may or may not be coincidental that America's most-recent recession seemed to accelerate immediately after the events of September 11, 2001. There were already signs of an economic slowdown, but after the World Trade Center and Pentagon attacks, the slowdown became a crawl. When that happened, many companies deferred investments, cut outside expenses, and laid off employees not deemed essential. Though many **management consultants advocate increasing, not decreasing, public relations efforts during slow economic times**, the reverse continues to be the rule, not the exception. Most CEOs are willing to risk a loss of momentum and even a short-term loss of identity and trust, simply based on short-term cost cutting.

In the new millennium, philanthropy has undergone fundamental changes. One is a much-tighter focus on strategic impact. For example:

> Companies have shifted their involvement from merely handing out annual checks to becoming directly involved in programs, and the results are encouraging. The best-managed companies are focusing their community involvement in areas that draw upon skills and resources they use every day in their businesses. The days in which companies arbitrarily reacted to the solicitations—or, worse, supported organizations because the CEO or his spouse liked them—have passed.[3]

Following are examples of worthwhile—and strategic—philanthropic programs by large corporations.

- Citigroup enhances financial literacy around the world. In tandem with nonprofit organizations, employee volunteers work with students on technology-driven simulated cases.[4]

- American Express raised nearly $2 million for restoration of the Statue of Liberty by donating a portion of its charge card transactions. Over the three-month period of the program, American Express card use increased by 28 percent.[5]

- When Joan Kroc, widow of Ray Kroc, founder of McDonald's, died in 2003, she left $200 million to National Public Radio. This bequest was the largest in NPR history and actually amounted to twice the size of NPR's yearly operating budget at the time.[6]

- The Timberland Company has a Path of Service program that commits up to 40 paid hours of an employee's annual time for community volunteerism. Twelve years after its launch, "The fully integrated program has now grown to give more than 200,000 hours of service through more than 200 social service agencies in…73 American cities spanning 30 states, as well as 18 foreign countries."[7]

- General Mills donated $2.5 million in cash and thousands of employee hours to an effort to convert the crime, drug, and gang-choked Minneapolis suburb of Hawthorne—just five miles from General Mills' headquarters—into a safe and livable community. The drop in crime rates and the demolition of crack houses to make way for a new elementary school are just a few indicators of success.[8]

CORPORATE FINANCIAL RELATIONS

Chapters 1 and 6 discussed some of the responsibilities of financial public relations. Depending on whether this function reports to the chief financial officer or the vice president of public relations, several factors make this job one of the most demanding—and perhaps the least forgiving—jobs in an organization. Reasons include

- Financial public relations serves many clients, including stockholders, financial analysts, pension fund managers, financial and business editors and reporters, the internal organization (CEO, CFO, controller, treasurer, investor relations director, general counsel, heads of business units, and others), the board of directors, and, in some cases, the Securities and Exchange Commission and the various stock exchanges (NASDQ, New York Stock Exchange, Tokyo Exchange, etc.). These audiences have widely varied expectations and always-tight deadlines.

- Financial public relations is quite literally a zero-defect operation. Typographical errors in earnings statements, news releases regarding mergers or acquisitions, annual, or quarterly reports—all carefully proofread by many internal and external reviewers—are unacceptable.

- The financial community speaks its own dialect, and a public relations practitioner who is not conversant with the language of a balance sheet or SEC filing will be at a distinct disadvantage.

- In a so-called bear market, with depressed stock prices reflecting a soft economy, financial public relations and investor relations professionals must deal with an increasingly anxious (even hostile) group of shareholders, sometimes called "the dissatisfied investor class."[9] The challenge is to persuade investors to ride out an economic slump *with* the company.

- Some of financial public relations' clientele may not check the company's stock price more than once a week. Others will check every hour, especially when the company has just announced news of some substance. Any time the stock price takes an unexpected dip of perhaps 3 to 10 percent, key clients will want to know **why**. It may result from an industry analyst writing a negative review of the company's earnings outlook. It could also be attributed to a large sell-off of stock (often called "profit taking") fueled by a recent rise in the company's stock price. Sometimes, however, the drop in the stock price can be attributed to something said (and perhaps misinterpreted) in response to a news media query. In this case, it doesn't really matter whether the "fault" lies with the public relations practitioner or the reporter.

- Financial public relations professionals have access to highly confidential and time-sensitive information that requires extraordinary discretion, lest the practitioner be guilty of insider trading or releasing information prematurely.

- The financial public relations manager is frequently chosen to answer media queries about the company CEO's compensation and perks. This may be the origin of the term "being between a rock and a hard place." Questions about "golden parachutes" (lucrative severance packages for departing CEOs) are especially difficult to explain to shareholders. So are questions asked in the context of "executive greed." The best of all worlds is to have the most profitable company *and* the best-paid CEO in an industry because his/her compensation is based on results. The flip side is having declining earnings when the CEO is collecting significantly increased base pay, bonuses, and stock options. All of this suggests that financial public relations managers need to be very "nimble."

- Another complex challenge is communicating about mergers, acquisitions, and divestitures. Loaded with SEC confidentiality implications and the need for formal shareholder approval, these situations require exquisite planning between two corporations, with numerous eventual publics to satisfy. The transactions often reflect good news for one party and not-so-good news for the other. Or, the "deal" may be good for both companies, though thousands of employees will lose their jobs when negotiations are consummated. In fact, when two companies of comparable size go through a merger, it is assumed that in two to three years, only 50 to 60 percent of the workforce will remain. And, there is growing evidence that mergers and/or acquisitions may not deliver the profits promised. In one study of 168 mergers between 1981 and 2001, takeovers by big firms were said to have "destroyed" $226 billion in shareholder value, whereas takeovers by small firms generated $8 billion in "shareholder wealth."[10]

Much of this section may read like a future obituary for a hard-working financial public relations professional. The good news is a definite flip side for those who succeed and master the world of financial communications. Those who prosper have a leg up on the competition for the next big communications job in the company. They have tackled some of the toughest tasks the company could dish out, and their victories are obvious. Some of the survivors will want to broaden their portfolio and parlay their communications successes into a job in one of the line business units. They may also find themselves in high demand by executive recruiters who never have enough outstanding financial public relations practitioners to present to their clients.

BUSINESS MISCONDUCT

It's unlikely the American corporate sector has ever had a rockier ride than what occurred in 2001–2003, with the legal—civil and criminal—implications continuing well beyond. Not only was there a significant economic recession and great unrest because of terrorism around the world, but also a large number of corporations and their leaders committed felonies and lost substantial levels of public trust. For each, there were dire public relations implications, along with severe questions about whether each company's practitioners were even factors in damage control.

The cases appear to have many similarities. Each began with a revelation of inaccurate SEC filings, earnings statements, or listings of debt. Then various government agencies announced an investigation to determine if laws were broken. When the government was confident its case was solid, various high-profile defendants were arrested, usually at about 6 A.M. at their residences, and led away in handcuffs—with the news media informed well in advance.

The arrest scenario has occurred so often that it is now known as the "Perp Walk." Next, the company's board files lawsuits against the management, their outside auditors, and anyone else responsible for the economic collapse. Eventually prosecutors and defense attorneys jawbone until there is agreement on a list of charges or a plea bargain that spares some defendants a trial. If the case goes to trial, the star witnesses are usually other company employees (or ex-employees), who themselves face criminal charges. In return for a guilty plea and agreement to testify against the "bigger fish," these lesser defendants cut years off their future imprisonment.

Following are short summaries of some recent cases (in alphabetical order).

Adelphia Communications Corp. John Rigas founded Adelphia in 1952 with $300 in capital. Adelphia eventually grew to be the sixth-largest cable television company in the United States and owner of a wide range of properties, including the National Hockey League Buffalo Sabres.

The company went public in 1986 and filed for bankruptcy in June 2002. In between, the Rigases went on personal spending binges with tens of millions of dollars in Adelphia funds. When John Rigas, sons Timothy and Michael, and two former

FIGURE 15.3

Used with permission. Courtesy Rex Babin, Sacramento Bee.

Adelphia executives were arrested on July 24, 2002, and charged with 24 crimes, the company's stock had plunged from $28.80 to 15 cents per share in just seven months, costing investors about $60 billion.[11]

The Rigases' alleged misdeeds began about 1999 and included: obtaining loans totaling $3.1 billion using Adelphia as the guarantor; artificially enhancing the company's balance sheet by adding 140,000 nonexistent cable subscribers; using $241 million in company funds to pay off personal loans; issuing inaccurate press releases and earnings reports;[12] buying more than 100 luxury residences in New York, Colorado, and Mexico; taking about $1 million per month in secret cash payments from the company in order to fund John Rigas' lavish lifestyle; and filing inaccurate financial reports in order to persuade investors that Adelphia was a better investment than was the case.[13]

During the defendants' trials in U.S. District Court in New York City, government prosecutors repeatedly returned to a common theme: The defendants had used Adelphia as their "personal piggy bank."

Arthur Andersen. If there is a corporate version of the death sentence, it aptly describes the fate of Arthur Andersen, once a respected Big Five accounting firm.

Enron relied heavily on Andersen for accounting and nonaccounting services. Ultimately, it was Andersen's involvement in helping craft some of the most troublesome business ventures and off-the-books financial dealings that eventually torpedoed Enron, too. The conflict of interest in establishing a business venture and then auditing its results apparently never occurred to Andersen.

When Enron came under intense public and government scrutiny, the Andersen team did a terribly ill-advised thing—they shredded thousands of documents investigators wanted to review. This ultimately led the senior Houston officer of Andersen, David B. Duncan, to refuse to testify before a House subcommittee without a grant of immunity. For this, Duncan was fired. Later, Duncan pleaded guilty to obstruction of justice and cooperated with prosecutors.

This pursuit was successful, as Andersen was convicted of obstruction of justice. Under U.S. law, this meant the firm could no longer audit publicly traded companies without special permission from the SEC. By that time, though, nearly 700 of Andersen's 2,300 audit customers had fired the firm.[14] Andersen's U.S. employment plunged from about 28,000 to several hundred, and about 100 of its 111 U.S. offices closed.[15]

Enron. This company had a wild ride from a small natural gas pipeline company, rapid growth through acquisitions, development of a highly aggressive corporate culture, star status on Wall Street, revelations that its accounting and other business practices were flawed, Congressional investigations, criminal indictments, employee savings plans vaporized, a decline in its stock price **from $84/share to 26 cents/share in under a year**, bankruptcy, and eventual disappearance as one of America's publicly traded companies.

In its heyday, Enron was a $200-billion-a-year company, with 20,000 employees and assets of more than $60 billion.[16] It had innovative business projects all over the world. Unfortunately, some of them were shams, and once media, Congress, and the SEC began investigating Enron, the downfall was neither pretty nor slow.

When Enron stock began its decline, Enron management froze the employee savings plan to keep its rank-and-file workers from selling their stock at a time when senior management was dumping their shares and salvaging several hundred million dollars. Portland General Corp., a subsidiary of Enron, purchased life insurance policies for all its employees, but the beneficiary of each policy was the *company*,

FIGURE 15.4

ENRON ELECTRIC PLUG CARTOON.

not the employees' survivors. Proceeds from these deals, known indelicately as "dead peasant" or "dead janitor" policies, provided about $80 million to a fund that provided bonuses and other benefits for its senior management team and directors.[17]

From a public relations standpoint, the Enron debacle was a classic example of all the wrong things to do. Key executives declined to testify in highly visible, televised, Congressional hearings. Others offered implausible mea culpas to a cynical public. Ex-CEO Jeffrey Skilling actually testified that as CEO he was unaware of many questionable practices that led to the investigations—at the same time other ex-Enron officials were testifying that Skilling knew precise details of the transactions.[18]

In mid-2004, Enron won approval from a federal judge to emerge from bankruptcy, sell assets to pay creditors about 20 cents for every dollar they were owed (shareholders will get nothing), and begin doing business under the name of **Prisma Energy International**—ironically returning to its roots as an energy and pipeline firm.[19]

Global Crossing Ltd. This firm was founded to cash in on the promise of fiber optic highways that would literally revolutionize communications around the globe. Several factors got in their way. The first was that Global Crossing (and others) badly overestimated the market for such capacity. The *New York Times* reported,

> Only a few years ago, the dream of striking it rich by transmitting Internet data and telephone calls across continents and under oceans, through endless ribbons of fiber optic cable, captivated one company after another. But rarely in economic history have so many people with so much money got it so wrong. Instead of a stampede of customers to fill up these fiber optic highways, the industry found itself with too many vacant lanes—way too many. What had once seemed like a brilliant idea—carriers' buy-

ing and selling future access on those fiber optic networks to meet expected customer demand—became a swap meet unto itself, with its own peculiar bookkeeping.[20]

Many companies engaged in "communications swaps" involving fiber optic capacity. Although the swaps themselves were legitimate, the way Global Crossing treated the transactions on its books led to financial disaster.

In simple terms, a firm might sell Product X for 12 payments of $50 each over a three-year period. But instead of recording that revenue (and any profit involved) as funds were received, the firm would log all three years' income at the beginning of the deal, thus misrepresenting, at least in the short term, their growth and profits.

This is essentially what Global Crossing did. Then, when it became apparent the SEC and others were investigating the practice, some employees apparently shredded crucial documents.

Soon, Congress began its own investigation, and more startling news emerged. Global Crossing's board chairman, Gary Winnick, grossed more than $700 million by selling his company stock before the price cratered. This came on the heels of Global Crossing acknowledging that it hid $4 billion in expenses, thus unnaturally inflating revenues and profits.

Winnick resigned as board chairman on December 30, 2002, but not before Global Crossing was flattened by $12 billion in debt. Two Asian companies eventually purchased a majority interest in Global Crossing for a paltry $250 million.[21]

ImClone Systems Inc. Sam Waksal, founder and former CEO of ImClone, currently resides at the Schuylkill Federal Correctional Institution at Minersville, Pennsylvania, after being sentenced to seven years in prison for conspiracy, securities fraud, and bank fraud.

Waksal's problems started when the U.S. Food and Drug Administration on December 26, 2001, declined to give a speedy review of test data on a new ImClone cancer drug, Erbitux. The company was counting on the quick approval and a profit windfall in 2002 and beyond.

Waksal knew the bad news would send ImClone's stock price tumbling the next day. In order to help his father and daughter and, allegedly, his friend Martha Stewart avoid financial losses, he arranged for them to learn about the prospects of the stock tanking. Several people close to Waksal sold about $10 million worth of their ImClone stock and avoided big losses when the FDA announcement came. The company's stock dropped 16 percent that day. Between December 2001 and June 2002, ImClone stock value declined by about 90 percent.[22]

Martha Stewart. The most well-known person to be charged was Ms. Stewart, CEO and primary shareholder of Martha Stewart Living Omnimedia Inc. The federal government charged that she committed securities fraud and lied to investigators about circumstances of her sale of ImClone stock worth $229,000 (see previous) based on insider information from Waksal. In February 2004, U.S. District Court Judge Miriam Goldman Cedarbaum dismissed the securities fraud charge, ruling that "No reasonable juror can find beyond a reasonable doubt that the defendant lied for the purpose of influencing the market for the securities of her company."[23]

Stewart and her former stockbroker still faced charges of lying to investigators. On March 5, 2004, the jury found Stewart guilty of conspiracy, obstruction of justice, and lying to federal investigators. She was sentenced to five months in federal prison and fined $30,000 on July 16, 2004, but the sentence was deferred pending outcome of Stewart's appeal of her conviction. Judge Cedarbaum acknowledged receiving some 1,500 letters from Stewart supporters. One letter said, "…It is apparent that you have helped many people outside of your own family and that you have a supportive family and hundreds of admirers." Addressing Stewart, Judge Cedarbaum said, "I believe that you have suffered, and will continue to suffer, enough."[24]

WorldCom Inc. This is another case of a fabulously successful small-town entrepreneur who ran afoul of the law and saw his/her empire disintegrate.

WorldCom founder Bernie Ebbers established the company in Mississippi. After paying $37 billion for MCI, WorldCom became the second-largest long-distance carrier in the United States with total 2001 revenues of $21.3 billion. Then disaster struck in June 2002, when it was learned that WorldCom had treated $3.8 billion in *expenses* as *assets* for accounting purposes. Then it was learned that Ebbers had borrowed $408 million from the company to pay off personal debts, and he was forced to resign as CEO. WorldCom was left with a raft of regulatory and Congressional inquiries and the tricky job of explaining how such a large company could make a $9 billion "accounting mistake."[25]

In July 2001, the company filed a $104 billion bankruptcy, and by the end of 2002, its stock price had fallen from a high of $64.50 to less than a dollar. When Ebbers appeared before Congress, he made a single statement about his innocence and then cited the Fifth Amendment in refusing to answer any questions.

Former CFO Scott Sullivan was the sixth WorldCom executive to plead guilty to criminal charges, and he agreed to testify against Ebbers, his longtime boss. By this time, additional discoveries had pushed the amount of WorldCom's "accounting" misdeeds to $11 billion.[26]

REMEDIES FOR CORPORATE MISBEHAVIOR

A combination of new federal legislation (The Sarbanes–Oxley Act of 2002) and Securities and Exchange Commission and New York Stock Exchange rules implemented since November 2003 has already provided some incentives and deterrents to ensure legal compliance by publicly held corporations. Some of the most-visible changes are

- "Separating the Siamese Twins" is a step to prohibit independent auditing firms from also engaging in business consulting assignments for the client. At Enron, Arthur Andersen collected $25 million per year in auditing fees, but $27 million per year in consulting fees—in effect, setting up the business operations, investments, and processes it would later examine as outside auditors. The conflict of interest was obvious, as was the case in dozens of other corporation–auditor relationships.[27]

- Creation of a Public Company Accounting Oversight Board is designed to ensure uniform legal behavior by companies' outside auditors.

- Quarterly and annual financial reports must be signed by a company's chief executive officer and chief financial officer, who are then personally accountable for any mistakes in the reports.

- Company loans to directors and officers are prohibited.

- Eleven types of financial crimes now carry statutory maximum sentences. For example, conviction on a charge of mail fraud or shredding/changing records in order to obstruct a federal investigation each can mean 20 years in prison and a fine of $250,000.[28]

Other remedies have not yet been implemented, though their logic is abundantly clear. For example,

- Make the financial penalties fit the crime. As the *Wall Street Journal* reported:

  > SEC fines don't pose much of a deterrent now, either. Consider the SEC's $7 million fine against Arthur Andersen last year [2001] over its botched audits of Waste Management Inc. In the settled complaint—in which Andersen neither admitted nor denied wrongdoing—the SEC accused the firm of committing financial fraud by certifying financial statements that it knew were false and misleading. The commission's public-relations arm touted the fine as the largest against an accounting firm in U.S. history. But that $7 million was less than 10% of the $79 million that Waste Management paid Andersen in 2000 for audit and other services.[29]

- Several opinion leaders have advocated requiring any corporate executive or director who prospers financially from illegal behavior to **forfeit the entire amount of his/her gain**—perhaps with a penalty tacked on.

- Some Congressional hearings have discussed ways to reward "whistle-blowers" who take courageous stands and play a key role in ending criminal behavior. One incentive would be to pay a percentage of ill-gotten gain to the whistle-blower. A reporter described the reasons for the new, stricter rules like this:

  > The accounting scandals of the past two years undermined the most valuable commodity in the U.S. stock market: trust. For many investors, the accounting fraud at companies such as Enron, WorldCom and Tyco broke their belief in a system in which corporate leaders are supposed to honestly boost shareholder value, auditors are supposed to ensure the accuracy of financial reports, and boards of directors are supposed to make sure everyone is doing their jobs.[30]

RESTORING PUBLIC TRUST

Restoring public confidence in the nation's investment system will take years. Public relations practitioners can either view the task as hopeless—or as a once-in-a-career opportunity to really turn things around. Corporations will need the best thinking of public relations and other resources, as will stock exchanges, regulatory agencies, and individual officers and directors. (See Exhibit 15.1 for one company's strong code of business conduct.)

Apparently it can be done. The trade publication *PRWeek* chose a unique effort as its 2004 Campaign of the Year. The principals were Weber Shandwick, one of the largest public relations consulting firms in the world, and Foley & Lardner, a national law firm. The campaign was entitled, "The Corporate Governance Price Tag—Sarbanes–Oxley at What Cost?" Its fundamental objective was to clarify the confusion that reigned when the new federal legislation was enacted. Most important, the campaign emphasized what companies *could* do under the new law—not just those things that were prohibited.[31]

TERRORISM AND CORPORATE SECURITY

In the first decade of this century, concerns about terrorism and corporate security are tightly entwined. The aftermath of the 9/11 attacks, suicide bombers in multiple

EXHIBIT 15.1

UPS CODE OF BUSINESS CONDUCT

Public relations practitioners are no strangers to corporate mission and value statements. Either they write the documents, oversee writing by an outside consultant, or sit on a company committee that hammers out a draft that then goes through a lengthy clearance process leading up to, and including, the board of directors. Unfortunately, many (if not most) such documents are full of passive language, platitudes, and buzzwords and attempts to satisfy every imaginable stakeholder group the company deals with.

A refreshing change is the Code of Business Conduct at UPS, the "brown" delivery company. The entire document can be found on the company's informative Web site (www.ups.com), but a review of the key elements is useful to future practitioners who may someday be doing the writing, with clear messages for would-be violators:

1. A brief, one-paragraph statement introducing the code of conduct.

2. A description of the reason for a code of conduct, including ways it relates to other company policies.

3. A message from Michael L. Eskew, chairman and CEO of the company, including this warning, "Employees who get results at the cost of violations of laws or through unscrupulous dealings do more than violate our standards—they challenge our ability to grow our business and undermine our reputation."

4. A statement of corporate values and management philosophies.

5. A "Checklist for Leading with Integrity" asks a dozen questions employees should consider as they create an ethical work environment.

6. A description of the way the UPS Business Conduct Program is administered.

7. Encouragement to raise questions and voice concerns about possible violations of company policies, including access to a UPS Help Line that is available around the clock, seven days a week.

8. A clear statement about retaliation, or the fear of retaliation, for those who raise questions or voice concerns.

9. Additional statements on workplace environment, equal employment opportunity, workplace health and safety, substance abuse and workplace violence, among others.

10. Policies on conflicts of interest, giving and/or receiving gifts and nonincidental entertainment, customer relationships, doing business with governments and dealing with confidential information.

11. Antitrust and insider trading policies.

12. Policies on intellectual property, proprietary company information, and protection of trademarks.

13. A description of company political activities, processes and contributions.

---

nations of the world, continuing resistance to regime change in Iraq, and vulnerability of many U.S. industrial and other public facilities should have brought corporate security to a high state of readiness. Because companies and governments, for good reason, do not publicize their security precautions and contingency plans, one can only speculate about the amount of preparation given to possible terrorist acts that could cripple sectors of the U.S. economy or cause trauma to the populace.

Public relations practitioners will recognize a number of significant challenges in the war on terrorism and concern about homeland security:

- There has never been a time when crisis planning is more necessary. Though corporations are quick to say they are ready for "any contingency," experience shows that CEOs and other senior officers consider the chances of such misfortune to be very remote.

- Employees must be made aware of the reasons for annoying but necessary increased security precautions at company buildings and manufacturing operations. They must also feel assured the company is atop the concerns, so that productivity is not hampered.

- The best time to develop contingency plans and practice them in realistic crisis drills is when the terrorism threat is at a low point. When the Homeland Security needle showing the risk of terrorist attack reaches the orange or red levels, it is virtually too late to begin developing a crisis plan and/or capability.

- One fear of homeland security and White House planners is that a preoccupation with terrorism might make firms so risk averse that they will forego expansion plans and/or cease entry into foreign markets. This would have negative effects on the U.S. economy in the long run, but what CEO would invest several hundred million dollars in an unsettled part of the world in today's conditions?

- Security and crisis planners must recognize that terrorism risks come in many forms other than Al-Qaida. Antiglobalization organizations, though seldom responsible for deaths, are quite adept at destroying property and disrupting operations through massive demonstrations. Animal rights activists, for example, continue to protest against corporate uses of test animals such as rats and mice—even those tests required by government regulations. A favorite tactic is to break into a laboratory at night and turn all the test animals loose, thus destroying research work done up to that point.

Dr. Murray Weidenbaum of Washington University, St. Louis, Missouri—distinguished educator, author and public servant—has written extensively since 2001 about terrorism's threats to international business. Some of his observations highlight the challenges to public and private organizations—and their public relations teams:

> The 1993 bombing of the World Trade Center killed six and injured more than 1,000 people. The cost to the conspirators, however, has been estimated at less than $50,000 in bomb materials and other expenses. The cost to the terrorists of the far more deadly September 11, 2001, attacks is estimated at $500,000—compared to over $135 billion of property losses, cleanup costs, and government bailouts that resulted.[32]

GLOBALIZATION

At the heart of many protests against multinational companies today is a growing sense among activists that the globalization movement is benefiting only the rich, with no noticeable gains for the poor in the developing world. Consider these statements by an Indian publication:

> Of the 100 largest economies in the world, 51 are now global corporations and only 49 are countries. The combined sales of the world's top 200 corporations are far greater than a quarter of the world's economic activity. The top 200 countries' combined sales are bigger than the combined economies of *all* [emphasis added] countries—barring nine. That is, they surpass the combined economies of 182 countries.[33]

One crucial challenge to America is that the country is not nearly as revered and respected as it was in previous decades. John Paluszek, former national president of the Public Relations Society of America and senior counsel at Ketchum Public Affairs in New York City, told the Southern Connecticut Chapter of PRSA:

[C]liché though it may be—there is truth in the axiom that perception is a form of reality. And, folks, America has been *perceived* in many places around the world as dominating. Our powerful economy and our military strength, our post-modern secular culture and our global communications capabilities—all taken together have a displacement effect in world affairs that is unavoidable.[34]

Paluszek also cited Benjamin Barber's book, *Jihad vs. McWorld*, in describing the current global unrest as:

[N]othing less than the clash between globalism and tribalism that is reshaping the world. He [Barber] characterizes these two forces as creating a destructive "pincer" movement on the nation-state (especially those Middle Eastern and African states artificially created by the fiat of Western diplomats some 80 years ago, in the aftermath of World War I).[35]

Globalization is a weighty topic of current debate. Although public relations people may not provide the economic and social solutions to the gulf between the haves and have-nots, they may be able to sensitize managements and host governments to the mutual benefits of multinational capital, technology and management skills providing jobs, a manufacturing-based economy, and export prospects for operations in less-developed countries.

One solution to the widening gulf, according to Paluszek, is to develop a "reformulation" of globalization that might be called "Responsible Globalization." This would create a natural link with corporate commitments to social responsibility and sustainable development while reducing fears about American domination.[36]

NOTES

[1] Nelson D. Schwartz, "Inside the Head of BP," *Fortune*, July 26, 2004, 68.

[2] Karen Lowry Miller, "The Teflon Shield," *Newsweek* (International Edition), March 12, 2001, 26.

[3] Paul Ostergard and Benjamin R. Barber, "Should Corporations Be Praised for Their Philanthropic Efforts?" *Across the Board*, May/June 2001, 44.

[4] Ibid.

[5] Daniel Gross, "A Company Scrambles to Keep its 'Strategic Philanthropy' Going," *The New York Times*, November 12, 2001, G-26.

[6] Jacques Steinberg and Elizabeth Olson, "Billions and Billions Served, Hundreds of Millions Donated," *New York Times*, November 7, 2003, E1.

[7] Marc R. Benioff, "The End of Philanthropy: A New Model for Globalization," *Nonprofit World*, September/October 2002, 31.

[8] Michelle Conlin and Jessi Hempel, with Joshua Tanzer and David Polek, "The Corporate Donors: Business Week's First Annual Ranking of America's Most Philanthropic Companies," *Business Week*, December 1, 2003, 92.

[9] "Investor Relations—Taking a Fair Share of the Responsibility," *Strategic Direction*, July/August 2002, 13.

[10] William A. Niskanen, "The Real Governance Challenges," *Chief Executive*," December 2003, 46.

[11] Peter J. Howe, "Adelphia Founder, 2 Sons Arrested on Fraud Charges; Rigases Accused of Stealing Hundreds of Millions from Cable TV Company," *Boston Globe*, July 25, 2002, C1.

[12] Bill McAllister and Jennifer Beauprez, "Adelphia Founder, Two Sons Arrested in $60 Billion Swindle," *Denver Post*, July 25, 2002, A1.

[13] David Ho, "Adelphia Fraud Trial Under Way," *Atlanta Journal-Constitution*, March 2, 2004, C1.

[14] Grant Ringshaw, "End of the Road for Andersen: The Giant Accountancy Firm is Doomed, Says Grant Ringshaw," *The Sunday Telegraph* (London), June 16, 2002, 2.

[15] Lee Hockstader, "Andersen Hit with Maximum Penalty; Judge Fines Firm $500,000, Puts It on Probation," *Washington Post*, October 17, 2002, E1.

[16] Allan Sloan, "Lights Out for Enron," *Newsweek*, December 10, 2001, 50.

[17] L. M. Sixel, "'Dead Peasant' Policies Benefit Top Executives," *Houston Chronicle*, April 24, 2002, 1.

[18] Gail Russell Chaddock, "The 'Inquisitors' Who Will Frame Enron Story; Tone and Import of Hill Probe is the Dictate of a Powerful Few Congressmen," *Christian Science Monitor*, February 12, 2002, 1.

[19] Kristen Hayes (Associated Press), "Enron Start-over OK'd," *Deseret Morning News* (Salt Lake City, Utah), July 16, 2004, D12.

[20] Simon Romero and Seth Schiesel, "The Fiber Optic Fantasy Slips Away," *New York Times*, February 17, 2002, 3.

[21] Christopher Stern, "Global Crossing Chairman Resigns; Winnick Still Faces Shareholders' Suits," *Washington Post*, December 31, 2002, E1.

[22] Justin Gillis and Ben White, "ImClone Scandal Tarnishes Biotech," *Washington Post*, August 9, 2002, E1.

[23] Thomas S. Mulligan, "Judge Drops Most Serious Stewart Charge," *Los Angeles Times*, February 28, 2004, C1.

[24] Constance L. Hays, "5 Months in Jail, and Stewart Vows, 'I'll be Back,'" *New York Times*, July 17, 2004, A1.

[25] Pia Sakar, "Year in Review; People in Crisis; WorldCom Unravels; Ex-CEO Bernie Ebbers Flew High, Fell Hard and Took the Telecom Giant with Him," *San Francisco Chronicle*, December 27, 2002, B1.

[26] Jayne O'Donnell, "Workaholic Sullivan Turns on Former Boss; Ex-WorldCom CFO Seen as an Enigma," *USA Today*, March 3, 2004, B3.

[27] Steve Liesman, Jonathan Weil, and Michael Schroeder, "Accounting Woes Spark Calls for Change—Suddenly, Everyone has a Fix for a Tarnished Industry," *Wall Street Journal Europe*, February 7, 2002, 3.

[28] "Maximum Penalties for Crimes Under the Sarbanes-Oxley Act of 2002," *Journal Record* (Oklahoma City, Okla.), July 31, 2002, 1.

[29] Liesman, Weil, and Schroeder, 3.

[30] Rafael Gerena-Morales, "Sarbanes-Oxley Act Aims to Restore Trust Among Investors," *Knight Ridder Tribune Business News*, August 3, 2003, 1.

[31] *PRWeek*, "PRWeek's Campaign of the Year 2004," March 8, 2004, S5.

[32] Murray L. Weidenbaum, *Business and Government in the Global Marketplace* (Upper Saddle River, NJ: Pearson Prentice Hall, 2004), 163.

[33] "India: The Power of MNCs over the Global Economy," *Businessline*, September 11, 2001, 1.

[34] John Paluszek, "How America and Her Companies are Viewed Overseas or the End of Superpower Hegemony," speech to the Southern Connecticut Chapter, Public Relations Society of America, October 23, 2001.

[35] Ibid.

[36] Ibid.

ADDITIONAL SOURCES

Building Trust—Leading CEOs Speak Out: How They Create It, Strengthen It, and Sustain It. New York: Arthur W. Page Society, Inc., 2004.

Golin, Al. *Trust or Consequences: Build Trust Today or Lose Your Market Tomorrow.* New York: American Management Association, 2004.

Manheim, Jarol B. *The Death of a Thousand Cuts: Corporate Campaigns and the Attack on the Corporation.* Mahwah, NJ: Lawrence Erlbaum Associates, 2001.

McLean, Bethany, and Peter Elkind. *The Smartest Guys in the Room: The Amazing Rise and Scandalous Fall of Enron.* New York: Penguin Group (USA) Inc., 2003.

Schwartz, Nelson D. "Inside the Head of BP," *Fortune*, July 26, 2004, 68.

Smith, Rebecca and John R. Emshwiller. *24 Days.* New York: HarperBusiness, 2003.

Tapscott, Don, and David Ticoll. *The Naked Corporation: How the Age of Transparency Will Revolutionize Business.* New York: Free Press, 2003.

Weidenbaum, Murray L. *Business and Government in the Global Marketplace*, 7th ed. Upper Saddle River, NJ: Pearson Prentice Hall, 2004.

GOVERNMENT AND PUBLIC AFFAIRS

A popular government without popular information or a means of acquiring it is but a prologue to a farce or tragedy, or perhaps both.

—James Madison

Government public relations specialists—specifically called public affairs officers in the United States and information officers in most other countries—are the critical link between the people and the government. The diversity of technical skills, organizational goals, and public activities of the function of government public affairs is far greater than of specialized and/or traditional public relations practices. And the paramount difference is the public advocacy role played by government communicators to government decision makers. Today's public affairs practitioner must possess a solid mix of communicative arts skills linked to a comprehensive understanding of the organization's culture, policies, practices, and constituents. Though it may be considered mere "wordsmithing," public affairs

This chapter was written in collaboration with George D. Lennon, National Director of the Office of Communication, U.S. Department of Agriculture Forest Service, Washington, D.C. Prior to retiring as Lieutenant Colonel in the U.S. Army, he served as a strategic plans officer in the Office of the Secretary of Defense (Public Affairs).

practitioners' believe their expanded responsibilities as well as performing under statutory restrictions justifies a distinction in name.

Whereas one public affairs specialist in the Internal Revenue Service conducts an information campaign explaining new user-friendly forms, another conducts an enrollment drive for pregnant women to take WIC (Women, Infants, and Children) nutrition education classes. Yet another practitioner writes an op-ed article describing the U.S. Department of Agriculture's "enhanced surveillance plan" to reduce consumers' anxieties toward "mad cow" disease in the U.S. beef industry. Simultaneously another practitioner prepares "infomercials" seeking to gain public compliance for stricter inspection measures launched by the Transportation Security Administration (TSA) to thwart terrorism. No matter the level of government in which one is engaged, a public affairs officer is available to inform the public about an elected official's programs or bureaucracy's doings.

In a very real sense, the purpose of public affairs itself closely matches that of democracy. Abundant and accurate information is used by effective democratic governments to maintain responsive relationships with constituents, based on mutual understanding and continuing two-way communication.

■

THE GOALS OF PUBLIC AFFAIRS IN GOVERNMENT

Government touches every aspect of society, and virtually every facet of government relies on, or is closely tied to, public affairs. (See Figure 16.1 for examples of related program materials.) The overall goals for government public affairs, regardless of the level and, to some extent, type of government, have at least seven purposes in common:

1. Informing constituents about the activities of a government agency.

2. Ensuring active cooperation in government programs—voting, curbside recycling, as well as compliance with regulatory programs—mandatory seat belt use, antismoking ordinances.

3. Fostering citizen support for established policies and programs—census participation, neighborhood crime watch programs, personal health awareness campaigns, support for disaster relief efforts.

4. Serving as the public's advocate to government administrators—conveying public opinion to decision makers, managing public issues within the organization, encouraging public accessibility to administration officials.

5. Managing information internally—preparing organization-focused newsletters, electronic bulletin boards, and the content of organization's Internet site for employees.

6. Facilitating media relations—maintaining relationships with local press; serving as the organization's conduit for all media inquiries; educating the press on the organization, its practices, and its policies.

7. Building community and nation—using government-sponsored public-health campaigns and other public-security programs and promoting a variety of social or development programs.

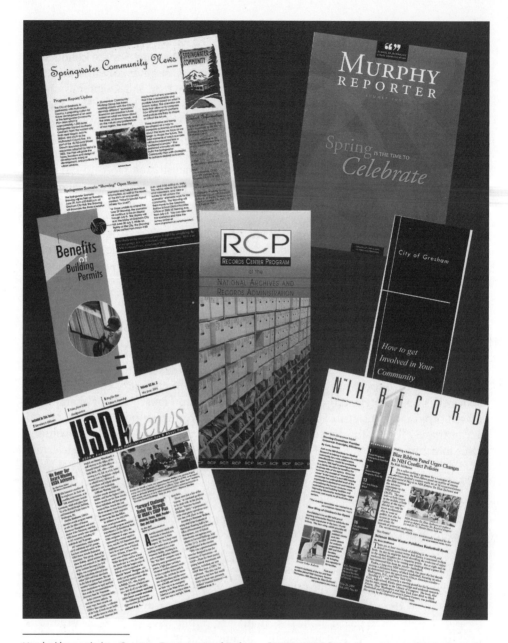

Used with permission. Courtesy Department of Defense; "USDA NEWS," U.S. Department of Agriculture; City of Gresham, Oregon; University of Minnesota School of Journalism and Mass Communication; NIH Record; and National Archives and Records Administration Records Center Program.

INFORMING CONSTITUENTS

The primary job of government public affairs practitioners is to inform. A multitude of other roles and responsibilities—many of enormous importance and scope—are assigned to specific governmental practitioners, and ensuring the constant flow of information to persons outside and inside government is generally the top priority. And the information function can be global, as the need to inform could well extend beyond the nation's borders to allies or to warn enemies. Bear in mind, however, that political systems may enable or constrain this particular role, especially when communication efforts are directed outside a nation.

For the United States, every federal department and agency retains a public affairs function, ranging from a single individual information service to organizations as large, aggressive, and sophisticated as a New York public relations firm. Regardless of size, their focus is to prepare and inform general and specific audiences on the services of their organization. Usually, these activities are accomplished through external, internal, and general information services. These information transfers are predicated on informing and educating the public, not one of lobbying for a desired outcome. Likewise at levels below the federal government, public affairs activities are usually combined to adjust for locale and budgets. The focus remains the same for all—to inform constituents about governmental activities and services. The exception of informing versus influencing a constituency occurs when information services are intended and disseminated to overseas audiences.

U.S. Department of State

On October 1, 1999, the United States dramatically changed how it manages the flow and purpose of its overseas informational services. The U.S. government, consistent with the Foreign Affairs Reform and Restructuring Act of 1998, transferred the functions of the United States Information Agency (USIA) to the United States Department of State. A multiagency reorganization plan submitted to Congress on December 30, 1998, had presented a rationale for that transfer: "The infusion of USIA's strategic approach to diplomacy, open style, close ties with non-governmental organizations (NGOs), technology for open communications, and skillful Internet use will make U.S. foreign policy more agile."[1]

An Overseas Presence Advisory Panel, established by the Secretary of State, later weighed in, reporting in November 1999,

> The United States needs to revise and reform the methods by which it operates overseas to reflect and accommodate a more complex environment. In short, we need a new design that will address the demands of the 21st century as effectively as the old model addressed those of the past 50 years.[2]

The USIA had, since its creation in 1953, interpreted public opinion in more than 200 locations in more than 140 countries and provided analysis and commentary on overseas trends to the federal government. And that function was justified by government's creation and management of media pools, the selective granting of media credentials, and the use of technology of image management to cultivate their desired global images, to advance their foreign policies, and to explain or defend their actions.[3]

USIA functions have been transferred largely to three bureaus and a bureau-equivalent office within the Department of State: the Bureau of Educational and Cultural Affairs (ECA), the Bureau of Public Affairs (PA), the Bureau of Intelligence and Research, and the Office of International Information Programs (IIP). All report to the Secretary of State. (By contrast, the USIA, an independent foreign affairs agency in the executive branch, formerly reported directly to the U.S. president.) A new position, Undersecretary of State for Public Diplomacy and Public Affairs, has immediate responsibility for ECA, PA, and IIP. The IIP is the principal U.S. government organization for

> engaging, informing, and influencing key audiences around the world about U.S. policies, principles, and values—to provide a context for understanding U.S. policy, to help set the international agenda, to forge consensus on common approaches to global challenges, and to help shape the preferences of international actors.[4]

To achieve their purposes, ECA and IIP use personal contacts, speaker programs, the Internet, print media, radio, television, film, libraries, books, the arts, and exhibits to communicate the U.S. message abroad. To facilitate two-way communication, their programs include cultural and educational exchanges of scholars, journalists, students, and cultural groups around the world. In much of Europe and in the developing world, ministries, agencies, and institutes, similar in organization to that of the U.S. Department of State, are charged with the triple responsibilities of image making, news gathering and dissemination, and information posturing to counter negative developments that have national or international implications—or both.

Globally, the former USIA was known as the United States Information Service (or USIS). In American embassies, the chief USIS officials were public affairs officers. They advised ambassadors and other diplomats on relevant public relations issues affecting U.S. interests and policy and on embassy operations and relationships within host countries.

International Broadcasting

The international broadcasting functions of the former USIA are managed by an independent executive branch: the Broadcasting Board of Governors (BBG). BBG's nonmilitary international broadcasting reaches an estimated 100 million people each week in about 130 markets worldwide. BBG oversees the International Broadcasting Bureau, which in turn operates the following federal entities: the Voice of America, Radio/TV Marti, and WorldNet Television. It also manages Radio Free Europe/Radio Liberty and Radio Free Asia, both of which operate as independent, nonprofit corporations, and program initiatives such as Radio Sawa, Radio Farda, and Afghanistan Radio Network. Consistent with the Act of 1998, the BBG and the Secretary of State must respect the professional independence and integrity of the International Broadcasting Bureau and its services. The Secretary sits on the board, providing information and guidance on foreign policy to the BBG and coordinating its efforts.

In February 2004, BBG launched Alhurra, a 24-hour Arabic-language satellite television news network in Springfield, Virginia; it also broadcasts from studios in the Middle East. The network broadcasts to at least 22 Middle Eastern countries in hopes of winning support for U.S. foreign policy in that region. BBG also planned a U.S. Department of Defense project in Iraq, the Iraqi Media Network, to serve as a symbol of a free press in that country.

The USIA was perhaps best known for its radio broadcast network, the Voice of America, which began in World War II and was responsible for providing information to American troops and citizens in war areas. Its mandate was and remains to

1. Serve as an authoritative, accurate, objective, and comprehensive news source

2. Represent America by presenting a balanced and comprehensive projection of significant American thought and institutions

3. Present the policies of the United States clearly and effectively and present responsible discussions and opinions on those policies[5]

Jess T. Ford, director of International Affairs and Trade, in testimony before a House subcommittee, said that concerns have been raised, even among public affairs officers at the Department of State, about insufficient resources to conduct public diplomacy effectively.[6] Similarly at issue are treating public diplomacy in the Department of State differently from other functions;[7] reversing trends in audience decline, particularly in high-priority markets; using modern broadcast techniques to reach large audiences; allocating resources to focus on high-priority broadcast markets; and questioning the overall efficacy of U.S. international broadcasting efforts in helping the United States achieve its mission overseas.[8]

All in all, the public affairs practitioner, whether working overseas striving to responsibly expose American cultures and value or as an agency representative focused on new policy direction, seeks to provide the targeted publics with the most up-to-date and accurate information available.

ENSURING ACTIVE COOPERATION IN GOVERNMENT PROGRAMS

How do citizens expand their knowledge about their civic obligations and duties? What actions should citizens take to fulfill them? Why is it important for citizens to comply with government regulations? And what changes in regulations are in the offing? These are some of the questions that frame governments' use of communication campaigns to remind Americans about the importance of, say, having vaccinations shortly after birth or filing tax returns each year—and about changes that may have been made in a particular year.

Without an informed and active citizenry, elected and appointed officials may lose touch with the true needs and interests of their constituents. Programs costing millions of dollars may be undertaken to address public needs that have been overestimated, while more pressing needs remain hidden. Special-interest politics may dominate decision making. Citizen discontent may linger just beneath the surface, then suddenly appear and be fueled by simplistic rhetoric in place of a deeper understanding of issues.

Even in emerging nations where governments tend not to be as directly responsive to citizen interests, public affairs is still used as a tactical information tool—albeit in much more constrained ways. The point is that the use of public affairs as a two-way symmetric activity—in which practitioners use public affairs to guide understanding of their publics—is a reflection of the nature of a nation's media freedom. The more independent the news media are of governmental control, the more freedom government public affairs specialists have to conduct public affairs responsively.

Reporters Without Borders produced the "World Press Freedom Ranking," which labeled media practices in most developed societies as "free"; those in much of the developing world were described as either "partly free" or "not free." The point is that the freer a media system is, the more it engenders an environment in which public affairs practitioners may conduct their activities without undue government restrictions. Advances in the practice of public affairs have, therefore, tended to occur in countries in which media and communications are less under governmental interference and where civil order is not an issue.

The collapse of the Soviet Union led to the birth of 21 republics, a number of which, including Armenia, Azerbaijan, and Ingushetia have had civil strife and in which "several barriers... stand in the way of public affairs maturation and growth."[9] In those new republics, "public affairs practitioners—often the 'new kids on the block' who are staff workers outside formal lines of authority—face uphill battles in gaining status within high-power-distance societies."[10]

The problems and pressures of society increasingly strain the machinery of government. Government is intended to provide services that would otherwise be impractical for individuals to provide, such as police and fire protection, wildlife preserves, civil and national defense, transportation systems, justice systems, social programs, and national museums. These programs, although administered by government officials, are responses to needs originating with ordinary citizens. As the needs of society have expanded in scope and complexity, government at all levels has also grown. Now some see government as no longer an extension of the people but as rather an adversary or "big brother." A labyrinth of bureaus, offices, departments, agencies, divisions, authorities, commissions, councils, boards, and committees has developed. Thousands of forms and reports are generated annually, most containing technical terms and jargon that inhibit many citizens' understanding and confidence in working effectively with government.

Much of the expansion of government in the United States may be attributed to two basic trends: First, increased population, social movements, business and economic activity, and technology have created new problems and issues that require regulatory attention and accompanying new procedures for the public. An example is the TSA's public-education campaign to inform airline passengers of new security procedures in the aftermath of the terrorist attacks of September 11, 2001.

Second, U.S. citizens have increasingly grown to expect more from all levels of government. What may start as an offhanded remark such as, "There ought to be a law against that!" often leads not just to new regulations but also to agencies set up to ensure that the new laws are obeyed. In the simpler times of our agrarian past, neighbors often worked together to build community projects, families were extended to include elderly grandparents, and food was grown locally. Today, government is viewed more than ever as the primary mechanism to address injustices and inequities in virtually all human activities. Examples of governments' responsiveness to protect their citizens include the Fair Housing Act, which prohibits discrimination in the sale and rental of housing; labor laws that address discrimination in employment; and government-approved services such as Medicaid.

FOSTERING CITIZEN SUPPORT

Specific public affairs objectives will vary from agency to agency, but the basic justification for government public affairs rests on two fundamental premises: (1) that a democratic government must report its activities to the citizens, and (2) that effective government administration requires active citizen participation and support. Even the staunchest critics of "government propaganda" concede that the first justification is a valid one, in that as government becomes more complex and ubiquitous, the challenge of maintaining citizen involvement and ensuring government responsiveness to societal needs becomes more difficult. Elected officials often claim credit for their election on their ability to keep a finger on the pulse of constituents. However, because of the sheer magnitude and complexity of the job, much of that responsibility falls to government public affairs specialists. In *Communicating for Results in Government*, James L. Garnett discussed the importance of straightforward communication with citizens:

> As with planning, budgeting, program evaluation, and other managerial tools, communication is important because it affects people's control over government. It influences employee morale and productivity and permeates all facets of government. Because government decisions and actions often affect more people and with greater consequences, communicating in government tends to be more important and often more difficult than communicating in business.[11]

Thus governments use communication to seek public understanding and their participation in assisting the less fortunate or disenfranchised as a measure toward building community. For example, the United States resettled thousands of Hmong refugees from camps in Southeast Asia and also declared them eligible for aid disbursed by the U.S. Department of Health and Human Services and by state governments. This effort required public affairs practitioners to operate simultaneously cross-culturally, multiagency, and at a neighborhood level as they sought to reduce residents' anxieties regarding the absorption of 60,000 Indochinese refugees into local communities.

The complexity of public affairs work is thus apparent in local government, which provides much community support for the new residents. This level is closest to its constituents, both in the services it provides and in the accessibility of elected and appointed officials. Moreover, the growing influence of neighborhood-level activist groups places a unique burden on local governments:

> Although the neighborhood associations are infrequently direct initiators of new agenda items, they play an important secondary role in creating a policy-making environment that will be hospitable to some kinds of proposals and unkind to others. They incrementally alter agendas, force initiators to anticipate their preferences, and play a vital role in the planning process at both the neighborhood and citywide levels.[12]

Public Participation

Another example is the frequently overlooked responsibility of government practitioners in soliciting and motivating involvement of citizens in governments' decision-making processes. In the Federal Advisory Committee Act (FACA) of 1972, Congress formally recognized the benefits of seeking advice from, and assistance of, citizens. Federal government agencies are empowered to establish, sponsor, or manage advisory committees, which now number more than 1,000.

Although FACA is not a public participation statute, its perhaps unintended effect might very well achieve just that. FACA stimulates discussion of important public issues with private individuals, nongovernmental organizations, or the public at large. Thus, FACA allows for collaboration as a means of obtaining public involvement in a broad range of issues affecting federal policies and programs. Federal agencies establish or sponsor advisory groups (or committees) that (a) provide advice that is relevant, objective, and open to the public; (b) act promptly to complete their work; and (c) comply with reasonable cost controls and record keeping requirements.

Often the major obstacle to such public involvement is internal, because elected officials and administrators may be reluctant to have their carefully formulated plans altered by the multitude of interests and viewpoints citizen involvement inevitably generates. In *Policy Studies Review*, Mary Kweit and Robert Kweit discussed the trade-offs inherent in encouraging citizen input:

> In the ideal bureaucracy there is no place for citizen participation. Citizens lack the technical expertise, are unfamiliar with bureaucratic routines, and are emotionally involved in issues rather than being detached and rational. Citizens are outside the hierarchy and therefore hard to control. As a consequence, participation may increase the time needed to reach decisions as well as the level of conflict.[13]

Public Opinion Surveys

Scientific surveys, which provide snapshots of public opinions, are used increasingly in government. Politicians, especially those running for national office, have long relied on the Roper and Gallup polls, as well as privately commissioned surveys, for guidance in formulating campaign strategies. More recently citizen surveys have been used for identifying priorities for government. In addition, surveys are being used as the bottom line for government, whereby citizens' ratings of various services are the barometer of organizational success.

When used to set goals and priorities, citizen surveys prove to be an equalizer against well-funded special interests and lobbying groups. "The greatest strength of citizen surveys is that they have the potential to sample the viewpoints of all citizens—not simply those who choose to participate."[14] However, citizen surveys can be counterproductive when they are not properly administered, as when surveys that ask citizens about subjects on which they have little or no knowledge—how best to design a major highway or how to solve complex financial problems facing government. Not only could the results be meaningless, they may cause problems.

> A second serious problem with citizen surveys is that they can have some serious political repercussions. The public may express a negative view of whatever services are dutifully provided. Pressures may develop to enact whatever recommendations the public might suggest. And then, apart from the issues of effectiveness and political advisability, there is always the issue of cost. With budgets getting ever tighter, a citizen survey might easily seem like an unnecessary frill. The costs could be particularly onerous to small governments.[15]

Increasing involvement in programs and activities leads many government practitioners to use other tools and tactics often identical to those of private public relations firms and advertising agencies. Many of these efforts go beyond increased communications, which often achieve additional scrutiny by both Congress and the press resulting in more oversight versus less.

SERVING AS THE PUBLIC'S ADVOCATE

Governments may be public institutions, but they are characteristically bureaucratic, riddled with labyrinths of process, and often contradictory to their nature of service. Except for campaigning, elected officials are routinely shrouded behind the machinery of their administration, rarely interacting with and understanding the day-to-day issues of their constituents. The public affairs officer bridges the desires of the official for accessibility with the people and in turn represents the people's values, opinions, and interest to that official. Public affairs officers provide the front-line "face" for an administration before the public through polling, interviewing, and maintaining constant contact in the community.

The practitioner straddles the need for communicating the organization's agenda and the need to communicate the public's desires, conflicting as they may be, back to the organization. For example, in the aftermath of the September 11, 2001, terrorist attacks in New York and Washington, U.S.-based airlines and the government took restrictive steps regarding passenger movement through airport terminals. Initially the public accepted the protracted screening process as a necessity for better security, but in time sentiment soured to outright complaints of governmental bungling. Public affairs officers in the Department of Transportation and TSA, the targets of this backlash, brought to their officials a well-researched argument to review the status quo despite accusations of being "soft on security." Management listened, and the screening processes were modified, which resulted in restoring TSA's credibility.

Similarly, public affairs officers at the Consumer Product Safety Commission advocated consumer well-being by assisting in crafting and issuing a recall of 150 million toy bracelets and necklaces that have lead concentration by weight as high as 69 percent. (Paint with lead concentration of more than 0.06 percent by weight is prohibited from sale.) At the same time, they were communicating the overarching mission—the safety agenda—of the commission.

With the support of their officials, these government public affairs officers performed their traditional public information role, namely, disseminated objective information about their agency (public-information model), and, to a slightly lesser extent, used research to develop a basis for advising officials about the need to make changes internally (two-way symmetrical model). This mix of models suggests a mixed-motive approach in which organizations seek to balance their own interests with those of their stakeholders.[16]

For example, when the Forest Service surveyed its publics about their values with respect to public lands the results indicated two categories of mutual interest:

1. Socially responsible individual values—respondents have a strong orientation toward environmental protection.

2. Socially responsible management values—the public holds a moderately strong conservation and preservation ethic.[17]

Cast against the background of what the Forest Service knows about the values of its publics vis-à-vis use of public lands on a national scale, the agency's Lake Tahoe Basin Management Unit conducted several studies of Americans' outdoor use preferences in the Pacific Northwest. The findings indicated, for example, that residents in communities close to the Zephyr Cove Resort Campground on the eastern shore of South Lake Tahoe would like not just a closer recreational facility, but one that catered to their eclectic interests: hiking and biking trails and Internet and television use. A Forest Service–private interest partnership was established to raise funds to cover the renovation project, which demonstrated the reach and value of government public affairs. The agency also sought upgrades on water quality in the area, and, as a by-product of that effort, added water controls and containment ponds, which improved the overall visual experience for campground visitors.

The public affairs office at the Management Unit used public relations research techniques to determine the public's needs and then used the findings for planning the recreation facilities. Zephyr, then a run-down camping facility in a prized location, now has numerous upgrades that include improved water quality, Internet and television hook-ups, laundry, and shower facilities. For an effective response to customers' needs, the Management Unit received the 2003 "Best in the Basin Award" from the Tahoe Regional Planning Agency.

ELECTRONIC GOVERNMENT AND CITIZEN PARTICIPATION

Governments in developed democracies, more so than those in developing countries, view information as a rights issue: that citizens are entitled to information on the workings of their government. In 2000, Sweden became the first country in the world to adopt a policy that promotes the civic and political uses of information and communication technology to enhance democracy.[18] That national policy will aid Sweden's focus toward becoming an electronic information-sharing society using the latest technology to communicate between each other and their government.

Even though the United States officially may not be an "information nation" in the same vein as Sweden, its federal government uses information and communication technologies to deliver a range of services and benefits to the American people and to encourage citizen participation in governance—electronic government ("e-gov" for short).

The Forest Service has a handful of e-gov initiatives underway, two of which will have major implications for how the agency, and eventually all of government, will enable citizens to participate in governance: (1) delivering Web-based information to internal and external constituents on demand, and (2) improving public access to Forest Service services by responding quickly and accurately to information requests, including those made under the Freedom of Information Act and those for commonly requested products, records, data, and documents. The public accesses Forest Service research publications through online "Treesearch" (www.treesearch.fs.fed.us) for locating and delivering publications by the agency's Research and Development scientists, as well as papers written by its scientists but published by other organizations in their journals, conference proceedings, or books.

But there is an area in which e-gov may not be a reality for a while in the United States—in the exercise of a citizen's fundamental right to participate in the nation's democratic process. For example, electronic voting for six million military service personnel and other Americans living abroad remains far-fetched. Secure Electronic Registration and Voting Experiment, a voting initiative, has been criticized for design weaknesses and security flaws that make it an easy target for saboteurs, yet the current paper voting system does not serve the interests of U.S. voters abroad, if it prevents or discourages them from voting.[19]

MANAGING INFORMATION INTERNALLY

Communicating internally is yet another major function of government public affairs. Although such communication per se is common in organizations, it assumes a unique significance in government for two key reasons. First, because of the near-instantaneous public dissemination of an organization's statement, policy pronouncement, or action, it is critical that all echelons of the organization be aware of and conversant with the issues. Second, rumors or half-truths may be destructive or counterproductive to any organization, but it is absolutely disastrous to governmental organizations.

All federal agencies, even the Central Intelligence Agency, maintain a public reception area or information room staffed by information specialists at their office locations. These frontline employees meeting the public must be fully familiar with the organization's policies, proposed changes, and practices, and not merely focused on the local available services. Employees must be apprised of organizational developments not so much because they may have to field questions from the media—a responsibility primary for the media staff—but because they work in the public domain and can better respond to public requests or concerns if they are current on the issues of the day. Their knowledge of issues fosters an immediate dissemination of key messages directly to a using or inquiring constituent.

The Department of Defense has no equal when it comes to managing internal information, which only further strengthens its external image. Each base, post, ship, and camp has what is commonly referred to as a Command Information (CI) program. The CI staff gathers the most current local information of the day and provides it to military members and their families through newspapers, closed circuit/cable access television, Web sites, bulletin boards, and/or daily briefings. Nearly all military organizations have weekly newsletters, newcomer's magazines, and special announcement papers, and many are using an "in-house" electronic information service or intranet. Military members, their families, and on-base civilian employees are kept well informed on the local, national, and global issues of the day, prepared and provided by fellow service members. This top-driven, timely information reduces rumors and anxieties associated with not understanding the current situation. And it provides ready mouthpieces to the public explaining policies or action in "their own words."

Additionally, government agencies work in partnership with one another; therefore, keeping up to date on interagency activities has a symbiotic, interagency significance.

Forest Service employees, for example, collaborate extensively through the intranet with other agencies such as the U.S. Department of State and the U.S. Department of Interior—particularly the latter's Fish and Wildlife Service and its Bureau of Land Management. Forest Service employees, as well as those in Interior, must be well informed about predictions relevant to movements of wildfires, regional threats to specific endangered wildlife, or mitigating environmental damage due to human activities. Such knowledge enables all to play meaningful roles as partners in service to communities, to interest groups, and to the nation.

FACILITATING MEDIA RELATIONS

Democratic traditions require that a nation's governmental agencies be accessible to the news media, hence media relations is a fundamental function of public affairs officers. The very nature of governmental programs makes their stakes so high that media interest is also high. Political theorist Jodi Dean succinctly captured the essence of that interest: "Democracy needs media."[20]

The National Media Desk of the Office of Communication in the Forest Service was created specifically to meet media outlets' expectation for timely and accurate information about Forest Service policies, programs, and activities. The media desk directly supports the agency management objectives by facilitating opportunities for the press to participate in Forest Service programs that include wildfire suppression, timber extraction, and research venues through well-planned efforts and local coordination. It uses frequent media contact and early sharing of information to keep the attending press well informed about agency issues, resulting in more balanced and informed accounting by the journalists covering the agency.

BUILDING COMMUNITY AND NATION

Because the public affairs practice emphasizes relationship management,[21] much interest has been demonstrated in its role in community and national development and in regional interdependence.[22] Governments use national campaigns for development—in promoting health, fostering tribal or ethnic relations, creating an environment for international investment, providing opportunity for acquiring job skills, expanding international trade, and advancing international relations.

U.S. Programs

In the United States, the federal government launched one such campaign in response to the national prevalence of obesity: More than 64 percent of U.S. adults are medically overweight or obese, with nearly 31 percent—more than 61 million people—meeting criteria for obesity. Yet an estimated 44 million people lack health insurance, and an additional 36 million have no access to any form of health care because their communities have no physician offices or clinics. As a result, health communication on obesity becomes even more critical as perhaps the only channel to address an escalating public health issue.

To tackle what the U.S. Food and Drug Administration calls the "nation's obesity epidemic," the U.S. Department of Health and Human Services launched "Steps to a Healthier U.S.," a bold initiative to promote healthful lifestyles in communities. Several communities across the United States have information- and practice-delivery partners: faith-based organizations; employee worksites; "patient navigators," who assist the uninsured and rural families access health care; kids' networks; and other nonprofit organizations, all of which advocate and promote health and prevent disease.

In a similar vein, the U.S. National Cancer Institute launched a "5 A Day" national campaign in California as an interagency effort to increase consumption of fruits and vegetables to at least five servings daily. The campaign increased public awareness of the importance of eating five or more servings of fruits and vegetables and provided consumers specific information on how to include them in their eating patterns. The national multimedia effort included a *5 A Day* logo, "*5 A Day* Month," subject matter experts available in the produce departments of grocery stores, television and radio spots, news releases, visits to churches and schools, dissemination projects, pitch letters, and fact sheets.

Other Nations

Globally, the United States and several other countries are also engaged in nation-building efforts in countries such as Afghanistan, Iraq, Haiti, Sierra Leone, Bosnia, and Kosovo. Public affairs play an overarching role in those efforts, perhaps more extensively in Afghanistan and in Iraq than in other countries. Communication programs and counterpropaganda measures are being used to restore public safety and to reorganize security forces; to rebuild schools, colleges, and universities; to rebuild infrastructures; to organize grassroots democracy and representative government; to assist in skills building, particularly among Afghan women; and to imbue Iraqis, Afghans, ethnic Albanians, and Serbs with a new level of much-needed patriotism that transcends ethnic, tribal, and religious-sect boundaries. There has been progress, even as such nation-building efforts have been an incredibly difficult, if not a disheartening, undertaking because in those countries "nation-building has come to mostly mean the comprehensive occupation of collapsed or defeated states, the remaking of entire societies and sky-high, endless costs."[23]

On a continental scale, government public affairs is even more critical to the effectiveness of the European Union (EU), which admitted 10 additional member states on May 1, 2004. This union of 25 nations has vexing challenges that have major implications for government public affairs. Those challenges include the following.

1. Tensions that are building up around borders of new member states.

2. Concerns that the big three—Germany, Britain, and France—will dominate the Union, threatening the sovereignty, culture, and identity of poorer member states in Central and Eastern Europe.

3. Ideological debate over harmonization of EU tax policies that have already led to charges of "dumping" and to concerns about higher corporate-tax countries losing jobs and investment to the East, where the average corporate tax rate is significantly lower.

4. Divergence in economies arises from differences in the robustness of member-states' economies. The 10 new members have per capita incomes about one-half those of the original 15 members.

5. Policy of a free movement of tourists and workers across national borders, as well as income gaps and disparate employment levels, may result in a flight of skilled workers and a drain on social-security benefits.

A key message in the union's information campaign is that the EU's membership provides a combined population of 450 million citizens—an enormous market for the movement of goods, services, and capital. And as an aid toward promoting trust and understanding in the union, and between it and the rest of the world, the Center for Transatlantic Relations at the Paul H. Nitze School of Advanced International Studies at Johns Hopkins University in the United States publishes a bimonthly publication, *Transatlantic: Europe, America & the World*.

In parts of the developing world that are ravaged by diseases, government-sponsored health campaigns use a variety of communication channels—public service announcements, radio soap operas, billboards, slogans, posters, singing groups, skits, murals, and social encounters—to inform citizens of the life-threatening consequences of HIV/AIDS or malaria and their implications for their national economies. Government-sponsored HIV-prevention programs in Uganda, one of a handful of success stories in sub-Saharan Africa, use an easily recognized national slogan as the centerpiece of a massive campaign to stem the spread of the disease.[24]

Malaysia uses communication campaigns in a variety of nation-building programs to foster interethnic relationships among its people of Malay, Chinese, and Indian ancestry.[25] And it uses nationally sponsored programs, development projects, and nationalist rhetoric, in light of the nation's history of ethnic conflicts, particularly those that came to a head between the Malays and Chinese in 1969.[26] Begun in the mid-1980s, the nation's Department of National Unity launched a Neighborliness Campaign to improve awareness on public safety and about social goals and to foster cooperation with other races at work, in communities, and in pursuit of national unity.

Similarly, one of the objectives of the Public Relations Organization of the Philippines—a professional organization of government information officers—is to assist the government to meet public needs, provide direction to the government's development-oriented information programs, and achieve national development.[27]

BARRIERS TO EFFECTIVE GOVERNMENT PUBLIC AFFAIRS

Public affairs practitioners in government shape much of the meaningful dialogue necessary to make democracy work. Their work carries with it a civic obligation to serve as intermediaries between elected officials and staff and their citizen constituencies. Yet three major issues hamper the work of building and maintaining government and citizen relationships: questionable credibility, public apathy, and legislative hostility.

Questionable Credibility

The public's perceived believability and trustworthiness of public affairs practitioners in general, and governments in particular, have been an irksome issue for decades. Whenever communication practitioners are perceived to have questionable ethics, then it is logical to expect that the organizations they represent reflect practitioner values and ethics. Too often government public affairs is variously referred to as "just PR" or "propaganda machines" and its implementers as "spin doctors" or "flacks." These pejorative labels notwithstanding, the public affairs officer is often the first and probably only contact for a citizen seeking information about a program or relief from a problem or shoddy service.

Accentuating the perceived questionable credibility of public relations practitioners in general is the inevitable association of government information programs with the word *propaganda*. Americans have long been deeply suspicious of anything with that label, particularly because this powerful technique has been used in other countries to gain and hold despotic control. Thus, public suspicion of information as "nothing but propaganda" is especially strong when the information comes from the government. This is reflected in a fear that government communication could become little more than tax-supported propaganda designed to persuade taxpayers to spend even more tax dollars. To shore up its credibility among citizens, the U.S. federal government recently took two key actions.

First, it approved the Electronic Freedom of Information Act Amendments of 1996 to harness technological innovations; to further open government to public advocacy groups, the news media, scientists, scholars, and others engaged in research; and to enhance public access to computerized government information.[28]

Second, it passed the Data Quality Act in 2001 that requires federal agencies to develop standards for using and disseminating substantively accurate, objective, and credible information and to develop supplementary guidelines for reviewing and disseminating scientific research information.

An example of government actions that could fuel the perception of questionable government communication was the assertion by some Western governments that Iraq had weapons of mass destruction (WMD). Professor Edward Lordan argued that "the WMD claims have inevitably reduced the administration's credibility, nationally and internationally, at a time when trust is at a premium."[29] He further stated that the U.S. government's reinterpretation of its earlier statements on WMD exerted pressure on various administration units that resulted in new messages that had subtle shifts from earlier positions and were sometimes contradictory.

Perhaps nowhere was such a shift more apparent than in the aftermath of the release in July 2004 of U.S. and British government reports on their intelligence-gathering activities before the start of "Operation Iraqi Freedom." The perceived credibility of government information among citizens was that both governments may have fallen short of exercising their full responsibility to question the veracity of amassed intelligence. That failure may have further eroded citizens' doubts worldwide about the credibility of government-disseminated information.

Also perpetuating concerns about credibility is the double standard that many citizens have for government and private enterprise. The public generally accepts the propriety of business publicizing and advertising, even though the customer pays for it. On the other hand, many people regard government information work as a waste of tax dollars; they see no need for government to promote itself or its products and services. Some politicians think they win votes when they flay "government propaganda," adding to public skepticism of the value of government communications. As a reflection of public perceptions of government communication, apathy looms large—the subject to which we now turn.

Public Apathy

Unlike most business operations, government practitioners usually cannot target small segments of broad publics to achieve desired results and ignore the rest of the people. An automobile manufacturer, for example, may be satisfied with 10 or 20 percent of the car-buying adults in a country. Government seeks to serve **all** taxpayers, or at least as great a portion as possible. This is an extremely difficult task, complicated by the lack of interest among many citizens.

An occasional wave of public apathy is an indisputable fact of public life. The percentage of eligible voters who participate in major national elections is invariably low, and the percentage of those voting in state and local elections is even lower. Only 49 percent of adult Americans voted in the 1996 presidential election, and slightly more than 51 percent voted in the 2000 elections. One writer wrote that public apathy is a "groundswell" among Americans:

> The hard fact is that most Americans are contemptuous of politicians and cynical about the motives of government and business. The U.S. now ranks 23rd in voter participation

among Western democracies, and the share of adults who vote in presidential elections has dropped 20 percent since 1960.[30]

City councils, county boards of supervisors, citizen advisory boards, and commissions all struggle with apathy each time a public hearing is scheduled, frequently cutting meetings short when few, if any, citizens show up to voice an opinion. Local government agencies that appoint citizens to serve on advisory boards often have woefully few candidates from which to choose.

Contributing to public apathy are citizen frustration and a general sense of impotence toward government at all levels. Correct or not, the popular perception of government is one of gridlock, a maze of red tape, special interests, corruption, ineptitude, and partisan politics. A law degree is virtual prerequisite for elected officials at the federal and state levels. The system has grown too complicated for most citizens either to understand or to gain access to services easily. Simply adding a room or a back porch to a home often requires the help of an architect or development consultant to ensure that proper permits are acquired and that no environmental regulations are violated.

Paying taxes, especially to the federal government, creates citizen hostility that spills over into other areas of government not related to the collection of taxes. Despite the annual rhetoric calling for simplifying the filing of personal income tax forms, millions of Americans still must seek the assistance of accountants and tax-preparation experts. Beginning in late 1997, the public outcry reached a peak when the Internal Revenue Service became a target of public and legislative scrutiny because of charges of intimidation, invasion of privacy, and favoritism. In Senate hearings "hooded witnesses told horror stories about IRS abuse, and the agency was depicted as a heartless cell snatching money and property from regular working folks."[31]

Facing citizen hostility is not unusual for many government agencies, even when they are simply fulfilling their most basic responsibilities. Consider the challenges faced by wildlife park management officials in controlling the growing deer population. In the Gettysburg National Military Park, the deer population is about 12 times what the local forest can reasonably maintain, resulting in deer–human collisions and fatalities. Due to restrictive administrative rules, the National Park Service is limited in the steps it can take to reduce an obvious hazard, regardless of common sense demanding such action. There and elsewhere deer contribute to the spread of Lyme disease and cause damage to crops and grazing lands. Despite what many believe are humane actions to control the deer population, wildlife management opponents have been effective in promoting their cause in allowing deer to roam with few restrictions.

Legislative Hostility

The public affairs function has been established longer in government than in any other field of practice, yet it has never been totally effective or given the respect enjoyed by practitioners in the private sector. In government, as in other organizational settings, public affairs is a legitimate management function that helps make agencies, departments, and other public entities responsive to the citizens they serve. However, government practitioners often face more hostility and suspicion than do other practitioners. They have had a rocky status at the federal level, where Congress has been hostile to information activities in the federal executive branch.[32] This hostility stems from four fundamental and long-standing conflicts embedded in our democratic government:

1. The continuing struggle between the press, fighting for "the people's right to know," and the officials of government, who insist upon discretion in certain sensitive areas of the public business.

2. The unrelenting struggle for the balance of power between the legislative and executive branches of government. This contest is present whether it is between mayor and council, governor and legislature, or president and Congress.

3. The continuing struggle for power between the major political parties. The "out" party fears the power of an army of "propagandists" in keeping the "ins" in and the "outs" out.

4. The protests of industries, institutions, and other vested interests when threatened by proposed legislation or government regulation. They often disparage the use of public funds and government machinery to carry the day against them.

Government public affairs had been handicapped by opposition legislators who prevent maximum effectiveness and accurate accounting of the function's cost and ascertaining corporate value. Attacks on public affairs programs by legislators are less frequent than those by the press but perhaps more damaging.

Legislative opposition is often stimulated by other sources of hostility. The formidability of early federal public relations practices shocked the Congress and highly placed interest groups at the turn of the nineteenth century. Beginning in 1905 through 1909, the Forest Service—an obscure, newly established agency led by its first chief, Gifford Pinchot—aggressively and successfully curried the favor of key newspapers and special-interest groups to move his message of conservation and protection of the nation's public forests. Pinchot and his "press officers" took the conservation debate straight to the people and clearly reshaped the nation's attitude toward unchecked logging and use of public lands. Finally, the Roosevelt–Pinchot campaign for land conservation sparked congressional reaction, thanks largely to the efforts of spokespersons of lumber interests, mine operators, and cattle grazers who had been exploiting the nation's public lands. Congressman Franklin Mondell of Wyoming, spokesman for sheep and cattle ranchers, won adoption of a 1908 amendment to the agricultural appropriation bill dealing with the Forest Service, which read:

> That no part of this appropriation shall be paid or used for the purpose of paying for in whole or in part the preparation of any newspaper or magazine articles.[33]

Thus, the first effective use of public relations to promote acceptance of an administration's policies brought congressional restriction of the function in the executive branch. Congressional ire erupted next in 1910, when Joseph T. Robinson, a representative from Arkansas, demanded an investigation of the Census Bureau for employing a special agent at $8 per day in 1909. The agent was to explain to the public the purpose of the 1910 census. Census Bureau Director E. Dana Durand insisted that it was essential, if the census was to be complete, that all citizens and aliens be reached—through newspapers, the foreign-language

FIGURE 16.2

**"ALASKA" EDITORIAL
CARTOON (CIRCA 1910)**

Circa 1910 illustrating Gifford Pinchot's powerfull use of the press to lobby for protection of Alaska's forests.

Courtesy Bushnell, circa 1910.

press, and agricultural weeklies—and be assured that their replies would not be used for taxation purposes. The committee, after hearing this, tacitly approved.

By 1912 the number of "publicity agents" employed by executive departments was growing, and some campaigns were not beyond reproach. In May 1912, Rep. John Nelson of Wisconsin gained passage of a House resolution to investigate meat inspection in the U.S. Department of Agriculture's Bureau of Animal Industry. Early in the hearings, Nelson was angered by a circular criticizing the resolution and defending the department; the pamphlet had been published before the hearings opened. He charged that the department was using publicity to discredit one of its accusers, and he introduced a House resolution to investigate "the expenditure of public moneys for press bureaus, postage, stationery, and employees by the Department of Agriculture and by other departments; and that said committee be directed to make recommendations to the House as to what steps are necessary to protect public funds from newspaper exploitations."[34] The resolution did not pass.

A year later the Civil Service Commission advertised for "a press agent to help boom the good roads movement" in the Office of Public Roads. The circular called for a "publicity expert" whose "affiliations with newspaper publishers and writers are extensive enough to secure publication of items prepared by him." The circular prompted Rep. Frederick H. Gillett to offer an amendment to an appropriations bill specifying that no money could be spent for publicity unless specifically authorized by Congress. It passed.

The 1913 Gillett Amendment remains embedded in law. It is only one of six restrictions on the function that has been written into U.S. codes and is a source of much confusion. As one government public affairs officer observed, "The amendment does not prohibit the use of publicity; it merely states that such funds be clearly identified."[35] He said that the 1913 amendment continues to intimidate those who work in government public affairs.[36]

Legislative opposition to the function at all levels has led to legal restrictions, circumvention of budgetary procedures, and wasteful practices designed to conceal legitimate government functioning. Legislative hostility and self-serving posturing by elected and appointed officials also causes many competent professionals to shy away from government service.

GOVERNMENT–MEDIA RELATIONS

Since the very beginning of American government, the First Amendment to the Constitution has guaranteed freedom of the press. This freedom was vital to the founders of the new nation, so much so that Thomas Jefferson said, "Were it left to me to decide whether we should have a government without newspapers or newspapers without government, I should not hesitate a moment to prefer the latter."

Media Access to Government

In more recent times, the constitutional freedoms guaranteed to the press have been expanded and clarified. Access to government information, in addition to the freedom to speak out or write freely about government, has been codified in freedom of information legislation and "sunshine laws." Except for well-defined areas, such as national security, litigation, certain personnel records, and so forth, virtually every piece of information maintained by the government is open to inspection by the press, and by the public for that matter. In most cases, a reporter can demand to see unfinished drafts of reports and handwritten notes if the reporter has specific knowledge of these and can request them with adequate specificity.

The right of access to government information and meetings is of paramount importance. Beyond just informing citizens about the official actions of government, the indispensable role of the press as the watchdog of government helps guarantee accountability, reduce corruption, and crystallize public issues and opinions, and it places the press in the position of being the citizen's representative in the broad system of checks and balances. Almost by definition, government–press relationships are adversarial. Government frequently argues that any large organization is more effective if it has a degree of privacy in formulating strategies. For example, in labor and contract negotiations or the purchase of land, privacy is needed to avoid giving the other side, often exempt from freedom of information laws, an unfair advantage. The press counters that the public's business should be conducted in the open to ensure that all activities are conducted ethically and in the public interest.

The idea of the news media having responsibilities beyond simply providing the facts and offering a few editorial columns is becoming more accepted. Sometimes labeled "public journalism" or "civic journalism," a more activist form of news coverage is being used by a growing number of media covering government agencies and programs.

Editors at the *Spokesman-Review* in Spokane, Washington, and at the *Virginian-Pilot* in Norfolk, Virginia, are examples of news media unabashedly seeking to affect the agenda of political and governmental discourse. The editors have convened public forums in their communities to discuss the same issues being discussed by legislative bodies, have sought out nonjournalists to write columns, and have generally attempted to increase the number of options and entities involved in government decision making.

The new role of these news organizations is not without criticism. Many government officials condemn the effort as ignorant of the basic principles of representative government. Many assert that American democracy is founded on the idea that most ordinary citizens—who do not have the time, expertise, or interest to fully research and understand complex and numerous issues facing governments—elect persons they trust to conduct the public's business. Reaching consensus, they argue, is a difficult, arduous process already criticized for its snail-like pace. Injecting additional entities with tremendous publicity powers but no legal accountability is counterproductive. Likewise, many journalists are fearful that by becoming newsmakers themselves, reporters and editors may lose the objectivity, independence, and courage to report on public issues.[37]

Government Dependence on Media

The relationship between journalists and government is simultaneously an unquestioned necessity and an obstacle to government communication with citizens. A shortage of media attention is rare, but it usually comes when government agencies want it least. On the other hand, when government agencies want media attention, journalists may decide that the information is not newsworthy or they are so busy working on other stories that they fail to notice a government news release.

The standards used by reporters and government communicators to define news are usually quite different. It is not surprising that much information considered by individual agencies to be of vital importance gets lost in the mountains of information generated by public affairs staffs. Besides, the news media do not have resources to cover all that is the public's stake in government, in part because there are not enough journalists on news media payrolls to adequately track all the activities and developments in the many agencies at all levels of government.

Despite those difficulties, government still relies heavily on the news media to pass on important information, as exemplified in the U.S. military's decision to embed journalists in combat units during the Iraq war. Granted, such a decision had

FIGURE 16.3

DONALD H. RUMSFELD, SECRETARY OF DEFENSE AND GENERAL RICHARD B. MYERS, CHAIRMAN OF THE JOINT CHIEFS OF STAFF, FIELDING MEDIA QUESTIONS ON MILITARY OPERATIONS UNDERWAY IN IRAQ

Courtesy Department of Defense.

been criticized for its potential to compromise the objectivity of news reports filed by embedded journalists, to discourage journalists from expanding their reporting beyond that to which they have been official embedded, and to create a climate conducive to "groupthink" that encourages journalists to march lockstep in their reporting. But the U.S. Department of Defense, which organized the program, argued that giving journalists a front-row seat in a war zone would give them get a bird's-eye view of war operations and lead to fuller and more comprehensive coverage. In the 1991 Gulf War, journalists relied on reports from a few (detached) stringers.

Historically, the concern was that journalists could undercut national security interest by giving "too much information to the enemy on the home front of public opinion,"[38] as Retired U.S. Army Colonel Robert Rigg wrote in reference to the Vietnam War. He also wrote that overcovering the details of that war resulted in "giving hope and misleading information to our enemy by publicizing 'the trees of minority attitudes' as against the forest of majority opinion, effort, and sacrifice."[39]

Is embedding journalists in combat operations necessarily tantamount to a public relations advantage or political leverage for the U.S. government? Does it result in reports essentially framed by government's efforts to tout their messages to achieve specific objectives? Journalists' experiences have been mixed. Christiane Amanpour, CNN news correspondent, thinks that embedding made the press uncritical of the administration: "I think the press was muzzled and I think the press self-muzzled. I'm sorry to say but certainly television, and perhaps to a certain extent my station, was intimidated by the Administration and its foot soldiers at Fox News."[40] Susan Carruthers also cites a danger of such journalistic restraint:

[S]elf-censorship is as real a threat to the free circulation of opinion and images in wartime as anything enacted by the state. Hence one increasingly visible anomaly, for "consumers" of news, is that our visual experience of war appears to be contracting even as the technological capacity to convey higher-definition images with greater immediacy expands.[41]

Some of the journalistic failings in the coverage of wars such as the Vietnam War and the Gulf War are apparent in more recent wars and conflicts. A content analysis of four U.S. newspapers—the *New York Times*, the *Washington Post*, *Los Angeles Times*, and *Chicago Tribune*—shows the following major results:

1. Embedded journalists' newspaper stories about the military, its units, and personnel were more decontextualized and episodic than those of nonembedded journalists.

2. Embedded coverage of "Operation Iraqi Freedom" was more favorable in overall tone, both toward the military generally and toward its personnel, than that of nonembedded coverage.

3. Overall tone of embedded reports during "Operation Iraqi Freedom" was not more positive than that of other conflicts—"Desert Storm" and "Enduring Freedom"—that had limited use of embedded journalists.[42]

Thus, based on this study, embedding journalists in military combat influences both the nature and the tone of news coverage. More important, two implications must be noted. The first is that embedded journalists must conduct self-censorship, which could force them to abandon objective reporting and information disclosure. The second implication is that episodic framing of news, that is, absent contextual reporting, is not necessarily a plus in that it could pressure journalists to ignore the broader, fuller news events. Process or contextual reporting that delves into meaningful details of war would be more advantageous to both the government and citizens.

Media Reporting of Government

In days gone by, news of government was a relatively simple matter of personalities, oratorical political campaigns, trust busting, and the like. It was entirely different from reporting international trade and outsourcing, world affairs, nuclear energy and waste disposal, mental health, space travel, issues affecting equal opportunity, the environment, and terrorism. Interpreting the complexities of government requires trained specialists and often takes more time than news media deadlines permit. Hence, government public affairs specialists play an essential role in working with journalists to communicate with citizens.

The media have made much progress in their reporting of governments, but the need for governments to strengthen and supplement today's reporting by the media is greater than ever. Problems in media coverage of federal government are not always the fault of either the media or individual journalists. Rather, shortcomings in coverage are due to the magnitude of the task, as the size of the job is staggering. Washington dominates the nation's news system. News organizations, write Michael Grossman and Martha Kumar, "have become one of the principal forces on the national political scene, influencing the other major forces—the President, Congress, the bureaucracy, the parties, and the pressure groups—and in turn being influenced by them."[43]

Some in government do not think that the media measure up to their task. At no time in history did this point come through as clearly as during the news coverage of the Clinton administration. Allegations of past marijuana use, draft dodging, questionable real estate dealings, and other issues early in the Clinton presidency served as merely a warm-up for what was to follow, ultimately leading all the way to impeachment by the House of Representatives and trial in the Senate. The issues centered not on the job performance of the president but on his purported liaisons with a variety of women close to the White House and his comments regarding the accuracy of those allegations. All of this came at a time when the country was at peace, the economy was strong, and the president's approval ratings in the national polls remained near historic high levels.

Instead of reporting on the president's relationships with foreign heads of state, every major news organization repeatedly led with stories about Clinton's affairs with former government employees such as Paula Jones and Gennifer Flowers and White House intern Monica Lewinsky. Many questioned the role of the press in making activities that had once been considered too sensitive—and perhaps too insignificant—the dominant issue in the nation's headlines.

The increasing emphasis on sex and scandal in media reporting of government has been widely criticized.[44] Yet, such emphasis is unlikely to go away. For one thing, the proliferation of television news and information programming has spawned saturation coverage, which, to fill time, nourishes itself on speculation, rumor, and the opinions of a staggering array of "reliable" sources and "experts."

For another, investigations and preparation for trial in civil and criminal cases can take years, during which there may be other parties involved with vested interests to keep the story on the front page, that is, litigation journalism.[45]

FIGURE 16.4

CNN WAR COVERAGE

MILITARY PUBLIC AFFAIRS

Military public affairs is geared toward boosting public opinion about the armed forces, maintaining or improving personnel morale, procuring financial support for its programs, and nurturing public understanding and support. But the American public's view of, and relationship with, the military changed dramatically in the 1990s, threatening to weaken recruitment efforts and legislative support. Although the end of the Cold War offered renewed hope for a peaceful world, many internal issues facing the military made front-page news and lead stories for tabloid television programs. Some of the most noteworthy had little to do with national defense, security, nuclear weapons, or similar topics. Instead, the focus of many administrative and news media investigations was often on the sexual activities of members of the armed forces, from the lowest to the highest ranks.

Understandably, the military, like private-sector corporations, has had controversies and historical tensions with the media, "compelling the two actors to interact as antagonists."[46] How did the military respond to the vacuum in media coverage of its activities and programs and to the tension with the media? For one thing, it developed a Statement of Principle for telling its own story to the American public, for projecting its own brand of public affairs, and for guiding military–media relations: "The American public must be informed about the United States' military operations, and this information must be provided through both the news media and the government."[47] For another, the military exemplified that principle by expanding its embedding policy during "Operation Iraqi Freedom."

Captain David Westover, a U.S. Air Force public affairs officer, and Margot Lamme, a professor of public affairs at the University of Florida, found that that principle, when applied to embedded journalism, resulted in broad accomplishments for the military: unprecedented access, better understanding of military life, reporters serve also as the link back home, greater trust that eased some tension, increased information exchange, and better military–media relationships.[48]

The military's programs and policies frequently are criticized in the news media. For example, gays in the military stirred considerable debate on the appropriateness of the "don't-ask-don't-tell" rule, an attempt to avoid discharging otherwise capable military personnel because of their sexual preferences. Perhaps posing a greater threat to the military's overall reputation was a series of news reports on scandalous episodes that brought into question the military establishment's moral character. In 1991, sexual misconduct at the Navy's Tailhook convention in Las Vegas captured the attention of the nation and led to high-level resignations. In 1997 it came to light that military trainers at the Army's Aberdeen Proving Ground had coerced female recruits into having sex. Soon after this, the base moved to address concerns and opened a hotline to allow complaints about sexual abuses to be logged anonymously. The result of one of the tips was that the commander of the facility was forced to retire after confirming that he had committed adultery five years earlier. That same year, the Navy relieved the commander of the Navy's supply system because of allegations that he had repeatedly propositioned one of his subordinates and created a work environment hostile to women. Also in 1997, an Air Force general lost his opportunity to become the chairman of the Joint Chiefs of Staff because of allegations of an adulterous affair more than 10 years earlier.

Public affairs activities were central to the case of Air Force Lieutenant Kelly Flinn. In 1995, Flinn was publicized by the Air Force as the first female B-52 pilot. A year later, she became the target of an investigation by the service that alleged she had committed adultery, lied to superiors, and engaged in conduct unbecoming an officer. Flinn went on the offensive, retaining a public relations agency and appearing on nationally televised news programs to tell her side of the story. Flinn ultimately resigned, but the military's handling of the case caused many public affairs professionals to question the service's strategy.

Beginning in January 2003, similar media interest, which was apparent during investigations into charges of rape filed by female cadets at the U.S Air Force Academy in Colorado Springs, led to nationwide investigations of similar charges in the armed forces, a policy to grant confidentiality to cadets who report being sexually assaulted, and the early retirement of the Superintendent of the Air Force Academy in Colorado Springs.

To avert a seeming media fixation on sex and trysts, or on debauchery, and the resulting antagonism between the media and the military, the latter has for at least two decades been carefully nurturing the professionalism of its public affairs staff and building better relations with its stakeholders. Many of the former journalists and the public affairs officers who fulfill the responsibilities of military public affairs were trained at the Defense Information School, Fort George G. Meade, in Maryland, or at universities offering undergraduate and graduate curricula in journalism and public affairs.

Some recommend that both military public affairs and journalism use a vigorous educational program to understand the other side, endure frustrations and setbacks along the way, educate each other on the peculiarities of each other's culture, and build on similarities and mutual interests.[49] Holm argues that the military's public wounds have been self-inflicted and concludes that "it is essential that the military abandon its self-protective, reclusive nature when responding to the press. In the absence of response, the American public will fill in the blanks, often not to the armed services' favor."[50]

GOVERNMENT AS BUSINESS

The 1990s brought significant changes to the way many government agencies integrate their activities into society. These new developments may have altered some of the basic philosophies of government. They included the following:

1. An increasing awareness among government entities of the need to compete with other government agencies in the public and political arenas for scarce funding resources.

2. A growing attitude among many observers that government should be run like a business, not a nonprofit charitable organization with unlimited resources.

3. The increasing need of federal officials and the nation to seek the advice and assistance of U.S. citizens led in part to new regulations, issued July 19, 2001, that exempted some advisory groups from FACA regulations.

Osborne and Gaebler point out that, unlike businesses, most public agencies do not get their funds directly from their clients or customers. Rather, funding decisions are made by city councils, legislatures, or elected boards. Agency heads therefore aim to please these bodies, not those they are designed to serve. Besides, their clients—unless they move to another city or state—have little choice for the services provided by government. Most businesses, on the other hand,

EXHIBIT 16.1

PUBLIC RELATIONS, NAVY STYLE

Rear Admiral T. L. McCreary
Chief of Information, U.S. Navy
Washington, D.C.

Navy public affairs apply identical skills, compete in the same markets and "approach" public relations in a very similar manner as the private sector. While we exercise the same basic public relations process: research, plan, implement, and evaluate, our work tends to be more complex because our structure spreads across the globe and our "bottom line" is more than simply satisfying stockholders and consumers. What sets us apart is that our actions can impact world events, and the fact that we are held accountable to the President, the Congress, and most important, the American people.

The primary mission for Navy public affairs is threefold: (1) keeping the American people informed about Navy operations, (2) coordinating Navy community relations programs and participation in special events, and (3) informing our internal audience. The internal communication function is strongly emphasized in our daily activities for one simple reason—the morale of our people and the degree to which they are kept informed directly impacts our combat readiness.

The issues that we deal with are vast in scope, ranging from the benign to combat operations. The topic *du jour* is often **not** known in advance, and depending on our level of ongoing operations, we regularly deal with events that might be considered a rare crisis in the private sector. Navy public affairs must be well prepared to manage this vast array of issues and act and react quickly to them all. To succeed in this

dynamic environment, we place great emphasis on establishing plans for any eventuality. Success also depends on Navy public affairs professionals having the trust and confidence of senior leadership in order to advise on immediate and longer-range actions.

In the international context, communicating the Navy's story clearly serves as part of the public diplomacy process. Information about the military and its operations around the world is used to deter potential adversaries, reassure friends, and if necessary, to respond to aggression. This demands from our public affairs professionals the ability to coordinate across organizational lines to collect and analyze the potential effects of communications, and to then provide strategic counsel to senior leadership. The stakes can often be enormous.

The embedding of media with operational units during Operation Iraqi Freedom underscored the military's fervent belief that a transparent process would spotlight our "products"—courageous, intelligent people and effective combat power. It also recognized that first-hand media reports would carry far more legitimacy than briefings away from the battlefield. The rapidity of information flow in words and visuals made it unlike any previous reporting on military events.

Today's environment requires professionals steeped in the practice of public affairs with a high degree of ethical standards, as well as a strong educational foundation. Only then can our Navy public affairs practitioners provide strategic counsel, operational planning and tactical execution of communications as a function of national objectives, joint combat operations and our navy mission.

Courtesy Rear Admiral T. L. McCreary, Chief of Information, U.S. Navy, Washington, D.C.

must remain competitive and attempt to please their customers just to stay in business.[51]

In several other aspects, government operates in a competitive, businesslike environment, one in which public affairs plays a key role. Many government activities are being funded by corporate sponsorships, and public–private partnerships are favored by politicians and taxpayers alike. States and cities launch massive promotional campaigns to attract tourists and conventions that bring millions of dollars into communities. These dollars support local businesses, which in turn pay more taxes and keep the general tax rates down for residents. State and local governments also compete to attract new industry through advertising, participation in international trade shows, and tax incentives, thereby creating more jobs and opportunities for their residents and diversifying their tax base.

PUBLIC AFFAIRS IN POLITICS

For as long as there have been leaders in society, there has been a love–hate relationship between the governed and the governing. Politicians often spend much of their careers in service to fellow citizens only to be crudely thrown out of office when the political environment or the local newspaper editorial policies change. At the same time, another politician may lack high ethical standards, or may even be guilty of serious crimes, and yet be returned to office when reelection time comes. Such was the case with Marion Barry, then-mayor of Washington, D.C., who was videotaped by police using illegal narcotics, yet returned as mayor of the nation's capital.

The challenge to lead and to serve in the midst of constant conflict is a difficult one for any politician or organization. Cynicism about public affairs in government is greatest when associated with elected officials, or "politicians." Within an environment of skepticism, many view communication from elected officials as mere propaganda. Often many wonder whether the work of government is at its roots purely politics and running for reelection. For example, members of Congress use their franking privileges (free mailing) merely to communicate to their constituents back home.

Similarly, voters decided in California in 1988 that many elected officials were taking advantage of their agencies' publications to gain recognition and popularity. Proposition 73 was aimed at limiting campaign contributions, as well as prohibiting elected officials from using public funds to gain political advantage. Included in the new law was a provision that prohibited government agencies from mailing newsletters and other mass-produced publications if the publication included "the name, office, photograph, or other reference to an elected officer affiliated with the agency which produces or sends the mailing." The California Fair Political Practices Commission, the agency responsible for enforcement, later clarified the law to prohibit any publication that "features" an elected official. This includes—by the Commission's definition—material that "singles out the elected officer by the manner of display of his or her name or office in the layout of the document, such as by headlines, captions, type size, typeface, or type color."[52] Elected officials' photographs and signatures were also prohibited.

In fact, politics and government cannot be separated. Likewise, the role of public affairs in politics and government is inextricably interrelated. At no level of government is public affairs more important than in our cities, where government provides schools, fire and police protection, safe streets and public transportation, recreation facilities and programs, housing, and other vital services. Yet, even with cities in crisis, public affairs has been slow to develop and is often the target of tax protesters and politicians looking for easy targets to exploit.

As the practice in government matures and becomes increasingly professional, however, it is demonstrating its ability to make government more responsive to citizens' needs and concerns, gain acceptance of necessary programs, and make services widely available to those who need them. In short, the public affairs function in government is increasingly recognized as a truly essential element of effective government.

EXHIBIT 16.2

CASE STUDY OF A GOVERNMENT PUBLIC AFFAIRS ISSUE: YUCCA MOUNTAIN, NEVADA

Richard K. Long, Professor
Department of Communications
Brigham Young University, Provo, Utah

When the United States dropped two atomic bombs on Japan in August 1945, World War II came to an abrupt end. That milestone also launched a 50-year "Cold War" in which the United States and the Soviet Union stockpiled nuclear weapons for use in case of a catastrophic war between communism and the Free World.

Many nations also began developing nuclear energy to produce electricity, initiating a decades-long opinion battle that has generated countless books, speeches, lawsuits, demonstrations, health studies, Congressional hearings, and TV documentaries designed to promote—or ban—nuclear power.

Except for scientists, few Americans seem to understand that nuclear energy creates highly radioactive waste and spent fuel that remains lethal to humans and other life forms for over 10,000 years. The U.S. will soon have nearly 80,000 tons (160 million pounds) stored at more than 100 sites. This is a potential risk to public health and the environment, but even scarier is its vulnerability to terrorist attack.

In 1982, Congress passed the Nuclear Waste Policy Act to develop a national program for permanent disposal of highly radioactive waste found in 39 of the United States. Since then, $8 billion has been spent studying sites for a $58 billion storage facility. Since the first list of potential sites was announced, state and local governments, advocacy groups and others have launched vigorous campaigns to

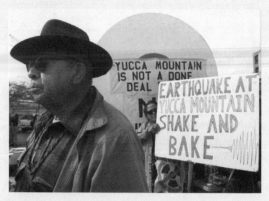

Courtesy Steve Marcus and Las Vegas Sun

avoid being selected. In 1987, Congress ordered the Department of Energy to focus its studies on a single site deep beneath Yucca Mountain, about 90 miles north of Las Vegas, Nevada. In the process, stakeholders of all stripes focused their efforts on the mother of all NIMBY ("Not in my backyard") battles.

Energy Secretary Spencer Abraham formally selected Yucca Mountain in 2002 as the final choice for the depository. As mandated by the political process, President George W. Bush was required to endorse the selection—which he did less than 24 hours after Abraham's announcement.

Nevada Gov. Kenny Guinn kept his promise and "vetoed" the Yucca Mountain selection. Then Congress decisively overrode Guinn's veto. Next came multiple lawsuits, while DOE began preparing documentation for the Nuclear Regulatory Commission, which must approve plans for construction and eventual use of the site.

continued on next page

NOTES

[1] "Reorganization Plan and Report," submitted to Congress on December 30, 1998. Available online at: www.state.gov/www/global/general_foreign_policy/rpt_981230_reorg1.html.

[2] U.S. Department of State, "America's Overseas Presence in the 21st Century: The Report of the Overseas Presence Advisory Panel," November 1999, 31.

[3] Michael Kunczik, *Images of Nations and International Public Relations* (Mahwah, NJ: Lawrence Erlbaum Associates, 1997): 230–233; Jarol B. Manheim, *Strategic Public Diplomacy and American Foreign Policy: The Evolution of Influence* (New York: Oxford University Press, 1994), 40–41.

EXHIBIT 16.2 (cont.)

The complex process has mega-billion-dollar implications, but DOE appears determined to use Yucca Mountain as early as 2010.

Yucca Mountain offers seemingly endless public relations challenges:

- Weapons complexes, nuclear-powered naval vessels, power plants and even hospitals created the waste that must be stored permanently **somewhere**.

- Leaving the waste at its current storage sites is unacceptable from a scientific, political, and environmental safety standpoint.

- Consensus on a single site to take 80,000 tons of radioactive waste is unlikely, (i.e., **nobody** wants the stuff, no matter how badly the nation needs to dispose of it).

- Transporting the waste will require thousands of specially designed trains, most of them traveling through cities such as Chicago and Salt Lake City. Waste will also be transported by truck convoys traveling mostly on the Interstate system, which critics describe as "mobile Chernobyls."

- The debate has created a form of "nuclear politics," where states with waste to store have been quick to embrace Yucca Mountain, whereas Nevada residents and many Californians vehemently oppose being a dumping ground for the whole country's radioactive garbage. Editorial opinions have clearly reflected the same geographic split.

As with many public relations issues worldwide, there is the prospect of litigation that may delay the whole project. In July 2004, a three-judge panel from the Federal Appeals Court for the District of Columbia ruled that the Department of Energy could not proceed with the project. The court ruled that DOE standard for protecting the public from radiation leaks at Yucca Mountain for at least **10,000** years was inadequate. Either DOE must raise its standards to **300,000** years, or Congress must rewrite the enabling legislation to change the protection requirements.

The core question is what to do with highly lethal waste that can't be left where it is, reprocessed, dumped into an ocean, fired into space, stored on an Antarctic ice sheet, or stored on some remote, uninhabited island—all of which have been studied and ruled out.

The longer the delays in implementing a viable plan, the more billions of dollars will be poured into a project that badly needs resolution but will **never** satisfy everyone.

Then, again, there might be something to be said for **really** "hot" dice in Las Vegas.

Courtesy Richard K Long, Professor, Department of Communications, Brigham Young University, Provo, Utah

[4] United States Department of State, "Public Diplomacy Worldwide," The Office of International Information Programs, Washington, D.C., n.d., 6.

[5] United States General Accounting Office, "U.S. International Broadcasting: New Strategic Approach Focuses on Reaching Large Audience But Lacks Measurable Program Goals," Report to the Committee on International Relations, House of Representatives, (July 2003): 6.

[6] Jess T. Ford, "U.S. Public Diplomacy: State Department and the Broadcasting Board of Governors Expand Efforts in the Middle East But Face Significant Challenges," Testimony before the Subcommittee on National Security, Emerging Threats, and International Relations; Committee on Government Reform; House of Representatives, February 10, 2004.

[7] U.S. Advisory Commission on Public Diplomacy, "Consolidation of USIA into the State Department: An Assessment After One Year," October 2000.

[8] U.S. General Accounting Office, "New Strategic Approach Focuses on Reaching Large Audiences."

[9] Hugh M. Culbertson, "Around Europe: An Introduction," in Donn J. Tilson and Emmanuel C. Alozie, eds., *Toward the Common Good: Perspectives in International Public Relations* (Boston: Allyn & Bacon, 2004), 129.

[10] Ibid., 130.

[11] James L. Garnett, *Communicating for Results in Government* (San Francisco: Jossey-Bass, 1992), 14.

[12] Jeffrey M. Berry, Kent E. Portney, and Ken Thomson, *The Rebirth of Urban Democracy* (Washington, DC: Brookings Institution, 1993), 113.

[13] Mary Grisez Kweit and Robert W. Kweit, "The Politics of Policy Analysis: The Role of Citizen Participation in Analytic Decision Making," *Policy Studies Review* 3, no. 2 (February 1984): 32.

[14] Gregory Streib, "Dusting Off a Forgotten Management Tool: The Citizen Survey," *Public Management* 72, no. 7 (August 1990): 17.

[15] Ibid., p. 18.

[16] Priscilla Murphy, "The Limits of Symmetry: A Game Theory Approach to Symmetric and Asymmetric Public Relations," in *Public Relations Research Annual, Volume* 3, ed. James E. Grunig and Larissa A. Grunig, 115–131. (Hillsdale, NJ: Lawrence Erlbaum Associates, 1991).

[17] Deborah J. Shields, Ingred M. Martin, Wade E. Martin, Michelle A. Haefele, "Survey Results of the American Public's Values, Objectives, Beliefs, and Attitudes Regarding Forests and Grasslands: A Technical Document Supporting the 2000 USDA Forest Service RPA Assessment," General Technical Report, RMRS-GTR-95. (Fort Collins, CO: USDA Forest Service, Rocky Mountain Research Station, September 2002): 22–24.

[18] Tobias Olsson, Håkan Sandström, and Peter Dahlgren, "An Information Society for Everyone?" *Gazette: The International Journal for Communication Studies* 65 (2003): 347–363.

[19] Shane Harris, "Voted Down: Why the Ultimate E-Government Effort Failed to Get Off the Ground," *Government Executive* (April 1, 2004): 34–38.

[20] Jodi Dean, "Making (It) Public," in *Public Affairs: Politics in the Age of Sex Scandals*, ed. Paul Apostolidis and Juliet A. Williams (Durham, NC: Duke University Press, 2004), 268.

[21] Robert L. Heath, ed., *Handbook of Public Relations* (Thousand Oaks, CA: Sage, 2001); John A. Ledingham and Stephen D. Bruning, eds., *Public Relations as Relationship Management: A Relational Approach to the Study and Practice of Public Relations* (Mahwah, NJ: Lawrence Erlbaum Associates, 2000).

[22] Maureen Taylor, "Toward a Public Relations Approach to Nation Building," *Journal of Public Relations Research* 12 (2000): 179–210; Maureen Taylor, "Media Relations in Bosnia: A Role for Public Relations in Building Civil Society," *Public Relations Review* (Spring 2000): 1–14; Hugh M. Culbertson and Ni Chen, eds., *International Public Relations: A Comparative Analysis* (Mahwah, NJ: Lawrence Erlbaum Associates, 1996).

[23] Morton Abramowitz and Heather Hurlburt, "The Shaky State of Nation-Building." *The Washington Post*, July 11, 2004, B4.

[24] Helen Epstein, "The Fidelity Fix," *New York Times Magazine* (June 13, 2004): 54–59.

[25] Taylor, "Toward a Public Relations Approach."

[26] Ibid.

[27] Zenaida S. Panol, "Philippine Public Relations: An Industry and Practitioner Profile," *Public Relations Review* 26 (Summer 2000): 237–254.

[28] Martin E. Halstuk and Bill F. Chamberlin, "Open Government in the Digital Age: The Legislative History of How Congress Established a Right of Public Access to Electronic Information Held by Federal Agencies," *Journalism & Mass Communication Quarterly* 78 (Spring 2001): 45–64.

[29] Edward J. Lordan, "Mixed Messages: The Bush Administration Public Relations Campaign in the Iraqi War," *Public Relations Quarterly* 48 (Fall 2003): 11.

[30] Mark D. Uebling, "All-American Apathy," *American Demographics* 13, no. 11 (November 1991): 30.

[31] Keith Elliott Greenberg, "A Taxing Challenge: The IRS Works to Improve Its Image," *Public Relations Tactics* 5, no. 2 (February 1998): 27.

[32] Mordecai Lee, "The First Federal Public Information Service, 1920–1933: At the US Bureau of Efficiency!" *Public Relations Review* 29 (November 2003): 415–425.

[33] Congressional Record, 60th Congress, House Rules Committee, 1st sess., 1908, vol. 42, 4137. Historical data provided by Felice Michaels Levin.

[34] U.S. Congress, House Rules Committee, Hearing on H. Res 545, Department Press Agents, 62nd Cong. 2d sess., 1912, 3–4.

[35] David H. Brown, "Government Public Affairs—Its Own Worst Enemy," *Public Relations Quarterly* 26 (Spring 1981): 4.

[36] Ibid.

[37] Christopher Conte, "Angels in the Newsroom," *Governing* 9, no. 11 (August 1996): 20.

[38] Colonel Robert B. Rigg, "How Not to Report a War," *Military Review* 49, no. 6 (June 1969): 15.

[39] Ibid., 14–24.

[40] Quoted in Ken Auletta, "Fortress Bush: How the White House Keeps the Press Under Control," *New Yorker*, January 19, 2004, 62.

[41] Susan L. Carruthers, *The Media at War: Communication and Conflict in the Twentieth Century*" (New York: St. Martin's Press, 2000), 275.

[42] Michael Pfau, Michel Haigh, Mitchell Gettle, Michael Donnelly, Gregory Scott, Dana Warr, and Elaine Wittenberg, "Embedding Journalists in Military Combat Units: Impact on Newspaper Story Frames and Tone," *Journalism & Mass Communication Quarterly* 81 (Spring 2004): 74–88.

[43] Michael Baruch Grossman and Martha Joynt Kumar, *Portraying the President* (Baltimore: Johns Hopkins University Press, 1981): 16.

[44] See, for example, Julie Yioutas and Ivana Segvic, "Revisiting the Clinton/Lewinsky Scandal: The Convergence of Agenda Setting and Framing," *Journalism & Mass Communication Quarterly* 80 (Autumn 2003): 571; Dean, "Making (It) Public."

[45] Carole Gorney, APR, "The Clinton Crisis: Public Relations vs. Legal Advice," *Public Relations Strategist* 4, no. 1 (Spring 1998): 14–15.

[46] Judith Raine Baroody, *Media Access and the Military: The Case of the Gulf War* (Lanham, MD: University Press of America, 1998): 3.

[47] Major Barry E. Venable, "The Army and the Media," *Military Review* 82, no. 1 (January–February 2002): 67.

[48] David S. Westover Jr. and Margot Opdycke Lamme, "A Qualitative Study of Military–Media Relations During the War in Iraq: Investigating Embedding, Discovering Relationship Theory in Action." Paper presented in the Public Relations Division, Annual Convention of the Association for Journalism and Mass Communication, Toronto, Canada, August 4–7, 2004.

[49] Colonel Barry E. Willey, "The Military-Media Connection: For Better or Worse," *Military Review* 78, no. 6 (December 1998-February 1999): 16–20.

[50] Jason Holm, "Get Over It! Repairing the Military's Adversarial Relationship with the Press," *Military Review* 82, no. 1 (January–February 2002): 65.

[51] David Osborne and Ted Gaebler, *Reinventing Government: How the Entrepreneurial Spirit Is Transforming the Public Sector* (Reading, MA: Addison-Wesley Publishing Company, 1992), 166–167.

[52] Information supplied by the League of Cities in a March 1990 letter to California city managers. Also see California Government Code Sections 82041.5 and 89001.

ADDITIONAL SOURCES

Althaus, Scott L. *Collective Preferences in Democratic Politics: Opinion Surveys and the Will of the People.* Cambridge, UK: Cambridge University Press, 2003. Focuses on the pitfalls of using polls to represent people's voices—or their collective preferences.

Artz, Lee, and Yahya R. Kamalipour, eds., *Bring 'Em On: Media and Politics in the U.S. War on Iraq.* Lanham, MD: Rowman & Littlefield, 2004. Presents an interplay among foreign policy, public relations, marketing, news media, and warfare within the context of the war in Iraq.

Berinsky, Adam J. *Silent Voices: Opinion Polls and Political Representation in America.* Princeton, NJ: Princeton University Press, 2004.

Bishop, George F. *The Illusion of Public Opinion: Fact and Artifact in American Public Opinion Polls.* Lanham, MD: Rowman & Littlefield, 2004.

Newland, Chester A. "Public Management and Reform in the United States." In *Public Sector Reform: An International Perspective,* edited by Brendan C. Nolan, 21–32. Houndmills, United Kingdom: Palgrave Publishers Ltd.

Smith, Jeffery A. *War and Press Freedom: The Problem of Prerogative Power.* New York: Oxford University Press, 1999. Discusses military–media relations from the French and American Revolutions to the Cold War.

Sriramesh, Krishnamurthy and Dejan Vercic, eds. *The Global Public Relations Handbook: Theory, Research, and Practice,* Mahwah, NJ: Lawrence Erlbaum Associates, 2003.

Thrall, A. Trevor. *War in the Media Age.* Cresskill, NJ: Hampton Press, 2000. Addresses media coverage of the world's major conflicts and discusses continuing government–press struggles.

17 NONPROFITS, TRADE ASSOCIATIONS, AND NONGOVERNMENTAL ORGANIZATIONS

Communities build nonprofits as vehicles through which people care for the vulnerable, demand civil and equal rights, find creative expression, preserve our heritages, and struggle for worldwide justice and peace.

—Jan Masaoka and John Kreidler[1]

STUDY GUIDE

After studying chapter 17, you should be able to

- Describe the role of public relations in the nonprofit sector.

- Outline some of the major changes affecting nonprofit organizations, health care, and education.

- List and briefly discuss major changes in recent public relations practice in nonprofit organizations.

- Discuss the changing role of public relations in health-care organizations.

- Outline the major purposes of associations, professional societies, and labor unions.

- List the major public relations activities of associations and professional societies.

- Describe the major purposes of public relations in the labor movement.

More so in the United States than in any other country, an array of voluntary nonprofit organizations provides many of the social, educational, cultural, and welfare services vital to society. In effect, the nonprofit sector fills the gaps in meeting the needs of society left unattended by the other two sectors—for-profit corporations and government agencies.

This chapter was written in collaboration with Jim McBride, president of McBride Communications and lecturer in the School of Communication at San Diego State University. He formerly served as director of Public Affairs and Communication for the Kaiser Permanente Medical Care Program, San Diego, California.

Recognition of the role and importance of nonprofit organizations in society highlights the need for effective public relations in the "third sector."

THE THIRD SECTOR

Nonprofit organizations did not always play such a large and significant role in society. There were only 12,500 charitable tax-exempt organizations not affiliated with churches in 1940, and only 32,000 in 1950.[2] In the United States today there are 1 million nonprofit organizations designated by the IRS as 501(c)(3) charitable agencies.[3]

Defining Nonprofit Organizations

Nonprofit organizations exist as a special category of organizations in the tax code in recognition that society is "delegating public tasks to private groups."[4] A definition of the nonprofit sector that can be applied in many countries includes five distinguishing features of such organizations:

1. *Organized.* In short, there is some institutionalized entity, meaning that the organization has a charter, regular meetings, officers, rules, or other indicators of relative permanence.

2. *Private.* Nonprofit organizations are institutionally separate from government, meaning that they are not agencies of or controlled by government, even if they receive government funding.

3. *Nonprofit distributing.* Nonprofit organizations do not attempt to generate profits for the owners or directors. This does not mean that nonprofit organizations cannot make a profit. Rather, it means that distributing the profits to those who manage or direct the enterprise is prohibited, hence the term *not-for-profit.*

4. *Self-governing.* Nonprofit organizations govern themselves and control their activities, meaning that they set their own procedures and are independent of external control. They have their own boards of directors and provide opportunities for citizen involvement without government control or direction.

5. *Voluntary.* At a minimum, there must be some voluntary participation in either the management of the organization or in the conduct of its program, meaning that there is some aspect of charitable contribution involved.

And although debate continues over whether or not the wide variety of charitable tax-exempt organizations truly represents a category that can be meaningfully defined, there is little question about the interdependence of government and the nonprofit sector.

For example, then President George H. W. Bush asked Congress for $425 million to support his "Points of Light Initiative" to help fight drug abuse, illiteracy, homelessness, and other critical social problems. President Bush recognized that nonprofit organizations are essential to the quality of life and in some instances the very survival of many citizens. The Clinton administration continued to emphasize the essential role of nonprofit organizations in "building a bridge to the twenty-first century," and President George W. Bush identified the importance of the church community in addressing pressing community needs by encouraging a "Faith-based Initiative."

Volunteerism and Philanthropy

In many nonprofit organizations, volunteers mean the difference between providing services and closing down the organization. Almost 40 million people volunteer (work without pay) each year at the 1.8 million nonprofit organizations in the United States. This figure includes private foundations reporting annual revenues of $20 billion and a broad range of nonprofit organizations raising more than $300 billion annually. Despite these impressive numbers, however, the number of volunteers and donated dollars are seldom enough to meet the increased demand for nonprofit organizations' services.

While the demand for services continues to outpace revenues, state, county, and local budgets have been cut, causing even fewer staff and reduced resources for social services. This focuses attention on the importance of philanthropic support — a key educational role for public relations to play. Fortunately, charitable giving in America has grown slightly. Since 1998, charitable giving has been 2 percent or more of the gross domestic product (GDP), whereas in 2003 it increased to 2.8 percent. Despite the terrorist attack on September 11, 2001, the war on terror, economic uncertainty, and an uneasy stock market, Americans gave almost $241 billion in 2003, with the largest segment coming from living individuals (see Figure 17.1 for contribution sources).[5]

According to Henry (Hank) Goldstein, chair of Giving USA Foundation:

> People are motivated to give because they value the cause, whether it is religion, education, health care, or international relief. Charitable giving above the 2 percent of gross domestic product is one demonstration of our nation's renewed commitment to the good works done by charities and congregations.[6]

The charitable giving was directed to several types of organizations, with religion and education being the largest beneficiaries. Figure 17.2 shows the types of organizations that received contributions.

Changing Climate

The nonprofit sector operates within a climate of change:

1. Government cutbacks continue to shift responsibility for public service and assistance to voluntary organizations.
2. Competition is intense among hospitals and charitable groups for financial donations and volunteer support.
3. Demand for social and support services exceeds available resources.

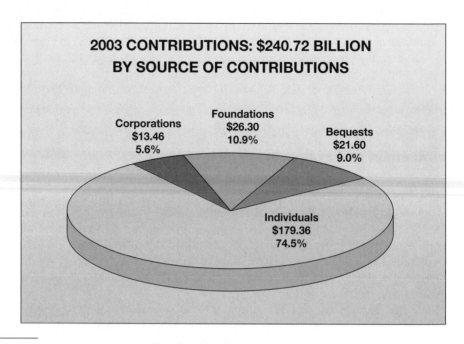

2003 CONTRIBUTIONS: $240.72 BILLION BY SOURCE OF CONTRIBUTIONS

Corporations
$13.46
5.6%

Foundations
$26.30
10.9%

Bequests
$21.60
9.0%

Individuals
$179.36
74.5%

FIGURE 17.1

CHARITABLE GIVING BY SOURCE

Courtesy Giving USA Foundation™, AAFRC Trust for Philanthropy 2004.

4. Diversity and cultural issues in the workplace and among target publics must be addressed.

5. There is growing public concern about the credibility and accountability of tax-exempt organizations.

6. To address social problems, nonprofits are building collaborative relationships and developing strategic partnerships with corporate donors and media organizations.

Charitable agencies within the nonprofit sector are still reeling from exposés of six-figure executive salaries and charges of financial mismanagement and lavish spending. Even the highly respected American Red Cross suffered significant criticism and negative publicity for failing to distribute in a timely manner the funds donated for the victims of the September 11 terrorist attacks. The reputation of the Red Cross was further tarnished when investigations revealed questionable accounting procedures at local chapters across the country. The Red Cross brought in a new CEO and subsequently announced sweeping changes in how disaster victims can access needed help and financial resources.[7]

Reform-minded critics and public officials call for more effective policing of all charitable fund-raising and fuller disclosure of how nonprofit organizations spend their funds. Public relations is charged with both helping rebuild credibility and

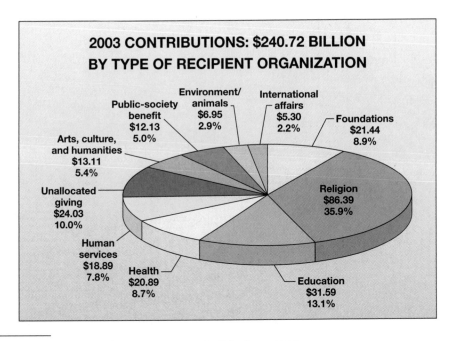

Courtesy Giving USA Foundation™, AAFRC Trust for Philanthropy 2004.

FIGURE 17.2

CHARITABLE GIVING BY TYPE OF RECIPIENT

maintaining or trying to restore public confidence in the many charitable agencies and voluntary groups that serve the needs of so many. Figure 17.3 illustrates one organization's rebuttal.

As health-care costs continued to rise through the 1990s, consumers, providers of health services and those who pay for health care—including the government—started demanding changes in the financing of health care. Some of these reform initiatives impacted quality of care and access to services, prompting the media to scrutinize the health industry. The nation debated topics like why health care costs so much, who will pay, who will be covered, what care will be available, and what are the roles of government, health insurance companies, health maintenance organizations (HMOs), private hospitals, doctors, nurses, and other caregivers. Public relations played a vital role in educating lawmakers and key target publics about health-care costs and the delicate balance between cost, access, and quality.

Questions about cost, access, and quality also dominated the public debate about education reform. Growing public concern almost caused a major change in California's educational system. Californians voted on a ballot initiative that, if approved, would have granted every parent an educational voucher worth about $4,000 per child that could be spent at either a public or private school. The pro-posal stimulated heated debate and was soundly defeated at the

FIGURE 17.3

**AMERICAN HEART
ASSOCIATION
CONTRIBUTION
SOLICITATION INSERT**

76% of every dollar we spend goes directly towards research, education and community service programs.

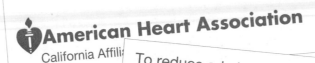

American Heart Association

California Affili

To reduce administrative costs, all gifts are processed at a central facility. Rest assured your contribution supports research and programs in your local area. For more information, please call your local American Heart Association. Thank you.

American Heart Association

Courtesy American Heart Association.

polls. Even though the ballot initiative failed, it spurred a serious reassessment of the education system and served as a wake-up call for public schools across the country.

At the national level, Congress passed the "No Child Left Behind Act of 2001" to ensure quality education by, among other things, increasing accountability among schools and teachers as well as requiring higher student scores—with financial consequences if performance standards are not met. Although many school superintendents across the country instituted standards of accountability, teachers unions and others lobbied for additional financing for schools as a better way to address educational problems. As the merits of the different reform proposals were debated, education administrators invited public relations specialists to work more closely with school districts, colleges and universities, and educational associations, as well as with parents and teachers.

ROLE OF PUBLIC RELATIONS IN NONPROFIT ORGANIZATIONS

In short, following a historic pattern, public relations is often added, expanded, and elevated in stature when organizations are confronted by outside forces, threatened with funding cuts or outright elimination, or otherwise pressured to change or reform. The nonprofit sector faces all these crises in an environment of increasing competition for donations, diminishing government subsidies, and increasing demand for services.

In most nonprofit agencies public relations aims to

1. Define or "brand" the organization, gain acceptance of its mission, and protect its reputation.
2. Develop channels of communication with those an organization serves.
3. Create and maintain a favorable climate for fund-raising.
4. Support the development and maintenance of public policy that is favorable to an organization's mission.
5. Inform and motivate key organizational constituents (such as employees, volunteers, and trustees) to dedicate themselves and work productively in support of an organization's mission, goals, and objectives.

Even though these objectives are common to most nonprofit organizations, the public relations tactics may differ greatly. For example, hospitals typically invest relatively more in public relations and associated programs such as marketing and development. In recent years, hospitals and health-care organizations have integrated public relations with marketing, as well as business development, government affairs, physician education, and even strategic planning.

To the extent that social and economic conditions require public support, public relations helps create the public policy environment, volunteer participation, and philanthropic support crucial to the survival of charitable organizations.

Health-care agencies, social service agencies, churches, educational institutions, and fine and performing arts groups all depend on public support (see Exhibit 17.1 for Principles of Fund-Raising).

The intense competition for limited resources in recent years has led to profound changes in how public relations is practiced in nonprofit organizations:

1. Integrating public relations with marketing, and management by objectives have emerged as important parts of the communication strategy.
2. Nonprofit sector leaders (boards of directors or trustees and program managers) have raised the standards and stepped up pressure to engage professional public relations assistance—either hiring staff or outside consultants.
3. Recruiting volunteers and obtaining donations are standard expectations of the public relations role.
4. Paid advertising has emerged as a major controlled communications tactic for nonprofit organizations, particularly for the health-care industry.
5. Strategic partnerships linking nonprofits with corporate donors and news media organizations have emerged to enhance the reputation of nonprofits and promote their services.

EXHIBIT 17.1

PRINCIPLES OF FUND-RAISING

Preparation

1. The five essentials of a successful campaign are a strong case, effective leadership, conscientious workers, prospects willing and able to give, and sufficient funds to finance the campaign.

2. Committee work and publicity work should be coordinated and spelled out in detail in advance.

3. The cost of a campaign, within reasonable limits, should be estimated in advance.

4. All campaign activities should be given a time limit and specific deadlines.

Committee Work

1. The originating group, whether a committee or a board of directors, should be a representative body.

2. Strong leadership is a necessity.

3. The effectiveness of the group depends on the degree to which individuals accept responsibility.

4. Committees are better at critiquing than creating. Before asking for ideas or suggestions for a plan, give each member of the group a copy of the plan to critique.

Publicity

1. The first objective of publicity is to sell the idea; the second objective is to sell the means of its accomplishment.

2. Publicity materials should appeal both to the emotions and to the intellect.

3. Publicity must have continuity, with all the elements of a campaign tied together with a theme of common appeal.

4. Publicity should proceed from the general to the specific. Interest in an idea proceeds from an appeal of general application.

5. Cheap publicity is expensive. Quality in publicity efforts pays dividends.

6. Publicity should be positive and not negative. Effective publicity always plays up elements of strength.

Campaign Operation

1. A campaign should solve immediate financial needs and lay a firm foundation for future campaigns.

2. Effective canvassing answers five questions: why, where, who, what, and how.

3. Campaigns should periodically reach milestones to arouse and maintain interest.

4. All canvassing, even for special gifts, should be conducted in an atmosphere of universality. Prospects typically ask, "What are others doing?"

5. Campaigns should be conducted under a steady and constant pressure and sense of urgency.

6. The time spent on a campaign varies directly with the size of the goal and inversely with the popularity of the appeal.

7. The direct appeal for help should be made when interest is at its peak.

8. There are four tests of the effectiveness of campaign operations: quality, quantity, cost, and time.

9. Campaign impact is determined by the degree to which the campaign objectives were achieved.

---

6. Technology, including Web sites and e-mail, has extended the selectivity and reach of communication, but has raised questions about ethics, privacy, and legitimacy.

Many social service agencies have neither the financial resources nor the expertise necessary to mount sophisticated public relations or marketing efforts. Some nonprofit organizations must rely on inexperienced practitioners, the executive director, or even volunteers who are not communicators to conduct their public relations programs.

Nonprofit organizations generate revenue from three major sources: **Private charitable giving** (gifts from individuals, corporations, and foundations), **govern-**

ment support or payments (grants and contracts or reimbursements for services), and **private fees and payments** (proceeds from the sale of services or products to the consumer). Nonprofit organizations in the United States generate 52 percent of their revenue from private fees and payment, 30 percent from government sources, and 19 percent from private charitable giving.[8]

It is clear from these data that nonprofits are dependent on multiple funding sources to meet the social, cultural, educational, and health-care needs of society.

FOUNDATIONS

Private and community grant-making foundations are part of the growing nonprofit sector. A foundation is a nongovernmental, nonprofit organization that uses its own funds to provide grants and financial assistance, primarily to other unrelated nonprofit agencies for educational, social, religious, cultural, or other charitable activities.[9]

Company-sponsored foundations either have an endowment established by a for-profit corporation or receive annual contributions from that corporation or both. **Independent** foundations are those established when an individual, family, or group contributes a significant sum to achieve a goal. **Community** foundations receive gifts from many different donors who are interested in funding programs in their own community. To comply with federal law, foundations must distribute at least 5 percent of their investment assets annually, making foundations one of the major sources of grants to other nonprofit organizations.[10]

There are about 62,000 active private and community foundations in the United States, with assets totaling $476 billion. The largest foundation, by size of assets, is the Bill and Melinda Gates Foundation, which has more $30 billion in assets. Lilly Endowment, Inc. is number two, with nearly $11 billion, and the Ford Foundation is third largest with assets totaling $10 billion. In one year, foundations give grants, scholarships, and employee matching gifts totaling more than $30 billion.[11]

In recent years foundations shied away from making as many major capital commitments and instead focused more on helping nonprofits sustain their operations in a more difficult economic environment.[12]

SOCIAL SERVICE AGENCIES

Nonprofit social service agencies, sometimes called human service agencies, fill a vital role in the health, safety, and well-being of millions of Americans. These nonprofit agencies and programs fill needs that other organizations are unable to meet by providing services and resources that either are not accessible or not readily available to those who need them. Social service programs typically are organized to provide parent and child programs, food and nutrition programs, shelter, services for the deaf and vision impaired, drug rehabilitation, services for the mentally ill or refugees, those suffering from depression, and much more. Programs like Medicaid or Food Stamps are generally considered social welfare programs.

Although federal and state governments spend hundreds of billions on social welfare and social service programs annually, it is still not enough to meet the demand for services. In many communities, budget deficits are requiring cuts in government spending on social programs. The burden of funding community nonprofit agencies shifts to American philanthropy, as nonprofit agencies strive to do more with less (i.e. recruit more volunteers and seek additional donations to fund programs and services). Given this situation, enlightened nonprofit social service agencies realize that public relations expertise is required to achieve organizational goals such as maintaining existing funding and attracting new philanthropy, building a committed staff and mobilizing volunteers, educating legislators and key community leaders to gain their support, establishing strategic partnerships, and so on.

A major challenge social service agencies face is whether to hire a public relations professional or contract with an outside firm for these services. Regardless of which choice is made, it is crucial for social service agencies to muster public support through a planned, strategic public relations program that will endure in good times or bad. Figure 17.4 shows the "United Way Wheel," graphically illustrating the components of United Way of America's public relations effort.

Beyond the fund-raising challenge, communicating with potential beneficiaries of social services can be a challenge. Without professional public relations assistance, it may be difficult to reach the people who need services. Many do not know how to access available services or simply do not know that services are available. In addition, because agencies must respect the privacy of clients, publicity and media coverage may be limited. In ethnically diverse communities, communication must address cultural and language differences, limited access to information, or low education levels.

FIGURE 17.4

UNITED WAY WHEEL

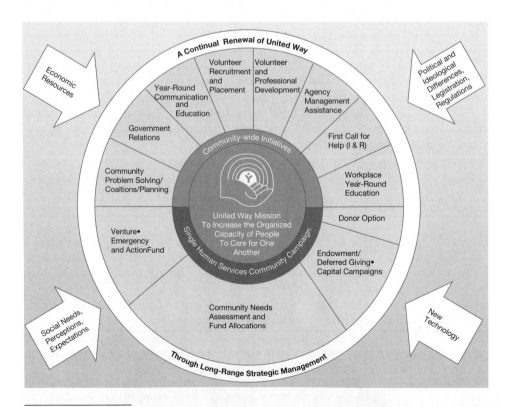

Courtesy United Way of America.

The role of public relations in social service agencies is rich with possibilities and variety. It includes counseling executive directors and boards of directors about the role of communication and developing a planned program to address organizational issues and achieve goals. Public relations supports recruiting of volunteers and fund-raising efforts. A key role is educating publics about the nature of the conditions their clients face and building trust in how agencies can help build a healthier community.

Currently, nonprofit agencies, news organizations, and corporate donors are creating strategic partnerships that help each achieve goals. Strategic partnerships often include a corporate donation used in part to fund a media campaign featuring a nonprofit agency. The donor gets positive publicity as a responsible corporate neighbor; the news organization gets the funds and enhances its image as a community leader; and the nonprofit agency receives significant media coverage to tell its story.

HEALTH CARE

More than a decade ago, Harris Wolford, a Pennsylvania college professor and Democratic state official, scored a stunning U.S. Senate victory over his White House–endorsed opponent by making health-care reform the centerpiece of his campaign—quality, access, and cost. In 2002, John Baldacci was elected governor of Maine on a platform of comprehensive health-care reform. Again, quality, access, and cost were among the issues.

The health-care system in America is in desperate need of significant reform. In the early 1990s, President Bill Clinton's complex proposal to expand access to health coverage for the uninsured and to control costs for those already covered, created significant resistance from the medical industry and never reached a formal floor vote in either house of Congress.[13]

Recent political strategy for reforming health care is to proceed incrementally with Congress and state legislatures focusing on a handful of smaller proposals to reform health care, such as expanding health insurance coverage—especially among vulnerable groups such as low-income Hispanic children and the disabled, encouraging greater use of generic drugs, adjusting tax credits, and exploring how information technology can improve health-care quality.

Still, despite years of analysis and health-policy debates at every level of government, the issues related to the quality, access, and costs of health care remain unresolved, and medical costs are accelerating at a much faster rate than the overall cost of living.[14]

Health Care in Crisis

The crisis in health care has been with us for so long, some would say we always will be in a state of crisis. Sherry Glied, Ph.D., of Columbia University summarizes it this way:

> In some senses we've always been in a health care crisis….We have a real conflict between how much money we're willing to spend on health care and how much we want for that money, and that's a perpetual conflict.[15]

Despite health industry efforts to exert downward pressure on rising costs, the costs continue to rise.

Factors influencing the continuing rise in health-care costs include advancing medical technology, skyrocketing medical malpractice rates, increasing government regulation, and surging costs of prescription drugs. Direct-to-consumer marketing of prescription drugs is creating demand where none previously existed.

According to the Kaiser Family Foundation, expenditures in the United States on health care have increased 87 percent since 1990, and in 2000 national health expenditures reached $1.3 trillion.[16]

In the meantime, 43 million Americans—including 12 million children—are not covered by health insurance of any kind. The total number of uninsured people increases by about one million a year.[17]

The uninsured issue has both financial and health implications. Delaying or not receiving treatment can lead to more serious illness. In California, for example, where 1 out of every 5 people is uninsured, hospitals provided $3.6 billion in uncompensated care in just one year.[18]

Assuring access to critical health services for the uninsured is a national priority. But it must compete for political attention and funding with numerous other major issues, including modernizing Medicare; attending to the special needs of the mentally ill and those with AIDS, Alzheimer's and Parkinson's; and preventing chronic conditions such as diabetes, obesity, and asthma.[19]

Health-Care Public Relations and Marketing

All hospitals must remain financially viable—whether they are nonprofit, in which case they reinvest net proceeds in health services, or for profit, in which case they pay shareholders. If they do not make money, they go out of business.

A major challenge in health care is responding to the decreasing reimbursement from third-party payers (insurance companies, HMOs, and the government). Less revenue means budget cuts, and layoffs and could potentially affect the survival of hospitals and health systems.

Another major challenge is responding to increasing government regulation of hospitals and health systems. Some regulations are mandated, but no funding is provided to implement required changes. For example, the state of California passed earthquake safety legislation that requires all acute-care inpatient hospitals to either be retrofitted or rebuilt to survive earthquakes. The price tag for this safety effort is estimated at anywhere from $24 to $41 billion, depending on what is included in the cost estimates.[20]

To survive in this complex, competitive, and rapidly changing environment, health-care leaders have turned to public relations and marketing for help. Marketing identifies the wants and needs of a hospital's constituents and guides the organization toward effectively satisfying those wants and needs. This can be challenging for three reasons:

1. Generally, the payer for health services—an insurance company—has limited control over the purchase or cost of service.

2. It is usually the physician or other provider—rather than the patient—who chooses a hospital or orders services.

3. The services rendered can be painful and unpleasant, clearly making a distinction between wants and needs.

Like marketing, health-care public relations has evolved into a highly regarded management function that is expected to contribute to the "bottom line." Today's public relations professionals must understand the business and financing of health care, know about health-care issues, have an ability to think and plan strategically, research skills to monitor consumers' perceptions, and be able work as part of a team, especially with the marketing department. The increasing overlap among many health-care departments requires a working knowledge of other disciplines to facilitate decision making and more effective communication.

Although public relations and marketing are distinct management functions expected to achieve different outcomes, they work closely together in today's health-care environment, utilizing their respective strengths in ways that enhance the survival of the health-care organizations.

Role of the News Media

Although health-care reform has been hotly debated for more than a decade, media coverage of health policy has increased over that time. Researchers at the Kaiser Family Foundation, in conjunction with Princeton Survey Research Associates, examined media coverage of four health topics—Medicare, the uninsured, health-care costs, and managed care. From 1997 to 2000, they found a 34 percent increase in news stories about health-care issues.[21]

The emergence of the Internet and availability of Web sites is causing a fundamental change in the nature of health-care media relations. Millions now use the Internet as a source of health information. Health-care organizations make their own news stories available to a worldwide audience by posting them on Web sites. Whether reporting on a breaking news story or just looking for story ideas, health reporters more frequently turn to company Web sites. Even news organizations have created their own Web sites, which is also changing the nature of health news reporting.

Even though technology offers many communication advantages to hospitals and health-care organizations, today's environment is still characterized by increased media scrutiny of health-care operations. According to Bruce Vladeck, president of the United Hospital Fund:

> Of all the tasks of leadership in healthcare organizations, maintaining communications between the organization and its communities is perhaps the most important.[22]

Although Web sites, paid advertising, community relations, interpersonal communication, publications, videos, and CDs all play a role in reaching target publics, the mass media still play an important role in setting the health-care agenda, explaining health-care issues, and shaping the reputation of hospitals.

Just as in other industries, honesty, rapid access to decision makers, and prompt response are the keys to good media relations in hospital or health-care settings. Most hospitals have an authorized spokesperson on call 24 hours a day to answer inquiries from the media. Journalists expect hospital administrators and senior leaders to be accessible—especially in crises. How the public relations staff responds to media needs in routine or crisis situations can have lasting impact on the organization's reputation.

Media requests for hospitalized patient condition reports, however, have strained relationships between the media and public relations practitioners. The Health Insurance Portability and Accountability Act of 1996 (HIPPA), which went into effect in 2003, creates strict rules governing patient privacy rights. One of

HIPPA's most notable restrictions is that the media must have a patient's first and last name before hospital officials can release patient condition reports. Without the patient's name, the hospital cannot even acknowledge that the patient is in the hospital.[23]

Many journalists are frustrated by HIPPA because it severely restricts their ability to obtain information for news stories involving accident victims or people hospitalized for other reasons, including celebrities or "public figures." Because the media were unprepared for HIPPA, the responsibility for educating the media fell on hospitals and health-care associations. The Californian Healthcare Association produced a booklet, "A Guide to Release of Patient Information to the Media," and made it available on its Web site (www.calhealth.org).[24]

HIPPA rules may prevent hospitals from responding to allegations made by disgruntled patients who take their complaint to the media (see Exhibit 17.2).

Whether adapting to legislation or responding to economic and social changes, public relations in the health industry has emerged in recent years as a vital member of the management team. Steven V. Seekins, a former vice president of the American Medical Association and an accredited member of PRSA, identifies an increasingly important role for practitioners in health-care settings: "To make public relations indispensable to senior management, practitioners must stake out issues management as an area of expertise."[25] No doubt the complex and hotly contested public debate on how to make quality health care both affordable and available to all those in need will continue for years. All parties in the debate will call on public relations practitioners to help set the agenda and to contribute constructively to shaping public policy in health care.

EXHIBIT 17.2

WHEN PATIENTS TAKE COMPLAINTS TO THE MEDIA

In a health-care environment characterized by diminishing public trust, increased litigation, a scrutinizing media, and a 24-hour news cycle, hospitals and health-care organizations find themselves the target of patient allegations about poor-quality care, denying access to care, failure to provide coverage of a procedure, and other issues.

When disgruntled patients take their complaints to the media, HIPPA restrictions on the release of patient information may have implications regarding the reputation of a hospital or physicians.

If a patient's complaint is compelling, and the media decide to do a story, what can the institution say in its defense? Unless the patient has a signed HIPPA consent form, the hospital cannot respond to the specific allegations, even if they are untrue. This is a public relations challenge.

Although HIPPA restricts the information hospitals can release about individuals, there are options for the public relations staff to consider. First, brief senior leaders on the situation and try to arrange a top administrator to serve as spokesperson. The spokesperson should express concern about the allegations and a strong commitment to look into them. The spokesperson can explain hospital policies and procedures or convey key general messages about quality of care or the expertise of the staff. The media may also appreciate general fact sheets about the medical condition faced by the patient, without saying anything specific about the patient making the allegations.

Although very little specific information can be released, a prompt response to the media helps journalists create a more balanced news report and assures consumers that the hospital takes these situations seriously.

EDUCATION

Education touches the lives of virtually every citizen. More than 74.6 million students, ages 3 and older, are enrolled in school.[26] There are 6.2 million teachers in the United States with about half (3.1 million) teaching at the elementary and middle school level. Federal, state, and local governments spent $410 billion dollars a year for elementary and high school education in 2001, an increase of $30 billion from the previous year.[27]

Accountability

Since the 1980s, policy makers, business leaders, professionals, and parents have challenged the efficacy of public education. The public has debated education reform ever since. The emerging consensus seems to be that major structural change is needed to fix the system. Growing public dissatisfaction revolves around the "value" proposition (i.e., the relationship between school performance and cost of education).

Virtually everyone is demanding that schools be more accountable. Demands for accountability have moved far beyond student achievement scores to include calls for teacher competency tests and the institution of merit-based incentive pay. Taxpayers and legislators reject the notion that schools and universities will improve if given more funds. Educators and schools believe that demanding change without reallocating or adding additional resources will not work.

Central to the difficult task facing public education is widespread concern that the money taxpayers spend on their schools and universities is not used effectively. However, that is not a simple issue. Education reform involves many more dimensions, including parental involvement, the physical and emotional health of children, cultural diversity, class size, relevant programming, how technology is changing learning, transportation and access issues, and many more.

Public Relations for Public Schools

The dilemma for public relations in this environment is that although the public values education and feels that it is a good investment, the public also feels that educational outcomes are not good and the costs are too high. The major objectives of public relations for public schools include the following:

1. To increase awareness of educational issues, especially funding issues, to dispel misinformation and rumor (see Figure 17.5).
2. To cultivate relationships with key constituents to build public support and help ensure adequate funding, including donations where appropriate.
3. To gain public acceptance of educational initiatives and support when making educational changes.
4. To enhance the reputation of schools among key target audiences.

Public relations for education is expanding in scope, concept, and utilization. It has taken on increased importance as officials try to persuade taxpayers to raise school levies to cope with inflation or to pass bond issues for new buildings. In

FIGURE 17.5

**PUBLIC SCHOOL
LITERATURE**

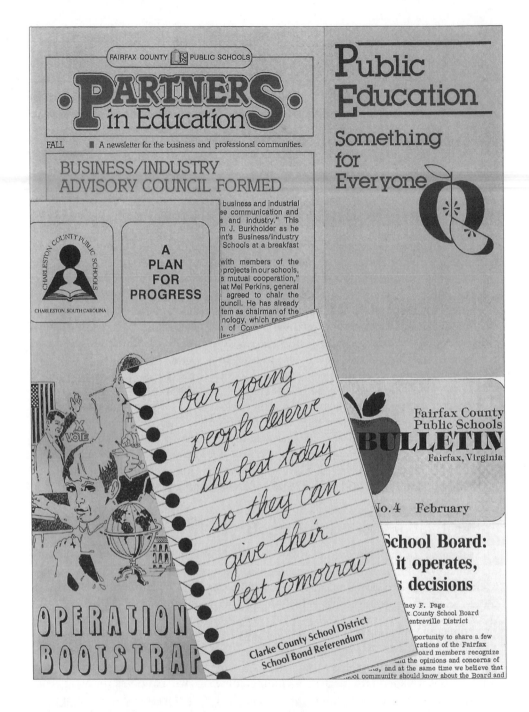

addition to helping schools address the financial issues, public relations directors help school officials deal with other crises. Some examples include: responding to the pledge of allegiance debate and the broader separation of church and state issue, determining when freedom of expression becomes hate speech, responding to the changing educational needs of society, incorporating technology in the classroom, and clarifying the role of the school in social issues such as sex education and providing condoms on campus.

The relationships between educational institutions and the communities they serve are many, diverse, and complex. Key target audiences for education include

1. *Parents play a key role in building support for adequate budgets.* Good relationships with parents start with frequent, frank communication between teachers and parents.

2. *School staff, from principal and teacher to custodian and school nurse, must become engaged in school public relations programs.* Many superintendents have organized advisory councils that include representatives from all categories of employees.

3. *Students may be the school system's most important public.* School executives should ensure that pupils are well informed about policies, that courses satisfy their needs and challenge their abilities, that individual attention is provided to those who need it, and that the overall atmosphere engenders pupil and parent pride in the school.

4. *Business community and school partnerships take many forms.* These can include adopt-a-school programs, resource sharing, consultation in management and technology, and advocacy with state and local governments to increase support for public schools.

5. *Community groups, such as neighbors, potential donors, and other concerned citizens.* These may be reached through Parent Teacher Associations (PTA) meetings, special events and forums, service clubs, church groups, Web sites, the media, etc.

6. *Local news media, cable television, and Web sites are key to informing the public about local school challenges.* To obtain strategic news coverage, schools must be creative and persistent in sharing information about educational curriculum and policies.

7. *Board of education members who can act as intermediaries between school publics and the professional administrators.* It is essential that board members agree on an adequate statement of public relations policy.

Higher Education

Enrollment in colleges and universities continues to grow, with more than 15 million people enrolled in college. The children of baby boomers are now graduating from high school and entering college, a trend that will continue for several years. In addition to increased numbers, the race and ethnic composition of college students is shifting with more African Americans, Hispanics, Asians, and foreign-born students enrolled in higher education.[28] The demand is increasing for more classes and newly added disciplines like information and technology science, as well as for more computers and Internet access. Although citizens do not want to spend more money on education, they also do not want to see classes cut. This creates financial and other challenges for higher education administrators as they hire faculty and staff, expand facilities, and add new technology.[29]

In recent years, many states have not increased higher education budgets enough to cover increased costs and demands for classes, research, and off-campus services. On many campuses, an increasing share of the cost is being covered by increases in student tuition and fees.

Higher education faces four continuing problems:

1. Financial support is insufficient and precarious.
2. Competition for qualified students is spirited and costly.
3. Government constraints and regulations make university administration difficult and costly.
4. Academic freedom and tenure are challenged by both internal and external stakeholders.

Higher education must "meet these issues head on," according to Gail Raiman, vice president for public affairs, National Association of Independent Colleges and Universities:

> Just as the media are being more aggressive in covering education, we must be more aggressive in educating the public and opinion leaders. We need to use clear language, not academic jargon. We have to go to these opinion leaders instead of waiting for them to come to us.[30]

Today, colleges face public relations challenges unlike anything in the past. One of the primary concerns in higher education is ensuring adequate funding. Public relations departments now align themselves closely with University Advancement and Alumni Associations to strengthen fund-raising efforts and increase donations and financial gifts.

In addition, a university's public relations staff must be prepared for potentially explosive issues such as challenges to its admissions policy, or campus crises such as crime, student alcohol or drug abuse, sexual harassment allegations, racial tension, closing academic units, and more.

To achieve public relations goals in higher education, programs typically target the following key publics:

1. *Students.* Students are both a university's most important public and its most important public relations representatives.
2. *Faculty and staff.* Faculty and staff are important internal publics because of their critical roles in education and governance, and their role as representatives of the university to external constituencies.
3. *Alumni.* Alumni contributions are the single most important source of voluntary support in higher education.
4. *Community groups and business leaders.* Many colleges and universities are turning to the business sector to build new, mutually beneficial relationships.
5. *Government.* Public relations must build understanding and support in all levels of government, especially in education departments.
6. *Media.* Building positive media relations is an investment that pays off over the long term. But centralizing and coordinating the news flow from the campus can be difficult to achieve. A college or university "speaks" with many voices—the president and other administrators, the public information office, the student newspaper and radio station, the faculty, and the athletic director and coaches, to name but a few.
7. *Parents and others.* Parents are a ready-made nucleus of support. Other publics include prospective students and their parents, current and prospective

donors, opinion leaders, philanthropic foundations, sister educational institutions worldwide, and professional organizations and scholarly societies.

College Presidents' Public Relations Role

Presidents must be effective communicators and mediators to balance the conflicting values and demands of key target publics. They must recognize that public relations is a required part of the job. Almost a third of university and college presidents say that they meet more frequently with their public relations officers than with any other member of the management team.[31] The president is the key to establishing the relationships and public support needed to fulfill higher education's mission in the new global society. As one former president said, "The president is the one best able to sell the entire institution."[32]

CHURCHES AND OTHER NONPROFIT ORGANIZATIONS

Space does not allow detailed analysis of all nonprofit settings. Brief descriptions of some of the issues and pressures on churches, libraries, museums, and arts groups will illustrate how the practice of public relations is both as complex and as essential in these settings as in other nonprofit settings. Public relations plays a role in advocating for nonprofit organizations (see Figure 17.6).

Religion and spirituality appear to be enjoying a revival in America. Findings from a Pew Research Center poll indicate that 71 percent of Americans believe in God and that 53 percent think prayer is important in their daily life. Both figures represent increases of more than 10 percent during the past decade.[33]

Religion is a strong and growing force in the way Americans think about politics and government. Its increasing influence on political opinion and behavior rivals factors such as race, region, age, social class, and gender. Those who say religion plays a very important role in their lives are more conservative, but there is little indication of a coherent pattern of liberal belief associated with any major religion or religious group.[34]

Organized religion is actively participating in social change efforts. For example, the nonprofit National Council of Churches has joined with 100 business leaders, religious groups, unions, insurers, consumer organizations, and provider groups to call on our nation's policy makers to dramatically overhaul the health-care system.[35]

Even in good times, however, the church is not immune from public relations crises. The child molestation scandal in the Catholic Church caused community outrage as well as shock and sadness among churchgoers and the vast majority of priests and clergy. The election of the Episcopal Church's first openly gay bishop created a crisis within the church, with conservative and traditionalist bishops raising the possibility that the church will split over this issue.[36] Some television evangelists and faith healers have been exposed as lavish spenders and frauds.

The September 11 terrorist attacks not only changed the world forever, but also had a strong impact on religion—both positive and negative. By 51 to 28 percent, Americans think the lesson of September 11 is that there is too little, not too much religion in the world. Questions have been raised about the Islamic faith and its teachings regarding violence. Although the public holds a favorable view of Muslims in this country, Muslims not identified as Americans get a mixed review. When

Meet J. Robert Anderson, philanthropist.

He's not a millionaire. In fact, he's not even rich. But he gives.

Most of the giving in this country doesn't come from the wealthy. Almost half of it comes from people who earn less than $20,000 a year. Everyday, ordinary people. Like the guy down the street. Or your next-door neighbor. Or 100 million others who, every year, give unselfishly just to help people.

And while those who give

may sometimes go unnoticed, their contributions don't. Because in this country, when a lot of people give, it adds up to a lot.

It helps fund important research. It helps run community church programs. It helps support local charities.

It helps people out.

There are so many things in this country that could use your hand. Your time, your tal-

ents, your money. What you give isn't so important. That you do give is. Because you don't have to

be rich to be a philanthropist. You just have to care.

A Public Service of This Publication & The Advertising Council

From the Advertising Council.

Courtesy Advertising Council.

Islam is rated, favorable responses outweigh unfavorable ones by a thin 38 to 33 percent margin.[37]

On top of such crises and activism, churches face increased competition for volunteer commitment and dollars. Slightly less than half the nation's population are regular churchgoers. Declining participation and the financial squeeze have underlined the importance of public relations to many church leaders. As a major force in society and social change, however, the church cannot avoid the spotlight. Virtually all the major denominations as well as many smaller churches and church-affiliated schools or hospitals have professional communicators on staff or public relations firms on retainer. With this professional help, churches are better able to respond to crises, convey strategic messages, enhance the image of churches, recruit new members, and strengthen the faith. The Church of Jesus Christ of Latter-day Saints, for example, used the 2002 Winter Olympics in Salt Lake City, Utah, to tell its story and improve understanding of the Mormon Church.[38]

Technology also is helping churches tell their stories. Church Web sites offer a broad range of content that tends to promote acceptance of the churches' missions.

Although apparently much less controversial by their very nature and missions, libraries, museums, and arts groups compete for public support in the form of volunteers, donations, and public funding. Many of these important institutions, which contribute so much to the quality of life, live in a financial straitjacket that does not permit adequate funding either for their programs or for professional public relations assistance.

Most public libraries in major cities have public relations departments, usually called public information departments. However, in smaller cities and suburbs, the public libraries may have very small staffs that do not include public relations expertise. At best, these libraries may take advantage of volunteer support and special events like National Library Week to achieve limited public relations objectives. To provide effective public relations support to its many small libraries, Wisconsin established the Coordinated Library Information Program, which provides the counsel of a public relations specialist to libraries in that state.

Like libraries, arts groups in this nation face a constant battle to keep the financial wolf from the door. In recent years, both foundations and the government have cut support of cultural institutions and museums.

Always confronted with the challenges of attracting individual volunteers and obtaining funding from donors and other public and private sources, nonprofit organizations recognize the importance of effective public relations and have come to rely on it. Without effective public relations, many nonprofits would have to close their doors, leaving the most vulnerable members of society with nowhere to turn.

ASSOCIATIONS AND SOCIETIES

A trade association is an organization dedicated to promoting the interests and assisting the members of a particular industry. Today, more than 147,000 associations exist in the United States, representing nearly every industry, profession, or special interest. Trade associations exist to advance the interests of their members by offering education programs, convention planning, Web site and e-mail communication among members, and public information activities. Americans active in associations devote more than 173 million volunteer hours each year—time valued at more than $2 billion—to charitable and community service projects.[39]

Types of Associations

Professional associations and **professional societies** typically represent individuals engaged in similar work based on common educational preparation or specialized knowledge. Examples include the American Nurses' Association, the American Bar Association, and the Public Relations Society of America. **Cause groups** and **special-interest groups** function as associations of individuals with a common interest or goal. Examples include the National Audubon Society and the American Automobile Association.

Membership in the more than 3,500 **trade associations** includes companies, firms, or other organizations engaged in similar activities. Business competitors associate in order to organize and implement mutual-assistance efforts and to expand or protect their industry. Examples include the American Automobile Manufacturers Association, with only three members, and the National Automobile Dealers Association, with approximately 19,000 members.

Producer associations and **commodity boards**, such as the National Dairy Promotion and Research Board, the National Livestock and Meat Board, and the Illinois Pork Producers Association, represent the interests of their members and promote consumption of their commodities.

Federations—also referred to as councils or institutes—typically include other associations. Examples are the Federation of National Associations, the National Cotton Council of America, and the Transportation Institute.

Federations of labor unions, such as the Teamsters and the American Federation of Labor and Congress of Industrial Organizations (AFL-CIO), represent many different occupational, trade, and craft unions. The AFL-CIO represents 13 million working people nationwide.[40]

Trade associations, professional societies, and labor unions advance the interests of their members in three ways: They provide information and services to members, they promote high standards of self-discipline, and they present the members' case to important publics and to government bodies. According to Christine Maurer and Tara E. Sheets, editors of *Encyclopedia of Associations*,

> Driven by the knowledge that they can achieve more through group efforts than they can individually, Americans have made associations one of the most powerful forces in the United States today.[41]

Well-known national associations include the YMCA of the USA with almost 17 million members and the American Tobacco Institute, which represents a relatively small number of corporations but is a powerful association. One of the most influential associations in the United States, the American Association of Retired Persons (AARP), flexed its muscle on behalf of 35 million members and contributed to the passage of a Medicare prescription drug bill.[42] The American Bar Association is an organization of 400,000 legal professionals that promotes improvements in the American system of justice.[43] The influential American Medical Association represents 250,000 physicians and medical students.[44]

At the state level, the California Milk Advisory Board promotes consumption of dairy products. Another statewide dairy association, the Dairy Council of California (DCC), conducts nutrition education programs financed by more than 2,000 California producers and more than 100 handlers of milk and milk products. In 2004, DCC had a budget of more than $5 million, 4 offices, 30 professionals working in nutrition education, and the services of the San Diego public relations firm of Nuffer, Smith, Tucker, Inc. Their educational programs are presented in secondary school classrooms and are directed to the medical and nutrition communities.

The resources dairy associations are able to direct to such activities illustrate the power of producer groups: Congress mandated that dairy farmers nationally contribute a 15-cent checkoff on every 100 pounds of milk produced to promote dairy products. Five cents of the checkoff goes to the National Dairy Promotion and Research Board, 5 cents goes to state or regional promotion organizations, and the remaining 5 cents (sometimes referred to as the "middle nickel") can go to either the national or state organization, depending on which one individual dairy farmers designate.[45]

The Problem of Serving Many Masters

In contrast to corporations and other organizations with clearly defined business interests, associations typically serve a variety of membership interests. Association staffs must attempt to meet membership demands and serve their interests externally but often must do so with little centralized power and authority. The challenge for public relations is to find the common ground and unifying positions that best represent member interests. Thus, associations are by nature limited to areas of action in which there is an obvious, predetermined unanimity of opinion or a substantial majority in support of any initiatives taken on behalf of membership.

Associations log nearly 200 million volunteer hours with activities such as organizing blood drives for the American Red Cross, contributing to the United Way, delivering meals, staffing hotlines, and more. Associations also protect consumers by ensuring high professional standards, disseminating accurate information to those who need it most, or providing educational background on health care, tax reform, product safety, and other issues affecting Americans.

Growing Importance of Public Relations

Association public relations practitioners design and implement programs to address a variety of challenges:

1. To provide members with helpful information (see Figure 17.7 for examples of association publications)

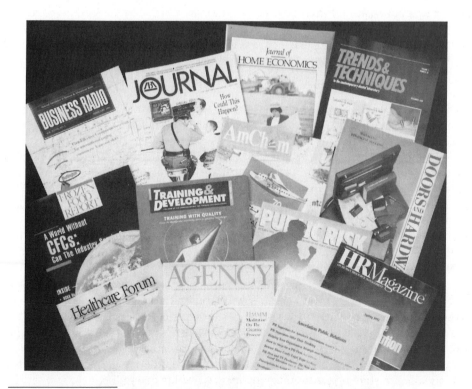

FIGURE 17.7

EXAMPLES OF ASSOCIATION PUBLICATIONS

Courtesy American Society of Association Executives.

2. To expand the association by recruiting new members

3. To harmonize member viewpoints by promoting positive positions

4. To promote the industry or profession

5. To influence government legislation and regulation

6. To improve products and services

7. To gain popular support and combat adverse publicity

8. To train recruits and provide continuing education for all members

9. To contribute to social progress by sponsoring public service programs

10. To promote behavior standards among members that will enhance credibility and stave off government regulation

To achieve these purposes, public relations practitioners in associations are playing increasingly important roles in dealing with issues in the news that affect their members. For example, when health-care reform dominated public debate, the American Medical Association public information staff responded to more than 1,100 calls a month, with about 75 percent of the calls from reporters:

> Associations have an advantage when it comes to dealing with the news media and other audiences. To the media and other publics, associations often have more credibility than individual companies or public relations firms because, correctly or not, they are perceived as less self-serving.[46]

The major goals of associations parallel those of public relations: to establish and maintain mutually beneficial relationships among internal publics and between the membership collectively and their many external publics (see Exhibit 17.3 for examples of Association Public Service Programs).

EXHIBIT 17.3

ASSOCIATION PUBLIC SERVICE PROGRAMS

The "Associations Advance America" Awards, sponsored by the American Society of Association Executives (ASAE), recognize associations and industry partners for innovative programs that improve the quality of life in communities across the country.

Following are some examples of such programs and the associations that sponsored them:

- "Dialogue on Freedom," American Bar Association
- "Sharing with Communities We Serve," American School Food Service Association
- "TechXplore," Electronic Industries Foundation
- "Teen Tobacco Use—Prevention and Cessation," Illinois Chapter, American Academy of Pediatrics
- "Drivers Education Outreach Program," Iowa Motor Truck Association

- "Operation School Bell," National Assistance League
- "Lunch Room Live," Ohio Farm Bureau Federation, Inc.
- "Disaster Recovery: A Guide to Financial Issues," American Institute of Certified Public Accountants
- "Helmets 4 Safety," American Society of Plastic Surgeons
- "Get Charged! Electricity and You Campaign," National Rural Electric Cooperative Association
- "Anthrax: Preparing and Protecting Your Family," Association for Professionals in Infection Control and Epidemiology
- "Fireworks Safety Campaign," Maryland Society of Eye Physicians and Surgeons
- "Hospice House," Peninsula Housing and Builders Association

The Nature of Programming

Much of what associations and societies do in the name of public relations follows an annual cycle: seeking new members, making reports to them, and holding conferences. Most associations engage in some of or all of the following activities:

1. Preparing and disseminating technical and educational publications, videos, and other public information materials
2. Sponsoring conventions and meetings, instructional seminars, and exhibitions
3. Handling government contacts and interpreting to members the legislative and administrative actions of government agencies
4. Compiling and publishing relevant statistics
5. Preparing and distributing news, information, and public service announcements to the media
6. Planning and implementing public service activities
7. Establishing and enforcing codes of ethics and standards of performance
8. Disseminating governmental and other standards to members
9. Conducting cooperative research: scientific, social, and economic
10. Placing advertisements on behalf of an entire industry, profession, or business endeavor; or on behalf of public health, safety, or welfare (see Figure 17.8 for example of American Medical Association advocacy advertising)
11. Promoting positive employee relations, accident prevention, and cooperation within an industry, profession, or other special-interest membership
12. Maintaining Internet and intranet sites serving current information needs of members and external stakeholders

Association trends include growing emphasis on public affairs and advocacy communication directed to external constituents and on the use of communication technology to meet the information needs of members.

LABOR UNIONS

Closely related to trade associations are labor unions. A labor union consists of a group of workers who organize to gain improvements in wages, benefits, and work conditions such as flexibility for meeting job and family obligations and a voice in improving the quality of products and services produced by the companies for whom they work.[47] Examples include the American Postal Workers Union, the International Association of Fire Fighters, the Screen Actors Guild, and the Communication Workers of America.

Organized labor unions, with a total membership of about 16 million in 2003, represent 12.9 percent of the American workforce, down from 13.3 percent in 2002. The union membership rate has steadily declined from a high of 20.1 percent in 1983, the first year for which comparable union data are available.[48] Still, organized labor symbolizes and speaks for working men and women in the United States. According to Lynn Williams, president of the United Steel Workers of America (USWA), suggestions that the labor movement is dead are exaggerated:

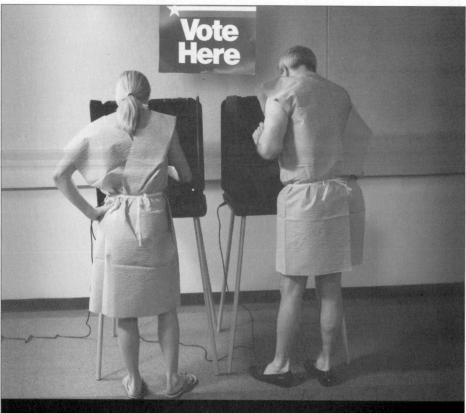

FIGURE 17.8

AMERICAN MEDICAL
ASSOCIATION
ADVERTISEMENT

There are about 200 million eligible voters.
ALL of them have a stake in the U.S. health care system.

Health care is the most important issue for many Americans ... because their lives literally depend on it.

Overwhelming numbers of Americans say their own physicians are "good" to "excellent," but our health care *system* has urgent problems that must be addressed.

As the Republican Party convenes in New York, the AMA calls on party leaders to consider the AMA's proposals for healing our nation's health care system.

Six critical issues need attention now:

- lack of health insurance and choice
- America's medical liability crisis
- patient safety
- strengthening Medicare
- financing care for low-income patients
- curbing managed care abuses

To learn more about the AMA's proposals to improve our nation's health care system, visit **www.ama-assn.org/go/HealingtheSystem**

America's physicians — together with America's largest voting bloc, our patients —
are eager to work with lawmakers to help heal our nation's health care system.

Let's work together to get it done.

American Medical Association
Physicians dedicated to the health of America

Courtesy American Medical Association.

The figures on unionization rates in the private sector are quite misleading. . . . When you look at the Northeastern states, such as New York and Pennsylvania, the percentage of the unionized work force is quite respectable by world standards. It's not the 90 percent-plus figure of Sweden or the 50 percent-plus of Germany or even the 40 percent figure of Canada. But at 34 percent, it's quite respectable.[49]

The American labor movement is credited with helping bring about many of the changes and legislation in civil rights, health, education, and employee rights that have occurred since the death of President Franklin Roosevelt. Labor's clout has diminished in recent years, however, because of changes in the workforce, a series of judicial rulings supportive of management, and declining public support of labor unions.

Still, organized labor has shaped national public opinion and policy. Labor has a rich history of fighting against employer abuses since the early part of the twentieth century and today still stands up for civil and human rights, voting rights, access to health care, better working conditions, protection for immigrant workers, and more.

But the development of a global economy and international trade agreements such as the North American Free Trade Agreement (NAFTA) has labor leaders concerned that jobs will be lost. Organized labor's strong convictions have led to the creation of powerful Political Action Committees (PACs). State laws restricting the use of union dues for political purposes, however, are challenging that power. For example, California Proposition 226, passed in June 1998, requires unions to obtain a member's written permission before it can use any portion of that member's dues to support political candidates. On the other hand, union support may have made the difference in electing President Bill Clinton twice.

The Role of Public Relations

Organized labor's approach to public relations has changed since the early days of George Meany, the first president of the AFL/CIO, who for 25 years was labor's clearly identifiable and unquestioned spokesperson. Today, the skills of public relations specialists and others have been augmented and honed to meet the needs of expanded, more sophisticated programs. The Digital Age and Globalization are forcing unions to better utilize public relations to mobilize members, tell their story, and gain public support. Public affairs management teams are now using research and the Internet along with the traditional means such as media relations, upgraded newsletters, and public service announcements (see Figure 17.9). A recent poll suggests that labor's efforts to advocate on behalf of workers are producing results. There has been an increase in the number of people who would support a union in the workplace—from 39 percent in 1993 to 43 percent in 1999.[50]

The Problem of Strikes

Following the bitter, 4-month strike by 70,000 United Food and Commercial Workers in Southern California against three grocery firms, the spokesperson for one of the companies said, "I think the lesson coming out of Southern California is clear. No one wins in a strike."[51]

AMERICAN FEDERATION OF STATE, COUNTY, AND MUNICIPAL EMPLOYEES' 60-SECOND TELEVISION SPOT, "SOCIAL SECURITY"

When I began working as a young man the government had just started Social Security.

Part of every worker's paycheck would be matched by the boss and sent to the government. When we retired, we'd get enough of our money back to help us get by.

It was sort of a contract between working people and the government.

Now the administration wants to cut out some of the benefits you'd get at 65. And at 62 they want to cut your benefits...from 80% to 55%.

Courtesy American Federation of State, County, and Municipal Employees.

Workers through the years have tried to improve living and working conditions by refusing to work—that is, go on strike—when their demands were not met. However, for a variety of political, economic, and social reasons, strikes are not as frequent as they were early in the twentieth century.

In the United States, the federal government and four out of five states ban their employees from striking altogether. In the private sector, employers can punish workers for striking by giving their jobs to permanent replacements. Labor has had problems sustaining a broad base of sympathetic support from the nonunion lay public.

Despite the inconveniences and costs involved, the strike weapon is considered essential to labor's success. Media coverage tends to feature picket lines, angry strikers, and vocal labor leaders. Management, on the other hand, is somewhat restricted by law as to what it can say and do. (Review the section in chapter 6 on the National Labor Act of 1935 and the Taft-Hartley Act of 1947.)

On the surface, it would be easy to advise unions not to go on strike because of the impact on public opinion and on relations with management. But, strategic public relations in the labor movement often calls for leveraging labor's position of power in ways that will not be universally popular but that will achieve labor's goals for members.

The Challenge for Labor

The challenges of public relations in the labor movement are similar to other sectors of the community: to establish and maintain mutually beneficial relationships with those upon whom success or failure depends.

For labor, that includes attracting the next generation of leaders with a special emphasis on females and people of color. To that end, the AFL-CIO launched "Union Summer," a summer internship program dedicated to uniting workers, students, and community activists to bring about social justice through workplace and community organizing.[52]

Some unions have been successful at cultivating mutually beneficial relationships with major employers. American Rights at Work, an educational and advocacy organization dedicated to improving the climate for America's workers, features four such companies that it says treat workers with respect. They are Harley Davidson, Inc., Cingular Wireless LLC, Ford Motor Co., and Kaiser Permanente, all of whom bring the notion of labor management "partnerships" to the workplace.[53] Recognizing that organized labor must change with the changing environment, David Pearce Snyder says:

> We in America are reinventing our corporations, reinventing government, reinventing labor relations, reinventing health care and public education. We are reinventing all of our great institutions, and when we are all done, we will have reinvented America. The other industrial nations are beginning to reinvent themselves as well. Eventually, the whole world will be reinvented.[54]

In labor unions, as in all other organizational settings, public relations will play a central role as organizations reinvent themselves and their relationships with publics. Change, in the final analysis, drives the public relations management function in all organizations.

NOTES

[1] Jan Masaoka, Executive Director, and John Kreidler, Chairman of the Board of Directors, CompassPoint Nonprofit Services, Annual Report 2003.

[2] Lester M. Salamon and Helmet K. Anheier, *The Emerging Nonprofit Sector: An Overview* (Manchester, UK: Manchester University Press, 1996), 33–42.

[3] Mark W. Everson, Commissioner of Internal Revenue, written statement presented to the Committee on Finance, U.S. Senate: Hearing on Charitable Giving Problems and Best Practices Tax Information for Charities and Other Non-Profits, www.irs.ustreas.gov/charities/ index.html.

[4] Peter Dobkin Hall, *Inventing the Nonprofit Sector and Other Essays on Philanthropy, Voluntarism, and Nonprofit Organizations* (Baltimore, MD: Johns Hopkins University Press, 1992), 13, 14, and 82.

[5] American Association of Fundraising Counsel (AAFRC), News Release, "Americans Gave Estimated $241 Billion in 2003," www.aafrc.org.

[6] Ibid.

[7] Sharyl Attkisson, three-part series: "Disaster Strikes in the Red Cross Backyard," "Red Faces at the Red Cross," "The Battle Inside the Red Cross," www.cbsnews.com, July 2002.

[8] Salamon and Anheier, *The Emerging Nonprofit Sector: An Overview*, 66.

[9] The Foundation Center (Online), Frequently Asked Questions/What is a Foundation? Copyright 1995–2004, www.fdncenter.org/learn/faqs/html/foundfun.html.

[10] Marina Dundjerski and Holly Hall, "Lilly Now No. 1 Among Foundations," *The Chronicle of Philanthropy* (Online), January 29, 1998; www.philanthropy.com/update.dir/givingusa.htm, March 9, 1998.

[11] The Foundation Center (Online), Researching Foundations/Top 100 U.S. Foundations by Asset Size, Copyright 1995–2004, www.fdncenter.org/research/trends_analysis/top100assets.html.

[12] "Foundation Giving Trends: Update on Funding Priorities" News Release, The Foundation Center's 2004 report, The Foundation Center (Online), 79 Fifth Ave., New York, NY 10003 Copyright 1995–2004, www.fdncenter.org.

[13] *Covering Health Issues: a Sourcebook for Journalists*, Chapter 8: Health Care Costs, Alliance for Health Reform, Washington, D.C. October 2004, www.allhealth.org/sourcebook 2002/ch8_10.html.

[14] Ibid.

[15] Sherry Glied, Ph.D., "Healthcare Crisis: Who's At Risk," (Online) Division of Health Policy and Management, Columbia University, www.pbs.org/healthcarecrisis.

[16] Kaiser Family Foundation, "Trends and Indicators in the Changing Health Care Marketplace 2002," Introduction, May 2002, www.kff.org/insurance.

[17] Kaiser Family Foundation, "The Uninsured and Their Access to Health Care," fact sheet, Health Insurance Coverage in America, 2002 Data Update (online), December 2003, www.kff.org/uninsured.

[18] California Health Care Association, Facts at a Glance, contained in News Kit titled "California's Hospitals, On the Front Lines of Care," 1215 K Street, Suite 800, Sacramento, CA 95814. Can be viewed online at www.calhealth.org.

[19] Remarks by HHS Secretary Tommy G. Thompson, Presentation of the President's Fiscal Year 2004 Budget for the Department of Health and Human Services, taken from a news release, Feb. 3, 2003, www.hhs.gov/budget/docbudget.htm.

[20] John Leighty, "Financial Jolt, Hospitals struggle to comply with costly retrofitting requirements" *Nurse Week*, April 19, 2004, www.nurseweek.com/news/features/0404/retrofit.asp.

[21] Mollyann Brodie, Ph.D., Drew Altman, Ph.D., LeeAnn Brady, Lindsay Heberling, "A Study of Media Coverage of Health Policy 1997–2000" Supplement to the January/February 2002 issue of *Columbia Journalism Review*.

[22] Quoted by David Kirk in "Briefings: Hospital Research Targets 'Key Leaders,'" *Public Relations Journal* 49, no. 3 (March 1993): 12.

[23] Daron Cowley, "HIPPA One Year Later," *The Public Relation Strategist*, Spring 2004.

[24] California Health Care Association, Press Room, Release of Patient Information, www.calhealth.org/public/press/relpatinf.html.

[25] Steven V. Seekins, "Forecast 1993: System Reform Looms," *Public Relations Journal* 49, no. 1 (January 1993): 21.

[26] U.S. Census Bureau, Facts for Features and Special Editions, July 6, 2004, www.census.gov/Press-Release/www/releases/archives/facts_for_features_special_editions/002263.html.

[27] U.S. Census Bureau, News Release, "School Districts in New York and New Jersey Spent Most Per Pupil on Education, Census Bureau Reports," March 11, 2003, www.census.gov/Press-Release/www/releases/archives/education/000816.html.

[28] U.S. Census Bureau, Fact Finder/People/Education "One in Four U.S. Residents Attends School," Oct. 16, 2003, http://factfinder.census.gov/jsp/saff/SAFFInfo.jsp?_pageId=tp5_education.

[29] Personal conversation with Jack Beresford, Marketing Communication Director, San Diego State University, 5500 Campanile Dr., San Diego, CA 92182, July 2004.

[30] Judith R. Phair, "1992 Education Report Card," *Public Relations Journal* 48, no. 2 (February 1992): 23.

[31] "'In' Box," *The Chronicle of Higher Education* 37, no. 47 (August 7, 1991): A9. For the complete report, see Commission on Institutional Relations, Survey of College and University Presidents' Perceptions of the Public Relations Function (Washington, DC: Council for Advancement and Support of Education, 1991).

[32] Michael J. Worth and James W. Asp II, *The Development Officer in Higher Education: Toward an Understanding of the Role*. ASHE-ERIC Higher Education Report No. 4 (Washington, DC: George Washington University, Graduate School of Education and Human Development, 1994), 54.

[33] Associated Press, "Americans' Belief in God Grows," reported in *San Diego Union Tribune*, December 22, 1997, A–8.

[34] Pew Research Center for the People & the Press, Survey Reports "The Diminishing Divide…American Churches, American Politics," June 25, 1996.

[35] National Council of Churches, "National Council of Churches, Other Religious Groups Join 100 Organizations Urging Overhaul of Nation's Health Care System," July 20, 2004, www.ncccusa.org/news/newshome.html.

[36] Sandi Dolbee, "Hunting for a healer, San Diego Episcopal Diocese Must Carefully Choose a New Bishop at a Divisive Time for the Denomination," *San Diego Union Tribune*, March 25, 2004.

[37] Pew Research Center for the People & the Press conducted in association with the Pew Forum on Religion and Public Life, Pew Center, "Americans Struggle with Religion's Role at Home and Abroad," March 20, 2002.

[38] Eric Arnold, "PR Has Essential Role in Advancing Mormon Mission," *PR Week*, April 28, 2003, p. 10.

[39] American Society for Association Executives (ASAE), Washington, DC, Fact Sheet, "Associations in a Nutshell," July 2004. Current information available at www.asaenet.org/asae/cda/index/1,1584,ETI17733_MEN3_NID4067,00.html.

[40] AFL/CIO (Online), "About the AFL/CIO," 2004, www.aflcio.org/aboutaflcio/.

[41] Christine Maurer and Tara E. Sheets, eds., *Encyclopedia of Associations*, 33rd ed., vol. 1 (Detroit: Gale Research, 1998), vii.

[42] Barbara T. Dreyfus, "The Seduction; AARP's Support for Last Fall's Medicare Bill Shocked Many Democrats—and Thousands of the Group's Members. But If They'd Known This History, They Wouldn't Have Been Shocked at All," *The American Prospect*, copyright 2004.

[43] "American Bar Association Nominates New Leadership," American Bar Association, *PR Newswire*, Feb. 9, 2004.

[44] Michael Romano, "Back to Basics; AMA Simplifies Philosophy on Membership," *Modern Healthcare,* Jan. 5, 2004.

[45] From "Wisconsin Milk Marketing Board 'Middle Nickel,'" unpublished 1993 case study, Morgan and Myers (public relations firm), Jefferson, WI.

[46] Helen Frank Bensimon and Patricia A. Walker, "Associations Gain Prestige and Visibility by Serving as Expert Resources for Media," *Public Relations Journal* 48, no. 2 (February 1992): 16.

[47] AFL/CIO (Online) All About Unions/How and Why People Join Unions, 2004, www.aflcio.org/aboutunions/joinunions.

[48] U.S. Department of Labor, Bureau of Labor Statistics, Washington D.C. News Release, "Union Members in 2003," Jan. 21, 2004, www.dol.gov.

[49] Data on union affiliation found in the January issues of *Employment and Earnings*, published monthly by the U.S. Department of Labor, Bureau of Labor Statistics, Washington, DC.

[50] Guy Molyneux, Hart Research, reported in *PR Week*, Jan. 29, 2001.

[51] David Washburn, "Lessons from Grocery Dispute Here Sink in Elsewhere," *San Diego Union Tribune*, July 11, 2004.

[52] AFL/CIO (Online), "About Unions/Union Summer," 2004, www.aflcio.org/aboutunions/unionsummer.

[53] American Rights at Work (Online), Resources/Fact Sheets/Fact Sheet: "A Profile of High Road Companies," May 23, 2004, www.araw.org/resources/facts/highroad.cfm.

[54] David Pearce Snyder, "The Revolution in the Workplace: What's Happening to Our Jobs?" *The Futurist* 30, no. 2 (March–April 1996): 13.

ADDITIONAL SOURCES

Andreasen, Alan, and Philip Kotler, *Strategic Marketing for Nonprofit Organizations*, 6th ed. Upper Saddle River, NJ: Prentice Hall, 2003. Outlines application of marketing principles and practices to churches, government agencies, schools, health-care organizations, and fine and performing arts groups.

"Association Public Relations," special issue of *Public Relations Quarterly* 37, no. 1 (Spring 1992). Features a collection of articles on professional, ethical, legal, and management issues in association public relations.

Ballot, Michael. *Labor-Management Relations in a Changing Environment*. New York: John Wiley and Sons, 1992. Covers the broad field of industrial relations, including the changing relationship between unions and employers, the future of organized labor, and public-sector unionization.

Cutlip, Scott M. *Fundraising in the United States*. New Brunswick, NJ: Transaction Publishers, 1990. Reprint of 1965 classic history of how fund-raising evolved to become big business, its early pioneers, and campaigns that had a major impact on society.

Dunlop, John T. *Industrial Relations Systems*, rev. ed. Boston: Harvard Business School Press, 1993. Presents a general theory of industrial relations, outlining the formal and informal ways management organizations, workers, and government agencies are organized.

Godfried, Nathan. *WCFL: Chicago's Voice of Labor, 1926–78*. Champaign: University of Illinois Press, 1997. Traces Chicago Federation of Labor's attempt to create a "voice of labor" by establishing Chicago radio station WCFL.

Heckscher, Charles C. *The New Unionism*, rev. ed. Ithaca, NY: ILR Press, 1996. Argues that the displacement of manufacturing and production line jobs by white-collar and service-sector jobs is eroding the influence of traditional unions slow to change from their nineteenth-century origins.

Henson, Keven D. *Just a Temp*. Philadelphia: Temple University Press, 1996. Presents history of rapidly expanding business of temporary help supply firms, portrays who temporary workers are and what they do, and suggests policy changes to improve working conditions for temporary workers.

Kelly, Kathleen S. *Effective Fund-Raising Management*. Mahwah, NJ: Lawrence Erlbaum Associates, 1997. First textbook to cover history, principles, theory, and process of contemporary fund-raising as a specialized public relations practice.

Kelly, Kathleen S. *Fund Raising and Public Relations: A Critical Analysis*. Hillsdale, NJ: Lawrence Erlbaum Associates, 1991. Argues that fund-raising should be a part of the larger public relations function in charitable, educational, and other nonprofit organizations, with the main purpose being to give these organizations the autonomy they need to achieve goals.

Maibach, Edward, and Roxanne Louiselle Parrott, eds. *Designing Health Messages: Approaches from Communication Theory and Public Health Practice*. Thousand Oaks, CA: Sage Publications, 1995. Contributing authors synthesize communication and health behavior change theory and research findings from AIDS, cancer, and other health promotion campaigns.

Masters, Marick F. *Unions at the Crossroads: Strategic Membership, Financial, and Political Perspectives*. Westport, CT: Quorum Books, 1997. Analyzes "institutional health" of the 28 unions in the United States with 80 percent of all union members and control over two-thirds of all union wealth.

Robinson, Archie. *George Meany and His Times: A Biography*. New York: Simon and Schuster, 1981. Details the life and personality of the man who shaped the American labor movement and the political events and social changes during his 63 years in labor unions.

Tilly, Chris. *Half a Job: Bad and Good Part-Time Jobs in a Changing Labor Market*. Philadelphia: Temple University Press, 1996. Explores why part-time employment has increased, where part-time jobs exist, and how organizations choose to use part-time instead of full-time workers.

INDEX